My Life is the Cinema

My Life is the Cinema

Жизнь моя—Кинематограф

Esfir' Il'inichna Shub

Translated and Edited
by Keith Sanborn

Sticking Place Books
New York

Compiled by
A. I. Konoplev

Executive Editor
S. V. Drobashenko

Introduction
S. I. Yutkevich

This book is composed of the articles, speeches, plans, scenarios, and correspondence of Esfir'
Shub in *Жизнь моя — кинматограф* [*Zhizn' moya — kinematograf*] (*My Life is the Cinema*),
published in 1972 by Iskusstvo Editions. Her memoir *Крупным планом* [*Krupnym planom*]
(*In Close Up*) was published by Iskusstvo Editions in 1959. The 1959 edition was published
with notes and an introductory essay under the general editorial supervision of I. Vaisfel'd.
The 1959 edition was designed by V. F. Stepanova and V. A. Rodchenko. We have omitted the
introduction and notes of the 1959 edition.

The English translations of Shub's correspondence with Alexei Gan are published here for the
first time. "She's No Dziga Vertov," and "On *Esfir Shub: Pioneer of Documentary Filmmaking*
by Ilana Shub Sharp," by the translator, have been added to the materials of the 1972 edition.

The photographic images in the chapter on Mayakovsky are by Alexander Rodchenko.
The origins of the other photographic images in this book are unknown.

This translation by Keith Sanborn was made in collaboration with Masha Godovannaya.

Shub's texts are believed by the publisher to be in the public domain, 50 years having elapsed
since her death. Good faith efforts to locate the descendants of her correspondents—all
deceased—have been made. None have been successful.

© Keith Sanborn
© Sticking Place Books 2025

ISBN 979-8-89976-041-9

Contents

Part II: Articles and Statements

Part III: Unrealized Projects

Appendices

The translator at Gosfilmofond, February 2008.
Photo: Peggy Ahwesh.

Translator's introduction

My dear friend Masha Godovannaya was my research collaborator and the primary editor of this translation of *Жизнь моя — кинематограф* (*My Life is the Cinema*), Shub's memoir and collected writings. She has refused the title of co-translator many times, but this work would not have been possible without her unstinting efforts, unflagging enthusiasm, and canny navigation of archival complexities. Tatsiana Zamirovskaya provided a critical review of several sections of the translation and corrective historical and cultural insights. Anton Ginzberg kindly reviewed my translations of the Vertov material in my own essay. Early on in the process of my exploration of Shub's work, Anastasia Osipova provided live and lively translations of the intertitles for screenings of *The Wings of a Serf*, edited by Shub, and *The Great Way*, Shub's own work. These screenings took place at an intimate theater at the Film Study Center of the Museum of Modern Art, New York, thanks to the generosity and good offices of Charles Silver, who is so sorely missed.

Yuri Tsivian and Daria Khitrova answered several questions about the language of the translation and the historical context in which Shub worked. Anton Vidokle, Matvei Yankelevich, and Professor Polina Barskova helped me untangle several Russian cultural and linguistic perplexities. Naum Kleiman provided extremely helpful information about Shub's relationship with Sergei Eisenstein and Eisenstein's library, allowing us to visit the Eisenstein apartment in Moscow and giving us access to a photograph of Eisenstein at work editing *Strike*. Paolo Vampa generously shared his deep knowledge of the historical intricacies of the Italian language. Aykan Safoğlu and his mother, Nevin Safoğlu, kindly provided critical information about Istanbul, its culture, and its environs.

Peggy Ahwesh offered support and enthusiasm for this unending project throughout its course, in the wake of my disenchantment with the academic publishing system. She put me in touch with Jake Perlin, who offered his support and ultimately connected me with Paul Cronin, the publisher of this volume, whose encouragement, support, and sage advice have been invaluable.

My parents, Keith and Wanda Sanborn and my grandparents, Jay and Lola Sanborn, supported my many forays into education with untiring support.

Several archivists shared information about their Shub holdings and their enthusiasm for her work, in particular, Adelheid Heftberger, formerly of the Austrian Film Museum. Funding for travel to the Shub archival holdings at the Russian State Archive of Literature and Art, Gosfilmofond, and the Russian State Documentary Film and Photo Archive was provided twice by the Program in Visual Arts of Princeton University. The staff at each of those institutions in the Russian Federation were helpful and efficient in aiding Masha and I gain access to materials critical for this work. Richard Witt generously and repeatedly opened his home to us in Moscow and provided numerous cultural insights. Philip Cavendish, Ian Christie, Su Friedrich, Tom Gunning, Stephen Herbert, Hellin Kay, Stuart Liebman, Luke McKernan, Rachel Moore, the late P. Adams Sitney, Gennady Shkliarevsky, Charlotte Mandell, Elena Gorfinkel, Lou Thieblement, and the late Aleksandr Borisovich Konoplev all helped in various ways. Jed Rapfogel of Anthology Film Archives and Anke Hennig of New York University allowed me the occasion to present some of the material of my afterword in an early form. John Klacsmann of Anthology Film Archives consulted on technical aspects of film material and terminology. Finally, I would like to sincerely thank Ewa M. Thompson, Professor Emerita of Slavic Studies at Rice University, for her rigorous and intelligent example. There are, undoubtedly, others, whose names my memory has refused to summon. For that I apologize, pleading only that this project has taken so many years to reach this stage, that my memory has failed in unpredictable ways.

This work was also supported in part by a Fulbright Fellowship to the former Smolny Faculty of Liberal Arts and Sciences of St. Petersburg State University, in the Russian Federation.

I must acknowledge my debt for deciphering linguistic material and cultural mysteries to contributors to the Russian Wikipedia, csdmuseum.ru, DeepTranslate, Reverso.net, lingvolive.com, and translate.academia.ru, the online version of Dahl's monumental dictionary, as well as printed sources too numerous to mention. In every case where I have used digital resources, I have evaluated them critically: I have crosschecked them, interpreted them, and when in doubt, relied on my intuitions as a translator and the review of trusted collaborators.

Following Benjamin's lead, my stylistic motivation in making this translation has been transparency, while maintaining readability, and faithfulness to the multi-faceted styles of Shub and her friends. My cultural motivation has been to make this material available to anyone interested in the history of documentary film and its unsung heroines, as well as to scholars of the period who might not have access to the primary texts, or who would like to include materials for teaching non-Russian-speaking students. For this reason, I have increased the size of the scholarly apparatus, i.e. the many footnotes, by several multiples of the original Russian notes. Specialists in the period may find this unnecessary, or may find ways to improve, or correct the notes, which I welcome. Film theorist Brian Henderson once remarked, that footnotes indicate stress points in a text; this being the case, you will notice many occasions on which a rabbit disappearing down his hole engaged me in stressed pursuit. To limit such adventures, I have left the missing dates of death in the Russian editor's notes as they were in 1972.

My ultimate motivation: I did this because I thought it needed to be done. In some measure, it is the repayment of a debt to one of the founders of the genre of films made from other films, a genre to which a great deal of my own work in film and that of my friends belongs.

Specialists will know, that this work is far from an exhaustive account of Shub's life and contributions to film culture and to Soviet culture. Much remains in the archives to be published and some remains in the hands of Shub's family in Esfir' Shub's extensive personal archive. But this is, I hope, a solid beginning for the English-speaking world. My hope is to stimulate further efforts and better access to her work, especially her films, which have been denigrated and marginalized in her own country by scholars who should know better. Elsewhere, however, Shub's work is beginning to receive some of the attention it deserves and, unfortunately, some of the blind admiration it does not.

As anyone who has undertaken the translator's task will know, each language has its own qualities, not always congruent with the language into which one would like to bring it. In the case of Russian and English, we have what I call a grammar-intensive language (Russian) and a syntax-intensive language (English). This means, that Russian can and does pile on modifiers across syntactic boundaries in a way English cannot. Though English can be quite flexible, often syntax, or word order, determines meaning: *Kristi shot her dog* vs. *Her dog shot Kristi*. In Russian, the case of the noun, whatever the word order, would immediately identify the shooter and the one shot. Having three genders of nouns and six cases (and remnants of a seventh), not to mention several kinds of participles, inflected by two verb aspects, Russian is considerably more flexible in what goes where in a sentence. In addition, there are cultural conventions, which determine what is meaningful and acceptable, and word-play, which disputes those conventions via slippages of sound and meaning. Maya-kovsky, for example, brings all of these resources into play and into collision.

In this book, there are many different writers, each with a personal style. While I have, because of my limitations, lost some nuances of style, I have tried to preserve meaning and rhythm. And, when in doubt, added footnotes. Word order may some-times seem strange to native English speakers, though I hope it will remain compre-hensible, within a Latinate Elizabethan range of syntactic play. The distinctive vocab-ulary of the era, which I have tried to represent in at least some of its defamiliarizing strangeness, may also occasion some head-scratching. I have tried to contextualize—if not to eliminate—this effect by means of footnotes, sometimes, for the perplexed and sometimes, for experts. There will also be various kinds of mistakes on my part. I ask for your curiosity and whatever tolerance you can muster; I also welcome corrections.

Some readers will note what might seem to be a surfeit of commas in this translation. There are several reasons for their large presence. First is the issue of untangling the complexities of grammatically-rich but more syntactically flexible Russian into the more rigidly rule-governed resources of syntax-rich English. Second is the very nature of Shub's style. She places many image-rich phrases in apposition to one another, creating a montage of details, as she does in her films, which accumulate into a larger, descriptive landscape. To keep each image in individual relief, I have used commas to separate them, as she does. As several of her correspondents comment, Shub writes the way she speaks. This includes dramatic pauses and a free-flowing association of ideas and images. Third, it is my predilection as a translator to try to preserve the rhythm of a text along with its meaning; for me, commas are the best way of doing so, once other linguistic resources have been honed as finely as possible. Commas guide the reader to parse the rhythm of a phrase along with its meaning. I try to use commas in prose, the way a poet might use line breaks.

Translating Russian poetry presents other complications. A poet like Mayakovsky, for example, a master of the grammatical resources of Russian, can relocate words in a phrase and enhance meaning in these dislocations. In such a case, I simply try to do the best I can to preserve the meaning and a general sense of the poetics of the line breaks. Finally, attempting to preserve rhymes in poetry from one language to another, for me, is simply a fool's errand; the coincidence of sound and meaning, which creates the joyous discoveries of rhyme, will always be lost. So, I opt for attempting to preserve the rhythm, as I do with prose. For wordplay, I try to do the best I can and, when in doubt, as previously noted, resort to footnotes.

Readers will know, that Russian uses Cyrillic characters and English, Latin characters. Several systems of transliterating Russian into English exist, both scholarly and popular. Since this book is directed to both a more scholarly and a less scholarly audience, I have used a hybrid system that I hope will respect both. For proper nouns, I have used popular versions of famous names: Chaliapin instead of Shalyapin, Dostoyevsky instead of Dostoevsky. For names of interest mostly to scholars, I have used a system that Russian speakers will easily see through. Those with little sense of Russian orthography might rely on intelligent agents to aid them in their follow-up searches. For common nouns, or phrases of uncommon interest, I have favored an English translation in the main body of the text, with a footnote for the curious containing the original in Cyrillic characters, and, when necessary, further explanation. When I consider a word not easily captured by a translation or paraphrase, I have also given a transliteration. As with Classical Greek, sometimes a word is transliterated, sometimes given in Greek, with or without an explanation by footnote or by context.

For the titles of films listed in the Russian editor's notes, I have tried to provide the English language or international release titles listed in Jay Leyda's *Kino*, the IMDB, or elsewhere. In cases where no English release title is listed, or was unobtainable by me, I have tried to give an accurate idiomatic rendering of the title. Russian scholars may consult the original film, though, as they well know, films were sometimes released under several different titles. In cases where the English-language release title has little resemblance to the Russian release title, I have given the English release title, followed in square brackets by the Russian release title followed by a rendering of the Russian release title into English, enclosed within parentheses. Thus: *New Horizons* [Выборгская сторона (*The Vyborg Side*)]. *New Horizons* is the English-language release title. *Выборгская сторона* is the Russian release title. *The Vyborg Side* is an accurate translation of the Russian release title.

The curious will note, that the edition of the Shub materials on which this translation is based was edited in 1972 by one Sergei Vladimirovich Dobrashenko, formerly Editor in Chief of Iskusstvo Editions. It seems that in 1958, he had been relieved of that post, when it was learned that his father had owned 200 hectares of land and his mother, who came from a noble family, was accused of aiding and abetting the enemy in her capacity as a doctor during the Great Patriotic War. In the vigilant and conservative Brezhnev era, one can imagine, that an editor such as Dobrashenko, having once fallen from grace for inherited sins, might well take a cautious approach to important historical figures in film and the arts. And while there does not seem to be any evidence of tampering with the statements, or the unrealized projects, the careful reader will note a fair number of unexplained ellipses in the memoir and ellipses enclosed in square brackets, acknowledging omissions by the editor in the correspondence.

Shub also regularly says in her correspondence, that there are things she cannot put in a letter, occasionally pleading her inarticulateness. In letter #37 of 1935 from Fadeev to Shub, Fadeev alludes to a film to which Shub had declined to attach her name. Fadeev reproaches her for this gesture, since it would be "useful" to her "in a social sense." In 1949, Shub declined to attach her name to a film called *От чистого сердца* (*With Heartfelt Sincerity*), a paean of praise to Comrade Stalin, "our Leader and Teacher." Shub doesn't give her motivation in either case, at least in the present material, but she was clearly taking a risk—on behalf of her legacy, perhaps—by declining to attach her name to a film praising Stalin on the occasion of his birthday. It is also curious, that the editor chose the version of Shub's contribution to the debate on cinema conducted by *Novy LEF* as published originally in the issue of *Novy LEF* devoted to that debate, rather than a version corrected by Shub, which was the subject of her letter of protest to Tret'yakov. Curious, since the failure to publish a corrected version of her contribution led to her, as well as Eisenstein's, break with *Novy LEF*. Shub learned to navigate the Stalin era carefully and her texts sometimes echo the burden of the skills she acquired in so doing.

Finally, any errors or misinterpretations of these collective efforts are entirely mine. I am humbled by the time, intelligence, and care shared with me. No expression of thanks could ever suffice, but I thank here and now, anyway, all who have contributed, for helping me to allow some of the genius and the demons of Esfir' Shub to shine forth in all their fiery, complex brilliance.

Keith Sanborn
Catskill, NY
September, 2025

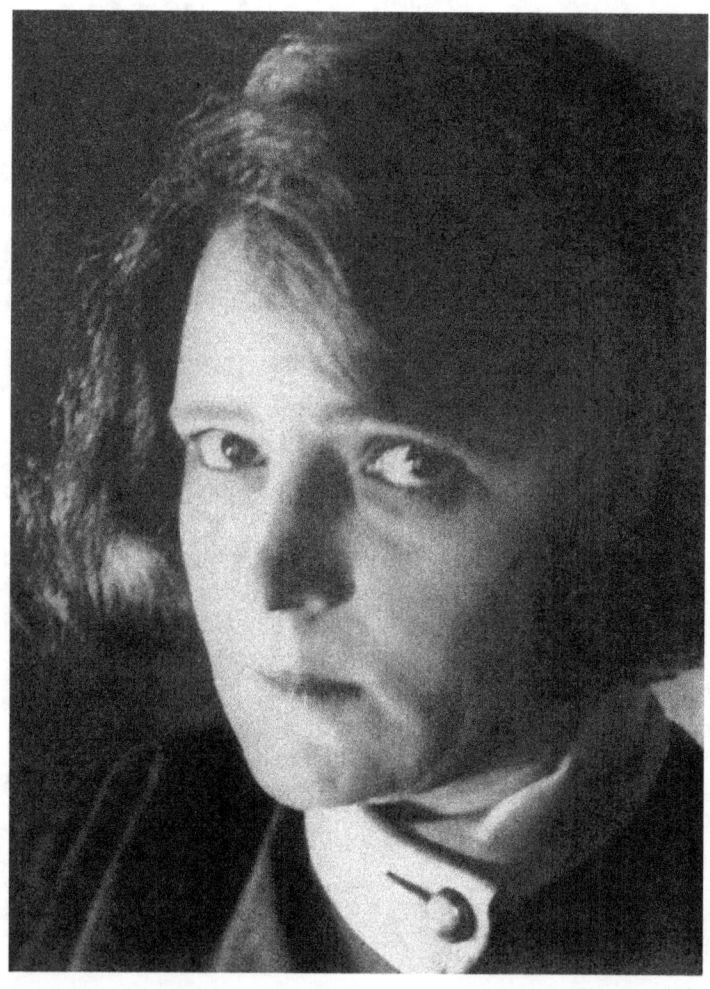

Sorceress of the Editing Table
by Sergei Yutkevich

Summer, 1927. Moscow. For the first time, I was one-on-one with the footage, which had been shot for my first film *Lace* [*Кружева*], in a little editing room of the 1st Goskino Factory on Zhitnaya ulitsa.

A warm evening. The windows looked out onto the dark courtyard, where on the cobblestones lay the squares of light from the windows of the lab. There, squeaking wooden wheels were turning, on which film was drying, that they were still processing by hand.

Generally, the technology in this small studio (formerly the Khanzhonkov studio) was still quite antediluvian, but precisely here, Soviet Cinema had already been born.

Precisely here, in a not very spacious glass studio, already *Strike, The Battleship Potemkin, Bay of Death, The Death Ray, Bed and Sofa* had been shot.

On the editing table lie rolled-up lengths of film. I am supposed to join them together according to some sort of law, as yet unknown to me, in order to construct a film out of them.

I turn the rewinds. I am confused.

I don't know how long one piece or another should be, in what order I should put these shots, that I had taken separately.

I hadn't yet caught on to the art of montage.

So, I run to the editing room next door. There, leaning over a plate of frosted glass, is a beautiful woman, with her hair cut short, in the style of the 1920s.

She, just as I, deep in the night, is examining with her intelligent, attentive gaze, the same sorts of pieces of film, though not ones shot by her, but by other directors and camera operators. In her editing room, they are wound onto a reel on the rewinds, but in a unique, determined, strict order, known only to her: shot after shot, roll after roll. And precisely from her, only from her, am I able to find out all the secrets of the mysterious and powerful process, known as "montage."

She isn't surprised. She's happy about my popping up, though it is rather late. After all, she generally likes people. She's friendly, sociable. She's always ready to help filmmakers and especially beginners like me.

I'm begging you, tell me, Edi—that's how her close friends called Esfir' Shub—tell me why I should put this shot here and not there, how many meters should I cut off of this wide shot? one meter? two? and why exactly that much? Reveal to me the secrets you possess.

She smiles.

There is no secret. Nor any rules. You need just one: you have to have the *feel of the piece* of film.

Oddly enough, this rather unscientific definition calms me down. I go back to my editing room, I desperately wave my scissors, I cut various pieces, I glue them together, intuitively guided by this mysterious "feel of the piece," but only tomorrow, will I able to see the results on the screen.

After all, at that time at the factory, we didn't even have a simple device like a Moviola for going over a rough cut.

The next day, Esfir' Shub was shown to be correct. Only when the first shots you had edited together ran by on the screen and when—not just as their author—but as their first viewer, with acutely heightened attention, with the mobilization of all your feelings, do you grasp their rhythm, only then, are you able to feel, whether or not you've correctly figured out the editing structure of the sequence. Here, you understand, that it's necessary to shorten, or to lengthen things, how to create contrasts, how to bring into collision these up to now dead pieces of celluloid, in order to bring them to life on the screen. And joined together, not only by the astringent pear-scented essence of film cement, but through the magical living water of montage, were they transformed into a production of art: a motion picture.

"Montage"—this word, in the early years of our cinematic youth, possessed an almost magical significance. It sounded like an incantation, like an "open sesame," granting access to the cavern of all cinematic treasures. And the possessor of these secrets, with undisputed, unconditional authority, was the sorceress of montage, Esfir' Shub.

People love to tell everyone within reach succinct stories about great discoveries. Thus, it is widely known, that an apple, which fell from a tree, helped Newton to formulate the law of terrestrial attraction. We say, "simple, like Columbus and his egg," in memory of the exploit of the famous navigator.[1]

For cinema, the celebrated "Kuleshov effect" was the same, when he edited a close up of Mozzhukhin alternating with three other pieces of film and through those very pieces of film, not only painted the actor with distinct emotions, but, from such simple montage combinations opened up the unlimited possibilities arising from them in the perception of the viewer.

---

[1] [Trans.] An apocryphal story claims, that to discredit his critics who said finding a new trade route to the East was no great feat, Columbus challenged them to stand an egg on end. When their attempts failed, he demonstrated a successful method by tapping the egg on the table to flatten its point.

And just after these experiments had entered into history, a new and genuinely astonishing discovery entered the cinema, inseparably connected with the name of Esfir' Shub.

Today, when for several decades already, on the screens of the world, films have been appearing, which were edited together out of old and new newsreels, when this genre, in various ways and imprecisely called, sometimes artistic-documentaries,[2] sometimes journalistic-newsreel pictures, is universally recognized and has gained millions of viewers, and when Joris Ivens, Frank Capra, Paul Rotha, Erwin Leiser, and Frédéric Rossif reap their laurels, when venerable creators of artistic canvases count in their biographies this kind of montage film, it is fitting once again to appreciate the courage and talent of the pioneers. And here, the names of Dziga Vertov and Esfir' Shub will be found, at the very beginnings of this significant phenomenon.

How this came about is being told in this accomplished, yet, at the same time, modest book, that you are now about to read.

From its pages, as if from the shots of a film, will rise up in front of you the film of a life, saturated to the limit with searches and encounters, successes and failures, hopes and doubts, where the joy of accomplishment will be mixed with bitterness for the lack of recognition. In one of those moments, Esfir' Shub wrote:

> Unfortunately, among us, the creative people in the cinema—and not only in the newsreel—are distinguished by one very problematic characteristic. They lack a sense of [historical] continuity. There is no sense of taking up the baton in the relay race of art. All the same, it is important, while not bringing to a standstill—even for a minute—the forward movement of art to daring new discoveries, not to forget the founders and their place in this movement.

No, we are not forgetting about them. For this reason, this book has come out, and once again, we turn towards the biography and the experience of Esfir' Shub, in order to find strength and wisdom in them for the uninterrupted forward motion of revolutionary, socialist film art.

And so it seems, everything began very simply.

In revolutionary Russia, the cinema passed from the agile hands of wheeler-dealers and merchants to the leadership of the young Soviet government. There were very few domestic films, practically none. Kuleshov, in his workshop, demonstrated "films without film stock," because there wasn't enough film stock. Dziga

---

[2] [Trans.]: In the original: художественно-документальных. The word translated here as "artistic" connotes, in its various forms, a feature-length work with a distinct author. It will be translated in various ways throughout the remainder of the book, including "feature" and "feature-length," among others. I have used this literal translation here to alert the reader to its many valences.

Vertov was editing his first *Kino-Pravdas* and newsreel camera operators seemed to be shooting on leftover print stock. On movie screens, big-budget films[3] from abroad were making a lot of noise. They had to be adapted, somewhat, to the perceptions of the new spectators.

This menial and unnoticed work was taken up by a young woman from a family of the intelligentsia, who, by this time, came not only with an education from a Gymnasium but with the experience of a community of the masters of revolutionary art. You will find portraits of A. Lunacharsky, V. Meyerhold, V. Mayakovsky and other figures from the worlds of theater and poetry in the pages of this book.

In these portraits, not only is there an interested and observant description of the theatrical-literary milieu of that time, but what is most important is, that the worldview of the future artist was being formed by the atmosphere of great changes, the life-giving breath of the revolution.

In the beginning, Esfir' Shub studied diligently, observed carefully, while gluing together pieces of other people's films, not fully suspecting, at the time, the power contained in these rolls of celluloid.

She herself remembers this period this way:

> Gradually, at the editing table and in the viewing room, I acquired the knowledge essential for every director. I learned how to properly assess the construction and composition of a shot. I cultivated a memory for shots, for the content and motion within the frame, for the rhythm and pacing of things as a whole. I interiorized when it was necessary and appropriate to change from a wide shot to a medium shot, from a medium shot to a close-up and back again. I understood the magical power of the scissors in the hands of a person possessing mastery of the grammar of montage. I began to try to make the changes imperceptible, so that one shot would replace another in a continuous motion. All this was basic, but I realized it and conceptualized it myself.

Shub soon mastered all the secrets of the craft. Re-editing foreign pictures no longer satisfied the insistent demands of independent creative thinking and she offered her skillful and agile hands to help directors making their first feature films, whose knowledge of the area of montage was utterly lacking.

She attentively examined the experiments of Kuleshov and Vertov. She made use of their very important observations about the miraculous power of montage in her work, just how pieces [of film] shot by the directors of the first Soviet feature films, in the majority of cases, were in need not only of simple splicing together, but of new,

---

[3] [Trans.]: боевики. This could also mean blockbusters, or, more narrowly, detective or cops & robbers films.

and not only of rhythmic, but of dramatic organization. Here, creativity began. Here, the foundations of the profession were laid, which would later take its legitimate place in production under the designation of "director-editor."[4]

The reader of this book will find in it interesting pages devoted to work on the film *The Wings of a Serf*, where the performance of the leading role of Ivan the Terrible by Leonidov, acquired new qualities, heightened expressiveness only because it occurred to the cunning and restless female editor[5] to use shots, which even the director considered defective.

The celebrated narrowing of the eyes of Leonidov's Ivan the Terrible—which became the reference point for the entire role—owes more to Esfir' Shub, than to the director, Yuri Tarich.

The renown of the sorceress of the editing table spread throughout the young Soviet film industry.

Sergei Eisenstein, at the beginning of the 1920s, still only in his apprentice-ship to the new art, spent day and night in Shub's editing room. Gingerly sitting on the edge of his seat, he observed with admiration, how she transformed Fritz Lang's two-part expressionist, big-budget film *Dr. Mabuse, the Gambler*.

The Vasil'ev brothers rightly considered themselves students of Esfir' Shub, and there was practically no young filmmaker, who did not turn to her in a difficult moment for good advice. But all this was only the beginning.

Her breakthrough came later, when the young woman, who was keen on the experiments of Dziga Vertov—which had given the leading role to fact, to document (not for nothing, did she herself call him an artist, who had exerted a great influence on her)—took the risk, relying on her entire cumulative experience, of constructing the first full-length film,[6] consisting entirely of archival material: footage from pre-revolutionary newsreels.

The working title of the film was *February*, but it entered the history of world cinema as *Fall of the Romanov Dynasty* and was released for the tenth Anniversary of the October Revolution.

The archival footage of this picture, for the first time in the history of world cinema, was not simply spliced together in consecutive order. It was compared, constructed, bound together by the integral thinking of an artist. A creative, *authorial* principle was displayed in the film in all its brilliance and force.

---

[4] [Trans.]: In the original: «режиссер-монтажер» ["rezhisser-montazher"].

[5] [Trans.]: In the original: монтажерша [montazhersha]. This seems to be archaic industry jargon for referring to a woman, who is an editor. Both then and now, the term монтажер, which is grammatically masculine, is used indifferently for male and female editors in screen credits, though as Masha Godovannaya informs me, some independent female filmmakers have used the term монтажерка [montazherka]. This term is not accepted in the industry and is subjected to male ridicule there.

[6] [Trans.]: In the original: полнометражный фильм, quite literally "full-length film," meaning a feature-length film.

One mustn't think, that the process of the creation and distribution of the film came about easily. Precisely at the beginning of her career as an author, she was dismissed when her innovative work appeared.

The administration of the film industry at that time did not recognize what was most important about it: the independent and original thinking of the artist.

The work was qualified as purely technical. It was said: How can you talk about authorship or being a director, when Shub herself didn't shoot anything, but only spliced together pieces of other people's films…?

The scandal concerning I. I. Trainin's decree and the discussion, which ensued, are well described in the book.

But Esfir' Shub, while fighting for her rights, was not entirely aware of the entire significance of her breakthrough—and not only for contemporary, but for future cinema.

Above all, she justly gave their due to the newsreel camera operators—the pioneers of Soviet documentary film—who in those years tenaciously pursued their modest but important work. She wrote:

> What most expressed our era in art? What did the spectator go to see, what did he look forward to, and embrace with particular feeling?
>
> It was the newsreel.
>
> The newsreel. True, it was still a small thing, quite meager, but it honestly and truthfully set down in the record an entire series of historical events of world significance: October, the Civil War, the reconstruction of the national economy, the social and political life of the Soviet Union.
>
> This managed to be filmed, because as a legacy from the cinematic past, we inherited a first-class group of camera operators, who took the lead through mastery in reporting. From the first hours of the victory of the October Revolution, they began to work for the Land of the Soviets, in the name of the Soviet Power of workers and peasants. The names of A. Levitsky, P. Novitsky, N. Kozlovsky, E. Tissé, G. Giber, E. Slavinsky, Yu. Zhelyabuzhsky, A. and G. Lemberg are well known to Soviet film-makers.

All of these camera operators, whose service to Soviet Documentary Cinema is truly difficult to overestimate, filmed their day to their utmost capacity.

Their material was in the hands of Esfir' Shub, and through her, a more ambitious and at the same time polemical vision, took hold. If such masters as Eisenstein and Pudovkin were able to reproduce the history of the country and of the revolution using the method of staging actors,[7] then why shouldn't she have a chance, as a

---

[7] [Trans.]: In the original: методом игровой инсценировки, literally: using the method of acted

confirmed supporter of the all-powerful newsreel, to attempt to enter into competition with them, having demonstrated the possibility of the synthesis of historical facts through the new method of the documentary montage film?

And so arose the concept of *Fall of the Romanov Dynasty.*

For its realization, it was necessary to carry out not only cinematographic, but historiographic research work, requiring not only the possession of the films, but the intuition, the patience of an archivist, an historian, and of a fact-gatherer.

Esfir' Shub went to Leningrad, where, almost accidentally, she managed to uncover the personal film archive of Nicholas II and a great deal of other previously unreleased material.

She remembers:

"Over the course of two months, I looked at 60 thousand meters of film. I selected 5,200 meters. 1,500 meters went into the film.

A whole series of historical documents, newspapers, and objects was shot by me and laboratory treatment of a whole series of shots was carried out."

It would seem possible to be satisfied by this. But that was not Esfir' Shub's character. She found out, that a wide range of valuable newsreel footage, taken during the first years of the revolution, had been sold to America. She was able to buy it and get it back. Within it, some extremely precious shots of V. I. Lenin were to be found.

The film *Fall of the Romanov Dynasty* was released during the days of celebration and had a huge success with viewers, one completely unexpected by the distributors. And to this day, it remains a remarkable example of this hitherto unprecedented genre of world cinema.

But Esfir' Shub was not thinking of resting on her laurels. Right then, she drew conclusions, the significance of which has not been lost even in our own day.

Her appeal for the shooting of more newsreels sounds today more like a cry of alarm:

It is essential to understand, that each piece[8] of a newsreel shot now should be regarded as a *document* for future days. This consciousness should determine the purpose and the content of events and occurrences filmed, the form, the montage, and treatments, the dating of pieces of film. Without material of our days, the future will not be able to understand and comprehend our present.

---

staging or production. In the terms of the era, the critical distinction is made between Eisenstein, Pudovkin et al., the fiction filmmakers and Shub, Vertov et. al, the documentarists, using the terms: игровая фильма [igrovaya fil'ma] (acted film). and неигровая фильма [neigrovaya fil'ma] (non-acted film). I think it interesting to note in passing, that фильма [fil'ma] in the 1920s was a feminine noun. It is now a masculine noun and spelled фильм [fil'm].

[8] [Trans.]: In the original: каждый кусок.

What is more, while working on her next film, concerning revolutionary events —*The Great Way*—she again and again insistently reminded [us]:

> Our cinema, above all, must reflect the greatest historical era, whose
> contemporaries we have the fortune to be. And this can only be done
> on the condition of the systematic accumulation of newsreel material.
> When this is comprehended with sufficient force, then, not in words, but
> in deeds, the technological and material conditions of the newsreel will
> be transformed and normal conditions for workers, innovators, experi-
> menters in the cultural film will be realized.

These truths, which are today obvious, were not immediately recognized. Conflict played out around them, not only with those who did not understand the political and artistic significance of Vertov's and Shub's breakthroughs, but with those who, having reduced their postulates to extremes, complicated the normal development of Soviet Cinema, that is, primarily, with the theoreticians of "Constructivism" (not to be confused with the movement in poetry headed by Il'ya Sel'ninsky, which arose in the middle of the 1920s).

As is well known, the main proponents of factography were in those years associated with the LEF[9] group. But in their practice, they created an odd mixture of the verses of Mayakovsky and Aseev, the prose of Babel, and the theatrical spectacles of Meyerhold and Eisenstein, along with manifestos rejecting poetry, the theater and the novel. The leadership of LEF, who had rejected film production with actors,[10] nonetheless worked as story editors and scriptwriters for the film studios which made feature films,[11] in particular the film factory "Mezhrabpomrus," which was the stronghold of commercial cinema.

But even further left at LEF were the "Constructivists," with their small number of adherents.

Echoes of these theories can be heard in an early article of Esfir' Shub "The non-acted film"[12]: "We don't need studios, we don't need actors, we don't need set

---

[9] [[Trans.] In the original: *ЛЕФ*, the journal of and an acronym for a loosely formed avant-garde group called the *Левый фронт искусств* [*Lefy front iskusstv*] (Left Front of the Arts). The journal ran from 1923 to 1925 and had a second run as *Новый ЛЕФ* [*Novy LEF*] (*New LEF*) from 1927–1929. Contributors included Mayakovsky, Eisenstein, Vertov, Shub, Alexei Gan and other innovative Soviet artists and critics.

[10] [Trans.]: In the original: *отрицавшие игровую кинематографию*.

[11] [Trans.]: In the original: *на киностудиях художественных фильмов*. In Russian, feature-length films are generally referred to as "artistic films," which normally means they are fiction films with actors. Shub uses this terminology, but sometimes uses as an alternate "*большие фильмы*" or "big films," which I have usually translated as "feature-length films."

[12] [Trans.]: In the original: *неигровая фильма*.

designers and property shops, we don't need scenarios. Literary classics teach us nothing, nor do the use of color and the compositional methods of the masters of painting."

But Esfir' Shub quickly understood the ultimate limitation of these slogans, especially when she herself embarked upon shooting material for her documentary-journalistic films. She certainly made use of the entire wealth of artistic culture, taking from it whatever would enhance the political and emotional impact of her picture. For this reason, she later wrote:

> At first glance, my statement that documentary films are not only socio-political, but epic and tragic in form, will appear paradoxical. It is clear which role the artist's design must play, and in the event, it cannot be the tasteful splicing together of shots.

And still later she states with complete impartiality:

> The difficulty with non-acted films is generally the same as with acted films, but in documentary material it is more intensely tangible.
> That is: the lack of precise, dramaturgically intense, efficient development of the action.

Thus, from the refusal of a scenario, Shub came to the assertion of the necessity of dramatic construction[13] in the non-acted film, constructed, of course, according to new principles, proper to this genre.

Through all of her subsequent practice, Esfir' Shub would confirm the correctness of these stances, in time, feeling the necessity of further elaboration and deepening of her method, she entered into collaboration with writers (one good example would be the scenario of *Women*,[14] written by her together with Boris Lapin), and in her graphic decision-making, she began to make use of the entire wealth of the culture of painting, which allowed her to create not a few expressive and pointed compositions.

Esfir' Shub was a genuine poet of the screen. The lyricism of her films, which arose from her deep personal love of Soviet reality, gives her much in common with Mayakovsky, to whom, in this book, she devotes numerous inspired pages. Not entirely by coincidence, when Mayakovsky broke with LEF, and there remained at the head of the journal Sergei Tret'yakov—the talented dramatist and poet, whose theoretical views, however, were circumscribed by the circle of the almost fanatical defenders of the idea of factography—Esfir' Shub also left LEF.

---

[13] [Trans.]: In the original: драматургия. This can be rendered either as "dramaturgy" or "dramatic construction."
[14] [Trans.]: In the original: *Женщины.*

In the journal *Novy Lef* (№ 11–12, 1927) a stenogram was published of a public discussion of the theme "LEF and the cinema." One of the main speakers, Osip Brik, asserted: "The question has been posed concerning what we consider it necessary to do regarding film production.[15] And we say: above all we strive in the cinema for the same thing we do in literary work, that is, to educate people to value facts, documents, and not to value artistic fiction concerning these documents."

S. Tret'yakov said:

> The treatment of material is already its unilateral use. I'm referring to the film *The Great Way*. This is an "acted film,"[16] but there is only one character: Esfir' Il'inishna Shub. Her abuse of discretion is artistic,[17] her selection of material is purely aesthetic, directed so that, by way[18] of the alternation of montage attractions, she achieves a specific emotional charge in the audience… Not so stupid was a remark of one spectator, who, having seen Shub's film *Fall of the Romanov Dynasty*, sympathetically said: "Too bad, there are empty places; they should stage and insert what's needed." This man didn't really care about the authenticity of the material, but he valued the charge the film had given him, and in the name of that charge he wanted to plug up the empty places with inauthentic material.

Victor Shklovsky objected:

> You say: here is an acted film: this is Kuleshov and Eisenstein and a non-acted film is Shub and Dziga Vertov. They were all part of the same group and non-acted[19] Shub studied montage and the acted[20] director studied how to edit newsreels…
>
> So the distinction itself is erroneous, in creating a rule at all.

The disputes of this public discussion reflected in the stenogram became so entangled, and the juggling of terms led so far from artistic practice, that Shub was compelled to intervene:

---

[15] [Trans.]: In the original: кинематография [kinematografiya]. This word, depending on context and time period, can range in meaning from the film industry, film production, the cinema broadly understood, or even the cinematograph, referring to the technical apparatus of motion pictures.

[16] [Trans.]: In the original: игровая фильм, i.e. a fiction film.

[17] [Trans.]: In the original: художественный. Though it means "artistic," he is also playing on the sense of художественная фильма, i.e. a feature-length fiction film.

[18] [Trans.]: In the original: путь, meaning "path," "way" or "means," echoes the title of Shub's film *Великий путь* (*The Great Way*).

[19] [Trans.]: In the original: неигровой: non-acted, i.e. non-fiction.

[20] [Trans.]: In the original: игровой: acted, i.e. fiction.

The entire question lies in what we should film now. As long as just this is clear, the terminology is not important—acted or non-acted film.

However, Shub's intervention was included in the journal *Novy LEF* with such distortions, that she and Eisenstein were compelled to make a declaration of their break with this faction, as had Mayakovsky somewhat earlier.

Of all the LEF theoreticians of that time, perhaps, the one closest to the truth was V. Pertsov, who in his article "'Acting'[21] and Demonstration," included in that same issue of the journal, wrote:

> The concept has spread among many filmmakers, that the non-acted film cannot and must not take as its objective, the imparting to the spectator of a specific emotional charge. Influencing through the emotions is considered somehow appropriate only to the fiction motion picture.[22] As if it were possible without emotion to watch a peasant woman, who has become hardened to the endless wait for the train at Kursk station during the years of devastation (*The Great Way*), as if the spectator doesn't know with whom to sympathize, when he sees a General of the White Guard receiving a bread and salt welcome in Yalta, or Chapaev with his detachment, as if his true class essence were not defined by the direction of this sympathy!
>
> What Vertov was intending to do in *A Sixth Part of the World* and what Shub did in *Fall of the Romanov Dynasty* and *The Great Way* corresponds to political journalism or agit-prop oratorical statements, accomplished in the language of cinema. Non-acted, extra-aesthetic, *emotional* influence is a completely real fact, demonstrated by these pictures.
>
> Why do they consider that the emotion expressed in a non-acted film, thereby transforms that picture into a phenomenon of an aesthetic order.

We have presented these disputes in such detail, in order to make it possible to imagine the atmosphere of the struggle on several fronts, that it was necessary for Esfir' Shub to carry out.

In addition to the theoretical discord in the cinema, difficulties arose once again in mastering a specific language of the screen, as well as new difficulties, such as the problem of the spectator, which, by the way, remains not completely resolved up to the present day.

---

[21] [Trans.]: In the original: "Игра" и демонстрация.

[22] [Trans.]: In the original: художественной картине: feature-length, implicitly fictional film; in other contexts it can refer to a film of high artistic quality, or even feature-length documentary, but unless otherwise specified it refers to a fiction film.

This precise observation by Esfir' Shub might contribute to the contemporary discussion about the spectator, about "intellectual" and "mass" cinema:

> You already possess some kind of culture, when you watch an acted film, it is the culture of the spectator. Unfortunately, this culture does not exist for the non-acted film. And the spectator bears no guilt in this. In this, we are guilty.... Our works must be looked at differently. In them, there is no plot, or story, as there is in an acted film; the material works completely differently... Acted filmmaking is directed for the most part towards the emotions of the spectator, and we direct ours towards his intellect. The viewing of our works should entail not an emotional depth but an intellectual one, only that can afford the possibility of accurately evaluating a picture.

Long before Berthold Brecht, Shub formulated several features of contemporary aesthetics and grasped them not only theoretically, but most importantly, in her practice.

These thoughts she expressed in connection with her next film *Lev Tolstoy and the Russia of Nicholas II*, where she succeeded in creating from very scanty material not only an informative, but an emotional film, in which she set herself the complicated objective of giving an assessment of Tolstoy's philosophy and of his preaching of non-resistance to evil.

She wrote: "So expressive and remarkable are the newsreels of that time, that they alone by themselves express the delusional quality of this preaching and the utter loneliness of Tolstoy."

Esfir' Shub, with characteristic modesty, forgets to say, that it was not only a matter of the singular shots of Tolstoy, but of her talent, which helped her create this genuinely impressive poem about the loneliness of this great old man.

In E. Shub's next montage film, *Today* (1929), the journalistic direction of her gift becomes, as it were, more muscular, intense, pointed. Shub widely, diversely, and courageously draws on material from foreign newsreels and bringing into collision and confrontation shots of the economic and spiritual crisis in America with the victories of Socialist Construction in the USSR, lays out a panorama of the struggle of the two systems, a struggle, about the final result of which, the artist has no doubt, taking up, as always, the position of the struggle, of the Party and of art.

And here, for the first time, in the shots of marches of the Ku Klux Klan, the theme of Fascism appears. From then on, hatred, contempt, the analysis of the historical doom of Fascism, the struggle with it becomes one of the dominant themes of Esfir' Shub's creative work. It reaches its culmination in the unforgettable film *Spain* (1938), where, in collaboration with the writer Vs. Vishnevsky and the composer G. Popov, on the basis of stunning, unique shots taken by R. Karmen and

B. Makaseev, Esfir' Shub creates a cinematic poem about the heroism of the Spanish people.

Shub's important theoretical propositions about the unexplored possibilities of documentary film in the realm of epic and tragic impact, receive practical and inspired realization in this film. They were developed and borne out later, when the entire Soviet People, and with them their art (and in particular the films of E. Shub during the period of the war), were mobilized for the decisive struggle with German Fascism.

But in the meantime, after her film *Today*, Esfir' Shub took the next decisive step from editing documents shot by others, to turning to shooting herself. Her first sound film, *KShE* (*Komsomol: In Service to Electrification*), becomes not only the next expression of her creative principles, but at the same time, a good school for her as an artist. In particular, she carried out a bold experiment, the genuinely innovative significance of which, was only recognized later. Thirty years later, foreign theorists have begun to admire the breakthroughs of the "direct" cinema which uses the synchronous reportage of Leacock and Drew, Rouch and Marker, forgetting about the brilliant experiment of Esfir' Shub, daring with heavy, unwieldy sound and lighting equipment to carry out a synch sound shoot of a factory meeting. This is not a bureaucratic display, but a painful and self-critical dispute by Komsomol youth, wrestling with the deadline for fabrication of a turbine for Dneprostroi; its participants are not posing in front of the movie camera and not yet, of course, factory kids "educating themselves" with the help of a psychoanalytic film interview. Its creative result is the collective portrait of the generation of the 1930s, alive, unadulterated, and for that reason, a very precious account of the unique enthusiasm of the first Five-Year Plans. Shub shot this event without the "hidden" camera method (then not only did this term not exist, but neither did the technology for its realization) and so much the greater is her pure directorial merit, since she did not stage anything, nor "reconstruct" the meeting, she managed to bring it to life as a real, actual fact, and then to record it with the utmost precision and the keen power of observation of a documentary filmmaker.

I had the good fortune to show several excerpts from the film *KShE* during an evening of Soviet Cinema in Ankara, especially arranged for the President of the Turkish Republic, Mustafa Kemal, and the auditorium was over-capacity with representatives of the local community who were seeing Soviet Cinema for the first time.

It was in the fall of 1933, not long after the first visit of the Soviet Governmental Delegation to Turkey.

The program thus consisted of fragments of feature films, such as *Golden Mountains*, *Outskirts*, and *Counterplan*, and I can testify, that the work of Shub made a great impression on the president and the entire audience, not only through the persuasiveness of the facts about the growth of the industrial might of our country, but through the mastery with which the director delineated these phenomena of Soviet reality.

For this reason, it was by no means coincidental, that a subsequent invitation soon appeared for Esfir' Shub to direct a full-length film about the New Turkey. The work was never finished, not because of anything done by Shub, but more precisely, because of the whim of the producer, a wealthy private entrepreneur and the proprietor of a movie theater, who feared a lack of commercial viability for a documentary film.

The later path of Esfir' Shub was not, as they say, "strewn with roses." Since it was necessary for her not only, as in former times, to struggle against the extremely tenacious tendencies of the undervaluing of her chosen genre, but also, the time itself made new demands. For her and for the entire Soviet Cinema, Socialist Art of the middle of the 1930s presented special tasks. They touched, above all, on the singularly important problem of Man on the screen.

Esfir' Shub defined this new stage, as always, with precision, and so these, her thoughts, have not lost their meaning for us today:

> It is now, no longer necessary to prove that documentary film—either historical or contemporary—is an artistic phenomenon, a phenomenon of art. However, not all of us have learned how to film one of our contemporaries in a new way, though only this can alter the monotony of documentary films. The question of the biographical film must be worked out in an entirely different way. It must not only be concerned with those who have passed away, but with those living now. A film about a political figure, a worker, a kolkhoznik, a doctor, a teacher, a person in the arts must be worked out in a different way. I think, that in this direction, only discoveries lie ahead. It is necessary to be bold and then, we will manage to express more vividly our socialist era of today, we will see our culture, art, and nature in a new way.

And that is how Esfir' Shub proceeded in all her subsequent works. Formerly, she encountered incomprehension even among those, it seemed, who were fighting alongside her on the same front; having been forged within the narrow framework of a craft understanding of the newsreel, they did not in any way aid in the creative advancement of this artist-innovator.

In this regard, the discussion published in this book with R. Katsman, who persistently called upon Shub to return to the well-beaten paths of short newsreel subjects, is instructive. Because of this, those then in the administration of the cinema received theoretical confirmation and, thus, did not help Shub realize her extremely interesting project of a full-length film called *Women*.

But the tireless artist persevered at the same time in strengthening her theoretical positions, especially important at that period, when the danger of the over-aestheticization of documentary material, formalistic play with it, became perceptible in the films of western "avant-gardists," not only in the gifted ones, such as Walter Ruttman and Hans Richter, but in the mere charlatans of the type of the White Guard émigré Evgeny Deslau,[23] who released a whole series of short "experiments" where pieces of industrial reality were deformed in abstract opuses, robbed of any social content. Esfir' Shub wrote at that time:

> It is necessary to edit documentary films *simply and in a way their meaning* is clear. A spectator must not only be able to see people and events clearly, but to remember them. Those who love cheap montage effects, should remember, that to edit simply and in a way that meaning is clear is not at all easy, but quite difficult.

What a good lesson for many contemporary would-be innovators, who attempt to hide their lack of thought behind intellectual editing exotica!

And if one of the founders of the "New Wave," the French director Alexandre Astruc, let fly the wingèd phrase (which later became nearly the symbol of belief of contemporary *auteur* cinema) about how the filmmaker should use the camera as a writer does his fountain pen, and "the camera is a pen," then Esfir' Shub quite a bit earlier and more elegantly formulated this thought: "How many unexpected decisions come about, when you are holding the strip of film in your hands. It is just like a word: it is born on the tip of a pen."

Shub dedicates brilliant pages to one of her closest friends, S. M. Eisenstein. She remembers how in one of his lectures he said, you need to edit joyfully, "that one's mental state changed the relationship one had with one montage piece or the other, that it changed one's selection of takes." And she later writes, "He never stopped reminding his students, that shots, which had already been realized in shooting, look completely different than one had imagined they would when you look at them on the editing table, when you take them in your hands... He under-stood better than many others, that one had to approach the practice of art with a pure soul,[24] without deceiving oneself.

That's the way Esfir' Shub, a person with a crystal clear mind, an artist of great talent and principle remains in our memory.

If that first advice, which I heard from Esfir' Shub then, that night at the Goskinofabrika, touched upon the feeling of the piece, what we understood after-wards, was that she possessed a great deal more. It was not only the feeling of the film,

---

[23] [Trans.] I believe the Russian editor has in mind Eugène Deslaw, a Ukrainian filmmaker, born Levhen Slavchenko, who emigrated to France after the Revolution where he became known by this name.

[24] [Trans:] In the original: "с чистой душой." Literally: "with a pure soul." Another possible transla-tion is "with a clear conscience" or "with a clear mind."

but above all the feeling of life, the feeling of everything new, the feeling of truth. And above everything else is the feeling of that Revolution, that made her a remarkable and singular artist of her time.

Part I
In Close Up

1. The bayonet of the Red Army man made it possible

2. To raise the crimson flag of October.

3. Only the bayonet of the Red Army man preserved this banner,

4. It secured the October Revolution for us.

5. Only with the help of the Red Army men, this banner

6. Will we carry until the liberation of the entire world.

7. So, everyone work hard

8. In honor of October at strengthening the message of the army.

A Second Birth
(1918–1921)

The Spring of the Revolution

Moscow is the city of my adolescence and youth. The year is 1918. The first spring after the Great October Revolution.

The sidewalks and streets are full of people. From years of war, the cobblestone streets are heavily damaged. They mercilessly rip up shoes. Everyone goes about on foot. I can't remember other means of transportation, though there probably were. Many happy young voices. We walk until dawn.

Around the clock candles burn at Iverskaya Chapel and on the side wall of the former Moscow City Duma, next to Iverskaya, in capital letters has been inscribed: "Religion is the opium of the People."

Sounds of this song can be heard: "Boldly we go forth to battle for the power of the Soviets…" and workers with rifles march in line under the command of Drill Instructor Vsevobuch.

There are many shops without signs, particularly, where under the double eagle there had once appeared "By Appointment to the Court of his Imperial Majesty."

In a row, in front of the closed shops, stand the "has-been's." They are selling the devil knows what and every kind of food. Young people are not buying. It's disgusting. And besides, there's no money.

Along the cobblestone streets of Red Square, endlessly cart wheels rumble, coachmen, isolated automobiles pass through.

On the site where today the House of the Soviet of Ministries stands, there stretches an entire quarter of single-story hovels. A church rises, having retreated from the sidewalk to the pavement. Opposite, the famous Okhotny Ryad,[1] with shops right out to the sidewalk.

Traveling peddlers[2] scurry about.

On the street lies a dying horse. Isn't it the one Mayakovsky caught sight of and wrote about in his poem "Good relations with horses." Near the horse, a crowd has gathered. There are great ladies in fancy dresses and hats, carrying handbags, a student, a woman wrapped up in a scarf, men in straw hats, and the first couriers for Soviet Institutions, who have stopped for a moment.

---

[1] [Trans.]: In the original: Охотный ряд (Hunter's Row), a street near Red Square, a locale in pre-revolutionary Russia for luxury food shops.

[2] [Trans.]: In the original: мешочники: "People with bags," shuttling between city and country, exchanging or selling food or cheap goods. Shub pictures them in her film *The Great Way*, along with the "has-been's" and the dying horse.

At Nikitsky Gate, there is a ruined house. A vertical hole gapes from the first up to the fourth story. The house stands as a memorial to the battles of October. Memorials to the tsars and generals have been removed from the squares. Alone, forever inviolable, stands the monument to Pushkin. He stands on Strastny Boulevard, great and immortal.

> Renowned shall I be, as long, in this sublunary world,
> As there remains alive even a single poet.

With the signature of Vladimir Il'ich Lenin, a list was published of distinguished people selected to have monuments set up for them in Moscow: Marx, Engels, Pestel, Ryleev, Tolstoy, Pushkin, Belinsky, Mochalov, Komissarzhevskaya… We cherish the belief, that these monuments will be erected and adorn the magnificent prospects and gardens of the new Moscow.

Those were days of hunger in Moscow. Days of devastation, blockades, days of heroic struggle for the power of the Soviets with internal counter-revolutionaries, with interventionists. With unbridled hatred, enemies encircled with a fiery ring the world's first worker and peasant state. Demonstrators often marched through the streets, they carried signs: "Hands off Soviet Russia!" "We are not the Ruhr!" On the squares, meetings take place.

Automobiles scatter leaflets. Pedestrians pick them up.

In the "ROSTA Windows"[3] from October 1919 on, Vladimir Mayakovsky's posters appear. They call out to you to stop. You look and you remember both the drawings and the words. Here is a poster devoted to Party Week:

> If, in answer to the call of Party Week,
> millions come from factory and field,
> workers will prove in deed,
> that a Communist fears no one.

> A grinning skull over the Volga. A laconic title:
> > "In Russia there is hunger."
> Figures of hunger and destruction. The title:
> > "Destruction helps hunger."
> A Worker carries a banner. The title:
> > "Urgent measures are needed."
> A worker with a rifle. The title:
> > The bayonet of the Red Armyman made it possible
> > to raise the crimson flag of October.

---

[3] [Trans.]: ROSTA: Российское телеграфное агентство. The Russian Telegraph Office.

And many others.

That's how I remember Moscow. And in the following years, shots from documentaries have reinforced it that way in my memory. A time of hunger and destruction, a time of intervention and subversion within the country, but also a time of great hope, of great belief in the indestructible strength, courage, and heroism of the People who had risen up and achieved victory, a time of great belief in the genius of the leader of the revolution, Vladimir Il'ich Lenin.

Vladimir Il'ich was always everywhere alongside. Everyone had the opportunity both to see and hear him. On Red Square, before the walls of the Kremlin, he addressed the huge crowd surrounding him: "Comrade Workers! We are going to the final decisive battle." And in answer to these words, into battle went the many thousandfold masses of workers and peasants, who had trained beautifully to wield their rifles. The first army in the world of workers and peasants. The Red Army.

Remembering these days, I always hear the multi-voiced chorus of the song:

The White Army, the black baron
Once again are readying the throne of the tsar for us.
But from the taiga to the British Seas
The Red Army is the strongest of all.
    So let the Red one
    seize with command
    Its bayonet with calloused hand,
    So should we all
    Unbowed
    Go to the final, deadly battle!

I remember especially the Moscow of the spring of 1918, her green squares and boulevards in bloom and fragrant. During these months, there were young people studying: students, male and female, were preparing for their exams. But then, there weren't so many of us, who were preparing for exams. We are all different from one another. For various reasons, not everyone of us can sit attentively for lectures. The street draws us. We are excited. The days go by in passionate conversations.

What are we speaking of so passionately, what are we arguing about, we young girls and women, in light colored blouses, with buttoned collars, with the obligatory hats on our heads?

A Digression (A tribute to my youth):
Moscow Women's Advanced Studies

We studied next to Devich'e Pole,[4] in the building where the Lenin Pedagogical Institute is now located. The Director of Studies was Professor Chaplygin, an enlightened humanist, an advocate of higher education for women. He was treated with universal respect and love.

I personally came to be a student at Moscow Women's Advanced Studies only thanks to him. In spite of the fact, that I graduated from the gymnasium with distinction, my name did not appear on the list of admitted students. I started my studies after the New Year, exceptionally, as the result of a personal meeting between my father and Professor Chaplygin. To become a student in the Historical-Philosophical Faculty was my cherished dream. I decided on the Department of Literature. Specialty: Russian Literature.

We attended lectures on Russian National Literature, both folk literature and *belles-lettres*, from its very beginning to the present day. The Symbolists are mentioned in passing, and, of course, not a word about Mayakovsky. He's a Futurist. He goes around in a yellow smock. But for many male and female students in advanced studies,[5] this young poet, starting out so brilliantly, was *our poet*, the poet of our generation. And we loved to recite his verses aloud.

Besides lectures on Russian National Literature, we were required to attend the following lectures: Introduction to Comparative Linguistics, Historical Grammar of the Russian Language, General History of Literature, Literature of the Renaissance Period, Literature of the Era of the Enlightenment, the History of Greek Literature, the History of Roman Art. In History: the History of Russia, the History of France, England and Germany, the History of New Philosophy, Logic, Psychology, Pedagogical Psychology. Lectures on Literature were given by Professor A. N. Veselovsky, P. N. Sakulin, A. E. Gruzinsky, M. N. Speransky, F. G. de la Barthe and many others. Besides the lectures, we did practicums in seminars.

When Professor Sakulin gave his lectures, the huge auditorium was full to overflowing; he enjoyed a special popularity among the students.

My seminar work, besides a paper on Old Russian Literature, was on Dostoyevsky—his earliest period of creativity, ending with *The House of the Dead*—Heine, and Dante. In the large auditorium, I gave a paper, where I criticized the "intuitive method of Eichenwald." Sakulin commended the work, although, as I now under-

---

[4] [Trans.]: In the original: Девичье поле (Maiden Field).
[5] [Trans.]: Shub's more concise terminology requires explanation. At this historical juncture, а студент [student] is a male student who went to a university and а курсистка [kursistka] is a female student who at the time would not be admitted to a university, but might pursue advanced studies in special institutes for women. From here on I will simply say "male and female students."

stand, it was youthful enthusiasm that was being singled out, more than genuinely considered critique.

My thesis topic was The Pushkin Pleiades. My supervisor was Professor A. N. Veselovsky. Once every two weeks, I would come to see the professor at his apartment. He lived in one of the side streets in the Patriarch's Pond part of the city. The apartment was professorial. He had a leonine mane of gray hair. He had bulging light blue eyes. He was heavy-set and when he got upset, he got crimson red. And he frequently got upset. He was strict and it was interesting to work with him, but I wasn't at ease with him, I didn't feel comfortable.

It went quite differently with the work on the seminar papers with Professor Sakulin and Gruzinsky. We would also go to work with them at home. They were demanding, but we got along more easily with them. We freely shared our difficulties with our work. Conversations proceeded freely and you always left enriched with additional knowledge and a list of books they would recommend as required reading.

The women enrolled in the Courses of Advanced Studies, completing their educations on the eve of the revolution, for me, now clearly fall into three distinct groups, according to their aspirations and tastes.

The largest group did not define themselves politically, but were generally freedom-loving, and I would say, were disposed in favor of the revolution. Having grown up in Chernigovskaya Governate from the age of 13, I remember the estates of the landowners in flames. Along with the People fighting for their freedom, we hated the bloody regime of autocracy, the tsar, his ministers, the ruling, exploiting classes, the aristocracy, the landowners, the bourgeoisie, the Liberal Party of the Kadets [Constitutional Democrats]. We considered the greatest shame of Russia to be Rasputin, his followers, and the Black Hundreds organization. "Purishkevich"[6] was the most offensive word [one could utter].

We greedily seized upon everything that spoke of the decay of this abscess, of underground revolutionary organizations, of the spreading of revolutionary consciousness and of the resistance of workers and peasants. We wanted to do something useful. But at the same time, we rather indecisively recited the words: "Fight for Freedom." How to bring our understanding to the People, how to carry this out was the subject that most concerned us.

In our free time, we never failed, with cheap tickets or sometimes without them (by sneaking in) to attend concerts, literary evenings at the Polytechnical Museum, exhibitions. This enriched, extended, and broadened our understanding.

---

[6] [Trans.] Vladimir Mitrofanovich Purishkevich, a right wing extremist under tsarist rule. His views were ultranationalist, anti-semitic, and tsarist. He played an important role in the violent extreme right paramilitary Black Hundreds movement, known for pogroms and attacks on political protestors.

I would attend the theater very little. I did go to one: the Art [Theater].[7] I cannot forgive myself, that I saw the great Yermolova at the end of her theatrical activity in only one production and that I heard her only once reciting verse. I think that my lack of interest in the theater is due to the fact, that until I was 16, I had been in a professional theater barely once. I finished the Gymnasium in a small provincial town in Chernigovskaya Governate, where there was no theater, and I spent summer vacations at my father's place in the backwoods, thirty-six versts[8] from the railroad. Fairground booths, traveling circuses, puppet shows, the carousel were my only entertainments until my arrival in Moscow. Aside from that, at home I often listened to music: the violin, the piano, singing. And in Moscow, I was, for the most part, drawn to music.

I didn't miss symphony concerts; often I found my way in for free to morning general rehearsals. The concerts of Rachmaninoff and Scriabin were unforgettable. I would attend the opera…

The Art Theater on the eve of the Revolution was in crisis. Besides productions of Chekhov and the plays of Andreev, Goldoni, Turgenev, Dostoyevsky, there were memorable new productions: "Pushkin Spectacles" (*Feast in the Time of Plague*, *The Stone Guest*, *Mozart and Salieri*), *Autumn Violins* by Surguchev and *There Will Be Joy* by Merezhkovsky.

A special mood would come over me from the first moments in the comfortable foyer of the Art Theater. Now, I would see and hear Stanislavsky, Moskvin, Leonidov, Kachalov, Lilina, Knipper. I would now go to see genuine art. Excitedly, my thoughts and heart went to work. I wanted to be better, more pure. And nothing would prevent me from sinking into the mysterious world of genuine creativity. The curtain comes down in total silence. There is no applause. You gaze for a few instants at the white seagull suspended on the theater curtain, then, silently, as if under a spell, you slowly move through the noisy foyer.

For the student-aged population, visits to the Tret'yakov Gallery are obligatory. The Museum of Alexander III, the Tsvetkov picture gallery, the Armory Chamber, the palaces of the Kremlin and the Kremlin cathedrals. We wouldn't miss the annual exhibition of the Wanderers,[9] the "Mir Iskusstvo"[10] [World of Art].

---

[7] [Trans.]: In the original: Художественный: Shub refers by its original name to what became known as the Moscow Art Theater, founded by Stanislavsky and Nemirovich-Danchenko.

[8] [Trans.]: A verst is an old Russian measurement, slightly more than a kilometer.

[9] [Trans.]: In the original: Передвижники [Peredvizhniki], a group of mid-19th-century Russian realist artists, who left the Imperial Academy of the Arts to form a cooperative. The name by which they are known references the traveling art exhibitions they organized of their work.

[10] [Trans.]: An avant-garde art movement with an *art nouveau* aesthetic. Members included Diaghilev, Stravinsky, Bakst, Altman, and Tatlin. They had a journal of the same name. Their interests ranged from Watteau to folk art and puppet theater.

Not without effort, a group of youthful students manages to wind up in Shchukin's mansion. The owner himself is our guide. We walk through an entire suite of richly furnished salons and drawing rooms of the mansion. Shchukin acquaints us with his celebrated collection of paintings by western artists. He converses with us about impressionism, expressionism, about the works of particular artists. Matisse, Renoir, Cézanne, Van Gogh, Gauguin, Toulouse-Lautrec amaze us. All of this is so new to us.

Picasso. He is interesting and not entirely comprehensible. But we don't have the capacity to admit it.

To Shchukin himself, to all appearances, none of this was particularly remarkable. For me, it remains a riddle, why this capitalist, an amateur numismatist, was so passionate about French Impressionism, about left-wing currents in the field of painting. But the main thing was how subtly and with such passion he spoke about the masterpieces in his collection.

What was characteristic of Moscow in the pre-revolutionary era in the area of art? Patronage by a particular educated group of the prominent merchant class. Aristocratic patrons were supplanted by the millionaire merchant Ryabushinsky, the patron of the Symbolists, the publisher of the journals *The Golden Fleece*[11] and *The Balance*.[12] Mamontov spent lavishly on the opera, to put Chaliapin on the stage. The existence of the Art Theater is connected with the name of Savva Morozov. At the "Abramsevo" estate formerly called Aksakov, and subsequently belonging to Mamontov, many outstanding Russian artists worked, such as Repin, Serov, and Vrubel'. Shchukin assembled a world-famous collection of French painting. And alongside this, that same exact rich merchant class promoted in architecture, in painting, in literature and in poetry, the most decadent and tasteless of all styles: the decadent *style moderne*.[13] Then, in our youth, it was difficult for us to understand and explain this phenomenon. Later, while working in the Theatrical Department of Narkompros[14] (TEO), many things in the field of art became newly intelligible to me. It became understandable why precisely in the final years before the Revolution, there prospered a tasteless decadent style, mysticism, eroticism bordering on pornography.

There were very special visitors to the Conservatory and to the Hall of the Nobility (now the House of the Unions[15]). The music lovers came there. The symphonic concerts were remarkable. At one of these concerts, on the parterre, I caught sight of Sof'ya Andreevna Tolstoy. She was in a black evening dress, peaceful

---

[11] [Trans.]: In the original: *Золотое руно*.

[12] [Trans.]: In the original: *Весы*.

[13] [Trans.]: In the original: стиль модерн a transcription of the French *style moderne*. It bears formal resemblance to *Art Nouveau* in France, *Jugendstil* in Germany, "Modern Style" in the UK and "Tiffany Style" in the US.

[14] [Trans.]: In the original: Наркомпрос. An acronym for Народный комиссариат просвещения (People's Commisariat for Enlightenment).

[15] [Trans.]: In the original: Дом Союзов[Dom Soyuzov].

and immersed in the music that had just come to an end. Without hesitating, I came very close and for several minutes did not take my eyes off her. The wife of the great Tolstoy. Thoughts rushed by in a whirlwind. The memories came… "I cannot remain silent." Non-resistance to evil… His flight. Death. Sof'ya Andreevna's suicide attempt. The funeral of Lev Nikolaevich Tolstoy. I was then very far from the thought, that I would make a film about precisely this topic.[16]

One day, during intermission, a young lady approached me. She had a gentle face, sparkling hazel eyes, a charming smile. She was dressed quite simply, in the style current in the capital. "I dreamed about you today. Let's get to know each other. I am Lelya Ertel'." Elena Aleksandrovna Ertel'. The daughter of the writer Aleksandr Ivanovich Ertel'. She was my dear friend for many years.

For a few days, we had conversations—a kind of exploration—on various topics. Because of them, we decided to prepare for exams together. Thus, I found my way into the home of the quiet writer Aleksandr Ivanovich Ertel'.

The entire house bore the stamp of his tastes, his literary connections, and his views. A. I. Ertel' is the author of two great novels: *The Gardenins* and *The Strukovs' Career*.[17] His novel, *The Gardenins*, was impressed upon my memory. It is one of the best novels of the 1880s about post-reform peasant life. Ertel' had an admirable knowledge of peasant life. Lev Nikolaevich Tolstoy highly esteemed this work. He considered Ertel's use of peasant language striking for its fidelity, its beauty, and its variety. This novel, in both its artistic and informative aspects, in my opinion, should enjoy success with Soviet young people as well.

His later years were not devoted to literature, but once again, as he had in the days of his youth, he became an estate manager, this time, for even bigger estates.

The Ertel' family lived at the corner of Vozdvizhenka and Mokhovaya, in the same building, where later, our never-to-be-forgotten All-Union headman[18] Mikhail Ivanovich Kalinin would receive visitors. The entrance to the apartment was on the Vozdvizhenka side. I would go up in the elevator. A maid in a smart white apron with a starched lace cap on her head would open the door to the great entrance hall. I became acquainted with Mar'ya Vasil'evna Ertel'. This Moscow woman was a very capable lady. She looked quite young. It was hard to believe she had grown children. Her eldest daughter, Tat'yana Aleksandrovna, is considered the best translator of Dostoyevsky and Chekhov in England.[19]

---

[16] [Russian editor's note]: E. Shub would begin work on her film *Lev Tolstoy and The Russia of Nicholas II* in 1927.

[17] [Trans.]: In the original: *Карьера Струковых*. Shub slightly misquotes the title. It is actually, *Карьера Струкова* (*Strukov's Career*).

[18] [Trans.]: In the original: Всесоюзный староста: the term refers at once to his role of titular head of state in the late teens and to his peasant origins. Kalinin was one of Stalin's inner circle.

[19] [Trans.]: In England she translated under the name Natalie Duddington.

All the rooms are arranged for comfort. The quality of the bookcases leaps to your eye. They are in every room. This huge library (made up, for the most part, of Russian and English books) was assembled by Aleksandr Ivanovich.

Mar'ya Vasil'evna, her daughter Elena Aleksandrovna and her foster daughter, Elena Goncharova, a student in advanced studies in the Historical Faculty, speak with one another in English. Elena Goncharova is the daughter of a doctor, a friend of Aleksandr Ivanovich, who ended up committing suicide.

My ignorance of English embarrasses me. I'm not comfortable with foreign languages. I study French and German only for the compulsory exams. My embarrassment limits me to Lelya's room; that's how I called Elena Aleksandrovna, just simply as a girlfriend.

A charming room. All of the furniture is covered with thick fabric embroidered with red carnations. A door is open onto the balcony. There is a view of Vozdvizhenka. Opposite, a strange mansion. The building is no longer there. In this mansion was the state archive of the Collegium of Foreign Affairs. The poet Dmitry Vladimirovich Venevitinov worked here; he was one of the most prominent Moscow poets of Pushkin's time and belonged to the group in literature known as the "Young men of the Archives."[20] This was a circle of brilliant and talented young people of Moscow: D. V. Venevitinov, I. V. Kireevsky, S. P. Shevyrev, S. I. Sobolevsky and others. They would meet in this mansion and not just for work. Here, they would hold freewheeling conversations about philosophy, art, politics. The soul of this society was the young poet Venevitinov. Leli and I would talk about him, about his unhappy, hopeless love for the noted beauty Zinaida Volkonskaya. The most outstanding people of the art world of that time would meet at her salon and she herself was a talented singer. Pushkin, Mitskevich, and Nekrasov sang her praises.

> Sorceress! How sweetly didst thou sing
> Of the sticky land of enchantment.
> Of the hot country of beauty!
> How I loved your memories.
> How greedily I attended to your words...

(D. Venevitinov)

...Our favorite game was to recite verses to one another from memory, catching the lines on the run like a ball. Now, my memory for verse is bad. My memory for shots of film has killed my memory for the word. I can remember quite well a composition, a rhythm, movement within the frame.

When we said goodbye, Lelya gave me portrait of Venevitinov. He was very handsome, with the Romantic beauty of youth.

---

[20] [Trans.]: In the original: Архивные юноши.

We prepared for our exam. I would alternate: one day I would work in the Rumyantsevskaya Library or in the library of the Historical Museum. Another day, at Lelya's. Sometimes, I would be at her place every day. Our exams went splendidly.

It was embarrassing to me, that at one o'clock in the afternoon, I should be sitting in the dining room for a formal luncheon and in the evening for a no less cere- monious dinner. There were many people around the table. Three older ladies—one of them was Aleksandr Ivanovich's mother. Guests were the rule; frequently the English people who lived with them. They were professors, students, good acquaintances of Aleksandr Ivanovich (he had lived in England for a long while).

Gordon Craig[21] lived with them when he staged *Hamlet* at the Moscow Art Theater. Lelya showed me an enormous quantity of drawings he did with a single stroke of his hand. They were done in pencil or in ink on small scraps of paper; they were very expressive. This was his pattern: as he went out, he would leave behind notes for the household. These drawings were as easily read, as words. There was a distinctive semantic montage of the drawings.[22]

My ignorance of the English language embarrasses me. I stop coming to the Ertel's. My absence upsets Lelya. After a short time, Lelya comes to me with piteous words and once again I begin to visit them regularly. They are accepting of me and gradually I will come to learn all their domestic joys and the romance of the house- hold.[23] I like Tat'yana Aleksandrovna a lot. She would visit every year with her husband. On her arrival, the house would liven up; it was really interesting to chat with her. Elena Aleksandrovna and I were very romantic and we not only prepared for exams, but would talk about love. Whenever the hour of our intimate conversa- tions would arrive, Lelya in her memories would return to the time when her father was alive, and we spoke about him a great deal. She would recount in detail their trips together abroad.

This is how I imagine A. I. Ertel' on the basis of Elena Aleksandrovna's stories.

This was a man in love with life and possessed of a rare talent for living. Very capable, energetic, strong-willed. He considered creative work the greatest joy of his life. An open heart and a huge imagination were his distinguishing characteristics. He was always in search of the meaning of life. In his youth, he was a believer; he was close to revolutionary young people and ended up in prison. He was friendly with Uspensky, Zlatovratsky, Garshin, Chertkov, corresponded with Korolenko. He was a widely educated humanist, in the range of his views, close to Tolstoy, though never a Tolstoyan. In his time, a strong impression was produced on him by Tolstoy's *A Confession*, though the withdrawal Tolstoy contemplated for himself, close to despair, was foreign to A. I.

---

[21] [Trans.]: A visionary avant-garde British theater director; he asserted, that actors were essentially marionettes in the hands of the director, "the true artist" of the theater.

[22] [Trans.]: In the original: Своеобразный смысловой монтаж рисунков.

[23] [Trans.]: In the original: романтика дома.

Ertel'. He considered that science and art brought benefits to people. He valued the great writer L. N. Tolstoy above all others in Russian Literature. Every word of Lelya about her father breathed tenderness and the unrelenting pain of loss.

One day, Lelya told me, that at the table I would set eyes on V. G. Chertkov. He would necessarily be speaking about god, about truth, about good and evil, and Lelya warned me, that I should be ready to answer him, about how I was preparing for life and for serving people. This was his favorite topic for conversations with young people. It was too late to run. Mar'ya Vasil'evna tried to calm me: "Vladimir Grig-or'evich loves young people, he loves to speak with young people about what you are preparing to do in life."

Lelya, Elena, I, and a student named Agamalov represented youth at the table, but this conversation had apparently taken place earlier for Lelya and Elena.

V. G. Chertkov was L. N. Tolstoy's closest friend. At that time, I did not know about N. Gorky's pronouncements about Sof'ya Andreevna, I hadn't read the memoirs of Il'ya L'vovich and Sergei L'vovich, I wasn't familiar with the correspondence of Lev Nikolaevich, but Chertkov's interference in the personal life of Lev Nikolaevich and Sof'ya Andreevna was widely known, though the main thing, that was widely known was that he was so demanding, he had forced Lev Nikolaevich to make fateful decisions. It seemed ruthless to me to be so demanding towards a person, who was in such a painful mental state as Lev Nikolaevich in the final months of his life. All this had already put me on my guard beforehand.

At the table sat a tall, heavy old man with traces of former beauty on this face. His eyes were bright and cold. His voice was lacking in tender emotions. Vegetarian food was prepared specially for him. He really did ask Agamalov and me questions, to which it was outright difficult, or impossible to respond. All this conversation was very little instructive for the young people sitting around the table. We knelt down before Tolstoy, the literary genius. Tolstoyism and its followers did not interest us. This just didn't excite us then. It was the eve of the Imperialist war. The years of Black Reaction. An orgy of vulgar decadence in art, the poetry evenings of Igor' Severyanin, the infatuation of some young people with the theory of art for art's sake, the first Futurist Manifesto: "A Slap in the Face of Public Taste." Young people were absorbed in reading Leonid Andreev, Sologub, Artsybashev, Pshibyshevsky, Oscar Wilde and Mirbeau. Elena Aleksandrovna and I were also reading these authors. But in the home of A. I. Ertel', the tradition was preserved of reverence before the great classics of Russian and Western European literature, reverence for democrats, for educated people who were not aristocrats.[24] For Gorky and Chekhov. Here, music and painting were strongly valued. And this household played a great role in the formation of my literary and aesthetic tastes.

---

[24] [Trans.]: In the original: разночинец [raznochinets].

I remember, how sad it was for me, when the books and paintings were packed up, the apartment sold. All this was "moved" to a small estate, known as "Ertelevka," in Voronezhskaya Governate. After the October Revolution, Elena Aleksandovna organized a House of Creative Work[25] there for Soviet writers. She later turned over the house and grounds to the administration of the Soviet Writers Union.

And so, the years of my adolescence and young adulthood came to an end. Elena Aleksandrovna remains connected to me through the memories of the exams, the disputes about art and politics, reading verse aloud, walks around the city, where I was always captivated by Lelya's special love of nature, inherited by her from her father, and the happy days in the Ertel' home.

The last thing, that I vividly recall in connection with that house, happened after the February Revolution: Mar'ya Vasil'evna took me with her to the Morozov mansion. This was not a two-story house, peculiar to the architecture on Vozdvizhenka near Arbatskaya Square, but a different kind, alongside them, a one-story mansion behind a grillework fence. We were going to meet Breshko-Breshkovskaya.

We walked through suites of luxurious rooms, furnished with antique furniture. There were many paintings, carpets, cabinets of antique porcelain and crystal. I don't remember everything the gray-haired old lady said. The basic theme was the necessity of fighting to the victorious end. I remember quite well those listening. There were living faces, well known to me from the canvases of Repin and Serov. There were Maklakovs, Korzinkins, Botkins, Chetverikovs, well-known professors, lawyers.

I examined these people with interest, because I understood already quite well then, that I would never catch sight of them again, that this Moscow was passing away forever.

My good friend and fellow student, Nina Kolomeeva, helped me to understand all this. She and a small group of students were sharply different from the general mass. She was older than me, reserved in behavior, but at the same time, kind. Her seminar work was distinguished by its thoughtfulness, its endeavor to interpret all literary phenomena socially and politically, connecting them with the contemporary situation. She was married and breast-fed her infant. I was jubilant when one day during the break between lectures, going out to feed her baby, she took me with her.

She lived not far from where classes were given, on a side street, in the courtyard, in a wooden outbuilding. A large empty room. A wooden table, heaped with books, lecture notes, and right there as well: cups, bread, sausage. Two narrow iron beds, chairs, and a baby, lying in a large oval straw basket. The room was bright, sunny with a freshly washed unpainted wooden floor. Her husband was at home as well as a small group of students, his comrades, in print kosovorotkas[26] and student pea

---

[25] [Trans.]: In the original: Дом творчества [Dom tvorchestva]. A kind of artists' residence.

[26] [Trans.]: A long traditional Russian shirt, reaching down to mid-thigh, with a collar that buttons on the side, worn by both peasants and town dwellers. Also called a tolstovka because Tolstoy wore one

coats. I took advantage of every opportunity to visit them. Often, I happened in upon heated arguments. These arguments carried the stamp of the Prague Conference which expelled the Mensheviks from the ranks of the RSDLP.[27] For the first time, I began to clearly understand the difference between the Bolsheviks and the Mensheviks. Lenin, Plekhanov—these were the names, incessantly repeated in the arguments. As a result, I began once again to re-read Herzen, Dobrolyubov, Chernyshevsky, for the first time I began to read Plekhanov-Bel'tov and was able to gain access to V. I. Lenin. I read *The Manifesto of the Communist Party.*

Conversations with Nina helped me to properly evaluate the significance of the February Revolution, to acquire an ironic attitude towards Kerensky. In the period from February to October, when the party of the Bolsheviks continued its work on the further development of the revolution, Nina explained to me, with an extremely clear logic, why the Bolsheviks were in favor of discontinuation of the Imperialist war, were in favor of a break of revolutionary elements with social chauvinism.

In the February days, I remember myself in the midst of a huge crowd, pressed against the wall of the Moscow Hotel building, opposite the City Duma (now the V. I. Lenin Museum); the crowd moved in an endless stream from the Nikitskaya ulitsa[28] side. A sea of red cotton banners. Red armbands on people's sleeves, red ribbons on people's chest. Many thousands of cries and songs: "Hostile whirlwinds are blowing upon us,"[29] "Arise, you branded with malediction"[30] Impromptu public meetings went on, one speaker continuously replacing the other. Representatives of all the parties would state their views: Kadets, SR's, Mensheviks, Bolsheviks; workers, students, people in military uniforms would state their views.

I remember one unusually warm Easterweek evening after the February Revolution. Holy Saturday. Red Square was overflowing with people. The Temple of Basil the Blessed[31] was open to all. Candles were burning, divine services were taking place. We made our way to the Kremlin, to the cathedral. The square in front of the cathedral was also overflowing with people.

---

in his later years.

[27] [Trans.]: In the original: РСДРП: *Российская социал-демократическая рабочая партия* (Russian Social Democratic Labor Party).

[28] [Trans.]: Ulitsa translates as street.

[29] [Trans.]: This the first line of the "Варшавянка" ["Warshavianka"] ("The Woman of Warsaw") song, popular among early 20th-century revolutionaries. Originally written in 1879 in Polish by the poet Wacław Święcicki while imprisoned in the Warsaw citadel. This line is sometimes translated into English as: "Whirlwinds of danger are raging around us."

[30] [Trans.]: This is the not very literal translation into Russian of the first line of the Internationale: "Debout, les damnés de la terre"; literally, "Arise, you damned of the earth," often translated into English as: "Arise, you wretched of the earth."

[31] [Trans.]: This is the Russian name for the church, known in English as St. Basil's Cathedral, the iconic 16th-century onion dome cathedral on Red Square.

An endless stream of carriages were pulling up, dandified coachmen with fancy open horse cabs[32] on inflated tires, automobiles were rare then. The associates of Kerensky, Milyukov and Maklakov pulled up, in top hats and tails, with them, alongside them, were ladies in luxurious spring fashions, with large hats with ostrich feathers, soldiers, generals with unbelievable plumage on their headgear. They all had red armbands on their sleeves, or red ribbons on their chests. This was the final parade of the future White Guard.

The crowd on the Kremlin square unceasingly moved, made noise, laughed. There was none of the religious tone of previous years. People were becoming different, it must have been, because of all those burdensome years of war for the country.

"Have you been hanging around with your boys without pants again?"[33] That's how my fellow student Zinaida Zikeeva called my new acquaintances. A little about her. She was also a typical figure by which to define one stratum of young people on the eve of the revolution. She was very pretty. If it weren't for her features being a bit too large, one could have called her a real beauty. She had green eyes. Chestnut curls piled up in a knot in classical style. She dressed according to the latest Decadent fashion. A very tight dress outlining her entire body. An open neck and sleeves open to the elbow. She was studying painting. In the midst of the general mass of demurely dressed female students, were some, who by the way they dressed, and especially by the way they wore their hair, scented themselves with delicate French perfume, gazed mysteriously and smiled, resembled Zinaida. Who were they? Many of them came to the lectures in their own private carriages, or in fancy open carriages; some in normal

---

[32] [Trans.]: In the original: лихачи, which refers to coachmen, who would drive a fancy carriage and charge two or three times the normal fee for speedy arrival at fashionable locations where normal cabmen were not even allowed. In current Russian, it means a daredevil, or reckless driver.

[33] [Trans.]: In the original: «Вы опять были со своими мальчиками без штанов?» Here, I believe, that the fashion-conscious Zinaida is alluding to the fact that the young friends of Nina wear kosovo-rotkas, long shirts, which are worn out and go down below the knees, such as might be worn by young boys quite literally without pants. It implies that her male acquaintances were immature, crude and of dubious judgment, ragged and penniless. It also references a phrase meaning either to be "caught with your pants down" or to "end up losing your shirt," only in this metaphor, you lose your pants. It could also be a sarcastic allusion to the Saltykov-Shchedrin short story, "Мальчик в штанах и мальчик без штанов" ("A Boy with Pants and a Boy without Pants"), from a collection of travel impressions called За рубезом (Abroad). It takes the form of the report of a dream by the author while traveling in Germany. The dream is set in a German village. This story then takes on the form of a play, or dialogue, between the boy with pants, an obsequiously well-mannered German peasant boy, who wants to live his life without upsetting his parents or the social order, and the boy without pants, an ordinary rebellious Russian peasant boy, who jumps out of a Russian puddle, that suddenly appears in the middle of the cobbled street of the dream German village. The Russian boy's speech is peppered with lively familiar phrases and contentious comments on the social order of both Russia and Germany. The German boy responds with incomprehension, a defense of German customs and culture, a pointed critique of Russia, and horror at the familiar language used by the Russian boy without pants.

horse cabs. They rarely visited the evening seminar sessions. In the majority of cases, they were the daughters of rich or famous Moscovites. "Decadents" we rightly called them. But Zinaida, who appeared so much like them, lived in a tiny modest wooden house, in the Bozhedomka district. She, her younger sister, and her brother were artists. Their paintings had no content. They were strange still lives or mysterious compositions built up of colorful, heavy dabs of paint with titles, that were no less strange. The room smelled of the fresh tuberoses, which stood on a little table, of perfume and of cigarettes. In the corner was an easel. Their elderly mother fed us food bordering on the beggarly.

Zinaida also loved verse. She loved the poet V. Khlebnikov. She told me stories about David Burliuk. She was a futurist and was in love with the Symbolist Likoardo-pulo, who was on the editorial board of *The Golden Fleece*. She showed me the jour-nals *The Golden Fleece* and *The Balance*.

One day, she took me to the meeting of a literary-artistic circle. It took place in a luxurious mansion on Bol'shaya Dmitrovka. There were a lot of paintings. For a long time, I examined a beautiful painted portrait of the quiet actor and director of the Maly Theater, Lensky. Quite an elegant crowd. Many Moscow celebrities.

What was most memorable in this entire evening was the utterly hysterical statement of the long-haired Berdyaev, who hated everything that signaled the eve of the great revolution. He spoke for a long time and about once a minute would poke out his long fleshy red tongue—not at all "the wise sting of the serpent."[34] All of this frightened me and called forth disgust. Then Andrei Bely spoke. He was young, made violent gestures, had a huge professorial forehead, piercing pale eyes. He was outwardly stiff, but his voice was so wrought-up, that in the upper pitches it reached almost a whistling sound. And each and every word was pronounced distinctly and uniquely. Incisively. He spoke about Symbolism and about his mystical presentiments concerning the coming revolution. I don't remember it in detail, but after Berdyaev, his statement had the sound of a breathing space. It became possible to come back to one's senses, to manage the physical disgust. Bely interested me and it was because I knew: he was a friend of the poet A. Blok.

Somehow, in those years we experienced together: reverence for Pushkin, Tolstoy, love for Gogol, Lermontov, Nekrasov, Tyuchev, Turgenev, Dostoyevsky, Blok, and a passionate response to everything that Maxim Gorky and Vladimir Mayakovsky wrote.

Vladimir Mayakovsky was the poet of our generation. He was us. Our thoughts, our revolutionary aspirations, our lyrics. Reading Mayakovsky and Gorky, we thought about one thing: "A storm! Soon a storm will break out!" And even sooner, let the revolution break out! The great proletarian revolution!

It broke out. It was victorious. We were happy, that there would be no more capitalists and landlords. That workers and peasants would take power into their

---

[34] [Trans.]: Shub is citing Pushkin's poem "Пророк" ("The Prophet").

own hands, that the end had come for the aestheticizers, and what is essential, for the counter-revolutionary intelligentsia. And we argued, what should we do? Should we write our diploma work or go to work, immediately to work...?

The Way to the Choice of a Profession

After the October Revolution, my singular, passionate desire was to work in the field of literature. My course work had come to an end. My end of term exams and seminar work were turned in, only my thesis was left.

I found out, that at Savva Morozov's mansion, at the corner of Vozdvizhenka and Arbatskaya Square, classes were being given for a group of proletarian poets. I headed there carrying my student photo ID card. They allowed me in. There was a formal entranceway, then an entrance hall. A suite of rooms, which had preserved the mansion's furnishings, trim, and the decorative work on the walls, stained glass, chandeliers, the mosaic by Vrubel'. It all bore the stamp of the decadent style. It all seemed tasteless to me, in spite of its pomp, especially in comparison with the appointments of the more moderate mansion that stood nearby, where Mar'ya Vasil'evna Ertel' had taken me.

I open the very first door, because of the voices that reached me. And, to my surprise, I had stumbled upon the class given by the Symbolist Andrei Bely for a group of proletarian poets. No one paid any attention to me. I sat there until the end of the class. All of it was of interest to me: the proletarian poets and everything that the Symbolist-mystic Andrei Bely presented to them in the class about prosody and the ease with which the conversation proceeded. One designation captivated me: "proletarian poets."

I began to attend the class rather regularly, but quickly understood, that for me work was not to be found here. I was not a poet, nor a theorist, nor an art historian. I was overcome with despair.

I decided to go to work in any kind of Soviet institution whatsoever. Unexpectedly, I found out that the Theatrical Division of Narkompros (TEO) had moved from Petrograd to Moscow. Workers were needed there. I wasted no time in heading over there.

The TEO had set up temporarily at the "Metropole." The entrance was located on the side with the monument to the First Printer, not far from the access gate on Nikol'skaya ulitsa.

They spoke with me at length. It was their sort of exam. We talked about literature, dramaturgy, poetry. As a result, they proposed to me, that today I should record in detail at today's meeting, as stenographically accurately as possible, but above all, thoughtfully, the statements of those present.

The poet Vladimir Mayakovsky was to read his play *Mystery-bouffe*. Well-known directors, theater historians, and critics would be in attendance.

I was concerned. Meeting the poet concerned me and the fact that I was going to be listening to him reading his own play. I was concerned about whether I would

succeed in thoughtfully recording the statements by people of diverse tastes, of diverse tendencies in art.

Fall 1918. A warm sunny day. A large room. A writing desk and a small table for conducting the proceedings, chairs along the wall. The noise from the street can be heard. The room gradually fills. I approach and discreetly ask the surnames of those prominent figures of the pre-revolutionary theater who had been unknown to me until this moment.

The directors present are: Nikolai Popov, someone, I don't recall whom, who was one of the directors at the MKhAT [The Moscow Art Theater], Fedor Komissarzhevsky (thin and dark, his face resembling that of his sister V. F. Komissarzhevskaya), A. A. Bakhrushin, S. A. Polyakov, N. E. Efros… Mayakovsky appears. And I mean appears.

Until this day, I had seen Mayakovsky only one time. One day at the Polytechnical Museum, when Igor Severyanin was reading, or rather, singing his "poetry," like recitatives, in the distance, high above the tribune, in front of the door, Mayakovsky appeared in his yellow smock.

> It's good, when in your yellow smock,
> Your soul is bundled up against inspection.

The protest of youth against hateful bourgeois society with its false morality, with its hypocrisy—that's how we understood this then.

The "troublemaker" stood quietly in front of the door. In his yellow smock of cotton cloth, there was nothing picturesque. The shirt was a shirt. He quietly stood for a time, listened, and noiselessly departed.

Now into the TEO came the poet, "mobilized and called up by the revolution," the poet who had created "A Cloud in Trousers," which had brought the great Gorky to tears, the poet, who had created the brilliant poem "Backbone-flute," written with the blood of his heart, a heart that was young, large, romantic, and passionate. Everyone knew his latest poem "War and peace"—an inflammatory protest against the imperialist war.

> People!
> loved,
> unloved,
> known,

unknown,
in a vast procession, pour out those doors.
And him,
free,
I'm hollering about him,
the man—
he's coming,
believe me,
believe!

Only now, we understand, what the path was of the poet in his movement forward, towards revolution, towards socialism and communism, everything forward, to the last hour of his life, a life that's now really forever young. Before our eyes, his step became more firm and he rose up in a spiral to the height of his creativity—so that he speaks in a loud voice to us and to generations to come in the far off communist "distance."

He was handsome, courageous, optimistic. He exuded strength; his way of reading, speaking, defending himself against criticism unacceptable to him was inimitable. His laughter was infectious even when he was extremely sarcastic.

He read the first version of *Mystery-bouffe*. A. V. Lunacharsky, having listened to the entire play at Mayakovsky's reading, defined it this way: "Mayakovsky's first revolutionary play was also the first deeply meaningful and, in the final analysis, the first artistic-revolutionary play."

Everything seemed electric in this revolutionary satire in praise of the October revolution: and a remarkable poetic solution, the monumentality of everything, the devastating wit, and flagrantly bold theatrical innovation.

The responses were cautious, verging on critical. For the most part, they maintained, that the Proletariat would not understand the content; they spoke about the difficulties of bringing it to the stage. A. V. Lunacharsky evaluated it differently: "I saw the impression this thing produced on workers: it fascinated them…" It was curious, that the older man Bakhrushin was entirely in favor of staging this first artistic-revolutionary satire, and Fyodor Komissarzhevsky conducted himself ambivalently: he admired it and resisted it at one and the same time. It is interesting to remember, that in 1921, V. E. Meyerhold[35] arranged a lively public debate about the staging of *Mystery-bouffe*. Mayakovsky recounted what ordeals this play underwent in the course of the two and a half years of the attempt to bring it to the stage. The following resolution was unanimously adopted:

---

[35] [Russian editor's note]: *Meyerhold, Vsevolod Emil'evich* (1874–1940). Theatrical director and actor. He staged V. V. Mayakovsky's play *Mystery-bouffe* in 1918 on the first anniversary of the October Revolution.

We, having gathered together on the 30th of January in the RSFSR First Theater, having listened through to the end to the intelligent and truly proletarian play of Vladimir Mayakovsky, *Mystery-bouffe*, and having recognized its accomplishment as an agitational and revolutionary work, formally request its production in all the theaters of the Republic and its printing in the greatest possible quantity of copies.

87 Communists took part in the voting.

My minutes of the TEO meeting, in which Mayakovsky in the fall of 1918 for the first time gave a complete reading of *Mystery-bouffe*, were approved and I was accepted into the staff of workers of the TEO of Narkompros.

Again, in November 1917, a decree by the Soviet Government was published concerning the transferal of theaters to the leadership of the Department of Art of Narkompros, and in January 1918, the TEO was organized. The general administration of matters relating to theater entered into its activities in wide-ranging fashion. It issued decrees of a general character concerning the management of matters relating to the theater, promoted the unification of all creative and research agencies, organized conferences, contests, courses, public debates.

It was necessary to create a new type of theater, reflecting the struggle of the Soviet Government for socialism, for communism. The theater was called upon to educate spectators conceptually and artistically. The TEO was charged with the preparation of new theatrical cadres.

The TEO was based in a house opposite the Kremlin Wall and Aleksandrovsky Garden. It was apparent, that rich people had lived here earlier. In the large receiving room, we covered the table with green cloth. This was used for the reception of visitors and as a conference hall.

From this room, a door led into the office of A. V. Lunacharsky. From that office, another door led to the office of the Information Bureau. In these three rooms, I spent almost 3 years. Besides me, the following individuals served in the secretariat: the academic secretary M. D. Eikhengol'ts, an art critic and, subsequently, a professor on the Historical-Philological Faculty of Moscow University, the actor Mgrebrov from the Komissarzhevskaya Theater, an expert in the theater and its history, and P. A. Markov a student, who had just completed his studies at the Literary-Philological Faculty and had not yet completed his thesis. He had taken a wide variety of university courses and was passionately interested in all questions related to the theater. He was very young, with a light, unusually quick gait. When he took the floor at meetings, he became flushed and he defended his proposals with youthful fervor.

My work, besides responsibility for the minutes of the nearly daily meetings, included the compiling of materials on the current work of the Moscow and Leningrad sections of the Information Office, for which I was responsible. Materials were summarized and, together with articles by the workers of the section, were transmitted to the editorial staff of the magazine *The Theater Bulletin*,[36] at the TEO. Besides that, it was my duty to prepare for the reception of visitors—directors, actors, impresarios, writers, dramaturgs, who literally filled up the reception room.

At first, it was difficult for me to distinguish whom to admit right away to the TEO management, whom one must not ever admit, and how to determine this. It was especially difficult for me, when V. E. Meyerhold assumed the administration of the TEO. I worked with him for around two years. I was his personal secretary, I sat in his office and, as a result, saw and learned a great deal. Meyerhold was a great artist, an innovator; he worked for the creation of a theater capable of expressing the revolutionary era. He labored around the clock. His achievements and his errors are worthy of the most attentive scrutiny. V. V. Mayakovsky turned over to him the staging of his plays. K. S. Stanislavsky, just before his death, called him to the MKhAT [The Moscow Art Theater].

Vsevolod Meyerhold.

---

[36] [Trans.]: In the original: *Вестник театра.*

I want to recount one event that happened in the course of the daily reception of visitors.

Now, this memory brings a smile to me. This is as it should be: the days of one's youth recall everything, the smiles and the pain. But then, I cried for the whole day.

In the morning, I was warned not to allow any visitors to enter the office: there, they were preparing some kind of report. Everyone had to be made to believe, that there would be no reception of visitors, that there was no one in the office. As ill luck would have it, the reception room was overflowing. Some of the visitors remained all the same, having decided to wait. In walks Vl. I. Nemirovich-Danchenko. As always, exquisitely elegant, with a light, hardly discernible streak of gray in his well-cared-for goatee, on his intelligent face, well known to all of us. He says hello and goes directly towards the door of the office. I start to explain: "Unfortunately, there will be no receiving of visitors and there's no one in the office..." and I stupidly demonstrate to him that the door is locked. In response, I receive his strong, piercing gaze. He turns around, and without saying goodbye, walks out of the reception room. After a few minutes, they call me into the office, and, to my surprise, I see Vl. I. Nemirovich-Danchenko sitting there. It seems, that he knew, as well as I did, that there was another door, leading into the office from the dark hallway. Meyerhold is playing a part... Right in front of Vladimir Ivanovich, I received a thorough dressing down. I was forcefully told, that the door to the office is always open to Nemirovich-Danchenko, that there was always time free for him. And quite a bit more in the same vein. Worst of all, was Nemirovich-Danchenko's exit from the office, of course, through the door leading to the reception room. He said goodbye to me as if nothing had happened. The visitors saw him off with approving laughter, looking at me derisively. Right there, I burst into tears out of the injustice of it all, since I considered, that I had carried out my instructions exactly. Vsevolod Emilevich looked at me kind of sideways and slyly smiled.

I remember one gray day as winter was approaching. It was cold in the reception room. K. S. Stanislavsky walked in. Tall, sturdy. His head was magnificent. Thick silver hair, wide black eyebrows. Some eyes sparkle and almost smile. I cannot tear my admiring gaze away from him and at first, I don't really understand what he is saying to me.

That same day, two very unusual visitors came to the TEO. Fyodor Chaliapin came in. He is dressed up so artistically, that it seems a concert is beginning right now. He sits down and lays his wide-brimmed felt hat on his knee and on top of it, his light-yellow leather gloves. A tuft of light-colored straight hair falls across his forehead. How faithfully Serov portrayed him in his famous portrait! He sits in the waiting room in a relaxed and picturesque pose. You look and you think, "A great artist"; no other conclusion is possible. Earlier, I had listened to him at a concert at the Conservatory. The hall was filled to overflowing with new spectators. How they listened to him! How they took him in! After "Song of the Volga Boatmen" an unprecedented thunder of applause resounded, people called out, they cried out his name. I will never, to the end of my days, be able to understand how Chaliapin could live and die, so far away from the People who so deeply adored him.

The second visitor was Maxim Gorky. I was seeing him for the first time. He was quite cold. He did not remove his overcoat. He was hunched over. His eyes were sad. He coughed frequently and gave the impression of being a sick man. Many years later, I caught sight of him at the First All Russian Writers Congress, and again later—when he had invited a group of Soviet film directors to his house on the outskirts of the city. He appeared healthier and younger than he did on that cold and gloomy day. With him came Mariya Fedorovna Andreeva, who at that time had taken over the administration of Leningrad theaters. Alexander Blok assisted her in this. She was very pretty and looked young, her dark hair was streaked with gold.

What brought all these remarkable people to the TEO in the first years after the revolution? That Department, as well as all of Narkompros, was administered by A. V. Lunacharsky, basing his activities on the direct orders of V. I. Lenin. During those first months, it was difficult for me to understand and to conceptualize why, among the workers of the TEO, there were so many artistic figures of the pre-revolutionary era. The presence of the Symbolists—A. Bely, V. Ivanov, V. Bryusov and others—and the old theatrical critics seemed especially strange. You don't construct the foundation for a new theater with them, I thought. Many years passed, before I could work through

Lenin (left) with Lunacharsky (glasses).

the confusion of my thoughts and impressions of that time. Just then, the figures of the so-called "Left Front" triggered a huge interest in me. It was my thought, that only this tendency in art was capable of expressing the revolutionary feeling of those years. And the standard bearer of everything new for me was Vladimir Mayakovsky. Many young people regarded him as such, among those just beginning work in the arts.

Anatoly Vasil'evich, in conversation with V. I. Lenin, expressed the thought, that the new spectator and the very time were forcing even the most conservative theaters to gradually change, that the change would come about relatively soon, but that to introduce a direct break at this point was dangerous...

V. I. Lenin responded, that it was necessary to continue to follow precisely this line, while not forgetting to support what is new, that is born under the influence of the revolution. Even if, at first, it is weak; in this, one must not take a single aesthetic position, otherwise, an old one, a more mature one on art, will hamper the growth of the new, and the position itself will change, but more slowly, the less it is in competition with youthful phenomena.

How was the TEO structured?

In the beginning, the sections for repertoire and directors were the primary ones. New plays arrived here for evaluation and, here, pre-revolutionary plays and European classics were considered for publication. The Director's section was headed by Evgeny Bogrationovich Vakhtangov. His arrival at the TEO was met with great interest; great hopes were placed upon him. Everyone knew, that he was the favorite student of K. S. Stanislavsky, that his activities as a director, in spite of his youth, were marked by maturity, exceptional talent, and innovation. His personal charisma was enormous. All of us experienced it. A. V. Lunacharsky considered him the most brilliant and promising person in the field of theater in Russia.

"What would one want to work for in the TEO?" E. V. Vakhtangov wrote in his diary:

> 1. The TEO must precisely and with nuance give every type of theater to understand, that their future life is on a path laid out for them: in the best sense, the best, new page of their old life. That the revolution has brought to an end the growth of theaters as they existed up to now. It has, so to say, hewn out new possibilities upon the old, and perhaps, solid tracks; and if they don't want to become "old theater," museum theater, they must *abruptly* change something in their life. Theaters, which by the date of the revolution had managed to reach their culmination, will be put in a museum and will occupy honored places there and in the encyclopedia of Russian art (Small and Artistic Theaters). The ones, who have not managed to evolve, will die.

This means, that it is necessary to give people to understand, that if they want to create the new, they must bury what of theirs is beautiful and old and leap forward once again to create the new. If this is not possible, given the condition of human nature generally, then let them live out their days, let them do what they know how.
2. The New is the new condition of life. One must understand, finally, that everything old has come to an end. Forever. The tsars are dead. The landowners will not return. Capital will not return. There will be no factory owners. One must understand, that we are finished with all that...

Whatever is not overheard in the soul of the People, whatever is not guessed at in the heart of the People can never be of enduring value. One must go to "listen" to the People. One must blend into the crowd and incline the ear of the artist to its pulse. One must gather one's creative strength among the People. One must contemplate the People with one's entire creative being.

No sort of public debates, discussions, conversations, lectures, and reports will create a new theater.

Subtle and daring artists must emerge, who have a feeling for the People. They must emerge from among the People themselves, or they must be People, "who have heard the voice" of god, the People. That is when a new theater will arrive.

It will take time for persons to emerge from among the People themselves. Perhaps, a great deal of time. For this, it is necessary to patiently create sites from which they can emerge. In order for this to happen, if the creators of the new are those who, at the dawn of the revolution, happened to be part of the old art—it will be necessary for them to understand how harshly people lived until then, the beauty of what now is being accomplished for humanity, that all of the old is at an end.[37]

E. B. Vakhtangov did not remain in the Theatrical Department long because of an illness, which ended catastrophically. Nor did the Director's Section exist for very long. In its place, an Experimental Division was organized. The Repertoire section was also abolished and the Workshop of Communist Dramaturgs was created (Moskomdram).

I do not consider it my objective to accurately describe the entire organizational structure of the TEO; I will elaborate on only those sections, whose work I recall most vividly.

---

[37] [Footnote, presumably by Shub, which appears at the bottom of the page with an asterisk.]
E. Vakhtangov, "Notes, Letters, Articles, Moscow Leningrad," Iskusstvo, 1939, p. 199.

The Historical-Theatrical Section. It replaced the old Historical-Theoretical section. It was concerned with the development of issues concerning the history of the theater and the popularization of knowledge in that area, studied archival materials, and developed a working plan for theater history. N. E. Efros, A. A. Bakhrushin, S. A. Polyakov, P. A. Markov and others took part in the work of the Historical-Theatrical Section. I. G. Ehrenburg briefly worked in the TEO at Narkompros.

The most colorful figure was A. A. Bakhrushin, previously a rich Moscow merchant. A tall, erect old man, with an intelligent, stern gaze. A passionate theater-goer and a subtle judge of Russian theater, he created a theatrical museum, famous not only here but in the entire cultural world. This supremely rich, interesting museum was his entire life's work; it now bears his name. In February 1919, by the decree of the Soviet Government, the administration of this museum was transferred to the TEO. By the direct order of V. I. Lenin, Bakhrushin was named director of the museum for life. Aleksei Aleksandrovich was won over by frankness and spoke freely and famil-iarly with anyone, regardless of their position. He was outwardly severe and exacting towards himself in the fulfillment of his responsibilities; he was just as exacting towards his closest comrades at work. His stories about the past of the Russian theater, about the luminaries of the stage were laconic, but interesting, especially when he would eval-uate the artistic and educational significance of the theaters of the past. He treated with interest everything new that the revolution had brought into the field of the theater. He was one, among the first who heard *Mystery-bouffe*, to highly esteem its innovation. His outward severity concealed a person who was kind, attentive, and sensitive to those around him. I know that well from personal experience.

The Symbolist poet Vyacheslav Ivanov was an interesting individual to observe. His first wife was the writer Zinoveva-Annibal. In Petersburg, in their apartment, various groupings of Symbolists and religious seekers would cross paths in literary disputes. His verses were rationalistic and polished and carried the stamp of mystical anarchism and decadent Hellenism. He was widely educated. He spoke with a profes-sorial dispassion, with a bit of a feeling of superiority over his interlocutor. V. Ivanov seemed to me estranged from, or at best, indifferent to the events of the revolution. I can't forget, how in the presence of a rather large group of co-workers at the TEO, he read verses, dedicated to an individual lady, who had some influence on the business of theatrical art.

Here is a line from that poem: "…the profile of a Borgia proud"… In those years what a madrigal that was![38] After that, I could not refer to him except by saying "the profile of a Borgia proud." His person was best suited to the Catholic cassock, in which he finally ended up attiring himself, when he received the promotion, it seems, to Vatican librarian. Mystical anarchism, Hellenism, and the Roman Pontiff! All at once…

---

[38] [Trans.]: In the original: мадригал. "Madrigal" implies a love poem of excessive refinement dedi-cated to an individual lady.

In 1919, the Department of Workers and Peasants Theater was established. It was to help worker and peasant theatrical circles and to awaken interest in theatrical creation through the organizing of productions and lectures. In essence, it was the beginning of the amateur performances, now so widely practiced. A. V. Lunacharsky responded rather critically to the results of the work of this department. He considered, that for a theatrical performance you needed a professional actor and, of necessity, a talented professional giving his entire effort, all of his time to the mastery of acting. Otherwise, the results are amateurish. From his point of view, this department should have given greatest attention to folk choral and song performance and to the development of circles for folk dance. A section for mass performances was also created. Here, plans were made for the realization of popular mass celebrations—the joyous First of May celebration, the great Anniversary of October, tree planting ceremonies, and others. But plans were also made for monumental mass spectacles in the open air, in which professional actors, singers, orchestras and choruses would take part. This necessarily involved a systematic attempt at the inclusion of the mass of spectators in the course of events. The work of this section ran more to research and had no tangible practical results, except for a few mass productions, among them, the extremely well known "Storming of the Winter Palace" performed on Palace Square in what was then still Petrograd in the fall of 1920.

On the other hand, the Circus Section was highly effective. The circus was and remains the favorite spectacle of the broad popular masses. And this is understandable. The daring, supreme dexterity, and the expressivity of the bodies of acrobats and gymnasts are beautiful and give great pleasure. The precision of the work of the jugglers and the strictly calculated movements of the vaulters give delight; the attractions, humor, the "popular jokesters"—the clowns— call forth an instant response. The elegant equestrians, the colorful circus costumes, the bold greasepaint, the ceremonial entrance parade[39] of the performers, pantomime—the spectator responds noisily and enthusiastically to all this.

The Moscow Circus, at that time, could boast of wonderful performers, who were born and raised in the circus arena, acquiring their mastery from their parents. One could say, that the circus possessed celebrated dynasties of circus performers, who spent their entire lives in lively communication with the popular masses. Sharp social criticism, sometimes politically pointed, would resound in the arena of the circus, even during the blackest days of reaction.

The Circus Section was charged with the supervision of circus matters for the country and the construction of new circuses, working out model circus programs, carrying out the nationalization of all circuses in the republic. It was the duty of this section to supervise the Central Administration of the Moscow State Circuses. This

---

[39] [Trans.]: In the original: парад-алле, possibly from the French, "parade allée," or "parade, allez."

section was also charged with the education of new cadres and the creation of short satires with a political resonance and new revolutionary humor.

The section was headed by N. S. Rukavishnikova, the wife of the poet Ivan Rukavishnikov. She was extremely young. Tall, statuesque, with a head of black hair on a short neck, elongated gray eyes, with thick, downy eyelashes. She had a large mouth with a strange smile on her wide face. They said, that she had spent her childhood and youth in a traveling circus. The poet Rukavishnikov took her away, at the age of sixteen, to his estate on the Volga. She was taciturn. She knew by heart almost all of Rukavishnikov's poetry as well as the poetry and the plays of A. V. Lunacharsky. She considered them works of genius.

She had a strange way of listening: inclining her head a little to one side and quietly swaying her body in time to the words of her interlocutor. She had enormous power over animals, almost hypnotic. She fearlessly picked up young tigers, lions, and bear cubs. Dogs and cats would cling to her. She would bestow her love on white rats. But she especially loved horses—they were her friends. Greeting them, she would kiss them, stroke them; she rode beautifully. She would spend whole days and nights at the circus, often ignoring the working hours of the section. In order to keep things going, meetings of the section would be transferred to the circus building. This building is no more—its site is now occupied by the Theater of Satire.

In addition to my other work, I was named Executive Secretary of the Directorate of Moscow Circuses. It was my duty to be present once a week at a meeting and once a week to be on duty at one of the evening performances (all the members of the Directorate did this). In this way, through me, precise information would be collected about the activities of the Moscow Circuses, to which V. Meyerhold attached so much significance.

From my childhood, fairground booths, the circus, Petrushka (the puppet theater) have been my favorite things to watch. Working in the circus for me was completely fascinating. A relation of comradeship was established with my circus performers. I loved Vladimir Durov. Coming into the TEO and sitting down in order to speak with me, he frightened me, when he let loose on the table a white mouse called Mashka, which he had brought with him inside his shirt. He tried to explain to me, how untruthful the usual representations of mice were. He himself found them intelligent and clean. All the same, I was wildly frightened and he did not inspire love in me. His stories about beasts of prey and other animals were not only interesting, but instructive. Vitaly Lazarenko was a wonderful clown. In performance, before an audience, a clown always had either his face dusted with white power and wore a clown costume, or wore a red clown wig. Vitaly Lazarenko would appear in makeup, which gave his face the look of rose-colored porcelain, and the straight, black, bushy outlining of his eyebrows gave him a lively youthful appearance. Handsome in a colorful costume based on drawings by Boris Erdman, he drew the enthusiastic applause of the spectator from the first moment of his appearance in the arena. The young clown Dmitry Al'perov (who performed with his father), the musical clowns the Brothers Tanti, and many others were very good.

It ended up, that Nina Rukavishnikova and I decided to write a circus panto-mime, in which all the best circus performers would take part, performing their best acts. People liked it. P. A. Markov praised this production in *The Theater Bulletin*.

Who were the most outstanding individuals working at the TEO?

The majority were representatives of the old Russian intelligentsia. Thanks to the skillful policy of the Soviet Leadership, the best of those working in art before the revolution remained in Soviet Russia; they worked with great interest and transformed themselves before one's eyes. Of course, there were also some very painful exceptions.

In these cold and hungry years—years of destruction, when factories gaped with emptiness, when profiteers and bloodsuckers did their black business—in Moscow an unprecedented number of public debates, discussions, and conversations took place.

Theater attendance was huge. There were days, when in Moscow six Shake-spearean plays were running at the same time and, on the outskirts of the city, in workers' theaters, the great Yermolova was appearing on stage (her name, at that time, was already legendary). She was the pride of Russia. In 1920, V. I. Lenin was at the Maly Theater at the celebration of Yermolova's 50th year of theatrical activity. The awarding to her of an official rank was announced that very day. She was the first person to receive the rank of People's Artist of the Republic. Excerpts from the third act of *Woe from Wit*[40] and the scene of the two queens from *Mary Stuart*[41] were performed. Sadovsky, Yuzhin, and others were appearing at workers' theaters. The new spectator—especially the popular spectator, not having attended the best theaters until the Revolution—eagerly familiarized himself with theatrical culture. A. V. Luncharsky, carrying out the directives of the Party, made every effort to meet the cultural demands of the revolutionary spectator. Dialogue with outstanding personalities of the pre-revolutionary theater greatly aided in this.

Theaters were subsidized by the State. At the beginning, performances were announced as free. Tickets were not sold, but distributed at Moscow plants, facto-ries, and institutions. Passes for performances were produced at the TEO. It was my responsibility, though not for long, it is true, to see to it, that they were prepared in the appropriate quantity and properly distributed. The tickets were printed using typewriters on long narrow sheets, with an indication of the production, row, and seat number. A stamp with my last name was prepared and it was put on mechanically at the end of the sheet. But it was discovered rather quickly, that it was very easy to fake my signature—and several spectators would turn up for the same seat. After that, some conventional sign was adopted—which one, I no longer recall.

---

[40] [Trans.]: by Alexander Griboyedov.
[41] [Trans.]: by Friedrich Schiller.

A . V. Lunacharsky attempted to preserve the theatrical heritage of past years and attentively, as they said then, maintained a respectful attitude towards state theater. However, everything new in the field of theater elicited great interest and support from him, especially if a new phenomenon found a response with the broad popular masses.

In these first years after the Revolution, a full variety of artistic tendencies took shape. All the disputes around the theater, the struggle for this, or that objective were concentrated around the TEO. It is not my objective to give a detailed critique of the tendencies that took shape. Historians and theorists of Soviet theater have studied this and continue to study this. I will limit myself to a brief overview.

The most widely held point of view, having affirmed that it was necessary to preserve outstanding pre-revolutionary theaters—their culture—found it indispensable to integrate these theaters into the new objectives that had arisen from the new conditions.

In reality, The Bolshoi and Maly Theaters in Moscow, the Marinsky and Aleksandrinsky in Petrograd were theaters of enormous artistic value. The theaters were connected with the great names of Shchepkin, Yermolova, Glinka, Mussorgsky, Tchaikovsky, Borodin, Chaliapin…

In each one of these theaters, a directorship was appointed. It was comprised of the principal group of creative and technical workers. They were given the right to direct the internal life of the theater. By special resolution, these theaters were transferred to direct administration by Narkom Education,[42] that is, by A. V. Lunacharsky. That, in itself, provided for the full preservation of the theaters and wide possibilities for their work.

Just think about it! In the severe winter of 1919, in the midst of a brutal fuel crisis, at the meeting of Sovnarkom,[43] the matter of heating state theaters was presented.

Even the MAT[44] was included in this group.

In these years, the MAT lived through many difficult days. There was no fuel. None of the former personal comfort, cleanliness. The new spectator was troubling. K. S. Stanislavsky said, that they "found themselves in a helpless state with the kind of masses which had flooded into the theater."

The new spectator imperiously presented the theater with the question of revisions to the repertoire. The new spectator needed to be won over with the same force

---

[42] [Trans.]: In the original: просвещения, which can mean either education or enlightenment.

[43] [Trans.]: In the original: Совнарком. An acronym for Совет народных комиссаров (The Council of People's Commissars), the highest executive authority in the Soviet Union. Their decrees had the force of law. They were responsible for the general administration of the State, responsible only to the Congress of Soviets.

[44] [Trans.]: The Moscow Art Theater.

with which the spectator—for the most part, the intelligentsia—of the pre-revolutionary period had been won over.

The revolution put questions of enormous importance before The [Moscow] Art Theater. Here's approximately how A. V. Lunacharsky conducted his conversation with V. I. Lenin on the [Moscow] Art Theater:

> I remember quite well the day and the time, I ensured that the MAT— a private enterprise—would not longer exist as such and that it would be transformed into a state theater... Vladimir Il'ich, although he thought there should be nothing surprising in my asking for his instructions in the matter, was just amazed: "How could it be otherwise? If there is any theater from the past, which, at any cost, we should save and preserve, this, of course would be the MAT."

In spite of the fact that the [Moscow] Art Theater, in the eyes of Lunacharsky, possessed enormous merits, his favorite theater was the Maly and he treated it preferentially. He considered, that the Theater of Griboyedov, of Gogol through to Ostrovsky was nearly the only actors' theater and he maintained, that proletarian theater should begin from the technique of the Maly Theater.

A. V. Lunacharsky would reproach the [Moscow] Art Theater for its aestheticism, for its predilection for Symbolism, for Impressionism. But at the same time, he always underscored, that this theater distinguished itself by its artistic conscientiousness and that Stanislavsky reached artistic heights in everything. He said, that the [Moscow] Art Theater was the theater of Chekhov. And he considered Chekhov, in spite of Chekhov being a sophisticated writer, to be a capitalist. Besides that, in my view, he didn't like Chekhov as a dramatist and considered him a dramatist of the "twilight era." He said that at the [Moscow] Art Theater, only the productions of Dostoyevsky were remarkable for their gigantic force. And, besides that, he maintained, that in all its activities, the MAT was distant from the inner culture of the People. But Stanislavsky he considered a genius and found the sophisticated taste of Nemirovich-Danchenko and the actors to be amazing. And at the same time, he would reproach the production designers[45] and actors for the "imitation of life."

The so-called left front was concerned with the new tendencies of the time, at the head of which was V. E. Meyerhold. The strongest tendency was the group of theater figures called "Theatrical October."

Here are a few of their slogans:

---

[45] [Trans.]: Here the word постановщик is used, implying the person responsible for staging, rather than режиссер, which, can encompass both that function and the directing of actors. In practice this could easily be the same person.

October of the Arts is the overcoming of the hypnotism of false traditions, which conceal their rejection of new forms, of harmful stagnation, and frequent hostility to the principles of Communist construction.

October of the Arts is the struggle with hackneyed pedantic traditions, which violently drag the proletariat into the captivity of the ideology of feudalism, serfdom, and the bourgeosie.

October of the Arts explicitly establishes a Marxist approach to the arts in the field of its relations of production.

October of the Arts is the research of forms for the vulcanizing content of the contemporary.

In practice, this came down to the following: 1. The left front completely rejected pre-revolutionary theatrical art. 2. It rejected the continuity of art as a whole. 3. The left front, first and foremost, set itself the objective of abolishing state theaters; it considered that these theaters were not able to reflect the new, revolutionary era and that, in their very essence, were incapable of creating revolutionary art.

It got to the point, that at a meeting of Sovnarkom, it was proposed by someone that the Bolshoi Theater be closed. The statement of V. I. Lenin, that the heritage of bourgeois art should be placed in the archive early, determined the failure of this proposal (this is well known from the statements of P. Lepeshinsky).

Here are some remarks of Lenin on this question recorded by Klara Tsetkin: "Why is it necessary for us to turn away from what is truthfully beautiful, to reject it as a point of departure for further development, simply on the basis that it is 'old'? Why should we prostrate ourselves before the new, as if before a god, to which we must submit, simply because it's 'new'? This is nonsense, utter nonsense! Here, there is a great deal of hypocrisy and the unconscious obeisance to artistic 'fashion,' that reigns in the West."[46]

What was characteristic of "Theatrical October"? Before all else, the search for pure form, theatrical spectacle, a Constructivist treatment of the platform[47] (as the stage was called), an enthusiasm for biomechanics. An almost acrobatic mastery by the actors. An approximation in theater to the dynamics of the cinema, to the attractionality[48] of the music hall. The director did away with the curtain and, before the eyes of the spectators, temporary wooden constructions were rigged instead of sets. It was preferred, that the actors do away with make up, replacing it with burnt cork, and instead of expensive costumes, they worked in industrial uniforms,[49] colored with

---

[46] [Russian editor's note]: Cf. "Lenin on Culture and Art," Moscow, Iskusstvo, 1956, p. 520.

[47] [Trans.]: In the original: площадка [ploshadka].

[48] [Trans.]: In the original: Аттракционность . One could say "attraction," but аттракцион [attraktsion] exists as a separate term, notably in Eisenstein's монтаж аттракционов (montage of attractions).

[49] [Trans.]: In the original: Прозодежда [Prozodezhda]. A Soviet Era neologism, a portmanteau word combining "production" "Произведение" [Proizvedenie] with "clothing" "одежда" [odezhda]. Vavara Stepanova was a leading designer of this clothing for industrial and theatrical use.

aniline dyes. Worst of all were the imitators of these currents. Among them, were a great number, whose work bore the stamp of the decomposition of bourgeois art on the eve of the Revolution.

The first spectacle to be realized of this tendency was *The Dawn* by Verhaeren.[50] Some were delighted, others irritated. It underwent Party criticism. N. K. Krupskaya wrote in *Pravda*: "A wondrous folk tale has been transformed into a vulgar farce—all the charm of *The Dawn* has disappeared."

In that brief period, when the administration of the TEO was headed up by a representative of the LEF tendency—Meyerhold—the attack on State theaters was conducted with a great deal of energy.

Here are some of the arguments that were advanced first: the time and the material conditions of the country dictate the rejection of lavish, costly staging. And the fundamental thing was that all the art of these theaters was archaic, it bore the stamp of the decomposition of the aristocratic and bourgeois classes and was unnecessary to the revolutionary, victorious People. Subsequently, the figures of this tendency themselves returned to costly and luxuriant forms of staging, to the classical repertoire, to leading roles for actors on the stage. Right then, the meetings on these exciting questions were transferred from the TEO directly to the theaters. The attack and defense took place in an extremely excited atmosphere.

I remember, we were returning after a meeting at the Bolshoi Theater late at night. V. E. Meyerhold and others, who were with him, were walking arm in arm, shoulder to shoulder, forming a wall, in order to stay a bit warmer. We were walking in the middle of the pavement, because there was so much ice, walking on the sidewalk was dangerous. We were all in knee-high felt boots, wrapped up in kerchiefs and warm scarves; the majority of us were going to cold apartments. But we felt lively and cheerful. In cold and hungry Moscow, as in the entire country, which the Interventionists and the White Guard were ripping to pieces, laughter could always be heard. It seems to me, that people never laughed with so much youthful enthusiasm, or so contagiously, as in those years, that there were never so many laughing, happy faces in theaters, at the cinema, in the crowds of workers, Red Army men, and young people.

The implementation of the liquidation of the State theaters did not proceed. Lunacharsky personally took charge of them. He was given every resource for creating the best conditions for the strongest of the theaters, outstanding in their cultural and artistic accomplishments. He endeavored to carry out Lenin's fundamental directives, he avoided crude authoritarianism in the administration of art, preserving the cultural heritage of the past, while at the same time, aiding in every possible way every genuinely new phenomenon in the field of theater.

---

[50] [Trans.]: *Les aubes* by Émile Verhaeren, Belgian poet and playwright (1855–1916). The original in French and the Russian translation is in the plural.

Now, of course, this occasioned visits to the TEO by Stanislavsky, Nemirovich-Danchenko, Bryusov, Chaliapin, Gorky, Adreeva and many other outstanding figures.

In this connection, I would like to speak in more detail about A. V. Lunacharsky and Narkom Education. I will try to resurrect his image in my memory, as I was able to observe him in the course of the first three years after the revolution. He was a Russian revolutionary of the intelligentsia, a man of encyclopedic education, an outstanding orator, dramatist, researcher, and journalist. His aesthetic tastes were famously polemical, but quite well established. He possessed a great gift: his knowledge in the field of art, and it was vast, which he communicated both in abstract terms and in terms of emotional coloration.

When he took up the task in earnest of administering the theaters, at the request of his fellow-workers at the TEO, he addressed the issue: "What purpose does the theater serve."

This was a wide-ranging presentation. He began, at a great remove, with Dionysian Festivals. These festivals laid the foundation of the great Greek tradition. He analyzed in detail the great creations of Aeschylus, Sophocles, Euripides, Aristophanes. He, then, went on to the Middle Ages, to the Mystery Plays, to the Spanish Theater of Lope de Vega, Calderón, to the theater of Shakespeare, Goethe, Schiller, Hugo; he ended with the productions of Griboyedov, Gogol, Chekhov, Gorky. He maintained, that as a playwright, Gogol had two souls: one was Romantic—hence his love of romantic fairy tales; the second soul compelled him to write the brutal truth about reality. He spoke about all this in detail, because he considered that we needed to know this.

He ended his presentation by specifying which paths were leading towards a new theater. He attached enormous importance to studio practice; he considered, that by means of studio training, remarkable results could be achieved, that there, the *new* actor would be born. A proletarian knows quite well, that "the affairs of the master are to be feared," and loves nothing so much as mastery. A new dramatic art, with new content, reflecting the great events of our days, the new actor—in that, he saw the beginning of the construction of a new theater.

He often repeated and deeply believed, that the Proletariat assigned its intelligentsia on the Front of Art the task of creating a new theater, together with progressive figures from the old theater. In any case, mass open-air pageants were not the prototype of the future. It was imperative to know the history of human culture, the old classical repertoire—this would lead to knowledge.

Anatoly Vasil'evich was very accessible, kind, and skillful at listening with interest and at the same time observing his interlocutor. But there were days when he was distracted and cold.

He had a very developed sense of humor. Subtly observing a person's internal beauty and gifts, he would make comical remarks. With a single short phrase, or sometimes with a single word, he knew how to delineate one, or another impression of his, giving his observation the form of an unexpected and brilliant summing up. He was especially sharp at observing how the behavior of a person was dictated by his collision with the constraints of his circumstances.

On several occasions, I was at his apartment in the Kremlin. At the common table, Anna Aleksandrovna, his wife, would always very persistently feed me, by the way, very rich food. At that time, the family of their friend, G. V. Kristi, lived with them. Now, their son Leonid Kristi is a talented film director, my younger comrade at the documentary film studio. At that time, he was a little boy with big, sad eyes, quiet, especially side by side with another little boy, the handsome, noisy, and brilliant Anatoly, son of Lunacharsky. Anatoly fell in battle on the front in the Great Patriotic War.[51]

I always left with a large package for my dear little daughter. This was always done with such tact, that it was impossible to refuse.

I remember one story from a dinner table conversation, a brilliant impromptu story by Anatoly Vasil'evich, about Felix Dzerzhinsky. One apprehended the figure of Felix Edmundovich by attending to the sum of his inner beauty. While, at that time, one didn't utter the words "knight of the revolution," this flowed out from what was said, as the most accurate characterization. These unspoken words resounded in the entire subtext of his story.

The evening is vividly imprinted on my memory, when the Lunacharsky family took me with them to see Comrade Tsuryupa. In his apartment in the Kremlin, some fifteen or twenty people were gathered. In a large room, with a low ceiling, we sat in a semi-circle around a grand piano. Meichik, the pianist, played. That evening, he played splendidly. Others appeared on the program, but my memory does not preserve their names. What was preserved is only that feeling of extraordinary immersion in the music. I remember how those present gave themselves up to the magical force of the sounds. But in me, this feeling sparked an awareness as well: What people these are! What a huge responsibility to the country, what intense daily occupations and this capacity to immerse themselves in the world of sounds, in the world of the most emotional art, how much I valued and even now value music.

I will always preserve in my memory the sight of the Kremlin covered deep in snow and snowdrifts. Its majestic beauty and silence, I would say its calm, during these days that were so harsh for our people. And the special excitement from knowing, that I was in the Kremlin, where Comrade Lenin was living and working. Vladimir Il'ich. Il'ich. How simply and lovingly the entire Soviet People would utter his name.

He was always somehow close by. Knowing, that he was putting in an extra work day on Saturday, we considered ourselves morally obligated, we considered it our patriotic duty to put in an extra work day on Saturday. In those working Satur-

---

[51] [Trans.]: World War II.

days, V. I. Lenin saw the factual beginning of communism. He considered, that only in laboring together with workers and peasants could we be real communists.

He laid the cornerstone of the monument to "Emancipated Labor" and, on that same day in Sverdlov Square, the monument to Karl Marx. Crowds of workers surrounded his car. Their hands stretched out to him found a handshake in return. He saw off to the front the Red Army men in Red Square. He spoke from the balcony of the MosSoviet with the many thousands in the hushed crowds. He went regularly to the factories, he found time to meet with the members of the Komsomol, with students from Vkhutemas, to attend the theater, where Yermolova appeared.

All the decrees signed by him, all the articles, all the words spoken by him were the shining sun of our youth; they awakened an inexhaustible belief in the victory of the great achievements of October.

I remember with what trepidation I accepted the call for Lunacharsky to the telephone for a conversation with Comrade Lenin. The telephone of the TEO was located in the information section above my desk. I quickly cleared out everyone from the room. I didn't walk, but ran for Lunacharsky. The enormous feeling swept over me that here, to us, the workers of the TEO, Comrade Lenin had come; that he had found the time for this.

After [several] such calls, an entire series of critical decisions concerning the theater were made.

During these years of my life, the most joyful event came to pass. I had the great fortune to happen to be present at the Bolshoi Theater for a speech by V. I. Lenin. The main hall of the theater, as always, was magnificent in a festive way and noisy with excitement. From the overflowing loges of the upper tier, the stage was perfectly visible. All around were new people, looking not at all like the spectators, who had attended this theater before the revolution. The eyes of those seated never left the stage, fearing they might miss the first instant of the appearance of V. I. Lenin. And indeed, this appearance was sudden and dazzling because of the rapture of the greeting, which filled the hall like a storm. Lenin moved to the front of the stage swiftly, extending his hand several times, trying to stop the storm of sound, then silence came. It was the first time in my life, I heard such a silence: a collective silence with breath held, a silence ringing with the utmost collective attention. Lenin spoke, throwing his head back somewhat, rather loudly, moving in a limited area around the front of the stage. His coat was open and his fingers were laid along his vest, at the sleeve. His head towered above his somewhat short, agile body, with the huge brow of a philosopher, marked by genius. At moments, through a narrowed gaze, the watchful eyes of an exceptional mind would shine with a smile. In return, the faces of those listening would light up with happy smiles. Everything about him was, quite simply, great. Titanically vast. It seems to me, that they not only were listening to him, but were drinking in his words, for the ages. He was joined with each one of them. He was in them. He and his listeners were as if a single entity. As for me, this was the happiest day of my youth, because of the feeling of joy and from the consciousness of my second birth.

Many have found, that Lunacharsky showed excessive liberalism, a spirit of conciliation towards the left front in art, but curiously, the figures of the so-called "left front" charged him with inadequate attention to them. He recognized great talent in many of them, but at the same time, he was repulsed by them because of the residues of futurism and, as he thought, the unsuppressed influence of bourgeois bohemianism.

He preferred a theater saturated with ideas, with great feelings, expressed in simple, clear, convincing, and deeply realistic forms. It is precisely this kind of theater, in his opinion, that satisfies the People as well.

The struggle of these two tendencies found expression not only in the theater but in painting. Impressionism and Expressionism were considered outdated. They were replaced by Cubism and Non-objective Art.[52] The artists V. Tatlin, L. Popova, A. Rodchenko, V. Stepanova, A. Vesnin and G. Yakulov worked in the theater.

Bryusov, Yesenin, Shershenevich, Mayakovsky would perform at the "Poets' Cafe."[53]

Mayakovsky criticized the Symbolists, the Acmeists, the Imaginists, and the Futurists as well. Public debates went on at the Cafe "Pittoresque,"[54] colorfully and "uniquely" designed by the artist Yakulov.

Evenings devoted to the question of Art at the Printing House[55] on Nikitsky boulevard were interesting and, very likely, the best attended. Even workers attended these evenings. I remember one presentation by A. V. Lunacharsky in the Printing House. Up until this presentation, he had been criticized for an inadequately attentive attitude towards new currents, for underestimating the emerging left tendencies in art. On this particular evening, he was somehow quite irritated; he responded with brilliance as always, and not without sarcasm. It fell especially hard on one Constructivist, who was dressed in jodhpurs made of thin material and a double-breasted jacket of a military cut. Critiquing Lunacharsky, he said he was speaking on behalf of the bakers union. A. V. Lunacharsky, in answering him was especially devastating; to the general laughter of the hall, he designated him the "baker in jodhpurs."

---

[52] [Trans.]: In the original: беспредметное: literally "without an objective," or "without a subject." It can also mean "pointless." In this case, it may refer to the Tenth State Exhibition in Moscow in 1919 called "Беспредметное творчество и супрематизм" ["Non-objective Creation and Suprematism"]. Participants included Malevich, Stepanova, Vesnin, Davydova, Klyun, Menkov, Popova, Rodchenko and Rozanova (posthumously). Anything from Kandinsky to Constructivism would currently be understood by the term беспредметное искусство: non-objective art and the term was later adopted by Russian artists in the 1970s.

[53] [Trans.]: In the original: кафе поэтов.

[54] [Trans.]: In the original: Питореск.

[55] [Trans.]: In the original: Дом печати.

For work, it often happened that I would be at the Printing House for meetings of the Section on Questions of the Theater. Once, when it was already rather late, after the meeting, I was walking through the large auditorium. The stage, with the curtains raised, gaped open like a desert. The chairs stood in perfect order, unoccupied by anyone. It was quiet in the auditorium and almost dark. A shaft of light came out of some half-open door. Leaning against the wall, sat Yesenin. I recognized him immediately by the wild hair on his young head. He was sitting slumped over and must have been there already for quite a while. I'm sure, that evening he wasn't drunk. Something touched me, from his posture and his face, which was somehow exceedingly lonely, disordered. I wanted to say something to him, but I couldn't find the needed words. I stood next to him for a minute, and remaining silent, walked away. When I found out about his tragic death, I remembered that evening.

A lot of people would gather at the Palace of the Arts.[56] It was set up in the former mansion of the Countess Sologub, on Vorovsky ulitsa, where the Writer's Union now operates. The external appearance of this house has changed little, but the internal one in no way recalls the charming suite of rooms in the receiving hall and the drawing rooms of that time.

On the landing of the stairs, stood a knight in armor. The door on the left led into the drawing rooms and the receiving hall furnished with antique furniture, paintings, carpets. The entire mansion bore the stamp of great taste. From the red drawing room, the walls of which were covered in woven Chinese silk, two white doors encrusted with gold led to the grand, marvelous, white receiving hall. The furniture in it was white and gilt, on the windows were bright portraits woven in gold. Here, the evenings of the Palace of the Arts took place. Leading out from the red drawing room was a suite of rooms: green, rose, yellow… their walls were covered in green, rose, and yellow silk, and there were portraits in each of these colors.

There were two more charming rooms: one Chinese, with black lacquer furniture with mother-of-pearl inlay, with ancient Chinese arms, masks, Chinese Buddhas, jade objects, embroideries, and porcelain. In the Venetian room, the walls were interwoven with antique brocade, embroidered with gold. On the wide divans, were great cushions, covered with this same brocade. In this room, were many paintings by Italian artists and wonderful objects of Venetian glass. From this room, a long, narrow balcony looked out onto the courtyard. Under the balcony, grew trees with miniature Chinese apples. In the courtyard, was the private chapel. In it, they said, Natasha Rostova[57] was married. What could they mean, saying this name: who was the prototype for Natasha Rostova?

I have described this house in such detail, so that it will be understood, what an antique oasis it was in Moscow in these hungry years.

---

[56] [Trans.]: In the original: Дворец искусств [Dvorets iskusstv].
[57] [Trans.]: A leading character in Tolstoy's *War and Peace*.

The poet I. S. Rukavishnikov[58] was in charge of this Palace. He had fallen in love with this house and he protected it. Somehow, he managed to heat the receiving hall and the red drawing room, so that those who came to the evenings there could surrender their outer garments to the coat racks. In the fireplace in the green drawing room sometimes a few logs would burn, or lumps of coal would smolder.

The poet Ivan Rukavishnikov was a unique and interesting man, with an unusual life story. The son of a Volga millionaire and himself a millionaire, he was not at all in thrall to gold. He was tall, thin, with a narrow wedge of a blonde beard, straight blonde hair and bright eyes, pensive, with a kind smile; in him there was something that simultaneously resembled an ikon painting and Don Quixote. He managed to spend the major portion of his fortune before the revolution. On what? He dressed modestly and did not indulge himself on food. I know that he drank a lot and traveled a lot, but, above all, he loved the country, the Volga countryside, Russian song, old Russian clothing, and everything created by the hands of men: architecture, sculpture, antique furniture, brocade, handwoven fabrics. He was captivated by color in things and combinations of colors. He maintained, that manufactured articles lost their charm, because the force of color was lost in them, that objects made by machines, and not by the skillful, human hand, lost their individuality, their unique identity, their beauty.

Perhaps, he was so in love with the building of the Palace of the Arts, because there, on each object, lay the stamp of the singular talent of the Russian People, the talent of the Chinese and Italian Masters. Above all, he hated everything that bore on it the stamp of the Decadent style. When he would look at objects of this style, his eyes somehow disappeared, he would cover them with his hands, blind himself, and then, with a strange smile, full of pity, he would turn away.

He was not a Symbolist, but the Symbolists would participate in all the events at the Palace of the Arts. On these evenings, Bryusov and Bely would present, even Balmont would present.

It was there, that I first saw Balmont. He read his verse, lisping, in a sing-song voice; there was something rubbery about him for me. At his readings, the actress Agness Rubinchik would appear: dark-skinned, dark-eyed, dark-haired, with an African coiffure. My surprise was quite great, when one day, on one of the evenings, the poet Balmont approached me and presented me with a small brochure "Am I a Revolutionary or not?" in which, of course, he demonstrated, that he was a revolu-

---

[58] [Russian editor's note]: In the archive of E. Shub, a humorous message in verse by the poet I. Rukavishnikov was found, evoking a memory of the times when he was in charge of the Palace of the Arts:

…And the white house with a smile I remember,
And the noise below and the silence above,
And the triolet service in verse.

tionary. In the brochure, there were poems dedicated to me, printed on a typewriter but in cursive letters. The little book, in my view, was simply counter-revolutionary and it was surprising that they printed it. After this, I began to avoid him.

Even stranger was my meeting with F. Sologub. He was on that evening with his wife Chebotarevskaya; she was short, with a spiteful, cruel and at the same time, sad face. She was quite a bit younger than him. Sologub had a puffy face, a bare skull, piercing cold eyes. He spoke and read masterfully. And while I was listening to him, I would silently utter his verses: "The devil swings on a swing…" During the break, I. Rukavishnikov introduced me to him and Chebotarevskaya. Ever since that moment I can remember his cold regard, his bloodless lips, uttering these strange words: "You are the bride. I have known you for a long time. A very long time. Ages ago, you were the bride." This was all both strange and incomprehensible and his artificiality was repellent. I saw, that he gave himself airs. And it was repulsive.

On some evenings, Antokol'sky, Yesenin and others read their verses. There were sometimes lovely evenings of music. I remember one evening, when the receiving room was lit with candlelight, as there was no electricity from the generating station, and the music in this illumination sounded especially impressive. I remember quite well two evenings in the large white receiving room, when Lunacharsky read his plays *Chancellor and Locksmith* and *Oliver Cromwell*. The hall was full to overflowing.

Who attended these evenings? Poets, writers, artists, musicians, young listeners attending daytime lectures on literature and versification (subsequently, when the Palace of the Arts was liquidated, they became the first students of the Advanced Literary-Artistic Institute, directed by Valery Bryusov). Workers also came to these evenings, but one must say quite directly, that they were few in number. Lunacharsky read his plays expressively, with great mastery, especially *Oliver Cromwell*. A. V. Lunacharsky loved *Cromwell*, considering, in addition to its literary merits, that the play was lively and had a revolutionary character. It was staged in the Maly Theater and played with success, though it was strongly criticized. A. V. Lunacharsky defended himself against the criticism; he maintained, that artists should not create some kind of art especially for the People, or more precisely, something that was half-art (A. V. considered his dramatic work genuine art). I personally was on the side of those, who found, that in *Oliver Cromwell* they talked too much about god.

One day, Lunacharsky unexpectedly came to my one-room apartment with its soot-blackened makeshift walls. At that time, I was baking the usual Lenten cakes. He had come, in order to take me to a debate at the Polytechnical Museum. There, a presentation was to be given by the priest Vvedensky, the ideologue of the new church, who was enjoying great popularity among believers. In the overcrowded car, on the road to the Polytechnical Museum, A. V. Lunacharsky, managed to tell me, that today it would become clear to me, what he fervently believed in and that this belief of his was stronger and more indisputable than a belief in god.

The Auditorium was full to overflowing, all of the aisles were occupied by people. The handsome Vvedensky spoke for a long time, and not without oratorical skill, about god, about the soul, about eternity, about purification, about good and evil and all this was interwoven with quotations and commentaries of idealist philosophers, who maintained the existence of god. Lunacharsky's presentation was shattering. He made short work of Vvedensky and his Hegelian dialectics. He spoke about dialectical materialism, about Marx's philosophy. His comprehensive knowledge of idealist philosophy and the history of religious cults—from pagan to Christian— helped him bring down all of Vvedensky's propositions with such acuity and force, that after his presentation, he was rewarded with thunderous applause.

Sometimes in the evenings, I would find Anatoly Vasil'evich in one of the two smallish rooms occupied by I. Rukavishnikov and his wife Nina Sergeevna on the entresol of the Palace. One arrived there by a dark, narrow staircase. Sometimes Lunacharsky would appear unexpectedly. He would appear noisily; on the way, he would already have taken off his fur coat and he would share some kind of literary, theatrical, or political news of the day. Everything he said would bring into the room a fresh breeze, bursting with life.

One day he asked Rukavishnikov to read through his book *Triolets*, that had only just come out. I. Rukavishnikov read softly, in a sing-song manner, somewhat hoarsely, in an "ecclesiastical" voice, frequently coughing. During one pause, A. V. Lunacharsky took the volume of verse from his hands and began to read it himself. It was a marvelous reading. *Triolets* began to sparkle, at times, acquiring a new meaning, which the reader would embed in the verses. In the room, there were a number of people and they all experienced the power of the reading. Ivan Rukavishnikov as well. And Nina Sergeevna gently rocked back and forth in rhythm to the verses and on her lips a smile began to take shape, that was well known to us all, but not understood.

Rukavishnikov loved and valued old Gypsy[59] songs. He collaborated with Kruchinin,[60] helped him assemble some gypsies celebrated for their voices living somewhere in Sokol in the village of Vsekhsvyatsky and in the large white hall, a chorus of gypsies gave a concert of ancient Gypsy songs and dances. I remember how the Gypsy songs overwhelmed me. I was listening to them for the first time, everything was new: the peculiar Gypsy costumes, the jingling of the necklaces, the strange throaty screech at the moment the chorus began to sing, setting fire to their songs, and the striking, spirited dancing. It is clear, that Pushkin and Tolstoy loved ancient Gypsy songs and Gypsy themes clearly appear in the verses of Blok.

---

[59] [Trans.]: I have chosen to keep the period equivalent of цыган [tsigan] and its derivative forms, rather than changing them to "Roma." There is no small measure of exoticism involved and well-intentioned or not, it should be preserved, for better or for worse.

[60] [Trans.]: Valentin Yakovlevich Kruchinin, a Soviet composer of operettas, suites, and film music. Decorated Worker in the Arts.

I remember two meetings with Alexander Blok. I knew him through portraits and the stories of I. Rukavishnikov, who said, that his head was of antique beauty, and that his face was the color of copper, his curls were bronze shot with gold and his eyes were light blue and almost too elongated. How did I see him? Tall, thin, with a narrow, weary face, a pointy nose, with thinning, dyed hair. His eyes were beautiful as was the shape of his mouth. He read his verses in an inimitable fashion. Just as Mayakovsky's way of reading was inimitable, but utterly different. He read, never raising his voice, at a single invariable tone, stamping out each word, or more precisely, making a barely noticeable pause after each word, so that, in spite of his soft voice and the monotonous sounding [of each word], each word lodged itself in one's memory in three dimensions; it functioned emotionally, like music. His way of reading was magical. Late at night, we sat at a round table in his living room in front of the fireplace where coal was smoldering. There were several people there with us. I remember that he said, that of late he heard the revolution as a powerful symphony in a major key. He said, that he was becoming aware of a major mode inside himself and that it would undoubtedly find expression in his new poetry. Every word was to be believed. This was a heart-to-heart talk for the most part with I. Rukavishnikov. They spoke to one another confidentially and confided this conversation to us, who were listening. The quiet, unhurried conversation went on. It was striking how he sat: too utterly motionless, straight up. He gave the impression of a man with a deep interior secret. As we were saying goodbye, I very shyly asked him to read some of my favorite poems during the evening at the Polytechnical Museum, scheduled for the next day. In return, he asked simply: "Which ones?" I named a selection from *Retribution* and some lyrical verses.

The next evening in the overflowing hall of the Polytechnical Museum, Alexander Blok read his verses. He read endlessly, because they kept summoning him endlessly back. This was the final farewell meeting of revolutionary Moscow with the beautiful poet of pre-revolutionary Russia, who had been born and had expressed himself at the juncture of two eras.

That evening, it seems to me, he was not only excited, but, perhaps, even happy from the consciousness, that he was a contemporary of great events, that his meeting with new listeners was joyous, and that he was ready to stride forward together with them into the days of struggle and victory.

I was touched, that he found the opportunity to recite a few of the verses I had asked him to the evening before. Nina Sergeevna and I started off to say goodbye to him and to thank him for the evening. We said goodbye to one another, as if many joyful and significant meetings lay ahead. There were to be no more of these. Blok died soon after. Who could have thought that? He spoke so unforgettably that evening at the Palace of the Arts about his internal major mode ("major": that word, that would always remain in my memory). This music inside him, it seemed, had merged with the music that was sounding in the depths of the soul of the People—those were the meaning of his words.

It seems to me, that no one so precisely conveyed his interior and physical image the way Maxim Gorky did. In his series *Portraits of Remarkable People*, his account of the poet A. Blok should undoubtedly be ranked alongside his inspired portraits of L. Tolstoy, V. Korolenko, and his account of his last meeting with Yesenin.

Ivan Sergeevich Rukavishnikov showed an extraordinary interest in and I would even say tenderness towards the sculptor, Konenkov, one exceeded only by what he showed for Blok. The sculptor, Konenkov, was already at that time quite colorful and interesting. I encountered him often at the Palace of the Arts. Ivan Sergeevich and his younger brother, the sculptor, Mitrofan Sergeevich, were friendly with him. I personally did not happen to have a lot of close contact with Konenkov. I knew from what the Rukavishnikov brothers said, that he was an exceptional master, quite original, who brilliantly expressed the gifts of the Russian people. They took me to Konenkov's studio (this was shortly before his departure for America). He was organizing an exhibition in his studio somewhere in Presnya. It was located in the courtyard of a one-story wooden building. It was evening when we arrived at the studio. There were many visitors there invited by the sculptor. If my memory does not deceive me, at the entrance above the door a sculpture was fastened: the hands and wings of a fallen, broken angel. All the visitors were, for the most part, crowding around a statue of Paganini. The face of Paganini was marked with inspiration and the stamp of genius. An extraordinary gift could be felt in the sculptor, who had created this statue. It was the first time, I had seen wooden sculptures with color. Many had the air of Russian folk tales and legends.

Konenkov arranged a small exhibition of his work at the circus. I would really have liked to have had any one of them, but I could never make up my mind to speak to Konenkov about it. Rukavishnikov did this for me. Unexpectedly for me, they brought me a small painted wooden sculpture: the head of an old man, entwined with leaves and clusters of grapes. This was the head of a destitute and deranged old man, who walked the streets of Moscow in the cruel frosts with a bare head, with his long, curly hair for a thick cap.

For me, the single most incomprehensible person in the Palace of the Arts was the poet Velemir Khlebnikov, who actually lived there for a while. He was young and silent. He would converse—and that very quietly—with Rukavishnikov alone. I knew from Ivan Sergeevich, that under his clothing, Khlebnikov wore chains. As people said, he didn't wash and did not comb his overgrown, uncut ashen hair. His eyes were congealed ash. He was capable of sitting for hours in the Venetian room by the door which opened onto the balcony, without uttering a single word. I would have liked for him to talk with me, but, at the same time, I feared this. It seemed to me, that I wouldn't find the words with which to respond to him. Sometimes, he would go out onto the balcony and observe the cheerful young people clustering there. He slept, without undressing, in the Venetian room on the great cushions covered with strange embroidery. Then, he disappeared. Rukavishnikov became bored without him and waited for his return. But I never saw him again at the Palace of the Arts. And thus, shortly before his death, the "chairman of the earthly sphere," as he called himself, "the signalman[61] on the paths where the past and future meet," was writing down the commands of the "solar world" in mysterious calculations. How did he end up at the Palace of the Arts? No one knows… What could have connected him with Rukavishnikov? Nothing… He ends one of his decrees with these words: "It's boring in the world." It must have been, that at this time he was already bored in the world, there must have been no future for him. I cannot imagine him next to Mayakovsky. I can't imagine, how their conversation about poetry, about manifestos must have gone: "Between Mayakovsky and me: 2,809 days…." Only that? Two extreme poles, two worlds, opposed to one another. The poet of the Revolution, Mayakovsky, was always on the attack, engaged in the struggle:

> I
> believe
> in the Lenin
> of this world
> and celebrate
> my belief.
> I would not be a poet,
> if I
> did not sing this—
> in five-pointed stars, the heaven
> of the measureless vault of the RCP.[62]

In quiet, contemplative "other worlds" is Velemir Khlebnikov.

Many years had elapsed when I met the artist Tatlin in the home of some friends. The entire evening he recited by heart the verses of Khlebnikov; he recited, entranced by their sounds. They recalled fortune-telling, witchcraft.

Towards the end of 1921, it became clear to me, that I would not find my profession in the Theater Department. Professional theater did not enthrall me. I didn't love it so passionately. I loved reading plays and they always seemed more meaningful to me while reading them than on the stage. I didn't get much enjoyment from the circus work either. Someone suggested, that Rukavishnikov invite the

---

[61] [Trans.]: In the original: стрелочник на путях встречи прошлого с будущим. The word стрелочник also means "switchman," "scapegoat," and "lightning rod."

[62] [Trans.]: In the original: РКП (Russian Communist Party).

producer Goleizovsky[63] to the circus, in order to help with the design of a production by the artist Kuznetsov. A great deal of effort and funds were expended and the result was a lavish and not terribly jolly spectacle. In design, it was close to the theatrical, but in the performances of the actors, it was closer to ballet, in which the pure circus numbers became lost. V. E. Meyerhold was extremely embarrassed. He was very displeased, that I didn't warn him. All of the attempts of authoritative experts in the art of the circus to convince Rukavishnikov, that this was not the right path for the circus, failed. In 1922, I stopped working there.

Just at this time, I met Sergei Mikhailovich Eisenstein.[64] He had just returned from the front of the Civil War and came to the TEO, intending to start out as an artist in the theater and to engage in preparation for directorial work. He dreamed of becoming a student of V. E. Meyerhold.

He was young and had a striking face. A large head, with a beautiful forehead framed by thick, wavy hair, streaked with gold. Somehow, it always stood straight out. His gray eyes under dark, delicately outlined eyebrows, looked out somewhat mockingly. V. E. Meyerhold worked with him a lot on his voice and he acquired a low, steady, baritonal inflection. The movements of his smallish hands were unusually expressive. We immediately began chatting about everything in the world: literature, painting, theater. Somehow it happened quite simply, that I told him, that I wanted to work in the cinema, that only there did I see the possibility of beginning my studies once again, that the cinema could become the new art, that only it could truly become the communist educator of the multiple millions of the masses (I already knew V. I. Lenin's statement about the cinema). And even though he himself wanted to work in the theater, he listened to me with interest. We decided to meet each other again. And thus began our great friendship, which continued to the final days of his life.

---

[63] [Trans.] I believe that Shub has in mind, the choreographer Kas'yan Yaroslavich Goleizovsky. She uses the word постановщик to describe him, an extremely general term ranging from production designer to producer.

[64] [Russian editor's note]: *Eisenstein, Sergei Mikhailovich* (1898–1948). Film director. While still a theatrical director at Proletkult, he became interested in Shub's work in re-editing. In 1924, together they re-edited the film *Doctor Mabuse, the Gambler* by the German director F. Lang (in the Soviet version *Gilded Decay*). From then on, the creative and personal friendship of E. Shub and S. Eisenstein continued through out the course of their entire lives.

First Years in the Cinema[65]
(1922–1930)

My Film School

To work in film production. In this field precisely, I wanted to make myself a professional.

The cinema is a new art. Or more precisely, everything made up to the year 1922, cannot be called "art," in the full sense of the word. Everything must be re-interpreted. To find the means of expression for everything, that the Great October Revolution has brought. The Old World has perished, ended. A New Life is beginning. New People will construct this life. And in art, the road is open. Forward! Innovators! Seekers of new ways!

The cinema is the art of future.

I needed to study once again. Perhaps, I should have tried to find a place for myself at the First State School of Cinema.[66] V. Gardin,[67] O. Preobrazhenskaya,[68]

---

[65] [Trans.]: In the original: The word used is кинематограф [kinematograf], the same as in the title of the entire memoir. This word can refer to the historical invention of the Lumière Brothers, the *cinématographe*, but most commonly for Shub, it means film production or even the film industry. It can also mean what we might call "the cinema": the whole of the institutions of production, distribution and exhibition, which is also referred to by the word "кино" [kino]. Kino, in turn can also mean a movie theater, or even the movies, as in "Why don't we go to the movies?" A filmmaker as such is a кинематографист [kinematografist], a term Shub rarely uses. She typically refers to the role of the director режиссер [rezhisser] and when it is necessary to distinguish a film director from a theater director, she uses the term кинорежиссер [kinorezhisser]. If there is a need to distinguish a movie theater from a place where live theater takes place, we have a similar doublet: кинотеатр [kinoteatr] and театр [teatr]. The term режиссер is clearly a loan of the French *régisseur*. In translating this work, I will use whichever term seems appropriate in its context. The curious may refer to the original.

[66] [Russian editor's note]: "*I should have tried to find a place for myself at the First State School of Cinema.*" In September 1919, shortly after the signing of the directive of V. I. Lenin concerning the nationalization of the film industry, the First State School of Cinema opened, establishing the basis of cinema education in the country. Then, after a series of reorganizations and reforms, it became the All Union State Institute of Cinema.

[67] [Russian editor's note]: *Gardin, Vladimir Rostislavovich* (1877–1965), Director and actor. People's Artist of the USSR. Head of the first Goskino school. He directed more than 60 films, among them *Anna Karenina* (1914), *A Nest of Noblemen* (1915), *Hammer and Sickle* (1921), *Locksmith and Chancellor* (1924), *The Poet and the Tsar* (1927). He performed more than 50 roles. Among them: Napoleon in *War and Peace* (1914), Master Babchenko in the film *Counterplan* (1932), Iudushka in *Iudushka Golovlev* (1933).

[68] [Russian editor's note]: *Preobazhenskaya, Ol'ga Ivanovna* (b. 1884), film director and actress. Decorated Worker in the Arts of the RFSFSR. She became popular for her roles as Liza (*A Nest of Noblemen*), Elena (*On the Eve*), Natasha Rostova (*War and Peace*). In 1916, she directed (together

L. Kuleshov,[69] V. Turkin,[70] F. Shipulinsky,[71] L. Leonidov[72] and others taught there. Perhaps, I should have tried to get into L. Kuleshov's workshop, from which many first-class actors and directors entered the cinema: V. Pudovkin,[73] B. Barnet,[74] V. Fogel',[75] A. Khokhlova,[76] S. Komarov,[77] P. Galadzhev,[78] and many others.

---

with V. Gardin) the film *Miss Peasant.* Her most well known films are: *Women of Ryazan* (1927), *And Quiet flows the Don* (1930), *Paths of Enemies* (1935), *Stepan Razin* (1939). Almost all of the films were directed in collaboration with I. Pravov.

[69] [Russian editor's note]: *Kuleshov, Lev Vladimirovich* (1899–1970). Film director, artist, and educator. People's Artist of the RSFSR. At the beginning of the 1920s, he created an experimental school for acting technique, which produced V. Pudovkin, B. Barnet, M. Doller, A. Khokhlova, S. Komarov, V. Fogel', and others. He directed the following pictures: (silent): *The Extraordinary Adventures of Mr. West in the Land of the Bolsheviks, The Death Ray, By the Law,* and others; (sound): *The Horizon, The Great Consoler, Timur's Oath, The Siberians.*

[70] [Russian editor's note]: *Turkin, Valentin Konstantinovich* (1887–1958). Screenwriter, critic, and educator. One of the first professional screenwriters. He began to work in the cinema even before the revolution. The author of the screenplays of these famous Soviet silent films: *The Taylor from Torzhok, The Stationmaster, The Girl with the Hatbox, The Ghost that will not Return.* The author of *Dramatic Writing for the Cinema* [Драматургия кино] (Moscow, Goskinoizdat, 1938). Professor, Founder Department of Screenwriting of the VGIK.

[71] [Russian editor's note]: *Shipulinsky, Feofan Platonovich* (1876–1942). Cinema historian. Author of books on Foreign Cinema: *The History of Cinema* (Moscow, GIKhL, 1933).

[72] [Russian editor's note]: *Leonidov, Leonid Mironovich* (1873–1941). Actor. People's Artist of the USSR. First roles in the cinema were in the films *The Pangs of Love, Iron Heel.* Principal roles: Ivan the Terrible in *The Wings of a Serf* and Gobsek in the film of the same title.

[73] [Russian editor's note]: *Pudovkin, Vsevolod Illarionovich* (1893–1953). Film director, actor, cinema theorist. People's Artist of the USSR.

[74] [Russian editor's note]: *Barnet, Boris Vasil'evich* (1902–1965). Film director and actor. Decorated Artist of the RSFSR. Director of the films: *The Girl with the Hatbox* (1927), *The House on Trubnaya Square* (1928), *Outskirts* (1933), *By the Bluest of Seas* (1936), *The Scout's Secret* (1947), *Alenka* (1961).

[75] [Russian editor's note]: *Fogel', Vladimir Petrovich* (1902–1929). Actor of Soviet silent cinema. He appears in the films: *Chess Fever, By the Law, The Girl with the Hatbox, Bed and Sofa, The House on Trubnaya Square.*

[76] [Russian editor's note]: *Khokhlova, Aleksandra Sergeevna* (b. 1897). Film actress and director. Decorated Artist of the RSFSR. She began to appear in films in 1916. Her most famous roles are in the films of L. Kuleshov. Lecturer in Directing at the VGIK.

[77] [Russian editor's note]: *Komarov, Sergei Petrovich* (1891–1957). Film actor. Decorated Artist of the RSFSR. One of the leading actors of the experimental workshop of L. Kuleshov. He also appeared in the films *The End of Saint Petersburg, Outskirts, Shchors, Minin and Pozharsky, Secret of Two Oceans.*

[78] [Russian editor's note]: *Galadzhev, Petr Stepanovich* (1900–1971). Actor and cinema production designer. Decorated Artist of the RSFSR. He appeared in the films *The Extraordinary Adventures of Mr. West in the Land of the Bolsheviks, The Death Ray, The Great Consoler, Treasure Island,* and others. In the capacity of production designer, he participated in work on the following films: *The Old Courtyard, Timur's Oath, The Cruiser "Varyag," Private Aleksandr Matrosov, When the Trees were Tall, By the Lake.*

But I didn't go to the Cinema School, nor to the workshop, but to the Film and Photo Department, soon reorganized as Goskino, and I asked to be directed to the employment office of Goskino in charge of re-editing and editing intertitles for films, being prepared for release at that time. This would later turn out to have been the right decision for me.

…The Civil War and the Foreign Interventions were then beginning.

It was essential to restore the collapsed armaments industry and agricultural production, to heal the wounds suffered in the struggle by the Soviet People defending their freedom and independence.

The time of the New Economic Policy (NEP) ensued. I didn't understand the purpose and the significance of what had occurred. Until I worked through it all, until I understood, that it was the inevitable, singularly correct decision of the Party, I was not at peace with myself.

I saw Moscow in a strange and unimaginable way.

The slime of the past began to surface on the precious streets of the city where I was born. Once again, hanging shop signs, luxury goods stores, restaurants, cabarets, casinos, late night dives, "NEPgirls,"[79] "NEPmen."[80] The scum of the past, which it seemed, had gone away for good.

Some of the names of the stores broke my heart: "Liberté": cloth of the highest quality of all sorts; "Comfort": a complete line of apartment décor; "Salon de Paris" and the perfumes Guerlain, Houbigant.

Luxury women's and men's footwear: Zelenkina. Kishevsky: I buy and sell diamonds, gold, silver. Wines of the firm of Peter Smirnov.

The restaurants: the former "Maxime's," Gypsy and Romanian Chorus. The former "Yar," Gypsy Chorus. The "Zaveril"[81] Tavern. Traditional Russian cuisine by Testov. "Casino" open until 10 in the morning.

And everything else of that sort.

I once found myself in a strange apartment somewhere on a small lane crossing Tverskaya (now Gorky ulitsa). A comrade at my new job decided to feed me, as he said, "once and for all." We were met by a done-up lady in diamonds with the "high society" manners of a *madame* of a questionable "salon." She conducted herself, as if we'd known her for a hundred years, as if she'd only just been waiting for us. We walked into a large room, heaped with mahogany, carpets, crystal, porcelain, tropical trees in planters. Taken together, it resembled the random objects of an antique store. Closer to the wall, there was an oval table with comfortable chairs around it. On the table were the daintiest of hors d'oeuvres, wine, and vodka. Then, a meal began that was nothing less than sumptuous.

---

[79] [Trans.]: In the original: нэповки [nepovki].
[80] [Trans.]: In the original: нэпманы [nepmany].
[81] [Trans.]: The name means something like "Certified."

Those who sat around the table, it must be said, were all famous actors. They had money. This was a painful time, painful pages in the biographies of many. The time became notorious and it was a life of hackwork.

We left quickly. I asked my comrade, how much the meal cost, how much I owed him, whether he had managed to settle up. He burst out laughing. He paid; this lady did everything touching on payment adroitly and discretely. To all appearances, one might think, that the hospitable proprietress entertained her dear guests at her own expense. And that I didn't need to settle up with him. This one meal cost as much as my entire monthly salary. I never went into such a place again, but I understood a lot and there was a lot to think about.

This was one side of life, inevitable with the arrival of the NEP. But we very quickly understood, that this was temporary. The NEP was also a struggle, a means of struggle with devastation and hunger. This was a struggle for the foundation of a period of reconstruction. Life, new forms of life would increasingly appear and they would triumph.

And the front of art lives life in many forms. In searching, in struggle, in arguments, in fights. New books, films, new ways of staging plays make their appearance. As before, the new spectator is exacting and wants to examine, to understand, to accept, to reject for himself.

There were lines at the ticket booths for the movies: "lines around the block." All the cinemas were full to overflowing. In the first years after the revolution, there were few movie theaters and they didn't operate every day. Now, there were more of them. Movie theaters appeared, that could hold a greater number of spectators: the Mirrored "Hermitage" and the "Colossus" movie theater, the Great Hall of the Conservatory.

The distribution offices of Goskino and Sevzapkino were on Dmitrovka, "Moscow" cinema was across from MosSoviet (the building is no longer there). Rus' (on the corner of Sadovaya and Tverskaya) had just barely enough time to produce films from the pool of domestic and foreign pre-revolutionary pictures, editing them over again.[82] New films were shot. They were turned out in make-shift studios, or, as they called them then "ateliers."

A flood of so-called "psychological" dramas came out—tasteless examples of the worst sort of decadence.

The Rus' film organization, which had brought classic themes to the screen, such as *Polikushka*, *The Thieving Magpie*, *Snowstorm*, was planning to shoot *Aelita*, based on a scenario by A. N. Tolstoy. There, from 1923 on, the eminent director of the pre-revolutionary period, Ya. A. Protazanov, worked.[83]

---

[82] [Trans.]: In the original: заново.

[83] [Russian editor's note]: *Protazanov, Yakob Aleskandrovich* (1881–1945). Film director. Decorated Worker in the Arts. His directorial work began in 1909. He directed some of the best pre-revolu-

Films ceaselessly replaced one another on the screen. On fences, on the sides of buildings, on the façades of cinemas, posters screamed out. The street became gaudy with them. *Infinite Sorrow* with Maksimov, *Slave of a Woman*, *Heart of a Woman* with Mia May, *A Fairy Tale of Precious Love* (*Be Silent, My Sorrow, Be Silent*), and others of the sort. Just then, one of the first Soviet films with actors appeared on the screen, directed by a non-professional, P. Voevodin. Posters were plastered all over Moscow, with the image of a lily, then this text: "New! Original! Breathtaking!" — "In the whirlwind of the Revolution."

But this did not define the cinema. No matter how hard wheeler-dealers of every stamp tried to get their hands on the dainty little pieces of profit of the Soviet screens, to dictate their tastes, not shrinking from any means of control — from counter-revolutionary agitation, acts of sabotage and wrecking production to the destruction and concealment of film stock, cameras, and films — they were not able to halt what was for them the inexorable course of events.

The development of Soviet cinema went in another direction and inevitably this scum was swept away.

I remember a cautionary poster of V. Mayakovsky. On thin little legs with a huge belly in a black coat with tails, a head covered with a scarf and on top of the scarf was a top hat. Enormous paws. One clutching a knife, ready to strike. Under the drawing were the words:

> Capital still lives and still is capable
> of trying to bully

And how they tried!

And here again, are the words of the poet from his poem "Kiev," thoughts and words near to all of us then:

> Let
>
>   the wolf's cry
>
>   from Kreshatik [street]
>
> still cut deep:
>
>   "I give and take your ten-ruble notes"

---

tionary Russian films: *The Queen of Spades* and *Father Sergius*. In the Soviet period, he created the films *Aelita, His Call, The Forty-first, The Case of the Three Million, Don Diego and Pelagia, Without a Dowry,* and others.

Our strength is

truth,

yours is

the jingling of laurels.

Yours is

the smoke of incense.

Ours is

the smoke of the factory.

Your might is

the ten-ruble note,

ours is

the red banner.

—We will seize,

occupy

and triumph.

As far back as August 1919, by the decree of Sovnarkom,[84] the cinema had been transferred to the authority of Narkompros. Narkompros had the right to nationalization. But for three years, little was done and with the institution of the NEP, things got worse.

All the ateliers wound up in private hands. Once again, their former owners took charge of them. The single exception was Khanzhonkov,[85] who operated honestly within Soviet institutions and helped to carry out the establishment of Soviet power.

Having acquired the ateliers, the wheeler-dealers by no means hastened to launch new productions. Seizing control of the distribution of films was their goal.

What was new, exciting in these years of the NEP? What most expressed our era in art? What did the spectator go to see, what did he look forward to, and embrace with particular feeling?

It was the newsreel.

---

[84] [Russian editor's note]: *"As far back as August 1919, by the decree of Sovnarkom…"* On August 27, 1919, V. I. Lenin signed the "Decree concerning the Transfer of Photographic and Cinematographic Commerce and Industry to the Authority of the People's Commisariat of Enlightenment."

[85] [Russian editor's note]: *Khanzhonkov, Aleksandr Alekseevich* (1877–1945). One of the first Russian cinema entrepreneurs. He began to work in the cinema in 1906. He played a foundational role in the development of domestic cinema.

The newsreel. True, it was still a small thing, quite meager, but it honestly and truthfully set down in the record an entire series of historical events of world significance: October, the Civil War, the reconstruction of the national economy, the social and political life of the Soviet Union.

This managed to be filmed, because, as a legacy from the cinematic past, we inherited a first-class group of camera operators, who took the lead through mastery in reporting. From the first hours of the victory of the October Revolution, they began to work for the Land of the Soviets, in the name of the Soviet Power of workers and peasants. The names of A. Levitsky,[86] P. Novitsky,[87] N. Kozlovsky,[88] E. Tissé,[89] G. Giber,[90] E. Slavinsky,[91] Yu. Zhelyabuzhsky,[92] A.[93] and G.[94] Lemberg are well known

---

[86] [Russian editor's note]: *Levitsky, Aleksandr Andreevich* (1888–1965). Camera operator and educator. He entered the cinema in 1910, being an artist-photographer. One of the creators of the School for Soviet Film Industry Camera Operators. To A. A. Levitsky we may attribute a series of shots of V. I. Lenin.

[87] [Russian editor's note]: *Novitsky, Petr Konstantinovich* (1883–1940). Camera operator. He began to work in the cinema before the October Revolution. He recorded newsreels of the Civil War and the most important events of the first years of the Soviet State. He filmed V. I. Lenin. He took part in the shooting of the documentary films *Chelyuskin, Heroes of the Arctic* and *The Sibryakov.*

[88] [Russian editor's note]: *Kozlovsky, Nikolai Feofanovich* (1887–1939). Camera operator. In 1908 with A. Drankov, he shot the first Russian feature film *The Free men of Ponizovo* aka *Stenka Razin*. After the October Revolution, he worked on films with A. Panteleev, I. Perestiani, A. Dovzhenko, G. Roshal'.

[89] [Russian editor's note]: *Tissé, Edouard Kazimirovich* (1897–1961). Camera operator. Decorated Worker in the Arts of the RSFSR. He took part in the creation of all the films directed by Eisenstein.

[90] [Russian editor's note]: *Giber, Grigory Vladimirovich* (1893–1951). Camera operator. He began his activities in the cinema in 1913. In Soviet times he worked in the field of newsreels, documentary and feature film production. He took part in filming V. I. Lenin.

[91] [Russian editor's note]: *Slavinsky, Evgeny Iosifovich* (1877–1950). Film director and camera operator. Director of the film *The Young Lady and the Hooligan* with V. V. Mayakovsky in the principal role. Camera operator for the film *Locksmith and Chancellor, Bay of Death* and others.

[92] [Russian editor's note]: *Zhelyabuzhsky, Yuri Adreevich* (1888–1955). Film director and camera operator. He began working in cinema in 1915. He shot a newsreel of the Civil War. He took part in filming V. I. Lenin. In 1920, he shot one of the first popular scientific pictures about hydraulic peat extraction. Among the feature films, in the creation of which Zhelyabuzhsky participated, the most famous are *Polikushka* and *The Stationmaster* [*Kollezhsky registrator*]. He made a series of popular scientific and art historical pictures. He taught at the VGIK for many years.

[93] [Russian editor's note]: *Lemberg, Aleksandr Grigor'evich* (b. 1898). Camera operator. He began to work in the cinema in 1914. He filmed at the front during World War I. He shot a series of film portraits of V. I. Lenin. He participated in the shooting of these documentary films of Dziga Vertov: *Kino-Pravda, A Sixth Part of the World*. He was the camera operator on a series of feature films (*Ukhtomsky the Engineer* and others).

[94] [Russian editor's note]: *Lemberg, Grigory Moiseevich* (1873–1945). Camera operator and director. He worked in cinema from 1908 on. After the October Revolution, as a newsreel camera operator.

to Soviet filmmakers. Close contact with such exacting artists, as A. Levitsky and E. Tissé showed themselves to be, was the best school for me in the mastery of shooting.

The works of A. Levitsky, even then, were distinguished by the compositional brilliance of the framing. He possessed a beautiful mastery of tonal range and treated close ups in the best traditions of Russian painting.

E. Tissé I observed at work, not only with other directors, but I myself filmed with him. This gives me the right to say, that he was equally strong as a master of fiction film, where, in creative collaboration with S. Eisenstein, he attained world-wide recognition, and as a newsreel cameraman-reporter, he was courageous, knowing no fear, instantaneously orienting himself in any circumstances, with the ability to select the most characteristic and typical event from a whole series of them, having been present with his movie camera on many battle fronts during the Civil War.

What also captivated me about Levitsky and Tissé was their love of nature, of the Russian landscape. It was impossible for them to shoot stereotypical nature shots. The shots they took never tended towards the pretty postcards that typically appeared in the cinema of those years. Levitsky and Tissé strove to express, in both the composition of the shot and in the handling of light and shade, the unique beauty of the vast expanses, the woods, the rivers, the seas of our homeland: in the brilliance of the sun, in a quivering gust of wind, in rain, in mist, in a snowstorm.

In spite of all the difficulties of that time — there was never enough equipment, film stock — the newsreel cameramen, in a spirit of self-dedication, filmed the most important events of the political life of our country. Novitsky, outwardly sullen, seemingly immobile, without waiting for instructions, always found a way to place the camera where it was possible to record the events, having not transient, but undoubtedly historical significance as well as the people participating in them. More than once, he showed me his albums of film frames. These shots were the film history, the film chronicles of our country, recorded with skillful hands and eyes. His stories about the shoots were interesting as well.

G. Giber was a nimble, joyful wiseguy. He was interested in shooting everything: newsreels and fiction films. He willingly carried out any assignment by the director. He even loved for the director to right next to him. Being together was more fun, made it easier to come up with a lot of things, you could talk things over as you went along and at the same time, do the essential wise-cracking. Yu. A. Zhelyabuzhsky was a man of great cinematic culture and directorial finesse. Old man N. Kozlovsky was surprisingly sharp and fair; he inspired particular respect and trust.

Our archive preserves motion picture images of the pre-revolutionary period starting from 1906. Already during these years, camera operators Novitsky, Giber, Lemberg, father and son, Ermolov[95] shot many historical film documents. The inci-

---

[95] [Russian editor's note]: *Ermolov, Petr Vasil'evich* (b. 1887). Camera operator. Decorated Worker in the Arts of the RSFSR. He shot newsreels of the revolution and the Civil War. He worked as a camera

dents and occurrences of life, which characterized pre-war reality, the way of life of the bourgeois property owners. Old Moscow and Petersburg were shot beautifully. These shots also reflect the social conflicts of the capital (there are remarkable shots of Khitrov Market, of Boloto, of Verbny Bazaar).

There are shots of the city, of villages, of estates, of factories. The tsarist government is shown, the Duma, demonstrations by the Black Hundreds. There were even shots of the arrests of revolutionaries and Alekseevsky Central Prison. The imperialist war was shot in various facets and expressively, the front and the rear. The February Revolution in Petrograd and Moscow.

The Great October of 1917 arrived. A new world was born. Workers and peasants became masters of the country. In these great days, the newsreel workers set down on film the first days of the revolution: the new social restructuring of the world, the struggle of the workers and the peasants for their freedom under the leadership of Lenin, the genius, and the Party created by him.

Neither devastation nor hunger, nor encirclement by the White Guard could stop the courageous work of the cameramen. The cameramen worked on film, often positive print stock, in damp conditions, in cold laboratories, as did the editors; they were a new, self-dedicated detachment in the ranks of Soviet filmmaking.

Tens of thousands of meters of film preserve the exciting events of the Civil War, the NEP, the first years of the Construction of Socialism, the first steps of the young proletarian society, the new conditions of labor, the new way of life, the solemn days of proletarian celebrations, the ferocious statements of the masses protesting against their enemies, against the threat of international counter-revolution.

While the film documents are few, all the same, they set down on film the immortal image of Vladimir Il'ich Lenin and his closest comrades-in-arms.

In 1922, the Tenth Congress of the Soviets turned the most serious attention of all organizations of Soviet Power, including Narkompros, to the enormous agitational and educational importance, which the cinema could and must acquire for the broad masses of the population.

A. V. Lunacharsky would recall the momentous conversation he had with V. I. Lenin about the cinema, and the moment when he said to him: "Among us, you have the reputation as a champion of the arts, so you should keep firmly in mind, that of all the arts, the most important for us is the cinema."

Here are the instructions of V. I. Lenin on the question of the cinema, given to A. V. Lunacharsky: "...the production of new films, imbued with Communist ideals, reflecting Soviet reality, must begin with newsreels..."[96]

---

operator on the feature films *On the Red Front*, *The Forty-First*, *The Childhood of Maxim Gorky*, *Among the People*, *My Universities*, *Timur and his Squad* and others.

[96] Cf. *Lenin on Culture and Art*, p. 529. [In original this is noted with ** and is one of the few footnotes at the bottom of a page. Almost all others are endnotes.]

If you have good newsreels, serious and educational pictures, then it won't be important, that, for engaging the public, there are some of the usual sort of pointless films. Of course, you will need censorship all the same. Counter-revolutionary and immoral films must have no place.[97]

It's well known, that from time to time, Vladimir Il'ich would inquire of VFKU what was being made for the broad masses.

In theaters and on city squares, events, which had only recently been filmed, were screened: the fifth anniversary of October, maneuvers of the Armored Divisions of the Red Army. The 1st of May, 1922, Komsomol Day, shots of Uralkhim, Kashira Electric Power Plant, the flight of passenger airplanes, the seizure of ecclesiastical treasures, the trial of the SR's, Mostorg, Mosselprom, motorcycle races, and many other things. The newsreel entered the consciousness of spectators, as the artistic phenomenon, which reflected most truthfully the life of the country, the life of the popular masses. And now, remembering that time, summing up, reflecting on the role the newsreel played in the development of Soviet Film Art, I can say, without fear of exaggeration, that the influence of the newsreel was enormous.

The newsreel, with its veracity, with its passionate pursuit of vividly reflecting our reality, unquestionably conceived a new, socialist film art. And I do mean "conceived." It had very little, with which to serve the needs of the screen. For the most part, foreign films appeared on Soviet screens.

From 1922 to 1925, it was my job to re-edit and to make intertitles for some 200 foreign films, imbued with bourgeois ideology.

The 12th Party Congress of 1923 formulated its outlook on the distribution for the Soviet Screen of foreign films, mostly American and German films, in the following way:

> During the time of the New Economic Policy, the number of movie theaters and their capacity has increased in great measure. In so far as the cinema has made use of old Russian pictures, or pictures of Western European Production, it has, in fact, become transformed into a proponent of bourgeois influence, or corruption of the laboring masses. It is imperative to develop film production in Russia, both by means of the aid of special allocations by the government and by means of attracting (foreign and Russian) private capital, subject to the full guarantee of ideological supervision and control by the government and the Party.[98]

---

[97] [Trans]: Ibid. [In original this is noted with ** and is one of the few footnotes at the bottom of a page. Almost all others are endnotes unless otherwise specified.]

[98] [Trans]: This is another footnote (rather than end note) marked with an asterisk: *KPSS in resolutions and decisions of meetings, conferences and plenary sessions of the CC*, 7th ed., part 1, 1953, p. 741.

The first film, which I prepared for the screen, was an extended American adventure-detective serial, of something like 50 reels, called *The Gray Ghost*. Some interesting silent film actors took part in it: Harry Carter and Eddie Polo, as well as others. Lines about the *Gray Ghost* found their way into the poetry of V. Maya-kovsky:

Dawn.
> Rising like the shade of the Seine,
> like the cinema's gray ghost.

Gradually, the adventure and cowboy serials of Ruth Rolland and the detective films of Pearl White would come into my hands for re-editing and intertitling as well as films starring Mary Pickford, Douglas Fairbanks, Priscilla Dean, Edna Purviance (later the heroine of Chaplin's *A Woman of Paris*), Pola Negri, Asta Nielsen, Lillian Gish, Jannings, Wegener, Conrad Veidt, and many others, so many you couldn't count them all.

S. M. Eisenstein—already at that time a theater director at Proletkult—was very interested in my work in re-editing.[99] More than once, he came to my editing studio and viewing room. There, for the first time, we would screen huge reels of mixed pieces of film, which would turn out to be newsreels of the events of February [1917] in Leningrad and Moscow.

This material made a huge impression on us. I returned to it when I became a director of documentary films, and in Eisenstein's case, in his film *October*, the scene of the events of July in Leningrad was unquestionably worked out under the influence of this viewing.

Serial films had one particularity: each successive [episode of the] serial began with a quick summary of the previous one. The summaries were edited together out of very small bits of film and each one contained shots of various episodes. I would cut out the introduction, so that in the process of re-editing, many shots would drop out. When rather a large number of these short reels from various films would accumulate, Sergei Mikhailovich and I would engage ourselves over at my place (in my apartment at that time there was an editing table and a small projector) in thinking up new studies, elaborately splicing together the shots once again. This was a useful and lively activity, borrowed by us from L. V. Kuleshov.

Later, Eisenstein and I re-edited a German adventure-detective film about stock-market speculators, cardsharps, courtesans, and aristocrats. The film was called *Dr.*

---

[99] [Trans.]: In the original: перемонтаж [peremontazh]. The Russian word does not emphasis repetition, but rather the sense of through or across. The Russian word for translator переводчик [perevodchik] uses this same prefix. Though the idiomatic translation is re-edit, the sense of *peremontazh* is more "transformative montage," giving the sense that a work undergoing *peremontazh* is being thoroughly repurposed.

Mabuse. We had to re-work[100] it several times. Instead of multiple episodes,[101] it became a two-part film and then, we reduced it to the length of a normal program. Even the title *Dr. Mabuse* disappeared; the film was called *Gilded Decay.*[102] A long title introduced the film. This, by the way, was considered obligatory and necessary in almost all re-edited films. I will cite it in its entirety, since it gives an idea about the direction the work took. The distribution of foreign films was unavoidable, since our own Soviet films were very few in number and did little to distinguish themselves from pre-revolutionary films, either in their content or their execution.

Here is the title:

> International slaughter brought Imperial Germany to division and capitalist collapse. And at that time, when the working class was making incredible efforts to maintain its existence and to repel foreign and internal predators, people who did not participate in the war and in its hardships, having accustomed themselves during wartime to an idle life, to speculation and adventurism, after the war, continued to occupy themselves in the same way, leading licentious and reckless sorts of lives.

As you can see, this is rather primitive, agitational, and confrontational, not to mention, that this title occupied twenty-four meters of film! It lasted more than a minute. And in the silent cinema!

Gradually, at the editing table and in the viewing room, I acquired the knowledge essential for every director. I learned how to properly assess the construction and composition of a shot. I cultivated a memory for shots, for the content and motion within the frame, for the rhythm and pacing of things as a whole. I interiorized when it was necessary and appropriate to change from a wide shot to a medium shot, from a medium shot to a close-up and back again. I understood the magical power of the scissors in the hands of a person possessing mastery of the grammar of montage. I began to try to make the changes imperceptible, so that one shot would replace another in a continuous motion. All this was basic, but I realized it and conceptualized it myself.

And what else was clear to me was this: the necessity of a particular kind of behavior for the film actor in front of the camera, as distinct from the behavior of the theatrical actor. Different laws of mastering through mimicry, through the body, of

---

[100] [Trans.]: In the original: переделывать.

[101] [Trans.]: In the original: Многосерийного. The Lang film is broken down into Acts, but it was never a serial. It appeared as a two-part film. Part One was released on April 27, Part Two on May 26 of 1922. Both parts were quite long so, perhaps, she assumed it was a serial because of the number of reels. Perhaps she is using the term "serial" quite loosely, or perhaps a serial version, unknown in the West, was offered for Russian distribution. Tom Gunning informs me, that the term "serial" was used quite loosely at the time.

[102] [Trans.}: In the original: *Позолоченная гниль.*

movement within the frame, of behavior in specific surroundings with acting partners, and in working with objects. Everything is different. A different expressiveness, a different means of creating an effect, and montage, as the strongest means of eliciting the objectives set by the director. Montage is the most vivid means, that is, of eliciting everything emotionally, which lies within the material which has been shot. In the silent cinema, everything which brought the performance of the actor closer to theatrical solutions, even down to makeup, was perceived as false, as untruth, as tedious.

What was most interesting in my work was to reconstruct, with neither a script, nor intertitles, an intelligible film out of scattered, numberless little reels of film. That is, in essence, to create a scenario for a film, which had already been shot. Since so many such films accumulated in the state rental offices (for some reason they would call them "silent" films), after a time I became somewhat famous in this line of work. From Goskino, I moved over to "Kino-Moskva" and the Vasil'ev brothers, Sergei and Grigory,[103] went to work as editors at Goskino. This was their film school too. I even worked at "Rus'." It was lovely to work there, because Moisei Nikiforovich Aleinikov[104]—the director of production of the artistic collective "Rus'"—was a man of good taste, not a wheeler-dealer; he understood quite well, that he should compel me to come to work with a little notebook in hand, to describe in detail the shots that had struck me, to keep an account of the length of shots in well-edited scenes. He was always attentive and, as a highly qualified specialist, would tactfully approach to help in difficult circumstances.

I remember my consternation when presented with a few small reels with Charlie Chaplin, without the title of the film, without the script, and without intertitles. I put together the disparate reels, which had no numbers indicating their order, on the basis of what happened in them, and called the film *Carmen* and made intertitles, which parodied the opera. Everything went well and the spectators laughed a lot. This was one of the early films of Charlie Chaplin and it was practically the first film in which he acted to appear on Soviet Screens. Later, when I had become a director, when I was in Berlin, I figured out the title of this film; I had a look at the script and the intertitles. I was glad, that many of the ones which I had found for it, were quite close to the real ones.

But this work was not my only form of schooling. I was interested by the activities of L. Kuleshov and his collective. Kuleshov not only directed fiction films, but

---

[103] [Russian editor's note]: *The Vasil'ev Brothers*: pseudonym of the directors, Decorated Worker in the Arts of the RSFSR Grigory Nikolaevich Vasil'ev (1899–1946) and People's Artist of the USSR Sergei Dmitrievich Vasil'ev (1900–1959), who, in collaboration, directed the films *Chapayev*, *The Defense of Volochayevsk* [*Volochaevskie dni* (*Volochaevsk Days*)], *Fortress on the Volga* [*Oborona Tsaritsyna* (*The Defense of Tsaritsyn*)], *The Front*, and others.
[104] [Russian editor's note]: *Aleinikov, Moisei Nikiforovich* (1885–1964). One of the most senior figures of the Russian pre-revolutionary and Soviet cinema; film producer, historian of cinema, and man of letters.

also worked in newsreels. He shot with the cameramen P. Ermolov and E. Tissé on the Eastern and Western Fronts during the Civil War. From the material shot, he edited together several news films: *The Urals, Tverskaya Governate*, and his famous agitfilm *On the Red Front*.[105] Having returned from the front, Kuleshov created his school. He and his comrades trained themselves to work in the cinema in a new way: to shoot in terms of montage, to determine in terms of montage the role of the *kinonaturshchik*[106] (cinema-model) (that's how they referred at that time to the film actor). But they thought little, at that time, about the new content dictated by Soviet reality.

I was to visit laboratory training sessions of his workshop, rehearsals for certain study projects, and small film productions. One of these productions, called "The Venetian Stocking," and based on a scenario by V. Turkin, was of undeniable interest for that time. Everything was subordinated to the intentions of the director. The accuracy of the actors with space and time was magnificent. I was especially struck by the work of V. Pudovkin, A. Khokhlova, B. Barnet, V. Fogel', and S. Komarov. When I remember Khokhlova, it is always painful to me, that her life's work in film production received no official honors. As an actress, she was easily comprehensible and full of eccentric devices,[107] always elegant and daring, and with an original, lyrical quality. She would carry out any task given to her by the director with easy, virtuoso precision, expressive to the very limit. I also used to drop by Kuleshov and Khokhlova's apartment.

A. S. Khokhlova was born a Botkin, of the family of the famous medical doctor Botkin. In the apartment was a lot of lived-in, antique family furniture made of mahogany. I would always think, that, possibly, this furniture was in existence at the time the Botkins would be visited by their friends: Turgenev, Nekrasov, and the poet Fet. Khokhlova minutely resembled her childhood portrait painted by the famous artist Serov. On the table would be slices of black bread and some greens. We all lived modestly and made no effort to live better. The monstrous aspects of the NEP passed us by, but never touched us. We were absorbed by one thing: the desire to work in filmmaking outside the traditions of the old filmmaking and, through our work, to prove, that the cinema was a new domain in the arts. And, in reality, the first films of Kuleshov, *The Extraordinary Adventures of Mr. West in the Land of the Bolsheviks*, based on a scenario by N. Aseev, and *By the Law*, based on a scenario by V. Shklovsky—which adapted a story by Jack London—were received as the foundation of a new development in filmmaking. The treatment, the performance of the actors, shooting according to a preplanned storyboard, the daring use of various kinds of

---

[105] [Russian editor's note]: *On the Red Front*, an adventure agitfilm, made by Kuleshov in 1920. Alongside acted episodes, shot by Kuleshov and his students A. Khokhlova, L. Obolensky, A. Reikh, into the film went war newsreels shot by Kuleshov on the Polish Front.

[106] [Trans.]: In the original: кинонатурщик [kinonaturshchik].

[107] Trans.]: In the original: эксцентриада [ekstsentriada], which comes from a technical aesthetic register: a theater or circus act based on eccentric devices.

shots, and finally, the post-production film montage were all newly discovered and implemented in practice. Kuleshov's actors aided him in this.

As is well known, his student, the eminent director Vsevolod Pudovkin, pursued his research on a completely different path—going farther and deeper than his teacher. He belongs to that group of innovators, who laid the foundations of Socialist Realism in the art of cinema.

I used to come over to Kuleshov's place in the evenings, after his and my work-days. I often found him at the "Kinap" projector, running little 25 meter rolls, and sometimes even shorter ones, experimenting, testing each and every montage variation, in front of me, as he went along, splicing and changing one and another montage study. This was a visual school of montage. Decisions about filmic space had many aspects. It was extremely interesting how Kuleshov had the ability to transmit the simultaneity of events, to create the impression of unity of place with shots, taken in various places, to find montage connections. He possessed an astonishingly accurate sense of the length of alternating shots, taking into consideration the movement within the frame as the basis of rhythm and tempo. All this was demonstrated and made clear visually, willingly, in a spirit of comradeship, simply and cheerfully.

I return once again to Aleksandra Sergeevna Khokhlova.

There should have been scenarios written for her and special films produced. It's laughable to remember now, that directors then preferred the saccharine beauty of the talentless Malinovskaya and that Khokhlova did not work in pictures for years because her face did not conform to the cliché ideal of cinematic beauty. It's possible, that in her creative fate, as in the fate of the director Kuleshov, their enthusiasm for scenarios distant from the life of our country, and, as well, their enthusiasm for detective themes played a negative role. It is interesting, how Khokhlova's talent was seen by such a celebrated master of Soviet filmmaking as S. M. Eisenstein. He wrote: "Khokhlova needs be given the proper treatment, corresponding to her pointedly Soviet repertoire. Decisively casting away her demonic woman, adventuress, et al., I would braid up her pigtails, dress her up in a peasant pinafore[108] and would unleash the first female eccentric actor on the screen (*Dun'ka in the GUM, Dun'ka on the Bus* or something of that sort)."

In my estimation, she would make a good director. Consider even now, how many years later, she shot a short film based on a work by Gorky, *The Affair of the Clasps*, and it will become clear, that we permitted ourselves an unpardonable extravagance: we did not help a genuinely talented human being in any way.

In 1925, I was transferred to the 3rd Goskino Factory (studios were then called "factories"). It was located on a side street right by the Kiev Station Square.

---

[108] [Trans.]: A sarafan.

The directors Yu. Tarich[109] and E. Ivanov-Barkov[110] assigned me to edit a film shot by them called *Trouble*.[111] This was extremely interesting to me. I considered this work a step forward, a new stage in my acquisition of the necessary knowledge for the profession of directing. For the first time, I held in my hands a strip of film with many takes, shot according to a scenario with a Soviet theme, with Soviet heroes.

This small studio was living a fulfilling life. In the course of a year, I edited, though with no credit, the following films: *First Fires*, about the electrification of the country, directed by Yu. Tarich, *Twice the Smoke*,[112] directed by O. Frelikh,[113] *The Skotinins*,[114] the first work in film by the director G. Roshal',[115] *Abrek Zaur*, directed by B. Mikhin,[116] *Father*, a film about life on a kolkhoz directed by L. Molchanov,[117] *Wings of a Serf*, directed by Yu. Tarich (in the role of Ivan the Terrible is the celebrated artist of the Moscow Art Theater L. Leonidov) and others. At that very time, Kuleshov was shooting his film *By the Law*, based on a scenario by V. Shklovsky.

V. Shklovsky also did a great deal of work on K. Shil'dkret's scenario for *Wings of a Serf*. His participation in the reworking of the scenario already in production, his presence on the set, his creative and comradely collaboration with the director unquestionably helped make this film a noteworthy phenomenon of the young Soviet Cinema.

---

[109] [Russian editor's note]: *Tarich, Yuri Viktorovich* (1885–1967). Film director. Decorated Worker in the Arts of the RSFSR and BSSR. One of the founders of Belorussian Film Production. He directed the following films: *First Fires, Darkness* (in collaboration with E. Ivanov-Barkov), *Wings of a Serf* aka *Ivan the Terrible, A Tale of the Woods, The Captain's Daughter, Hatred,* Путь корабля (*The Path of a Ship*), and others.

[110] [Russian editor's note]: *Ivanov-Barkov, Evgeny Aleksandrovich* (1892–1965). Film director and screenwriter. Decorated Worker in the Arts of the Turkmen Soviet Socialist Republic. He began work in the cinema in 1919. His first production as sole director was *Heroes of the Blast Furnace*. His best known films are *Dursun, Darkness*, and *The Distant Bride* aka *Under Sunny Skies*.

[111] [Trans.]: On the film, the title is given as Две силы (Морока), meaning: *Two Forces*, though posters show only Морока.

[112] [Trans.]: In the original: Два дыма. Also known as Девушка-Героя (*The Girl Hero*).

[113] [Russian editor's note]: *Frelikh, Oleg Nikolaevich* (1887–1953). Film and theater actor. Known for his roles in the following silent films: *A Spectre is Haunting Europe, Locksmith and Chancellor,* Хозяин черных скал (*The Master of Black Rocks*), and others. His final works in the cinema were the role of the professor in the film *Zhukovsky* and the role of [U.S. President Franklin Delano] Roosevelt in *The Fall of Berlin*.

[114] [Trans.]: In the original: Господа Скотинины.

[115] [Russian editor's note]: *Roshal', Grigory L'vovich* (b. 1899). Film director. People's Artist of the USSR. He directed the following films: *The Skotinins, Salamander, Petersburg Nights, The Paris Commune, Ivan Pavlov, Musorgsky, The Sisters, 1918, Gloomy Morning, A Year as Long as Life* aka *Karl Marx* and others.

[116] [Russian editor's note]: *Mikhin, Boris Aleksandrovich* (1881–1963). Film director and film producer, one of the most senior figures of Russian pre-revolutionary and Soviet film production. Director of the film *Abrek Zaur*.

[117] [Russian editor's note]: *Molchanov, Leonid Mikhailovich*, film director. Director of the film *Father, The Sound of Pine Trees,* Полесские робинзоны (*The Robinsons of Polesie*).

I will never forget my first day at work at the 3rd Factory. The editing room, such as it was, had no editing table, no normal rewinds[118] with properly functioning reels. The young editor Tanechka Kuvshinchikova met me in a state of confusion. Since then, she has pursued a glorious path of labor for many years. She is now known to everyone as the respected comrade Tat'yana Nikolaevna Kuvshinchikova. For many years, she has worked at the documentary film studio. Always, when I run into her, we invariably, more mentally than anything else, as we exchange smiles, recall my first day at the 3rd Factory.

In a little room, without much light, with a single window onto the side street, we would lay a flannel blanket out on the floor and we would throw onto the blanket all the trims and would begin to select the film necessary to fill out the pieces of the rough cut selected and cut out by the directors. At that time, it was widely and falsely believed, that the more frequently in the scene the shots changed and the shorter the shots were, the more expressive and dynamic was the film. Movement within the frame was not taken into account. This frequently resulted in utter absurdity. The endless movements of the actors' faces were perceived as unintelligible and purposeless.

In order to correct this, we would splice back in (and by hand) pieces of film, which had been cut out, to the corresponding shots. We wound up the film on the towering rewinds with only one reel. There was no second reel. There was also no storyboard from the director. I got verbal approval from the director for everything I intended to do. From that time on, I have felt a deep gratitude towards Tarich and Ivanov-Barkov for trusting in my ability to aid them, for entrusting the fate of their film, for allowing me, in essence, to reconceive their film in the editing. They entrusted me with a directorial function. This was the beginning of a very important stage for me.

Within a few months, I was managing a beautifully-equipped editing studio. In a large bright room stood five editing tables, well-illuminated with electric lights, with proper rewinds and reels. Yu. Tarich's assistant directors (V. Korsh[119] and I. Pyr'ev[120]) would often come by to see me in the editing room. A student of

---

[118] [Trans.]: In the original: моталка [motalka]. Usages of the word in the text and images of the period I have seen lead me to believe that a *motalka* was essentially a set of rewinds, though it may designate rewinds and a viewer. Мотать пленку [motat' plenku] means to wind film; перемотать пленку [peremotat' plenku] is to rewind film.

[119] [Russian editor's note]: *Korsh-Sablin, Vladimir Vladimirovich* (b. 1900). Film director. People's Artist of the USSR. One of the founders of Belorussian Filmmaking. He directed the films: *The First Platoon, Seekers of Happiness, My Love, Konstantin Zaslonov, Red Leaves* and others.

[120] [Russian editor's note]: *Pyr'ev, Ivan Aleksandrovich* (1901–1968). Film director. People's Artist of the USSR. Actor in Meyerhold's theater. His path to the cinema began as an assistant to Yu. Tarich. He directed the silent films *The Other Woman, The Civil Servant*. Wide popularity was enjoyed by *Party Card, The Rich Bride, Tractor Drivers, The Swineherd and the Shepherd* aka *They met in Moscow, We Will Come Back* aka *The District Secretary, The Idiot, The Brothers Karamazov* and others.

Vs. Meyerhold, Ivan Pyr'ev would always storm in with his propositions, defend them somewhat temperamentally, argue, think up things, and I had no doubt even then, that he, with his distinctive, somewhat eccentric views about various aspects of our craft, was a future director.

One day, unexpectedly for me, a distinguished guest visited the editing room: Henri Barbusse. The head of the studio, M. Kresin, and a translator accompanied him. Barbusse had the look of a sick man. I immediately recognized him, although his face was badly aged, with deep furrows. Only the eyes on his austere face were deeply alive. He did not smile even once. We spoke for rather a long time. He inquired of me about the content of the films that I was editing. Films about Soviet realities especially interested him.

The most meaningful lessons for me were the trips with Shklovsky to the Kolomena rural settlement, to the place where *The Wings of a Serf* was being shot. Often, Shklovsky and the staff script writer of the factory B. Leonidov[121] would ride back home with me and together we would work on the director's storyboard for one scene or another that was about to be shot.

It was memorable, how, at the time of the screening of all the takes, the shots of the Moscow Art Theater artist Leonidov produced a strong impression on me; it was his eyes, or rather, the relentlessly threatening expression of his face with a slight narrowing of one eye at the moment the take began, when the light from the lighting equipment flared up. This footage at the beginning of a shot, would usually be cut out, as a matter of course. I began to realize that this facial expression of the artist could be used meaningfully in particular moments of the film. What remained was to see how Leonidov would take this. He worked a lot on this part, he rehearsed carefully before a take, and for the take he demanded a lot of himself. He was extremely interested in the editing of the film. I invariably showed him all the edited scenes, conferred with him about the choice of takes and was utterly overjoyed when he not only accepted, but even encouraged me for the use of these shots, which were not in the director's storyboard. Truly, an added, extremely distinctive coloration was given to the image imagined beforehand. It became customary for other directors to invite me to the studio during shooting. As for the film *By the Law*, I made use of every occasion to be present for rehearsals and for the shoots. It proceeded very much according to plan, professionally, intelligently; there was a great deal to be learned there.

This year came to an end with what was for me a noteworthy event. S. M. Eisenstein proposed that I work with him on the shooting script[122] for *Strike*. It

---

[121] [Russian editor's note]: *Leonidov, Boris Leonidovich* (1892–1958). Screenwriter. Author of the scenario for the films: *The House in the Snowdrifts, The Parisian Cobbler, Bay of Death, Katerina Izmailova, The Forty-First.*

[122] [Trans.]: In the original: режиссерский вариант сценария.

Leonidov's squint.

was proposed that after this I would become part of the production team. This determined my subsequent career in filmmaking. We were by that time the greatest of friends. We were brought together by the common views on filmmaking we held. We worked for at least two months at my home on *Strike*. The shooting script was approved and accepted for production. But I did not become part of the production team.

In *Strike*, Eisenstein set for his goal to make a film, where the principal actors should be the workers' collective of a factory, a film about the struggles of the workers for their political and economic rights. In the process of shooting, Eisenstein changed his conception of the scenario and reworked specific scenes spontaneously on the spot while shooting. *Strike* was criticized for the eccentricity of some of the scenes, for the superficial performances of the actors, for the lack of memorable, exciting images of specific heroes. But the fundamental treatment of *Strike* might be regarded as agitational. Everyone agrees that *Strike* was undoubtedly an advance for Soviet Filmmaking, that this was the first proletarian film. The beautiful camera work of cameraman Eduard Tissé is still remarked upon.

On April 28, 1925, the workers of Moscow saw *Strike* at the Colosseum theater. The reception was a warm one. Only a few young workers criticized the film for lacking heroes; they complained, that the director had made only the factory collective the principal hero of the film, that there were no people acting individually. Some critics maintained, that the best parts of *Strike* were realized under the influence of the work of Dziga Vertov.[123]

This is how Vertov himself wrote about the film: "We consider *Strike* an experiment in the inoculation of the feature film with some of the methods of *Kinoeye*. Close to the Kinoks are: the montage construction, the choice of shots taken, the construction of intertitles in this picture. Alien are: actors, everything theatrical and circus-like, everything deriving from fiction film. On behalf of the Kinoks, D. Vertov."

But everything approved of by the Kinoks was not what was generally at stake in *Strike*.

And this did not define the significance of this first directorial work of S. M. Eisenstein.

I was distressed, that I was not part of the production collective of *Strike*, but now I think, that perhaps, this was helpful. What interested me most of all in art, was its connection with our reality, everything that reflected and strengthened it. I was finding my own way. At that time, I became acquainted with Dziga Vertov; I became interested in his activity.

Dziga Vertov

I do not intend to remember my comrade, as would an historian. Yes, and not everything I intended to write could be a part of the history of Soviet filmmaking…
Dziga Vertov was my close comrade; his activity helped me to determine the path, on which I should search for my place in filmmaking.

He was an innovator, an inventor, a searcher after new ways and means of expression in the newsreel. And although there was much about which we did not agree, about which we vehemently argued, and because of which we attacked one another, our argument was that of a student and a teacher. The student, of course, was me. Because of this, I need to be careful, in the face of disquieting memories about him, in order not to lose objectivity in assessing his place in Soviet filmmaking.

---

[123] [Russian editor's note]: *Vertov, Dziga* (Denis Arkad'evich Kaufman) (1896–1954). Director of newsreel-documentary cinema, one of the founders of a school of Soviet social-political journalism in film. [Trans.]: This somewhat diffident estimation of Vertov compared to other less important filmmakers is an index to the low estimation to which Vertov had been relegated in official circles at the time. He had been strongly condemned by those enforcing the reigning canons of Socialist Realism. Considering Vertov's blanket dismissal of some of Shub's most important work, she is truly bending over backwards to be fair. In fact, she is taking a risk on his behalf for the judgment of history.

From the beginning of 1923 to 1926 our meetings were frequent. I was able to observe him both at work and in close personal interactions. All of our conversations, our arguments, the plans which were born as the result of the arguments, bore in them the stamp of youthful passion, of an interest in our own affairs.

In 1923, he was still quite young: 25, with a determined character, happy, in love with Soviet life, full of plans, a swirl of activity.

He understood quite well the necessity and the significance of varied shots, taken from a variety of angles, of Soviet reality. At the same time he was a visionary, a poet. He knew and loved Mayakovsky and Whitman. He was very musical, symphonic music in particular would seize hold of him, with its powerful, polyphonic, orchestral resonance, musical rhythm, tempo… You would need to have seen Vertov during the process of mixing the sound for his first large-scale documentary films at the facilities of the [State] Committee for Radio Broadcasting, in order to understand, that he put the entire force of his talent into the objective of carefully selecting music that would merge with the visual content of the shot, the rhythm and theme of the film. Music directors and arrangers understood this characteristic of his, respected him, and willingly submitted to him.

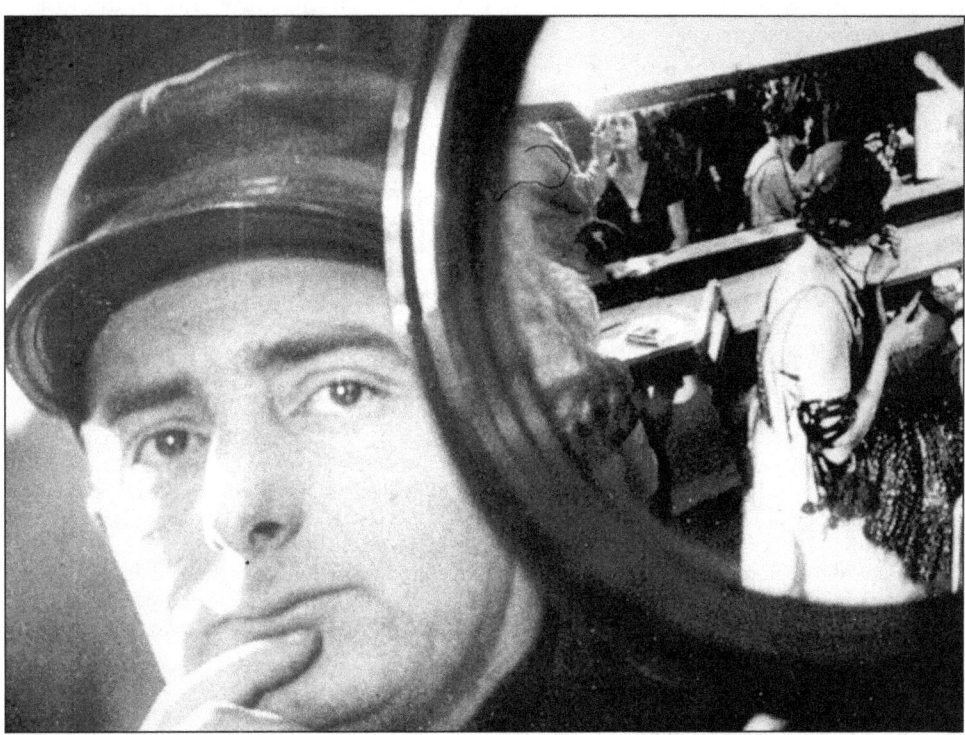

From 1923 to 1925, Dziga Vertov put out *Kino-Pravda* every month,[124] laying the foundations for the newsreel: revolutionary and Soviet in its content and new in its form.

The Kinoks,[125] as Dziga Vertov's group called themselves, and the Kinoconstructivists (the group, who edited and published the journal *Kino-Fot*),[126] declared war on "acted,"[127] as they then called it "aesthetic"[128] filmmaking. They considered it indispensable, that the movie camera be used for shooting new modes of social life and its dynamics and through montage to transfer to the screen the truth of our reality.

They made it their objective to show to the spectator the new stirrings of socialist modes of life, to show simple genuine people in everyday life. To shoot not only parades and public meetings, but everything without exception, whatever transpires in the course of the day, from early waking to late at night, the daily vortex of labor, the evening hours of free leisure time.

They considered, that such films should be finished productions. They said, that it was not enough to connect separate moments, separate scenes by means of montage into a single motion picture, unified more or less by means of appropriate titles. Seizing on unexpected happenings, developments, events, comparing them, discovering the organic connection among them, it was necessary to know how to disclose their innermost essence.

Besides that, the "Kinoks" denied the necessity of a preparatory shooting and scenario plan, considering, that this was necessary only for "acted" cinema. [129]

---

[124] [Russian editor's note]: *Kino-Pravda* was a film journal of Goskino, which appeared from 1922 to 1925. During this time, 23 issues appeared under the general title of *Kino-Pravda*, except for the following: №13: *Yesterday, Today, Tomorrow*, 1923; № 16: *Spring Pravda*, 1923; № 19: *The Black Sea—The Arctic Ocean—Moscow*, 1924; № 20 *Pioneer Pravda*, 1924; № 21 *Leninist Kino-Pravda*, 1925; № 22: *Lenin is Alive in the Heart of the Peasant*, 1925; № 23: *Radiokinopravda*, 1925. The film journal was made with Dziga Vertov as director, and author of the scenario outlines and intertitles. The camera operators were: M. Kaufman, A. Levitsky, A. Lemberg, P. Novitsky, E. Tissé, I. Belyakov, E. Bushkin, G. Giber. The artist A. Rodchenko took part in the graphic design of the subtitles of certain issues.

[125] [Russian editor's note]: *The Kinoks* were like-minded followers of Dziga Vertov, who formed a group under his direction. The group included: M. Kaufman, I. Belyakov, A. Lemberg, the editor E. Svilova, the so-called "secret agents" I. Kopalin, P. Zotov, and others. The name of the "kinoks" derives from the word kino objective [i.e. lens], that is "kinoglaz" [kinoeye] or "kinooko" [kinoeye] in the terminology of Dziga Vertov. The platform of the "kinoks" is laid out in the manifesto by Dziga Vertov: "The Kinoks. A Revolution," published in the journal *LEF*, Moscow, 1922. № 3.

[126] [Russian editor's note]: *Kino-Fot*, a journal of filmmaking and photography (the publication of the Constructivists; Moscow, 1922). Editor-in-Chief A. Gan (№ 1–4). In the journal were published: V. Mayakovsky's declaration about filmmaking (1922. № 50), Dziga Vertov's manifesto (1922, № 1), and a piece by Lev Kuleshov (1922. № 1).

[127] [Trans.]: In the original: игровой.

[128] [Trans.]: In the original: эстетической.

[129] [Trans.]: In the original: игровая кинематография.

They shot events, developments, the life of the country, even Vertov himself. The first works of D. Vertov were also made from these newsreels. But the quality of the shots was insufficient for him, neither was their content, that is, in the conception of what was shot, either in form, or in the painterly visual qualities of the shot.[130] Because of this, he himself began to direct the shoots.

I could, as has been done up to now, busy myself with citations from his manifestos, in which the stamp of the youth of the artist and the "childhood disease of Leftism" may be found. I'm not going to do that. I'm not doing that, because it does little to contribute to an understanding of D. Vertov and his significance in the Soviet newsreel. His practical activity, his work is what characterizes him most vividly.

I will never forget Dziga Vertov, standing on the dais of the great studio auditorium, overflowing with people working in newsreels. With an agitated voice, he responded to the attacks of his comrades, who had already accused him of formalism in the postwar years. He responded simply, with profound honesty, from the heart.

This was the meaning of his words: why do you want to take me back to the childhood of my creative path, to my theoretical errors, with which I have long since finished, which I do not love and which make me ashamed to remember. In all my works, in all my activities of the years following, I have tried to demonstrate that.

What, in essence, are the lasting contributions of Vertov to the newsreel and what are the practical and ideological errors of some of his directives?

The group of the "Kinoks" consisted of the camera operators Kaufman,[131] Lemberg, Belyakov,[132] the directors Kopalin,[133] and Svilova.[134] Vertov was appointed by them as their leader.

He was the first to understand how deep the connection must be between the director of a newsreel and the cameraman in realizing his idea. He, as no one else, understood, that material satisfying to the director does not fall from the sky, is not the result of long and, to a greater or lesser extent, speculative conversations between the director and the cameraman. One must take action, that is, one must be present with the cameraman where the shooting takes place. One must stand with

---

[130] [Trans.]: In the original: живописной образности кадра; this might also be rendered "the pictorial visuality of the shot."

[131] [Russian editor's note]: *Kaufman, Mikhail Abramovich* (b. 1897). Camera operator. Decorated Worker in the Arts of the RSFSR. He worked with Dziga Vertov for many years.

[132] [Russian editor's note]: *Belyakov, Ivan Ivanovich* (b. 1900). Camera operator. Decorated Worker in the Arts of the RSFSR. He worked in newsreels starting in 1924. Did camera work for Vertov's pictures *Kino-Pravda, Kino Calendar, Kino Week*, and was a camera operator for Vertov's films *Stride Forward, Soviet!* and *A Sixth Part of the World*.

[133] [Russian editor's note]: *Kopalin, Il'ya Petrovich* (b. 1900). Director of documentary cinema. People's Artist of the USSR. Began to work in cinema in 1925 in the "Kinoks" group of Dziga Vertov.

[134] [Russian editor's note]: *Svilova, Elizaveta Ignat'evna* (b. 1900). Director of documentary cinema. Wife of Dziga Vertov; worked with Dziga Vertov on Documentary films for many years.

the cameraman at the lens of the camera. One must know how, at the location where shooting takes place, to give instantaneous instructions. He especially valued the work of a cameraman using a portable, mobile camera in his hands, which at that time was the "Kinamo." With Kaufman and other cameramen of his group, he would go to many places in the Soviet Union, shooting everything most lively, everything connected with the period of reconstruction, with the great construction projects of the Five-Year Plans. He would go to kolkhozes, sovkhozes, recording along the way the new growths of the socialist mode of life, shooting the most crucial moments in the life of the country.

He maintained, that the lens of the camera perceived the world in a more multi-faceted way, from more distinct visual angles and more completely than the human eye. And for that reason, there was never an end to his imagining, where and how to direct the lens of the camera: the "eye of the cinema."[135]

He knew how differently people perceived industrial sites, landscapes, and objects from how they shot them: from the highest points and from the lowest, with a stationary camera and one in motion. He boldly took upon himself the decision about the point from which one shot, or another, should be taken.

He knew, as did no one else, that the correct understanding of cinematic space and time determine the expressiveness and the power to influence of a shot. And in this, his imagination was limitless.

He saw all phenomena in terms of dynamics. He limited himself to a single intrinsic motion, but made the lens of the camera move together with the motion within the frame—moving closer and farther away, and in parallel motion. He would shoot from moving cranes, from any moving points, in this way, expanding space even from points above. He was always busy with experimental technical research. I can say, without exaggeration, that very little has likely been done in that direction since that time, either in the newsreel or in the feature film. Now, remembering all his experiments, I would say, that he avoided the static more than was necessary. He did not always take into consideration the force and expressiveness of a properly used static shot.

In the newsreel, new material made its appearance: short, dynamic pieces [of film] with pointed, compositional solutions, with multiple variations in shot: wide, medium, close-up.

Kaufman the camera operator accomplished everything with supreme mastery. Working with a small portable camera, the "Kinamo," or even with the cumbersome static cameras of that time, he always strove, in any circumstances, towards mobility. He helped Vertov to shoot life unawares, especially people, never disturbing their natural behavior.

---

[135] [Trans.]: Shub evokes the formulation киноглаз [kinoglaz] with the phrase "глаз кино" [glaz kino].

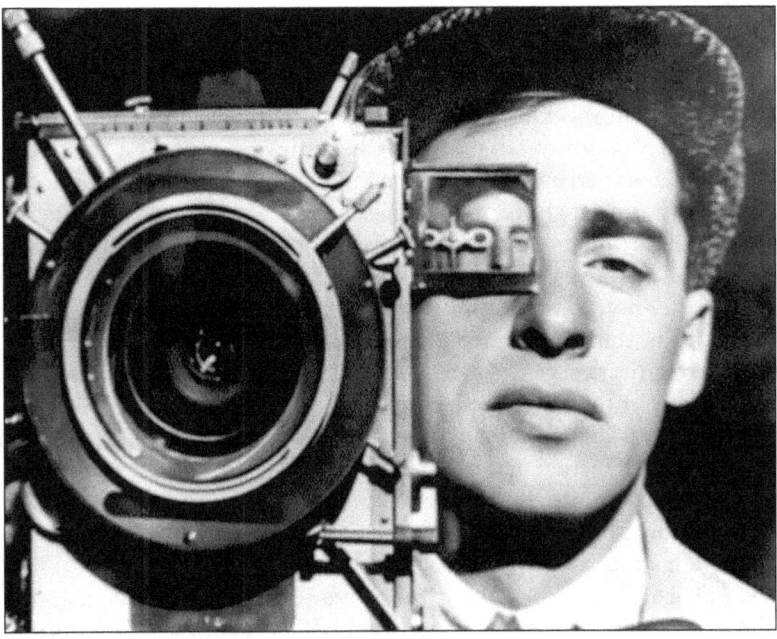

Kinok camera operator Mikhail Kaufman.

"Life unawares"[136] without acted moments, without the premeditated and unnatural behavior of a man in front of a camera. To aid a man, not an actor, to be natural, to strip him of his inhibitions because of the mere gaze of the lens directed at him.

This system, undoubtedly valid for film reportage, contained extremes, which led Vertov towards purely formal solutions. But this was also its positive side. It forced creative people working in newsreels to seriously think about how to work out the correct methods for shooting people genuinely carrying out their activities, without disturbing their genuine natural behavior.

Vertov's montage was the most experimental part of his work and in many ways the most formal. Conceiving montage in time and space anew, in the process of

---

[136] [Russian editor's note]: "Life unawares" (*Kinoglaz*), a film of an experimental character, made by Dziga Vertov and his group the "kinoks" in 1924. In the creation of several specific episodes of the film, the method of film-observation, theoretically laid down by Dziga Vertov in his articles and manifestos, was employed. One of the most important devices of the kinoks was shooting "life unawares," which in contemporary cinema is known as shooting with a "hidden camera." This device also gave the film its title. [Trans.]: In the original: Жизнь врасплох. This was the subtitle to the film: *KINO-GLAZ: On its First Reconnaissance Mission 1st series of the cycle "Life Unawares."*

working, he shortened alternating pieces of film to two frames or even a single frame. His assertion that a closeup being seen several times in precise alternation can be shortened in length each time, that such a shot can be remembered visually even at two frames, was correct, but this kind of montage helps the conception of the scene very little and leads the spectator to fall in love with the device itself.

The assertion was erroneous, that one kind of montage can be applied to any content; the enthusiasm for shots of machines, details, and objects was excessive. The absence of people impoverished the contents of the frame. The enthusiasm for montage principles lead the kinoks to contradiction, to the annihilation of the conceptual meaning of the shot, to the annihilation of documentation. Outside of montage, the shot expressed nothing, it became a sign, a segment of a montage phrase. A fact was used with no indication of the location of the action, outside of time. Individuals genuinely carrying out their activities were stripped of their first and last names. The fact, stripped of the assignment of a date, was aestheticized and distorted. All the same, the artist working with factual material, should clearly understand, that in art what is important is not the fact in itself, but the relation of the artist to the fact, his vision, his conception "according to the Party" of factual material. Even D. Vertov understood this quite well in his final works.

One of Dziga Vertov's first outstanding works was *Kino-Pravda*; appearing in 1925, on the anniversary of the death of Vladimir Il'ich Lenin was *Leninist Kino-Pravda*.[137] This three-part film (Lenin's actions, Lenin's funeral, Lenin is alive) was accomplished by Vertov magnificently, in the spirit of the People. The film had a great influence on all of Soviet cinema.

S. M. Eisenstein, who denied the influence of Vertov's work on *Strike*, with the probity and honesty of a great artist, more than once said to me—I am certain, that he said it not only to me, but to his students at the GIK—that one of the best dramatic scenes of *The Battleship Potemkin*—the public meeting before the corpse of Vakulin-chuk—was done under the direct influence of this production of Vertov.

A great and interesting work was *A Sixth Part of the World*.[138] The film was commissioned by Gostorg as an advertisement. It was shot under Vertov's direction

---

[137] [Russian editor's note]: *Leninist Kino-Pravda* was a film poem about Lenin. It appeared 1925, the 21st issue of *Kino-Pravda*. Dziga Vertov is the author of the outline and intertitles and is the director. In the film, shots by the following newsreel camera operators are used: G. Giber, M. Kaufman, A. Levitsky, A. Lemberg, P. Novitsky, E. Tissé and others. Its creation by Dziga Vertov can be considered as anticipating his film *Three Songs about Lenin* (1934).

[138] [Russian editor's note]: *A Sixth Part of the World*, a film done by the "kinoks" group in 1926 at the Kultkino, Goskino, and Sovkino factories. Author-manager: Dziga Vertov, principal camera operator: M. Kaufman, additional camera operators: I. Belyakov, S. Bendersky, P. Zotov, N. Konstantinov, A. Lemberg, N. Strukov, Ya. Tolchan; location scouts: A. Kagarlitsky, I. Kopalin, B. Kudinov. [Trans.]: The Russian editor omits E. Svilova's credit: "Ассистент режиссера Е. Свилова," (Assistant to the director, or even Assistant Director, E. Svilova).

by many cameramen in various locations in our great Motherland. And immediately, during the process of montage, D. Vertov expanded the assignment. Along with the advertising film, came the first journalistic documentary film. The film was decidedly poetic. The intertitles accompanying the shots, showing the richness of the Soviet Union, the new way of life, the most remote outlying regions, state commerce, the broad possibilities for exports, in what can only be called a poetic sequence, were as if a prolongation of the shots, flowing together with them, prolonging and deepening them, bringing a poetic resonance to the film. *A Sixth Part of the World* was visually graphic poetry. This, of course, was new. It also awakened creative thought.

In 1929, the film *Man With a Movie Camera*[139] was created by Vertov. In this film, there was not a single intertitle. The shots, conceived through montage, according to Dziga Vertov, should speak for themselves. He made it his objective in this film to affirm the practices of the kinoks. He attempted to show, that the *kinoglaz* [*kino-eye*] of the lens of the camera, could penetrate into every corner of human life. He observed secretly, he listened secretly, he seized life unawares. The whole film was accomplished with the device stripped bare. The principal hero of the film is the cameraman M. Kaufman. He is quick and inventive. He sees and shoots much that the unaided eye cannot. Vertov considered that the lens of the camera was able to disclose to the spectators all the complexity of the contradictions of life.

Vertov made use in this film of the full arsenal of his montage devices, in order to make a film that was captivating and rhythmic. In it, was much that was brilliant, much that was thoughtful, but also, an extensive formal sophistication, which impaired the force and truth of the document.

Critics maintained, that this film was simply formalistic. Nonetheless, even in this film, the force of revolutionary reality was victorious.

I want to tell the story of a screening of this film in a large theater in Berlin on the Kurfürstendamm. The theater was full to overflowing with figures in the arts and leading members of the intelligentsia.

At the beginning of the screening, D. Vertov spoke. He spoke in German. He spoke briefly and concisely about his native land, about the goals established by the group, which had realized this film. The screening proceeded with great success. All the newspapers remarked upon the revolutionary quality, the innovation and daring of this film. After the screening, which Il'ya Ehrenburg attended, Ehrenburg invited Vertov and me to go to a restaurant with him. It was some kind of ballroom, over-

---

[139] [Russian editor's note]: *Man With a Movie Camera* a kino-feuilleton in 6 reels [or parts], a production of the Kiev factory of VUFKU. Author-manager: Dziga Vertov, Principal camera operator: M. Kaufman. Assistant Director: E. Svilova. The film was made in 1929 immediately after the film *The Eleventh Year*. In aiming for a "purity of film language" Vertov did not make use here of intertitles: in the film, the movie camera predominates, all the possibilities of which are used for the fixation of the phenomena of reality. [Trans.]: Svilova's actual credit in the film is Ассистент по монтажу [Assistant in Editing].

flowing with people, gaudily decorated in gold with a large number of mirrors, where they danced the foxtrot the whole time. From time to time, the ceiling would slide open to reveal the starry heaven high above. We spoke for a long time about another heaven, about other people—our own people. We spoke about our native land.

Some historians of the cinema end their analysis of Dziga Vertov's activities in filmmaking with this film. All the same, after this, Vertov created *Symphony of the Donbass*,[140] *Three Songs about Lenin*,[141] *Lullaby*.[142]

At the invitation of a film organization, Dziga Vertov brought his film *Symphony of the Donbass* to Berlin, Hamburg, Breslau, and Hannover, then left for Basel. Everywhere the film had a great success, but everywhere because of pressure from the press, within 24 hours, Vertov would be invited to leave the city. From Switzerland, he left for London. At the time, Charlie Chaplin lived there. He invited Vertov to come to his place and show the film *Symphony of the Donbass*.

After the screening of the film, Chaplin wrote Vertov the following letter:

I never knew that industrial films could be arranged so that they came out so beautifully. I consider this film one of the most exciting symphonies I have ever heard. Dziga Vertov is a musician. The professors should study with him and not quarrel with him.

Accept my congratulations,

Charlie Chaplin, November 17, 1931.[143]

---

[140] [Russian editor's note]: *Symphony of the Donbass* (*Enthusiasm*), Dziga Vertov's first sound film, made at the beginning of the sound era, in 1930. Before the author lay still unresolved technical and aesthetic problems, to which Vertov responded as a bold experimentalist. In Professor Shorin's laboratory, an apparatus was created, which permitted synch sound recording on location. Enriching the imagery with a background of real sounds, the author set the task for himself of creating a symphony of labor. Camera operator on the film B. Tseitlin, sound operator P. Shtro, Assistant Director, E. Svilova.

[141] [Russian editor's note]: *Three Songs about Lenin*, Documentary sound film, a Mezhrabpomfilm Production (1934). Author-Director [Автор-режиссер] Dziga Vertov; assistant [ассистент] E. Svilova; camera operators D. Surensky, M. Magidson, B. Monastyrsky, as well as newsreel cameramen, who had filmed V. I. Lenin, whose shots were used in the film. This classic documentary film, which brought glory to Soviet film art, was informed by all the previous creative activity of Dziga Vertov, his research, experiments, discoveries. Vertov addressed the theme of Lenin repeatedly in many of his works: one might say that it never left him: he identified Lenin with the life of the country and the fate of its people. The influence of the film *Three Songs about Lenin* on the film art of the world is difficult to overestimate.

[142] [Russian editor's note]: *Lullaby* a documentary sound film, created by the author-director [Автор-режиссер] Dziga Vertov in the "Soyuzkinokhronika" [Union Newsreel] film studio in 1937. A film poem about the happiness of Soviet women who are mothers. Co-director [Со-режиссер] E. Svilova, camera operator D. Surensky, Music by Dm. and Dan. Pokrass, Text by Dziga Vertov. Sound operator I. Renkov, Songs by V. Lebedev-Kumach.

[143] [Russian editor's note at the bottom of the page]: Original letter from C. Chaplin to Dziga Vertov

I, myself, after the Great Patriotic War, by chance managed to see some selected reels of *Symphony of the Donbass*. The impression was great; the film not only withstood the test of time, but achieved significance as a chronicle of the time. In the montage, Vertov succeeded in making visual material flow together with words, music, and sounds recorded in documentary fashion. All this gave the artist the right to call the film a symphony.

Three Songs about Lenin was one of the best of Vertov's works, being done with great enthusiasm. The film ably combined archival documents and newly photographed shots with songs, music, sounds. The entire lyrical make-up of the film was poetic, moving, and of the People. It deeply, truthfully expressed joy and grief; it made beautiful use of the recordings of the speeches of the shock workers of Dneprostroi.

Now, looking back on Vertov's creative path, I am sorry, that this talented artist, the world's pioneering founder of documentary film, in the subsequent years of his life made no other feature-length pictures.

He was a remarkably sincere human being, unselfish, without a hint, without a speck of narrow-mindedness in questions of art. In all the subsequent years, D. Vertov, once a month created an installment of the periodical in film *News of the Day* [*Novosti Dnya*]. He returned to the work of the early years of his youth. He did this diligently, demanding a great deal of himself. For him, as for any genuinely talented person, there could be no distinction between "big" and "small" projects. Everything is important; everything is to be taken seriously.[144]

Unfortunately, among us, the creative people in the cinema—and not only in the newsreel—are distinguished by one very problematic characteristic. They lack a sense of [historical] continuity. There is no sense of taking up the baton in the relay race of art. All the same, it is important, while not bringing to a standstill—even for a minute—the forward movement of art to daring new discoveries, not to forget the founders and their place in this movement.

Some of us think, that the history of Soviet filmmaking begins only with his own works.

M. Gorky and V. Mayakovsky are great examples of a different sort of relationship with their contemporaries. Maxim Gorky's book about remarkable people, his correspondence and personal ties with writers are all striking examples.

---

preserved in the archive of E. Svilova. Published in I. P. Abramov's book *Дзига Вертов* (М. Изд-во АН СССР, 1962, стр 124) (*Dziga Vertov*. Moscow. Academy of Sciences of the USSR Publishing House, 1962, p. 124). [Trans.]: This is actually a slight mistranslation of the original letter, which reads: "Never had I known that these mechanical sounds could be arranged to sound so beautiful. I regard it as one of the most exhilarating symphonies I have heard. Mr. Dziga Vertov is a musician. The professors should learn from him, not quarrel with him. Congratulations." As quoted by Jeremy Hicks, *Dziga Vertov: Defining Documentary Film* (I.B. Tauris, 2007), p. 126.

[144] [Trans.]: Shub suffered a similar fate: after a distinguished career in feature-length documentaries, she was allowed to make only a few short films, and finally, only to edit newsreels.

Just as leading figures in the theater honored and continue to honor their contemporaries: Stanislavsky, Nemirovich-Danchenko, Vakhtangov...[145]

Dear Dziga Vertov! How beautiful, great, and majestic is our native land that you loved so much.

So many captivating journeys with a movie camera around the boundless space of our country remain to be accomplished, around cities and kolkhozes, factories and industrial complexes, around new construction and new highways, new seas and around millions of hectares of tilled, virgin, and fallow land! How many beautiful, simple people the movie camera will film.

Creative thought moves forward, grows, and broadens.

Soviet power, our Communist Party help us to grow, to dare, to be bold, to place before ourselves ever more crucial tasks, and to fulfill them with great artistic force.

Among us in the documentary cinema, there are wonderful camera operators. There are people who you can shoot with. Each day brings significant themes, which can resound most brilliantly in the documentary cinema.

How many beautiful works lie ahead!

And in all that has been done, that is done now, in all tomorrow's discoveries, your labor will not be lost. It will remain a part of it forever.

---

[145] I believe these unexplained ellipses might be completed with other names, such as that of Meyerhold, who was cleared of espionage charges only in late 1955, some 15 years after his execution. Writing in 1953–55, Shub does not shy away from describing her relationship with him. Fadeev mentions overhearing patients in the sanatorium where he had been discussing Meyerhold's possible rehabilitation and indicates in a letter of November 1955 the strategic necessity of a mention of Meyerhold in the book she is writing. See Letter #51 in this volume.

Trip to Berlin in 1929

In 1929, at the time Dziga Vertov was showing *Man With a Movie Camera* in Berlin, a large group of Soviet workers in filmmaking traveled there as well.

The director Erofeev[146] was shooting a film called *Berlin*, Alexander Dovzhenko[147] came in order to prepare his film *Arsenal* for its release in Germany. The screenwriter Natan Zarkhi,[148] the directors E. Chervyakov[149] and K. Eggert,[150] celebrated for his film *The Bear's Wedding*, and I. Trainin,[151] the head of Glavrepertkom, were all in Berlin. I was sent there, in order to realize, in collaboration with the German Communist organization "Weltfilm," the production of a film with the working title *Two Worlds*. Subsequently, this film came out here with the title *Сегодня* (*Today*) and in Germany, it was called *Tractors and Cannons*.[152]

D. Vertov, A. Dovzhenko, I. Trainin, and I lived in the Soviet guest house.

Berlin was lovely in those days. A lot of greenery, on the balconies red carnations, asphalt roadways worn so smooth by automobiles that they sparkled like a

---

[146] [Russian editor's note]: *Erofeev, Vladimir Alekseevich* (1898–1940). Documentary film director. He shot pictures about foreign countries and about the Soviet East: *Afghanistan*, *To a Safe Harbor* (*Berlin*), *The Wings of the World* (*The Pamir Mountains*), *The Heart of Asia* and others.

[147] [Russian editor's note]: *Dovzhenko, Alexander Petrovich* (1894–1954). Director, screenwriter, author. People's Artist of the RSFSR. Author of the films: *The Diplomatic Pouch*, *Zvenigora*, *Arsenal*, *Earth*, *Ivan*, *Aerograd*, *Shchors*, *Michurin*. Using scenarios by Dovzhenko, Yuliya I. Solntseva, after Dovzhenko's death, directed the films *Poem of the Sea*, *The Enchanted Desna*, *The Story of the Flaming Years* and others.

[148] [Russian editor's note]: *Zarkhi, Natan Abramovich* (1900–1935). Screenwriter. Author of the scenarios for the films *Mother*, *The End of St. Petersburg*, and others.

[149] [Russian editor's note]: *Chervyakov, Evgeny Veniaminovich* (1899–1942). Film director and actor. He played the roles of A. S. Pushkin in the picture *The Poet and the Tsar*. He directed the film *The Girl from a Far River*, *My Son*, *Cities and Years*, *Prisoners*, and others. He died heroically in 1942 in a partisan detachment.

[150] [Russian editor's note]: *Eggert, Konstantin Vladimirovich* (1883–1955). Actor and film director. As an actor, he took part in the films *Aelita*, *Chess Fever*, *The Bear's Wedding*, *It is Forbidden to Enter the City*, and others. He directed the films *The Bear's Wedding*, *The Ice House*, *The Lame Gentleman*, *Nasten'ka Ustinova*, *Gobsek*, and others.

[151] [Russian editor's note]: *Trainin, Il'ya Pavlovich* (1887–1949). Director of the 1st Moscow Film Factory, one of the executives of Sovkino. In the 1930s he moved into scholarly work in the field of law.

[152] [Trans.]: It remains unclear to me whether the American release of the film was *Cannons and Tractors* or *Cannons or Tractors*. Brad Chisholm in *Jump Cut* (no. 37), refers to it as *Cannons or Tractors*. German Censorship documents refer to the work as both *Kanonen oder Traktoren* and *Kanonen und Traktoren*. Shub says the title in Germany, which she gives here only in Russian, was *Тракторы и пушки* [*Cannons and Tractors*]. Given the pointed opposition of the "two worlds" discourse of the film, this confusion is somewhat frustrating. Having never seen a copy of either the American or German release of the film, I cannot resolve these differences.

black mirror, as if water had just been poured onto them, and in the evening, they reflected the lights of the city. I liked it.

They took me to "Werder" over a forty-kilometer-long asphalt highway. Above the river, among the blossoming apple trees were people out for a stroll. Many were drunk, but no coarse words were to be heard. They ate sausages and drank wine endlessly. On the return trip, we stopped by *Sanssouci* in Potsdam.

One evening, Mar'yanov, the husband of the daughter of the philosopher Einstein, took me to see the grandson of the great Tagore. A youthful, beautiful face, he lived modestly; at his home were guests, [among them] an Indian dancer dressed in her national costume of rose-colored muslin. On her forehead was a red circle. She was not very pretty and was quiet, yet somehow touching and made an impression.

I talked a lot with Alexander Dovzhenko. Our meeting in Berlin was the beginning of our friendship. He told me about the content of *Earth*, on which he was working. I will never forget how he could describe things quite clairvoyantly. What I saw on the screen was utterly identical with what he had described.

In the screening room of Weltfilm, they showed my film *Lev Tolstoy and The Russia of Nicholas II* several times. The film was seen by Max Hoelz and his comrades, the artist Moholy-Nagy, the architect Gropius and his wife, and the chairman of the Society for Russo-German Cultural Relations (he was already showing Russian films at the "Russian Court"). Everyone liked the film. And good notices appeared in the press.

Every day, I would take the train to Neubabelsberg. A translator would accompany me. We would arrive at the entrance security checkpoint by way of a beautiful woods. There, our studio passes would be waiting for us. I would work in the editing department, looking at negatives of newsreels from capitalist countries, for the most part from America, and from colonialist countries. I would choose the shots I needed for my film. They would make me a lavender print—a dupe negative.[153] I would allow it to be screened only once in the viewing room. Material I lacked, I would look for at the "Emelka" firm. At break time in Neubabelsberg, I would go to the directors' canteen to have a snack. One day, I found myself next to the actors' canteen, which

---

[153] [Trans.]: In the original: лаванда—дубль-негатив [lavanda—dubl'-negativ]. Lavender print лаванда [lavanda] is an outdated term for a fine grain master positive or a dupe negative, black and white intermediate printing materials in the post-production process. The name "lavender print" derives from the purplish tint of the base of the film stock. Shub specifically glosses this lavender print as a dupe negative дубль-негатив [dubl'-negativ]. By context, one can infer, that when Shub uses the word лаванда [lavanda] by itself, without this gloss, she means a fine grain master positive. What is noteworthy, here, is that, she is looking at negatives rather than positive prints and that she screens this intermediate material at all, as it is soft and easily scratched and low in contrast, making it less than ideal for projection. Shub does speak elsewhere about screening negatives, which is just not done by professionals now. Screening negatives or intermediate material may be due to budgetary constraints, for quality control, or to quickly verify the correct elements have been printed.

was filled with Russian voices. I recognized them as White Russian emigrants taking part in the shooting of a Russian film adaptation of a story by L. Tolstoy. Mozzhukhin[154] was playing the hero. Well-proportioned, in a smart, white Circassian coat, his thin waist cinched with a belt chased in silver; he had a dagger and on his head, a white Astrakhan wool hat.[155] He came into the directors' canteen and went up to the bar to get a drink. He struck up a conversation with my translator: "Where are you from?" "From Leningrad." Then I heard these rude and insulting words: "I don't know of any such city. You must mean 'Petrograd.'" Silence. "Introduce me to Miss[156] Shub…"

"Convey to Mozzhukhin, that I don't wish to be acquainted with him."

He left at once.

At five o'clock after work, when I go through the woods to the train station, a luxurious car drives by alongside me. In it is Mozzhukhin. He sees nothing around him. In the car, sits an old man, a wreck with lifeless eyes.

I meet the actors Gzovskaya[157] and Gaidarov.[158] They are among the elite at the Trade Mission. Gzovskaya is still quite nice looking. Vertov and I dine at their place. Then, we go to the film club. There, everyone is drunk, they are dancing the foxtrot, nothing of interest.

One evening, at the home of one of our workers from the Trade Mission, Gzovskaya reads some verses and selections from some of her roles quite beautifully. She and Gaidarov are to leave for the Soviet Union any day.

---

[154] [Russian editor's note]: *Mozzhukhin, Ivan Il'ich* (1888–1939). Actor in pre-revolutionary Russian cinema. He emigrated after the revolution. [Trans.]: this is a terse and deliberate understatement. Mozzhukhin was one of the most popular and versatile actors of Pre-revolutionary Russian cinema. Not by accident, did Kuleshov choose footage of him for his famous editing experiment, which became known as the Kuleshov Effect. After emigrating, he quickly became a popular silent film star in France, as an exotic romantic lead.

[155] [Trans.]: Papakha: a wool hat worn Cossacks, Turkmenistanis, and Azerbaijanis among others.

[156] [Trans.]: The form of address Mozzhukhin uses is the pre-revolutionary "gospozha," "Miss," but slightly more formal, implying someone of a non-peasant, but non-noble background. The form then current in revolutionary Russia would have been "tovarishch," "comrade," a gender neutral form of address, or possibly "grazhdanka," closer to "Citizen," a gendered official form of address sounding very much like *Citoyenne* from the French Revolution.

[157] [Russian editor's note]: *Gzovskaya, Ol'ga Vladimirovna* (1889–1962). Theater and film actress. She acted at the Maly Theater (1905–1910), the Moscow Art Theater (1910–1918), and other theaters as well as in films.

[158] [Russian editor's note]: *Gaidarov, Vladimir Georgievich* (b. 1893). Actor and director. Decorated Artist of the RSFSR. He played at the Moscow Art Theater, the Leningrad Pushkin Academy Theater of Drama, and others. He also acted in the cinema (*The Battle of Stalingrad Part One* and others).

Mozzhukhin in *The White Devil.*

In the evenings, I go to a tiny little theater where they are showing Chaplin's films. I saw a number of his short pictures. Among the features, I watched *Circus* and *The Gold Rush* twice. They make an enormous impression.

I meet the artist Hans Richter. This leftist artist is interested in filmmaking. At the same time I meet Moholy-Nagy. He is creating theatrical productions, staging Brecht. I see Brecht's *Threepenny Opera.* It makes a great impression.

Moholy-Nagy is absorbed by photography. He gives me a portrait of Mayakovsky as a gift. He makes an invitation to visit him. A. Dovzhenko, D. Vertov, and I come over. Coffee and Russian vodka together with liquor are served. Everyone is having a lovely time. Some kind of Dadaist-pianist, quite serious, raises the lid of the grand piano and plays on the strings and strikes the keys with his feet. I barely manage to keep from bursting out laughing. To all of us, this is strange and unnecessary.

Mar'yanov, Vertov, and I visit Hans Richter. He lives outside the city in the Grünewald. There are a lot of people making toasts. Among them, we all very much like the artist-photographer Greiffs.[159]

Gropius the architect invites Vertov and me over as guests. He receives us in a beautifully appointed apartment. Contemporary furniture. In the apartment, there are lots of flowers: lilies, irises. Then, he conducts us to his studio and shows us the maquette of a new theater. It's interesting.

With Vertov, I saw my first sound films: *Submarine*[160] and *The Singing Fool*.[161]

At the Piscator-Theater we saw his production of *Rivalen*[162] and *Asphalt*. When the Fascists came to power, Piscator and Hans Richter briefly lived in Moscow and worked in the "Mezhrabpom" studio.

Original Production of *Threepenny Opera* at Theater am Schiffbauerdamm.

---

[159] [Trans.]: In the original: Грэффс. Possibly Werner Graeff, who was a friend of Richter and co-wrote and stars in Richter's film *Ghosts Before Breakfast*.

[160] [Trans]: In the original: *Сумбарина* [*Sumbarina*]. This appears to be a typo for *Субмарина* [*Submarina*], i.e. *Submarine* (1928), directed by Frank Capra.

[161] [Trans.]: (1928), directed by Lloyd Bacon starring Al Jolson.

[162] [Trans.]: In the original: *Риволен* [*Rivolen*]. The seems to be a slight mistransliteration of *Rivalen*, which Piscator staged in 1929.

Gaidarov and Gzovskaya in *Crime and Punishment.*

We saw a lot of pictures: *Jeanne d'Arc, The Godless Girl,*[163] the pictures of von Stroheim, *The Man and the Masses,*[164] *The Big Parade,*[165] *Wedding March,*[166] pictures with Greta Garbo.

For my film, I made additional shots of Berlin; I took with me the footage purchased and material I had shot and returned to our homeland for a big shoot.

We shot a lot of things: Karelia, Lake Kivach, villages with wooden peasant huts with wonderfully painted carvings. We shot the burning South, the tea plantations of Chakva, Baku, ports, the unloading of tractors and combines, kolkhozes, industrial complexes, and many other things.

As always, L. Felonov[167] worked with me. By this time, he could be called a second director. I assigned him responsibility for shooting. He acquitted himself beautifully.

A screening of the finished film took place in Berlin without me in the "Stella-Palast." There was a large crowd, larger than the three-thousand-seat theater could hold. A lot of people tried to get into the theater who couldn't. A scandal. Intervention by the police. They showed my film *Today* under the German title *Tractors and Cannons.*

The *Berlin am Morgen* daily gave the following review:

Tractors and Cannons. Marxist montage. For the first time at the "Stella-Palast" Mezhrabpom offers the opportunity to envision how it is possible to create an integral, living work out of various documentary shots on the basis of its structural configuration. One must say, that this montage form is new and a very important kind of art... This film shows a profile in documentary fashion of today's world. Five sixths and one sixth of the world stand opposed to one another... It is a flight through all strata of capitalist society at a breathtaking pace and with artistic restraint. The sequences so tightly and consistently transition from one to the other, that they are as tightly connected visually as they are intrinsically. This is five sixths of the world and, on the other side: Socialist Construction, documents of the dedication of the masses, the Five-Year Plan, and the creation of a new world.

---

[163] [Trans.]: Directed by Cecil B. DeMille (1928).

[164] [Trans.]: This is a literal translation of the title. I'm not sure of the English title of the film, but perhaps it is based on Toller's *Die Masse-Mensch,* or this is Shub's not quite accurate translation of *Ein Mensch der Masse,* the German title of King Vidor's *The Crowd* (1928).

[165] [Trans.]: Directed by King Vidor (1925).

[166] [Trans.]: Directed by von Stroheim (1928).

[167] [Russian editor's note]: *Felonov, Lev Borisovich* (b. 1900). A close associate of E. Shub, at first an editor, and later an assistant director. At present, a lecturer at the VGIK.

From the Far East to the burning South and tea plantations. Frames from *Today*.

This film is not made in the service of petty pacifism. Cannons are needed to defend the tractors.

 The film is instructive and you will watch it carefully until the final moment. It arouses you without dancing girls, it grabs hold of you without detectives, it is exotic without Indian dances, and romantic without recourse to dreams.

The *Film-Kurier* newspaper wrote:

 …the production *Tractors and Cannons* about economic construction in the USSR and the Five-Year Plan once again presents a convincing example of the virtuosity of the Russians in the art of montage. The film has a splendid conception of the profile of the capitalist world. An optical review (an overview): tractors against cannons. Silent images begin to speak.

 The film is made brilliantly and produces an impression thanks to the strength of its convictions…

From Karelia to Baku, the old and the new. Frames from *Today*.

And finally, *Welt am Abend*:

> The most exciting, gripping, intense, staggering [example] of anything
> in recent years to be shown on the screens of the world is *Tractors and
> Cannons*. It is a documentary overview. It is precisely its documentari-
> ness,[168] that elevates and increases the value of this work astronomically.
> No one can say, that everything shown is untrue. Here, no one can deny
> it, no one can correct it. No one can speak of tendentiousness. What
> is shown, simply *is*. Many are swept away and completely ignore the
> inexpensive means of persuasion of the film. The dialectically precisely
> formed montage of the film seized hold of everyone.

The public screening of the film *Today* was arranged in Moscow at the "Ars"
film theater on Gorky ulitsa. The screening enjoyed a great success. This was my last
silent film.

---

[168] [Trans.] In the original: документальность [dokumentalnost']. One could say here: its quality as a
document, or documentary quality.

The Beginning of the Renown of Soviet Cinema

At the beginning of 1924, S. M. Eisenstein left Proletkult. An essential divergence was beginning to show between him and the administration of Proletkult.

It was said, that in the production of the film *Strike*, there was an unsound Proletkult-style treatment in the understanding of the "masses": of the collective and of the roles of individuals in the collective, as well as a harmful disavowal of the art of the past as a whole. The Party and social assessment of the merits and deficiencies of *Strike* played a role in healing [from this]. These pronouncements had great significance for Eisenstein.

S. M. Eisenstein began work on a grand monumental film on a commission by the Jubilee Commission of the Presidium of the Central Executive Committee of the USSR in celebration of the 20th anniversary of the Revolution of 1905. The working title of the film was *1905*. The scenario was assigned to N. F. Agadzhanova.[169] S. M. Eisenstein prepared to begin shooting in Moscow, Leningrad, Odessa, Sevastopol, Tiflis, Baku, Batumi, Central Asia, in the Caucasus, in Siberia, in Tambovskaya Governate, in Ivanovo-Voznesensk and in many other places. As before, he considered, that the united revolutionary masses of the proletariat would be the main character.

The concepts of the film were very complicated in terms of the technical set-up for shooting: fires at night, railroad strikes, shots of the fleet, the battle of Tsushima, a peasant movement, and other extremely complicated sequences. It was initially planned, that besides E. Tissé, A. Levitsky, of whom Eisenstein had a very high opinion, would be a camera operator, but Tissé alone shot the film.

This sealed a creative comradeship for many years to come, which had begun with *Strike*.

The Jubilee Commission of the Central Executive Committee assigned great significance to this film, and understanding all the difficulties for the realization of the work, it decided to allow shooting the entire year, but stipulated the condition that at least one completed episode would be screened on the 20th of December 1925 for the celebration of the 20th anniversary of the 1905 revolution.

On the 23rd of November, it was reported in the newspaper *Kino*, that Eisenstein had returned from his expedition with his assistants Shtraukh[170] and A. Levshin[171]

---

[169] [Russian editor's note]: *Agadzhanova, Nina Ferdinandovna* (b. 1889). Screenwriter. Author of the scenario for the film *The Battleship Potemkin*. Other scenarios: *In the White Roses* [*В тылу у белых (Behind White Lines)*], *The Sailor Ivan Galai, Deserter*.

[170] [Russian editor's note]: *Shtraukh, Maksim Maksimovich* (b. 1900). Theater and film actor. People's Artist of the USSR. S. Eisenstein's assistant on the films *The Battleship Potemkin, October, Old and New*. He played the role of Lenin in S. Yutkevich's films *The Man with the Gun, Yakov Sverdlov, Stories about Lenin, Lenin in Poland*.

[171] [Russian editor's note]: *Levshin, Aleksandr Ivanovich* (b. 1903). Film director and actor. Student of S. Eisenstein in theater at Proletkult. Assistant director on the films *Strike, The Battleship Potemkin, October*.

and at once began editing. Just before his arrival in Moscow, scenes were shot on the Battleship "Potemkin," the story of the events on which the plot of the film was based. Shooting took place in Odessa and Sevastopol. His assistants G. Alexandrov,[172] A. Antonov,[173] and M. Gomorov[174] remained behind with the cameraman Tissé to shoot continuity for selected edited pieces of film. In all, 5,200 meters of film were shot. Editing and the continuity shoots in the studio by Eisenstein at the time of editing were done in Moscow; this took twenty-one days.

Eisenstein fulfilled his obligation: on December 21, *The Battleship Potemkin* — that's how this film was called by its director — had its premiere at the Jubilee evening in the Bolshoi Theater. The commission was brilliantly fulfilled. Eisenstein never returned to his original plan.

At the beginning of 1926, the film was released on the screens of the Soviet Union.

These were the dates of the realization of this outstanding production of Soviet filmmaking. From that moment, a turning point began in the history of Soviet cinema. A film of great revolutionary force, responsible for a great revolutionary impact, was accomplished with inspiration and courage by an artist-innovator.

This production played an enormous role in the development not only of Soviet, but of world cinema. Its procession across the screen was not limited only to the Soviet Union, but was a triumph in every country.

So much has been written about *The Battleship Potemkin*, that it's difficult for me to say anything new. This immortal production is beloved by the Soviet People even now, not withstanding how far we have advanced. In the intervening years, film-making has been enriched with sound and color. We are on the eve of a time when our films will be shown in widescreen, when sound and images will be stereoscopic. A thousand more wondrous discoveries lie ahead for the filmmaker. We stand on the threshold of these things. But *The Battleship Potemkin* will remain the first stage of this splendid path and the red flag on the mast of the victorious battleship, tinted red by order of the director, will always mark the beginning of this victorious procession

---

In 1928 he directed the films *Chinese Mill, Panic* [*Переполох*] (both based on scenarios by I. Babel).

[172] [Russian editor's note]: *Alexandrov, Grigory Vasil'evich* (b. 1903). Film director and actor. People's Artist of the USSR. S. Eisenstein's assistant on the film *The Battleship Potemkin*, co-director [сопостановщик] on the films *October, Old and New, ¡Que viva México!*. He directed the films *Jolly Fellows, Circus, Volga-Volga, Tanya* [*Светлый путь* (*The Shining Path*)], *Springtime, Encounter at the Elbe, The Composer Glinka* and others.

[173] [Russian editor's note]: *Antonov, Aleksandr Pavlovich* (1898–1962). Film actor. Decorated Worker in the Arts of the RSFSR. He played the role of the sailor Vakulinchuk in the film *The Battleship Potemkin*, and was assistant director on that film as well as on *Old and New*. He played more than 50 roles in silent and sound cinema.

[174] [Russian editor's note]: *Gomorov, Mikhail Sergeevich* (b. 1898). Actor and director. He appeared in *Strike*, and *The Battleship Potemkin*. For those films as well as for *October, Old and New, Bezhin Meadow*, he served as assistant director. He was the assistant to V. I. Pudovkin on the films *Menin and Pozharsky* and *Suvorov*.

of Soviet Cinema. The directorial realization of this film is coupled with the name of Eisenstein alone. *The Battleship Potemkin is* the director S. M. Eisenstein. Thus, began a new stage in the history of Soviet Cinema.

A few months later, Soviet Film Art was enriched by yet another outstanding production. In October of 1926, there appeared on the screens of the Soviet Union the picture *Mother*, the screen adaptation of the classic work by Maxim Gorky. The film was also about the revolutionary movement and its cruel repression by tsarism. The scenario was created by Natan Zarkhi, who departed from us untimely. The director was Vsevolod Pudovkin and the magnificent young cameraman was Anatoly Golovnya.[175]

The impression made by this film was enormous. The actors N. Batalov,[176] A. Chistyakov,[177] V. Baranovskaya[178] stirred our emotions with their inimitable, realistic performances, they held the spectators in suspense from the first to the last shot. It became clear at once, that in the person of V. Pudovkin, we had a master of the first order, who had created inspiring images and elicited from the performance of the actors the most complex psychic processes. Besides that, he showed himself to be an artist of the first order in the composition of shots and in montage. The film was a new universal triumph in Soviet filmmaking. Soon thereafter, the second film of V. Pudovkin, N. Zarkhi and A. Golovnya appeared: *The End of St. Petersburg*, in which the outstanding actor I. Chuvelev[179] participated, executing the role of the ignorant peasant fellow, who travels the difficult path to revolution, to participation in the struggle for its victory.

---

[175] [Russian editor's note]: *Golovnya, Anatoly Dmitrievich* (b. 1900). Camera operator. Decorated Worker in the Arts of the RSFSR. One of the founders of the Soviet Camera Operators School. He worked continually with the director V. Pudovkin, with whom he shot the films *Chess Fever, Mother, The End of St. Petersburg, Storm over Asia* aka *The Heir of Genghis Khan, Deserter, Victory, Minin and Pozharsky, Suvorov, Admiral Nakhimov*. Professor. Head of the Department of the Camera Operator Master Course at the VGIK.

[176] [Russian editor's note]: *Balatov, Nikolai Petrovich* (1899–1937). Theater and film actor. Decorated Artist of the RSFSR. His most famous roles were in *Mother* (Pavel Vlasov), *Road to Life* (Sergeev).

[177] [Russian editor's note]: *Chistyakov, Aleksandr Petrovich* (1880–1942). Film actor. He performed his most famous roles in the films *Mother* (the father), *Storm Over Asia* aka *The Heir of Genghis Khan* (head of the partisan detachment), *Life is Beautiful* [Простой случай (*A Simple Case*)] (Uncle Sasha), *A Great Life* (Secretary of the Communist Party District Committee), *The Return of Maxim* (the worker Mishchenko), *New Horizons* [Выборгская сторона (*The Vyborg Side*)] (the worker Mishchenko).

[178] [Russian editor's note]: *Barankovskaya, Vera Vsevolodovna* (b. unknown–1935). Actress at the Moscow Art Theater. She acted in these films of V. Pudovkin: *Mother* (Nilovna) and *The End of St. Petersburg* (the wife of a worker).

[179] [Russian editor's note]: *Chuvelev, Ivan Pavlovich* (1897–1942). Film actor. Decorated Artist of the RSFSR. He acted in the films *The End of St. Petersburg* (peasant fellow), *The White Eagle* (the snoop) *Cities and Years* (the artist Startsev), *Thunderstorm* (Tikhon), *Captain Grant's Family* (Ayerton) and others.

In the years from 1925 to 1928, a series of films appeared, which laid the foundations of the shining path of Soviet Revolutionary Filmmaking. First of all, there was *Zvenigora* by Alexander Dovzhenko. The film bears the stamp of a particular originality, marked by a sense of humor and inexhaustible imagination, a poem by Alexander Dovzhenko about his Motherland. *Leninist Kino-Pravda* by D. Vertov passed onto the screens of the Soviet Union followed by *The Battleship Potemkin*. Soon thereafter, the film *The Club of the Big Deed*, based on a scenario by Yu. Tynyanov[180] by the young directors G. Kozintsev[181] and L. Trauberg,[182] appeared on the screen. This film was pleasing not only because of the talent of the directors, who had overcome the formalist infatuation of their preceding films (*The Devil's Wheel* and *The Overcoat*) but also because of the talent of the young film actors who played the main roles: S. Magarill,[183] P. Sobolevsky,[184] S. Gerasimov,[185] Ya. Zheimo,[186] O. Zhakov[187] and others. Clearly, remarkable for their talent as well were the first works of Fridrikh Ermler.[188] *The Parisian Cobbler* enjoyed a great success with Soviet viewers.

---

[180] [Russian editor's note]: *Tynyanov, Yuri Nikolaevich* (1894–1943). Writer, literary historian, screenwriter. Author of the scenarios for the films *The Overcoat*, *The Club of the Big Deed* (in collaboration with Yu. Oksman), *The Tsar Wants to Sleep* [Поручик Киже (*Lieutenant Kizhe*)].

[181] [Russian editor's note]: *Kozintsev, Grigory Mikhailovich* (b. 1905). Film director. People's Artist of the USSR. He directed a series of films in collaboration with L. Trauberg. By himself he directed the films *Pirogov*, *Belinsky*, *Don Quixote*, *Hamlet*, *King Lear*.

[182] [Russian editor's note]: *Trauberg, Leonid Zakharovich* (b. 1902). Film director. Decorated Worker in the Arts of the RSFSR. Together with G. Kozintsev he directed *The Overcoat*, *The Club of the Big Deed*, *New Babylon*, *Alone*, the Maxim trilogy and others.

[183] [Russian editor's note]: *Magarill, Sof'ya Zinov'evna* (1900–1943). Film actress. Decorated Artist of the RSFSR. She acted in the films *The Club of the Big Deed* (Marina Vishnevskaya), *New Babylon* (an actress), *Enemies* (Tat'yana), *Masquerade* (The Baroness Shtral') and others.

[184] [Russian editor's note]: *Sobolevsky, Petr Stanislavovich* (b. 1904). Film actor. He appeared in the films *The Club of the Big Deed* (Lieutenant Sukhanov), *New Babylon* (a soldier), *Alone* (the teacher's fiancé), *Minin and Pozharsky* (Anokha), *Admiral Nakhimov* (Ostreno), *The Secret of Two Oceans* (Druzhinin) and others.

[185] [Russian editor's note]: *Gerasimov, Sergei Apollinarievich* (b. 1906). Film director, actor, and screenwriter. People's Artist of the USSR. He began to work in the cinema as an actor in the films of Kozintsev and Trauberg. He directed the films *Seven Brave Men*, *City of Youth* [Комсомольск (*Komsomol'sk*)], *The New Teacher*, *Masquerade*, *The Young Guard*, *Quiet Flows the Don*, *Men and Beasts*, *The Journalist*, *By the Lake*. Professor. Head of the Acting and Directing Master Course at the VGIK.

[186] [Russian editor's note]: *Zheimo, Yanina Boleslavovna* (b. 1909). Film actress. She appeared in the films *The Fourth Wheel*, *The Overcoat*, *New Babylon*, *Song of Happiness*, *China Express*, *Wake up, Little Lena!*, *Red Army Days*, *Three Women*, and others.

[187] [Russian editor's note]: *Zhakov, Oleg Petrovich* (b. 1905). Film actor. People's Artist of the USSR. He appeared in a large number of silent and sound pictures. His most significant roles were in the films *Seven Brave Men*, *Great Citizen*, *Baltic Deputy*, *The Invasion*, *By the Lake*.

[188] [Russian editor's note]: *Ermler, Fridrikh Markovich* (1898–1967). Film director. People's Artist of the USSR. He directed the films: Катька — бумажный ранет (*Kat'ka's Rennet Apples*), *The Parisian*

I am speaking about those films, which, because of various factors, were cherished by me and forced me to reconsider my notions, incorrect in many ways, about the path Soviet Filmmaking should take. The question of the necessity of "acted"[189] feature films—that is, those in which actors participated—was decided for me once and for all.

I remember a public screening of *The Battleship Potemkin* at the Art Cinema[190] on Arbatskaya Square.

The entrance to the theater was decorated. A large battleship was fastened to the façade of the building. The whole group, except for S. M. Eisenstein, were in sailor's costumes. A huge crowd had gathered around the building. Even making your way into the building was difficult. After the end of the screening, I stood in the foyer for a long time without managing to calm down, my heart was pounding because of the film. I was overjoyed by the knowledge, that I had been present at the birth of an outstanding artist and I had seen a magnificent feature film of enormous revolutionary, Bolshevik intensity. I was practically the last one to leave the theater building. At the door stood S. M. Eisenstein; he was looking at me intently. After *Strike*, we hadn't seen each other for a long time. Inwardly, I was wounded. But somehow, all by itself, it happened, that, upon seeing him, I walked up to him and squeezed his hand, I spoke a few disconnected words of admiration. S. M. Eisenstein was very pleased. He told me, that he had been standing and waiting for me, that now his joy was without any shade of gloom, "It means friendship once again, and without any resentment." And so it was. We learned how not to resent one another even under circumstances very difficult for our friendship.

A group of people working in film and critics, enamored of the so-called "psychological drama," maintained that *The Battleship Potemkin* was difficult of reception for a wide audience, especially for the understanding of peasants.

A screening was arranged at the House of the Peasant.[191] The critics were beaten. Twenty peasant petitioners[192] who were staying there gave high marks to the film; they

---

Cobbler, Fragment of an Empire, Counterplan aka *Shame, Peasants, Great Citizen, No Greater Love* [Она защищает Родину (*She Defends the Motherland*)], *Unfinished Story* and others.

[189] [Trans.]: In the original: игровый фильм [igrovy fil'm] (acted film). It's interesting, Shub feels the necessity to clarify that she means, "one in which actors participate." Perhaps it is because the terminology is somewhat archaic at this point and because of the double sense of acted and played for игровый. "Feature film" is a translation of художественный фильм [khudozhestvenny fil'm]; it carries the connotations of both feature-length production and something of the notion of the *film d'auteur*.

[190] [Trans.]: In the original: Художественный кинотеатр in this context means "Art" (used as an adjective, as in the "Moscow Art Theater") or "artistic." This is the actual name of the theater.

[191] [Trans.]: In the original: Дом крестьянина [Dom krest'yanina], an educational and cultural center for peasants and farmworkers.

[192] [Trans.]: I am informed by novelist and journalist Tatsiana Zamirovskaya, that in the early years of the revolution peasants would travel to visit Lenin with petitions. They were called крестьяне-ходоки (peasant-petitioners).

affirmed, that they had more than understood it. They considered, that it was especially important to show this film in the countryside, since many peasants couldn't
imagine how the revolution took place in the cities. Besides that, they remarked, that
the film "was very beautiful, it shows the sea, the sailor's life, calling up a surge of
emotion, even calling up tears." And what was especially interesting and surprising
was the assertion that "the peasants need it more than the workers." An account of
this screening was published in the *Kino* newspaper of March 16, 1926. All this made
S. M. Eisenstein very happy. One plan after another was born within him.

So the recognition was natural, that this was a period of innovative discoveries in filmmaking, that Soviet filmmaking was a genuine and great art, accessible to
the wide masses; the youthfulness of talented comrades, who were passionately and
successfully working in the cinema, gave birth in me to the desire to test my strengths.
Five years of labor, of training in filmmaking, somehow gave me the right to this.

What was to be done, then? What should be taken on?

It was clear, that not just the newsreel alone had the right to express our era.

It was clear, that work in the newsreel, too, should be an artistic labor. Besides
that, the newsreel could become an historian, a profoundly Party-oriented chronicler
of our era.

It was clear, that a whole series of such things could be most vividly expressed
by the newsreel.

But how could this be corroborated? Just now, Eisenstein and Pudovkin had
reenacted in their films the events of 1905; they created unforgettable images and
showed the destiny of the people who had carried out the revolution and of those who
cruelly repressed it.

But the newsreel... Even if the February Revolution, under the difficult conditions of those years, was shot in dull gray, with static discharges on the negatives, even
if very little was shot of Great October, this is authentic film shot of those days. Its
historical significance is difficult to overestimate.

And so, before me lay what I had found after painstaking research: the list of
newsreels of pre-revolutionary Russia, beginning with 1905 and ending with the First
Imperialist War. In my hands were the lists not only of Russian newsreels, but those
of Pathé, Gaumont, Éclair, American newsreels. There were branch offices of these
firms in Russia. And what was completely unexpected for me, I found out, that the
last Russian tsar had his own movie camera operator and that a lot of film of him was
shot. But where were these newsreels? How could one find them? What was shot?
How could one get access to the newsreels disclosed in these lists? How could one get
permission to search without knowing where the materials were located?

At about this time, I was transferred from the 3rd Factory near Bryansky (now
Kiev) Railroad Station to the 1st Factory on Zhitnaya ulitsa. There, as well, was the
tiniest little film production studio, looking more like a photo studio. The Director

of the factory, I. P. Trainin, a former academic, responded to all my proposals with a "no." He couldn't imagine how it would be possible to make a thematically intelligible film from assorted pieces of newsreels, taken in various years and by many different organizations. I ought to continue editing acted feature films, I should explore the possibilities, while shooting films with actors.

I headed over to Sovkino, to see P. A. Blyakhin.[193] The film *Red Imps*, based on his scenario, had come out in 1923; it was splendid for that time. It had brought us a great deal of joy. V. B. Shklovsky was working with him.

Our conversation was a long one; I came back several times. They were interested in my proposal and considered, that it would be worth it to give it a try. They made the decision to help me and help they did. They convinced I. P. Trainin. And right there my search for material began. There were days of disenchantment and of unexpected and happy discoveries.

They allocated to me a room of my own. In the course of a day, I would go through many meters of positive and negative at the editing table. L. B. Felonov, who became my devoted and close assistant on all my subsequent works, would bring me container after container of material. In this way, I looked at all the newsreels I found in Moscow. This was not enough for the film. By talking to camera operators, I established which newsreels remained undiscovered by me and where it might be possible to find them.

At the end of the summer of 1926, I traveled to Leningrad. There, it was even harder.

All the important negatives and positives of the war-time and pre-revolutionary newsreels were being stored in a damp basement on Sergievsky ulitsa. The containers were covered with rust. At many places on the film strip, the emulsion had become detached because of the dampness. Many shots that appeared on the lists, in actual fact, were not to be found.

Not one meter of negative or positive of the Leningrad newsreels of the February days was to be found and they refused my request to issue a document, saying that the February newsreels were not in Leningrad.[194] A number of old people who used to work in film, all the same, maintained, that shots from the newsreels of the February Revolu-

---

[193] [Russian editor's note]: *Blyakhin, Pavel Andreevich* (1887–1961). Short story writer and author of the scenario for *Red Imps*. He did a great deal of work in the organization of Sovkino, Glavrepertkom, The Central Committee of the Profsoyuz [Professional Union] of Film- and Photo-Workers.

[194] [Trans.]: [Trans.]: In the original: Ни одного метра негатива и позитива ленинградской хроники февральских дней не обнаружено, а между тем на мое требование выдать мне документ, что февральской хроники в Ленинграде нет, мне ответили отказом. Apparently Jay Leyda misunderstood Shub's text in *Films Beget Films*, which he translates as "Not one meter of negative or positive on the February Revolution had been preserved, and I was even shown a document that declared that no film of that event could be found in Leningrad." The 1959 edition of Shub's text which Leyda uses, and the 1972 edition used here, are identical.

tion should exist, and that, presumably, part of them were located in private hands. I made this known to I. P. Trainin and Sovkino undertook measures to help me uncover all film material in private hands in Leningrad. The work took a turn for the better.

All the historical newsreels I had collected were immediately transferred to a dry location (the Vladimirskaya ulitsa office of Sovkino). In my search for material, I managed to establish, that part of our newsreels had gone off to America. In Leningrad, an old newsreel worker, comrade Khmel'nitsky, helped me a great deal. At once, in a comradely way, he began to help me with everything. Together, we hung up strands of film with damp emulsion and patiently dried them out. He did everything possible to uncover newsreels in the possession of archives in Leningrad. One day, he brought me a stack of containers. "This is an old, tsarist, counter-revolutionary newsreel," he said. "I don't know, whether it will be of any use to you. We have a lot of containers like that."

This turned out to be the personal archive of the last, small and angry tsar Nicholas II, who had wallowed in the blood of the People. The newsreels (for the most part, negatives) turned out to amount to around twenty thousand meters. Everything was beautifully shot. Nicholas and his spouse loved to be filmed. They were filmed in domestic settings, in parades, on manoeuvres, inspecting the regiment of the guard, with the fleet, in Moscow, Petrograd, Yalta, on trips abroad, on trips around the country, at the dedications of monuments, along with ministers from the Black Hundreds, in hysterical religious processions, even at the Sarov monastery.

Out of all the material I examined, I was allowed to print and take with me only the most limited quantity of negative with the commitment to make certain use of it. I promised to do so.

Leningrad. The great city of Lenin. I was there for the first time after the revolution. In my free time, I walked around all the historical sites: Smolny, the Winter Palace Square, the Finland Station, the Marsovo Pole [Champs de Mars], the Kshesinskaya mansion. I walked along the embankments, I spent a long time at the Stock Exchange, on the bridges, at the Engineer's Castle, and went to the Russian Museum and the Hermitage.

Leningrad in early autumn is uniquely beautiful. In this way, it became my custom, from that time on, that when I would come there, I would avoid trams, busses, and cars. An extraordinary train of thought would take hold of me. I would walk along, delighting in grandeur and beauty. On this trip, I did not yet have any comrades, or friends in Leningrad. That happened later. All of these walks I completed in solitude. I would sometimes catch myself mentally reciting verses by Pushkin—they would come to me by themselves, uninvited.

During these two months, I watched sixty thousand meters of film. For the film I selected five thousand two hundred meters. Fifteen hundred meters went into the film. I had a whole series of historical documents, newspapers, and objects filmed and a whole series of shots given laboratory treatment.

The film consists of seven reels and with intertitles is one thousand seven hundred meters long.[195] Sovkino took all the necessary steps, so that the newsreels, which were shot by the Skobelevsky Committee[196] and by the All Russian Photo-Film Department and sold in America, were repurchased and brought back.

The film was ready in time for the tenth anniversary of the February Revolution. Its working title was "February." I never showed it before it was finished. M. Z. Tseitlin,[197] a researcher at the Museum of the Revolution, consulted on the film and did the intertitles for it; I. P. Trainin edited the intertitles.

In editing, I endeavored not to abstract from the newsreel material, but to affirm the principle of its documentariness.[198] Everything was subordinated to the subject matter. This gave me the opportunity, in spite of the well-known dearth of filmed historical events and facts, to connect material meaningfully, so that it would bring back to life those years before the Revolution and the February days.

And then the day arrived for the review of the film. I. P. Trainin came—he must have been the only head of a studio, who never demanded screenings from directors of their films for him, until the directors themselves thought it feasible. But somehow, for him, I was a beginner. In the screening room were S. M. Eisenstein, V. I. Pudovkin, and many friends. I was so agitated I don't remember anything. I don't remember even a single remark. What I remember is the applause after the part of the film, which goes with the title "A global slaughter." Everything was in order. The film was approved.

Right there, Trainin gave the film another title—*Fall of the Romanov Dynasty*—and he came up with a large poster for the ads: the two-headed eagle, crossed-out with two thick red lines. Eisenstein was as happy as if it were his film that had been approved. He maintained this ability to rejoice in the success of his comrades to the end of his days.

---

[195] [Trans.]: Oddly, the filmography in this volume, while it also says the film consists of 7 reels, gives the length of the film as 2,080m. This could be accounted for by knowing the projected length of the film in time and wrongly assuming a projection speed of 24fps, instead of 16fps. However, this is pure speculation on my part. Leyda points out that Shub's negatives were constantly pillaged, so without detailed in-person research in various archives, the completeness of any existing copies of the film is nearly impossible to establish. I have taken up this matter in my essay at the end of this volume.

[196] [Russian editor's note]: *The Skobelevsky Committee*: "Under Imperial Patronage" the Skobelevsky Committee in 1914 founded a War-Film Department for the production and distribution of feature films and for the filming of newsreels at the Front. This is the first film enterprise in Russia, the mission of which was political agitation by means of the cinema.

[197] [Russian editor's note]: *Tseitlin, Mark Zakharovich* (b. 1902). Screenwriter and editor, one of the oldest Soviet documentarians. His amical collaboration with E. Shub began during his time as a researcher at the Museum of the Revolution when he consulted on *Fall of the Romanov Dynasty*, for which he wrote the intertitles. He took part in the creation of several films by E. Shub.

[198] [Trans.]: Документальность [dokumentalnost']. One could also say "its quality as a document."

Right at this time, a big crate of Soviet newsreels were received that had been purchased by Amtorg in America. I immediately went to work examining the material. Among various newsreels, possessing significance as chronicles, I suddenly uncovered a negative with hitherto unknown shots of V. I. Lenin. It is to be supposed, that some of these were taken in Moscow by an unknown American cameraman. The shots consisted of the following:

1.) V. I. Lenin speaking—close, filling the entire screen, shot at his office in the Kremlin.
2.) V. I. Lenin in his office, at his writing desk.
3.) V. I. Lenin, with some visitor (close).
4.) V. I. Lenin sitting on a divan beside N. K. Krupskaya. In his arms is a pussycat.
5.) V. I. Lenin alone on a divan, chatting with someone. In his arms is a pussycat.
6.) V. I. Lenin in the foreground, standing at a window.

My joy was tremendous. These shots revealed in such a lively way the image of Vladimir Il'ich during his working hours and his rare minutes of leisure.

I. P. Trainin immediately phoned the V. I. Lenin Institute. All of these shots, after they had been copied onto a dupe negative were turned over to the Institute along with an inventory and formal declaration. They were first widely seen in my film *The Great Way*. The film was released on the screens of the Soviet Union for the tenth Anniversary of the Great October Revolution.

And then, what were the decisive days for me arrived. Huge posters were plastered all over Moscow, in newspapers this ad appeared:

FALL OF THE ROMANOV DYNASTY
A work by Esfir' Shub
Starting March 11 in all major motion picture theaters in Moscow

There were lines at the box offices.

There was a private screening at the head office of Sovkino. In attendance were representatives of the Agitprop Department of the Central Committee, of Comintern, the Director of the Museum of the Revolution, the Deputy of the People's Commissariat for Foreign Affairs[199] (M. M. Litvinov), old Bolsheviks, representatives of the Press. The picture was received with excitement. M. M. Litvinov said: "A remarkable film. It must absolutely be sent abroad." Those in attendance at the screening assessed the film as a significant event in Soviet Cinema, as a new victory for the newsreel.

---

[199] [Trans.]: In the original: Наркоминдел [Narkomindel], an acronym for Народный комиссариат по иностранным делам.

A. A. Fadeev also expressed his opinion about the film in his report to the Congress of Proletarian Writers in 1928:

> How are we to apply the theory of "the precise fixation of facts"[200] in practice? There is this director, Dziga Vertov. In all probability, he is a talented person, but, in creating his picture *A Sixth Part of the World*, he, as an orthodox follower of LEF, avoids all philosophy and instead of *A Sixth Part of the World*, he presents an eccentric mishmash, such a superficial mixing together of facts, that the result is simply a boring picture… The LEF group loves to refer to the beautiful film work of Esfir' Shub, which presents a montage of old pre-revolutionary films. But the LEF group sees, that Shub has taken the line of art and not the simple fixation of facts, because she has brought facts into a well-defined system, she has taken the most typical ones and turned those very ones into artistic symbols…

When preparing this statement for press, A. A. Fadeev addresses himself to his readers in the following words:

> Readers, please take note. The author would like to advise, that a passage followed further on, according to which he would see "nothing wrong" were Esfir' Shub to supplement the incomplete moments in old newsreels for the "integral representation of the fall of the Romanov dynasty," with performances by actors.
> This attests, that the author in those years already understood some things, and completely misunderstood some things, and for this reason, he does not include this passage, which brings discredit upon him and not upon E. Shub.[201]

When sending me this statement, he told me in a letter: "I'm using the same version of this passage; for the sharpness of my characterization of Vertov, I apologize."

I walk to the movie theater and I can't tear my eyes away from the auditorium. I'm not looking at the screen. The film I know by heart.

The Soviet spectator. How will he receive my first work? I am checking myself against him and I am studying him. He, the spectator, is now deciding whether or not I have fulfilled the task set before me. The film was liked. I felt a deep satisfaction.

---

[200] [Trans.]: In the original: Точная фиксация фактов, a reference to *Novy LEF*'s factography.
[201] [Russian editor's note]: The Letter from A. Fadeev and the cited excerpt are preserved in the archive of E. Shub.

People and Events

Vladimir Mayakovsky

At the beginning of 1927, when *Fall of the Romanov Dynasty* was having its run in theaters, one evening the phone rang.

I go over to it. I hear the voice of Valdimir Mayakovsky. He invites me to come over to his place on Gendrikov pereulok,[202] without delay, without hesitation. "No reason to be shy. You know everyone. Come over right now." I grab a cab. I go. My fast approaching first meeting with my favorite poet makes me happy.

Thousands of Muscovites and visitors from every Republic of our native land and visitors from abroad know well this not very large apartment in quiet Gendrikov pereulok (Mayakovsky ulitsa in Taganka District).

Now, it's a museum. With the stamp of quiet of a museum and infrequent quiet voices. Or so I think. I've never been in this museum even once, so as not to violate in any way my memories of this home. Everything in it was seething to the brim with life, youth, and daring. And everything in it was particularly modest. In the first room was a square table, around the table were chairs. Over the table was the bright light of a lamp under a lampshade and against the walls were benches covered in cotton fabric. There was a small cupboard of some sort with dishes and an armchair in the corner. From this room, a door led into the small office of the poet. A Swedish writing desk, a bookcase, a divan covered in leather, an armchair. That's all. On the walls, no decorations whatsoever. Around the table were about twelve to fifteen people. Maya-kovsky was cheerful, his big, kind eyes sparkled, his voice was soft, deep, low, almost a murmur. He preferred to listen to others. All of this was unexpected to me. That is, that he could be that way. I remember O. M. Brik, L. Yu. Brik, the poet N. N. Aseev, S. M. Tret'yakov,[203] V. B. Shklovsky, A. M. Rodchenko, S. I. Kirsanov, V. O. Pertsov, V. F. Stepanova; the utterly youthful Klava Kirsanova, the blue-eyed Ksana Aseeva and Ol'ga Tret'yakova were there... Basically, it was *Novy LEF*, almost the entire staff.

Lilya Yur'evna Brik arrested my attention: rosey hued, with light brown eyes, fiery golden hair, the nervous movements of the fingers of her expressive hands. I watch her. The modest food on the table seemed festive, the apartment, cosy. Lively, uninterrupted conversation went on. People moved deftly from one interesting topic to another.

Lilya Brik knew how to listen to others. With a smile, a single word, an expres-sion of the eye, a sometimes somewhat nervous laugh, she would bring out the

---

[202] [Trans.]: A pereulok is a side street, sometimes translated as "lane."

[203] [Russian editor's note]: *Tret'yakov, Sergei Mikhailovich* (1892–1939). Screenwriter, prose writer, poet. Author of the scenarios for *Eliso* and *Salt for Svanetia*.

meaning of words spoken by anyone. A cup of tea, received from her hands, seemed very tasty, you had never drunk such tea. She would touch things and it was as if the contour of the thing had only now been sculpted out by her.

In the center of everything for everyone was the poet Vladimir Mayakovsky.

This evening verses were being read. Mayakovsky didn't read his own verses. They ladled out from a crystal bowl some kind of drink with slices of fruit in it. They drank to the commencement of my activity as a director.

O. M. Brik, N. N. Aseev, V. B. Shklovsky explained to me why, what I was doing was good. I was happy: they spoke to me as comrades, [observing] how this film underscored the significance of newsreels, considering, most likely, that while working on them, I had not set an objective for myself. It stuck, that Mayakovsky told me more, or less, the following: You interpreted all the material well; it was especially good, that you turned material that was counter-revolutionary in its essence (he had in mind the tsarist newsreels), so that it resounded with a revolutionary denunciation.

From that evening on, almost every week, I would drop by Gendrikov pereulok.

I am trying, as difficult as it might be, to present an image of the poet in the circle of those nearest him and his comrades during the period of the greatest blossoming of his creative power—just after the publication of his poem of genius "Vladimir Il'ich Lenin."

Vladimir Mayakovsky expressed himself perfectly in his creative work. Upon all his labor as a poet lies the imprint of genius, of innovation, and great interior truth.

For us, he stood in the same rank as Pushkin, Lermontov, Nekrasov. We were proud of him. On the paths of our life, just as they were, he was our companion.

The fundamental content of his poetry is the Socialist Motherland, the People, the great Party, the Communist future, the role of the poet, his organizational participation in the People's labor system.

He hated everything reactionary, all of our enemies—those open, those hidden, and those who masquerade. His satire on the enemies of the People, the platitudinizing, the narrow-mindedness, was a crushing blow.

"I want to make Socialist art," wrote the poet as far back as in his early autobiography.

The interests of the workers, the new life, being created under the direction of the Party by workers, peasants, by the entire People, socialist labor—this is what filled his day.

A beautiful and lyric poet: fervent, passionate, joyful, tragic.

Every feeling in him was immense. There was room for everything in his heart. Both an immense love, forever-energetic, and a stormy, incinerating hatred towards the enemy, a sun-lit presentiment of future days.

He was big, he walked around the streets, the squares, and the boulevards of Moscow as if he were walking around his home: "The street is mine; the buildings are mine!"

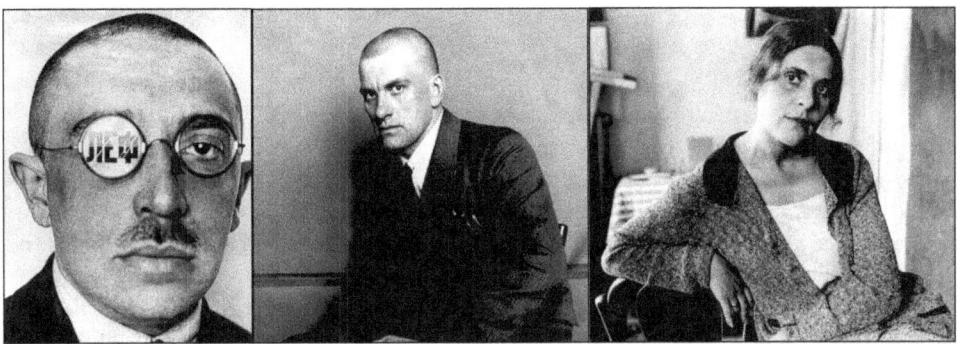

Ossip Brik, Vladimir Mayakovsky, Lilya Brik.

His voice resounded in overflowing auditoriums, in factories, in clubs, in vacation resorts for workers and peasants, not only in Moscow, but in many cities of our Motherland with the strength of a many-voiced orchestra, the power of a choral, the majestic resonance of an organ.

The nuances of his voice were limitless. Everything was within him: powerful exhortation, joy and hatred, sarcasm, jokes, and a manly lyricism.

He was young and he was the favorite poet of everything youthful, eagerly constructing a new life, with a fiery belief in our tomorrow.

And so, even now, there is no event, which stirs our people, in which his poetic lines may not be found, as if written today, an hour ago.

And so, here, this great man, with his complicated poetic world of genius, walks around his not very large apartment, among those near to him, among his comrades, the rooms seem small because of his enormous size. But it's fine for everyone in them. There is room for everyone. There is an attentive gaze for everyone and a smile and a subdued and vibrant voice. No fuss. No stiffness. He is different and yet, the same as what the People see in listening to him and reading him.

There is always a sincere attentiveness to the work and the words of his comrades. A special interior purity.

He is direct, exacting, and severe to those surrounding him. In spite of that, everyone always had a sense of conviviality in close dialogue with him.

We would gather every week at Gendrikov pereulok. Almost the entire editorial staff of *Novy LEF* would gather there. Although I was never part of the editorial staff, they would call me and I would often come.

Both S. I. Yutkevich,[204] when he was still a production designer, and Lev Kassil' would come there.

What did they talk about?

Everything that was most important and significant, which had taken place during the course of the week, in politics, in literature, in the cinema, in painting was the subject of conversation around the table. Everything was of interest, which characterized the life of the country: the great processes of transformation, facts, and events. Conversations and assessments would go on concerning new productions in literature and poetry. The content of the next issue of *Novy LEF* would be planned.

And there was always an analysis of newspaper, social, and political journalism, feature articles: did they correspond to the truth of life, or not? This would especially attract the attention of the poet. Conversation flowed freely. Without a chairman. Popular phrases and replies full of humor could always be heard and conversation was often interrupted by loud, youthful laughter. Almost always, verses were read. Aseev, Kirsanov, Tret'yakov, Mayakovsky himself, and others would read.

Mayakovsky would listen in a striking way. Slightly inclining his head in the direction of the one reading, never taking his eyes off them. Just as a lot of musical people scrutinize the score during the execution of their favorite musical compositions. Not one false note escaped his scrutiny. With his entire being, he would apprehend the content, the composition, and orchestral execution and while apprehending the playing of all the instruments of the orchestra in their unity, at the same time he would listen, with utmost precision, to how each particular instrument would carry its theme.

Mastery of the highest class of mastery: that is what he tried to attain in his poetic labor as a poet-agitator and propagandist. He sought out mastery as well in the labor of his close comrades. Sometimes, he would ask to have a poem read through to the end a second time, or for some particular parts of it to be repeated. More than all of the others, Nikolai Aseev gave him joy. They understood one another from the slightest hints. Being older, he would listen to Kirsanov and sometimes, while critiquing him, he would answer his youthful excitement with a friendly excitement, not less youthful and always cheerful.

Two presentations by the poet at the Polytechnical Museum will forever stand out in my memory.

With some comrades, I stopped by the poet's second apartment on Lubyansky passage, in order to pick up a pass for his presentation.

---

[204] [Russian editor's note]: *Yutkevich, Sergei Iosifovich* (b. 1904). Film director, production designer, film theorist. People's Artist of the USSR. In silent cinema, he directed *Lace* and *The Black Sail*. Among his best-known sound films are *Golden Mountains, Counterplan* (in collaboration with F. Ermler), *Man with a Gun, Yakob Sverdlov, Othello, Stories about Lenin, Lenin in Poland, Subject for a Short Story*. He worked in documentary film (*Liberated France*) and in animation (*The Bathhouse*).

It was a cold evening. The apartment was overflowing with people, who had come to get passes. Mayakovsky stood in front of a large writing table in a topcoat flung wide open. Excited by the coming presentation, with sparkling eyes, he wrote out the passes. The door would open continuously, allowing in visitor after visitor, and he, joking lightheartedly, would greet those who entered and write out pass after pass.

The apartment seemed cold, haphazard, not lived in. It was strange to see on the table a large bowl on a high pedestal, filled up with fruit. It seemed stuck into this room like a still life. This fruit you didn't pick up with your hand, you didn't bite into them. It was decoration, nothing more. The appearance of someone living there. This bowl of fruit gave the impression of the haphazard refuge of a lonely man. He asked me and my comrade to wait for him. We left with Vladimir Vladimirovich. At the entrance to the Polytechnical Museum stood a great crowd who couldn't get in to the auditorium, which was already at the point of overflowing. And so, closely surrounded by this great crowd, Mayakovsky walked up to the stage itself, and took us with him.

The entire evening remains in my mind as the utmost mobilization of the spiritual force of the poet. This was a battle, in which the question of honor would emerge the victor. He spoke about poetry and about his relationship to art, he read his verses, he responded to endless commentaries, he responded devastatingly and without a minute's hesitation to malicious remarks.

He was doing his great work. This was his great, inspired labor. He even took off his jacket, so that nothing would hinder him. He hurled into the auditorium the fire of his words and the auditorium, especially the young, seized upon every word. They took in every word as the expression of their thought. As their heart's desire.

> I know the force of words, I know the alarm bell of words.
> They are not the ones applauded from the boxes.
> From words like those, coffins tear themselves away
> To trot off on the team of their four oaken legs.

The second time I heard a presentation by Vladimir Vladimirovich from the auditorium of the Polytechnical Museum was not utterly in the usual circumstances. The artist Alexander Rodchenko, whom Mayakovsky loved and esteemed, calling him "the remarkable Rodchenko," was a man, who possessed golden hands, who had constructed a radio receiver by himself. This was virtually one of the first presentations of the poet to be transmitted by radio. The Briks and a few more people headed over to the tenth floor of the Vkhutemas Building (of course there was no elevator) on Myasnitskaya to the studio of the artist Rodchenko and his wife Varvara Stevanova, to listen to Mayakovsky.

Being conscious of the fact that, along with them, tens of thousands of Soviet citizens, who loved the radio, were listening to the poet, and that this invention, which was entering into Soviet existence, infinitely increased the size of the auditorium, brought a joyous exhilaration into our small circle of people, who had gathered near the radio receiver.

Alexander Rodchenko was "even more" agitated. How would the receiver behave towards those gathered around it, would it let them down? Nearly the entire time the audibility was good. Rodchenko's hands moved around the knobs. The noise of applause and laughter reached us. We also laughed, while listening, at how Mayakovsky parried those who tried to attack him. Very soon after his presentation, Mayakovsky arrived where we were.

Well, how was it?

Good...

This meant for him that thousands and thousands more citizens could hear him well.

Then, all at once, he stretched out on the divan. I was sitting on one corner of the divan, his head was near my eyes, and it was clear, just how incredibly tired he was, what an expenditure of strength this evening had cost him. He lay there with his eyes nearly closed, his face had an adolescent youth and sculptural peace. We talked together quietly. We talked about what we had won and time and space and light and sound. There were a million inventions ahead and all of them in our hands, within the scope of our possibilities. It was necessary to take chances. To be courageous, not to fear experiments, not to fear the difficulties in overcoming obstacles on the road to conquering the unknown, while standing at the threshold of a breakthrough.

Vladimir Mayakovsky considered, that our Soviet Filmmaking was a great breakthrough, but, that in order for it to become a genuine art and propagandistic revolutionary achievement, a difficult path still lay ahead.

He showed an unflagging interest in filmmaking. In the early years of the revolution, he wrote scenarios and even appeared in them himself as an actor. None of it was in any way remarkable; they were sloppily produced things. The only thing remarkable was, that Mayakovsky appeared in them.

Once, I held in my hands a strip of film of the movie in which the poet appeared: *The Lady and the Hooligan*. "Sentimental, made-to-order garbage" is how Mayakovsky himself described this film.

Vladimir Mayakovsky, shot in close up in this film from 1918, with almost no makeup, and this is the only such film image of the poet in those years. I really wanted to use a single shot in my film, *The Great Way*, but the management of Sovkino would not permit it. It turned out, that they were even more concerned than I was, about destroying the documentary quality of the film, by showing Mayakovsky acting. But truthfully speaking, they didn't want there to be included in a film for the tenth anniversary of the Great October Revolution, a film portrait of Mayakovsky, whom they didn't understand and they feared. Mayakovsky did not spare the management of Sovkino. Mercilessly criticizing their activities, he said directly, as they say, to their faces, in front of the entire nation:

> They say, here's Mayakovsky,[205] if he's a poet, just let him sit in his dumpy little poetic corner store... They spit on the fact that I'm a poet. I'm not a poet, but someone who, above all, has put his pen in service, you will note, in service to the present hour, to current reality, and to their guide: the Soviet Government and the Party.
>
> I want to make my word into a guide to the ideas of today. If, as I understand it, the cinema serves the millions, then I want to introduce my poetic capabilities into filmmaking, since the craft of the screenwriter and the poet, at their core, have one and the same essence...
>
> ...Why is the deciding word[206] in artistic questions left to the administration?
>
> Why, after so many decisions concerning art, are they giving up and find themselves in the position of the character in the children's fairy tale:
>
>> He opens up the little fishy's mouth,
>> but what it's singing can't be heard.
>
> Why are the bookkeepers of culture the deciding voice, and those, who practice art and culture, not even consulted by the bookkeepers?
>
> ...Why is it that the scenarios of the pictures being shown are so crappy, that creativity in screenwriting limits itself to the use of dead people, and that every inventory of every film enterprise reveals the unsold merchandise of the acceptable and scenarios which are unfit for anything whatsoever?
>
> There is one consolation for workers in the cinema.
>
> Management passes away; art endures.

In those years, he wrote scenarios, in which actors were supposed to take part, but he considered, that the most important aspect of filmmaking was the newsreel, that they shot a criminally small amount of them, that for workers in the newsreel normal conditions of work had not been established. He said, "The newsreel orders

---

[205] [Russian editor's note]: "*They say, that here is Mayakovsky...*" From a speech by V. V. Mayakovsky in the public debate *Пути и политика Совккпо* [*The Paths and Politics of Sovkino*], October 15, 1927. Published in *Полное собрание сочинений В. В. Маяковского* (М. «Художественная литература», т. XII, 1959, стр. 358) (*Complete Collected Works of V. V. Mayakovsky*), Moscow, Khudozhestvennaya Literatura, vol. XII, 1958, p. 358.

[206] [Russian editor's note]: "*Why is the deciding word...*" Ibid., p. 355.

real things and facts. The newsreel must not be haphazard, but organized and it must organize things itself. The newsreel is a newspaper. Without those kinds of newsreels, it's impossible to live."

He not only spoke, but he struggled for it. My relationship with Mayakovsky provided crucial support for my first three works: *Fall of the Romanov Dynasty*, *The Great Way*, and *Lev Tolstoy and the Russia of Nicholas II*. He not only spoke to me about them in comradely conversations, but stepped forward in front of the public, struggled with the leadership of Sovkino for my position within film production. Here is yet another excerpt of his presentation in a public discussion at Sovkino of October 15, 1927:

> *Mayakovsky*: They point to Eisenstein, to Shub. But they don't say, that these film directors are the pride of our film production and that they became that almost in spite of Sovkino. They sent out *The Battleship Potemkin* on its first release only to second-rank theaters and only after the German press heralded it, did it go to first-rank theaters. They spoke about Shub's victory. She is a filmmaker properly understood[207] because in its foundation, the strip of film rests on a completely different principle. The montage of real shots without the least shooting of additional material. What does Sovkino do? They refuse to give Shub authorship. You shot little fragments; even we could do that.[208]

> *Trainin*: That's not so... [That was so. — *Esfir' Shub*.]

> *Mayakovsky*: With your signature the factory was ordered to give out some kind of honorific designation, but authorship was denied. I am speaking on the basis of facts, about which any journalist can speak. I am saying in relationship to Shub, what they told me about this directive. But even if all this were not true, Shub as a director was able to make this picture, not thanks to the existence of a scenario, but only because in its foundation, it rested upon a completely new principle in the character of montage and making another such a picture wouldn't be possible, because Sovkino doesn't shoot newsreels.

---

[207] [Trans.]: In the original: Она художественная. My translation is a paraphrase of the multifaceted implications of the term художественная [literally "artistic"], which had previously been used only to designate the directors of full-length fiction films. It implies the idea of directorial authorship, but does not explicitly say that.

[208] [Trans.]: In the original: Оно отказывает Шуб в авторских. Вы снимали кусочки—это и мы можем сделать.

My film, *The Great Way*, I made in more favorable circumstances. In this, I was helped first and foremost by the political and social recognition for my first film, *Fall of the Romanov Dynasty*, but no small part was played concerning my situation at the studio and with Sovkino, by help on the part of Vladimir Mayakovsky and Sergei Eisenstein. I received the right to be considered the author of the film *Fall of the Romanov Dynasty*, I received the title of director, and I was given the possibility of shooting, or rather, of shooting additional material for my next film, *The Great Way*, for the Tenth Anniversary of the Great October Revolution. Besides that, newsreels of current events in Europe and in America were purchased for me.

And so, here I am at the lens of the movie camera. I shot delegations of foreign workers, institutions of advanced industrial education. The Communist University of the Toilers of the East in Moscow, Moscow factories, sovkhozes, Sun Yat-sen Communist University, the Lenin Institute, day care centers, laboring children in the Colonies, the existence and socialist education of Red Army men, the Don Region, the factory for agricultural machinery in Rostov-on-the-Don, the construction of workers' developments. The Volkhovskaya electrical station, cotton farming, the tractor and locomotive shops of the Putilovsky factory, the new development for the workers of the Putilovsky factory, and historical locations connected with the Great October Revolution and with the name of Vladimir Il'ich Lenin.

At the end of the summer of 1927, I was living in Leningrad, in the "European" Hotel. Also living there was the crew shooting the film *October*. I would shoot all day long, but in my time off from work in the evening, without fail, I would attend Eisenstein's shoots at the Winter Palace. Shooting with him was G. V. Alexandrov, already in the capacity of [co-]director of the film *October*. The camera operator was E. Tissé.

Sergei Mikhailovich, after the shot and the lighting were set up, would always beckon to me to come over to the lens and, while he was directing one of the pre-shooting rehearsals, would let me look at it through the lens. He would always ask for critical remarks and loved to say: "And please, don't pull any punches." And there were no punches to pull. I was sincerely delighted with everything. The plastic quality of the shot, the intelligence of the content, the movement within the frame, the storyboard, the tracking shots all delighted me. On Sundays, Sergei Mikhailovich would take me along to scout locations. It was unfortunate, that Sergei Mikhailovich didn't happen to finish the film on time.

The Great Way I did manage to finish. Comrades Voroshilov, Yaroslavsky, Podvoisky, and many others attended the screening at Sovkino.

But first, the entire work was seen by Sergei Mikhailovich Eisenstein. Arrangments were being made for accelerating the distribution of *October*, for finalization of the script, and for additional shooting. Afterwards, the screening of my film was initiated. I remember my unbounded joy when K. E. Voroshilov proposed showing

The Great Way in Leningrad at the anniversary conference of the Central Executive Committee of the USSR. He repeated a few times, that it was just unfortunate, that there were no shots in the film portraying Sergo Ordzhonikidze. A few film portraits of S. Ordzhonikidze from the time of the Civil War were subsequently found in archives in Baku and Tbilisi.

Sergei Mikhailovich, who was sincerely distressed that he did not manage to finish *October* on time, with the generous heart of a great artist, was happy for me as a friend, congratulating me after the screening. He, of course, knew very well, how much I myself was distressed by the delay in his work.

So there I am with my film in Leningrad. The session of the anniversary conference opened in the Uritsky Palace (the former Tavrichesky Palace, where in tsarist times, the State Duma was seated). Members of the anniversary conference, members of the Central Executive Committee traveled to Leningrad. The session was attended by representatives of workers' organizations of Leningrad.

The Palace was decorated with flags, posters with greetings in Russian and other languages. In the conference hall, a great bronze bust of V. I. Lenin was installed.

On the wall, charts were hung, which illustrated the growth of the National Economy of the USSR.

A large box had been allocated for the diplomatic corps.

At the conference, M. I. Kalinin, A. V. Lunacharsky, V. V. Kuibyshev, S. M. Kirov, and others gave presentations.

I listened eagerly and I remember all the presentations.

On October 20, after the evening session, in the very hall where the session took place, a screening of my film was arranged for the delegates. The auditorium reacted to the film in lively fashion, which brought to life again on the screen various stages of the heroic struggle of the proletariat, which led it to victory. The hall reacted with special enthusiasm to the film portraits of the great Lenin, especially to those, which were shown for the first time in my film.

On November 4, in the grand "Titan" movie theater, the second public screening took place for members of the Central Executive Committee of the Party; besides that, I attended screenings and presented my work in many workers' clubs. During that trip, I got to know the outskirts of Leningrad well, the outlying workers' districts. The New Leningrad entered my life for the first time. This was the beginning of numerous trips of mine to the great city of Lenin with film production equipment. On this trip there, I found new comrades: G. Kozintsev and F. Ermler.

In November 1927, *The Great Way* was shown on the screens of Moscow and of the entire Soviet Union. The film was well regarded by both the Party and the Soviet press and by many comrades from abroad. It was singled out for recognition by the Agitprop Section of the Central Committee.

Here is how Mayakovsky wrote about the film:

The best advice for Soviet Cinema for the Tenth Year of the October Revolution is to deny funding to abominable productions such as *Poet and Tsar*, and give the funds, vainly squandered on such pictures, to the shooting of our Revolutionary Labor newsreels. This will support the making of such beautiful pictures as *Fall of the Romanov Dynasty*, *The Great Way*, etc.

I avail myself of the occasion of a discussion about the cinema to protest once again in every conceivable way against the staging of scenes of Lenin using various look-a-likes in the Nikandrov style [in Eisenstein's film *October*, Nikandrov had played the role of V. I. Lenin— *E. Shub*] It is abominable to watch, while a man assumes poses like Lenin's and makes body movements resembling his; and behind all this outward appearance an utter emptiness is felt, the utter absence of thought. One comrade said utterly truthfully that Nikandrov didn't look like Lenin, but like all the statues of him.

We want to see on the screen not the performance of an actor on the theme of Lenin, but Lenin himself, who, in the few shots, which exist, all the same, is watching us, from the fabric of the cinema screen. This is the likeness to be valued in our filmmaking.

Let there be newsreels!

In his turn, Sergei Mikhailovich Eisenstein was critical of the poem "Good" ["Хорошо"]. He said that, he was waiting for a monumental epic from Mayakovsky, with a force comparable to the poem "Vladimir Il'ich Lenin," which he esteemed highly. He didn't like the poem "Good."

One of the evenings of September 1927 on Gendrikov pereulok has always remained in my memory. Mayakovsky read "Good." There were more people than usual there. Lunacharsky, Fadeev, the poet Svetlov, and others were present. The small dining room couldn't hold them all. The door to the poet's study was open wide. It too was overflowing. From behind the door of the room, I watched those sitting around the brightly lit table, which had been extended. Everyone was clearly visible in the frame of the door. The aging Lunacharsky whose eyes had lost their luster. His eye disease must have been evident already. Fadeev, lean, tall, in jodhpurs and a long shirt cut like a military uniform, without a single gray hair, with bright eyes in his sunburned face.

The usual table conversation went on, but everyone was anxious for the reading to start. And then the first verses of the poem began to sound:

Time

    is a thing

        extraordinarily long.—

There were times—

        which passed like bylinas.[209]

Neither bylinas,

      nor epics,

        nor epopées.

By telegram,

    you must fly,

       strophe!

With your lips   on fire,

      bend down

        and have a drink

from   the river

    whose name is "Fact."[210]

In spite of the fact, that Mayakovsky did not read with the full power of his voice, the complex intentionality, the diverse nuances, the comprehensibility of every word powerfully filled the apartment, extended the walls of the apartment. It seemed as though, along with us, thousands of people, were sitting right there, behind us, although they were invisible.

The words resounded about the great days of October, about Lenin, about the years of the intervention, about hunger, cold, and devastation.

I will never forget the range of elevated feelings, the inexhaustible belief in the future, and the great thoughts, which illuminated the youthful and courageous face of the poet.

Sometimes, his gaze would seize hold of the faces of those listening. But more often, he would turn to the side, where Lilya Yur'evna Brik was sitting. The ability to listen for the hundredth time, as if for the first, giving profound attention to every word—this was clearly the gift of L. Yu. Brik. And this especially attracted Mayakovsky.

---

[209] [Trans.]: In the original: былинные, an adjective from былина [bylina] a genre of oral Russian folk epic.
[210] [Russian editor's footnote at the bottom of the page]: V. V. Mayakovsky, *Полное собрание сочинении* [*Complete Collected Works*, Moscow, Khudozhestvennaya Literatura, 1959, v. XII, p. 147].

And so, offending no one, in this severe and joyous poem, these lyrical verses sounded:

If
    I
        have written anything,
    if
    I
        have said anything—
then it is the fault
                of those eyes which are heaven,
    the beloved
            of my
                    eye.
Round
        and chestnut,
    burning
        to a cinder.

Everyone received the poem ecstatically. Lunacharsky spoke about it enthusiastically. He spoke a great deal, expressing admiration for a whole series of things.

He said that this poem was a memorial to the great days of October and that in it the deeds of Lenin rise up with the same power, as in the poem "Vladimir Il'ich Lenin."

Only Fadeev treated it adversely; it appeared to him, that it was an inadequately realistic expression of the reality of those days. He did, however, like one theme of the poem, which began with the lines:

I've
    wandered astray
            in many warm countries.
But only
        this winter

did an understanding

come

to me

of the warmth

of love

of friendship

and of family.

The others strongly attacked Fadeev: N. Aseev, O. Brik, V. Shklovsky. Maya-kovsky was clearly upset by Fadeev's remarks.

One day, I happened to be present, when Fadeev spoke about this poem. He remembered both that evening and what he had said. He said, that now this was his favorite poem by Mayakovsky and that it reminded him, that it was as if, it had been written about our days by the poet through a kind of presentiment. All of this had come to be accomplished in our days.

For me, precisely this distinctive trait of the poet was always so precious. Today, Tomorrow, the Future, Communism: seeing them as an integrated wholeness of accomplishment.

Already in 1928, a split had become evident in the meetings of the members of LEF at Gendrikov pereulok. The meetings grew more gloomy. It was no longer possible to agree upon how to leave behind the atmosphere of seclusion of a closed literary circle grouped around Mayakovsky.

Over *Novy LEF* hung the inescapable sensation of isolation from the larger life of the country.

The positions of *Novy LEF* on art were contradictory, but the main thing, was that they were not popular with the great masses. They became unconvincing, even for Mayakovsky. While speaking out against the art of the past, Mayakovsky, when he spoke of Pushkin, Lermontov, Nekrasov, Gorky, spoke of them, as the summits of our art, and in his own creative work was connected with them by the blood ties of succes-sion. Any critic of art could easily establish this.

While speaking against the theater and acted cinema, Mayakovsky wrote plays and scenarios. O. Brik and V. Shklovsky did the same thing. How was it possible for them to be against acted cinema, while at the same time, praising to the entire world the art of Soviet Cinema: Sergei Eisenstein, Alexander Dovzhenko, Vsevolod Pudovkin.

The position of the applied arts and of photography together with painting was hanging in the air. The relationship to photography was fuzzy and imprecise. Maya-kovsky was the first to understand this. His position came down in the end to this: that not only the fact was important, but our relationship to it, our conception of it.

Novy LEF did not succeed in gaining social recognition; it did not succeed in gaining wide readership. Mayakovsky could hardly fail to notice this, since all of his poetry and social actions were connected with the masses.

I had the feeling, that the poet lived two lives: one in the great auditoriums, responding to every event in the life of the country; the other, among those close to him, where each day he felt more and more alone. He was sullen and taciturn. He would listen to everyone, yet draw no conclusions.

In the summer of 1928, on a Sunday afternoon, I traveled to Pushkino, to the dacha of Mayakovsky and the Briks. Everything seemed bleak to me: both nature and the dacha. A lot of people, a lot of typical dacha fuss, and a taciturn Mayakovsky. From the morning on, he would play cards. As with everything he did, he gave himself over entirely to the game. At lunch, he was silent, distracted. L. Yu. Brik tried to enliven the group gathered around the table, but little came of this. Right after lunch, Mayakovsky would once again sit down at cards. It became boring and I left. In the train car, his sister, Lyudmila Valdimirovna, who had just arrived at the dacha that day, turned up beside me. All along the way, she would recite to me from memory fragments of his verses, which, in her opinion, held a distinctly autobiographical character; they were called up by the days of his youth in the Caucasus. For me, this was inspired and moving.

For New Year's, we gathered at L. V. Kuleshov's place. There was no "holiday table" in the usual sense of the word. On various small tables, scattered across two adjoining rooms, were bottles of wine and very modest hors d'oeuvres. The whole time we would drink hot black coffee out of little cups. The room was decorated for the holidays with balloons of various colors, tied together into a huge floor-to-ceiling bouquet, which stood in the corner. From the movement of the air, they would constantly twirl around. The guests would constantly dance around in circles. The whole time, coming in and out, were scenarists, actors, cinematographers, set designers. L. Yu. Brik taught everyone how to dance the foxtrot, which was just then coming into fashion. She would hold her partners at a respectable distance from her. She danced with reserve and elegance; on the whole, her dancing obtained a dove-like purity, little resembling the vulgar way, which one usually saw.

Unexpectedly, a bit after midnight, Mayakovsky appeared. He was not drunk that night, although he clinked glasses and wished everyone a Happy New Year both as a group and individually.

He wanted to dance. He walked up to Lily Brik and whirled around with her a bit. Then he walked up to me. But I didn't know how to dance the foxtrot. Then he pulled me away from the floor and all the same began to circle around the room with me. "Now, that's the foxtrot!" he said. Shortly after that, without saying goodbye to anyone, he left. For where?

The meetings of the LEF group in Gendrikov pereulok ceased. One day, the principal editorial staff of *Novy LEF* gathered at the place of one of the members, S. Tret'yakov. S. Eisenstein and I were invited. This was not long after the Party conference[211] devoted to the question of filmmaking. Everything was business-like and dry. Vladimir Vladimirovich, for the most part spoke with Sergei Mikhailovich Eisenstein, as did the other members of the group. Again and again they argued, that he should not break with LEF. And Sergei Mikhailovich again and again explained, that he saw LEF as lacking in prospects. I was completely in agreement with him. Not long after that day, V. Shklovsky send me a note: "Esfir', your view is highly developed. It would be easy to refute, but your error is useful for the cinema."

But then, the issue of *LEF* came out, and what surprised me most of all, what distressed me was the inaccurate stenogram of my presentation, which appeared. I could not believe, that my words which criticized LEF could be discarded and it would come out that I had endorsed it. I know that Vladimir Vladimirovich valued my straightforwardness. I couldn't imagine how they could publish my presentation in *LEF* in such an inarticulate fashion, so erroneously in meaning, without even basic "conversational" logic. It was necessary for me to write a letter to the editorial staff. I asked, that the text of my presentation be given to me to correct and that it be published again, if possible, with a note from the editorial staff. This didn't happen. This ended my relationship with the *Novy LEF* group. But this didn't alter my relationship with the poet Mayakovsky. I continued to go to his presentations and I would drop by Gendrikov pereulok.

A change of singular importance took place in the life of the poet. He became part of RAPP [The Russian Association of Proletarian Writers].

Here is how he himself described this act of life-changing importance, in a presentation at the MAPP [The Moscow Association of Proletarian Writers] Conference on February 8, 1930: "...I enter RAPP, in order to enter the place, which affords me the opportunity to change my task to work in an organization of a mass order." In a presentation at the Komsomol House on March 25, 1930, he said: "I became part of RAPP, the organization of proletarian writers, in order to demonstrate my serious and urgent desire to change over in a great number of ways to mass work."

So, he sought the path towards the unification of all the forces of proletarian literature. He sought and thought, that in joining RAPP, he, perhaps, had found his solution. Could it have been so? To my way of thinking, not completely. In 1930, RAPP, although it had not yet reached the demagogic position, which led to its liquidation, the slogan "ally or enemy" had already been put forward and writers who were Party members strongly opposed those who were not.

Vladimir Mayakovsky and RAPP...

---

[211] [Russian editor's note]: *not long after the Party conference*. The First All-Union Conference took place March 15–21, 1928.

Mayakovsky with his deep commitment to the Party, with his life, merged with the life of the Soviet People, with his untiring stride among the ranks of workers, shoulder to shoulder... I think, that for him this brought no small number of bitter moments.

Sometime on the eve of the twentieth anniversary of the beginning of his literary activity, I came over to Gendrikov pereulok a bit early, long before dinner.

On the table lay a huge quantity of newspaper clippings. Mayakovsky wasn't wearing a jacket; he was wearing a vest over his shirt. With scissors in hand, he was gluing newspaper clippings onto large pieces of paper. He was working nimbly and seriously.

In essence, this was the geography of the travels of the poet across the entire Soviet Union. Only Pushkin had traveled across his Motherland to as great an extent. Mayakovsky would sometimes read aloud to me selections from the material about his presentations. For some reason, as I was looking at him, I clearly imagined him to myself, when he was working for ROSTA.[212] He would ask me in detail about filmmaking, about news, about what people were doing. Mayakovsky accorded enormous importance to Soviet Filmmaking as a new form of artistic labor. *The Battleship Potemkin, Mother, The End of St. Petersburg*, the poetic creative work of Alexander Dovzhenko, documentary films, which in those years for the first time were appearing on the screens of the Soviet Union, defined for him the new path of Soviet Filmmaking.

He deeply wanted to work in filmmaking. This didn't come to pass, just as our desire to shoot film of him, to record his voice never came to pass. It all seemed as if there were a great deal of time ahead. If only he could have gone on living. His creative powers were flourishing. We would always have time to shoot him on film, to record his voice. We didn't have time. For this, we stand guilty before the poet.

On February 1, 1930 there was an opening for an exhibition of his. He made a summation of his activities. Here is what he said to the youth of the Krasnopresnensky Region about his exhibition: "The idea of this exhibition is to show that the writer-revolutionary is not a renegade, whose little verses are written down in little books, which lie on the shelf and gather dust, but the writer-revolutionary is a human being, a participant in the routine, daily life of the Construction of Socialism." At that very exhibition he recited the entirety of his most recent poem, "At the top of his voice."

I know that Vladimir Mayakovsky was very distressed that his close comrades did not come to the opening of the exhibition. Knowing his mental vulnerability, one can imagine what whirlwind of thoughts must have taken possession of his brain in those hours.

---

[212] [Trans.]: ROSTA was the Russian Telegraph Agency, the official News Agency of the Soviet Union. Mayakovsky designed many posters for them, which became quite well known.

I had managed to get permission to shoot Vladimir Mayakovsky in connection with the twentieth anniversary of his literary activity, to get a camera operator and film for the shoot. The artist Alexander Rodchenko was supposed to be making a whole series of photographs for an album commemorating that date.

This was my last conversation with Mayakovsky by telephone about four or five days before his impossible end. I said to him, that I wanted to shoot film of him on his favorite Moscow streets, in outlying factory areas, in workers' clubs, in the Polytechnic Museum and every place he had the habit of being. I told him, I was going to try to edit these shots in parallel with the text of the last part of his poem "Good." I was happy, that I was going to shoot film of him, my favorite poet. But I was nervous, would I be able to manage the shoot, would I know how? He responded to me, that I would certainly manage, that in a few days we would surely meet and come to an agreement about everything. He was glad, that I would be working with Alexander Rodchenko.

The meeting and the shoot never took place.

In the "Podlipki" Sanatorium in the summer of 1953, Aleksandra Alekseevna Mayakovskaya, the mother of the poet, was undergoing treatment.

She was small and frail. On her slender shoulders was her large head; she was beautiful, with the beauty of the wisdom of age. Her face was surprisingly calm, with stillness and concentration. A quiet and kind voice. And only occasionally, would the fiery, mobile gaze of her big dark eyes appear. The face of the son resembled that of his mother. Now the face of the mother recalled the son.

On the day of the sixtieth anniversary of Mayakovsky's birth, I was sitting next to her beside an open window. She spoke: "You know, Volodya was against monuments, against heavy weight bronzes," and quietly she quoted his verses:

> …let's let
>
> the principal monument
>
> constructed
>
> in our struggles
>
> be socialism.

"All the same, now I would like to live until the day, when the monument is erected in Mayakovsky Square. They talk and talk, projects and young sculptors. I think, that they might find a way." Her eyes welled up with tears and her voice was shaking…. "There are people now in literature, who don't like Mayakovsky. They are not above interfering now, either. Nothing can come of that. He is alive and strides ever forward. Who cares if they don't like him…" She looked off into the distance, into the tree-lined allée. And she and I together caught sight of the inimitable Maya-kovsky, forever alive, walking along the allée:

> In my soul, there's not one streak of gray,
> nor any senile tenderness!
> Having stunned the world with the power of my voice,
> I go: handsome,
> twenty-two years old.

Sergei Eisenstein

> Sad and happy, I walked into
> your studio, sculptor.
>
> A. Pushkin[213]

My agitated memory of Sergei Mikhailovich constantly draws me to record those facts of his life, where he showed himself to be a distinguished artist, a master.

He loved this word. And he always accepted being addressed with the word "master" as the greatest gift, as the acknowledgment of the labor of his life. He was a great hard worker with a fiery imagination; he was an inventor and researcher, combining in himself the ability to analytically and synthetically compare phenomena and to summarize them. This ability of his has led some to think of him as a cold, intellectual artist. For me, he was always an artist of enormous, fiery incandescence. And not only for me.

This was his private studio. Here, all his activity began.

Sergei Mikhailovich's apartment on Potylikha, not far from the [Mosfil'm] studio, reflected the essence of his multifaceted interests. The entire ambiance spoke to the artist's inimitable taste. A lively testimonial to him in terms of objects.

He loved light: the sun. The room where he worked immediately gave you the feeling, that you were permeated by the warm rays of the sun.

This was created mostly by the bright yellow color of the wall of the room and the window, which ran the length of the entire wall, beyond which could be seen the green expanse of a small woods. Bright rugs were spread out on the floor. His work table ran the full length of the window. On it, were books, manuscripts, reproductions. Everything he needed for his work.

---

[213] [Trans.] From the poem "Художнику" ["To the Artist"].

On the table, always at hand were the books of Lenin, the books of Marx...

The furniture in the room in which he worked was bright, metallic, light-weight, movable. And right there, was an antique armchair, with frayed raspberry colored fabric.

He loved music. Against the background of the yellow wall, a polished grand piano stood out.

He knew the force and the charm of combinations of colors of various shades, various textures and various densities. The grand piano was covered with a red Chinese brocade, embroidered with gold. Everywhere there were masses of figurines and toys: some from Vyatka, some Mexican, and some Negro[214] ones. There was a

---

[214] [Trans.]: In the original: негритянских [negrityaskix], a potentially diminutive adjective from the noun негр [negr] ("Negro" or "nigger"). In the historical context, this is not considered racist. I have chosen not to change the terminology to something more acceptable today in order to keep a parallel with American English usage of the period and to remind the reader of a problem which has not gone away. The word is still in use and is as varied in its meaning as the French word "nègre." In Russian, however, this word is considered acceptable by some in everyday use. Some biracial Russians find the word uncomfortable, others do not. There are some offensive terms related to it,

Negro Madonna in porcelain. The clothing was white with gold, but the face of both the Madonna and child were black.

All this together created a range of colors, superbly selected by the artist.

In this room, he would write, would work on a script, and would prepare for lectures to students at the VGIK.

Books. Books were his best friends.

A second room was a library.

He valued communication with people in the arts worldwide. On the wall hung portraits with personal inscriptions by Charlie Chaplin, Paul Robeson, Einstein, Abel Gance, Asta Nielsen, and others.

The room was crammed with bookcases with wide shelves along the wall. Books were packed in, two or three rows to a shelf.

The room couldn't contain all the books. They were lying everywhere, in every room in bookcases, and unsorted in boxes.

There were several thousand volumes in Russian, English, German, French, Italian, and other languages. He spoke the languages fluently, as perfectly as his native Russian. This afforded him the possibility of giving lectures and presentations on art at Cambridge University, in Paris, in New York, and in Hollywood. The facility, with which he spoke in the language of whatever country in which he happened to be, astonished his listeners.

There were many unique books. Literature, poetry, monographs about the painting of every nation. Many monographs about the art of China, India, and Mexico. Books on architecture. As a civil engineer, he was especially interested in new construction. In the middle of the course of lectures at the VGIK, he took a leave to travel, at the invitation of Betal Kalmykov to Nal'chik, which was being rebuilt. Eisenstein, with the rigor of a great artist, would criticize what was being done. It seemed an

---

such as литературный негр [literaturny negr] ("literary nigger"), i.e. ghost writer. This is clearly a borrowing from the French "nègre littéraire," which has wide currency, but betrays its origins in slavery. Others argue, that there is a positive meaning attached to the phrase работать, как негр [rabotat', kak negr] ("to work like a nigger," meaning to work hard), as hard work is an honored Russian value. Diana Muromtseva, self described "black Russian, vegan-activist and feminist," in a post on Quora.com dated June 9, 2018, says, "I'm black Russian. I was born in Moscow and lived here all my life. So I don't identify myself as 'Afro-Russian.' I really don't like this label. Most of Russians don't mean anything bad when they use word негр (negr). But it's an unpleasant and offensive word for me. In my opinion, the better words for black people in Russian language is темнокожие, чернокожие, черные." The terms she prefers could be rendered as "dark-skinned (ones)," "blackskinned (ones)," and "blacks." Taras Shun'ko adds to the discussion, that the terms "afroamerikanets" and "afrikanets" (African-American and African) also exist. The former is sometimes applied indiscriminately to persons from the Americas of the African Diaspora and to persons from Africa, who understandably, do not appreciate it. Ironically, the word черные (Blacks) is more widely used as a negative way of referring to people from the Caucasus, i.e. the original "Caucasians," as well as to Arabs, Georgians, Armenians, Chechens, Azerbaijanis, and others.

anachronism to him to construct Soviet palaces and housing blocks using Florentine, feudal structures, in the style of Piranesi and Bibbiena. "Why do we need palace-fortresses? What are we defending ourselves against in our palaces of culture and art?" he would invariably ask. Because of his insistence about the construction of Nal'chik, the architects A. Vesnin and M. Ginzburg were invited, with whom he had become acquainted and with whom he would meet at my home.

He showed a great and profound interest in the study of philosophy and psychology.

Everything was studied deeply. None of his books were without his personal notations and extra sheets of paper inserted in them. His phenomenal memory and his unique ability to synthesize from what he had read made him a rarity as an educated person.

The library. This room was his intellectual laboratory. He would spend many hours reading. The room had walls painted dark-blue, soft red carpets, which dampened one's steps, a round table covered with green brocade embroidered with gold, and an antique English armchair and divan. Above the divan, a Mexican straw mat. The distinctive pattern allowed light to pass through. Everything in this room, both the serene tones of the paint and the glittering spines of the bindings of the books, were conducive to thoughtful reading, to quiet conversation, to reflection. More than once he said to me, that the most precious thing in his life were books. They were his companions in life. With them, he was never alone. Some of those closest to him caused him to experience the feeling of loneliness. Books never betrayed him.

I was always delighted when he would take me with him to bookstores in search of books. The booksellers greeted him like an old acquaintance. They knew his tastes. They put aside for him editions that rarely came onto the market. They would phone him about book finds. For him, a book-buying day was a celebration. Upon returning home, he would prepare a celebratory tea. We would leaf through and evaluate the new friends at length before placing them on the shelves.

His bedroom was completely unexpected. There, he gave free play to the eccentric, to humor, to the grotesque. He had all this within himself. He wielded these capacities brilliantly and in happy moments knew how to entertain and make his comrades laugh.

In the middle of the bedroom was a wide daybed, covered with a Mexican rug with a fanciful design. Above the daybed there was the same sort of rug. On the walls were masks: Japanese, Javanese, Mexican. A wooden Negro sculpture. In the corners of the room were little angel heads with little wings extended behind them. In front of the wide window was a tall, antique, seven-piece candelabrum from a church, hung with neckties of every color.

From every expedition, he would bring back some kind of example of folk art: Georgian embroidery, antique Ukrainian handmade skirts.[215] The black fabric had bright embroidery of colored silk and glass beads of such beauty, that it was difficult to tear your eyes away from the patterns.

And so many more wonderful works of Russian folk art, of Negro and Mexican art were lovingly collected by him. He loved to surprise his comrades with a rare new book, a monograph, one of his own drawings, or a new acquisition for his collection of fanciful objects.

In his home, he would take part in and conduct creative discussions with other film directors. Those closest to him among the film directors were the ones from Leningrad.

He was very proud of the Vasil'ev brothers, he was proud of their success all over the Soviet Union, he was proud of them as students, who had outstripped their teacher—that's how he talked about them with his kind, sparkling eyes. With Sergei Vasil'ev, he had a personal friendship. He maintained that there was a close line of succession between *Battleship Potemkin*, *Chapaev*, and the film *We Are from Kronstadt* by Vs. Vishnevsky[216] and E. Dzigan.[217]

He highly esteemed the Maxim trilogy by the directors G. Kozintsev and L. Trauberg and the film *Yakov Sverdlov* by S. Yutkevich. He was extremely close creatively with Grigory Mikhailovich Kozintsev. They could talk for hours on end one-on-one, not only about filmmaking, but about literature, about painting—about art in the wider sense. He was friendly with Sergei Yutkevich, often meeting and working passionately with him. Their meetings were devoted to cinema history and theoretical questions concerning the art of filmmaking.

Sergei Mikhailovich greatly esteemed the film *The Great Citizen* by F. Ermler and *Lenin in 1918* by M. Romm[218] based on a scenario by A. Kapler.[219] In speaking

---

[215] [Trans.]: In the original: плахты [plakhty], which can refer either to the traditional skirt or the striped or checked handmade woolen or cotton fabric from which it is made.

[216] [Russian editor's note]: *Vishnevsky, Vsevolod Vital'evich* (1900–1951). Writer, screenwriter. Author of the scenario *We Are from Kronstadt*, *We, the Russian People*, *The Unforgettable Year 1919* (in collaboration with M. Chiaureli and A. Filimonov). Author of the scenario of the documentary film *Spain* (directed by E. Shub).

[217] [Russian editor's note]: *Dzigan, Efim L'vovich* (b. 1898) film director. People's Artist of the USSR. He directed the film *First Cornet Streshnev* (in collaboration with M. Chiaureli), *We Are from Kronstadt*, *Dzhambul*, *Prologue*, *Torrents of Steel*, and others. Professor at the VGIK.

[218] [Russian editor's note]: *Romm, Mikhail Il'ich* (1901–1979). Film director and screenwriter. People's Artist of the Soviet Union. He directed the films *Boule de Suif*, *The Thirteen*, *Lenin in October*, *Lenin in 1918*, *Dream*, *The Russian Question*, *Secret Mission*, *Murder on Dante Street*, *Nine Days in One Year*, *Ordinary Fascism* and others. Professor at the VGIK.

[219] [Russian editor's note]: *Kapler, Alexei Yakovlevich* (b. 1904). Screenwriter. Decorated Worker in the Arts of the RSFSR. Author of the scenarios for *Lenin in October*, *Lenin in 1918*, *Kotovsky*, *No Greater Love*, *Two Lives* and others.

about this film, we would always pause to dwell in detail on the remarkable performance by Shchukin,[220] which had created an image of Lenin.

More than once, these rooms resounded with the din of happy young voices. He would always bring into his home especially gifted students and rehearse with them assignments he had given.

Of all the Muscovites, he was closest with Vsevolod Pudovkin. He communicated in person very little with A. P. Dovzhenko, but considered him the artist closest to himself. We were together at a public screening of the film *Zvenigora*. The impression this film made was so strong, that upon arriving home, he phoned me twice that night, in order to share his thoughts about this film. He said that, Alexander Dovzhenko showed himself to be an innovator and an accomplished master, that the combination of legend and fantasy with reality, with Ukrainian history, was beautifully resolved. That the image of the "grandpa," which had come down through the ages, had been rendered poetic. *Shchors* he considered one of the best films of Soviet art.

There was not a single major event in film art, which did not draw his rapt attention and response, regardless of whether or not he had a personal relationship with the director, regardless of style and genre, which were sometimes distant from him personally.

In Sergei Eisenstein's apartment, many creative meetings and conversations took place with Soviet writers; those closest to him were Vsevolod Vishnevsky, Aleksandr Fadeev, Petr Pavlenko and others.

Here, his friend Ivor Montagu and his wife would stay as guests. And I never will forget the evening when Paul Robeson so movingly sang the songs of his People in Eisenstein's study. Some of the songs came with the voice of the singer accompanied by an orchestra, recorded on records, which intensified the impression. Eisenstein, when he introduced me to Robeson, called him the "Black Mayakovsky;"[221] this was the highest expression of good feeling by Sergei Mikhailovich towards the remarkable singer.

Eisenstein did not have the capacity and did not like to conduct conversations in a circle with numerous interlocutors. He loved one-on-one communication. He very rarely had very many people over. As a matter of fact, I personally remember two such evenings. One was when he had over a group of filmmakers from Georgia. He proposed, that I act as the hostess for the evening. And the second was when the Vishnevskys came over for the first time.

---

[220] [Russian editor's note]: *Shchukin, Boris Vasil'evich* (1894–1939). Theater and film actor. People's Artist of the Soviet Union. He appeared in the films *Flyers, Generation of Victors* aka *Generation of Conquerors, Lenin in October, Lenin in 1918.*

[221] [Trans.]: In the original: Черным Маяковским. Eisenstein uses the word, which translates literally as "Black."

One-on-one with a person who interested him, he would be utterly open. He not only knew how to listen attentively to his guest, but also loved to stimulate an interest in himself, in his thoughts about art, his general views, his plans for the future.

I used to call those encounters "hours of enchantment" or "sorcery." He would laugh, though he liked this, and in response to my question, "Well, were they enchanted?" would invariably follow a detailed account of the conversation. What a pity, I didn't record all this at the time. Only a few people would come by his place.

But he loved being at noisy gatherings at the homes of his comrades. The First of May and the Seventh of November were at the Vishnevskys'. For New Year's we would gather at G. Roshal' and V. Stroeva's[222] place. He loved holiday tables, a lit-up Christmas tree, noise, laughter, the horseplay of talented young people. There were a lot of them at these evenings. He would speak little himself. He did not make toasts, but was happy to observe; he would exchange banter with someone in a few, often wingèd words, which would invariably invoke laughter.

And he loved to dance a bit. He danced like a clown. His movements were indescribably lively and musically rhythmical, but all this verged on the grotesque: partially a satire on fashionable dances, partially on himself, partially on the credulity of the lady, who would humbly submit to all these seemingly impossible dance positions.

Besides bookstores, he would take me with him to the theater and to concerts. These were not only hours of leisure and entertainment, but necessarily included asides to me about his evaluation of the spectacle as it went along. For him, indispensable for a fully shared viewing experience was the knowledge that the person accompanying him saw everything through his eyes.

If over an extended period, I would fail to agree with him, he would invariably say, "You have been damaged by extended contact with the Symbolists." He had in view, the years of my work in the Theatrical Department, where the Symbolists really were numerous. My surprise was great indeed, when posters were plastered all over Moscow concerning a lecture by Andrei Bely at the Polytechnic Museum to be presided over by S. M. Eisenstein. Without letting him know in advance, I came and sat in the first row. As he presided over things, he would slyly look over at me, but after this, there were no more conversations about the influence of the Symbolists on me. He kept in communication with Bely and after the presentation, Bely would come over to his place, and he would drop in at Bely's. He valued Bely's books *Kotik Letaev*, *Notes of an Old Eccentric*.[223]

---

[222] [Russian editor's note]: *Stroeva, Vera Pavlovna* (b. 1903). Film director. Decorated Worker in the Arts of the RSFSR. She worked in collaboration with G. L. Roshal'. On her own, she directed *Generation of Victors* aka *Generation of Conquerors*, *Boris Godunov*, *We, the Russian People* and others.
[223] [Trans.]: Shub apparently misquotes the title of Bely's *Notes of an Eccentric* [Записки чудака] (1922), which she calls *Notes of an Old Eccentric* [Записки старого чудака].

Together we watched all the theatrical events in which Mei Lanfang, whom Eisenstein admired, played a role; several times we saw Meyerhold's staging of *The Queen of Spades*, which had been brought to Moscow from Leningrad. At one of the performances Meyerhold was there. He would follow very attentively the impression the staging would produce on us. I remember a long, nighttime walk with him along Gorky ulitsa after a performance. Vsevolod Emil'evich shared with us his own very interesting concepts for creating a theater piece based on the "Bronze Horseman" of Pushkin.

Eisenstein and I never missed a theatrical event, staged by his friend, the director E. S. Telesheva.[224] We would attend concerts in which Prokofiev, Shostakovich, Musorgsky would be played, concerts where Gilel's would play.[225] Although Eisenstein maintained, that he understood music badly, he was one of the most enraptured listeners of music. As is well known, he even staged the opera *Die Walküre* at the Bolshoi Theater with the artist Williams. He had his favorite actors and directors: Stanislavsky, Meyerhold, and the young Vakhtangov. "In your creative work, you resemble the young Vakhtangov," Telesheva said to him and this made him happy. He brought me an unpublished book by V. Aksenov[226] to read, mainly, so that I could read, how once, Sergei Mikhailovich, during his years of study, had presented his directorial étude to Vsevolod Meyerhold, who then became gloomy. This frightened Eisenstein; he decided the étude had been badly done. The Meyerhold theater actress Zinaida Raikh sent him a note with approximately this content: "When a student is not only equal, but better than the teacher, he should leave." So Eisenstein acted accordingly, convinced, that this was what the teacher wanted.

His favorite actors were friends of his youth, Shtraukh and Glizer; at one time he would often meet with Livanov. He highly esteemed the acting mastery of Cher-

---

[224] [Trans.]: Elizaveta Sergeevna Telesheva (1892–1943). Soviet Russian actress, director and teacher. Decorated Artist of the RSFSR. Telesheva acted in and directed numerous productions at the Moscow Art Theater. She also acted as Stanislavsky's assistant on other productions and taught at the Moscow Art Theater. She appeared in the first version of Eisenstein's ill-fated *Bezhin Meadow* as the Chairwoman of the kolkhoz. Filming was interrupted and after a review of the work print by the General Management of the film industry, the material which had been shot, was discarded. In the second version of the film, her part was eliminated. She remained as an adviser on the film and also participated in the filming of *Alexander Nevsky* as a consultant on working with actors. According to the Russian Wikipedia entry, perhaps not the most reliable source, her relationship with Eisenstein was so close, that many of their circle considered her his legal spouse. They went their separate ways some time after the release of *Alexander Nevsky* in 1939. Shub's apparent discretion and the Russian editor's silence on her are telling, though perhaps in different ways.

[225] [Trans.]: Most likely the highly regarded pianist Emil' Grigor'evich Gilel's.

[226] [Russian editor's note]: *He brought me an unpublished book by V. Aksenov.* An essay, which served as the basis for this book, was written in 1933 and published in shortened form under the title "Сергей Михаилович Эйзенштейн (портрет художника)" ["Sergei Mikhailovich Eisenstein (a portrait of the artist)"] in the journal *Iskusstvo Kino* (1968, № 1).

kasov, Maretskaya, Okhlopkov, Ranevskaya, Lyubov' Orlova, Babanova, Il'insky, Kachalov, Leonidov, Khmelev, and Birman.

Sergei Eisenstein considered, that the great masters were distinguished by their individuality, their school, and the quantity of students produced by this school. Stanislavsky had many students, as did Vakhtangov and Meyerhold: Garin, Il'insky, Zharov, Tsarev, Samoilov, Bogolyubov, Okhlopkov, Yutkevich, Pyr'ev, and others. The School of Kozintsev and Trauberg produced many splendid actors: Magarill, Kuz'mina, Zheimo, Sobolevsky, Gerasimov, Kostrichkin, Zhakov... and Eisenstein himself had many students. With his name are connected the Vasilyev Brothers, Shtraukh, Glizer, Alexandrov, Yanukova, Kadochnikov, Pipinashvili, Nizhny, Rostotsky, Filippov. How many precise, unique characterizations of their creativity it was my fortune to hear, how many words about the joy of creative collaboration with them.

Eisenstein was enraptured by Ulanova; he considered her a wonder and saw *Giselle* many times.

Complicated and full of twists and turns was the path of S. M. Eisenstein as a director. Success did not always accompany him. He took on difficult subjects, the fundamental subjects of his time. He wanted to express the thoughts and feelings of his people, to find new, visual solutions, appropriate to the cinema.

In fact, the only unqualified success here as well as on the screens of the world, which came to him and continues up to now, is *Battleship Potemkin*. His other films always touched off impassioned debates. On them, lay the stamp of the relentless searching of an artist. There were great successes alongside failures. But even the errors of these films were instructive. One trait unquestionably distinguished his films. The impassioned relationship to his choice of subject, the impeccable composition of the frame, the profound artistic treatment of the subject. Every shot filmed by Eisenstein, in its lighting design, in its composition, was a complete and beautiful picture. Every film was a search for new montage solutions, which would best express the subject emotionally and conceptually. And Sergei Mikhailovich understood best of all, that in his films, his greatest successes and greatest failures occurred alongside one another.

I would like, after having enumerated those films done by him after *Battleship Potemkin*, to speak about them, without referring to the critical articles in the years of their release. I do not intend to reminisce about his personal relationship to them, but to attempt to recall my conversations with Sergei Mikhailovich about his works, to make use of his public presentations and give his personal evaluations of the successes and failures of his work.

He was extremely demanding towards himself. Enduring his failures with difficulty, he was skillful at not putting himself at ease through the ill-considered praise of his enthusiastic admirers. He thought everything through to the end and mercilessly rooted out the reason for his failures. Arriving at well-defined conclusions, he would take on the new work, setting for himself ever more demanding, more difficult tasks.

October, the film by S. Eisenstein and G. Alexandrov, was late for the date of the anniversary, the tenth anniversary of the day of the Great October Socialist Revolution. Eisenstein was distressed. After a year of intensive labor, Sergei Mikhailovich gave the impression of a person who was exhausted. *October* was completed and delivered only in 1928. All the same, after delivering it, Sergei Mikhailovich had the feeling that the film was still not fully ready. Out of his rigor towards a purity of the montage phrase, he considered, that not all the repetitions had been eliminated, that the rhythm necessary for the entire film had not been completely established. He accorded great significance to the professional luster of a work.

He himself did the editing. He sat at the editing table, completely wrapped up in film, with scissors in hand, checking his montage discoveries on the Moviola. This was for him the most interesting time. There were so many possibilities for resolving this or that episode. What a joy to break down the resistance of the material, to subordinate it to his design, to devise and find solutions for montage objectives, which until then, had never been put forward by anyone. Not only to find solutions for them, but to know that through precisely these solutions, he would strike the spectator in the heart and in the imagination!

Sometimes, he would phone to call me to his editing room, or to the screening room, in order to test a sequence he had just completed on me. At those times, in a friendly way, he would call me his "hunting dog." He demanded rigorous assessments. Again and again, he would show me an episode, impatiently compelling me to say everything: both about what I considered unassailable and about what was still unclear to me and wanted thinking through to the end.

More than once he repeated to me, that on the film *October* lay the patina of some kind of negligence and not only from fatigue or lack of time. It wasn't just this, that he found damaging to the integrity of perception. No, not just this.

He considered the fundamental shortcoming to be, that methodology got the upper hand over construction and, at the expense of the whole, it fractured the fundamental content of the object. In this, he found the tragic flaw of the director of *October*.

In spite of the ruthlessness of his self-criticism, he never said what was fundamental. It continued to hurt, like a bleeding wound that will not heal. What was fundamental was not the failure with the image of Lenin, and this always tormented him. He understood, that in the attempts at "typage" lay his fundamental error. Without Lenin, there could be no *October*.

And all the same, the film was realized in an innovative way and much in it was splendid: it advanced cinema art. Pudovkin said, that the works of Eisenstein were impossible to describe, or to picture, or to imagine on the stage, but could only be seen on the screen. That *October* was a remarkable film: people would not only watch it and memorize it, but they would make notes on it and learn from it. This, in fact, did happen, in spite of all the errors of *October*.

N. K. Krupskaya wrote in the *Kino* newspaper of March 20, 1928: "This is an unsuccessful representation of Il'ich. He is somehow too fussy. Il'ich was never like that. What is good, if you please, are the legs of Il'ich, which correctly transmit his involuntary gesture of impatience. If it isn't possible to represent Il'ich otherwise, then it would be better to leave him out entirely, although this, of course, would not accord with historical truth." This sounded to Sergei Mikhailovich like a condemnation and even the following words of Nadezhda Konstantinovna Krupskaya: "…but already one can say, that the film *October* is a stage on the road to a new art, the art of the future" could not bring peace to the master. This demanded a leap forward.

Forward, again and again.

And the road chosen was difficult: *The General Line*, directed by S. Eisenstein and G. Alexandrov.

Collectivization. The first years of collectivization in the villages. The old, monstrous, village way of life. The superstition, the spite, the hatred in the kulaks. In order to keep intact their land, their plot, their property, they were prepared to do anything. Their ruthlessness in relation to anything new knew no limits. And alongside them were the poor peasants. They were prepared to hitch a cow to the plow, to drag the harrow themselves, though it broke their backs.

But consciousness grew. It was necessary, it was possible to achieve new forms of labor. The poorest, illiterate peasants, with the support of the Party, came to realize, to understand, how to achieve new conditions of labor and that meant a new and better life.

And so, a small milk cooperative grew into comradeship in mechanized livestock production. A tractor begins to till the earth. Electric power comes to the stalls for the cows.

The dull, everyday struggle goes on of the old with the new, of the new with the old. In the struggle, new people develop.

Before beginning this work, the crew would visit Rostov, Baku, they became familiar with the sovkhozes[227] and plemkhozes[228] of Ryazanskaya Governate.

Near Moscow, instead of sets, real cow barns in a new architectural style were constructed by the architect A. Burov. Bright, white buildings, that looked more like sanatoriums. The breeding stock was there. Electric milking took place. Before the beginning of the shoot, Sergei Mikhailovich took me all over the newly constructed

---

[227] [Trans.]: A *sovkhoz* (a contraction of *Sovetskoe khozyaistvo*) is a state owned farm where workers are explicitly working for the state. In theory it was distinct from a *kolkhoz* (a contraction of kollektivnoe khozyaistvo), which is a farm collectively owned by its workers, though after the forced collectivization of agriculture under Stalin, the difference was moot.

[228] [Trans.]: A *plemkhoz* (a contraction of *plemmenoe khozyaistvo*) was a state-owned farm dedicated to breeding quality livestock.

architectural facility. He was pleased with my mute amazement and kept repeating the whole time, "This, this is how our village will be."

Yes, everything was accomplished. The dream of Eisenstein, the artist, became reality. And the accomplishment of a dream was realized within his lifetime.

But then, I was stupefied by the sight of the new alongside the old, wretched, and miserable village.

The heroine was Marfa Lapkina. She was not an actress. She was a peasant and that was her real name: Marfa Lapkina. They didn't find Marfa right away. They searched in the production plants and factories, at employment exchanges, they looked at thousands of women, and found her at the Central Exchange. They taught her how to drive a tractor. She carefully learned the regulations of the Collective Farm Milk Cooperative. She herself looked after the breeding bull. The bull was huge, purebred, and had a mythical appearance. A symbol of fertility, everlasting eternal life, he was filmed in surroundings celebrating nature.

Marfa performed the scene with authentic dramatic tension, in which she learns of the death of the bull, mutilated by the kulaks, and expiring as a dog howls in the night. Her eyes and her dry, whispering lips were full of hatred for the enemy and human grief over the loss. Before us stood the new human being, who had understood, that the old way of life was no longer possible. It is necessary to struggle, it is necessary to build a new life, it is necessary to achieve victory.

For the second time, an error had been committed. Instead of a character, created by a talented actress, there was "typage."[229] A real peasant woman, but all the same, "typage." And in a whole series of crucial scenes, she was helpless and even physically repulsive.

After a screening of this film attended by Henri Barbusse, he wrote in the *Kinogazeta*, of March 12, 1929: "The new film by the Eisenstein group reproduces the change from past to present-day peasantry. The outrageous destitution under the oppression of the old regime and the old methods. The human being crushed by the land, and later, his subsequent and brilliant victory in collective labor."

Henry Barbusse remained silent about the inadequacies of the film. And there were more than a few of them. The release of the film was delayed. Eisenstein carried out a series of substantial modifications to the film. The group went to shoot additional material of the sovkhozes at "Gigant" and elsewhere. Even the title of the film was changed. The film appeared under the title *Old and New*.

In connection with the work on *The General Line* some extremely important events took place in the lives of Eisenstein and Alexandrov. They were called in by members of the government headed by I. V. Stalin. I will never forget the happy face of Sergei Mikhailovich after this meeting. His face was overflowing with youth. Thick

---

[229] [Trans.]: In the original: типаж. In *typage* a person is selected for a role based on their external characteristics representative of a social type.

golden curls over the large, serene brow of a philosopher. His hair, it seems, was also electrified with joy. Everything in him was sparkling, bubbling. He made plans. He fantasized. What a pity, I don't precisely remember the story of this meeting. The picture was subjected to friendly criticism. It was explained to them, what the general line of the Party was in the villages. It was clear, that they had not succeeded in saying everything correctly, even in their great artistry.

After the delivery of the film *Old and New*, Eisenstein and Alexandrov were given a trip abroad to Europe and then to America to gather material for creative work.

America: this was a new stage in the creative life of Sergei Mikhailovich. Years of creative ferment and great spiritual experiences. This was the end of youth, the beginning of maturity. And once again, searching…

America. This was the time when Chaplin, Flaherty, Griffith captivated us with their creative work. Hollywood was attractive as the place, where the available technology of a studio afforded the possibility of realizing any kind of cinematic project.

New York struck Sergei Mikhailovich with its extraordinary tempo of movement. At first, this seemed to be efficiency, but soon after the efficiency, he glimpsed hustle and bustle and anxiety. "Transferring your gaze from quickly striding legs to faces and eyes, you see uncertainty, concern, disquiet."

Sergei Mikhailovich met Griffith in passing. He would often meet with Charlie Chaplin and Flaherty. Meeting with them strikingly revealed to him the life of great artists under the circumstances of capitalism.

In New York, Sergei Miklailovich stayed in the noisiest part of the city. In a hotel on Broadway. From his room, he had the possibility of observing and recording in his memory the most characteristic aspects of this city. This is how he describes his meeting with Griffith[230]:

> Griffith… A first meeting with a first rank film classic. It seemed like a shot from one of his early films. Five or six o'clock in the morning. I am returning to my hotel, full of impressions from the Negro neighborhood of New York, Harlem… Right here my meeting took place with Griffith, who had remained faithful for thirty years to the place he had fallen in love with.
>
> So then, five or six in the morning. A gray dawn on Broadway. Metal trash barrels. They are sweeping the streets. A vast empty lobby. In the morning light, it seems as if there is no window and the emptiness of Broadway pours out into the sleeping hotel. Overturned armchairs. Rolled up carpets. They are cleaning. The desk clerk with the keys is

---

[230] [Russian editor's note]: *he describes his meeting with Griffith*. Later, E. Shub will quote Eisenstein in an article published in the newspaper *Kino* (1932).

lost in the depths of the lobby. Near him is a figure in gray. Gray stubble sticks out of the gray skin on his face. The gray gaze of bright eyes. The sharp gaze fixed motionlessly on a single point: among the overturned armchairs and rolled up carpets is a stretcher. On the bare pavement are two medics. Behind them a policemen. On the stretcher is a man covered in blood. A bandage. Blood. Alongside, they are sweeping away the dust from a palm tree. Under the windows they are sweeping up mountains of paper. There was a knife-fight someplace. They carry the man into the hotel. They bandaged him up. They carry him off. Gray street. Gray people. And a gray man in the depths. How many times he—Griffith— reconstructed in front of us, authentic scenes of American gangsterism... It seems like you are seeing all this on the screen: color disappears: a single range of gray tones from the white splotches of paper on the street to the almost complete darkness, where the stairway of the hotel goes up. We recognize each other immediately, from photographs. We introduce ourselves. I shake the hand of the creator of remarkable pictures. But the author doesn't want to talk about them: "Half of my pictures are *trash*[231] (roughly as we would say 'schlock'). I made them, so that I would have the money for directing, for covering the losses of my favorite films, or to have the opportunity to make the things I really wanted to..." The first ones brought in heaps of gold, the ones in the second group were solid losses. The losers were *Broken Blossoms* and others, which Griffith remembered lovingly... Here and now... he has been nursing the thought of shooting a film about corruption around the dry law.[232] "I'm looking for money. No one wants to finance that kind of subject. But it seems to me that it might be possible to convince some rich widow. I've been working on this for the past two weeks already..."

A remarkable master. One of the founders of cinema. A man, who went gray at this work. An old man. And being compelled to run after stupid rich women, wasting his days on persuasion, humiliation, contrivance, just as it is for any youthful beginner, whose name no one knows, whose productions have not yet been applauded in all corners of the globe, as have the films of Griffith! In the end, the foolish woman, it seems, did not agree, the film was not produced, and the name of Griffith has not been seen on movie screens for a long time.

Here's a characteristic letter of Eisenstein to me from that time:

---

[231] [Trans.]: In English in the original.
[232] [Trans.]: i.e., Prohibition.

...we are doing four or five hundred kilometers a day,[233] racing around the most interesting part of America—the Negro part. The automobile makes it possible to linger and to become familiar with everything worthy of attention—and there's so much that is. Now, we will see each other soon and in a bit more colorful terms I will tell you about all this... I gave a speech at a Negro university this morning in... Charleston (yes, yes, the very same place where the dance comes from). I gave a presentation on the [Soviet] Union (in particular, about the family, about abortion, and other such questions) in... a Negro Baptist church! (on the occasion of Easter Sunday). Tomorrow we will be in Washington and then New York...

But we didn't see each other so soon.

He met Dreiser and began to work with him on a script for *An American Tragedy*. He wrote to me: "...You wrote me such a good, such a remarkable letter...[234] (I heard it directly, like I was accustomed to hearing you regularly on the telephone) and since that time I have not written: but this is not out of thoughtlessness, but, on the contrary: I don't want to answer it "on the fly," but there really just isn't any time to answer properly. We are working intensively on the script for *An American Tragedy*; today we are leaving for New York for a conversation with Dreiser. Write me what you think about this, but *only after you clearly imagine to yourself how I am going to do this. You know me well enough for that...*" My answer to him is not preserved. But I remember, that I asked him not to work on this, convinced as I was, that his interpretation and understanding of *An American Tragedy* would not be produced. And so it happened. He intended after this production to quickly return to the Soviet Union. But no, he did not quickly return.

Having signed an agreement with "Paramount" for a production of *An American Tragedy* by Dreiser, he left for Hollywood. There, he met Flaherty. We had come to know and to love him through his films *Nanook* and *Moana*. Impressed by him, Sergei Mikhailovich wrote, that

he would stop for anyone, though he hardly knew them, and was prepared to tell stories for hours, which were endlessly fascinating and long, about remarkable events and stories for the screen, which were in no way inferior to *Nanook* or *Moana*. He would invariably finish his story

---

[233] [Russian editor's note]: *we are doing four or five hundred kilometers a day...* Letter from Eisenstein to E. Shub from the USA dated March 28, 1932. The original is preserved in the personal archive of E. Shub.
[234] [Russian editor's note]: *You wrote me such a good, such a remarkable letter...* S. Eisenstein's letter from the USA is undated. The original is preserved in E. Shub's personal archive.

this way: "I make a gift of this to you." It was the only thing he could do. Not only would no one give him even a meter of film, but no one wanted to lend him the means for even one of these remarkable pictures, which he would have been able to release ten at a time. He was compelled, alas, to do them not with vast "creative" delays but… with financial ones.

A widow, or a fur company, a junkman grown rich, or the temperamental owner of a water pipe company: in their hands lie the fate of the art and culture of cinema in the West. And when you don't meet up with a widow, or a furrier, or a speculator grown rich, the fate of any great artist resembles the fate of Flaherty.

It happened that Eisenstein broke off with the "Paramount" company. Upton Sinclair, together with a group of leading intellectuals, got hold of the means for a film about Mexico; Sergei Mikhailovich set off there with his collective. Before his departure from Hollywood, he managed to do a talk on the widescreen format to a gathering of directors, camera operators, and entrepreneurs. He demonstrated, that the widescreen format opened up enormous possibilities. It created ideal proportions, it afforded the opportunity, which was completely unique, to construct a shot simultaneously vertically and horizontally, it afforded the possibility of conceiving the content of a shooting script in a totally different way. There were people who wanted to do the technical work on the realization of the widescreen format. An estimate was drawn up of six hundred thousand dollars. This didn't happen.

When he arrived back in the Soviet Union, he put forward this question there, but at that time, we didn't have the possibility of thinking about it. It is interesting, that almost at this same time, A. P. Dovzhenko began talking about the widescreen format.

Here is Eisenstein's first letter from Mexico[235]:

…considering things cinematographically, I am presenting to you my nearest neighbor: a pyramid. Telotsotlan[236] in montage segments from a wide shot to a close up in four camera set-ups: this is the pinnacle of refinement in montage thinking in America. The ways of the Lord are mysterious… and so now, I find myself in Mexico. I think, that my leaving Hollywood was better than anything I could do there! In light of the political situation, it was pretty much unthinkable for me to have done anything with those people. Now I am making a Mexican *Kulturfilm*—a travelogue. And as you see, the examples here are worthy of attention.

---

[235] [Russian editor's note]: *Here is Eisenstein's first letter from Mexico…* Letter written on four postcards, undated. The original is preserved in E. Shub's personal archive.
[236] [Trans.]: Perhaps a faulty transcription of Tepoztlan, the location of the archaeological site known as Tepozteco, which contains a small pyramid.

Flaherty got me excited about Mexico, and I, in return, got him excited about the Soviet Union. The old man (he's completely gray) got very excited and left to see his family for Christmas with the firm resolution to work in the Soviet Union on a series of films, devoted to national minorities. He is remarkable and you, of course, will love him. My vacation ends in February, and I don't think I'll be late getting back—unless I linger a bit in Japan on the way. Here, things are quite remarkable and powerful: starting with the bullfight—which I went crazy for—cock fights and dances of pagan Indians honoring Catholic saints. I'm thinking about traveling around the entire country.

But the most remarkable thing was the meeting of Sergei Mikhailovich with Charlie Chaplin. They became acquainted while Chaplin was working on, or actually, as he was finishing *City Lights* and Eisenstein was often present during shooting. How many interesting stories Sergei Mikhailovich would tell about Chaplin, some about the man, but for the most part about the artist. I didn't write it down and much has faded from my memory.

Some Western European scholars on Chaplin see in his creative work the stamp of philosophical reflection of especial depth. Charlie Chaplin is a great artist and a truthful one, he organically and accurately reflects in his productions the alogicality and absurdity of what happens in America and in other capitalist countries. Sharply and truthfully, he shows all the contradictions of this world. His films echo with great and profound thoughts. Sergei Mikhailovich said, that to some degree, the same thing happened with him as with Balzac. It's well known, that, in assessing the creative works of Balzac via the classics of Marxism, it has clearly been demonstrated, that the picture of capitalism so sweepingly and truthfully seized upon by Balzac sometimes works against his personal political judgments. The films of Chaplin give a truthful reflection of the capitalist world and this has the proper influence.

Sergei Mikhailovich spoke a great deal and with great interest about Chaplin's humor, about the childlike spontaneity of his humor and about how in his creative work there is an infantile approach towards a great number of things. He would laugh at external facts, at situations, never going deeper into what brought forth the laughter. (Sergei Mikhailovich himself, in my opinion, "suffered" to some degree from infantilism.)

Eisenstein used to tell his students at the GIK[237] about one particular conversation with Chaplin. In one of his meetings with him, Chaplin told him, that the homeless and neglected children[238] in the Soviet Union strongly interested him. Sergei Mikhailovich began to explain to him that the main problem in our country was the re-adaptation of these homeless orphans to normal life. But this didn't interest Chaplin. Chaplin said, "I would like to produce a picture drawn from the lives of these hoodlums." What attracted him in this subject was not the conception of a phenomenon, nor a sense of tragedy, but it was their funny black snouts at the asphalt boilers that interested him, and what they did there.

When Sergei Mikhailovich went out on Chaplin's yacht, the following conversation between them took place. The sun was setting, they were sitting on the deck, the yacht was swaying back and forth. The conversation turned to the swaying backs of elephants. Chaplin said, that the elephant was a stupid beast and could crush anyone it pleased with its legs. Someone asked what animal he liked best. He responded: wolves. Sergei Mikhailovich would say, that if he were to write a memoir, he would write, that Chaplin's gray hair and cold gray eyes at that moment reminded him of a wolf.

In Mexico, Eisenstein's group fell under constant political surveillance by the authorities. In no time at all, Sergei Mikhailovich was under arrest. Elaborate sabotage of the shooting began.

Eisenstein had planned to realize an ethnographic film to which sound would later be added. Shooting took place in regions of Mexico, where no one had ever been with a movie camera. The Eisenstein group was to visit particular locations in old Mexico, in tropical Tehuantepec, where at that time there still remained intact an untouched form of matriarchy. They shot the ancient pyramids and the remains of the culture of the ancient Aztecs, knowing their historical significance. In Mérida, in the Yucatan, a bullfight was filmed.

It was supposed, that the USSR would get this film for free. Eisenstein and Alexandrov wrote to Soyuzkino from Mexico:

> The picture will be interesting for the [Soviet] Union and exceptional in its material. It is difficult to work, many difficulties with organization, various languages, general lack of understanding of film work by the local public, etc.

---

[237] [Trans.]: The abbreviation for Государственный институт кинематографии (The State Institute for Cinematography). In 1938, it became the VGIK: Всесоюзный государственный институт кинематографии (The All Union State Institute for Cinematography). In 1986, it became the Всероссийский государственный университет кинематографии имени С.А. Герасимова (ВГИК) (The S. A. Gerasimov All Russian State University of Cinematography [VGIK]).

[238] [Trans.]: In the original: беспризорные [besprizornye]. Tatsiana Zamirovskaya informs me that this term refers to homeless children orphaned by the Revolution, World War I, and the Civil War, or runaways. It implies not being looked after. They enjoyed a reputation for criminality. She notes, that a number of them, after re-adaptation, became KGB agents, loyal unto death.

The tropical sun torments us more than bad weather days in Moscow. It is often necessary to stop shooting because of the heat, because everyone is collapsing on their feet and cannot work.

The form of the picture is an attempt at visual creation through tensions and powerful impressions, just as in *Potemkin*; an artistically realized chronicle.[239]

We are making an overview of the country and in this overview are interwoven with each other… five stories: the Indian, the Spanish, the Military, the Revolutionary, and the typically Mexican. These five stories through their composition will allow us to show, in a single picture, the south and the north, the way of life and the life of the country, and besides that, to create the tension which is essential for a good picture.

At the same time, in the French newspaper *Le Monde* the following communiqué from Upton Sinclair about Eisenstein's work appeared:

Eisenstein is now working in Tetlapayac, a hacienda (farm) in the State of Hidalgo. Around him are gathered actors of all colors and all races. The female leading role of the poor Indian woman is being played by the artist Isabel Villaseñor.[240] The male lead is being played by a horse groom, who has never been filmed before. The owner of the hacienda, Don Julio Saldívar,[241] is also engaged as an actor, and a senior member of the film crew, Nikolai Kunets, has gotten a major role.

A large part of the inhabitants of the small town of Tetlapayac[242] and Apam has also been taking part in the work, by portraying their usual occupations: horse grooms, carters, peasants, small vendors. All showed themselves to be, in Eisenstein's words, magnificent film actors.

Eisenstein had already been in Mexico for five months without any sort of uproar and sensation. As the result of some misunderstanding, he was obliged to spend two days in police custody. His only crime involved his being a Soviet Citizen. Then, after his release, he got to work. To begin with, he spent two months studying the various celebrations in Tehancos-

---

[239] [Trans.]: In the original: хроника [khronika], which can mean "newsreel" as well as "chronicle."

[240] [Trans.]: In the original: Изабелла Билаюкор [Izabella Bilayukor]. Hard to say whose mistake this is.

[241] [Trans.]: In the original: дон Жуан Сальзивар [don Juan Salzivar]. Saldívar comes from Marie Seton's biography of Eisenstein, p. 195. The Russian spelling seems to be an attempt to approximate the Spanish sound phonetically in Russian, rather than to transliterate it. A phonetic rendering is typical in Russian for words in foreign languages.

[242] [Trans.]: In the original: Питлараяк [Pitlarayac]. The correction is also suggested by Seton's book.

Indian[243]; then, headed towards Acatán, where he devoted himself to the study of the ancient tribe of the Maya. In Mérida, he shot a bullfight; in central Mexico, he shot historical scenes from the time of President Díaz.

As always, Eisenstein was accompanied by Alexandrov and Tissé...

So far, the plot of the new film remains unknown. Even Alexandrov and Tissé don't know the details. Editing will begin after departure from Mexico...

Around this time, I received a letter from Sergei Mikhailovich, which contained the following:

...We wandered from top to bottom across the map of Mexico.[244] Pushkin also wrote about us, "the rains wash them, dust covers them."[245] Work is complicated, difficult, multi-lingual, but fascinating as hell.
I don't think about the final results: after *General*,[246] I do not consider myself competent to judge the quality of my own work. I didn't think I would survive after the fate it suffered and time is even prolonging all sorts of wounds and perhaps the only trace that remains of it is, that I am interested in everything except... cinema.

Cinema is engaging as a "small experimental universe" in which it's possible to study the laws of much more interesting and meaningful phenomena than current pictures, which are nowadays accompanied by deafening noise and tiresome chatter. Maybe this is a quite logical period of "purification" for a cinema, which is advancing, a complete re-configuration is required, not a stone will be left upon another stone of our dearly departed ones, sorry... [our] work. I am surrounded by living ethnography, more fascinating than any fiction film and even any documentary. There is a colossally interesting shift taking place in the viewer psychology of the USSR. I am receiving very scanty material, but even by means of it, the most curious changes in the viewer's pulse are making themselves felt...

What are you doing now? Do you think, that the prospect also lies before *your* line of thought for a colossal revision, even if it is along

---

[243] [Trans.]: In the original: Теанкос-Индиан. Perhaps a mistranscription of Tehuacán, at the time renowned for its religious festivals and the culture of its women.

[244] [Russian editor's note]: *We wandered from top to bottom across the map of Mexico...* From a letter from Eisenstein. The letter is dated July 4, 1931. The original is preserved in the personal archive of Esfir' Shub.

[245] [Trans.] This is a line from Pushkin's poem "Песнь о вещем Олеге" ["The Song of Wise Oleg"].

[246] [Trans.]: Eisenstein in referring to the criticism he encountered for *The General Line*.

the same tracks… Don't make a tactical error by conducting a Bacchic funerary feast over the ripped-open belly of the feature film.

Sometimes, I feel like I would like to stage things in a theater. In a good one, a genuine one. My reaction to the cinema is just that strong. Although it seems that I have never worked more earnestly than here and now.

The problems of montage do not occupy me in any way any more, and I'm afraid to say, sound occupies me even less.

It's interesting what comes of a picture shot in such circumstances.

Things didn't turn out the way Sergei Mikhailovich had planned with this film. He wanted to finish editing and do his sound work in Hollywood, and bring it back to the Soviet Union in a finished state. He had intended, that his route back to the Motherland would be by way of China. He wrote me about that. China was a longstanding dream of his. To see China, to get to know the life of its people, and upon returning to the Motherland, to create a scenario and then, go back again to China with a movie camera. To film China! He spoke about this as his most passionate desire. For hours on end he would force his comrades to sit and listen to Chinese popular, ancient, and revolutionary songs. He had a rare collection of Chinese records.

But things didn't turn out that way. Eisenstein returned without having finished work on *Mexico*. And then complicated conversations began about sending the material which had been shot to Moscow… In the end, Eisenstein didn't even edit his film himself. In those circumstances, this was especially important, since the film was shot without a scenario, as were the majority of the semi-documentary films of that time. It was important to transmit the author's handling of the material which had been shot, to properly resolve the conceptual structure of this artistic chronicle. It goes without saying, that in those circumstances, montage by the author had nearly a decisive importance. It was even more frustrating, that it did not turn out that way, because Eisenstein considered this work, after the *Battleship*, to be the most significant stage in his creative life.

The film was finished by some stranger's hand. There was not even a director's consultation *in absentia*. Vsevolod Vishnevsky saw this film in a tiny theater on the outskirts of Paris. In Paris, the film had nearly five different runs. Vishnevsky said, that the absence of the synthesizing thought, of the eye and the hand of Eisenstein, weighed heavily on this production… And all the same, the impression made by the film was enormous. The shots of real people, ancient historical monuments, the conception of individual episodes, nature, the bullfight were fascinating… Tissé shot everything magnificently.

S. M. Eisenstein never caught even a glimpse of this film.

I know, that several Mexicans—workers in the arts—said: "Eisenstein revealed Mexico to us."

In Moscow, once again. Eisenstein, with his characteristic understanding, that the creative fate of an artist is decided by his labor, by his creations, like any great master, did everything he could to cope with the dissatisfaction, which tortured him, because the plan for *Mexico* was not brought to completion. Upon returning to the Soviet Union, he rushed out in search of a scenario and did everything within his power to meet with Gorky as soon as possible. At this time, the first sound film, *The Road to Life*, which was directed by Ekk,[247] was playing in theaters. Gorky, during his meeting with Sergei Mikhailovich, singled out this work for strong criticism. He considered, that the problem had been touched upon in insufficient depth, superficially, sentimentally. He was seized with the thought, that a film should be made in response. The issue of homelessness among children interested him and he wanted to compare the past with the current day. He read through his notes for the theme of a scenario with Sergei Mikhailovich. They spent the entire evening together. Sergei Mikhailovich was deeply excited by the conversation with the great writer. A number of episodes in what Gorky had read, reminded him of biographical sketches from the life of the writer in childhood. Everything was touched upon with a critical social attitude. There were remarkable comic scenes of the way of life of the homeless orphans.[248]

We, Eisenstein's comrades, were distressed by his prolonged absence. These were the decisive years of industrialization and collectivization. The atmosphere among his comrades, which greeted Sergei Mikhailovich, was harsh. His fault was the extended period of time he spent outside the borders of his Motherland, his enthusiasm for various exotic countries, in the years when, in his Motherland, shifts of enormous historical importance were taking place. This was a concern for the artist. It seemed impossible, inconceivable—not having lived through all the events in the life of the country alongside the People and the Party—to view them correctly, to interpret them correctly. Was imagination, mastery, the keen eye of a great artist enough for this?

I addressed him with these misgivings. It was striking how attentive he was to what people said to him. Our relationship as friends was not impaired. To make a film on the subject of Soviet Reality was also, above all, his personal and passionate desire. And that's how *Bezhin Meadow* originated.

---

[247] [Russian editor's note]: *Ekk, Nikolai Vladimirovich* (b. 1902). Film director. He was the director of the first sound film (*The Road to Life*) and the first color motion picture (*Nightingale, Little Nightingale*).

[248] [Trans.]: In the original: беспризорные [besprizornye], the neglected children living on the street, sometimes homeless, sometimes not, often engaged in begging or criminal activity. They had been orphaned by the Revolution, WWI, or the Civil War. Sometimes they were runaways. Shub explores their situation in her script for *Women*.

Before me lies a small brochure,[249] published by Iskusstvo Editions in 1937: *Concerning the film* Bezhin Meadow *by Sergei Eisenstein. Against Formalism in Film Art.* On it in red pencil is written: "To my dear friend Esfir'" and the palm of a hand is sketched there. The attraction, which follows on this occasion, is not a happy one. On the palm has been drawn the "line of art" (as in chiromancy), which is broken in several places. Out of the line comes an arrow and "ha-ha" is written there. A straight red "line of fate"—and an arrow once again—and "ha-ha." It is signed "July 20, 1937." As if he were mocking himself. But no, this wasn't self-mockery. He greeted his failure with this film as a great creative disaster.

Now, there is little interest in what the authors of this brochure wrote. What was said did not stand the test of time, but the article by Sergei Mikhailovich is moving even now. Rather than give extracts of this article, I want to resurrect in memory, what exactly happened with this film.

The basic plot[250] of the film was class struggle in the countryside in the period of Socialist Reconstruction. The struggle of the new people with the kulaks and podkulachniks.[251] The subject was taken from reality. The struggle of a little Pioneer Pavlik Morozov with his own father and the podkulachniks. The father killed his son. In the film, the little hero dies in the arms of the head of the Political Agitation Section.

In embarking upon shooting the film, Sergei Mikhailovich once again repeated his fundamental error. In shooting his first version, he rejected accomplished actors taking part in the film. In the process of shooting, he began to realize that this was a disaster and arrived at the decision to do a re-shoot. He invited Khmelev, Telesheva from the MKhAT, and others. But other difficulties arose for Sergei Mikhailovich in working with the actors. His longstanding refusal to recognize the craft of acting, the desire to avoid "theatricality of the worst sort" in filmmaking took its revenge on him. Rzheshevsky's "emotional scenario" was said to be deficient. So the second version was never finished either. After a viewing of material from the first version and selected parts of the second version, shooting was halted. But Sergei Mikhailovich never attributed misfortunes and errors in his works to others; and above all, never

---

[249] [Russian editor's note]: *Before me lies a small brochure...* The brochure referred to is *About the film* Bezhin Meadow *by S. M. Eisenstein. Against Formalism in Film Art* (Moscow, Leningrad. Iskusstvo, 1937). In the brochure were collected critical articles of a journalistic stamp: "About the film *Bezhin Meadow*," by B. Shumyatsky, "The Theoretical Errors of S. M. Eisenstein" by I. Vaisfel'd, "The World and Life" by E. Veisman, "The Errors of *Bezhin Meadow*" by S. Eisenstein. E. Shub justly observes, that what was said in the brochure did not stand the test of time. The reconstruction in 1967 of the lost reels of *Bezhin Meadow* allowed modern film historians to evaluate the merits of the true artistic qualities of this production (see *Sergei Eisenstein, Selected Works*, vol. 1, introductory article by R. Yurenev).

[250] [Trans.]: In the original: сюжет (syuzhet)

[251] [Trans.]: In the original: подкулачники [podkulachniki]: a Stalinist neologism meaning the peasant underlings of the kulaks.

attributed these errors to the author of the scenario. He spoke about errors in the scenario as his own; he took responsibility for everything, considering that a director could not conduct himself otherwise.

This is what he wrote after the discontinuation of work on the film:

What is the basis of the disaster, which befell the picture, on which I worked for almost two years? The error is rooted in a single profoundly individualist illusion typical of the intelligentsia. In an illusion, which, starting from something small can lead to great and tragic errors and consequences. In the illusion, which alleges that it is possible to perform truly revolutionary acts "at one's personal risk," not in the body of the collective, not united in lock step with it.

…The pull of this [illusion] was the origin of what happened to me in my understanding of the doctrines of realism.

Through my own stylistic aspirations and my character, I have an immense pull towards society in general, towards the generalized, towards generalization. But is that generality, the general, the understanding of which, the Marxist study of realism teaches us? No. Because, the generalization in my work absorbs the particular… It was not so in *Potemkin*. Its strength would seem to be precisely, that through this particular, singular event, there was success in reaching a social conception of 1905, about the "dress rehearsal" for October. This particular episode managed to absorb into itself what was typical for that phase of the history of revolutionary struggle…

It didn't happen that way with *Bezhin Meadow*. The very incident, which forms its basis—its dramatic incident—is in no way a characteristic one. The murder by the kulak father of his son, the pioneer, is a possible incident, which one encounters, but not a typical incident. On the contrary, it is an exceptional, singular, and uncharacteristic incident. All the same, located at the center of the scenario, it takes on an independent, self-contained, generalizing meaning.

…The errors of generalization—in the break from the reality of a particular event—within the subject itself—stand out no less sharply in the method of its realization…

The shape of the kulak pushed its way into the foreground in sharp disproportion. The head of the Political Agitation Section[252] was pale, dull, and rhetorical.

…And at the same time, the Young Pioneer from the village reached exaggeration beyond all real limits of his social significance…

---

[252] [Trans.]: In the original: Начполит [Nachpolit].

This led to an exaggeration of expressiveness in the surroundings: a lair instead of a peasant hut; disfiguring foreshortening of the shots, deformations of lighting. Sets, framing, lighting play a role beyond that of the actor, instead of the actor. The same can be said in relation to the effect of the shaping of faces. A shape is no longer a living face, but a mask, as a limit of generalization of "typicalness" detached from a living face...

...I am writing about this with utter severity, because over the course of two years, I myself, inwardly, and with the aid of the unflagging criticism by cinema management came to overcome these traits. But I did not manage to completely overcome them. Having watched every piece of film which was shot, from the first scenes to the last ones, they noticed that a shift towards a realistic style was undeniable and the complex of "night" scenes already testified to the fact, that the author was moving away from the unsound positions, he had taken at the time of the work on the first version.

...But who is primarily at fault? And can it be said, that a political error is a catastrophe and the consequence of an error of creative method? Of course, not. A mistake of creative method is nestled within an error on the order of a world view.

Mistakes on the order of a world view lead to mistakes of method. Mistakes of method lead to objective political error and failure.

...Additional shooting and re-shooting could not save it. It became clear to me that the error was not only on the order of details, but in the conception of the thing as a whole. It grew from the scenario, but the interpretation of the director did not rise up against these elements and persisted in repeating the initial errors in spite of the opportunities provided by a second version.

What must I do?

Seriously work on my own world view, in greater depth, as a Marxist, to penetrate new subjects. Concretely studying reality and the New Man. Orienting myself towards a concretely chosen, solid scenario and subject.

There can be only one theme for a new work: heroic in spirit, Party-oriented, concerned with war defense in content, and popular in style: regardless of whether it is material from 1917 or 1937, it will serve the victory of the march of socialism.

He dreamed of creating a production of *We, the Russian People* by Vsevolod Vishnevsky. The author wanted this as well. This coincided with a time when their personal relations were anchored in mutual friendship.

In one of the rehearsal rooms of Mosfil'm, Vsevolod Vishnevsky was reading his scenario-novel *We, the Russian People* for directors, actors, set designers, camera operators, for the Artistic Soviet.[253] This reading is impossible to forget. Vsevolod Vishnevsky was unsurpassed as a reader. As he was reading the scenario with his subdued voice, he would play all the parts. The language of Russian soldiers was conspicuously present. The authorial asides were full of poetry, his summons, "We will fix our gaze upon their faces and we will memorize them for a lifetime," was an appeal by a Russian man with a great heart: a soldier and a poet. His reading and the images he acted out were not to be forgotten. Who could possibly forget Orl, Aleshka, Boier, and Ermolai. The authorial asides were moving and poetic and I saw tears not only on the faces of those listening, but on the face of the author of the scenario of the film-novel.

Sergei Mikhailovich was also moved and joyful. A film about the great Russian People, about its Civil War, about its imperishable history. Lenin, who was not shown in the film, was tangible, as if alive. He was alongside the Russian soldier. He was with the People at the most decisive moments on the front.

To work shoulder to shoulder with Vsevolod Vishnevsky, to feel his friendly assistance was what Sergei Mikhailovich passionately desired.

Here is an excerpt from his unpublished article[254] about this scenario:

> *We, the Russian People* is not only a joy of a powerful production, it is as well a victory of the principle of theoretical thought, the birth of an independent, original, class-national style and of its method in response to the specific thematic demands of epoch and class. The appearance of the object as a whole grows from unique premises towards a popular and mass cinema of its own, which was born in October and for which we fought, are fighting, and will fight from our screens.
>
> No production of the sort has yet been devised. To me, it seems to grow in concentric circles. Within it, are one, two, three, four patterns of such completeness in detail and relief, of such unexpected turns and so comprehensively elucidated, as have been hitherto unknown in our art of the scenario: these are the heroes "of the front ranks."
>
> A step away from them is the second rank. Equally distinctive, living people. But more sparing in traits. A smaller weight of details and coloration.

---

[253] [Trans.]: In the original: Художественный Совет [Khudozhestvenny Sovet]. It functioned as a review board for artistic proposals for various kinds. Its members would include leading figures in the arts, as well as government and Party officials, who would evaluate proposals on both their artistic merit and their conformity to ideological norms.

[254] In the original, an unnumbered footnote with the following citation: Статья вошла в сб. *С. Эйзенштейн. Избранные статьи*, М-. «Искусство», 1956, стр. 111–113. [The article appeared in the collection *S. Eisenstein, Selected Articles*. Moscow, Iskusstvo, 1956, pp. 111–113.]

The third circle. The drawing is still more lightly sketched in.

The further you go, the more this increases. And now there are people presented through two traits. Then through only one. And you don't notice how, from these protagonists, you moved into the midst of those who compose a unified body of the whole, of that whole, to which, in equal measure all these characters belong. So prominent, decisive and singular a trait, that it snatches out of the monotonousness of a wide shot, this character or another, this or that profile.

…It is impossible not to pause at the striking revelation of the distinction between the patriotism of the People and the "patriotism" of autocracy: It is given in the image of the enemy colonel. His patriotism, in its consistency, reaches the point of the betrayal of the land of his birth.

The images of people, of situations, of events cannot help but touch the heart of the spectator with their tragic elements. They cannot help but captivate his feelings and emotions through the beauty of their heroic exploits. They cannot help but conquer the reader with the breath of the true *socialist* patriotism of the country, which is the Motherland of all working people of the world. The country, for which all working people are ready to fight and to die, as they would for their own Motherland: from the blood spilled on the fields of Spain to the plains of China.

Sergei Mikhailovich did not receive permission to direct this. It didn't work out.

Then, at once, the desire arose to work with the writer A. A. Fadeev. Here is a letter from Fadeev.[255]

Dear Sergei Mikhailovich!

I'm very sorry I did not manage before your departure to get to know you a bit better and speak with you about your work in the cinema, which I esteem extraordinarily highly.

I got the impression—perhaps an incorrect one—that your creative well-being is influenced by the rumors and gossip of film people and people near the film world, when they say Eisenstein "has fallen silent, he's not doing any new pictures," and so on.

It seems to me that you should be completely unconcerned about this sort of conversation, for, as is well known to me, all these years you have never discontinued your work, which in the case of a great master, such as you, is tied to continuous research of the new. And in such cases (and you don't need me to tell you this), what is necessary, does not

---

[255] [Russian editor's note]: An undated letter from A. Fadeev to S. Eisenstein. A copy of the letter is preserved in the personal archive of E. Shub.

always immediately appear in one's work. What is important here is only, in my opinion, not to surrender to bare form, which, if you experiment with it, will begin to dominate in and of itself and transform itself into an obstacle.

I am very interested now in the new work you have conceived about Moscow. I cannot tell you, with what joy I would participate in this work, for I have no doubt, that I would gain a great deal from it. Precisely because, the road I travel in the field of literature, so little resembles the road you travel in the cinema. I would like to have closer contact with you. I've been told, that you would not be disinclined to work a bit with a writer.

I would advise you to get in contact with Pavlenko. He is a writer, who is unquestionably talented and in work is an organized person, but the main thing is: he's smart. In such collaborative work, it's important, for the writer, who is working with one director or another, to be able to thoughtfully "cross over" to the director's creative position in order to help him realize his plan according to his individual identity. In this connection, I would be able to be a good assistant for you, but, unfortunately, my own literary work and my work in collaboration with Dovzhenko, which interests me greatly, deprives me of this possibility. However, if you would bring me in, at any stage of your work on the scenario and generally acquaint me with your work, I would be deeply grateful to you.

I would like to say to you once again, how extraordinarily much you have given to Soviet and World cinema and, unquestionably, will give even more. So, you should take a brighter view of things.

With warmth and respect,

Fadeev

Aleksandr Fadeev's letter played a big role in those days. It set Eisenstein at ease. It helped him to collect himself mentally. From that point, Eisenstein and Fadeev's friendship began, and, invariably, in difficult moments of his creative work, he would seek out meetings with Fadeev. They spoke to each other familiarly. This was extremely rare.

The creative association of Eisenstein and Pavlenko brought to the Soviet spectator the magnificent film *Alexander Nevsky*. A few meetings with Pavlenko, the first read-through of the scenario, the review of the sketches by the costume designer K. Eliseev happened at my place. All this was new to me and unexpected. Pavlenko won people over with his commitment, in addition, he was an amazing master of storytelling.

Pavlenko's scenario took a literary approach and was very expressive in its imagery. He made it possible for Eisenstein to construct his film in his favored monumental and, at once, epic style. This film resurrected the distant past of our people.

Pavlenko and Eisenstein attentively studied the chronicles of that time and the latest work and research on that period.

At the insistence of E. S. Telesheva—a director at the Moscow Art Theater and the Red Army Theater—Sergei Mikhailovich, invited to play the role of Alexander Nevsky the actor Cherkasov, who was already well-known to the Soviet spectator through his role as Professor Polezhaev in the film *Baltic Deputy* and as the tsarevich Alexei in the film *Peter the First*.

There was talk that Eisenstein suppressed the personality of the actor, subjecting their acting to his own conception, which allowed for no critique. In this connection, there are some very interesting statements by the actor Cherkasov in his book *Notes of a Soviet Actor*[256] about his work with Eisenstein. Here is what Cherkasov wrote about this:

I won't deny that this time, I was vacillating. The grand epic style of the picture, the legendary quality of the image of its hero, the great remoteness of the historical events, which we had to resurrect: all this seemed to me a difficult obstacle to surmount...

The first tests were disappointing. The external appearance of Alexander Nevsky, his makeup, for a long time didn't work for me. It was finally worked out and defined and one must say, it was through the immediate assistance of S. M. Eisenstein. He was amazing in his attention to secondary details, which would seem to be small things, but would later take on great significance when close ups were being shot. In the Hermitage, he managed to locate authentic armaments from the XIIIth century and carefully used them for the fabrication of my armor; during the critical shoots, he would always visit me in wardrobe. I remember, once, that surrounded by tailors and costume people, he spent more than an hour with me adjusting some detail or other of my costume, to the point my legs were starting to give way, while, merrily, making jokes, he persisted to achieve the greatest expressivity in my attire.

...He would confidently persuade me to subordinate myself to the general epic style of the production, not to give detail to the characterization, to the specific traits of the psychology of the protagonist, to the particulars of character, but, on the contrary, to strive for a wide

---

256 [Russian editor's footnote at the bottom of the page indicated with an asterisk]: Н. К. Черкасов, *Записки советского актера,* М., «Искусство», 1953, стр. 125–126. [N. K. Cherkasov, *Notes of a Soviet Actor*, Moscow, Iskusstvo, 1953, pp. 125–126.]

generality. In the actor's art, as in any art, what should predominate is the feeling of the whole, the feeling of what is collective, the feeling of what is primary. S. M. Eisenstein insistently led me in that direction, of becoming accustomed to accomplishing collective, broadly understood directorial goals, to search out and to find my creative line within the strict limits of the established stylistic goals, and, in the case at hand, above all, within an epic perspective.

The distant past. Shots of winter during the heat of summer, as in, for example the "battle on the ice." The battles: instead of snow, the field of battle was sprinkled with naphthalene and salt. The participation of such magnificent actors as N. Cherkasov, N. Okhlopkov, and others, the fact that S. M. Eisenstein was rejuvenated, happy, excited by the work—all this made me very happy. I attended almost all the most critical shoots. The crowd scenes. Pskov, the dog-knights, the battles: everything was envisioned through the eyes of a great artist, decisively with enormous mastery.

An outstanding role was played by the music of S. Prokofiev. I was often present when the pieces of film edited by the director were handed over to the composer Prokofiev. Eisenstein and Prokofiev understood one another with hardly a word. They made concessions to one another. If it were indispensable for the expressiveness of the music, Sergei Mikhailovich would shorten or lengthen pieces of film, but also Prokofiev more than once, in order not to spoil the impression of the edited pieces of film, subordinated his music to the footage of the episode. The sound recording proceeded like a celebration. Prokofiev's music enraptured Eisenstein. It merged with the imagery, often deepening an episode. They rehearsed for a long time, exactingly. As is well known, the film *Alexander Nevsky* enjoyed a great success not only here, but all over the world.

Shortly before the war, S. M. Eisenstein was named artistic director of the Mosfil'm studio.

Stretched to the limits, he would, all the same, throw himself into his work with great interest and devote many hours to it. He would attend important shoots, go over the material which had been shot with the director. He was interested in everything: the scenario, actors, the set designer, the music, makeup.

On the day of his appointments, he would call me in. And would keep me there for quite a while. With me at his side, he would receive the directors. He wanted to verify whether the new things he wanted to introduce were good, or not.

The study, in which he would receive people, was arranged with his innate skill and disposed people to easy conversation. There was nothing governmental or institutional about it. There was neither a writing desk, nor a conference table.

There were books, maquettes, artists' sketches. The best shots from pictures made at the studio hung in frames on the wall.

First of all, he would listen to a director with great attention, without hurrying, and, above all, without interrupting. While speaking, he would move from one corner of the room to another, pointing something out. He and the director would both feel relaxed. It couldn't be otherwise. Eisenstein never imposed on others creative decisions, which were particular to them alone. Through his instinct as a great artist, he understood what the value and uniqueness was of each director, though that director might be foreign to him in style. The directors left satisfied, with a clear understanding about what needed to be done to move the work forward.

One thing that distressed me was, that hanging on the wall, under glass was a photograph of a working moment of *Bezhin Meadow*; Eisenstein was carefully explaining something to the schoolboy, who was playing the role of Pavlik and the boy was delighted. This was already after the great success of *Alexander Nevsky*, but *Bezhin Meadow*, all the same, was not forgotten.

When Eisenstein left the room with some director, right there I took this photograph and without waiting for him, I disappeared.

Here's his inscription on the photograph: "This photograph was swiped from me from my study in Potylikha. I am very touched by that and very happy."

He understood quite well why I did this.

Ivan the Terrible. Once again, the hero of the film is a military commander. A man of enormous will, fearless and merciless in the struggle for the higher interests of the State. A military commander smashing Boyar opposition, conquering Kazan, setting for himself the task of winning an outlet for Russia to the sea. "Henceforth and for the ages, the seas will submit to Russian sovereignty. On the seas, we are and will remain."

A part of the history of Russia, closer in time and better known than in *Alexander Nevsky*. There is a great deal of historical, pictorial material on the era of Ivan the Terrible, which there was not for the film *Alexander Nevsky*. For this reason, during the shooting of *Alexander Nevsky*, the director had to invent a great deal; from this derives the stylistic conventions of certain scenes.

In the center of this new piece was the tragic figure of the tsar Ivan IV. S. M. Eisenstein studied the era from all sides. He sent me the scenario with a note: "Esfir', dear, it is indispensable, that you read the scenario completely today. It is indispensable, that you do it attentively. And it is indispensable, that you bring it to me tomorrow at the factory. I anxiously await your opinion."[257]

Essentially, this was already a shooting script. I reacted badly to it. The stylized Slavonic-Russian conversational speech—and even more the blank verse—bothered me. But I believed in the director, I believed, that shooting would resolve everything;

---

[257] [Russian editor's note]. *I anxiously await your opinion.* A note from S. Eisenstein, sent to E. Shub along with the scenario of *Ivan the Terrible*. It is dated March 24, 1939. It is preserved in the personal archive of E. Shub.

the intent would find pictorial realization. It seemed clear to me, that the director would construct his film as a tragedy, that the episodes would be resolved in his favored monumental-epic style. The role of the tsar is to be played by Cherkasov. He was excited by the role. The artists selected were remarkable. Besides Cherkasov: Buchma, Zharov, Ranevskaya, Mgebrov. The role of Efrosin'ya Staritskaya in the film was played not by Ranevskaya, who was selected at first, but by the actress Birman. The film was approved for production during the first days of the Great Patriotic War. The director was granted every resource; it was a challenge in many ways.

Shooting took place in the Alma-Ata studio during the days of the difficult battles of the Great Patriotic War, in 1942. All of us from the Mosfil'm Studio were evacuated to Alma-Ata. The former Municipal Club was turned into a studio. The auditorium for theatrical performances became a relatively small shooting studio. That's where S. M. Eisenstein demonstrated his capabilities as an artist and an organizer.

He took the primary role in the design of sets, costumes, and makeup. Several camera operators worked with him; as always, E. Tissé and, for the first time, one of our best camera operators, A. Moskvin, who did the studio shoots. Eisenstein considered him better than anyone; he would often approach him, confer with him, joke with him.

I observed Eisenstein as he gave direct instructions, when they were doing Cherkasov's and Zharov's makeup. Ulanova's makeup was especially beautifully conceived and realized by him. Eisenstein dreamed of shooting her in the role of the tsaritsa Anastasia. The tests were striking for the youthful beauty of her appearance, the purity and singularity of expression of the eyes of the actress. Shooting Ulanova [in the part] was not to be realized. The role of the tsaritsa in the film was filled by L. Tselikovskaya.

All the shots of the film were sketched out in advance by Eisenstein and were selected for precision of composition. The graphic artist Shpinel' worked with him. He achieved complete historical accuracy in the costumes and in the environment surrounding the characters. He made sure, that the costume on the actor was "lived-in."[258] The beauty of the costume of the young Ivan in the episode of his coronation as tsar, the makeup of the young Ivan were all hit upon by an artist of the first rank.

During the shooting of *Ivan the Terrible*, as during all of Eisenstein's shoots, a celebratory atmosphere held sway. No hustle and bustle, silence almost. On a few shoots, for example, the episode of the coronation, there was almost solemnity. Eisenstein was seeking out the characteristic rhythm of shooting particular to him, the characteristic creative state in the actors. He was extremely attentive, strict, and exacting. He listened attentively to what the actors said. This elevated their mood. These conditions created a joyous state for everyone who worked as part of the collective. A gloomy severe face, a displeased glance, and a slightly raised voice were a rarity and

---

[258] [Trans.]: In the original: «обжитой».

were perceived by the entire collective and the actors as a sign of the most serious failure; screaming or shouting were out of the question. And help would arrive immediately. Everyone would strive only to adjust things so that once again, that rhythm of work characteristic only of Eisenstein would return. During the shoots, no one ever saw Sergei Mikhailovich tired. He always found time to joke, to say something witty, of which he was a great master. Sometimes he knew how to evoke not only a smile, but also laughter. A pause. And then once again tranquility, exigency, the sharp, all-seeing eye. No one would ever guess, how much mental and physical strength shooting cost him.

In Alma-Ata I was assigned a room in the apartment where Eisenstein and Sergei Vasil'ev lived. Somehow it would happen, that some really great people would gather in my room. They would drop by to cheer each other up, to chat about Moscow. Those who would drop by included Vsevolod Pudovkin, Nikolai Cherkasov, Marina Ladynina, the clever and the charming Sof'ya Magarill, Mikhail Astangov, the composer Gavriil Popov. Mariya Smirnova, Mikhail Zoshchenko, Aleksandr Rumnev and others. M. Zoshchenko sometimes in a quiet voice would recount little melancholy romantic stories. It seemed as if he were making them up as he told them. Tired after shooting, even Sergei Mikhailovich would drop by. Sometimes, this was long past midnight. Shooting took place at night, since during the day electric power was needed for industrial facilities. Tired, he would often drop by with a joke. One day, when he dropped by, he asked, "Have you been talking about me?"

—No.

"No? Well, then I'm going to sleep." That evening, he was tired to the point of exhaustion, but he knew, that we were living in apprehension for the Motherland, for near ones who were far away. And not stop by, he could not.

I found it extremely difficult to accept my existence in Alma-Ata. I struggled with the isolation from events, I felt like I had been driven into the mountains and there was no way out… There was anguish about Moscow. I didn't want the war to pass me by. I managed, with Eisenstein's help, to have them call me to Moscow. I dreamed about making a film with Vs. Vishnevsky about our great people, through incredible hardships, liberating humanity from Fascism. I received a letter from Vishnevsky. He could not help me. He was in Leningrad, which was blocked off.[259]

In Alma-Ata, Pudovkin was working (making a film based on some stories by Brecht[260]); Ermler was working (a film about partisans with Maretskaya[261]), the Vasil'ev

---

[259] [Trans.]: Masha Godovannaya informs me, that Shub uses a rather unusual word блокированный [blokirovanny] instead of блокадный [blokadny] in order to avoid a direct reference to the Siege of Leningrad in language prohibited at the time of her writing.

[260] [Russian editor's note]: …*was making a film based on some stories by Brecht… Killers Are On the Way* was never released. [Trans.]: Leyda translates this as *Murderers Are On Their Way*. The film seems to have been released after the publication of Shub's text.

[261] [Russian editor's note]: …*a film about partisans with Maretskaya…* F. Ermler's film, *She Defends the Motherland* aka *No Greater Love* in which V. Maretskaya plays the main role. The film came out in 1942.

brothers were working (*Front*). I was only giving some classes to students from the VGIK.

I missed the Moscow sky with its clouds; here, the sky was bright blue, burning hot already from morning on. I missed the little Russian birches; here, there were allées with tall birches and poplars, beneath them the irrigation canals would babble, but brought no coolness. I missed the smell of grass with morning dew, the smell of newly mown hay, of lilacs, and my particular favorite, the smell of jasmine. Here, there were huge bright flowers, but some of these flowers in the mountains were dangerous. If you touched them, they would burn you.

The Architecture of the new Alma-Ata is very beautiful. In the evening, the sky seems low, hanging over you, the stars are huge. And this is beautiful.

I want to go to Moscow. I want to work. When I. G. Bol'shakov [262] comes to Alma-Ata, S. M. Eisenstein speaks with him about me and they call me to Moscow for the production of a film.

I am very strongly reminded of one day in Alma-Ata. Before the coming night shoot, Cherkasov unexpectedly dropped by during the afternoon. At the time, Marina Ladynina was there with me. Cherkasov played his part in *Don Quixote* for us, which he had played just shortly before the war in Leningrad. In my little room, as he got more and more carried away, the soliloquies of the "knight without fear and without reproach"[263] resounded with inspiration. In the creation of the image, he correctly proceeded from the classical characterization by Belinsky: "Don Quixote is above all the most magnificent, noble human being, a true knight without fear and without reproach. In spite of the fact that he's funny from head to foot, inside and outside—not only is he not stupid—on the contrary—he is quite clever; but that's a small thing; he is a true wise man."[264]

Ladynina and I were quietly weeping in ecstasy. I have always preserved a feeling of gratitude towards that remarkable actor for that afternoon…

Ivan the Terrible—part one—played with great success.

Because I was ill, I didn't happen to see the second part of *Ivan the Terrible*. Eisenstein was planning to show me the film one-on-one not long before his death. But this never came to be. Comrades told me about the great successes of particular

---

[262] [Russian editor's note]: *Bol'shakov, Ivan Grigor'evich* (b. 1902). Chairman of the Committee for Cinema Affairs of the People's Central Committee of the USSR (1939–1946). Minister of Cinema of the USSR (1946–1954).

[263] [Trans.]: This phrase was used by Engels in section VII of his article "The Frankfurt Assembly Debates the Polish Question," which appeared in the *Neue Rheinische Zeitung* № 91, September 1, 1848. It refers to Pierre Terrail, seigneur de Bayard, a 16th-century French knight, considered the model of chivalry.

[264] [Russian editor's footnote at the bottom of the page]: *В. Г. Белинский, Собр. соч. в 3-х томах*, т. 2. М., Государственное издательство художественной литературы, 1956, стр. 816 [*V. G. Belinsky. Collected works, in 3 volumes*, v. 2. Moscow. State Publishing House for Literary Works, 1956, p. 816.]

scenes. Some scenes bore the stamp of sovereign mastery. They especially remarked upon the episode Eisenstein realized in color. This was the first use of color. With his characteristic instinct, Sergei Mikhailovich accurately foresaw the future of film art—that the time of color cinematography had come.

Such was the complicated path of the outstanding master of filmmaking. Successes and failures; ascents and descents.

Why was Eisenstein and why does he remain the outstanding Soviet artist? I think, it was because, he always strove for the new. He lived always in search of the new, he searched, he made mistakes, and searched once again. Because in these searches, he was invariably moved by love for the Motherland, by the desire of expressing our great era through an image worthy of it, the desire to exalt Soviet art for the glory of the Motherland, for love of the Communist Party.

Eisenstein as pedagogue
In order to imagine Eisenstein's creative life to oneself in the greatest depth, one needs to know his work of many years as a professor at the VGIK. This activity for him was more than a simple matter of instruction.

As a great artist-innovator, he attached great importance to the education of the younger generation of film directors. The tasks he set for himself on this path merit the most attentive study.

The stenograms of his lectures remain after him. There is a huge quantity of them, but at that time, they were taken down in a surprisingly unskilled way, carelessly, and crudely deciphered. He had intended to sit down and edit them; he intended to, but not enough time remained. He didn't manage. Various attempts made by comrades to decipher his lectures were not very satisfactory. Lost was the tone of the master, the liveliness of his expositions, the wit, the brilliance, and the humor. The lectures should be brought into order. An editorial board needs to be created out of such people as S. Vasil'ev, G. Kozintsev, S. Yutkevich, V. Nizhny, P. Atasheva,[265] G. Roshal', I. Vaisfel'd. These people understand well Eisenstein's style of expression, his tone. Others should be brought in, whose help they need. But to do this is essential. Only these people can analyze the huge quantity of stenograms and select the ones from among them, which at that time have not lost their meaning. This is essential both for the younger generation of students and for people who seriously intend to pursue the theory of the art of the cinema.

In the pre-war period (1933–1935), I happened to be working in Eisenstein's workshop. To give a course in practical montage with his students. Later, I was an advisor to graduating seniors on their shooting scripts, for example, the director Filippov on his screen adaptation of *Taras Bul'ba*, and I was a member of the State Examination Commission. I often attended the lectures of Sergei Mikhailovich and

---

[265] [Russian editor's note]: *Atasheva, Pera Moiseevna* (1900–1965). Director, wife of S. M. Eisenstein.

will write about what is preserved in my memory and what a few stenograms from those years, which I managed to have a look at, remind me of.

Eisenstein prepared no less for his lectures than he did for shooting. Each lecture had the character of a conversation. In the course of the lecture, students would ask questions. Eisenstein would listen attentively to the questions and to the exchanges of points of view among the students. Sometimes, he would intermingle two distinct responses to the same question. However, this was by no means a discussion. Having listened attentively, he would answer. His answer was to be taken by the students as the categorical and decisive point of view.

He prohibited students from catching him in the halls and in the breaks between classes, to ask him questions one-on-one. He demanded, that all questions, all doubts which arose, be resolved directly, there in the auditorium. He considered it his mission to widen the range of knowledge of the students, to make them into cultural and educational innovators, and not only professionals in filmmaking. He wanted to engender in them a love of literature and, first and foremost, of Russian classics. Pushkin, Tolstoy, Dostoyevsky, Gogol, Nekrasov, Gorky, Mayakovsky—in his lectures he would always refer to the works of these writers. Models from Soviet literature would also be examined. He acquainted his students with painting and, first and foremost, with the artists beloved by him: Surikov, Fedotov, Serov, and with several canvasses by Repin ("Religious Procession," "Zaparozhian Cossacks," sketches for the picture "State Council"), and with [works by] Vereshchagin. From European painting, above all, he would present the universal genius Leonardo da Vinci, Michelangelo, El Greco, Rembrandt, Daumier.

He valued those students who knew how to draw the compositions of the shots they had imagined.

He himself often accompanied his lectures by drawings quickly produced on the blackboard. They were expressive, evocative, and they visually corroborated this or that proposition of his.

He acquainted his students with the history of the theater. He spoke to them about the reciprocal influence of film and theater and, along with that, about the laws inherent only to the art of cinema and about the inadmissibility of the adaptation for the theater of the cinema.

In the cinema, as distinct from the theater, the design of a role is resolved spatially by different laws.

He spoke to his students about the significance of music in the cinema and, finally, about the philosophy of Marxism. Nor did he bypass Hegel, he spoke about the idealist understanding of art. Everything found its place in his lectures.

While he highly valued the emotional quality of a work, he demanded, that this emotional quality be meaningful, just as montage must be meaningful.

He knew, that without imagination it was impossible to work in art and he carefully observed which of his students possessed this happy peculiarity. He highly valued the ability to translate word into image. "Always try to name things visually," he would say to students.

He was critical in the extreme of a spiritless, mediocre solution to a given assignment. Eisenstein would accept nothing "tepid" in art. He was exacting of his students, so that they would not approach an assignment mechanically, for that would inevitably lead to a mediocre, that is to say, a non-creative solution. He said, that he expected of them solutions, which reached a synthesis, as the result of concrete and not contrived propositions.

In speaking about the work of the director, or the activity of the actor, he was exacting, so that on their work lay an imprint, giving the possibility for synthesis. So, the image is not to be found via the everyday, the naturalistic. Only the unity of the particular and the general yields the typical.

He acquainted his students with ancient art and would begin his lectures with citations from Marx about the Greeks, about the ancient world.

He constantly referred to the ancient world, establishing the differences between Ancient Greek and Roman art. He maintained, that the Romans solved creative problems arithmetically, that is, they repeated decisions they had arrived at countless times. For the Ancient Greeks, on the contrary, every single decision was unique and unrepeatable.

He often used as an example for his students, the creative work of Dovzhenko, Pudovkin, and Vertov. The works of Pudovkin and Vertov, he would compare with the Roman school. They edit mathematically, in a metric mode, with preconceived formulas. Himself and Dovzhenko he placed side by side with those artists, who subordinate shooting and montage to their internal sensations. He pointed out, that, in spite of their differences as artists, Dovzhenko was closest to him. He would say, half in jest, that they were continuing the Greek tradition, that they worked without preconceived formulas. That everything in their work was subordinated to vivid sensations, to vivid internal perceptions. In editing, they subordinated the splicing together of pieces of film and the length of pieces of film, to visual, emotional, and internal sensation.

Dovzhenko captivated Eisenstein with his connection to Ukrainian folklore (folk art) and his love of Ukrainian mythology. Eisenstein considered, that from that, came Dovzhenko's love of long, static, close-ups, almost unmoving and symbolic; and from that also came Dovzhenko's fairytale way of showing nature, and the feeling, which was his alone, for pictorial humor, with very much a national character.

He was demanding of his students, so that in finding solutions to directorial assignments, before everything else, they would imagine what idea they intended to put into this or that plot,[266] and, so that, in editing they would not come up with objectives, which were not founded in the filmed material itself, so that, they did not bring in concepts to the filmed material which were not inherent in its content. He demanded audacity in bringing together material of similar emotional expressiveness, even if the shots in question were distinct in their *faktura*.[267]

Sergei Mikhailovich's lectures on montage were brilliant. He attached enormous importance to montage as the culminating phase of all directorial work in film. He considered that a director, who did not edit his own film, had not fully realized his work as a director. Eisenstein said, that montage had to be done joyfully, that one's mental state changed the relationship one had with one montage piece[268] or the other, that it changed one's selection of takes. He never stopped reminding his students, that shots, which had already been realized in shooting, look completely different than one had imagined they would when you look at them on the editing table, when you take them in your hands. Sometimes they are more insipid, sometimes more interesting than one had imagined beforehand. It was unavoidable, therefore, that a new montage composition for the utilization of a shot would arise. He understood better than many others, that one had to approach the practice of art with a pure soul, without deceiving oneself. One must scrutinize the material, listen to it attentively.

He said, that montage was the explosion of the shot: the tension in a single shot reaches its limit and finds its full expression in being spliced together with another montage piece.[269]

The most difficult thing in montage, he considered to be the interruption of rhythm, or, as he would always call it *"deceleration."*[270] As an example, he would bring in the work of the red-headed clown in the circus. The red-head in the circus, after an act executed with magnificent technique by one sort of circus performer or another, would repeat this act, and, according to the rule, for him things would not work out. He would fall, when flying through the air, he would not reach the trapeze, he would not fall into the rhythm, as if he didn't know how to do anything… but in fact he was the most experienced and knowledgeable acrobat. His superb playing of ignorance was the result of perfect knowledge of the act.

---

[266] [Trans.]: In the original: сюжет [syuzhet].

[267] [Trans.]: In the original: фактура, here referring to the visual aspect of their materiality. The term is loosely related to the art historical use of "facture."

[268] [Trans.]: In the original: монтажный кусок [montazhny kusok]. One could say, "one piece of film used in editing" or even "shot," but Shub constantly prefers the more concrete "kusok," that is, "piece."

[269] [Trans.]: In the original: кусок [kusok]. One might say "segment" in this more abstract usage, but I have used "piece" to be consistent.

[270] [Trans.]: In the original: *торможение* [tormozhenie], which can also mean "braking."

Eisenstein attached enormous importance to the first shot edited into a film and to each separate element of the plot.[271] He called these shots "overtures," defining the content of the theme. I could write many pages about what S. M. Eisenstein said about montage during the time of the review of the student montage projects, which were done under my supervision.

For me it was easy and a joy to work with him, because our points of view coincided on a great number of things and because he worked with me with great trust. This collaborative work was enriching for me.

I would like to conclude this chapter with a story about a lecture, in which he analyzed the portrait of Yermolova painted by Serov.[272]

This lecture was connected not only with questions of montage, but of composition. As is well-known, Eisenstein found the compositional and montage principles closest to cinema in the poetry of Pushkin, Mayakovsky, and in the painting of Leonardo da Vinci. Moreover, Sergei Mikhailovich maintained, that these laws are general for all kinds of art. Eisenstein said, that the composition of the portrait of Yermolova was magnificently resolved by the artist. In looking through all the sketches for this portrait, and by studying them well, he became convinced, that this compositionally accomplished painting, which on first glance appears simple, is, in fact, constructed in an extremely complex fashion.

To make a portrait of Yermolova, a great tragic actress, was the task that stood before the artist. For this, every means of expression was put to the task. V. Serov attained perfection in composition by skillful "croppings"[273] of the canvas, namely in "croppings" of the portrait all means of expressiveness were employed, in defining the composition as a whole. The "croppings" in the portrait of Yermolova were, in essence, a regular sequential montage of shots: wide shot, medium shot, close-up.

The wide shot is Yermolova taken at full height, the "cropping" of this shot at the bottom almost pours out of the frame of the portrait.

Starting from the boundary of the floor is the medium shot.

Yermolova, reflected in the mirror, is the close up. It causes the head of the actress to stand out with particular force.

It stands to reason, that Serov was far from thinking about a cinematographic wide, medium, or close-up shot. But he did think about "croppings," and these could be seen, just as correctly, to be constructed as cinematographic shots. And they did define the composition.

---

[271] [Trans.]: In the original: Эйзенштейн придавал огромное значение первому монтажному кадру фильма и каждого сюжета в отдельности.

[272] [Trans.]: This was published in English as "Y. Yermolova" in the second volume of Eisenstein's selected writings *Towards a Theory of Montage: Sergei Eisenstein Selected Works*, Volume 2, ed. Richard Taylor (I.B Tauris, 2010).

[273] [Trans.]: In the original: умелыми «обрезами».

Portrait of Maria Yermolova by Valentin Serov (1905).
State Tret'yakov Gallery Moscow.

Serov knew how on this canvas to give the appearance of various points of view, the various distinct points of view of the lens of a movie camera. In the cinema, we realize the objective in similar fashion, when shooting an object from above, at eye level, and from below. In Serov's work, this is done within a single plane.

The floor does not recede in depth, but seems to move upwards. If you exclude the floor and move upwards, the figure of Yermolova in the black dress in the mirror stands out spatially from the blue-black wall, and a sensation of depth arises. Yermolova stands with her back to the mirror and, because of this, behind her figure an even greater depth is obtained; one senses a large space reflected in the mirror.

The corner of the molded ceiling along with the frame of the mirror forms a "crop," which, in essence, gives a close-up of the beautiful, proud head of the great actress.

Thanks to these "crops," and to the modifications in foreshortening, the impression of an "expansion" of the figure is achieved, which is significant in every image of the tragic actress.

In filmmaking, in order to realize this perception, it would be necessary to use a wide shot, taken from slightly above, two medium shots at eye level, and finally, a close-up taken from below. It is evident, that the borders of the ceiling, reflected in the mirror at shoulder level, cause the head to stand out with particular expressiveness. This portrait speaks to the fact, that Serov understood the laws of composition magnificently, but it is difficult to say decisively, whether the portrait was composed according to feeling, or by a method of conscious calculation.

Sergei Mikhailovich analyzed in detail with his students the composition of the portraits of Lamanova, the spouse of the banker Girshman, and the portraits of Gorky and Ida Rubenstein.

He would also analyze in detail the canvases of his favorite artists. Surikov's *The Morning of Streletsky's Execution*, or *Boyarynya Morozova*, or *Menshikov in Exile*.[274]

In the work of Fedotov, he remarked upon the keen powers of observation, the national coloration, the bitter sarcasm, and the sense of humor—all indispensable for an artist in the cinema. He analyzed *The Major's Betrothal*, *The Young Widow*, *The Store*, the portraits by Fedotov. Eisenstein described these works in terms of montage construction.

In analyzing the canvas, *The Visit of the Grand Duke Mikhail Pavlovich to the Camp on the Finland Field on July 8, 1837*,[275] he concentrated on the dynamic upward flight of the soldiers' caps.

---

[274] [Trans.]: Also known as *Menshikov in Exile in Berezov*, or *Menshikov in Berezov*.

[275] [Trans.]: Shub slightly misquotes the title of the work, which is actually *Встреча в лагере лейб-гвардии Финляндского полка великого князя Михаила Павловича 8 июля 1837 года* [*The meeting in the camp of the Life Guard on Finland Field of the Grand Duke Mikhail Pavlovich on June 8, 1837.*] The soldier's caps have been thrown into the air.

In front of me is the January 1939 issue of the journal *Iskusstvo Kino* [*The Art of Cinema*]. Included in it is an article by Eisenstein called "Montage, 1938." Here, Sergei Mikhailovich repeats what he said to his students about Leonardo da Vinci, a genius who always attracted him, as did the geniuses Pushkin, Gogol, Tolstoy, Shakespeare, Goethe. He quotes a fragment, he calls a "montage list."[276] What was designated by this filmmaking term? A note by Leonardo da Vinci about what one must do in a painting in order to depict a flood. Eisenstein found in this writing a brilliantly visual and expressive presentation of an *audio-visual* picture of a flood. I will cite only the beginning of this note.

Make visible, how the dark and foggy air is disturbed by gusts of opposing winds, pierced through by constant rain and hail, now here, now there, carrying along countless numbers of branches ripped from the trees along with countless leaves.

All around: old trees uprooted and smashed to pieces by the fury of the winds.

The remnants of mountains are visible, washed away by the torrents—the remnants, which come crashing down from them and block up the valleys.

These torrents *with a loud* [My emphasis. E. Shub] gurgling, spill out and flood the broad expanses and their population.[277]

At the tops of many mountains, can be made out various kinds of animals, frightened and grown tame in the society of the people, who have fled and gathered there, men and women with children.

Across the fields, covered with water, carried in on the waves are tables, bedsteads, boats and various kinds of equipment, used in a moment of need and fear of death.

---

[276] [Trans.]: In the original: монтажный лист [montazhny list]. This term corresponds approximately to a detailed treatment, a shot list, or storyboard. It is used to attempt to previsualize a film before shooting as it will look when edited. In Esfir' Shub's own practice, a montage list would contain no images but only verbal descriptions of shots. Montage lists had to be submitted prior to shooting, or prior to editing of a compilation film. A montage list had to be approved. The final film might not include every single shot specified in the montage list, but could not include any additional shots.

[277] [Trans.]: In the Russian original: Эти потоки с ш у м н ы м клокотанием разливаются и затопляют обширные пространства с их населением. In the Italian original: "li quali fiumi ringorgati allagavano e sommergevano le moltissime terre colli lor popoli." An English translation of the Italian would be: "these swollen [or pent-up] rivers flooded and submerged the many lands with their populations." с ш у м н ы м клокотанием is not a correct translation of "ringorgati." MacCurdy and Richter suggest "pent-up" or "swollen." This translation was confirmed by independent scholar Paulo Vampa. The Russian translator has either made a mistake or uses a different source.

On all of these objects are women, men, children *howling and weeping*, having gone mad from the furious wind, which, with its heavy gusts, swell and agitate the waters along with the bodies of the drowned.

There is no object (lighter than water), on which different animals would not gather, having reconciled amongst themselves, and are standing with the frightened crowd: wolves, foxes, snakes and other species, saving themselves from death. Waves, as they are hurling the ones swimming against the shore, strike them blows with various drowned bodies—*blows*, which kill those in which there had remained any sort of life.

It is possible to see the bodies of people, who with weapons in their hands defend the small clumps of earth remaining to them from lions, wolves and other animals seeking safety here.

O, how many *horrifying cries* fill the dark air, *rent with the furor of thunder* and lightning, which rush down in destruction on all who fall into their path!

O, how many people can one see, who stop up their ears with their hands, in order not to hear the *terrible sounds*, produced in the dark air, *by the howling of the winds* and rain, *the crashing of the heavens*, and the destroying bursts of lightning.

Others not only cover their eyes with a hand, but put hand upon hand, in order to more tightly close off from sight, the cruel massacre of the human race by an angry god...[278]

This is a project for a future picture and Eisenstein found this note to be "organized on a basis more characteristic of the 'temporal' arts [cinema, music. —E. Shub], than of the spatial ones." We know that Eisenstein, in search of new emotionally expressive means in the art of the cinema, proceeded through an entire series of frequently purely formalistic solutions. At the beginning of his activity, he considered, that montage, for the most part, defined an entire object as a whole. This was, of course, a formalistic position. At the end of his activities, he ceased to consider montage as "everything." He said, that each work of art should, before anything else, be coherent, sequentially recounting its plot, theme, actions, and the behavior of its heroes. This recounting should be a stirring, emotional story. He gave his students brilliant examples of how an incorrect understanding of montage dynamics of construction leads to the opposite impression. Towards the static. If in montage, short montage shots are endlessly repeated, using this as a purely technical device for the strengthening of the dynamics, if this is not dictated by the semantic course of the

---

[278] [Trans.]: Though there are some divergences in the Russian translation from the Italian original, Shub's other evocations of sound do appear to conform to the original.

episode, but is set up by the director as a purely formal objective, then this device will call forth nothing but irritation in the spectator.

In this regard, his point of view did change both with respect to shooting and in relationship to the close-up. In his later years, he often said to me, that he dreamed of shooting a film entirely with wide shots and the widest sort of medium shots, shots with "people from the knees up."[279] He intended to give up his favorite lens, which—possessing the property of highlighting the figure of an actor in a close-up—gives the maximum amount of space in the distance on the screen, when using a close-up.

He told me, how he conceived the montage of wide shots, about the mechanisms of moving from one wide shot to another. In essence, this would, in its effect, have the same impact, as what is now given by the widescreen format, to which Eisenstein devoted a great deal of thought. How little time was given to him to realize, to implement, to leave behind. And this impassioned individual, who was always preoccupied with projects, always in search of the new, many saw as a cold, intellectual, cloistered scholar!

I would like to tell about two "attractions" staged by S. M. Eisenstein, in order to give some pleasure to his friends. One day, he invited Sergei Vasil'ev to his class and, surrounded by the students at the VGIK, the young Sergei Vasil'ev, having dropped to his knees and lowering his head, took from the hand of Eisenstein—the teacher, who with a solemnal air, had raised his eyes towards the heavens—a diploma, in which the teacher congratulated the student upon the triumph of *Chapaev* and acknowledged, that in this film the student had outstripped the teacher. It is a pity, that Georgy Vasil'ev was not standing alongside him. The partnership of the Vasil'ev brothers was creatively full and fruitful. The very talented Georgy Vasil'ev was good-looking; he loved Russian songs and sang them very well. He was a passionate hunter, magnificent scenarist and actor. In the film *Chapaev*, he played the role of the officer of the White Guard.

Eisenstein got along equally well with both of the Vasil'evs.

The second "attraction" was staged for me. Sergei Mikhailovich called me to hear one of his lectures and precisely indicating the time, when I should arrive, said sternly: "Don't be late."

Having arrived at the appointed time, I was embarrassed, to find that the lesson had already been going on for around ten minutes. I knew, that Eisenstein did not like to be interrupted. All the same, I took the risk of opening the door, going into the auditorium and under the stern gaze of Sergei Mikhailovich, of taking a place by the door.

---

[279] [Trans.]: In the original: на съемках «людей до колен». Literally "using shots of 'people from the knees.'" This is the classic definition of what in the United States is called a "two-shot." French post-war critics recognized this as a peculiarly American shot, used frequently in Westerns, calling it a "plan américain," i.e., an "American shot."

Eisenstein bestows his blessing on Sergei Vasil'ev at the VGIK.

And suddenly, with a kindly smile, he turned towards his students: "This is the director Esfir' Shub; stand up and raise a cheer for her. From her hand, I took my first strip of film and she gave me my first lessons in montage."

The students stood up and cheered me. The lessons continued. Brilliant sketches in chalk completed in an instant on the blackboard accompanied the lecture.

I was embarrassed and happy. This was also a case, when the "student" had greatly outstripped the "teacher." Sergei Mikhailovich taught me so much and communicating with him greatly enriched me.

S. M. Eisenstein's creative path was highly complicated and contradictory. His intellectual life was multifaceted. His interests in the phenomena of life in various fields, it seemed, knew no limits. Perhaps, for this reason, he was so interested in the creative activities of Leonardo da Vinci, Goethe. In him, at once, were a glistening coldness, terseness, severity and at the same time, an almost childlike defenselessness and tenderness. But his favorite traveling companions in life were Pushkin and Gogol. He especially loved the passion, lyricism, and sunniness of Pushkin. In his later years, Eisenstein worked a great deal on Pushkin. His fervent desire was to realize a film about Pushkin. You could say, that he was one of the most exceptional experts in Pushkin's texts. He studied and knew magnificently not only the printed works but the manuscripts of the poet as well.

The variants of one verse or another were studied by Sergei Mikhailovich with the thoroughness of a Pushkin scholar. He knew all the literature, all the research devoted to the Russian genius of poetry. But his thought also operated in the direction of revealing the composition of sound and color in Pushkin's verse. And he analyzed them from the point of view of montage construction.

The scenario on Pushkin he conceived as developing three fundamental themes: Pushkin and the Decembrists (the meetings at the Davydov estate), Pushkin's secret love, and his death (the murder of the poet, planned in advance and carried out by members of the imperial court under the direction of Nicholas I).

These researches were pursued daily. He would phone me day and night. Pushkin's verses would resound, as would plans for the construction of the scenario.

Especially close to complete resolution were the themes of the secret love and death of the poet. He shared the point of view of Yuri Tynyanov, that the great hidden love of Pushkin from his younger years until the final day of his life was his love for Ekaterina Andreevna Karamzina, the wife of the poet and historian Karamzin. She was almost twenty years older than Pushkin. All the same, this love continued for the poet's entire life.

During the years when Pushkin was at the lycée, Karamzina was still a beauty. She was an educated, intelligent woman, who was assisting Karamzin in his work on the history of the Russian State. Pushkin never merged together the image of husband and wife. Between him and Karamzin, relations were cold.

Ekaterina Andreevna was close to the poet, his creative work, to all the events of his personal life. During the time of Pushkin's pursuit of marriage with Goncharova, in a letter to the poet Vyazemsky (Karamzina was the illegitimate half-sister of Vyazemsky), in informing his friend about his engagement, he wrote, "...but transmit to me her words—my heart is in need of them, it is not completely happy."

Eisenstein intended to use the elegy "The daystar has gone out," where in the lines "I remember the reckless love of former days," he refers to Karamzina, and the epilogue to *Ruslan and Ludmila*: "...O friendship, tender consoler of my sick soul," as well as "Bakhchisarai Fountain," a theme inspired by stories of Karamzina.

This love was mysterious, enduring, and hidden. "I remember such a gentle gaze and a beauty ever earthly" are the verses directed towards the already aging Karamzina. The dedication of the poem "Poltava" is very much addressed to her: "To you—but will the languishing voice of the muse touch your ear?"

"Poltava" was Eisenstein's favorite poem. He worked on it a great deal, especially on the image of Peter the Great. Sergei Mikhailovich intended to use the original text, "In the hills of Georgia" and, as did Tynyanov and Bondi, he considered, that these lines were dedicated to Karamzina:

> Everything is quiet; on the Caucasus, a nighttime haze.
> The stars rise up above me.
> I am sorrowful and at ease; my suffering is bright.
> My suffering is full through you...
> I am yours as before, I love you once again,
> Without hope and without desire.
> My love is pure as the sacrificial flame
> And mine is the tenderness of chaste reveries.

The first person, whom the poet wanted to see after the duel was Karamzina. They sent for her immediately.

Eisenstein wanted to create a film about a great love: constant and beautiful. He wanted to transform to the core the understanding of Pushkin as a Don Juan and everything he said about this was full of feeling, beauty, and agitation of the soul.

Of all the projects unrealized by S. M. Eisenstein, the most dear to him were: the film about the struggle of Communist China, the second part of *Ivan the Terrible*[280] and the film about Pushkin. The film about China, about its ancient culture,

---

[280] [Trans.]: Shub was writing before the release of *Ivan the Terrible, Part II*, after Eisenstein's death. Shub dates the writing of this book to 1953–1956 and Shub died on September 21, 1959. Some five weeks later, on November 24, 1959, *Ivan the Terrible, Part II* was released. The implication may be, that it was not completed in the way Eisenstein had ultimately wanted. It is also possible she is referring to Part III, the shooting of which was not completed at the time of Eisenstein's death in 1948.

about the struggle of the Chinese people for their freedom: this was always the next in line. The second part of *Ivan*, on which he continued to work and was preparing to re-shoot,[281] and Pushkin. The theme of the great love and tragic death of this genius unsettled the image of what many took to be this "cold intellectual."

The artist, who had spoken so much about attractions, about the *eccentriad*,[282] about intellectual cinema, in the personally decisive moments of choosing themes always thought about the Soviet present day, about great feelings and fatal passions, about revolutionary-historical themes, about distant themes of history, celebrating our great Motherland, the Russian People, about patriotism, about the consonance of historical themes with the tasks of the current day.

When I think about the human relationships dear to me, in the first rank of my friends stands S. M. Eisenstein. A faithful friend, comrade, generous with kind deeds and kind words. Paying me respect and wishing to know my point of view on his creative activities, on all the significant events of his life.

This enriched me. It elevated me spiritually. It gave me the opportunity to regard him, not only through the eyes of an exacting friend, but with the feeling of gratitude towards a teacher, who knew so much and gave so much to me.

I think that these feelings live in the hearts of all those, whom he admitted into his creative world of seeking, with whom he spoke, with his intrinsic directness about their achievements and about their errors.

Because of this, he remains, as does Mayakovsky, forever alive in our midst.

---

[281] [Trans.]: In the original: Вторая серия «Ивана», над которой он все время работал и готовился пересня́ть. Since she says, he was working on it the whole time, it seems logical to say, that he was preparing for retakes, but it's possible Shub did not know exactly where Eisenstein stood and thought he might have been preparing to re-shoot the whole thing.

[282] [Trans.]: In the original: эксцентриада [ektsentriada]. A theater and film aesthetic inspired by circus aesthetics based on the use of eccentric devices and eccentric acting. Within the circus, performers were referred to as "eccentric," as a term of art. Eisenstein was introduced to this aesthetic by Yutkevich, who was a member of the FEKS group Фабрика эксцентрического актера [Fabrika ekstsentricheskogo aktera] (Factory of the Eccentric Actor). It is said to have had an influence on Eisenstein's early theater and film work.

Vsevolod Vishnevsky

I was introduced to him and his wife, the artist S. Vishnevetskaya,[283] by Alexander Dovzhenko. He took me to their home on Kislovsky pereulok. It was interesting to me to become better acquainted with the author of *Optimstic Tragedy*.

There were a lot of people at their home. They were dropping in to chat, but didn't sit down. I remember dear Natan Zarkhi: he dropped in and with humor sparkling in his wide smiling eyes, told a story, and left.

Vishnevsky had the build of a sailor. Not too tall, compact, a fine physique. Small feet, small hands with expressive gestures. The swaying gait of a sailor. A robust face. Under his thick eyebrows was the attentive gaze of his black eyes: intelligent, sharp-sighted, taking in everything. Sometimes his eyes would narrow slyly. A strong, hard chin. A large mouth. Large, severely pursed lips. His face would unexpectedly light up with a surprisingly kind, lively, almost cunning smile. One had the impression of directness and spiritual purity.

He kept quiet and was extremely attentive to the words of others.

I was in their home several times.

Unexpectedly, I was sent to Turkey. The job there was big and difficult.

At that time I was shooting the construction of the Metro in Moscow.[284] We were shooting at the Revolution Square station. The camera crew and I were in industrial uniforms,[285] up to our knees in water. We were waiting for the moment when two construction brigades would meet up with one another. We were shooting day and night. Completely absorbed.

And suddenly they called. It was imperative to leave immediately for Turkey.

At the train station in Kiev, I met I. Ehrenburg and his wife Lyuba Mikhailovna. They were going to Paris; they were going first to Istanbul, then Greece, Marseilles, Paris. While waiting for the steamer, they would be staying over for a few days in Odessa.

It was a marvelous autumn. We went to see various places connected with Pushkin. The neglect of the site of the former Voronstov Palace was distressing. We left Odessa accompanied by music. With us on the steamer was a Turkish military delegation. There was a formal sendoff.

We left happy.

---

[283] [Russian editor's note]: *Vishnevetskaya, Sof'ya Kas'yanovna* (1899–1962). Artist, wife of the writer V. V. Vishnevsky.

[284] [Trans.]: In the original: *Моска строит метро* (*Метро ночью*) [*Moskva stroit metro* (*Metro noch'yu*)] *Moscow Builds a Metro* (*The Metro by Night*) (1934). See filmography for further details.

[285] [Trans.]: In the original: прозодежда [Prozodezhda]. A Soviet Era neologism, a portmanteau word combining "production" (Произведение) [Proizvedenie] with "clothing" (одежда) [odezhda]. Vavara Stepanova was a leading designer of *prozodezhda* for industrial and theatrical use.

To be a traveling companion with I. Ehrenburg was more than interesting. He noticed everything. His bright eyes sparkled with good-natured derision.

Every stopover was noisy. Little boats would sail up to the steamer. On the little boats they would sell fish and shag tobacco. Ehrenburg even managed to get hold of bouquets of flowers.

In Istanbul, we stopped in at our consulate on the main street Grande rue de Péra.

My first long stroll around Istanbul with Ehrenburg. Since Ehrenburg showed it to me—especially old Istanbul—the city still remains that way in my memory. I can no longer see it any other way; so precise were the choices of places for our walks and so expressive was everything that was said about those places.

And so, we are working for a Turkish entrepreneur. He had the idea of making a film about the New Turkey. He viewed us only as specialists. It was necessary to make the best possible use of us. I was the director,[286] Martov[287] the cameraman, the sound operator was a Frenchman, Bogé,[288] the remainder of the group were Turks, relatives of the boss, wanting to master a new specialty. The boss accompanies us everywhere. He often changes the theme of the film, cancels shoots that have been scheduled, and does not allow us to finish what we have begun.

In Istanbul we shot:

The ruins of the wall of the Byzantine [Fortress of] Seven Towers.

The granite hippodrome. The obelisk. The Serpentine Column.

The remains of the tripod from the temple of Apollo at Delphi.

The Golden Horn glistening in the distance. Slowly sailing past the dead city amidst Gothic façades made of poplar.

We shot a world which has passed. Topkapı Sarayı: the palace of the Ottoman sultans. The tall cypresses. The magnificent inner precinct of the palace. The intricate cupola of the palace kitchen. The terraced hanging gardens, the palace pavilions.

The marble terraces and magnificent tile work.

The Harem wall. An internal courtyard, resembling a fortress. How many bloody tragedies it saw! From the main building of the palace, the fairy tale view of the Bosphorus. The Princes' Islands. The Golden Horn.

The throne room. In it were gathered the palace treasures. The dazzling luster of precious stones. The throne: a mass of Persian gold work, encrusted with emeralds and diamonds. Emeralds the size of a fist; the largest suspended from the baldachin. Persian and Smyrna carpets.

From Istanbul we went to Smyrna by steamer.

As in a vision, we sailed past the Topkapı Palace (XVth century) and the banks of the Bosphorus with its sublime mosques of Hagia-Sophia, Bayazid, Süleymaniye (XVIth century).

Remarkable monuments of Byzantine and Ottoman culture. Here, there is calm, grandeur, solemnity, beauty.

Through Marmora and the Aegean Sea we sailed to Smyrna. In the distance, as we sailed past, the Isle of Lesbos. Thoughts of Sappho, of Troy.

---

[286] [Trans.]: The film had the working title *Идет Новая Турция* [*Idet Novaya Turtsiya*] (*A New Turkey is on the Move*). Production was halted by the Turkish producer with the film unfinished. The State Archive of Literature and Art in Moscow holds Shub's production journals for the film and production stills. The whereabouts of the material shot is unknown.

[287] [Russian editor's note]: *Martov, Zhosef Kliment'evich* (b. 1900). Camera operator. His most significant works are *Golden Mountains, Counterplan* (in collaboration with A. Gintsburg and V. Rapoport), *Ankara is the Heart of Turkey, The Man with a Gun, Yakov Sverdlov* and others.

[288] In the original: Боже [Bozhe]. Possibly Louis Bogé, a sound recordist active in France in the 1930s. Due to the large number of homonyms in French and Russian transcription practice, it's impossible to be certain without more information.

We shot a great deal. The indifference and boundlessness of the distances of the sea. The splashing of the water.

The deserted pathways.

And again, the splashing of the water. A chain of mountains in the dawn fog. Ravines, mountain lakes. On the banks of a mountain lake, zeybeks[289] sit in a half circle, in ancient, embroidered garments of striking beauty. They are playing instruments, recalling sazes.[290] And rhythmically dance a warlike dance.

The mountains pile up in range after range. The ancient Roman road.

We shoot fig and olive groves, grape and pomegranate orchards.

We shot Ankara: the new capital at the foot of two mountains with straight avenues with European architecture.

We shot during the time of the parade honoring President Kemal-Pasha Atatürk. The entire city repeats his figure in numerous monuments: he is everywhere, the victor, the "*Gazi.*"[291] And everywhere on the monuments in honor of the *Gazi* is the figure of the Turkish peasant woman. Her face is uncovered.

I even shot the residence at the edge of the city of Kemal-Pasha in his absence. There is a beautiful canvas there by our artist Polenov.

People are impoverished. I got the impression, that, for the most part, women work.

They, more than the men, and at the complex machinery of the cigarette factories. At the Smyrna raisin, fig, and tobacco factories, women work together with little girls. The tanned little fingers of children's hands zip around with incredible speed.

We shot the port of Smyrna. Slowly, a pan extending in an arc over the port of Smyrna. The masts of the steamers are brightly colored with the flags of the entire world. And there are a lot of them. Really a lot. From a steamer you see Smyrna: an old Turkish city. Houses run down from the mountains almost to the gulf. At the top of the mountain are the ruins of the fortress towers. On the embankments, we shot the tiny little wagons of horse-drawn trams. They seem exotic alongside the busses, the automobiles of the latest kind, and the cranes of the port.

We shot schools, academies, institutes.

The shoot at Pergamon (Bergama) made the strongest impression on me. Ancient myth. Hellas.

Magnificent ruins. Marble buildings. Columns. Numerous temples. The Circus.

The Temple of Aesclapius with baths, alcoves, with a theater for the entertainment of the sick. The subterranean temple. Here, the sick were treated by immersing them in complete calm and silence.

---

[289] [Trans.]: zeybek is actually the name of the dance, rather than the dancers.

[290] [Trans.]: A long necked lute-like instrument played with a plectrum. In the original, it seems Shub confused the group of musicians (sazandari) with one of the instruments they use, the saz, or tar.

[291] [Trans.]: *Ghazi* is an Arabic honorific for a great warrior, bestowed on Atatürk for his military prowess.

The magnificent Acropolis, in the complex of which, were included the royal palaces, the sanctuary of the goddess Athena, with a temple and library; on the western slope of the hill at one time was a theater for fifteen thousand spectators.

Two walls of pink marble slabs remain. Architects from every country, under the blazing sun, measure out the proportions of these walls.

An ancient aqueduct. There are statues: of emperors, citizens, noblewomen, gods. Mosaics. The entire life, the entire existence of the city—destroyed and buried for centuries—you can imagine through these ruins and the monuments, that have been preserved.

To what Cyclopean labor, what genius of humankind, which came millennia before, do these ruins testify. Without speaking, without human presence.

A high granite wall, covered with moss, surrounds this dead city of yellow-pink marble, like a fortress.

We shot the divine head of the god of love, Eros, made of pink marble. They poured water over the grayed-out mosaics, and by means of the water, bright patches of mosaics appeared and, slowly, the terrible head of Medusa was outlined in every detail with serpents instead of hair, with cold, hypnotic eyes. We shot beautifully preserved masks for religious festivals. The shooting went on under the blazing sun.

After shooting Pergamon, we went into the depths of Asia, to the tiny town of Ödemiş. The Turkish women there remain in my memory for some reason, in their bright sand-colored garments, with veiled faces, in spite of the *Gazi*'s prohibition, with narrow clay pitchers of water on their heads, or shoulders.

We returned to Istanbul. We outlined what we would shoot. There, the rains came. On the streets were roses, carnations, violets.

The rains.

In those days, the Soviet People were overtaken by great sorrow; Sergei Mironovich Kirov was killed.

It was painful to be far away from the Motherland. Istanbul was especially hard for me. I was living in the Soviet consulate. On the spire, the red flag was lowered and a period of mourning began. Members of the White Guard would gather at the gates, in jubilation.

But we members of the Soviet People spent entire days in the great hall of the consulate. We would listen to the radio and then together with our People, to the sound of funeral music, in our minds would advance towards the House of the Soviets, in order to pay our final tributes of love and gratitude to a magnificent Bolshevik, to a fiery Tribune.

And suddenly, I made out the calm voice, muted by grief, of Vsevolod Vishnevsky.

It was as if he was speaking to us face to face. His heart, overflowing with grief, was feeling our grief. He held back tears and clenched his fists. He demanded the same of us. To be strong, courageous, not lose our way, to be worthy of the memory of Sergei Mironovich Kirov, who had departed from us so early.

Each time the voice of Vishnevsky rang out, we would all get up from our places and listen to him standing.

After the funeral, I sent a telegram to Vs. Vishnevsky. And thanked him for the great thing he had given me, that allowed me to endure, in my grief, so far from the Motherland.

Soon after, I received a letter from him.

December 19, 1934
Moscow

Esfir' Shub

Greetings,

Thanks for your greetings and your response. These days, I have been receiving letters from Leningrad and from the Khar'kovsky oblast' (from the garrison) etc. I have been imagining the power of the nightly Moscow radio, the power of the country… and its radius of operation.

I'm working: 20% of my film is done. I'm afraid of jinxing it (ugh!)—that happened with Dzigan. Severely, in a big way. The sea, the Baltic is magnificent. This is the cold of the ocean, and not "the charming black sea natural landscape with loons."

On December 28, we begin in the studio. In February—in Azov— off to the gloomy sands and in May to the dunes and swamps of the Baltic. I have found a series of dynamic, powerful new places… I am responding to *Chapaev*.

In the cinema, it's festive. As far as I know, they will be feting Ermler, Dovzhenko, Eisenstein and some others.

Maxim's Youth has been approved. Eisenstein solemnly declared it "a good picture."

Medvedkin's *The Moneygrubbers* is an excellent picture. It's new, grotesque, a pamphlet…

Dovzhenko is working and cursing Potylikha. He has two new scenarios in his head *The Tsar* and *Paradise Regained*. The theme is the efforts of socialist humanity to bring back a tropical climate to the earthly sphere. That would be great!

Everyone is writing, shooting, staging things… January will be exceptional in film and theater. January 4, 1935 "Tairov celebrates his 20th anniversary" [in the theater]. They're having a fête!!! January 11 is the premiere of *Shaw is Shakespeare*.[292]

I write my prose and am happy: at least when the theater isn't tugging at me.

A public discussion on aesthetics has begun: sharp arguments are erupting, and it's all getting bigger… Conversations take place on the essence of things: about style… huge masses of material, ideas, insults, joy, all this is gathering strength in view of the January plenary session of Soviet Writers. Good: let's argue, fight, search, act! How are things with you? I'm convinced you'll succeed…

Scribble something down about your impressions, etc.

Vsevolod Vishnevsky

Greetings from N. Zarkhi

The rains. They forced us to delay shooting and to return to Istanbul. I hurried off to return to Moscow for the New Year. A fair amount had been shot and was very good, but not enough for a feature-length documentary film. Little had been shot of Istanbul. I believed, that I would return and finish up the work.

During this time, we helped create the first small film studio in Turkey with a laboratory, editing workshop, and sound department.

We sailed off on a windy, rainy day. The entire way, a heavy storm tormented us. The rocking back and forth was a torment. We arrived at Odessa in the evening.

We arrived too late for the Moscow train, we were too late to greet the New Year in Moscow.

The Trade representative, who was traveling with us, put us up in the Odessa office of the Trade Agency. The Motherland greeted me with great joy: I walked around the streets of Odessa heading for film screenings, workers walked by in organized columns, young people studying, office workers. In the wind fluttered red banners on which Chapaev was portrayed, they also carried portraits of the directors, the Vasil'ev Brothers. In this way, Odessa celebrated the nationwide triumph of this film.

And in Moscow I began to see Vs. Vishnevsky frequently and to become friends with him. These were the years of the prime of his creative power. The film *We Are from Kronstadt* was playing with great success. It had great success as well beyond the borders of our Motherland. Vishnevsky immediately went to work on his second scenario, *First Cavalry*.[293] He wrote the scenario for Dzigan and they began at once to prepare for shooting.

---

[292] [Trans.] In the original: Шоу — Шекспир. Daria Khitrova notes, this refers to the play *Египетские ночи* (*Egyptian Nights*) by A. Ya. Tairov, based on Shaw, Pushkin, and Shakespeare.

[293] [Trans.]: The film was completed in 1941, but for ideological reasons was not released. Its first public screening seems to have taken place in 1987.

He amazed me with the breadth and audacity of his views on art and riveted my attention with the originality of his entire outlook. He was genuinely interested in filmmaking. For him, writing a scenario, participation with the director in shooting was a matter of creative responsibility. For the majority of writers in those years, the work of filmmaking was incidental, they stayed in the background.

Here, for example, is something he wrote me at that time:

Dear Esfir'!

I consider, that it has become indispensable to express with complete clarity and in detail my views on working and the methods for it. As you know, I am deeply absorbed in questions of cinematic practice and theory. I am occupied by the interaction of literature and cinema. A new era has arrived, a new phase for the filmmaker; a phase of more active and decisive participation by the writer in the entire creative process.

The cinema for some thirty or forty years has greedily, unscrupulously, and hastily made its way by revealing the world in front of the lens. They have shot comic sketches, fairy tale spectacles, they have put novels on film, invented pure film theories, attempted to work directly from nature on the easel of the film material, they have taken a bruising, they have made new attempts…

All this was the era of primitive accumulation. Quite interesting, of course. But the genuine maturity of film art will arrive only with the phase, where they begin to correctly, scientifically, and truly merge together in the synthesis of a new art: ideological, literary-cinematic thought, a complete compositional-plastic system, a complete music-sound system, and most likely, a polychromatic color one.

I will not lay out for you all of the views on the contemporary state of our filmmaking. I will say only, that we are living through a manifestly critical transitional period. The director has understood, that he can no longer go it alone, "independently." The writer has not yet understood, that he is *obliged* to go into the depths of production. It is painful for the writer to consider the transformation of his intentions, the intermediaries, the variations, the misunderstandings, the coarseness of the methods of production, and so on, and so on.

The racing around, the hastiness, the crude techniques, the makeshift work, and so on, and so on…

But this misses the point. I see the significance of the work in the possibility of deeply examining and analyzing the essence of the new syntheses: writer—director—camera operator—actor…[294]

---

[294] [Russian editor's note]: Letter of V. Vishnevsky dated April 7, 1939. The original is preserved in the

He applied that same commitment to his work on the editorial board of the journal *Znamya* [*Banner*]. I would often find him reading manuscripts. He would invariably be sitting on his low wide divan behind a small, low table. Showing the way to writers just starting out—poets were his joy—and he would read me texts that he liked with particular warmth.

The events in Spain disturbed him.

To be there—to see everything with his own eyes, to struggle alongside the Spanish People, who were rising up for their freedom and independence, to be at the side of Dolores Ibárruri and José Díaz—that was what he wanted. He could talk about this endlessly. And there he went.

He considered, that people involved in art should be in the avant-garde of the struggle. Be the first ones in the attacking column. Art directs consciousness, the will to action. The strength of art was for him indisputable.

Vishnevsky applied himself to documentary film with great interest.

I began my work on the film *Spain* with Mikhail Kol'tsov. The idea for the film belonged to him. He wanted to realize the film with R. Karmen and me. He called us in to the editorial offices of *Pravda*. Karmen and I went to his home several times and he spoke to us in detail about the film. We looked over all the material that could be had in Moscow. The screenings were attended by people from Spain. It became clear, that there was very little material for the realization of a film. It was decided to contact some Spanish camera operators. Everything that he intended for the future scenario was interesting, captivating.

I completed the film with Vs. Vishnevsky. We were supposed to work with R. Karmen, but at that time, everything of pressing interest to him lay in China.

It was easy for me to come to an agreement with Vishnevsky. We were speaking a lot about documentary film and about the paths for its development. I will try to briefly outline our general point of view. We considered, that work in documentary film was an artistic labor. We did not consider it "second-class art." Therefore, our evaluation of what appeared on the screen was stringent and exacting, so that it would lead to the advance of documentary film.

We did not make use of the long outdated kinds of shots repeated in every film, nor lacking research into new means of expression, use paintings and photographs instead of film footage. They couldn't make up for the lack of film material. We did not make use of cheap symbolism. Many shots in the documentary films of that time bore the stamp of the endless repetition of devices long familiar. The feebleness of the compositional structures was painful. The people making documentary films were not deeply reflecting upon our era, upon our days. Everything was done by brute force, with no subtext, with none of the dramatic construction particular to documentary film. There was a lot of glossing over. There were songs, beautiful, well-dressed

archive of E. Shub.

peasant and working women in abundance, orchestras, speeches… they sang, they danced, but they were not creating a gigantic new world according to a plan.

And there was nothing of the land, no accurate view of nature there. Only beautiful places were chosen. Why these and not others?

Continuous celebration!

But the most troubling was *the banal directing*, which kills the trust of the spectator in the filmed fact and, thereby, in the documentary film.

Vishnevsky agreed to help me make the film *Spain*.

Before me lay two scenarios by Vishnevsky. The first, written after many viewings by us of the material taken by the camera operators Karmen and Makaseev. In the corner Vishnevsky had written by hand: "For E. Shub. Forward! Together with Spain!—Vs. Vishnevsky. 22 March, 1939. Moscow."

And the final version of the scenario, which we composed in the process of working, after we had managed to arrange additional footage realized by Spanish camera operators, the objectives of which were worked out jointly with us, and to obtain material, shot in Franco's Capital—in Burgos and other places, and bring it together with additional footage of mine.[295]

Vishnevsky helped me to establish connections with Spanish friends and film cameramen.

Working with Vishnevsky was very interesting.

He was exacting towards himself and towards me. We argued a lot, after which, we would reach a unanimous decision.

On the battle scenes, I did not argue with him and did only what he required and it always succeeded expressively and emotionally, although the material for editing was, for understandable reasons, extremely limited.

Vsevolod Vishnevsky and I decided, that the author of the scenario would recite the voice-over text. This led to a whole series of new revelations both in the text and in the editing.

Vishnevksy's voice-over text was unique and beautiful. It is spoken aloud, or rather, thought aloud for an auditorium. Besides the voice-over text, additional intertitles were made.

The music by the composer Gavriil Popov played a great role in the shaping of the scenario. He took as its basis a folk melody and made beautiful use of folk instruments and folk songs.

Vishnevsky recited the text himself, in a somewhat soft and subdued voice. A new result was achieved in personal emotional expressiveness. Those who understood this, very much approved.

---

[295] [Russian editor's note]: A copy of the scenario of V. Vishnevsky for *Spain* and the voice-over text for it dated March 2, 1939 is preserved in the personal archive of E. Shub.

Individual words were not utterly distinct. A second recording duplicating the whole was required. The sound engineer promised to arrange everything. Vishnevsky was with me the whole time in the sound-recording studio, prepared to work as much as necessary. He very much wanted to preserve the authorial voice.

But the administration of the studio decided otherwise. It was ordered, that Levitan be recorded. Levitan recited the text as best he could in Vishnevsky's style, but realized he couldn't do it. Levitan's beautiful young voice resounded beautifully, but over this singular text, which had been written for the author, hung the typical sound of a radio broadcasting center. An unnecessary pathos emerged alongside the scansion of individual words. Much was irrevocably lost.

How did Vsevolod Vishnevsky and I work together?

While the film was being edited, returning late from the studio, I would find a letter at my home from Vishnevsky. These were carefully worked through even after our general review of the proposal for editing and the rough draft of the voice-over.

I would like to cite only two letters.[296]

The first one:

9 April, 1939, 7:00 pm.
Draft of the "Ebro" scene.
    After a short rest in the village comes a signal: the call to battle.
    The movement of weary, exhausted soldiers. Dust…
    Asleep on the rocks… Artillery at the ready… Reveille… Hurried movements. The battle has begun.
    Gunshots, the batteries… A view of the Ebro… (A quick view: some small boats, or perhaps without them, then a bold, planned maneuver). Soldiers emerge directly from the water!…
    Fragments of the intense fighting. Soldiers lie down, then run across. They are pulling out some cable… —A bridging operation.
    A first bridge. Trucks going over the bridge… Ranks, advance! The powerful explosion of a bomb.
    —The general offensive. Masses of soldiers…
    They dig trenches. They fortify their positions. Battle trophies…
    —Dolores among the victorious troops… smiles, remarks…
    The victorious troops in the village.
    A meeting of the 11th Division. A speech by the Commissar. They are wiping out Fascist slogans.
    This is the approximate evolution of a battle at the front. It also needs *bold, planned actions*, in various places.

---

[296] [Russian editor's note]: The originals of the correspondence of V. V. Vishnevsky with the notations on the text by E. Shub are preserved in her personal archive.

To have a few tiny little boats on a quiet river is pointless. Let the spectator fill out the action himself.

The movement of the ranks causes an increase in tension. The activity of the artillery in parallel montage, as if supporting the advancing infantry. Then, at a given moment, a general "hurrah": let there be an increasing montage of running infantrymen and increasing "hurrahs."

Afterwards, it becomes quiet... The narrator speaks about victory, about fortification... Then: battle trophies, welcomes, meetings etc.

The letter which awaited me at home after the first screening of the completed edit of the film was extremely characteristic. This screening was done before the dubbing.[297] I can't read this letter without being moved. This tenacious quest for improving *his own text* for the author's reading before the recording session. I was supposed to answer him by morning. He wanted to know my opinion, before he set to work. He knew that all the tasks, which he set for himself, would force me to go over the edited scenes again and again with eyes and hands, considering the new nuances of the text.

His exactingness towards himself and towards me led to a genuine creative sharing and was always a joy for me.

Here are some excerpts from one of the letters:

To: E. Shub

Evening, 27 April, 1939.

Some considerations on 26 and 27 April, 1939.
My observations:
...Madrid. There's something that needs to be examined in the voice-over text. About Cervantes once again. It needs to be cleaner, better! [Vishnevsky is writing this to himself about his own text. And all the following remarks are also about himself, about his text. *E. Sh.*]
...*The voice-over text* that goes with the scattering of the leaflets *is inadequate*. Who exactly was rising up, what news were the leaflets communicating?... Here, all of the material can be presented: *the Party of the Popular Front and the legitimate government of the Republic are calling for striking back at the mutinous traitors!*
...about the barricades: the section about the 60,000 volunteers could be expanded, about the People, there you have people of various

---

[297] [Trans.]: озвучания. That is, the recording of a voice-over to correspond to the picture. Since music was also part of the sound track, this might also be understood to be the sound mix.

parties: Communists, Socialists, Republicans... This strengthens the theme of the Popular Front. (A few remarks about how in the film practically only the Communist Party is mentioned; that needs to be considered...)

...About Franco. Give him a strongly political character.

...A brief characterization of the Moroccans must be given. Right there. (Otherwise, these brave columns [of men] somehow don't quite work.)

Two or three words could be said about the Germans...

The Battles in Toledo. Maybe it's necessary to deepen the meaning of the struggle a bit (these Republican boys, the soldiers, are deterring Fascism, they are saving Democracy). It's absolutely necessary to say something about the Asturians: the miners, the dinamiteros...

...Something like: "These Asturians, the ones who set the example for the Spanish Working Class..." The theme of the slogan: "Hold on, Spanish Brothers, you are not alone!" and so on, rewrite it again...

Madrid... Perhaps for José, something more concrete: enemies are forcing their way through to Madrid, and so on. Strengthen, synch up the thought with the speech of La Pasionaria. Develop once more the theme of the Popular Front. The theme of the government.

The Fifth Regiment. A few details: what kind of regiment is it? ... About the international volunteers:[298] "Leaving families behind, they forced their way across mountains and frontiers in the name of solidarity, of aiding the People..." *This will be stronger!*

Perhaps a few words about the international volunteers leaving for the front?

Armored train? (Maybe say something about it?)

[Enemies]... Perhaps a few more words are needed.

Need to examine, to rewrite the text about the blessing.

About Fascist aircraft, something clearer: *"These are German planes"*...

...Madrid. Everything there *appears* to be in order... Rewrite the phrases about the attack...

Make a clear-cut verbal and montage transition to entrenching, to labor. "Stay strong! Get to work! Dig the trenches!" and so on.

Say it clearly: "Here are the Moroccans" and so on (for the shots of them).

...A stronger text for the troops (Guadalajara). A clearer, stronger text for the prisoners: "These wretched, ignorant Kabyles[299] hurled Fascism *against European culture...*"

---

[298] [Trans.]: i.e., the "International Brigades."
[299] [Trans.]: A Berber ethnic group native to Kabylie in the north of Algeria.

Spring. Be more clear about Líster and M. Zalka.[300]

"The army mastered its equipment…" Say something similar about anti-aircraft devices.

Stronger and more closely synchronized texts about the meeting of Líster and the peasants. The voice: louder, more expansive!…

About the young people: "The young did not want to be left behind by the grown-ups… They wanted to be worthy of their fathers." (Get rid of material about athletic organizations.)

…New title about Italian-German interventions… Not "the enemy" in general, but *specifically Italian-German Fascists.*

Leisure… maybe a still more lyrical, gentler text?

Signal. Say the remark about the Chapaev Battalion more gently, *more lyrically.*

…The title about the blockade: give the title more weight, *more strength.*

The blockade… Perhaps, even stronger, a more urgent appeal from the Spanish people about the opening of the borders…

Explain the reasons for the departure of the International Brigade…

Get rid of the drumming sounds during the march of the Republican Columns to the train station.

The departure of the Catalunyans… Don't repeat this at the French border: the Fascists approach the border, and so on, several times.

…*Fine tune the text at the finale.* Say a few words about treachery, about the statement of the "junta," about the temporary defeat and so on. "The Trotskyists, the right-wingers, treacherously plunged a knife into the back of the People. They tried to sabotage the alliance of the party of the Popular Front. They murdered the loyal commanding officers"… and so on, but later on a text about the People and their perseverance. Perhaps extend it a bit.

In the final part, after the flag, on the fade: "The End is yet to come!"

Those are just a few remarks and concerns in a practical vein.

V. Vishnevsky

---

[300] [Trans.]: Enrique Líster and Máté Zalka [Paul Lukács]. General Líster, a Spanish Communist, born in Cuba, trained in the Soviet Union, led the 11th Division of the Fifth Corps of the Republican Army; his troops took part in the defense of Madrid, but also helped destroy the Anarchist Government of Aragón. After Franco took control of Spain, Líster took refuge in the Soviet Union and fought in the battle of Stalingrad. Zalka was a Republican General who died in the line of duty.

I, of course, agreed to all the changes, but this meant, that it was going to be necessary to re-edit a lot of things, to bring in new pieces of film, to lengthen or shorten what had been prepared for the dubbing session.[301] There was little time. We worked nights in order not to have to cancel the dubbing session. Everything was ready at the appointed time.

I would like to pause on what were for me two especially rich scenes in the film *Spain*. These clearly demonstrate the utter originality of Vishnevsky's work on the texts for the film.

The texts were characteristically laconic and few in quantity. For a film of such great length—2,449 meters,[302] in ten reels—the amount of text is surprisingly small. There was neither exaggerated emotion in the voice-over, nor phrase-mongering.

There was absolute confidence in the viewers. It was the author's overwhelming desire, that all spectators be able to discern, to learn, and to preserve in their memories and in their hearts what was taking place on the screen. Vishnevsky demanded that I be attentive in the highest degree to his text. I would think about the emotional montage for this text.[303] I placed emphasis on whatever would suitably call forth the singular attention of the viewer.

The scenes filmed for *Spain* had no synchronous sound. People would speak to each other the way they do in silent films. For example: A peasant man and woman stand together and talk with each other.

—*Any word, compañero?*—asks the author of the film over this shot.

—*They say, that in Madrid the Cortes is in session, they are announcing new laws.*

Narrator.

But will the gentlemen allow it? Who knows...

A car quickly rushes along.

Narrator.

Madrid, Madrid! Onwards! Faster to that city!

The feeling is created that the author is in the car, that together with him, we are rushing towards Madrid.

The main square in Madrid. And right there, the narrator strengthens the impression, through this remark:

—*There it is, Madrid, a beauty of a city!*

There goes Dolores Ibárruri. Who doesn't know her? But the author demands particular attention, and so the narrator says:

—*Look! that's Dolores Ibárruri...*

---

[301] [Trans.]: In the original: озвучания.

[302] [Trans.]: At sound speed of 24 frames per second, this is about 89.5 minutes, long for a documentary at that time in the Soviet Union.

[303] [Trans.]: In the original: Думала бы об эмоциональном монтаже для этого текста.

A demonstration is in progress.
Narrator.
In the name of the People shot in Asturia!
In the name of the widows and orphans! The workers demand
The imprisonment of the Fascist ringleaders!
A mass-meeting at a factory.
The crowd screams in Spanish. The narrator speaks for it:
Put Gil-Robles and Franco in prison!
Put them in prison. Before it's too late.
Dolores Ibárruri makes a speech.
Narrator.
La Pasionaria calls for unrelenting struggle against the betrayers of the Republic.
To arms!
Fight for Freedom! ¡No pasarán!
The author speaks for the crowd. The demands of the crowd with the power of verse ring out from the screen in the Spanish language. I recorded the voices of Spanish emigrants who were present at the recording sessions.

An injured man is walking through the streets. He is supported by his comrades.

The "Toledo" episode was edited precisely according to Vishnevsky's instructions. The final shot is accompanied by the author, making his heartfelt farewell.
Narrator.
Hold on, Spanish brothers! You are not alone in your struggle!
The cameraman Karmen stands out in this shot by his masterly reporting and his fearlessness. He stands alongside those advancing.

The authorial text for the episode in Burgos—Franco's so-called capital—is powerfully decisive. For understandable reasons, there was scant material.
A religious procession goes by.
Monks pass by.
Monks and priests pass by.
Panning shot. Monks. Behind them stand gendarmes.
The religious procession enters a gate.
Monks are standing, speaking to one another.
Monks and priests pass by.
A square, crowded with people. The religious procession goes by.
Franco's troops move around the square.
Franco's troops pass by, seen from above.
A hand with a cross.
Franco's troops on their knees. A prayer takes place.
A priest with a cross.

Franco's troops on their knees.

Here is the narrator's text for these shots:

Narrator.

They offer up...

Priest with a cross.

Narrator.

...prayers...

Franco's troops on their knees.

Narrator.

and dispatch to Madrid... A hand on a cross.

Narrator.

their congregation... Soldiers on their knees.

Narrator.

...kulaks from Navarre.

A hand on a cross

(Panning shot) Franco's soldiers on their knees.

Narrator.

these thugs!

A priest with a cross.

The voice of the narrator resounds, like a remorseless verdict:

Murderer!

This entire text was written for a prayer sequence I had already edited without Vishnesvky's participation: Franco's kneeling soldiers, the cross in the hands of the priest. The priest endlessly blessing the soldier with the sign of the cross.

The flight of Fascist aircraft towards Madrid I also showed to Vishnevsky in edited form. He approved. The remark of the author strengthens the emotional impact of this episode: "Aircraft in the heavens."

Narrator.

You are now going to see some of the bestial deeds of Fascism.

Workers pass by with spades...

Narrator.

...And never forget this.

...On the sidewalk lies a murdered pregnant woman with a child.

Narrator.

This no one can forgive—ever!

And after a short pause, the narrator repeats:

Ever!

People are digging trenches around Madrid.

Fury and vengeance set Madrid into motion.

An old man at work. A young man at work.

Narrator.
With energy redoubled and tripled they answer the enemy.
A little boy at work. A group of men at work.
Narrator.
Get to work! Surround Madrid with trenches and do battle there...
Men at work. (Panning shot.) José Díaz at work.
Narrator.
They are all at work!
José Díaz is at work. Ibárruri is at work.

My most beloved theme:
(Panning shot.) The sky. Blossoming trees. A blossoming tree.
Narrator.
Spring...
A blossoming tree.
Narrator.
Quiet...
blossoming Trees. (Panning shot). The wounded pass by.
Narrator.
...The firmly established front...
A peasant plows the earth amidst blossoming trees. On the hill stands a young woman with children. (Panning shot.)
Against a background of blossoming trees, a tank comes by. Two fighters go towards the trenches.
Narrator.
Go, comrades, to the trenches.

These words Vishnevsky pronounced with an especial intimacy, directing himself towards each individual viewer. It was impossible not to respond. We went along with him on that long panning shot.

A guitar sounds: a Spanish folksong, beautifully arranged by Popov.

The trees were flowering. Against the background of flowering trees, the cavalry rode by.

Against the background of flowering trees a tank was passing by.

On the hill stood a young woman with a child in her arms. The sounds of a guitar could be heard.

Two fighters were heading towards the trenches and we couldn't help but go there along with them.

You could believe, that victory was near, that we were all on the threshold of great joy, youthful and sunny, like this spring day.

With the just the same intimacy, the author led us into the trenches towards the best commanding officers: El Campesino, Líster, towards Máté Zalka (aka Lukács). [304] The meeting with Máté Zalka, the Hungarian commander, made us glad. We all knew him so well and loved him.

A short remark… —*He died a hero's death*—wounded in the heart.

This is how economically Vishnevsky presented combat in the sky:

Narrator:

Republican bombers…

Panning shot of the earth from an airplane.

A squadron of Republican bombers.

A Fascist aircraft, which has been hit, falls from the sky.

The wing of an aircraft with a Fascist insignia in flames.

A Fascist aircraft.

Three bombs fall to earth.

Explosions on the earth.

Republican aircraft.

Narrator.

Against the Fascist air force, the Republic sent into action…

Republican fighter aircraft in flight.

Narrator.

…its Air Force, young, new…

Republican fighter aircraft in flight.

Narrator.

Ah, there they are, fighter aircraft.

Commander Líster and his comrades look to the sky.

A Republican fighter aircraft dives through the air.

A Fascist aircraft.

A Fascist aircraft, which has been hit, falls from the sky.

Narrator.

One down! That's for Madrid!

A Fascist aircraft, which has been hit, falls from the sky.

Narrator.

And there's another one! That's for Madrid too! Disappear from Republican skies! Die!

An explosion.

---

[304] [Trans.]: In the original: Компенсино [Kompensino], likely a misspelling of the Russian editor or Shub for El Campesino, the *nom de guerre* of Valentín González. Líster is Enrique Líster Forján. Born Béla Frankl, he assumed the name Máté Zalka sometime around WWI, during which he became a prisoner in Russia, where he subsequently stayed after the revolution. He assumed the name of Pavol Lukács when joining the International Brigades.

A bomber drop bombs on a bunker.
Republican fighter aircraft.
Narrator.
A Republican pilot is consumed with rage.
Forward!
A Republican fighter aircraft.
... Death to the Fascists!
An explosion.
A Fascist aircraft, which has been hit, falls.
Narrator.
...Drop from Republican skies...
A burning aircraft falls from the sky.
Narrator.
...That's right... like that... like that.
The final episode of the Spanish tragedy:
[Narrator.[305]]
Barcelona—that beauty Barcelona—bids farewell to the International Brigades.
Narrator.
...In Spain there were 25 thousand international fighters...
Fighters of the International Brigades pass by.
...Five thousand warriors remained in their graves...
The People bid farewell to the fighters. They give them flowers. Tears can be seen.
Narrator.
...pouring out their blood... it went deep into the earth...
Fighters of the Republican Army pass by. Leaflets fall down on them from above.
Narrator.
... it became a part of the Spanish earth...
Women with flowers.
Narrator.
... and because of this...
(Shot from overhead)... Through the streets of Barcelona go the International Brigades.
Narrator.
...the Spanish People will never forget...
(Shot from overhead)... Fighters of the International Brigades pass by.
Narrator.
...this great act of love and solidarity...
(Shot from overhead)... Fighters of the International Brigades pass by.

---

[305] [Trans.]: These words are spoken by the narrator. There seems to be an error in typography in the original.

Narrator.

…a great act, done out of this love

The Cervantes memorial. A square full of people.

The fighters of the Republican Army pass by.

Narrator.

… But whatever may happen…

Command Líster speaks.

Legs, going down the street.

Narrator.

…however difficult it was to pack their belongings…

Panning shot from the legs of horses to the cavalry going by.

Narrator.

…they are Spaniards true to their oath and true to their vow.

The cavalry goes by.

Narrator.

New regiments are going into battle…

The regiments pass by.

Narrator.

Yes, that's what the People are all about!

Narrator.

The People of Catalunya were betrayed.

Everyone leaves: old men, mothers and children.

Narrator.

People will not remain where the Fascists tread.

Old men and women hurry past with their belongings.

Narrator.

They are leaving… They are leaving deep in grief.

Refugees pass by.

Narrator.

But the People are implacable.

A signpost at the French border.

At the border gendarmes search the belongings of the Spanish refugees.

Narrator.

What are the gendarmes to them?[306]

---

[306] [This version of the text differs from the finished film. Entry 1106 of the montazhny list for *Ispaniya* shows what is confirmed on the sound track. The version of *In Close-up* has… Что им жандармы! (What are the gendarmes to them!) In the film this is: …Что им, жандармам! (What are they to the gendarmes!").

And here is how a postscript to the film was realized:

…We see Ibárruri. She speaks.

Narrator.

Our land has been trampled upon in bestial fashion, a heavy moment has arrived. After the massacre of the Catalonian people, the foreign aggressors—Germans, Italians, Fascists—will return to Madrid. We will meet the blow! Rise up, Madrid!

Fighters going through the streets of Madrid.

Narrator.

Listen to the voice of Spain, the cry
of the heart stripped bare of these People.
This proud and freedom-loving people will not be reconciled to this…

Fighters on horseback with sabers bared.

Narrator.

…to colonial dependency, it will not bow down…

Fighters.

Narrator.

…The Great Spanish People…

Fighters.

Narrator.

…knew the sunny spring days…

A single fighter.

Narrator.

… sowed the earth for themselves…

A single fighter.

Narrator.

… The Spanish People were masters of their own factories…

A single fighter.

Narrator.

…The Spanish People were masters…

A single fighter.

Narrator.

… of their own destinies…

Fighters with rifles.

Narrator.

The Spanish People took up arms
and defeated their enemies…

Commander Líster salutes.

Narrator.

…A People such as this will never…

Fighters with raised fists.

Narrator.

…be defeated…

Troops pass by.

The People greet the fighters.

Narrator.

…Let traitors open the gates of Madrid to Franco…

Republican troops pass by. The People greet them. (Panning shot.) A Square with people.

Narrator.

Let our best comrades be shot, the Defeat is temporary. The struggle will continue…

Narrator.

…Relentless…

El Campesino speaks.[307]

Narrator.

…and implacable…

Commander Líster speaks.

Narrator.

…in secret and in the open, day and night…

Troops pass through the city.

…at every time and in every place…

Troops pass by.

Narrator.

…the People will not be reconciled, it will never go down on its knees!

A Spanish flag waving.

After the screening of *Spain*, Vsevolod Vishnevsky began at once to think about the work to follow. At once, I received a letter from Vishnevsky.

---

[307] [Trans.]: In the original: Командир Камесино [Kommandir Kamesino], likely another mistake for El Campesino (Spanish for "The Peasant"), the nom de guerre of Valentín González González.

27 April 1939

E. Shub
Moscow

Dear Esfir'

These days I have been thinking about our next new work. (A pity, that for a good ten years we didn't work together... That's so...)

I believe in *Spain*. It is tightly put together.

Further. The most essential, universal subject of the day has been aviation. In the attached proposal and letter to Mosfil'm, I state the reasons for this. They are connected with the very subject, we have both been thinking about...

If we work with concerted effort, from spring to fall, we will be able to create a decidedly universal film.

Consider it, think about it, and then answer. (I won't send the proposal and the letter to Mosfil'm yet.)

I gave my agreement. The desire to work with Vishnevsky dictated it. Aviation. This is not really my subject. But I knew, that Vishnevsky would help and provide enthusiasm. So, right then, he sent the letter and the proposal to Mosfil'm.

To:
Mosfil'm Studio
Comrade Director Polonsky
Head of the Scenario Department
Comrade Trauberg

Esteemed Comrades,

You have *Spain* in your hands. We need to go further...

It is necessary, in all senses, to energetically and quickly advance our production, in accordance with the decisions of the XVIIIth Party Congress and the directives of the Party and the Government.

At the meeting, the prospects for the country are extensively discussed... In particular, questions concerning aviation are touched upon extremely extensively.

International cinema, and Soviet cinema, up to now have been lacking in authentic films on the history of aviation. *Mankind has still not seen itself in the air, has not considered all the consequences of the "air revolution," which has been observed by us for the past 35 years.*

Film production in the Soviet Union is uniquely capable of giving answers to the questions at hand. This must be an historico-philosophical documentary film. It must be filled with facts, with documents of extreme acuity... It must all be directed forward, aloft—it must be poetically musical. (It will require the best composer.) This film will explain to people, what aviation means in the hands of mankind as it progresses... This film must be in every theater in order to propagandize the great strength of aviation in the USSR.

The project, which I am proposing, requires *the mobilization of all of our film collections* and the purchase of some (newsreel) material abroad. The expense will not be great. The film will repay the expense a thousandfold.

I request that you promptly consider my proposal. And that we start on the project.

With Communist greetings,

Vs. Vishnevsky.

To this was attached an interesting proposal. It didn't go through. Here's the telegram I received after this from Leningrad:

GREETINGS THOUGH BITTER I AM GETTING OVER IT THIS IS A SUBJECT MORE IMPORTANT THAN PERSONAL PRIDE I MADE SUCH A GREAT WORK WITH YOU WISH YOU SUCCESS AND TIME OFF WARM GREETINGS VSEVOLOD

What brought us closer? Why did we seek to work together again? How did our points of view coincide about the art of cinema and the documentary film?

We considered, that the fundamental subject of the art of cinema should be the contemporary, that in the work of the writer and the director, their sense of well-being, and as well, *the relationship to it in consulting on the scenario*, play no small role.[308]

We considered, that an unrestrained field of action for the writer and director was necessary. Greater trust in the creative designs of people who are working together.

Vishnevsky considered, that writers didn't give a tenth of what they could give. He blamed the scenario departments for this, considering that they conducted themselves bureaucratically.

---

[308] [Trans.]: In the original: Мы считали, что основной темой искусства кино должна быть современность, что в работе писателя и режиссера, их самочувствие, а также о т н о ш е н и е к н и м с ц е н а р н о г о с о в е т а играют немаловажную роль.

And it seemed to me, that contemporary subjects still didn't get approved, because in the studios, the relationship to the film was determined by the cost estimates. For this reason, historical films, the ones costing a great deal, were considered suitable for the most responsible individuals, but films on contemporary subjects were allowed to be shot, for the most part, by young people. What did this lead to? It would seem, that this is where young people would need help. To afford the best opportunity of expressing this subject, you allow the best authors to do it. But this was not the case. The director with the "important" historical subject received all the best resources. This doesn't mean, that there weren't any good films on contemporary subjects, but they should have been a lot better.

With documentary films, the matter became both simpler and more complicated.

The view that documentary film does not require special attention, the freedom to experiment, was false. The talent of the director, the camera operator, the equipment with which they work, sound recording are all so important and such things should be taken into account, as in any other field of artistic[309] labor. What a struggle I had, in order to have Vishnevsky read the voice-over text and for the composer Gavriil Popov to write the music. In spite of this, at the last minute, having Vishnevsky as the reader of the voice-over had to be abandoned and Levitan was recorded.

And for a documentary film, you need a scenario. The subject must be current and pointed. This is necessary, in order to give credibility to the author and to the director, just as in the scenario, it is necessary to strive to give a picture of life in all its complexity and contradictions. The surface "gloss" added to several of our documentary films did not please us.

At the same time, no matter how your treat a contemporary subject—whether in a tragic vein, or an optimistic one—you must reveal it, so that there's the feeling of a new world, of its beauty, of its richness, of its complexity. Too often we avoid disputes, do not freely express our opinions on the work of our comrades, are afraid to fight, to argue, even when this is necessary.

How strange it is, that the first years of the Revolution are better recorded, for example, than the first Five-Year Plans. Why did this happen? Because during the initial period of the Revolution, large-scale documentary films were shot according to plans and a lot of prints were made, so that a lot of material was accumulated. Afterwards, they began to shoot short subjects of 30 meters and the accumulation of historical, chronicle-type material was reduced.

Often in the art of cinema, the production scheduling system cannot be justified, when the writer and director are faced with a subject assigned in advance. At the same time, the individual experience of a collaborating writer and director, their interest in

---

[309] [Trans.]: Here, "artistic" has a double meaning, as it refers in a general sense to work in the arts, but also, in particular, to feature-length fiction films.

a given contemporary subject, their finding of a pointed approach to a given subject, it seems to us, should come first.

It is necessary to change the attitudes towards artists, towards people, so that they can fully develop. This is what Eisenstein and Dovzhenko and many other comrades have thought about this.

Life is full of contradictions and diversity and it became our habit to repeat accepted techniques. And the result was as if we were listening to ready-made quotations repeated over and over. Visual material became illustrative of those quotations.

To be utterly truthful, one must say, that in the case of dull, uninteresting films, as a rule, it is the screenwriter and the director who are at fault. They consider it a waste of time to argue, to fight for their point of view, giving in to the editors of scenario departments by following the customary paths.

A difficult passage began in the life of Vishnevsky. His scenario "We, the Russian People," which Eisenstein very much wanted to direct, never went into production. Eisenstein subsequently headed for Central Asia. He and Pavlenko were preparing for production of a film about Fergana.

Shooting never got started on *The First Horse*.

Here is a letter from Vishnevsky from this period:

March 13, 1941

To E. Shub

Greetings Esfir',

We received your letter this morning… —Shklovsky came by again yesterday, he has grown thin, nervous, frequently exclaiming "There you go…" giving messages from Koslovodsk, jumping from one topic to the other: Kurbsky, Ivan the Terrible, Pudovkin and so on. Then promptly, catching the sound of his wife's footsteps, he darted off to her.

About us… Unendingly stressful, Moscow life goes on. Dzigan and I were summoned by the Committee. My changes were all accepted. "Start shooting immediately." Government order: "It will be on theater screens the First of May." We need to finish shooting and do retakes; as much as 1,000 to 1,200 meters. A month and a half of work at a breakneck pace…

I'm glad that I wrote everything necessary this past winter—1,500 meters almost from scratch, half of the thing. The encroachment of the war, a series of changes, and so on—painful difficulties in shooting (two rainy summers, withdrawals by the army, and so on) all affected the work.

In life there are difficulties… they have to be overcome. We hope we can finish up by May 1.

It's a pity, that everything now is trending more strongly towards the conveyorbeltization of the cinema. A stream of identical objects, based on identical decisions.

I saw *Maria Stuart*[310] at the Theater of the Revolution. It's monumental, a bit heavy-going… A lot of gold, a lot of glitter… Glizer[311] in places is quite strong, good. The others are weaker. But the sensation of an event taking place, is, unfortunately, not there… —For a long time a performance, which is *really* a noteworthy event in the theater,[312] has been lacking.

For Muffin[313] the victories are in the Children's Theater: *Twenty Years Later* (M. Svetlov[314]) is having a good run.

What else?… In our exalted literary circles, there is only silence.[315] There are rare meetings, in which rather unnecessary questions are resolved.

Eisen[stein] is rushing around the studio. He says, that he's not succeeding in understanding the material on Ivan the Terrible as he should. The subject is undoubtedly vast, Shakespearean… It needs to be resolved on the plane of historical tragedy. And simply having spirited battles at Livonian castles, we will admit to ourselves, is not really so new and fresh… We will hope that solutions can be found.

Eisen[stein] has been meeting about the *Horse* movie, snorting, and livening up from time to time, elegantly pointing with his little fingers to certain little pictures on a table, and speaking about the necessities of making nuanced decisions concerning montage… Who would dispute that…

All the same, when unconnected from all business matters, at times when you see Eisen[stein]—his paunch, and forehead, and little eyes—he seems fine. Well, in a word, just like you do, I see at times, that you in

---

[310] [Trans.]: *Maria Stuart* is a play written by Schiller and first staged in 1800.

[311] [Trans.]: Yudif' Samoilovna Glizer (1904–1968). Soviet stage and screen actress, made a People's Artist of the RSFSR in 1954.

[312] [Trans.]: In the original: спектакля-события.

[313] [Trans.]: In the original: Мася [Masya]. As Anton Vidokle informs me, this is a term of endearment, like sweetie, honey, et al., though it can also be a diminutive form of Мария [Mariya]. In this case, I believe he is referring to his wife, Sof'ya Kas'yanovna Vishnevetskaya, a set designer, painter, and writer, with whom Shub was close.

[314] [Trans.]: Mikhail Arkad'evich Svetlov (born Sheinkman) (1903–1964). Poet, playwright, journalist. Awarded the Lenin Prize in 1967 posthumously.

[315] [Trans.]: In the original: В литературных палестинах тишина, literally, "in literary palestines silence." For the history of this reference to Palestines in Russian, see: https://www.genon.ru/GetAnswer.aspx?qid=bb00948b-7ee9-4fc4-9700-09d32e02ae27. I owe the decipherment of this reference to Masha Godovannaya, Matvei Yankelevich, and Professor Polina Barskova.

Kislovodsk hear and see everything, and participate in these dramas and comedies of our lives.—That's all for now…

—Vsevolod

I was spending a few days in Kislovodsk, when I received an urgent call to return to Moscow; they proposed, that Vishnevsky and I make a film on Bessarabia.

We left immediately: Vishnevsky, Tissé, and I.

With Vishnevsky was his wife, the artist Vishnevetskaya.

And there began our thorough, attentive, and interested acquaintance with Bessarabia. We reached Soviet Moldava and drove on towards the Desna. The opposite bank was drowning in apple blossoms. A bridge had been built to the ancient fortress of Bendery. We drove all over Bessarabia, through burning sun, through dust, through endless fields of corn.

Early in the morning we would seat ourselves in the car, stopping only to eat. And went on that way until evening.

Vishnevsky kept silent in the car, keen-sighted, attentive. A short cue: "Esfir', pay attention to that…" and again, silence and attentive observation.

In Kishinev, we looked over all the Pushkin sites. The tiny hut where he lived. We stood before the Pushkin monument.

"Here, with lyre sounding, the Northern desert, did I wander…"[316]

Shortly before our arrival, at this monument stood, with head uncovered, Feodor Chaliapin.

What was he thinking about? Close by was the homeland. How painful… The homeland was close by.

We drove to Agievsky Monastery. We were met by monks with red ribbons on their cassocks. The abbot of the monastery, who was White Guard High Society, ran off, having seized the treasures of the monastery. He stole the ikons.

Pushkin visited these places. The Gypsies, celebrated by Pushkin, live here. A lot of them. They surrounded our car. Time had touched them little—they were the same as they were in Pushkin's time.

We drove through villages with mud-thatched huts, recalling places in distant Asia—the home of the Arabs. We drove through Bulgarian villages. On the necks of the Bulgarian women jingled necklaces of gold coins. We passed entire displaced villages of German farmers.

They brought to mind a single small town. We arrived there in the evening. Narrow little streets. Tiny little houses titling sideways. Tiny lighted shop windows. Signs, depicting what could be bought there. And people…

---

[316] [Trans.]: A line from Pushkin's poem "К Овидию" ("To Ovid"). Pushkin composed his poem in exile, in the same place where Ovid had been exiled.

Chagall, pure Chagall. It was them, these Jews, these signs, that the remarkable artist painted on the walls of the Jewish Theater in Moscow. He didn't make up any of it. We were so charmed, we didn't want to leave.

We visited the homeland of the legendary hero Kotovsky.[317]

We stayed a few days in Izmail. We spent many hours in fortresses, places, which were the glory of Russia.

We drove to Vilkovo, the Russian Venice, to the mouth the Danube.

On the canals is a city on pilings. Boatmen glide along the canals. Here and there, little tiny bridges are thrown across the canal; they serve as places to cross from one sidewalk to another. There is lots of greenery and trees.

In Vilkovo live Russian fisherman. Strong, stately, beautiful people. The fisher-women are especially beautiful. I saw some real Russian beauties.

An amazing sight is the departure of the fishermen to catch sturgeons. Their return with their catch, huge sturgeons, is exciting. The loading of fresh caviar into barrels.

There is no other landscape like the road to Vilkovo. Primeval nature. Knolls that resemble dunes. Greenery, trees, shrubbery, exciting one's fancy. Deep, burning, golden sand. A dream within a dream. And everywhere, huge storks standing motionless on one leg, unintimidated by cars.

The scent of the burning sun, of the greenery, of the burning sand, and of the coolness of the waves of the sea, coming from somewhere.

Our encounter with the Danube was beautiful. We went out on a small speedboat. The Danube is truly a blue beauty. Wide, deep, festive. A dome of dark blue sky lighting up the water with golden sparks.

Opposite us: the Romanian shore. Businesslike; everything on docks. From there, boats left uninterruptedly with citizens who had been detained. In exchange, we send Romanians from our shore. It is noisy, disorderly, merry. It never comes into anyone's head, that we are on the eve of Hitler's great treachery.

Still further in the distance, the shores of Bulgaria and Yugoslavia appear in rugged outline.

In the center is the "no-man's" river. Ships of all nations proceed, giving friendly salutes as they encounter one another.

We land on our shore in order to have a look at the monument to Count Rumyantsev.

It appears we are alone. No, previously unnoticed by us, a border guard appears.

We are having fun. We joke with the skipper of the boat, sing songs, and return only very late in the evening to Izmail.

Where didn't we spend the night! Under the open sky, often we slept on floors, and once we spent the night in a hotel, which had earlier been a house of ill-repute.

---

[317] [Trans.]: Grigory Ivanovich Kotovsky, a bank robber turned military hero of the Russian Civil War.

On the walls of the room, hung very detailed tables of rates for services involving the human body.

Soon we are in Chernovitsy.

Vsevolod Vishnevsky reads us his scenario.[318] We go to Moscow to get it approved, so we can immediately return to get to work on it. Here are some of the tasks Vishnevsky set for himself, while working on the scenario:

The theme of Bessarabia is its people. The history of this people must be told in its entirety: literally from the Paleolithic period until the present day. This is no exaggeration. These natural tendencies, along with Soviet Science and Art, to once again reveal to this people its own proper power and its glories.

The Carpathians, Bessarabia, the Danube. The Balkans…

These are the historical paths of Slavic Peoples towards the deep blue waters of the Mediterranean.

The film must be constructed with a lofty summons to struggle, the poetry of the roar of battle and of the tranquil sun, the corrosive salt of the sea, the dust of the steppes, where the ashes lie of the ancestors so precious to us. They have given us many precepts.

We had no doubt about our success.

But we had no success in realizing this scenario.

All the labors of Vishnevsky, his utter determination to finish writing the scenario in the shortest possible time, his search for new means of expression, his vast imagination, his emotional sensitivity, his fervent efforts to engage with E. Tissé and I through his scenario, all proved futile.

There are times in the lives of great and talented people, when what they especially value, does not fall into their hands. And so it was with Vishnevsky.

I would often go and visit him; in fact, nearly every day. After lunch, Vishnevetskaya would arrange for us to meet privately.

What did he talk to me about? He read a lot, he followed literature and politics. He had an excellent appreciation of the international situation. He anticipated the inevitability of the struggle with Fascism, and the inevitability of war. And was ready. He was a warrior. At that time, it seemed to me, that his things were already packed, that he would not delay even a minute and when the hour came, when war would break out, he would be on his way immediately. And so it happened.

He had a prodigious memory. He could quote pages of prose. He quoted the works of V. I. Lenin, as if he had met with him an hour earlier and were transmitting the words he had spoken in conversation.

This came to have powerful implications. It was troubling.

---

[318] [Russian editor's note]: The scenario *Bessarabia* was not realized. It is preserved in the personal archive of E. Shub.

For May Day celebrations and on the Eve of October, we would gather at the Vishnevskys'. Gorodovikov and Papanin would come, sailors from the Baltic Fleet, Johann Al'tman—a friend of Vishnevsky's and a man of the purest and most lofty sentiments as a communist—Eisenstein, Dovzhenko, Dzigan, Shklovsky, Kataev, Tairov, Koonen and many others.

Vishnevsky would keep quiet, he would listen attentively to everyone, with eyes screwed up in a kindly way, laughed heartily, if there was a reason to do so. He would dance. So it was hard to imagine, while observing him, that the quiet Vishnevsky, possessed such great strength as an orator from the tribune.

But this talent of his was particular. He would begin to speak, hardly parting the lips of his great, strong, sculpted mouth. His face was peaceful. His voice quiet. And suddenly, a break. He would gaze with his eyes opened-wide at those listening and strike them in the heart with his powerful words. His voice would acquire a many-sided, emotional power. An orator makes sense of events, makes demands, makes a summons to action.

I would like to offer two texts related to Vishnevsky and Mayakovsky. They concern the beginning of the Great Patriotic War and establish just how close were Vishnevsky and the poet to contemporary events.

July 9, 1941

…Yesterday at TASS, I was reading the first volume of Mayakovsky (1912–1921). I read a number of things for the first time. Some sharp impressions came to me: here were the thoughts, the beliefs, the zeal of the era of our revolution, youth—passion, illusions—high points… Now the situation is completely different and I cannot find in the book the needed, the applicable citations. Mayakovsky takes down the *Entente*, Wilson, England. Everything is ripped apart into bloody pieces with the cries of the struggle *within* the country. Everything is tense, hyperbolic. I read a number of things twice. This is already history…

The new poets are noticeably weaker.

The Mayakovsky Tradition is the tradition of active participation in the defense of the Motherland. Whatever Mayakovsky did, he always said, that he was indebted to the Red Army. We have always emphasized this debt and will continue to emphasize it. This is one of the directives of the Mayakovsky line.

Two letters from Leningrad under siege tell Vishnevsky's story better than I could.

Evening, May 1, 1942.
To: E. Shub
S. Eisenstein
E. Dzigan and Yesipova
Roshal' and V. Stroeva
and all our friends in the cinema

Greetings, friends, comrades,

It is now the evening of the First of May... There are two of us
here... Out goes the electricity. I turn on the storage battery, there is a
lamp the size of a matchhead... From the country, from the "mainland"
come gifts: English bitters (of domestic production), crackers, and other
things.... A sunny day with furious bombardments is over... Stalin's
order was read and understood: forward, *fight 'til the finish, 'til victory*.

Yesterday, A. Fadeev and N. Tikhonov spent the whole day with
us. They are wrapped in air of Moscow. We showed them our broken
glass, etc.

Sasha said to me: "Carabanchel"[319]... We remembered Madrid in
1937, I remembered you, Esfir', my friend, our difficult rebellious life,
I remembered Efim and Raisa, *We Are from Kronstadt*, and the dear
Roshal's, all the pangs of joy, the recognition and repudiation of
Eisen[stein], and on top of all that, above our heads a squall is raging.
Sof'ya Kas'yanovna and I are happy and proud that we are here... No one
knows what to say about Leningrad: may strength be sufficient, may my
soul be sufficient, my diaries and my strength, the diaries of my comrades,
in order to say...

In a letter I refuse to relate this naked, holy, pure epic... People
removed ice and snow by hand and cleaned up the layers of mud and
towards May they defeated the Germans once again...

They thought they could take us by storm—with tanks and planes.
We beat them back. They thought they could take us through hunger,
through the blockade. We stood firm, we beat them back... They calculated
the frosts (40–45°) would cause starvation, the Commune system would
come to a halt. We improved it. We stood firm. We beat them back... They
calculated (O, these "planners" from Berlin!), that, in Spring, we would die
in the mud... —We cleaned up all of that ahead of schedule—If you could
see these masses of people, tenacious to the limit and beyond all limits...

---

[319] [Trans.]: Carabanchel, a southwestern suburb of Madrid, witnessed bloody street battles during the
Spanish Civil War, with the Republicans enjoying the upper hand.

And women are in the forefront. People have been hardened phenomenally—now *nothing* can break them… Yes, the city has stood up to more, than anyone else in the world…

We emerged from the ice age towards the First of May… When they heard the screech of the first tram, people were stunned. Life. The grass was laid bare, the witness of the autumn, the witness of the combat, in which, *for the first time*, Hitler was stopped. Leningrad *stands* powerful, gray, beautiful… At night you hear the pounding of the machine guns; they are powerless against the granite and the soul of this great city…

Starting the 10th of April, the Germans began massive air strikes. The city picked off 30% to 40% of them right away and the Germans got quiet…

We see a lot… a little half-pint nine-year-old kid comes up to me: "I've been collecting money all winter, for dad, to welcome dad[320]… The Fascists killed dad, take the money, my piggy bank, for a loan… and teach me proper how to shoot."

A woman comes along, an invalid, 17 years old. It's impossible for her to work. She needs work. She's on her knees, because she can't stand on her legs, and on her knees she begins working: getting rid of trash, cleaning up the city… (the backdrop of air raids and artillery don't even figure in).

I went to the Vyborg Side, in order to continue with a tradition broken off by some comrades… A lively public meeting… In the Komsomol organizations, there is no longer anyone who knows how to go about it, they are all in the trenches… A speech about struggle is going on, then, at the table of the presidium, spontaneous enlistment in the Komsomol, that is, into the ranks of activists, into new regiments.

The Vyborg District does a great deal and, perhaps, in 1943, these guys will be crowned with a Nobel Prize in chemistry, or something of the sort…

Muffin and I are happy. We are seeing the innermost core of the highest point in the history of the People… Over the years, my hand had begun to twitch when I was writing; here, I have overcome that and I can write, speak, organize, work endlessly. Where necessary…

Sometimes, I miss the experience of friends, of chatter, of arguments, of turbulence, "news" from our art world… Well, what can you do? We will try to bring everyone together for the First of May in 1943, so we can discuss different topics, plans, travels, delegations…

---

[320] [Trans.]: Masha Godovannaya explains, that the child is imagining giving his dad a hero's welcome.

A flight of the soul, of thought does not close down, even for a
minute, the unrelenting searches, the tragic aspect of life... it affirms
that tragedy is optimistic... And when the theaters go to the trenches
(Comrade Brodansky continues resolutely with "outreach") the Leningrad Dramatic [Theater] and the Baltic Fleet [Theater] perform my plays,
and today—the First of May—Moscow is presenting my literary texts,
I realize: this is right: we must continue, unrelenting and move towards
victory... The idea is raging in my head, a second series of *We Are from
Kronstadt* at the scale of total war. And if light prevents it (darkness, that
is) and so on... we will bring them to submission... —Work, friends! ...
Our People is great, holy, almighty. Vast distances lie ahead.

The Leningrad Soviet Writers Union continues with their periodic
spoken and literary collections and they are often beautiful, in form and
rhythm, when the speaker says: "No bombs! (a bomb explodes) will stop
us and the living word (a bomb explodes) will resound in answer to the
enemy all the louder in the city of Lenin."

Once in a while, we receive news from the Fronts and from
Moscow...

Life will return to its normal course, we should shoot a film with
Efisha on Adolf's tomb, then have a look at a fountain in Rome... —
Then—I will tell the story of Leningrad to the USA...

For Eisen[stein] it will be enough to be closer to the everyday life
of the People—than, for example, to the Thirteenth or Sixteenth Century,
about which I have often spoken to him—so that he will reach the People,
perhaps he will go into the mud, the concrete, the blood of events—albeit
a bit "later"—and to his theories, he will bring all the corrections of our
powerful practice.

Esfir', I wish you happiness—I think, that the two of us will once
again record, embracing[321] the world together from different points
of view and with different instruments, and better than it was with
"Spain"... I have not yet had time to argue with Roshal' and Verochka, so
they can recognize, damn it, that I am right.

Salud, Vs. Vishnevsky[322]

---

[321] [Trans.]: In the original: обснимем, a portmanteau word combining снять (to shoot film) and
обнять (to embrace).

[322] [Russian editor's note]: A letter from Vs. Vishnevsky on May 1, 1942, written on the letterhead of
the Political Administration of the KBF, that is, the Краснознаменный Балтийский флот [Kras-
noznamenny Baltysky flot] (Redbanner Baltic Fleet)], the director of the operational group of writers.
It is addressed to "All friends in the cinema" in Alma-Ata. Preserved in the personal archive of
E. Shub.

August 4, 1942
E. Shub
Film Committee of the SPC of the USSR[323]

Dear Esfir'!
 I received your bundle of letters: both the Alma-Ata letter and the
Moscow letter of Vera Stroeva.

The sound of the Newsreel has been frightening to me: I am almost
allergic to the movies. I have been working like a wild beast (on "Leningrad under siege"). Based on the pattern, you can recognize the fleet and
the blockade, the German prisoners, and crosses ad infinitum and so on
and so on… All, by the way, based on my plan for the montage. I sat in
the studio and its broken down shack for days and nights… And after
that, the usual "flow" of film production: guest performers, etc.

But a great theme does not even allow one to have a conversation
about these rules, about this "practice"… Just so the film works—that's
absolutely the main thing. We'll leave the rest for after the war…

There are things that leave their mark on the rest of one's life…

…And in Leningrad, nameless cameramen stoically labor on… You
would see them in winter, in the studio on Krestovsky, when I would
have the initial conversations with them about shooting…

August 21st of this year, as we were defending Leningrad…

At such times, there are such upsurges of spirit and strength, that
you surprise yourself. I am writing by hand (before the war, my hand
would twitch, I couldn't write much, so I dictated), I'm writing three
times more than I did before the war… As a kind of creative report, I am
attaching the letter of a wounded fighter to me. (An excerpt of the fighter's letter is printed below.—E. Shub.)

The city has been tempered; it seems that nothing can any longer
surprise or frighten us… All has already been tested again and again…
The evolution of spirit, of nerves over the course of the year is most
astonishing… I have been keeping a diary since the beginning of the war
and these ten thick notebooks and I have been inseparable. They have
been everywhere… —I think this is the best thing I have ever written.

Leningrad is now full of energy. We are striving to help the South
and are doing what needs to be done… The other day, after some big
attacks, German prisoners were led around the city… Ragged, broken,
filthy… Women nearly tore these fellows to pieces, the guards had a hard
time of it.

---

[323] [Trans.]: Soviet of People's Commissars of the USSR.

The city stands united: it performs incredible labors… O, if only there were more camera operators and directors, to record this great feat of a city at war, of a Commune!

The rains have come, autumn is drawing near… —and so, we will meet another winter…

I think: there are 28 countries in the coalition. And Russia is fighting *alone*. Well, we will not be afraid, we will give it all our strength… Let the world see up close just what Russia is made of. But we will have the last word…

The cannon fire is raging once again… Gray, watery sludge. Leningrad is attacking the enemy.

Write. We will shoot a few shots, but I don't know how it will come out. Here you have to take the Eyemo camera around with you… Hugs,

Vs Vishnevsky

Greetings from Leningrad. Remember it. That's the fighter's motto…

Comrade Commissar Vishnevsky…

You, Comrade Commissar, have really deserved the thoughts of our Bolshevik Party.[324]

Comrade Vishnevsky, I ask you to read this my illiterate letter. Here's what forced me to write. I am located in a hospital and so I have only been able to hear your reports on the Radio and you only have to hear that Comrade Vishnevsky is going to broadcast, and right then, it's as if the pain is gone, and things get easy and good. All at once they yell: "Quiet down, comrades, it's the broadcast of Baltic Commissar Vishnevsky." Well, you don't reach everyone in their heart, but all the same, it's evident, from the silence and from the attention, how they listen so attentively and joyfully, that your talent raises the spirits of all the fighters…

…When I hear you speaking, I want to get out of the hospital all the sooner and help, however I can, as soon as possible to crush those miserable parasites… including that parasite Hitler…

…Goodbye, I want, only what you want, Comrade Commissar. I will anxiously await Your report. With greetings to You.

Senior Sergeant Prokofiev.[325]

---

324 [Trans.]: In the original: Вы, тов. Комиссар, действительно заслужили при нашей партии большевиков, чтобы о Вас думать. This sounds just as awkward in Russian as it does in English.

325 [Trans.]: My collaborator Masha Godovannaya suggests this might be a prank typical of this group of

After the war, I did not see Vishnevsky so often. But he often and unexpectedly would come see me at the Studio for Documentary Films and would call me down to have a chat in the lobby.

He would even come to my home. But these were sad meetings.

Already ill myself, the last time I came to see the great Vishnevsky was in Barvikha, where he lay ill.

I brought him lots of flowers. Like a child, he threw himself upon me and joyfully clutched the flowers to him. He could not speak. I tried to tell him everything, that might interest him.

He left us. He left us early, the dear and splendid comrade.

His memory is precious to me.

Documentary Film: Matters and People

To write about the outstanding people of an art, about one's exhilarating contemporaries is exciting. Especially about those, who astonished one with their sincere beauty, their talent, their human kindness, their boldness, their sense of self-respect, their originality. This they taught me to understand: that one must approach an art with incorruptible discernment and passionate love.

The most important close-up in my life took place in my work in documentary film. I consciously gave years of my life to *documentary* film. This work became its principal content. And how much this work gave to me! Not for a minute did I regret, that I chose this specialty and did not take up work in the theater, literature, in acted cinema.[326] The administration of film production, when I achieved the rank of director, insisted that I direct acted films.[327] I cannot say, that I engaged in newsreel films because they considered me inadequately prepared to direct a dramatic film with actors.[328] No, I chose this path by myself.

The path of my generation to work in the cinema had no connection with advanced cinema education. Essentially, there was none to be had anywhere.

For this reason, my universities were different: the editing table, camera operators, directors of feature-length films with actors, and *Dziga Vertov*. With time, we departed further and further from each other. We argued a lot and intensely. I recognized his talent and carried on a principled struggle with him, speaking out against the

---

people. In this case, the composer Prokofiev pretending to be a semi-literate soldier praising Vishnevsky.

[326] [Trans.]: In the original: игровое кино: i.e. fiction cinema.

[327] [Trans.]: In the original: игровые фильмы: i.e. fiction films.

[328] [Trans.]: In the original: игровый актерский фильм. Somewhat pleonastic: acted actor film.

manifestos of the "kinoks," as Vertov's group called themselves. I did not accept his repudiation of working according to a scenario.

I have already written about how much I was taught by the camera operators E. Tissé and A. Levitsky. The camera operator-documentarians deserve a book to be written about them. The creative biographies of other camera operators—Karmen,[329] Bobrov,[330] Efimov,[331] Levitan,[332] and others—for example, deserve full individual monographs. I regret my inability to undertake this.

We know that in every kind of art form, the authentic mastery of an artist may eloquently resound not only in monumental productions and large canvases, but in a miniature, and in a sketch, and in a short musical impromptu-étude, and in a play, and in a short story. And in many productions, right beside the principal hero, acting roles are depicted—often with the same artistic force—which emerge for a short time and leave the production, never to return.

In the cinema, the main thing is the ability to succinctly create images of people. The artist who possesses this ability is, undoubtedly, a talented artist. This is characteristic of the director and the camera operator, not only of acted[333] cinema, but of the documentary cinema as well.

Work in the documentary cinema, moving it forward, requires talented people, innovators.

There was a time when there were arguments about the roles of the camera operator and the director in documentary cinema. These arguments go on even now. It seems to me, that these are empty conversations. In my view, it depends on the director and it depends on the camera operator… I know quite well, that a talented director in contemporary documentary cinema is always considered to be working with the camera operator, leaves him free to exercise his initiative. Such a director does

---

[329] [Russian editor's note]: *Karmen, Roman Lazarevich* (b.1906). Cinema director and camera operator in documentary cinema. People's Artist of the USSR. His best known works: *Spain* (camera operator), *China in the Fight, Judgment of the Peoples, A Day in Soviet Russia* [*A Day of the New World*], *Berlin, The Caspian Story* [*The Story of the Oilmen of the Caspian*], *Blazing Island, The Great Patriotic War, Comrade Berlin.*

[330] [Russian editor's note]: *Bobrov, Georgy Makarovich* (b.1905). Camera operator and director. He shot the feature films *Prosperity, Life is Beautiful* [*A Simple Case*], *Broken Shoes* and others. He worked in newsreels. His footage became part of a series of documentaries on the Great Patriotic War (*Moscow Strikes Back* and others).

[331] [Russian editor's note]: *Efimov, Evgeny Ivanovich* (b.1908). Camera operator. He shot the film *If War Comes Tomorrow* and others.

[332] [Russian editor's note]: *Levitan, Arkady Yulianovich* (b.1911). Camera operator. He participated in the making of the documentary films *A Day in Soviet Russia* [*A Day of the New World*], *The Caucasus* [*The Battle for the Caucasus*], *The Fall of Berlin* [*The Battle for Berlin*], *Bulgaria, Defending Peace, Pushkin, Mayakovsky* and others.

[333] [Trans.]: In the original: игровое кино, i.e. fiction cinema.

not pretend to be the commander, but listens to the camera operator's advice. In cases such as those, creative collaboration is born.

A no-talent director finds it indispensable to "instruct" the camera operator, even though he himself is completely helpless when it comes to shooting, or at best clichéd. And to be fair, one has to say that our camera operators are well-mannered. In this regard, they act respectfully, they listen attentively, although they know perfectly well, that shooting does not at all proceed according to such instructions.

As far as newsreels are concerned, there, the success in filming a subject, as a rule, depends upon the camera operator, especially when the shoot has the character of an on-the-spot report. Not, on discussions at the time of the shoot.

One valuable quality distinguishes the majority of camera operators for documentary films. I loved the daily screenings of subjects for *Novosti dnya* (*News of the Day*) and of the rushes for feature-length films.[334] During the post-screening discussions, the camera operators would listen attentively, without resentment, to often extremely severe criticism. With directors, it isn't possible to speak this way: arguments would start and resentment. This ability of camera operators of documentary cinema to handle criticism and to emotionally, joyfully, openly accept praise taught me a great deal. This compelled me to respect the entire collective of camera operators and to want to seek out good comrades among them. This is the most joyous memory remaining for me of the Studio of Documentary Films.

I will now briefly describe one of the camera operators who set in motion an innovative attitude towards his work.

Mikhail Kaufman—a student of Vertov—at present, a director at the Educational Film Studio. What a huge force was this camera operator! Because of the leftist phrase "kinoks," which obscured his originality, it was not immediately recognized, nor did he himself recognize, where his strength was. But his strength was in filming people, in the ability to give them memorable characteristics. He filmed people of various ages and of various social strata. Everything that they did within the frame: adults, the old, and children, the expression of their eyes, the movement of their hands, smiles, tears, the way they worked—all this helped one to understand them, to remember them. Kaufman's medium shots and close-ups were beautiful. For the first time, such strikingly filmed people appeared in newsreels. Not the "kino-eye" but Kaufman's eye, his ability to make use of the lens of the movie camera determined this success.

Mobility, I would even say, dynamism, a well-known risk when shooting, distinguishes the work of Kaufman, an artist-camera operator of global stature. With a particular individuality, he beautifully filmed nature and urban and industrial environments, kolkhozes and sovkhozes, snow and rain, frost and wind, but most remarkable of all were his shots of people. What Kaufman began has been picked up—like the baton in a

---

[334] [Trans.]: In the original: снятого материала для больших фильмов. Literally: the material shot for big films.

relay race—by the camera operators of our documentary cinema; it has given them much for the development of this skill. And not only our camera operators.

Just as with Kaufman, I am close to my creative work, which unites us with the social-political activity of *Joris Ivens*.[335]

He came to us from the West quite young; he came from a country, which in those years, did not have its own film industry—from Holland.

He wanted to learn our attitude towards a few reels of film he had brought with him, but the main thing was, to draw close to the revolutionary film industry of the Land of the Soviets, unique in the entire world.

Already his first films confirmed that he was a principled worker in *documentary* film.

He brought us films which were, for the most part, on themes of construction: *Zuidersee* (four reels), *Pile Diving* (one reel), *The Bridge* (one reel) and one film étude, *Rain*. It might seem like very little. But no. These were works speaking to the obvious talent of the young Ivens.

He shot with a "Kinamo" and showed a great level of achievement in the work of a camera operator. The "Kinamo" in his hands proved to be a perfect film camera for that time. His framing was expressive and lively, no trickery, no beauty for the joy of beauty. His shots recalled those of Mikhail Kaufman, but were distinguished by greater austerity.

As the author-director of his films, he took pleasure in the selection of the proper lens for a shot. Nature, technological environments, work processes, and primarily people, their behavior—everything was selected expressively and sensitively. The handling of the montage of the shots—especially in the film étude *Rain*—was complicated, but at the same time, it was not formalism, as some thought at the time—no. The perception of the action gave a lively feeling of genuine and not "cinefied"[336] life.

Of course, his first works did not distinguish themselves in the social meaningfulness, which inheres in Soviet documentary films, but we believed that this would come to Joris Ivens and he has justified our confidence in his most recent works.

His films about Magnitka,[337] Spain, and China, about the congress of pacifists in Poland, and his most recent film, which, unfortunately I have not had the opportunity to see, have brought him universal recognition. His public actions gladden me and my hand is forever extended to him in comradeship.

---

[335] [Russian editor's note]: *Joris Ivens* (b. 1898, Holland). Director of documentary cinema. He has worked in many countries of the world. He directed the films *The Bridge, Rain, Song of Heroes* (about Magnitogorsk in collaboration with Soviet filmmakers), *Borinage, The Spanish Earth* (based on a scenario by Hemingway), *The 400 Million, Indonesia Calling, Peace Will Win, Friendship Triumphs* (in collaboration with I. Pyr'ev), *The Seine meets Paris, Pueblo en armas*, etc.

[336] [Trans.]: In the original: «кинофицированной».

[337] [Trans.]: The familiar name for the Magnitogorsk ironworks, the subject of his film *Song of Heroes*, aka *Komsomol*, aka *Youth Speaks*.

The significance of documentary film is now recognized by all. It was born in the Soviet Union. Nowhere else, but among us, could it arise. This was recognized by directors in the West and in America. What events of Soviet life shot on film during the first years of the revolution did a viewer see? He saw the exciting events of the era of the Civil War and the first years of Socialist Construction, new working conditions, the empowerment of women, festive days of celebration, the formidable statements of the masses protesting against internal enemies, against International Counter-revolution. Those contemporaries of these events appeared on the screen, real Soviet people, and this was the most exciting thing.

Unfortunately, we shot very little of the great V. I. Lenin and his associates. All the same, there are shots, which keep his image alive for future generations.

We, the first directors of documentary films, strove to give our films the form of completed works. The innovative character of this is now clear to me, as are the mistakes we committed.

The very nature of our work, the tasks and the goals, which stand before us, require of us comprehensive knowledge and the correct understanding of our reality. We must know everything, because the strengths of documentation lie not only in filming vital facts, but in the choice of events, in the ability to select what is capable of captivating and moving the spectator and his understanding by means of what is filmed. This labor is not fundamentally distinct from the labor of the painter, or the musician, who selects from among a variety of sounds, or colors of paint, precisely one instead of another.

A documentary film must be a completed work. The material filmed must give the director the possibility of choosing precisely those shots, which in montage can be elevated to the generalization of a fact recorded in them. To give not only the events of our time, but also the living images of people. The living images of the Soviet Peoples is what is most important and exciting.

It is now, no longer necessary to prove that documentary film—either historical or contemporary—is an artistic phenomenon, a phenomenon of art. However, not all of us have learned how to film one of our contemporaries in a new way, though only this can alter the monotony of documentary films. The question of the biographical film must be worked out in an entirely different way. It must not only be concerned with those who have passed away, but with those living now. A film about a political figure, a worker, a kolkhoznik, a doctor, a teacher, a person in the arts must be worked out in a different way. I think, that in this direction, only discoveries lie ahead. It is necessary to be bold and then, we will manage to express more vividly our socialist era of today, we will see our culture, art, and nature in a new way.

It is necessary to edit documentary films *simply and in a way their meaning is clear*. A spectator must not only be able to see people and events clearly, but to remember them. Those who love cheap montage effects, should remember, that to edit simply and in a way that the meaning is clear is not at all easy, but quite difficult. Everything must be done with artistic cogency.

A documentary film must above all excite the spectator *and montage* is one of the most important means of helping to realize this. It is necessary to know how to abandon everything superfluous, experience in montage instructs one in rigorous selection, in "filtering" many times what is selected.

At first glance, my statement that documentary films are not only socio-political, but epic and tragic in form, will appear paradoxical. It is clear which role the artist's design must play, and in the event, it cannot be the tasteful splicing together of shots.

The director of a documentary film must know how to edit. You may not shift the burden onto an assistant. How many unexpected decisions come about, when you are holding the strip of film in your hands. It is just like a word: it is born on the tip of a pen.

And our archives![338] I maintain, that they await the most urgent study, so that directors will not repeat the same shots from film to film and shots will not be pillaged from completed films and these films will not be destroyed. Each director will strive to make certain, that the shots chosen by him are appearing for the very first time.

Yes, the newsreel archives of the Soviet years are our past. But not only that. They are our present and our future.

My lengthy creative life in documentary film was not easy, it was filled with the struggle for what seemed to me to be the only true path. Funny things also happened. I remember, for example, the campaign against documentary film by the Director of the Chief Directorate of the Film and Photo Industry [GUKF], B. Shumyatsky, who expressed himself at that time in a "theoretical" polemic, regarding production.

In 1935, I submitted a proposal for the film *Land of the Soviets* and immediately an order followed, with the following content:

May 20, 1935
Under my immediate artistic and production supervision (scenario, screening of preexisting film material, selection and shooting of new material, montage, musical supervision, and graphic design) to begin preparation for release at the end of this year a feature-length documentary film, reflecting the greatness of Socialist Construction.

I hereby declare that the Creative Collective will consist of the following:
1. Artistic Director: B. Shumyatsky

---

[338] [Trans.] : In the original: летопись. For further commentary, see note 125 in the section "Articles and Statements."

2. Author of the scenario and editorial plan[339]: B. Shumyatsky
3. Camera Operators: B. Makaseev and M. Oshurkov
Presentation of the scenario: August 20 of the current year.

The film must be extremely economical. The full extent of the material is not to exceed 1500 meters.

—Dir. GUKF of the SNK of the USSR[340]
(B. Shumyatsky).

This order called forth laughter from all my creative co-workers. It was clear that the Director of GUKF wasn't going to be doing that. The time was lacking, not to mention other... knowledge.

It was invented, as a way to remove me from the project. The comrades I met with laughed with me. I laughed too, but to tell the truth, I wasn't really up for laughter.

My comrades, who were fiction cinema directors, convened an Artistic Soviet, attended by the Director of GUKF, B. Shumyatsky. The entire Artistic Soviet demanded that I be the one to make the film. They went to battle with Shumyatsky. He had to give in and the film was turned over to me with B. Agapov[341] as screenwriter.

I was lucky. Directors of acted films, with a few exceptions, were people who were really in love with their art, talented, putting their hearts into the creation of Soviet cinema. And while they differed among themselves quite a bit—they treated me with respect, and never tried to convince me to do acted films, instead, they chose me as a member of the Artistic Soviet of Mosfil'm.

Their relationship with me was defined by the fact, that I began my work in the cinema as an editor of feature films and I had edited some of their first films.

For seventeen years, I worked in a studio for acted films and made my long films there, except for the film *On the Other Side of the Aras*, which was directed by me at the Baku Studio.

This gave me the opportunity to observe the creative work of outstanding Soviet cinema directors (S. Eisenstein, in particular), who established the international reputation of Soviet cinema.

This was a splendid school for me.

I also had the occasion to meet with great Soviet writers in connection with my work. They wrote scenarios for me, many of which I shot, and I became friends with some of them.

---

[339] [Trans.]: In the original: Автор сценарно-монтажного плана.

[340] [Trans.]: Soviet People's Commissariat of the USSR.

[341] [Russian editor's note]: *Agapov, Boris Nikolaevich* (b. 1899). Essayist and screenwriter of documentary films. His first work in the cinema was the scenario, written together with Esfir' Shub, for her film *Land of the Soviets* (1937).

Soviet directors and writers, in their creative activity, strove to express the greatness of our era: the era of the Construction of Socialism and the films created by them were expressive in form, advanced in content. There was something to learn from them. Sergei Mikhailovich Eisenstein, an innovator in the cinema, tirelessly affirmed, so that I would remember, that the cinema is an art, a new art. And, that it was necessary to create documentary film as an art.

And we were all inspired by the huge importance that V. I. Lenin gave to the cinema. The Party helped us in every way possible from the very first days of October.

My seventeen years of work at a studio for fiction feature films,[342] on many occasions and quite vividly, gave me the opportunity to determine the interdependence and interaction between acted and documentary cinema. Personal meetings with the masters had a great significance…

Now, I remember…

The "National" café in the center of the city. From three o'clock in the afternoon on, it was overflowing with customers. There were so many. They would eat lunch. And until late into the night, they would drink vodka, wine, they would dance the foxtrot… at noon, it was quiet, sunny, clean, in the distance through the windows you could see Kremlin Square. It was the meeting place for writers and directors. The sweet smell of black coffee was in the air. Around the small tables were Kataev, Afinogenov, Olesha, the young and sluggish Khatsrevin: his elongated Eastern, very black eyes seemed even longer because of his habit of stretching out one and then the other of them with his fingers. His hair was black, smooth like lacquered wood. His speech was a touch ironical, his smile was gentle.

"Lapinikhatsrevin"[343]: the last names of these two friends nearly merged when they were spoken. Lapin rarely appeared. He was near-sighted, always somewhere outside of time and space, he spoke confusedly, at times you wouldn't understand what he was trying to say.

What such splendid, gifted people! From the first day of the war, they were at the front. And they died courageously.

Other writers would come as well.

In an endless procession, directors, who needed to see a writer, to chat about a scenario. It was a meeting place for creative conversations. Ladynina, when she was quite young, would often come there. The appearance of the girl and her dog with her sad, bright eyes. The ballerina Ol'ga Lepeshinskaya and Il'ya Trauberg, who was then the head of the script department at Mosfil'm, would come.

---

[342] [Trans.]: In the original: на студии художественных фильмов.

[343] [Russian editor's note]: *B. Lapin* (1905–1941) and *Z. Khatsrevin* (1903–1941), were writers who, as a rule, worked together. They were authors of a series of books for grown-ups and young readers, as well as scenarios. Both died at the Battle of Kiev at the beginning of the war. [Trans.]: This word means: Lapin-and-Khatsrevin.

This was where the scenario for my film *Women* was conceived in collaboration with Boris Lapin. It was a novella about the fate of Soviet Women. The scenario was written by Boris Lapin, he was witty and original. The hero of the scenario is a mulatto woman, a reporter for an American newspaper. She is observing Soviet women. Some very sharp reporting results. Right here, Yuri Olesha proposed that I make a documentary comedy film about the Tsar Nicholas. His whole concept for the scenario was extremely witty, original, and revealing. But I never had the chance to realize these concepts.

Conversations between writers and directors touched on literature, drama, poetry, current political events. There were also many personal, interesting things to remember.

So many concepts were born from these creative interactions! Many of these concepts were realized and came to life on the screen.

One day, our director, E. K. Sokolovskaya came to us, to see what was going on in this unofficial script department for the studio.

Remembering this time, I regret, that now there is no place, where writers and directors can chat with one another over a cup of coffee in peace.

The film *Land of the Soviets* was finished by me on time, but... it never appeared in the larger cinemas... There were good notices about it in both *Pravda* and *Izvestia*, and a splendid notice by Sergei Mikhailovich Eisenstein in *Kino* magazine and there were others.

Here's what A. Fadeev wrote about it in *Literaturnaya Gazeta*:

Soviet film director E. Shub has created a splendid film, *Land of the Soviets*. The film received enthusiastic notices in the entirety of the Soviet press. The November 28, 1937 issue of *Pravda* wrote of this film:

The success of director E. Shub and screenwriter B. Agapov consists above all, in that they managed to choose from a mass of rich factual material, what is most characteristic, colorful, exciting. Individual shots remind the viewer of the huge struggle and the labor of the Peoples of the USSR, which accomplished the socialist transformation of the land, under the leadership of the Bolshevik Party. And, what is most important are the people shown, Soviet People... One can say with confidence, that the documentary film *Land of the Soviets* will have a great success with the widest possible cross-section of Soviet spectators. The film is good, timely, needed...

The film created by E. Shub genuinely represents an uncommon phenomenon in Soviet film art. Making use of the richest newsreel material, Comrade Shub, whom the Soviet spectator knows well through her previous remarkable work in this vein (*Fall of the Romanov Dynasty, Lev Tolstoy*), has created an unforgettable film poem with an exceptional feeling for rhythm and accent. This is a picture of great mastery. Unlike in her previous work, Comrade Shub has to a significant extent augmented the newsreel material with material shot by her in various regions of the land, in keeping with the grand ideological design of the picture. For the person unfamiliar with how films are made, it will be difficult to determine, the way in which, from this huge amount of factual material, of separate bits and pieces, shot at different times by different people, a film could be composed of the utmost integrity, flowing like a rushing torrent.

…However… for reasons unknown to us, the film *Land of the Soviets* was assigned to the "second-class" category and released in second-class theaters. As a result, the film did not go to the best cinema theaters in Moscow and other cities of our Motherland. Millions of Soviet spectators will not see this film.

In whose interest does the official in charge of distribution work, by hiding from millions of spectators, a splendid film poem, singing the heroic path of struggle and the victory of our People, of our Party?[344]

Good notices in the press and the article by A. A. Fadeev did not help. But I didn't give up.

Nothing could force me to shoot a film with actors. I was interested in real people, not in people acting. To observe them. To take note of their behavior, to choose to shoot those moments, when their true characteristics would appear — this was a joy for me if the shot succeeded and distress if the lens of the camera hindered people's natural behavior. The activity of these people, their participation in social life, their labor most clearly spoke about our era. In this, under the direction of the Party and the great Lenin, they created a new world together. In this, they pursued his victorious journey towards socialism.

How many remarkable people I filmed: workers and peasants, Soviet youth and children, people in the arts and sciences, the Soviet intelligentsia.

How this enriched my life! But I made films rarely and this reined in my eagerness to film real people.

I often think, that people like R. Karmen, who spent a great part of their lives on the road, in many countries of the world and filmed real people everywhere, could

---

[344] [Trans.]: This lengthy quotation within a quotation is divided this way. The November 28, 1937 issue of *Pravda* confirms this. Fadeev was writing in *Literaturnaya Gazeta*.

write his best book, if he wrote about people, who in some way astonished him. His sharp journalistic pen would help him to do this with brilliance.

But for me this is difficult. All the same, I would like to record my meetings with a few remarkable people.

Meeting M. Gorky and R. Rolland

A sunny July day. A group of film directors go to M. Gorky's place outside the city for a meeting with Romain Rolland.[345] We are happy and in a festive mood. Around a long table we talk about the film industry. We are in the great room of an old villa; there are trees outside the window. Light passes through the leaves, patches of sunlight make the room particularly cozy.

Romain Rolland has a blanket around his shoulders. He was cold on this warm day. His face is rigid, he does not smile, under the burden of many years, the eyes in his gaunt face gaze attentively and sternly. Beside him is Maxim Gorky. He is tall, with stooped shoulders, symmetrical and manly. He wore his loose-fitting suit, with an almost elegant negligence. His face is lively, his eyes full of expression. His eyes are dark, dark blue, beautiful. They gaze sternly, attentively, and sadly; at times, they ignite with sparks of joy. He monitors with interest what impression those sitting around the table produce on Romain Rolland.

Romain Rolland likes the fact that, on the pictures he has seen lies the stamp of the spirit of the nation, the originality of the nation. He is charmed by shots in films of the Russian landscape. He criticizes a great deal. He is dissatisfied by the acting of the actors in many films, the work of the directors with the actors, the drawn-out quality. He is interested in talking about music. All the same, he would like to write for Soviet theater and cinema, since only within our art, within our possibilities, lies the path towards authentic realism. Only within Soviet filmmaking is it of interest to work on the problem of the scenario, the problem of economy of expression, the weight of the word in the cinema.

He and Maxim Gorky are dissatisfied by shots in documentary films, which are clearly staged (*Komsomol City* [*Город Комсомольск*][346] by the director Slutsky[347]).

---

[345] [Russian editor's note]: The meeting of R. Rolland with workers in the Soviet cinema took place on July 16, 1935 at A. M. Gorky's dacha in the City of Gorky [the name of Nizhny Novgorod from 1932 to 1990].

[346] [Trans.]: Perhaps an alternate title for *Комсомольск* [*Komsomol'sk*] (1934). It refers to the city Komsomol'sk-na-Amure "officially" built by the Komsomol, but mostly by gulag labor.

[347] [Russian editor's note]: *Slutsky, Mikhail Yakovlevich* (1907–1959). Director and camera operator in documentary cinema. Decorated Worker in the Arts of the Ukrainian Soviet Socialist Republic. Films: *China in the Fight*, VSKhB [*The All-Russian Agricultural Exhibition*], *The People of Sedovo* [*Седовцы*

Staged scenes make the film artificial, you watch without being convinced. Gorky considers, that only cooperation between writer and director can enrich Soviet film-making through the interest of the content of the scenario and through ideological films. Among the films they had seen, the strongest impression was produced by the picture *The Border*[348] and *Torn Boots*.[349] The latter film, they thought could only be made in the Soviet Union.

Around the table sit Alexander Dovzhenko, Mikhail Romm, Grigory Roshal'. Roshal' wants to direct *Colas Breugnon*.[350] He tells Romain Rolland how he is thinking of adapting this production for the screen. Rolland is pleased, Gorky's eyes sparkle gaily, he is satisfied. As goodbyes are said, Rolland gives Roshal' a signed copy of *Colas Breugnon*.

Gorky is distressed by how our directors work with actors. He calls for more observation, more truth in the behavior of a person. He says, it would be interesting, if the director, before rehearsals, imagines himself as his hero, when he is alone in his room: in front of the mirror, eye-to-eye with himself, when no one is observing. This is the key to his characterization.

I especially remember Gorky telling us about how, the evening before, some women aviators and parachutists visited him. Unaffected, brave, bold. In them, he saw the prototype of a new, excellent generation of the land of socialism. By means of his account, I clearly imagined this great room with the young girls and Gorky among them. In his words, in the expression of his eyes there was a love for the young generation, there was a belief in its future, a belief that the Land of the Soviets, the land of socialism, would certainly be the land of the New Man, gifted with many psychological qualities, as yet unseen.

His belief was so inspired and deep, that, lifted up by it, we left him, with the profound intention to more truly reflect contemporary man in our productions, as best we could.

Such meetings not only give joy, but deepen the sense of responsibility to one's people, to the Motherland.

1939], *A Day in Soviet Russia* [*A Day of the New World*], *Our Moscow*, *Soviet Ukraine* and others.
[348] [Trans.]: In the original: *Граница*, directed by Mikhail Dubson (1935).
[349] [Trans.]: In the original: *Рваные башмаки*, written and directed by Margarita Barskaya (1933).
[350] [Trans.]: A short novel by Rolland (1919), the basis for the opera by Dmitry Kabelevsky.

Portrait of Alexander Pushkin by Vasily Tropinin (1827).
National Pushkin Museum, St. Petersburg.

Yuri Nikolaevich Tynyanov

I decided to attempt to make a documentary film about Pushkin. Viktor Shklovsky advised me to meet with Yuri Tynyanov. Of course! You couldn't think of anyone better.

I go Leningrad, but it turns out, that Yuri Nikolaevich is in Sestroretsk. I head there. It was the first time, that I communicated in person with him—with the lovely, thin writer. I know and love his books. In 1939, I read his article in *Literaturny kritik* [*Literary Criticism*] called "Nameless Love." The article made a huge impression on me. This piece of research, in which Tynyanov very convincingly proves, that Pushkin's "secret" love was the wife of the historian Karamzin—Ekaterina Andreevna—who in 1817 was still a beauty and traces of this beauty remained even into old age. I told Shklovsky what an impression this article had made on me.

—Send Tynyanov a telegram. He'll be glad.

I did this.

Recently, a similarly strong impression had been made on me by an article about Picasso by I. Ehrenburg in *Inostrannaya literatura* [*Foreign Literature*]. This article shed new light on this artist.

Sestroretsk… And so, I go to the seaside with Yuri Nikolaevich. He speaks about Pushkin. Communicating with him was more than interesting. He is satisfied, that I am thoroughly acquainted with the biography, the poetry of Pushkin, that I am thoroughly acquainted with the poets of the Pushkin Pleiades. It is easy for us to come to an agreement. The possibilities of documentary cinema in the creation of this kind of biographical film interested him. Towards the end of the day, I received his agreement to write a scenario.

He travels to Moscow and in the office of the director of the studio, E. Sokolovskaya, he tells how he intends to undertake this project. Viktor Shklovsky is present at this meeting.

In essence, this is a scenario about the Motherland. Tynyanov wants to show how Pushkin saw it, in his forced destiny as a wanderer, how he connected with it, how he created images of it in his poetry. Wandering. Pushkin for the first time revealed for himself the vast dimensions of Russia.

Tynyanov[351] intended to begin the scenario with Tsarskoe Selo. The Lycée, The Elizabethan-Versailles-style gardens, which are also Catherine-the-Great-style and English style. The statues, referred to in Pushkin's verse, the monument to his ancestor, Gannibal, who stormed the fortress of Navarino. There is material about his friends and teachers at the lycée. Crimea. Bessarabia. Odessa. Mikhailovskoe. Trigorskoe. The verses of the poet all precisely describe these places. Dates can be found for some of the poetry. Petersburg. The Decembrist uprising. Georgia. Boldino. Pushkin's apartment. The fact, that the poet knew he would be murdered.

It was interesting imagining how to research Pushkin's epigrams on the tsar Alexander, Arakcheev, Vorontsov, Sturdza—"the serf of the crowned soldier"—even on Karamzin ("he proves to us, without the least partiality, the inevitability of autocracy and the charm of the whip"). Tynyanov wanted, although it was indeed difficult, as he

---

351 [Russian editor's note]: A transcript of Yu. Tynyanov's presentation on February 17, 1936, where he recounts the plan for the picture about A. S. Pushkin is preserved in the private archive of Esfir' Shub. He said, in part, "before us lies a fascinating challenge, but it is not so easily accomplished, as it seems, for example, the relationship of Pushkin to space and through this to each little landscape. It must be said, that in Pushkin's time, there was not the same degree of understanding of space as concerns the Motherland. Pushkin, for the first time, revealed Russia in its actual dimensions.… In work on the film one must be governed only by precise facts, because it isn't possible for you to think up something better—Pushkin's footsteps must be shown: the places where he was.… If, in the film, the connections between these places and Pushkin can be shown, then what is needed will have been done.…This film cannot compete with an acted Pushkin film: it must be artistic, but not acted. If you travel around these places and bring in Pushkin's works, everything will be clear. From this film, it will be clear that Pushkin not only wrote verse, but was also a political figure."

said, but also fascinating, to attempt to find a way to show the magnificent culture on which Pushkin was nourished. Besides the verses of the poet, Tynyanov was trying to research the folk songs of the Cossacks, the indigent, the blind, whom Pushkin recorded in the bazaar, which is preserved up to the present day. Georgian, Gypsy, Tatar songs.

Pushkin was a great poet, but he was also a great citizen of his Motherland. There was so much interest in Yu. N. Tynyanov's presentation, that the plan was approved and an agreement signed. That afternoon towards evening, we met again at Shklovsky's: Yu. Tynyanov, I. Andronikov and I. In a small dining room, over a cup of tea, specially prepared by Shklovsky, Tynyanov, who was sitting on the divan, read Pushkin to us, never raising his voice. He read in a slightly sing-song manner. He said, that it was in precisely that way verses were read in Pushkin's time. After that, he read Kyukhel'beker, Baratynsky and others. The remarkable Andronikov, looked at Tynyanov, his eyes full of love, and would occasionally read lines of verse by the poets of the Pushkin Pleiades. What a wonderful evening this was!

The work was moving forward. Once again, I traveled to see Tynyanov. We met at his apartment in the city. The scenario began to take shape in visual form. The texts of the poetry selected by Yuri Nikolaevich and the montage planned by him of these texts were beautiful. He left the possibility open for the director to create a visual transformation into a film of astonishing power. I was especially interested in Tynyanov's concept asserting the "documentariness"[352] of these texts.

Then suddenly, unexpectedly, I received a letter from Yuri Nikolaevich:

> … I am very seriously ill. And for a long time this will deprive me of the possibility of working to the degree, which would be required. For this reason, and only for this reason, I must give up the thought of collaborative work with you on your film. Trust, that for me this is a great disappointment and even a privation….[353]

Yuri Nikolaevich was genuinely, seriously ill. Nonetheless, we did not give up the thought of this project. We decided to realize a scenario according to Tynyanov's plan.[354] The scenario was supervised by Viktor Shklovsky. Professor Oksman acted as a consultant. Shklovsky and I went to Leningrad and spent many hours studying the places connected with Pushkin's name and in the Pushkin House Academy of

---

[352] [Trans.]: In the original: документальность. One could paraphrase this as: its quality as a document, or its documentary quality.

[353] [Russian editor's note]: From a letter by Yu. Tynyanov dated December 22, 1935. The original is in the personal archive of Esfir' Shub.

[354] [Russian editor's note]: The scenario, *По следам Пушкина* (*In the Footsteps of Pushkin*), written by Viktor Shklovsky based on the treatment [сценарный план] by Yu. Tynyanov, was not produced. A copy of the scenario is preserved in the personal archive of Esfir' Shub.

Sciences, we collected graphic materials connected with Pushkin's era. To see Pushkin's actual texts, his drawings, was interesting, exhilarating even.

Viktor Shkovsky wrote a good scenario. It was accepted by the studio. I very much wanted to shoot this scenario, but the schedule was delayed, and so, this film was not shot by me.

It seems to me, that until the creative proposals of both the writer and the director, discovered by them in creative collaboration, are taken into account in creative work, little will change. It must not depend only on the studio's plan. How frequently, an outline is the only result.

I met with Yuri Nikalaevich Tynyanov for only a short time, but my meetings with him gave me much that was beautiful. Once again, as in the days of my youth, I became involved with Pushkin's poetry and this meant so much. Yuri Nikolaevich wrote and spoke about Pushkin with inspiration.

Ekaterina Vasil'evna Belokur

In my work, I happened to shoot many of the skilled artisans among our People — persons, who brought renown to our People's creative activity. I shot women who embroider, wood carvers, masters of decorative painting, potters, the amazing furniture and woodwork of the Hutsuls. But Ekaterina Vasil'evna Belokur produced the most indelible impression on me. This is the record of my meeting with her.

We travel to the village of Bogdanovka, in the Shmakovsky region, Poltavskaya oblast'. It is a huge village. We ask those whom we meet, how to find Ekaterina Vasil'evna Belokur. Everyone knows her wooden hut and they show us the way.

We draw near. Behind a fence is a small garden, a few fruit trees, mallows, mountain ash trees. We enter the hut. There is a large room with a dirt floor, a stove with a place to lie down on top, and up there is an old woman, Mother Belokur. Near the stove is a wooden bed; by the window, in the other corner, is a wooden table without a tablecloth and narrow wooden benches.

Ekaterina Vasil'evna remains silent as she greets us. Her legs are bad and she wears felt boots. A scarf covers her head. The beautiful face of an older woman. Large stern eyes. No, she is not going to be filmed.

No, she has nothing to show us. She has bad legs, and she works little.

Quickly and unobtrusively, we send our line producer to the Party Committee to get the Secretary. The Party Secretary arrives. She tries to persuade Ekaterina Vasil'evna to be filmed. Silence. And we understand, that she is not going to be filmed.

Her brother has heard, that Ekaterina Vasil'evna has guests. And so, he comes over. We all sit down around a table, we are provided with some vodka. We are chilled, it is damp, it begins to rain. The camera assistant, Klavdiya Filippovna Krasinskaya, and I settle down for the night on the narrow benches at the window. The line producer and our wonderful camera operator Andrikanis[355] go to sleep somewhere else.

In the wooden hut, it is dark, outside the windows there is the rain. Klavdiya Filippovna and I hold a quiet conversation about our successes and failures, about people, about work. The rain is making us depressed. Ekaterina Vasil'evna is not sleeping either. Maybe she has understood, that it's hard for us, that we traveled to see her with the best of intentions. And suddenly, to our question about how she became an artist, we received the most surprising answer. Here it is.

From her childhood, she was attracted to drawing. She used to draw on the walls of her log hut, but her relatives planned to make her a village seamstress. Out of poverty, she entered the service of a rich landowner. The daughter of the landowner became friends with her and began to give her little books to read. Into her hands fell a thin volume by Gorky. In it, she read how in a small Volga town he went to see a rich merchant. In a large, dreary room, the walls of which were hung with oleograph reproductions and bad paintings, Gorky caught sight of a small painting, on which flowers had been drawn by the hand of a French woman artist. They were wonderful. He couldn't tear himself away from them. The merchant was pleased, that Gorky liked the painting and said, that he too had been astonished by the colors of this thing and so wanted to have it, that he paid five thousand rubles for it.

From that time on, Ekaterina Vasil'evna's dream became to do everything she must, to create a canvas, where flowers would be drawn with no less mastery. And when she succeeded, she would send the flowers to the great writer as a gift.

In order to achieve this and to become an artist, self-educated, she turned away from any personal life. She would work and work… And finally, the moment arrived. But Gorky was no longer alive and there was no one to whom to send this gift. She grew silent. And we understood, that we would leave without having achieved our goal, which was utterly impossible. That night, in some way, we became comrades.

Morning. Rain, endless rain. Rare patches of sunlight. A day where it would not be possible to shoot. We could shoot Belokur only in the little garden. We were shooting color film. But we still could not manage to get her to agree. Unexpectedly, during a brief sunny interval, she agreed to show us some of her works. She opened a low door, we had not noticed earlier, and we entered a tiny little room. There was a wooden floor, the room was filled with sunlight. This was her studio. And everything that we happened to see in this room was beautiful.

---

[355] [Russian editor's note]: *Andrikanis, Evgeny Nikolaevich* (b. 1909). Camera operator and director. Decorated Worker in the Arts of the RSFSR. He shot the films *Mashenka, Days and Nights, Oldtime Vaudeville, Przhevalsky, Othello, Stories about Lenin* (based on the short novella *The Final Autumn*), and others. He directed: *Northern Story* and *Executed at Dawn*.

By one of the windows in the room was a little table. It was completely covered with jars of paint. There were extremely thin, needle point brushes, sharpened at the tips. There were two easels. On them, were small format paintings that were covered. She showed us some finished paintings: all were flowers. They were outlined, like precious enamels, with these tiny brushes. The flowers were alive. You wanted to touch them. They were full of expression. There were wildflowers, that sang of youth, of love. There were roses, poppies, and on and on. This is maturity, the beauty of life. There were flowers like the setting sun. Above some of them, circled weightless butterflies. Their little wings were transparent with astonishing patterns. It was like a miracle. She uncovered a canvas on the easel. It was a complex composition. A huge wreath of flowers interwoven. A riot of colors. Within this circle is a table. On it are the fruits of the earth: cantaloupes, watermelons, apples, pears… in abundance. Then, she covers the paintings. I remember two in particular: the sky, just before evening, on the ground of the sky a simple wooden cradle is rocking. The thick cords on the cradle mount towards the sky. In the cradle is a child. He is sleeping. Butterflies are flying above him. It appears, that the cradle is rocking. The child's face is beautiful. His sleep is his wisdom, he knows more than we do, the grownups and those not sleeping. A secret hovers above him. There is also a young girl. A portrait down to the knees. A beautiful combination of colors. She is holding a jug of water. She is deep in thought and does not notice, that from the tilted jug, a transparent trickle of water is flowing. Flowing, flowing… Youth. The heart is open to love and to dreams.

The next morning there is sun. Finally, Ekaterina Vasil'evna's gives her agreement to being filmed. She doesn't want to go out into the little garden across the way, where we would have a few hours to work. No, she agrees to be filmed only in her own little garden, by the window of her studio. Ekaterina Vasil'evna's at her easel. She refuses to change into her national costume. She wears a gray blouse, with a dark scarf on her head. We have only a few minutes. The sun in this spot in the garden does not shine for very long.

Ekterina Vasil'evna Belokur is working. Suddenly, she pulls down her scarf—her eyes disappear and half of her face… The sun bothers her. We don't know what to do. Then, I walk up to her and with an abrupt movement uncover her face. Out of surprise, she stops working. For a moment she looks at me, but something in me causes her to grow silent and comply. The daylight runs out. We search for a place where we could shoot her hand at work. The painting we had shot earlier.

We needed to leave. Instead of one or two days, we had spent four in the village. We were not convinced that we had shot things the way we wanted. We figured, that the shoot was a failure.

We say our goodbyes with Ekaterina Vasil'evna. She understood, that in numerous ways, she had upset us. We are driving in an open truck across the endless steppe. The train station is far away. Behind us a light dust, behind that, there are storm clouds, the smell of dust, the wind of the impending storm, and the steppe. It grows dark. The storm catches up with us. There is lightning, thunder, a downpour. A wall of water pours from the sky. We quickly hide under a tarpaulin. The pouring rain beats against the tarpaulin. It nearly drowns us. All the same, we reach the station, utterly soaked.

In Moscow, we are happy. When the material is processed, we can see that we will be able to represent Ekaterina Vasil'evna Belokur nicely.

Nata Vachnadze[356]

Nata Bachnadze:
screen goddess and
Shub's trusted collaborator.

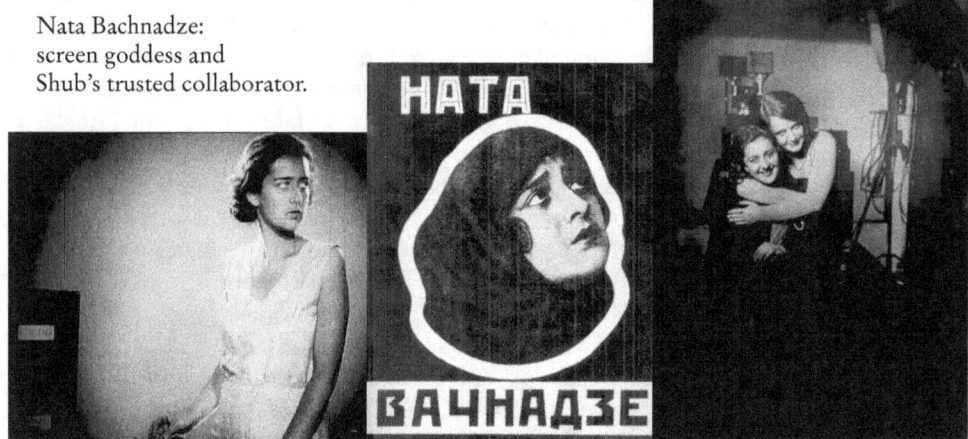

In the first Soviet films receiving recognition, both among us and abroad, directors would shoot young actresses, unknown to everyone up to that point, but they were always beautiful.

Yuliya Solntseva was really a beauty (*Aelita*, *The Cigarette Girl of Mosselprom*), Ol'ga Zhizneva (already a well-known theater actress, appeared in many pictures), Galina Kravchenko (*His Majesty's Soloist*, *The Happy Canary*), Raisa Yesipova (*Woman's World*, *Love*). After them, for some reason, they began to shoot women who were blatantly not beautiful: they were short-legged, snub-nosed, and in no way remarkable actresses.

---

[356] [Russian editor's note]. *Vachnadze, Natalya Georgievna* (1904–1953) film actress. People's Artist of the Georgian Soviet Socialist Republic, Decorated Artist of the RSFSR. She acted around 30 roles in films. She appeared in these films: *Arsen the Bandit*, *Three Lives*, *The Case of Tariel Mklavadze*, *Amok* [*Amok, Law and Duty*], *The Gadfly*, *The Last Masquerade*, *The Golden Valley*, *Qadjana* and others. She was the Assistant to E. Shub on *KShE*.

Among the beauties, Nata Vachnadze, was for me always noteworthy.

She shot films with directors like Barsky, Bek-Nazarov and others. I particularly remember her in a film directed by Perestiani called *Three Lives*. Through her charisma, her femininity, and beauty she won the love of all spectators of the Soviet Screen. Perestiani found this "princess" in Kakheti, on a tiny piece of land, cultivating grapes with her mother. She was, through her father, a Princess Andronikova, through her mother, she was of Italian blood (her grandmother was an Italian singer).

Life was hard labor and poverty, a peasant's lot.

Soon, she became the wife of director Nikolai Shengelaya.[357] Life became more difficult for her. She was condemned, because she left her first husband—Prince Vachnadze—and chose the amazing and fiery Shengelaya. Nikolai Shengelaya was a poet, a great admirer of Mayakovsky. In the evenings, he would climb a tree on the main street of Tbilisi—Rustaveli Prospect—and would gather people around the tree, while he read his verse and the verse of Mayakovsky. He was young, handsome, brave. He was funny in a youthful way, eccentric, he would do the unexpected in the extreme, he was passionate in his creative work. As a director, he became famous for his pictures *Caucasian Love* [*Eliso*], *26 Commissars*, and many others. He was passionate not only in his creative work, but in his love for Natasha.

I was quite surprised when in 1932, she phoned me at home. She needed to see me. She had a letter for me from G. Kozintsev and brought greetings from N. Shengelaya (we were good comrades).

—Come. At Once.

I will always remember the morning, when Nata Vachnadze, who was an actress well-known for so many films, came to my place.

Thin, in a modest white dress, shy, with a charming smile. The beautiful woman arrived. The long lashes of her wide-open eyes were fluttering slightly.

G. Kozintsev had written to me. Here is the gist of his letter: "They are not filming 'beautiful women' anymore. Vachnadze, of course, could become an assistant to any director of feature films, but she very much wanted to work with me... She asked me not to consider her past in 'acted' films, to trust her. She is extremely hardworking—he would vouch for the seriousness of her intentions."

That was enough for me. I was convinced, and although the crew was already assembled, I included Natasha in it.

I had just acquired the perfect assistant for a difficult job—the shooting of the film *Komsomol in Service to Electrification—KShE*.

---

[357] [Russian editor's note]: *Shengelaya, Nikolai Mikhailovich* (1854–1943). Director. Screenwriter. Decorated Worker in the Arts of the RSFSR. He directed the films: *Caucasian Love* [*Eliso*], *Twenty Six Commissars*, *The Golden Valley*.

The treatment[358] for the film had been approved by the Central Committee of the VLKSM.[359] During our work, the Central Committee of the VLKSM always came to our aid, requesting cooperation from the organizations in the places where we were filming. The film *KShE*, along with the films *Counterplan*, *Men and Jobs*[360] and others was one of the first sound films. It was supposed to reflect the struggle of the Komsomol Organization for the electrification of the People's economy. I recorded not only synch-sound footage, but as well, documentary sounds by themselves: the sounds of machines in factories, the sound of construction, water, crowds, echoes, birdsong, the sounds of gramophones mixed with the sound of water at the time American experts were swimming on the banks of the Dnepr, and a lot more. When the film was processed, I edited these sounds and the synchronous sound recordings together with the picture material. We filmed the greatest achievements in the field of electrical engineering, radio, the first attempts at television, the high voltage transmissions laboratory of Professor Chernyshev, and the laboratory of the academician Ioffe, and so on. We received the most active assistance from the Komsomol Committees, wherever our shoots took place. They even helped us choose what to shoot.

During the time of the Dneprostroi shoot in September 1931, we committed ourselves to traveling to Leningrad to shoot the factories in order to promote and move forward in every possible way the order for the generator and turbines to the Komsomol unit called "Komsomol'skaya Pravda." We succeeded in fulfilling the commitments we had undertaken. In connection with this, we began to shoot a series of exciting scenes of the delivery and receiving of the generator by the Komsomol team of Dneprostroi. We also had no small success in shooting people: Komsomolets Klimov, the American expert Cooper at Dneprostroi, the women's Komsomol unit at the Moscow Electrical Plant (in particular Paramonova, the job foreman).

Vachnadze wore work clothes,[361] and felt boots. She worked enthusiastically and passionately, not shunning any task. She was genuinely interested in documentary production and the fate of documentary film. She assured me, that this work was enriching to her. I acquired not only the perfect assistant who took initiative, but also a friend until the final days of her life. We made our way to the place we were to shoot at Svir'stroe on skis through deep snow, as there was no other way to reach it. In Leningrad we shot huge factories. It was still dark when we made our way there and we returned in darkness as well, when the lights had been lit for the evening, so that, in fact, we never saw daylight. In Leningrad, the majority of the evening location shoots

---

[358] [Trans.]: In the original: Сценарный план.

[359] [Trans]: In the original: ВЛКСМ: Всесоюзный ленинский коммунистический союз молодежи [All-union Leninist Young Communist League].

[360] [Trans.]: In the original: *Дела и люди.*

[361] [Trans.]: In the original: спецодежда [spetsodezhda] work clothes designed for the specific tasks of their wearers. Varvara Stepanova played a major role in their conceptualization and design.

took place at Medvezh'ya Gora under heavy frost. Returning to the hotel after work, everyone in the group would head to the restaurant, only there, did I clearly realize Nata Vachnadze's popularity. She was noisily welcomed, flowers, wine and fruit were sent to the table. Natasha felt awkward in my presence, since I was the director, but I asked her not to be embarrassed.

At DzaroGES [Dzaroget Hydro Electric Generating Station] we would get up early, at dawn. We put the equipment on a simple bullock cart and went away far into the mountains and would work until sundown. Vachnadze took an active part in the shoots. She always found beautiful mountain landscapes with electrical transmission lines and would stop peasants traveling through and others passing through on foot with particularly expressive faces for shots. The heavy sound equipment was carried by hand in shifts by members of the group, as they feared jostling it. The release of the water for the electric power station turned into a big celebration. The preparations for the shoot and the shoot itself were very difficult. All the same, we managed well. We recorded a lot of synch sound footage and documentary sounds. At sunset, tired, we would go back home. The entire group would sit down at a long, country table. Fragrant mountain herbs lay on the table in a heap. Lamb, cheese, wine skins filled with young wine and these herbs were our food. And almost always, Nata Vachnadze would begin to quietly sing Kakhetian folk songs at the table. She loved her native Kakheti as much as her children, as much as Nikolai Shengelaya. She was quiet and beautiful in these moments.

I shot a working moment, when Natasha stood at the control panel during the recording of some electro-music on the Theremin. I shot her without makeup. Many people liked this shot—a working moment during the shooting of *KShE*, N. Vachnadze without makeup.

The music for this sequence, as well as for the entire film, was written by the composer G. Popov. S. Eisenstein, after seeing *KShE* sent Popov, whom he did not know, this telegram: "I congratulate you on the magnificent sound-image creative victory in the film *KShE*.—Sergei Eisenstein."

I was friends with N. Vachnadze until the final days of her life. Shortly before her death, she brought her three sons to me. It was difficult to believe, that this woman, still quite a beauty, was the mother of such grown-up children. She had come to say goodbye just before the fatal accident. She was happy, excited, and worried. And then came the accident. When I read the newspaper article about it, and found out later, that the plane had crashed in mountains above the village, where Nikolai Shengelaya was born (and that all that remained of Natasha was her hand with her wedding band), my first thought was, that Natasha didn't perish. It seemed to me, that Nikolai had gone to the mountain top to pick her up.

Dear, beautiful, unforgettable little Natasha! Thank you for the love and the beauty of your soul…

○   ○   ○

V. Mayakovsky, S. Eisenstein, V. Pudovkin. Vs. Vishnevsky, Yu. Tynyanov, the short meeting with M. Gorky and R. Rolland strengthened my attitude towards documentary film production and to the truthful art of showing real people—our contemporaries, our people constructing socialism—and to the art of structuring the consciousness of the broad masses. They strengthened me in my conviction, that a documentary film must, of necessity, inspire trust in the reality of its shots. The spectator must believe, that these shots are not staged.

Not many people know, that Vsevolod Pudovkin during the war years taught documentary cinema for a semester at the VGIK in Alma-Ata. I was his assistant and ran the classes on montage with his group of students. The students listened to his lectures with excitement. They were interesting and instructive. Pudovkin considered, that staging was unacceptable. But there are some directors, who believe in their methods of staging using predetermined, desirable shots. Does this mean, that every sequence must be shot as reportage? Of course, not. The shooting of large-scale films requires structured preparation. Such preparation requires from the director a great deal of tact. Each of us has their own characteristic way of preparing for a shoot. The principal task, which we set for ourselves in this, is to manage not to shut people (or actors) down, not to infringe upon their natural behavior. The ability of the director plays no small role in choosing which people to shoot: people who won't "freeze" in front of the camera lens.

You can immediately sense staging. A man, playing himself, will cease to interest the spectator, just as will sequences with huge amounts of polish.

If difficulties are shown in such a way, that the spectator knows from the first shot, that everything ends perfectly, with a victory, this becomes annoying because the time spent is wasted. No, there is no place for staging in documentary film.

For this reason, we must film a great deal of our reality, film the kinds of facts and events that will not immediately be put to use, but will be preserved in the archives. Our best camera operators must be the ones to shoot and to shoot responsibly, and not off-handedly, and not only when they are unoccupied with shooting large-scale films.

Just as it is impossible for the authentic director of a feature fiction film, if he doesn't know how to work with actors—doesn't know how to shoot an actor in such a way that the spectator will believe in the truth of the image—it is inconceivable to me, that the director of a documentary film could succeed in this, if he is not able to discover opportunities and methods of shooting real people. And these possibilities and methods number in the thousands. One must research, one must study. To tell the truth, some newsreel camera operators, even when they are not shooting reportage, show people better than several comrades, who hold the rank of directors.

It has been necessary for each of us, because of the inadmissibly small amount of material, to reconstruct some events. But we do this unwillingly and don't brag about the method and are happy when what we have shot does not stick out in the film as a lie. As for polishing up reality, there, I think we have gotten a good lesson. We now know, what this leads to, especially in documentary cinema. And I believe, that shooting is now carried out more responsibly, with a full understanding of the necessity of truthfully reflecting our reality.

Given the significance I attach to documentary cinema, I believe, that there should be a studio for documentary films, along with an ongoing newsreel chronicle, closer to an archive. How much more varied will be the content of feature-length films and how much more active will be the participation in them of Soviet man—the hero of these films—when it will be required to turn more frequently to the archives, to see, whether a given hero has not already been filmed. And, if a film should have young people as its subject, how much more interesting will it be to show in it, how their fathers lived, when they were constructing socialist society.

The dramatic collision of events gone by with those of today presents many possibilities for making the content of a film more profound. For this reason, I consider obligatory, the presence of directors from every Republic of our Motherland, in the review of narratives.[362] This enriches the director's knowledge of life in the Land of the Soviets and a critical directorial review of narratives undoubtedly has great significance for camera operators, especially those who are working outside major urban centers, or in the newsreel departments of the National Republics. Among them are many gifted camera operators, but they don't always properly sense what in any given moment it is most important to shoot.

My creative life has taken shape in such a way, that I had to examine a great number of historical documentary film shots on negative. I held in my hands very old, pre-revolutionary rolls of film. Among them were shots taken on Lumière film stock—with only one perforation per frame.[363] *Fall of the Romanov Dynasty*, *Lev Tolstoy and The Russia of Nicholas II*, *The Great Way* were edited for the most part using historical newsreels. This work underscored for me, that history in documentary cinema—*the great history of our days*—must be shown responsibly, not by replacing history with acted history. It is not by accident, that the best documentary films possess lasting archival significance. For example: *Ukraine in Flames* [*The Fight for Our Soviet Ukraine*] by Dovzhenko and Solntseva. *The Battle for Sevastopol* by Belyaev, *Moscow Strikes Back* [*The Rout of German Troops near Moscow*] by Varlamov and Kopalin, *Stalingrad* by Varlamov, *Nuremberg Trials* [*The Judgment of*

---

[362] [Trans.]: In the original: сюжет [syuzhet].
[363] [Trans.]: Standard 35mm film stock has 4 perforations per frame. Lumière film stock would require a special reproduction technique for transfer to 35mm film for use by Shub in her films.

the Peoples] by Karmen, *On Iran* by Posel'sky,[364] the works of Kristi[365] and others. All these films are made by the best directors.

During the years of the Great Patriotic War, I looked at around eight hundred thousand meters of film. I systematized these shots.

A large number of things, a very large number of important things were not shot and a large number were shot badly. Simply badly planned. Among them, the first shoots of the beginning of the war were lacking. Besides that, the shoots were poorly thought-out—not as we understand this now, with the perspective of the years lived through by our Great Motherland. The further we go forward in time, the more responsibly the shoots were conducted. There was success in capturing on film the most important stages of the struggle, capturing [them] without staging. And in this, we see the contributions of the camera operators—many of whom perished heroically while shooting. In the perspective of the years, these filmed images[366] are acquiring a huge force of inspiration—the force of a document, unique in its significance and truthfulness. Such shots as these clearly demonstrate the heroic efforts of the entire Soviet People, who, under the leadership of the Party, emerged victorious from a titanic struggle.

What tasks did I set for myself in the organization of the archive material of the Patriotic War?

Shots from the archive are depleted, because the best shots in terms of content and camera work are stolen by film chronicles for large-scale documentary films. Edited shots are cut out and worn out in printing. I believe it is essential, that there be two negatives, two master positive of the best shots. All shots systematized by me were labeled concisely, precisely, and graphically. I dated them, gave them a number, observing thematic sequence. All material was grouped into episodes.

Upon examination, such treatment constitutes the recorded cinema history of the Great Patriotic War. I performed the same work on the description of the home front. To the description of the shots, I intended to attach the clearest articles and essays from *Pravda, Izvestiya, Krasnaya Zvezda,*[367] *Krasny flot,*[368] coinciding in

---

[364] [Trans.]: Iosif Mikhailovich Posel'sky (1899–1970). Soviet director of documentary films. Decorated Worker in the Arts of the Latvian Soviet Socialist Republic, Three Stalin Prizes. His films include *The Truth about the Red Army, Memories of Il'ich* and *The Renaissance of Stalingrad.*

[365] [Trans.]: Leonid Mikhailovich Kristi (1910–1984). Soviet director of documentary films. People's Artist of the USSR, Decorated Worker in the Arts of the Latvian Soviet Socialist Republic, Lenin Prize and two Stalin Prizes. His films include *Soviet Latvia, Circus Artists,* and *Three Springs of Lenin.*

[366] [Trans.]: In the original: съемки, that could be rendered "shoot," "shots," or in this case "filmed images."

[367] [Trans.] In the original: *Красная звезда* (*Red Star*). Created by the Politburo in 1923, it was the newspaper of the People's Commissariat of Military and Naval Affairs of the USSR. During WW II, it was a leading source of news across the USSR.

[368] In the original: *Красный Флот* (*Red Fleet*). The Soviet Navy's daily newspaper, created in 1938.

content with the description of the particular episodes in the archive. My work was approved by historians and by colleagues at the former Ministry of Film Production.[369] But, unfortunately, it was not completed.

In order to present an approximation of how I intended to describe shots of the Patriotic War, I would draw the attention of the reader to a record I made of the shots, capturing Lev Nikolaevich Tolstoy.

Poster for *Lev Tolstoy and the Russia of Nicholas II.*

---

[369] [Trans.]: In the original: Министерство кинематографии.

Yasnaya Polyana

In the summer of 1928, I shot Yasnaya Polyana for my film *Lev Tolstoy and the Russia of Nicholas II*. I shot the house, the rooms, where Lev Tolstoy spent his hours of work and leisure: the dining room, the living room, the study and the bedroom, the vaulted room on the ground floor, where he composed his novel *War and Peace*... The house was swimming in blossoming lilac, in a sweet-smelling white and lavender haze. The allées and the garden and the woods and the field all smelled sweetly. It was quiet and sunny. At our request, Tolstoy's niece played for us his favorite sonatas on the piano: "The Moonlight Sonata" and the "Appassionata" of Beethoven, Chopin and others. I filmed her at the piano, on which more than once, Lev Nikolaevich used to play his favorite things. I filmed the places where Lev Nikolaevich used to walk, his great tomb, the village which changed greatly during Soviet times, the lessons given in the new school, high upon the hill. The day of the visit to the house-museum, there were tourists: workers, peasants, students. Sunday evening on the banks of the pond beside a fire, young kolkhozniks relaxed and made merry and an old woman danced a Russian dance, the execution of which, would have pleased Lev Nikolaevich.

In the evenings after our shoots, a Tolstoyan, Igor' Il'ich Il'insky, would come to us. He softly sang the favorite Gypsy romances of Lev Nikolaevich, accompanying himself on the guitar. Nikolai Nikolaevich Gusev[370] was very attentive to the film crew and helped as much as possible.

By this time, I had already located all the film images of L. N. Tolstoy which had been preserved and I had located the old newsreels shot during the period from 1907 to the year of the death of the great writer. All these newsreels recreated the era of tsarist Russia in the final years of L. N. Tolstoy's life.

These were years of savage reaction, arrests, and mass executions without trial, a wave of atrocities by the Black Hundreds. The content of the material was exceptional, making it possible to reveal Stolypin's Russia.

During these years, L. N. Tolstoy's sermon on non-violent resistance to evil rang out.

But in 1908, in answer to the executions he published, "I cannot remain silent."

In 1910, after a long, difficult, painful struggle, he left Yasnaya Polyana forever and died in a small railroad station, until then unknown to anyone, called Astapovo, on the eve of the total disintegration of the monarchy.

To the millions of Soviet readers of the works of the great writer, portraits of Lev Nikolaevich, made by the artists Repin, Ge, Kramskoi, Pasternak, and others are well known—if not by the originals, then through reproductions.

---

[370] [Russian editor's note]: *Gusev, Nikolai Nikolaevich* (1882–1967). Literary scholar, a specialist on the creative work of L. N. Tolstoy. For a short time (1907–1909), Gusev was Tolstoy's secretary.

In these very years, the cinema was still at the dawn of its existence, when it captured the living images of L. N. Tolstoy. The filmed images were produced by the Drankov Cinema firm and were made by the experienced hand of an operator, who had beautifully mastered the camera. With the exception of the badly realized shots taken the day of his eightieth birthday celebration, all the remaining shots were very well filmed and represent enormous historical value. One can only feel distress, that the entire series of shots I found at that time, for the film *Lev Tolstoy and the Russia of Nicholas II*, have disappeared. The shots taken are so expressive, that they give a lively characterization of the great writer and the era.

I will give a description of the shots of L. N. Tolstoy, wherever possible, in chronological order. So, that, at least, the description of the shots will remain. I will give both the record by the writer in his diary for the days of the shoot and the comments of our great contemporary on the value of the cinema. The film ends in 1912. In the final shots, we see the tsar Nicholas leaping to the throne and doll-like courtiers running around—everything was actually shot—it is a formal reception in the throne room and a session of the Council of State. Since the shot was made without lighting equipment, the camera operator turned the handle of the movie camera slowly and unwittingly filmed bits of caricature. S. Eisenstein sent me a Japanese photograph of Tolstoy with the notation on it, that I had embarked upon the path of the attraction.

Description of the shots that capture L. N. Tolstoy.

1. Yasnaya Polyana. On a bench in the garden, with a flowerbed in the background, sits Lev Tolstoy. He is wearing a long, dark overcoat over his shoulders like a cape, boots, and a light-colored wide-brimmed felt hat. He is absorbed in the reading of a book. His face is severe, his bushy eyebrows tangled.

Most likely, Sof'ya Andreevna was also filmed that same day. She is wearing an elegant light-colored lace dress and a large, light-colored hat. On her hands are fingerless gloves. And as she poses before the camera, she cuts roses from the flowerbed.

2.–3. At the open door of the house, on the steps among his relatives, stands Lev Nikolaevich Tolstoy. Beside him are Sof'ya Andreevna and his grandchildren: a boy and a girl with a white bow on her head. Tighter framing: Lev Nikolaevich in profile, speaking with his son-in-law who is standing at the door. Smiling with a surprisingly gentle smile, he moves towards the camera.

4. A sunny day. Lev Nikolaevich and Sof'ya Andreevna appear in the distance on a path surrounded by flowers. Sof'ya Andreevna in a light-colored outfit, without a hat, with a tall coiffure, in her hands a lorgnette on a little chain. She chats endlessly with Tolstoy, smiling at the camera—she is posing. Lev Nikolaevich is clearly dissatisfied with the shot Sof'ya Andreevna has thought up. Already approaching the camera

more closely, gloomily, and sharply he pronounces a few words. Clearly the shoot is unpleasant. Most likely, he is submitting to Sof'ya Andreevna's persistence.

5.–6.–7. A cloudy, windy day. A little winding path beside the woods. Lev Nikolaevich moves towards the camera, with a quick, nervous, somewhat uneven gait. He is so fragile, that the wind rocks him. He is in a dark coat, drawn tight with a belt, in a round dark cap, tight on his head. In his hands is a folding walking stick. His head hangs at half-mast. His gray beard flutters in the wind. He walks, deep in concentration, without noticing the camera.

8.–9. Yasnaya Polyana, August 28, 1908. The day of his eightieth birthday celebration. There is Tolstoy. He is bare-headed, warmly dressed. He is covered with a plaid blanket, there is a cushion positioned for his legs. Next to him, Sof'ya Andreevna and someone else from among those close to him. Lev Nikolaevich rocks his head and smiles. His hands lie on the arms of his rocking chair. His fingers are constantly touching each other, moving in rhythm to some hidden thoughts.

10. On this same day, one of the daughters of the great writer is filmed. She is traveling around the village of Yasnaya Polyana. The village is so poor, miserable, and uncomfortable, like thousands of villages of tsarist Russia.

She is driving a horse [-drawn carriage].[371] At her feet there are boxes with candies and cookies. Village children are running after her. She distributes the sweets.

11.–12. The platform of the station. The train is approaching. Lev Nikolaevich, Sof'ya Andreevna, and those accompanying them head towards the train car. An elderly lady overtakes them; it must be his friend Shmidt. Tolstoy turns, sees her, and quickly goes to meet her. The lady extends her hand, curtseys, and kisses Lev Nikolaevich. The Tolstoys take their seats in the train car. The train pulls away.

1909. September. Krekshino. Lev Nikolaevich Tolstoy on a visit to his friend Chertkov.[372] This is an especially difficult time in the life of Lev Nikolaevich. Life became intolerable for him in the environment of wealth of the landowners' way of life. His personal relationships with his relatives became more and more complicated and painful.

13.–14. The front entrance to the house. Lev Nikolaevich is standing there. He is in a dark tolstovka.[373] On his head, a skull-cap. His hands are tucked inside a belt

---

[371] [Trans.]: The text is slightly ambiguous, but the Drankov footage clearly shows this scene.

[372] [Russian editor's note]: *Chertkov, Vladimir Georgievich* (1854–1936). A well-known follower and promoter of the teachings of L. N. Tolstoy. A close friend of the writer. In Soviet times, he participated in the publication of the Jubilee edition of the works of L. N. Tolstoy.

[373] [Trans.]: Also known as a *kosovorotka*. A long traditional peasant shirt with a line of collar buttons offset to one side, reaching down to mid-thigh. In the existing Drankov footage where Tolstoy drinks a glass of water at his front door, he is wearing an overcoat and a conventional western style suit and a hat with a brim. Though in other footage, where he stands at his front door, he wears a skull-cap and has a woolen sweater thrown over his shoulders, but it is difficult to say he is wearing a tolstovka, which he does in other footage, though they are always white. There are several discrepancies between

Has Shub conflated these two images, or is there additional footage, now lost?

around his waist. Over his shoulders, like a cape, is a knitted woolen sweater. Next to Tolstoy are a lady and a young boy. Lev Nikolaevich's face is sullen. Gradually people surround him. He drinks water from a glass.

15.–16. The day of his departure from Krekshino. Sof'ya Andreevna stands in front of a fence with a bouquet of flowers. On the side, is a photographer with a large camera on a tripod. Out of the woods come Lev Nikolaevich, Chertkov, Gol'denveizer[374] and others.

Lev Nikolaevich turns over to one of the ladies a bouquet of flowers, that had been presented to him. He does this with the elegance of an old man. Gol'denveizer can be seen. From out of the woods appears Sof'ya Andreevna. She crosses the road and hurries, limping just slightly, to join the group.

L. N. Tolstoy. Beside him is Chertkov and some others accompanying them. They walk to the woods in the background. Tolstoy is clearly agitated and upset. His hat is pushed back, his forehead exposed. (This trip to Krekshino likely coincides with the time of the writing of his will.)

---

her descriptions and existing Drankov footage. Either she is referring to footage, which no longer exists as she suggests, or her memory has conflated various pieces of footage. Unfortunately, her Tolstoy film is considered lost and this footage along with it. She says as much. It is difficult to doubt her keen eye for detail, her ability to memorize footage, and the fact that she saw better 35mm copies than the video footage available now, so this footage may be considered lost. However, some of the footage described here seems to have been preserved, perhaps abroad as Drankov is known to have exported some of his films and Tolstoy was certainly a figure of world renown in literature. A closer critical scrutiny of the existing Drankov footage and a comparison with these descriptions might eventually lead the way to a partial reconstruction of her Tolstoy film, though without the footage she shot for it, such a goal would remain elusive.

[374] [Russian editor's note]: *Gol'denveizer, Aleksandr Borisovich* (1875–1961). Composer, pianist and teacher, professor at the Moscow Conservatory. He used to visit L. N. Tolstoy at Yasnaya Polyana.

20.–21. The platform near Krekshino. Porters, passengers, those waiting for the arrival of the train to Moscow. Under the awning of the small train station, Chertkov appears. Behind him are L. N. Tolstoy, Sof'ya Andreevna, Gol'denveizer, and others. Suddenly, the entire platform empties out. Only Tolstoy and Sof'ya Andreevna, who grasps him firmly by the hand, remain.

The following shot is undoubtedly filmed at the insistence of Sof'ya Andreevna Tolstoy.

22. A warm, sunny day. The platform of the station. L. N. Tolstoy in a long dark tolstovka, with a little chain, in a wide-brimmed light-colored hat, in boots polished up to a sparkle. In his hands is a cane. His beard is combed carefully on each side of his face. He goes along holding himself erect. Sof'ya Andreevna grasps him firmly by the hand. In her other hand is a bouquet of flowers. They cast sharp shadows. There is no one on the platform besides them.

23.–24.–25. Lev Nikolaevich, Chertkov, and Gol'denveizer walk along the platform. The train arrives. Boarding. At the foot of the stairs to the train, Lev Nikolaevich bids farewell to those accompanying him and seats himself in the train car. The train pulls away.

September 1909. Moscow. The last visit of L. N. Tolstoy to Moscow.

26. The courtyard of the Tolstoy home in Khamovniki. On the left side of the frame is a dog kennel. At the entrance is a four-seat Landau. The coachman is wearing a thick overcoat cinched up with a belt and a coachman's top hat. From the doors of the entrance L. N. Tolstoy, Sof'ya Andreevna with a bouquet of flowers, and Chertkov walk out. They take their seats in the Landau. The horses pull away.

27.–28. The street at the gates of the house in Khamovniki. In the small crowd, which has gathered waiting for Tolstoy, there is a man around fifteen or twenty years old. There is a gentleman in a bowler hat, a youngster in the peaked cap of a student, but most are simple people wearing caps. The Landau exits with L. N. Tolstoy, Sof'ya Andreevna, and Chertkov seated in it.

29. The Landau travels along a cobblestone Moscow street in the direction of Kursk Station.

30. The Landau arrives at Kursk Station. L. N. Tolstoy is bare-headed (he is holding his hat in his hands) he responds to the greeting of the enormous crowd that has gathered at the station.

31.–32. Entrance to Kursk Station. An enormous crowd surrounds the great writer. Many male and female students. Many workers, many women in scarves. A few gentlemen in bowler hats, porters in white aprons. They are all trying to get a little closer to Tolstoy. They are all greeting him.

33. L. N. Tolstoy, Chertkov, and Sof'ya Andreevna, surrounded by the enormous crowd, remain where they are, so that they can all be filmed together for the

cinema. A young woman is memorable; she must be a student, who can't tear herself away from looking at Tolstoy. There is ecstasy in her eyes.

34. The platform of Kursk Station. An enormous crowd enthusiastically welcomes L. N. Tolstoy as he moves towards the train car.

35. The train pulls away. The enthusiastically screaming crowd runs after the train. A young woman screaming, in some kind of frenzy, running along the tracks is memorable.

1910. The final year of the life of the great writer. Winter. Yasnaya Polyana. The entry of L. N Tolstoy in his diary for the 7th of January:

> "State of mind, somewhat better, no helpless melancholy, only unceasing shame before people. Will I really end life in this shameful state? Lord, help me, I know what is within me, please help me. Got up late. The cinematograph people were shooting. This is nothing. The abject and the petitioners were there and [this is] also nothing. But along the road, we met a group of three who were well-dressed, they asked for help. I forgot about God and refused. And when I remembered, it was too late. I had a good chat with a pitiful, ragged youngster from Pirogov. I met Sasha and Varya and again the cinematograph man... So I did nothing. I went with Dushan... the cinematograph man again. Boring. Weakness came on. Time to rest."

On this day, January 7, the following shots were filmed:

36. Tolstoy in a long fur coat, unbuttoned, in a round warm cap, stooping over, running his fingers along something in his hands, is walking beside the house.

37.–38. Two peasants are standing at the side entrance. One tall in a wretched short fur coat, the other in an old peasant's sheepskin coat. Beside them a dog. Both peasants bow low to Lev Nikolaevich. The tall one approaches him closely, takes off his cap and speaks to him for a long time bare-headed. Tolstoy is clearly unhappy, upset. His face is gloomy, almost angry. There is something he does not agree to. At the end of the conversation, he reluctantly gives them some money. Turning abruptly, he leaves. Plainly, this is not a solution for him.

39.–40. The trunks of the trees on both sides of the road and the road are covered with snow. L. N. Tolstoy moves towards the camera. He is in a winter coat, with a scarf wound around his neck, on his head is a round cap. The winter wind rustles his beard and the flaps of his coat. He walks quickly with an uneven gait, deeply lost in thought, without noticing the filming.

Deeply lost in thought.

L. N. Tolstoy walks into the distance. He walks along an empty, snowy expanse. No sky can be seen. He walks more quickly than usual. The winter wind rocks him. Alone. The snowy expanse, the winter wind. Solitude.

Kochety. At the estate of Tolstoy's daughter Sukhotina. September 7, 1910. The entry for this day in the diary of L. N. Tolstoy about his approaching death: "As it is ordained on high, so let it be. It is already, but is not given to me to see."

This day, two months before his death, the final motion picture images of his life of the great writer were produced.

41.–42. Woods. Shadows and patches of sunlight. Along with a peasant, L. N. Tolstoy, greatly bent over, saws a thick fallen tree.

43. A break in the work. L. N. Tolstoy turns his head. He seriously and attentively looks at the camera.

44. –45. L. N. Tolstoy walks out of the woods. He walks with a weary gait, greatly bent over. His coat over his shoulders.

46. A sunny day. A semi-dark allée. L. N. Tolstoy is chatting with a young woman. Beside them, a white dog. Patches of sunlight glide across Tolstoy's dark coat. He leans on a cane. He speaks in a lively, attentive way. In his manner, the gallantry of an old man.

The person with whom he is speaking does not hear his last words. She hurries to leave, being camera shy. L. N. Tolstoy, smiling, almost with regret, takes leave of her, and goes off in the other direction.

November 1910. Astapovo. A cold autumn. All the shots filmed at Astapovo, are full of genuine drama.

47. A medium pan of the railroad tracks of the Astapovo station with train cars standing in the distance. The pan captures the station and the little house of Ozolin the stationmaster, who sheltered L. N. Tolstoy after he had fallen ill. After a long, painful struggle, L. N. Tolstoy at night, secretly, literally runs away from Yasnaya Polyana. He wants to hide his whereabouts from Sof'ya Andreevna.

48. In the shot is the train car, in which S. A. Tolstaya is residing. The whereabouts of the ailing Tolstoy could not be hidden and she traveled to Astapovo. She goes from the train car to the little house of the stationmaster. She moves slowly, born down by irretrievable grief, growing old at once. Her son and an unknown woman support her.

49. In the shot is the little house of Ozolin and the little steps leading to the front door. S. A. Tolstaya mounts the stairs with difficulty and knocks on the door. The door opens half-way and immediately shuts. It opens again. Someone who has been looking after the sick man comes out. There is a short conversation. The door is clearly blocked to Sof'ya Andreevna. They do not let her in. They quickly slam the door shut. Sof'ya Andreevna remains alone at the entrance with her head bowed low.

50. The window to the room where the sick L. N. Tolstoy is lying. Sof'ya Andreevna stands in front of the window by the fence, leaning against the trunk of a birch tree. She stands there stubbornly, for a long time. She then approaches the window and for an instant she leans her face towards it. Her son and the woman standing next to her try to convince her to leave. She won't listen to them, she is outside of time.

51.–52. In the frame there is a bed. On the bed is the dead L. N. Tolstoy. He is covered up to his chest with a white bedspread.

53. Close: head of the dead L. N. Tolstoy. It lies on a pillow. Around the head are delicate garlands and small bouquets of flowers. Dense gray overhanging brows cast a shadow on the eyes, now closed forever.

54. A great number of people, mostly peasants, crowd around Ozolin's little house, awaiting the carrying out of the body.

55. The carrying out of the coffin from Ozolin's house. The open coffin. Behind the coffin is Sof'ya Andreevna, those near to Tolstoy, and a great number of people.

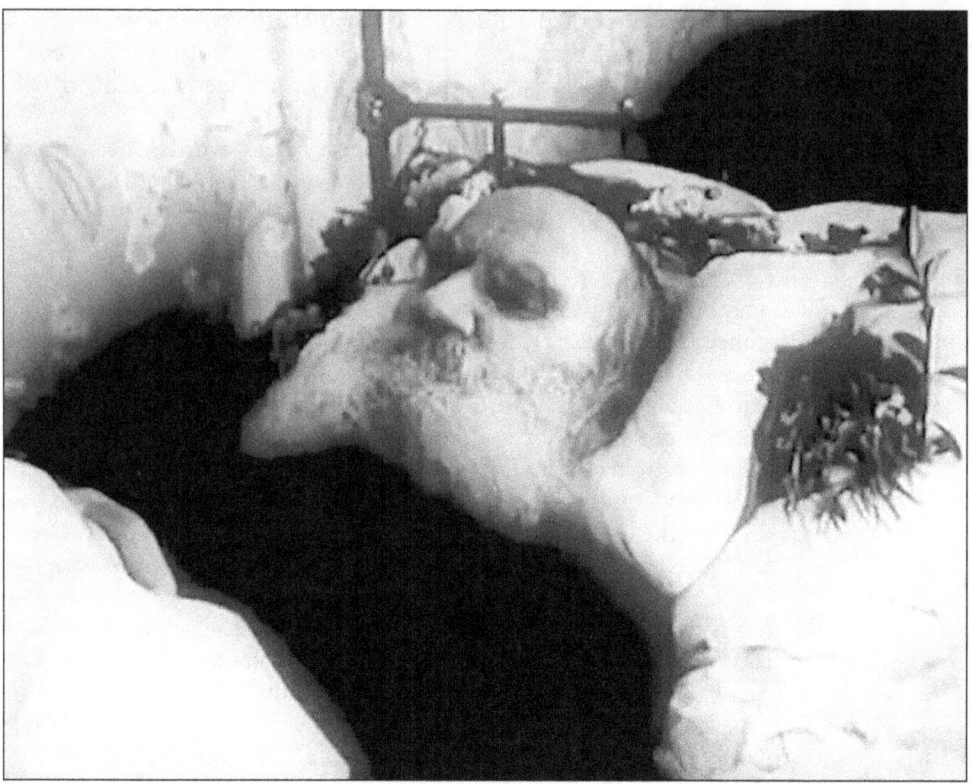

Eyes now closed forever.

56. The coffin is slowly carried into a freight car. A lot of fussing with the funeral wreaths. The doors of the train car close.

57. The road to the Yasnaya Polyana Estate. An enormous crowd moves behind the coffin. The Yasnaya Polyana peasantry carry a long white banner. On it is written: "Lev Nikolaevich, the memory of your goodness will live in our hearts eternally."[375] A great number of gendarmes and mounted policemen.

58. Pan of the approach of the procession towards the gates of Yasnaya Polyana and the entrance into Yasnaya Polyana Park.

59. The coffin is brought inside the house at Yasnaya Polyana.

---

[375] [Trans.]: While this banner is not shown in the current Drankov footage known to me, there is a shot of one illegible banner and another shot of a banner which reads: Левъ Николаевичъ! Память о твоемъ добрѣ НЕ УМРЕТЪ среди насъ осиротѣвшихъ Ясн. Пол. (Lev Nikolaevich! The memory of your goodness WILL NOT DIE among us, the bereaved peasants of Yasnaya Polyana.)

60. A huge crowd awaits the carrying out of the coffin. In the crowd, the poet Valery Bryusov can be seen distinctly.

61. The coffin is carried out of the house at Yasnaya Polyana. The huge crowd kneels. Only gendarmes and policemen remain standing.

62.–66. Opposite the ravine. A civil funeral at the place of interment. The coffin is committed to the earth. A huge crowd kneels. One gets the impression, that the crowd tries to get the gendarmes and police to kneel as well.

67. At the site of "the little green stick" stands the lonely grave of Lev Nikolaevich Tolstoy, covered by the first snow.

There are a whole series of shots not described by me, but they were no less significant, showing living images of L. N. Tolstoy at various times of his life.

The image of the great writer, fixed on a strip of film, gave a huge gamut of changes of emotion, of movements of the thought and behavior of Lev Nikolaevich at various moments of his life.

It was not within the power of the portraits even of the masters of the brush such as Repin, Kramskoi and Ge to give such an exhaustive completeness of expression.

In the film *Lev Tolstoy and the Russia of Nicholas II*, I used historical newsreels to complement this material. Each shot presented enormous historical interest. Real events and occurrences of these years, as well as those in the midst of which Tolstoy lived in those years, were successfully organized through montage, so that, the spirit of that era reached the Soviet spectator. The persuasiveness of real, non-staged material helped to eloquently reveal the utter loneliness of Tolstoy and the resignation of his sermons. This film was not preserved.[376]

The comments of Lev Nikolaevich Tolstoy on the cinematograph have come down to us. From them, it is obvious, what enormous significance he attributed to the new invention.

January 5–7, 1910, film screenings, organized by Drankov took place at Yasnaya Polyana. They showed *Working Life in Bombay*, *The Zoological Park in London*, and the acted film *The Power of Darkness*. Drankov's remarks about this screening are preserved: "It is essential," said Tolstoy, "that the cinématographe[377] capture Russian reality in its most diverse manifestations. Russian life must be reproduced just as it is…" From further conversations, in which T. L. Sukhotina participated, it is clear, that there was also a discussion of the kind of film adaptations, that would truly reflect Russian reality. L. N. Tolstoy expressed the desire to glimpse on the screen Russian writers and public figures who had been filmed. They showed him Leonid Andreev and also those shots filmed during the time of the latest visit of L. N. Tolstoy to

---

[376] [Trans.]: In the original: Этот фильм не сохранился.

[377] [Trans.]: In the original: синематограф [cinematograf], a transliteration of the French name for the device. The usual word would be кинематограф [kinematograf].

Moscow. This sequence, in the words of Drankov, made a strong impression on Lev Nikolaevich: "Oh," said Lev Nikolaevich, "if only I could see my mother and father now, just as I see myself?" This sequence,[378] by his request, was shown a second time.

In 1922, the Tolstoy follower I. Teneromo published the following thoughts by L. N. Tolstoy, commenting on the cinematograph:

"You will see," said L. N., "that this clattering little thing with the handle that turns round is going to change something in our life as writers. It is a campaign against our old ways of literary art. An attack. An assault. We will have to adapt ourselves to the pale half-tones of the screen, to the cold glass lens. A new way of writing is required. I like the quick changes of scenes. True, this is better than the drawn out, slicking up of the plot. This is closer to life, if you like. And there, changes and excesses flash and fly past and emotional experiences are like hurricanes. The cinematograph has cracked the secret of movement and this is great. When I wrote *The Living Corpse*, I tore my hair out, bit my own fingers in pain and frustration, because it's impossible to present a large number of scenes, a large number of pictures, it's impossible to switch from one event to another…"

In *Utro Rossii*[379] on April 29, 1910, a few months before the death of L. N. Tolstoy, the following words of Lev Nikolaevich spoken to Leonid Andreev, while visiting Yasnaya Polyana at the beginning of April 1910, were published.

L. Andreev told Lev Nikolaevich, that he had advised Drankov to arrange a competition for writers for creating film scenarios. "You know," [said Tolstoy] when he met Andreev the next morning, "I've been thinking all about the cinematograph. Even last night I woke up and was thinking it all over. I've decided to write for the cinematograph. Of course, it would be essential, for there to be a reader, like in Amsterdam, who would deliver the text, and without the text it would be impossible."

If this had been realized, it would be the first talking film, a precursor of the sound cinema.

We filmed little of the great Lenin and his associates. And none too much of Maxim Gorky. Vladimir Mayakovsky, Stanislavsky and others we practically did not film at all. How little we now pay attention to genuinely, intelligently and fully capturing our great contemporaries. This is something to think about for the Ministry of Culture and the Film Section of the Writers Union.

---

[378] [Trans.]: In the original: съемка. This might also be translated as a shoot, a shot, a series of images, filmed images, or even a sequence, depending on the context. Shub is not utterly rigorous in separating the process of shooting from that of editing.

[379] [Trans.]: In the original: *Утро Poccuu* (*Russia's Morning*), a Moscow daily newspaper.

I have tried to write a book of remembrances of a few of the remarkable people, whom I had the good fortune to meet in my work, of people, who passed through my life *in close up*. I strove to record what seemed to me to be of interest to society and perhaps of interest when read not only by my friends and comrades, but by any Soviet reader. Above all, it was my desire to tell young Soviet readers about the roads traveled by Soviet film production and about the people who created it.

I don't know, whether my ability was sufficient.

I have always been the enemy of dilettantism. I well know, that true ability in any field, is a matter not only of talent, or aptitude, but of labor. Unrelenting labor, proven by the years.

Russian Literature was my school, my university.

Soviet filmmaking, in particular, documentary, is the labor of my adult life.

At any hour of the day or night, I was ready to enter the screening room and tirelessly watch film shot but not yet edited, because that for me was the most interesting material coming from the entire Soviet Union. Shots fixing the life of our Motherland, her utterly rich and many-sided life, fixing achievements of labor by the simple people of our country and their passionate love towards their Motherland, the Party, the Government, always inspire me. I easily commit to memory the content within the frame of what is shot, I commit to memory the graphic characteristics of the shot. I am always drawn towards shooting, drawn to be with the operator and his camera. My hands and eyes are drawn towards the editing table. I know all of this.

But all this is behind me.

And here, there was no such certainty of *knowledge*, when I wrote this book. I am not a writer, so at once I decided to limit myself.

I wanted for this to be a record of a filmmaker, a simply truthful story, with no "literary embellishment." I wanted to write simply, like rigorous and truthful documentary shots, when taken by the able eyes and hands of a camera operator. If I have succeeded even a little, it means that my labor in this field, which is new to me, is not in vain.

I would like, for the conclusions drawn by me as the result of thirty-five years of labor, to merit close attention in themselves.

This story inevitably resurrects the paths of development of Soviet filmmaking.

Aleksandr Aleksandrovich Fadeev was the editor of this book.

It was to him that I first showed the plan I had conceived.

He made me believe, that I would write it. Through this belief, he brought new substance to my life.

He found the time to scrutinize each chapter.

He even accepted the style of my writing—not at all literary, but rather cinematographic.

All of his directives were permeated with good will in order to help me. When the work was approaching its end, he wrote to me, what he thought of my book. This letter gave me inspiration.

With deep respect and love, the final words of this book, words of gratitude, I dedicate to a magnificent writer of the Soviet land: Aleksandr Fadeev.

1953–1956.

Two faces of Aleksandr Aleksandrovich Fadeev.

Part II
Articles and Statements

About Myself (1929)

I have been working in the cinema since 1921. In the Photo-Cinema Committee, later reorganized as Sovkino, I was the secretary responsible for the Soviet of the Arts and Film Censorship Board. Wanting to work in production, I began with re-editing foreign films. I actively participated in the journal *Kino-fot*,[1] around which, a group of young people just starting to work were getting organized.

From my work on foreign films, I passed over to editing features, helping young directors.

In 1927, I began my own work using newsreel material.

My first picture—*Fall of the Romanov Dynasty*—was constructed from historical documents. The following work was a film celebrating the tenth anniversary of the revolution: *The Great Way*. For the hundredth anniversary of the birth of L. N. Tolstoy, I released my film *Lev Tolstoy and the Russia of Nicholas II*.

I have just finished the outline for a large work using authentic documentary material *Today* (*Capital and Labor*) based on a large-scale shoot.

The Woman of the USSR[2] will be my next work.

The Fabrication of Facts (1926)

One of the significant facts of our filmmaking front is the fact of the recognition of the non-acted motion picture.[3] This is not a declaration, or an article, or a resolution, nor even a decree: it is the fact of the real organization of actual production.

And this production base is to be called the factory of facts, in which the "kinoks" will work.

The "kinoks," to whom this production facility will be assigned and entrusted, of course, merited, or, so to say, earned this right. There is nothing to object to here. But it is impossible not to object to the monopoly of the "kinoks."

In non-acted filmmaking, it is not only those who in the USSR see through "kino-eyes,"[4] or those who know how to express Soviet construction as "passionate film-fighters," who want to work.

Various facts should make their way into the factory.

The latter should consider for this, getting rid of their futurist sign board and becoming simply a factory of non-acted filmmaking, where the editing of newsreels, revolutionary-historical films produced from newsreel film material, where scientific,

---

[1] [Trans.]: *Kino-fot* was edited by Alexei Gan who eventually became Shub's husband. Its six issues included contributions by Vertov, Mayakovsky, and Kuleshov, among others.

[2] [Trans.]: In the original: *Женщина СССР*.

[3] [Trans.]: In the original: признании неигровой кинокартины.

[4] [Trans.]: In the original «кино-глазом» [kino-glazom] alludes to Vertov's kino-glaz, or kino-eye.

industrial films, and, above all, cultural filmmaking could be accomplished, as a counterbalance to acted, entertainment films.

The factory of facts is not needed, if it is a fabrication of facts.

To Work! (1926)

In 1922, the first Constructivists in a series of articles in *Kino-fot* raised the slogan:

For the Newsreel!

Long live the demonstration of everyday life!

They conducted a struggle for shooting authentic, non-staged film documents, emphasizing, that only the newsreel can and should reflect our greatest historical era. This was taken by the film community, at best, as a childhood disease of leftism, at worst, as a demonstration of stupidity.

Now, on the ten-year anniversary of October, everyone is conscious of the significance of newsreels.

The work of Vertov's "kinoks," in the most difficult years of the struggle for the newsreel, my works, those of Kaufman, Karmazinsky, Kopalin and others in the following years established the non-acted film front with reasonable cogency.

But the struggle is not over.

The technological and material conditions for newsreels, industrial and scientific films continue to be difficult.

There is no opportunity to make experimental work. We are studying ourselves very little. We are studying others very little.

There are few workers.

We shoot little and not always what is needed.

What and how do we shoot?

The development of technique.

The problem of form.

The organization of film archives, organically connected with the newsreel factory.

We must work on that! and work! and work!

And then, the so-called *feature* film[5] will not only find itself in a tight spot, but its speculative essence, which deceives the consciousness of viewers, will be exposed.

---

[5] [Trans.]: In the original: «художественная» фильма, literally "artistic" film; at this point, only applied to acted films. To my knowledge, the feature-length documentary, with the possible exception of Vertov's *Годовщина Революции* [*Anniversary of the Revolution*] (1918) did not exist, though the limitations of that film might arguably deny it the sense of authorship also implied by *khudozhestvennaya*. It is interesting to note, that Shub omits mention of it here. Her *Fall of the Romanov Dynasty* (1927), on which she may well have been at work while writing this, is often polemically cited as the first feature-length documentary with a clear stamp of authorship.

Before *February* (1927)[6]

The non-acted Soviet film is the greatest phenomenon of our film industry. It is the most wide-ranging field of work, in which there can be no one-sided solutions and no devices established once and for all. It is a new undertaking and, in the realization of its fundamental task, various methods can and should be adopted, provided they are precise and clear.

Until now, attempts have been made to create a few such motion pictures, in such a way, that they were fully completed film productions. But these attempts have erred, in that, an extremely unclear method was employed in determining the goal of the work in non-acted films and in the work itself.

The lack of clarity of method announces itself above all, in that the authors, in attempting to create a new film-object[7] without a treatment, without actors, sets and other devices and accessories of acted feature-length motion pictures—nevertheless, are forced to make use of a series of devices, which have been and continue to be used in fiction, dramatic, and entertainment film production.

The motion picture *February* is constructed somewhat differently.

In this work, an attempt is made to bring to bear a precise and clear functional method.

The task is to show "February."[8] And since the essence of the cinema is not to tell, but to show, "February" must be shown in its complete historical truth. For this, nothing needs to be concocted, or made up.

It is necessary to understand events well, to thoroughly memorize the material at hand, and, making use of technology and of the mastery of montage, to connect it in a monolithic[9] form of political and social significance. Only in that way, is it appropriate to bring to the screen an historical chronicle. In order for it to be meaningful and convincing, it is unavoidable to use a series of technological devices, about which it is not appropriate to speak—they must be shown in the film-object itself.

---

[6] [Trans.]: *February* was Shub's working title for her film released by the studio as *Fall of the Romanov Dynasty*.

[7] [Trans.]: In the original: киновещь [kinoveshch']: a term used by Vertov and others with Constructivist interests.

[8] [Trans.]: I believe that here Shub is alluding to the events of the February revolution, rather than to her motion picture of that title.

[9] [Trans.]: In the original: монолитный.

[From my experience] (1927)

The picture *Fall of the Romanov Dynasty* (*February*) was made for the tenth anniversary of the February revolution. The February revolution is considered to be the uprising of millions of workers and peasants against the historically obsolete autocracy and a stage on the way to the seizure of power by working people in October 1917.

There are 3 themes in the picture:

"Tsarist Russia in the years of Black Reaction and Europe during these same years."

"World War."

"February."

All the material of the picture is taken from Russian and foreign film newsreels from the period of 1913 to 1917.

The condition of our newsreel archives complicated the work significantly. It was particularly difficult to find February material. Practically all of the negative material of the events in Leningrad was, as they say, "transferred" to America; some 500 to 600 meters of negative material of the February days in Moscow was preserved. The vast majority of the positive material, which I managed to find, came from the former storage facility of Kino-Moskva [Cinema-Moscow] and from the Moscow film archive of Sovkino. I hunted down around 60 meters of precious positive material (armored cars) at the Museum of the Revolution. All of the positive material turned out to be in such a technical condition, that for a whole series of pieces of film, it wasn't possible to create intermediate printing material and they had to be excluded. In the process of working over the course of two months, I had occasion to look at 60,000 meters of positive and negative material. For editing, 5,200 meters were printed (from negatives via intermediate printing material) of which some 1,500 meters were included in the motion picture. In the editing of this picture, I strove to uphold the principle of the documentariness[10] of newsreel material. Without abstracting the material, without specifying merely formal tasks (thematic content is the focus, form is only the means of expression) I employed the functional method of Constructivism. This allowed me the possibility of rigorously and systematically, despite the extremely limited range of historical facts recorded on film, all the same, to bring the material together into a complete film object, demonstrating[11] the well-known stage of the revolution.

The elaboration of a plan[12] and the emphasis of themes were realized by me in collaboration with the Museum of the Revolution. M. Z. Tseitlin, a research fellow of the Museum of the Revolution, worked as an advisor.

---

[10] [Trans.]: In the original: документальность [dokumentalnost'], that is, its quality as a document.

[11] [Trans.]: The notion of demonstration is another key part of Constructivist thought.

[12] [Trans.]: In the original: Выработка плана.

It is my belief, that the actual experience I underwent in the work on *February*, will convince many people of the necessity of immediately raising the question of the preservation of negative material and of making intermediate printing material from existing positive material. Existing material is decaying, drying out, becoming damaged. With each day, our chances grow fewer of succeeding in preserving for posterity entire pieces of film of the period from the February days to the October struggles (there are almost no negatives of this material).

It is essential to understand, that each piece of newsreel film shot now should be regarded as a *document* for future days. This consciousness should determine the purpose and the content of events and occurrences filmed, the form, the montage, and treatments, the dating of pieces of film. Without material of our days, the future will not be able to understand and comprehend our present.

["We do not reject the element of mastery"] (1927)

The entire question lies in what we should film now. As long as just this is clear, the terminology is not important—acted or non-acted film. It is important that we are LEF.[13]

We think, that in our era, we must film only newsreels, and in that way, preserve our era for a future generation. Only this. This means that we want to film the current day, the people of today, current events. [...][14]

It is important to us, that the camera film both Lenin and Dybenko.[15]

---

[13] [Trans.]: That is, The Left Front of the Arts.

[14] [Trans.]: This is apparently not Shub's redaction of the stenogram of the LEF conference on film, which appeared in *Novy LEF*, 11–12 of 1927. A slightly longer version is translated in *The Film Factory: Russian and Soviet Cinema in Documents,* edited by Richard Taylor and Ian Christie (Harvard, 1988). The sentence missing here I would translate as: "Whether Lenin or Rykov acts badly in front of the camera and whether this will be a moment of acting, does not trouble us in the least. It is important to us, that the camera films both Lenin and Dybenko, even if they do not know how to comport themselves before the camera, because this moment best characterizes them." There are also other minor differences: where Shub says "picture" she is recorded as having said "film," for example. Shub objected to this transcription of her remarks as inaccurate and demanded that a more accurate version edited by her be printed. See Shub's letter to Tret'yakov, #56 in this volume. When this was refused, both she and Eisenstein broke off relations with the *Novy LEF* group, though not with all of its members on a personal basis.

[15] [Trans.]: Pavel Efimov Dybenko. A controversial and mercurial figure of the early years of the Russian Revolution. He was, at one time, married to the feminist Alexandra Kollontai. He was tortured by the NKVD and executed as a traitor by Stalin in 1938. He was "rehabilitated" some 20 years later.

Why does Dybenko reach you in a way that's not abstract? Because it is Dybenko himself and not someone representing Dybenko. And it doesn't bother us that, if here, there is an acted moment.

Therefore, we insist, that you not eliminate this term: non-acted filmmaking. Let's speak about non-acted filmmaking. Suppose there are some acted moments. What does it mean when, for example, you watch a remarkable acted film, shot three years ago? You won't be able to watch it; it will simply be indigestible. And when you watch a non-acted film, this is not the case; it turns out to be interesting, because this is a piece of life, that has actually taken place. Whatever acted elements may be there.

But the whole matter is in the technology.

When you have good lighting equipment, when there are good technological means for shooting, then the element of acting will fall away.

Today, the struggle is no longer, whether we should shoot newsreels. On every street corner, in all the newspapers they are writing, that we need the newsreel. There's no longer any need to agitate in favor of the newsreel; our work agitates better than any article. It is now important to struggle for the possibility of working at a high standard. We are accumulating material; mastery comes with the years.

Why do you think, that we don't want to make emotionally moving pictures? The whole matter lies in the material we want to work with.

Do we really reject the element of mastery? We do not reject it. We are convinced, that with mastery in the non-acted film, it is possible to make better films than any feature acted films. It's a matter of method.

The Great Way (1928)

The Great Way (*10 Years*) was done by me using unstaged, authentic film documents. We, the workers in the non-acted film, believe with the utmost certainty, that the path of cultural-revolutionary cinema lies in the rejection of acting to reflect reality and that this very thing most deforms reality.

Our cinema, above all, must reflect the greatest historical era, whose contemporaries we have the fortune to be. And this can be done only on the condition of the systematic accumulation of newsreel material. When this is comprehended with sufficient force, then, not in words, but in deeds, will the technological and material conditions of the newsreel be transformed and normal conditions for workers, innovators, experimenters in the cultural film be realized.

But these conditions do not yet exist. In order to collect surviving pieces of film material, scattered in the most varied locations, it was necessary for me to undertake a tremendous amount of work.

Having collected the material, it was necessary to establish the content and date of the piece, to carefully transfer the dried-out negative and positive film, which had deteriorated from improper storage, to intermediate materials and, thus, to preserve the material from final destruction.

Much historical material perished, much precious material slipped away abroad by mysterious paths, many important moments of the struggle and construction are not recorded on film. It was difficult to comprehend and cement together the selected material in a thematically coherent fashion. While working on *The Great Way*, we knew all this, but we worked with enthusiasm, convinced, that these badly preserved pieces of film of low technical quality could authentically resurrect the great way we have traversed and preserve for the future generation *the truth* about the harsh and heroic era of struggle of their fathers for a brighter future in coming days.

First Work (1928)

Two hundred foreign feature motion pictures reedited by me, ten Soviet ones edited by me were my training school in montage. But my first independent work I accomplished using non-acted, newsreel material.

To get this work was difficult. The director of the factory didn't think I could do it.

At the end of August, 1926, I was commissioned to make a film chronicle for the ten-year anniversary of the February Revolution. To clarify for myself the goal of the thing and the method, which would be necessary in order to realize it, I immersed myself in the search for material. "To discover" material became a sport bordering on mania. There was no film archive in either the Leningrad or Moscow film factory. Precious historical material lay unaccounted for. Heaps of unnumbered boxes lay there mysteriously, but what was in them, no one knew.

In my hands were lists of old film newsreels; they didn't help me to orient myself amidst the utter chaos. It was established, with some effort, that negatives of the newsreels of the days of the February Revolution had long ago gone to America; bubbled up pieces of the tsar's newsreels went there in exchange for packages from the ARA.[16] Sovkino via Amtorg[17] bought back a portion of the material discovered in America, but I received it when I was already working on *The Great Way* (1927). In sorting out this material, a most precious discovery was made: *unknown shots on nega-*

---

[16] [Trans.]: The American Relief Administration was agency of the US Government formed in 1919 to give aid to Europe and later to post-revolutionary Russia.

[17] [Trans.]: Amtorg was the Amtorg Trading Corporation, a private company established in 1924 in New York, controlled by the People's Commissariat for Foreign Trade of the Soviet Union. It provided trade links for the exchange of goods between the United States and the Soviet Union.

tive of V. I. Lenin, close-ups, with a cat on his lap (pieces first shown in *The Great Way*) (1927). Material of the February Revolution was found, in part, in positive prints left in the warehouse of the former film organization Kino-Moskva, and, in part, in the Museum of the Revolution.

Fighting in Verdun and the Gaumont and Pathé newsreels of the time of the imperialist war[18] were found by chance in a warehouse of unknown material in the 1st Factory of Sovkino. The tsar's newsreels in Leningrad were stacked up in a damp basement and had not been studied by anyone previously.

The disparate negatives selected by me were carefully studied. It took a year to bring the shots into order. Sometimes, we succeeded in putting together an entire sequence, pieces of which had been scattered in various places. The theme grew out of the material organically. The theme and the material defined the form of the thing.

By connecting the scattered pieces of events through meaningful montage, the film *Fall of the Romanov Dynasty* presented an authentic film document of the recent past.

The purpose was not only to show fact, but to give to fact an evaluation from the point of view of the class that had been victorious in its struggles. This made the film, which had been edited for the most part from counter-revolutionary material, revolutionary and agitational.

The fact that the spectators were agitated by real environments, real people and events, given in historical sequence and with an accurate perspective, made the film not only agitational and propagandistic, but also emotionally infectious. Because there is no force more influential than the force of fact, presented creatively and with a clear purpose.

The conviction, that a truthful purpose, that only authentic, unstaged film documents can and should reveal the past *as well as our era*, helped to overcome all difficulties.

I knew, that if the effort to deliver an historical motion picture based on authentic material would prevail, it would serve as the most convincing *agitation for the newsreel*, for the necessity of preserving, systematizing, and studying the accumulated material.

I knew that, such a film should convince those doubters genuflecting before the acted film, that newsreel type pieces of film[19] were suitable not only for being glued into "cinema magazines," but, that from the material, it was possible to create a great thematic feature. In 1928 *this was already clear to everyone.*

I privately considered the victory of *Fall of the Romanov Dynasty* to be a victory of school and method.

---

[18] [Trans.]: This is the standard Soviet way of referring to what in the U.S. is called World War I.

[19] [Trans.]: The words Shub uses are хроникальные куски [khronikal'nye kuski]. There is no suitable one-word English translation which preserves the dual meaning of хроникальные, which refers both to newsreels as an adjective and more widely to chronicles.

During these two years, some kind of real results were achieved. The film archives of Moscow and Leningrad began to carefully collect and systematize material. Newsreels moved away from the standard practice: shots of October and May celebrations, public meetings, and physical culture.

The camera of the newsreel reporter slowly, and not always consciously, heroically overcoming difficult conditions, is striving to penetrate into the heart of political, social, economic, and everyday life.

Newsreel material is becoming charged... a squirt of camphor for acted filmmaking, whose strength is failing (now there is practically no acted film, that does not include newsreel sequences).

The non-acted film became a reality and even under conditions of unequal opportunities, is already conquering the large first-run theaters.

The road ahead for me and my work is to present a film of authentic material of today with the real activities in it of people in the daily struggle for a new life.

To learn how to film these people in their daily behavior—that is what I want to work on.

Lev Tolstoy and the Russia of Nicholas II (1928)

An endeavor to reflect one of the periods of time, in which Tolstoy was active, organically connected with his era, and to present his characteristics as a thinker, through the use of newsreel material, is a new endeavor and comes with extraordinary responsibility.

Any staging was excluded. The approach was to work with authentic, preserved film documents, to work with letters, manuscripts, the physical environment and objects, immediately connected with Tolstoy and his era. (Naturally, by virtue of the inadequate quantity of filmed material of Tolstoy himself and those years, the scope of the task narrowed.) But precisely this approach allowed for the possibility of resurrecting the authentic world of preserved facts, the living image of Tolstoy and not by means of speculative devices, but through a method of selection and organization of authentic facts, it allowed for the possibility of directing the consciousness of the spectator towards an accurate perception of Tolstoy and the principles of Tolstoy's thought. And my next work must fulfill another such task. It must seriously pose the question of the immediate neglect of our newsreels, which are not filming people in their activities, people, who are the brains of our country. We must film their work, their participation in political and social life, their everyday life, their domestic environments, their surroundings.

As for the objective and plan according to which the work will be conducted for the selection and organization of material, I would like to bring to bear the words of V. I. Lenin:

"...the correct evaluation of Tolstoy is possible only through the point of view of the class, whose political role and whose struggle at the time of the first outbreaks of these conflicts, at the time of the revolution, showed its calling as a leader in the struggle for the freedom of the People and for the liberation of the masses from exploitation..."

The theme of the film must reflect the era and the active forces influencing it, Tolstoy as an artist and moralist, and thus, his connection to this era.

Russia at the juncture of the break-down of the feudal-manorial way of life and emerging capitalism.

Vast spaces lacking even roads.
The country estates of the landed nobility.
Pastures, fields, and forests, etc.
And millions of peasants, the majority not serfs, "Freemen."
wretched
cold
hungry
death hanging over them
homeless lives
mud
superstition
in desperation crying out to god
seeking oblivion in vodka
Railroads, factories, mills under construction
Exploitation of peasants as cheap labor, as they flee
the countryside, major commerce and industry growing.
The cities of merchants, factory owners.
Poverty, suffering of the working masses.
The coronation of Nicholas II.
The family estate of Count Volkonsky: Yasnaya Polyana.
Tolstoy's ancestors were minions of the tsars, owners of serfs
Count Lev Nikolaevich Tolstoy was a contrite nobleman...
outwardly simplifying...
rejecting opulence
working for himself (not making use of the labor of others)
Continuation of the lifestyle typical of the landed nobility
of those surrounding him.
The village of Yasnaya Polyana, like any other village
Documents of the actions of S. A. Tolstaya, as landowner

In this situation, the protest of Tolstoy against autocracy,
state violence, exploitation (documents)
The protest against societal lies, wretchedness, suffering
of the working masses (documents)
The unmasking of Orthodoxy and priests (documents)

In those days when…

Documents	Events
Calendars, dates of massacres of revolutionaries, of all who rose up against violence, who dared to assert their personal freedom (members of sects).	And the tsar's mania for processions… hypocrisy, …bloody decrees, "to banish, to execute, and so on." Minions of the tsar carrying out his will, landowners, all powerful officials. the "Balalaikins."[20] The State Duma. The Press. And alongside this, the Orthodox police-run church, through the mouths of the priests, in the name of god and the cross, enforcing inequalities, violence, slavery, excommunicating Tolstoy from the church.
Response to all this of Tolstoy.	
Moral improvement. Creation of his own religion. The uselessness of education, of urban culture. And the sermon on non-resistance to evil.	Fragments of documents showing Unrelenting Poverty, the struggle for existence. The Tolstoyans as the same kind of popery. Drunkenness, superstition, savagery of the masses. Violent reprisals and preparations for the greatest violence, for war.

---

[20] [Trans.] Saltykov-Shchedrin created a character called Balalaikin, a lawyer and plotter of intrigues.

Tolstoy's outcry, the feeling of protest and indignation in "I cannot remain silent" (documents)

AND

revolutionary leaflets of that time.

The death and burial of Tolstoy.

The struggle of the millions, realizing where their enemy lies.

The end of autocracy (February to October).

The destruction of private ownership of land. The end of the domination of the bourgeoisie (factories and mills in the hands of the workers)

Instead of darkness and savagery of the masses…

Yasnaya Polyana…

In Yasnaya Polyana the elimination of illiteracy

Village life (nurseries, village reading rooms, community-mindedness)…

The rationalization of agriculture…

The House of the Volkonskys, of the Tolstoys, as a museum in memory of Tolstoy.

The familiarization of the masses with science… Higher education…

The goals, aspirations, and activism of youth towards collectivism, towards the Construction of Socialism.

This work cries out (1928)

Have S. Eisenstein and G. Alexandrov, with their picture *October*, fulfilled the task of the jubilee commission of the CEC,[21] as a social contract carrying the greatest responsibility received by these masters of filmmaking? Have they produced *Ten Days that Shook the World*? Have they made the people and things of ten years ago return and convince us, that, in precisely that way, *a fact of world significance* took place: the seizure of power by workers and peasants and that this is Lenin, who gesticulates on the screen, and that it is this *Vladimir Il'ich*, who through his great intelligence and through his will led the uprising?

No, *October* did not fulfill this task.

You must not stage an historical fact, because staging distorts a fact.

---

[21] [Trans.]: In the original: ЦИК (ЦЕНТРАЛЬНЫЙ ИСПОЛНИТЕЛЬНЫЙ КОМИТЕТ) (THE CENTRAL EXECUTIVE COMMITTEE).

You must not substitute for Vladimir Lenin an actor's performance[22] and a face, resembling Vladimir Il'ich.

You must not allow the millions of peasants and workers, who did not participate in the struggles, and those who will succeed us—the Komsomol and Pioneers—to think, that precisely according to *October* by Sergei Eisenstein and Alexandrov, that the events of those great days took place.

In such things, historical truth is needed, facts, documents, and the greatest rigor in execution; newsreels are what is needed.

And the very talented, very cultured Eisenstein, who has produced a whole series of remarkable, principled, formal solutions (but falling outside the task assigned), the talented Alexandrov, one of the best camera operators Tissé, the 100,000-strong army, who passed in front of the camera, and all the remaining singular resources are powerless to fulfill the task given them using their methods and their approach.

This work cries out: film in a more organized way, film newsreels, film events, facts, people participating in life, and not playing at life, because only film newsreels will preserve our great era for future generations.

The Newsreel, once again (1929)

Lev Tolstoy and the Russia of Nicholas II was my third work. As with the previous two, it was made from old material. My first works, *Fall of the Romanov Dynasty* and *The Great Way*, I made with great enthusiasm. Why do I return so insistently to old material? Because I work within the sphere of a specific school, the school of the Constructivists. The task of this school in filmmaking is to work with authentic, non-staged material. We are deeply convinced, that only the newsreel, only the non-acted film, only living material has the ability to reflect the great era we are experiencing and the people who are truly living and creating within it.

When they proposed to me to make a film about Tolstoy, I was in a very difficult position. The figure of Tolstoy is very controversial and complex and very little material is recorded on film. But I decided right there, there was an obligation not to abandon this work, that working on this was necessary. For the first time ever, an attempt was being made using non-acted material to show not the collective, but the individual, to give an assessment through the general political attitudes of Tolstoy. I was given an estimable, complex task of extremely great responsibility, that would have to be worked out in five to six months.

---

[22] [Trans.]: In the original: игра [igra].

How then, did I work…? There were 80 meters in all of Tolstoy. And so, based on these 80 meters, I set myself the task of making a film. Besides that footage, there were 100 meters of Yasnaya Polyana, 100 meters of Astapovo and around 300–400 meters of newsreel footage of the burial. And that is all. With material such as that, of course, I could not give an account of the religious-philosophical theory of Tolstoy. It was not only a matter of montage. Montage is absolutely the fundamental form of knowledge for workers in filmmaking. A person, who does not know montage, should absolutely not make pictures. In the same way, a camera operator, who does not know how to shoot, should not shoot, a director, who does not know how to work with actors, is not a director. These are the principal elements, without which, it is impossible to make a picture. It's not just a matter of montage, but of purpose.

I had, for the most part, materials relating to everyday life and newsreels of formal ceremonies. More than anything else, there were films about the tsar. Nicholas II loved to be filmed and there is around 40,000 meters of newsreels of the tsar. He had his own camera operator, a good camera operator, and frequently the quality of the material is quite good. The newsreels of the tsar are of inexpressible significance and meaning. And so my task was to select material, which I could repurpose,[23] that is, make distinctive. We succeeded in finding very interesting newsreels. You will see Sarovsky Hermitage, Moscow in 1906, the starving countryside of 1906–1907, Khitrov Market in 1906. All this material was very intriguing, interesting in its meaning and significance. That's how we succeeded in making this film. The task was to give an account of only one side of Tolstoy's activity: the non-violent resistance to evil. So expressive and remarkable are the newsreels of that time, that they alone by themselves express the delusional quality of this preaching and the utter loneliness of Tolstoy.

One request to the comrades, who will be seeing this picture. You already possess some kind of culture, when you watch an acted film, it is the culture of the spectator. Unfortunately, this culture does not exist for the non-acted film. And the spectator bears no guilt in this. In this, we are guilty. We have very few non-acted films, we are only beginning to work. Our works need to be understood as educational. We do not have the traditions, nor the opportunities, which exist for acted filmmaking. Our works must be looked at differently. In them, there is no plot, or story,[24] as there is in an acted film; the material works completely differently: in its documentariness, in its authenticity. Acted filmmaking is directed for the most part towards the emotions of the spectator, and we direct ours towards his intellect. The viewing of our works should entail not an emotional depth, but an intellectual one, only that can afford the possibility of accurately evaluating a picture. In our work, there are problems: We were very restricted in our possibilities, there was little material. The significance of the film is purely of an agitational order. It seems to me, that this film, which

---

[23] [Trans.]: In the original: переключить.
[24] [Trans.]: In the original: сюжет [syuzhet] and фабула [fabula].

shows Tolstoy, the man, who was born a hundred years ago, should cry out, about our utter lack of filming of our contemporary reality. And before the beginning of the 11th anniversary of October, if we wanted to make a film about Lenin, we would be faced with the fact, that we have no material whatsoever…

I have to say, that the school of Constructivism in no way intends to work only on old newsreels. I think, that for me, this is my last such work. If I were to do something similar, it would be in three or four years. I think, that with our method, it would be possible to make a wonderful comedy picture: *The Russia of Nicholas II*. I would like to carry out such a work with an old newsreel. I am now working on my next object[25]: *Ten Years of Comintern,* a feature-length film — not an historical one — about Comintern.

It was necessary to agitate for the newsreel, to demonstrate, that it is of enormous value. And in this connection, my film played a great role. We found newsreels in a basement, in such a horribly damp place, that the emulsion was peeling away from them. And these are newsreels of great historical significance.

It is necessary now to agitate for the newsreel of the present day. And to treat this need, not only as an instance of agitation. When we speak about acted and non-acted filmmaking, it isn't in any way, in order to abolish acted filmmaking. We see, that in the acted film there are enormous resources, the finest forces are at work there: the mastery of actors, of set designers, of highly qualified camera operators. But we have tiny little factories, no camera operators, no people working with ideological enthusiasm. And without that, it isn't possible to do anything at all.

At the current time, is it necessary to make such a picture with eighty meters of material? I think, that from the point of view of our approach, of our methods, we had an obligation to do this. In the Repertkom,[26] they were afraid, that this film would aid in the canonization of Tolstoy and that he would be canonized by whatever means possible. The most frightening thing would be if we were to canonize Tolstoy. Tolstoy is a complex figure… When I shot Yasnaya Polyana, I had to speak with Alexandra L'vovna Tolstoya. She is now the director of the museum. I asked her, whether some older Japanese people had seen a newsreel of Tolstoy. She told me that they did have this newsreel, but when she watched it, she noticed, that Lev Nikolaevich was a landowner like any other and she decided not to show it. Film doesn't lie, she said it for herself. And when I asked to examine it carefully, it had the persuasive effect of authentic film material. What is Tolstoy here? Look, how elegantly he wears his tolstovka, or his gesture when he drinks water. It is an aristocratic gesture. And these ways of walking… You need to watch this film very attentively. Tolstoy saws,

---

[25] [Trans.]: In the original: над следующей вещью, a most Constructivist turn of phrase using вещь, i.e. thing or object.

[26] [Trans.]: A Soviet era acronym for репертуарный комитет [repertuarny komitet] (repertory committee).

then quietly walks away, and the worker remains behind to saw. Is it possible not to judge this film? And take his walks… Tolstoy was really a figure with two sides. He suffered, but never walked away, because he didn't oppose evil. I spoke with some older peasants. They didn't speak too enthusiastically either about Tolstoy, or about that era.

This is the last thing I have to say. Our task was not simply to present a film. This is not interesting for us. Let feature acted filmmaking[27] do that. We think, that the cinema should be an organizer, an agitator, a propagandist. And this is how we intend to do this work. And when it is said, that it is necessary to present an anti-religious film, or one about the Soviet countryside, we will always say, that this is our work, and not feature acted filmmaking… I regret, that I did not show you the picture made about Tolstoy after his death by our great director Protazanov—*The Life and Death of Tolstoy.*[28] You would have laughed like lunatics. If you wish, I will show you, I will bring a few reels, so that you can see that's how it is. I will say further. You know, that Eisenstein filmed two thousand meters of Nikandrov, who played Lenin in *October*, but only used 10 meters in the film. When you look at Lenin, it convinces no one. We recognize Tolstoy as a great artist, we publish his entire body of work. For this reason, we affix our signature to the statement, that Tolstoy is the greatest artist, who reflects old Russia in his works… I repeat, that our pictures need to be looked at attentively. And perhaps, need to be seen not once, but twice…

A film about Tolstoy (1929)

My next film is a picture for the Tolstoy Jubilee. I am constructing the cinematic design of the subject exclusively with non-acted newsreel material. This next experiment is difficult and carries extremely great responsibility.

I am deeply convinced, that only material, which has recorded on pieces of film, the original environment, authentic events and occurrences, provides the possibility, with the correct montage organization, of presenting *the era* and of showing the actual characteristics of the people participating in it. Only this induced me to undertake the present work, in spite of the fact, that I knew in advance the difficulty of this task, since little material was filmed and even less of the film material was preserved. But the principal difficulty was hidden in the complexity and contradictions of the figure of Lev Tolstoy. To present the object with great thematic development, to show Tolstoy in all his complexity, this is the task I set for myself, though it was impossible.

---

[27] [Trans.]: In the original: художественная кинематография [khudozhestvennaya kinematografiya].
[28] [Trans.]: I can find no film by this title by Protazanov. I believe she is referring to the film called *Уход великого старца* [*Ukhod veikogo startsa*] (*Departure of a Grand Old Man*).

The design flowed organically from the material. I made this picture with early newsreels, which might be classified as the first film chronicles. The material was chosen by me consciously. In spite of the fact that there are more newsreels after 1912, I rejected them, since newsreels from 1897 to 1912 coincide in their historical content and aspects of everyday life with the final years of Lev Tolstoy.

Over two years I watched around a million meters of newsreels and from the selected material were edited:

Lev Tolstoy and the Russia of Nicholas II (a montage of newsreels from 1897–1912).
Fall of the Romanov Dynasty (a montage of newsreels from 1912–1917).
The Great Way (a montage of newsreels from 1917–1922).

Now, I want to shoot and edit the present day.

And so, into the picture about Tolstoy went material from 1897 to 1912, film images of Tolstoy from 1906 to 1910. The spectator is introduced to these years. These are the years of the executions of Balmashev and Kalyaev; the years of the defeat of the 1905 Revolution. This is the period, when in the first three months of 1906, 679 persons were executed without trial. These are the years of the most savage reaction and despotism and, in precisely these years, Tolstoy preached with greatest inspiration the non-violent resistance to evil. This is the period of his statement "I cannot remain silent," of his departure and death on the eve of the complete destruction of the monarchy.

All of the pieces chosen by me possess great historical and cinematic value. I drew a large part of the material from the archives of the Leningrad film archive of Sovkino. All of the shots belong to the years 1897 to 1905. For the most part, they were shot on Lumière, or old Gaumont film stock. It was necessary to prepare this negative material in order to transfer it to contemporary film stock. It was difficult to do this as the film stock had dried out, the emulsion of many pieces had peeled off. Our laboratory assistant Comrade Kulygin of the Moscow Sovkino Factory managed this task beautifully. The cinematic quality of these newsreels is often quite high and, as such, not only do they present great interest as historical film documents, but they are also beautiful visual histories of the film chronicle.

The persuasiveness of authentic, unstaged material genuinely brings into relief the spirit of the era; it shows, where and in what surroundings the final years of Lev Tolstoy elapsed. This material by itself quite eloquently discloses and helps to make known both the utter loneliness and resignation of Tolstoy's sermon. The task of showing this is dictated to me by the material itself and I want to bring it to the Soviet spectator.

These pieces [of film] should show, with tremendous force, the temporary "worth" of the greatest "big-budget"[29] acted historical film and the fact, that the persuasiveness of the newsreel never wears out, or grows old with time.

Since the struggle for the non-acted film is, for the most part, the struggle to determine on what material, making up our revolutionary filmmaking, we need to work. This is the struggle for the possibility of creating cinema-objects, not by simulation, but with authentic material, with material on which is recorded the pieces of our lives. This is the struggle for working under normal production and material conditions. This is the struggle for qualified and cultured production personnel, conscious of the significance of the work on this front. This is the struggle for the possibility of creating new methods of work, distinct from acted cinema, flowing from the very essence of non-acted cinema.

And I consider each of my works on old newsreels, an instance of agitating for newsreel-style shooting, for non-acted filmmaking in our day.

The non-acted film (1929)

Among us, it is acceptable to make acted feature and "Kultur" films... Into the understanding of "acted feature filmmaking" enter even such "specimens" of platitudinous vulgarity as *The Lame Gentleman*.[30]

This kind of filmmaking is served by nicely equipped film factories, directors, the best camera operators, an army of actors, screenwriters, set decorator-architects, prop- and other kinds of workshops.

A huge amount of money is spent on this kind of filmmaking.

To act out life, to transfer this *acted* life onto film, to construct films from this speculative material, which is supposed to emotionally affect and charge up the spectator: that is the matter, with which highly qualified film workers, busy themselves, genuflecting before the magic of art. *We think this kind of filmmaking is rightly called acted.*

The so-called "Kulturfilm"[31] does not exist. It was thought up by people, who have neither the ability, nor the desire, to establish a new kind of filmmaking. The *non-acted* film has become a reality for the present day, despite its minor successes. This came about, for the most part, because the demand for a kind of film, realized using a different method than the acted film, is the direct response to our tasks.

---

[29] [Trans.]: In the original: боевичной. Though slightly anachronistic, this carries a military overtone like "combative" and implies an expensive, large-scale production, not unlike "blockbuster."

[30] [Trans.]: In the original: *Хромой барин* [*Khromoi barin*] (1920), directed by Konstantin Eggert, also known as an actor. As an actor he appeared in *Aelita Queen of Mars* and *Chess Fever*.

[31] [Trans.]: *Kulturfilms* were popular science and educational films developed in Germany beginning in 1918.

Workers in the non-acted film want to *efficiently and genuinely* participate in the rigorous construction of the present day.

To make use of all the technological means and possibilities of the camera, in order to understand our quickly fleeting life, in all its diversity, in all its complexity — understanding, by recording it on film.

We don't need studios, we don't need actors, we don't need set designers and property shops, we don't need scenarios. Literary classics teach us nothing, nor do the use of color and the compositional methods of the masters of painting.

The real world composed of two hemispheres, real, natural, and technological environments, objects, people carrying out real activities, events of the day, accidents and incidents, a person acquiring scientific knowledge to move science forward, a person in an heroic struggle, mastering all the chance phenomena of the world: this is the material for our film productions.

To gather these facts and from these facts to organize objects, connected socially to science, technology, pedagogy, to the urgent tasks of the present day.

Nothing can be more convincing than a fact, scientifically verified, and *inventively* presented with a clear social purpose.

How quickly "blockbusters" wear thin, made by the greatest masters of acted cinema art, can be easily verified, by looking now at the productions of these masters, which are only five years old. That the value of non-acted material can never be destroyed was demonstrated best of all by my three historical documentary films: *Fall of the Romanov Dynasty, The Great Way, Lev Tolstoy and the Russia of Nicholas II.* Only this material allows for the possibility of resurrecting the era of tsarist Russia and the heroic days of the years of October and the Civil War. In these films, for the first time, the term a "montage of documents" was used. And if the significance of non-acted films in 1929, after the work of the "kinoks" Vertov, Kaufman, Kopalin, Svilova, after my historical documentary films, after *The Shanghai Document*[32] by Bliokh and Stepanova, is understood by everyone—in 1921–1922, when the "kinoks" had only just been given the possibility of working practically, and the Constructivists in the journal *Kino-fot,* in *Zrelishcha,*[33] […] were undertaking in a practical and theoretical way their project for non-acted film, this was classified at best as "a childhood disease of the members of the LEF group," and, at worst, as the demonstration of stupidity. This is how this project was defined by the same people, who now, it seems, sincerely defend the documentary film […].

---

[32] [Trans.]: Released in 1928, a Soyuzkino production.

[33] [Russian editor's note]: A weekly journal of the theater, music hall, circus, mass spectacles [массое действо], farces, and the cinema. Edited by L. Kolpakchi and published in Moscow in 1922, 1923, and 1924. [Trans.] In the original: Зрелища (*Spectacles*). It was the continuation of an earlier journal called Эрмитаж (*Hermitage*), published from May to August 1922 in 15 numbers. Articles were often published pseudonymously. Its editors saw themselves aligned with the LEF group.

…All this, up to the present day, remains a road yet to be traveled.

They say to us: the sight of the camera at the moment of filming transforms human nature as it is filmed. The naturalness of the behavior is disrupted. At times, it is necessary to make use of the demonstration of behavior before the camera; this means, there are moments of acting, bad acting in comparison with the work of professional actors. And so, shoot actors, write scenarios, reenact life.

This is what so-called "Kulturfilms" do, where alongside an authentic, scientific experiment, alongside real environments, objects and events, actors and directors sweat with all their might, attempting to connect the life of facts with acting out facts. This results in a complete breakdown. Acting alongside facts reveals the utter falseness of acting and the spectator ceases to believe even the facts. However, the complete confidence, that a film shows authentic pieces of life, authentic, scientifically verifiable experience is the necessary condition for such films to achieve their goals. Our films on alcohol can serve as a prime example, where, as a result of their eclectic method, they can never fulfill their intended purpose: agitation against alcohol. Or a film such as *Abortion*[34] and others "of the sort," the success of which stems from the same causes as those, which create the success of the films *Girls Seek Lodging*,[35] or *Behind Monastery Walls*,[36] and everything "of the sort," and even the advertisement "Children and those under the age of 16 will absolutely *not be admitted.*"

And there is one more distinguishing mark of almost all "Kulturfilms." This is an absolutely undisguised amateurism. The perception that a "Kulturfilm" can be cooked up, by knowing anything at all, in any old way, pushes towards this work, with few exceptions, people who either have absolutely no qualifications in production, or who are doing this temporarily, while waiting in line to get the opportunity of working in acted filmmaking.[37]

Our workers in non-acted filmmaking, not having in their hands all of the technological possibilities, which already exist in the West, shoot a real person in his everyday behavior. It doesn't bother us, that the sight of the camera disrupts the usual behavior of many, so that, *while posing in front of the camera, "acting," they demonstrate themselves*, and each of their "poses" is a true characterization of their personality. When working on my own films, I deliberately chose not to cut out those moments when a person, upon seeing the movie camera, prepares themselves for the shot. This is how I

[34] [Trans.]: In the original: *Аборт* [*Abort*] 1924 by Noi Galkin and Grigory Lemberg.

[35] [Trans.]: In the original: *Девушки ищут пристанища* [*Devushki ishchut pristanishcha*]. I could find no film by that title. Perhaps Shub had in mind *6 Девушки ищут пристанища* (*Sechs Mädchen suchen Nachtquartier/Six Girls Seek Lodging*) (1928) by Hans Behrendt, which was released in the Soviet Union that year by Sovkino. It was released in English as *Six Girls and a Room for the Night*.

[36] [Trans.]: In the original: *За монастырской стеной* [*Za Monastyrskoi stenoi*], an alternate title for *Белые голуби* [*Belye golubi*] (*White Doves*) also known as *Сектанты* [*Sektanty*] (*Cult Members*) (1917), directed by Nikolai Malikoff.

[37] [Trans.]: In the original: в игровой кинематографии.

showed Rodzyanko, and Kerensky in *Fall of the Romanov Dynasty*, comrade Dybenko in *The Great Way*, Countess Tolstaya in the film *Lev Tolstoy and the Russia of Nicholas II*. Every one of these pieces is capable of convincing the skeptical. The people are not "acting," they are not representing some unnecessary and famous "mom and dad," and as they prepare themselves for the shot, they transmit an exhaustive filmic characterization *all by themselves*, through their body movements, sometimes through a barely perceptible smile, sometimes through a statuesque motionlessness.

But even these indications have only a temporary significance. We know, that the growth of contemporary technology (equipment, high sensitivity film stock, new devices and methods for shooting, laboratory processes), open up an enormous possibility for penetrating into the very heart of life, without disrupting a person's behavior.

The development of methods of shooting, of course, plays an enormous role for the non-acted film. A profound adherence to principles is needed, conviction is needed, inventiveness is needed; much will be overcome along this path, and much has already been achieved.

A striking example: the brilliant camera work of the "kinok" Kaufman is the result of just such conviction. The enormous mobility, the keen vision, the ability to orient himself in any environment, the ability to catch the most telling moments of behavior, either through the use of a hidden camera, or through a surprise attack on human nature, gave Kaufman the opportunity to shoot such compelling footage as the girl with the bow next to the magician, the people in the beer hall, the homeless boy waking up, the girl disturbed on a bench on the street, the Vital Records Office,[38] the woman crying at the grave, the childbirth (shots from *Man With a Movie Camera*).

This footage and, as well, the picture as a whole, made by D. Vertov, brilliantly demonstrate, that even in our technological conditions, it is possible with a movie camera to seize life in all its diversity; all that is needed is conviction and the belief in one's task, the will to overcome all the difficulties of this work.

The role of the camera operator in the non-acted film and the production relationship with the author of a film, who assigns the task, are different from the relationship between the camera operator and the director of an acted film. Thousands of unexpected things, which are impossible to foresee in advance, confront the camera operator in any shoot, even one organized in advance. Only the complete creative cooperation with the author of the film affords the possibility, at the most unexpected moments, of recording material with the camera, which will be consistent in every way with the task as a whole.

The role of the newsreel camera operator carries even greater responsibility when the camera records situations, occurrences and events at maximum speed. To

---

[38] [Trans.]: In the original: загс, short for Органы записи актов гражданского состояния (The Offices of Records of Acts of Civil Status), the public records or registry office where births, deaths, marriages, etc. are recorded.

know how to quickly orient oneself, to mentally sketch out a shooting plan, to choose the significant moments to shoot, discarding everything accidental, and not to forget for a moment, that one must shoot with maximum cinematographic expressiveness— these are things the newsreel camera operator must master.

The role of the author-organizer[39] of a non-acted film is distinct from that of the director of an acted film. The lack of a scenario for the plot and of a shot list from the director, which are not necessary for a non-acted film because of its specific working conditions, is compensated for by the use of a working plan, in which it is essential to precisely formulate the end purpose of the cinema object one intends to realize, with precise indications for shooting the things on which the author is basing the cinema task, and the locations where the shooting will take place. Any other attempts to fabricate a scenario will turn out to be a waste of money, since there are no and can be no situations recorded in advance, in which the camera operator might find himself. The definitive thematic construction of the object by the final edited footage is already determined in the organization of the material. In this way, the author of the non-acted film is as well the singular writer of the scenario of their own object. Precisely this peculiarity dictates the necessity for the author and camera operator, before they embark on shooting, to acquaint themselves with the environment, in which shooting will take place, to observe, as soon as possible, the effect of this on the person who will be the object of the shoot. Such research is essential; it affords the possibility of concretely constructing a plan and, in unforeseen circumstances in the process of shooting, to immediately account for the changed circumstances and to continue the shoot according to plan for the task as established.

The author–manager[40] of scientific, technical, and normal pedagogical films on local culture, in both the establishing of a plan, as well as in the process of shooting, must work in full cooperation with scholars or scientific workers in the field whose subject is to be treated. Now, all these particularities require of the author of a non-acted film professional qualifications and the requisite ingenuity: political literacy, the ability to make any object socially significant; they require the author to be able to stand up to the level of cultural tasks put forward by the revolution.

In this way, *the tasks of montage of the non-acted film are unique.*

The ultimate purpose *of the acted film*—to reach its spectator through the path of emotional impact—also defines the devices of montage. To this end, both the classical devices of American montage and new devices, related to the imitation of literature and painting are employed, and often by appealing to crazy stunts. The close-up

---

[39] [Trans.]: In the original: роль автор-организатора.
[40] [Trans.]: There is a great deal of Vertovian and Constructivist language in this article. This is the exact title Vertov gives himself in *Man With a Movie Camera*: Автор-руководитель, though he adds эксперимента (of the experiment).

has been canonized for the most "pathetic" moments; this is cellular montage.[41] The composition of the frame, the problem of lighting are increasingly subject to a purely aesthetic treatment. Partially because of this, the monotonous use of the static frame in almost all acted pictures in recent times can be explained, because movement transforms the frame, it disrupts the initial painterly composition and initial lighting effect.

The problem of the montage form of the non-acted film is something new, as new and unique as the non-acted film. It knows no continuity [of tradition], no canons.[42]

The purpose is the fact, the purpose is not only to present the fact, but to turn it over for examination: after examination comes remembering, after remembering comes reflection, to provide space, to provide an environment, to provide a person in this space and environment with the utmost clarity, working by means of facts, to gather this material into the kind of reflective, associational, and broadly synthesizing series, which will vividly convey to the spectator the relationship of the author to the facts presented: these are the tasks of montage, which confront the workers in the non-acted and intellectual cinema.

The "kinoks" are now working on this, defining a form of montage for the most part through the kinetic essence of filmed facts, and the Constructivists, closely connecting the problem of montage form with the ultimate purpose of an object and with the material subject to treatment (the functional method).

And so, the new, emerging methods, in the devices of the camera operator's work and in the work of the author of the non-acted film, throughout their range, pose the question of the consciousness of the shot of the workers. Author-managers, camera operators, editors, laboratory technicians: these are what the non-acted film needs now, more than ever. There is a need to make use of the experiments of the pioneers in this matter and create at the GTK[43] a special course of study in non-acted film. Such attempts have already been made: the introduction of non-acted filmmakers[44] took place in two sessions at the GTK in December 1928. In subsequent meetings, it was proposed that non-acted filmmakers organize individual workshops and a department in the form of a scientific-research center for research work in non-acted filmmaking at the GTK. This would afford the opportunity to transmit its

---

[41] [Trans.]: In the original: клеточный монтаж [kletochny montazh], not to be confused with Eisenstein's montage cell: яйчека монтажа [yaicheka montazha].

[42] [Trans.]: In the original: Никакой преемственности, никаких канонов она не знает.

[43] [Trans.]: In the original: ГТК, the abbreviation for the Государственный техникум кинематографии [Gosudarstvenny tekhnikum kinematografii] (The State Technical Institute of Cinematography). It had begun as the State School of Cinematography (GShK) in 1919, became the GTK in 1925 and was to become the celebrated VGIK (the All-Union State Institute of Cinematography) in 1930. At various times, Kuleshov, Tissé, Eisenstein, and many others taught there. It exists today as the VGIK, but now All-Union has become All-Russian.

[44] [Trans.]: In the original: неигровик [neigrovik] a neologism she and Eisenstein use familiarly.

experience and working methods to young people preparing themselves for that kind of work; this also affords workers on this front to take stock of their experience. The situation is equally serious for the basis of production. In order to be effective, factories of non-acted film must be organized. In the factory, it is essential to create scientifically-equipped film archives. Shooting laboratories, experimental centers must aid in the development of non-acted film production. It must be understood, that instead of actors, what is needed is sophisticated technology in filming and lighting equipment, special film is needed. The Artistic Soviet must consist not only of administrators, directors, and camera operators, but of representatives of science and technology, economic-industrial and public institutions, and of personally invited participants in public life. Screenwriters, who speak importantly about a shot breakdown[45] of the scenario and of locating the junction between non-acted and acted footage, do not contribute with their scenarios to the practical planning of a shoot and do not eliminate amateurism. Workers in non-acted film must be materially supported in their work just as workers in acted films. The idea of the Leninist proportion must not be an empty formal statement, but a genuine distribution policy. Only under these conditions can non-acted cinema be set into motion.

---

[45] [Trans.]: In the original: монтажная кадровка. This is not current film terminology and seems to have been misguided terminology when Shub wrote, so it is difficult to say what the meaning is, let alone, what misunderstandings are to be discarded. It seems to imply a breakdown into shots according to a plan for editing, in this case recognizing the problem of joining acted and non-acted material. This could cover a range of meanings from shot breakdown to shooting script to storyboard, none of which are typically the province of the screenwriter. Yuri Tsivian suggests "continuity script" as an alternative in this context.

Towards the arrival of sound in the cinema (1929)

The new invention: the *Tonfilm*, the sound cinema, excited everyone working in the cinema.

A victory, or a defeat?

To work with it, to study it, or to be its fierce opponent?

For workers in the non-acted cinema, there was no doubt. We know, that the sound film and the radio-screen[46] afford the non-acted film the possibility of being truly the most advanced instrument of international communication.

We want to direct all our energy towards seizing control of the invention, to making it serve us, without yielding the positions won by the silent cinema.

We know, that our first experiments are destined to be "comic" material for future workers, as the first cinema films are for us. But we are proceeding consciously towards this apprenticeship, study, experiment.

For us, the non-acted filmmakers, the most important thing—before anything else—is to learn thoroughly, authentically how to shoot sound, tone,[47] the voice, noise and so on, with the same maximum expressiveness, with which we have learned to shoot authentic, unstaged nature as it happens.

For this reason, we are little interested by what happens in the studio, in those hermetically sealed, theatrical boxes with microphones, amplifiers, and so on. What interests us are the experimental laboratories of scientific worker-inventors, and it is there we want, first of all, to direct our camera operators and ourselves, the future organizers of sound.

At the present time, we are confident only of the fact, that sound film[48] must not be an acoustic illustration [for a film], that sound will be of the same order of organic material as film material, that in this work an entire world of remarkable discoveries awaits us.

---

[46] [Trans.]: In the original: радиоэкран [radioekran]. It is unclear to me, whether Shub is speculating about something like television, or metaphorically referring to the technological possibilities of radio. The only other time she uses this term in her published writings is in "First Impressions," where she places it in parallel with sound cinema. Vertov's *Man With a Movie Camera* offers a vision of an ear and an accordion superimposed on a radio loudspeaker. In his essay "Radio-eye" of 1925, he refers to the transmission of pictures by radio (which had been accomplished as early as 1909), though in a later essay on *Man With a Movie Camera*, he glosses radio-eye as the audible kino-eye transmitted by radio.

[47] [Trans]: In the original: тон [ton]. Here, seemingly in a technical register: musical pitch, emotional coloration, or some other quality of sound. In "First Impressions," she describes the crude post-dubbing of Stroheim's *The Wedding March* as killing the ironic tone.

[48] [Trans.] In the original: звучащая фильма, an early attempt at creating a term for the new technology. Currently, sound film is звуковой фильм.

First Impressions (1929)

Among cinema workers abroad, there is confusion.

At the largest German factory, Neubabelsberg, at the height of the production season, shooting has been almost completely suspended.

Sources say, that Chaplin, Fairbanks, Mary Pickford and others have temporarily stopped working in cinema.

They are all waiting.

The actively working avant-garde of filmmaking has switched to a new way of working.

The tremendous invention of the *Tonfilm*, the sound cinema,[49] weighs heavily upon the film industry.

An invention, we still do not know how to make use of.

An invention, which has brought to a halt the triumphal procession of the "silent" cinema.

A new, technological cinema in the West, falling immediately into the hands of speculators and businessmen.

A victory and a defeat at the same time.

In Berlin, I managed to see and hear almost all the *Tonfilme* made in Germany, as well as two American ones, *Submarine*[50] and *The Singing Fool.*[51]

We Russian directors didn't manage to get into a shoot in a studio, or a laboratory, or receive exhaustive information from workers in the *Tonfilme*. This is all "The Holy of Holies." Everything is kept secret.

My impressions relate to the immediate perception of films on the screen.

The American films clearly testify to the fact, that the businessmen are exploiting this new invention. And that depressed me.

Submarine is an average love film, with well-shot scenes of a doomed submarine. Sound was added after editing. The musical accompaniment, the chatter of the sailors' voices, the banging and the noises were not organically connected to the thing as a whole. The tone is metallic, deafening, unclear.

Stroheim's *The Wedding March*, remarkable in many ways, had sound added after editing, which kills the tone. The subtle irony of the film is killed by the deafening, crude sound added later. The German films are even worse in the clarity of their sound, than the American ones.

---

[49] [Trans.] In the original: звуковое кино.
[50] [Trans.]: 1928, directed by Frank Capra.
[51] [Trans.]: 1928, directed by Lloyd Bacon, starring Al Jolson.

A short *Revuefilm*[52] deserves a separate mention. The author of this film attempts to approach sound,[53] the same way we approach [visual] material which is shot. He tried to shoot sound[54] not only as an acoustic illustration of actions. He made an attempt to shoot and edit the sound, so that the latter became the same kind of organic material for editing, as the cinematic material. In this way, it was not oversimplified and was not reduced to a bare cinema exercise. In some way, he undoubtedly succeeded.

That's almost everything.

There is still something I must repeat, which makes me discouraged. But not discouraged. This is not a defeat, but rather an incorrect usage.

The future, undoubtedly, belongs to the *Tonfilm*.

A few decades of labor and inventiveness yielded the creation of a complex, distinctive language of cinema, distinct from other forms of artistic labor. Decades have yielded the creation of montage: the fundamental organizing feature of the film-object.

But, in a few months, they want to conquer a new invention and force it to serve them. They have immediately set themselves a tremendous task. They have decided to make a *Tonfilm* of two thousand meters!

This is fundamentally incorrect.

Qualified cinema workers understand quite well the importance of the study and the mastering of methods. We must not approach the work of the *Tonfilm* amateurishly. It requires study. Going off to the laboratory to experiment. To master the technology, to thoroughly learn to shoot and edit sound and tone[55] with the same maximum expressiveness, with which we learned to shoot and edit live action[56]; this is the path for our work.

We must set small tasks for ourselves and solve them inventively.

We must not become discouraged by failures: they are inevitable.

The confusion of cinema workers in acted filmmaking will not create panic in the ranks of those working in non-acted filmmaking. We are convinced, that the greatest inventions—the sound cinema and the radio-screen—will elevate all cultural cinema work to a higher stage of development in filmmaking, which must become the most advanced instrument of national and international communication.

---

[52] [Trans.]: A *Revuefilm* was a genre of short musical or dance films, usually romantic comedies, sometimes based on contemporary theater productions. It flourished in Germany and Austria from the beginning of the sound era to as late as the 1960s. It was especially popular during the Nazi era.

[53] [Trans.]: In the original: тон. She seems to be using this as a transliteration of the German "Ton."

[54] [Trans.]: In the original: снять звук (snyat' zvuk). It could even be translated as "take sound," but снять is the normal verb referring to shooting photographs or motion pictures. I believe this slightly awkward phrase reflects the reception of sound recording by Shub at the time. Later записать [zapisat'] becomes the standard word for recording sound.

[55] [Trans.]: In the original: звук и тон.

[56] [Trans.]: In the original: действующую натуру. "On location" would be an alternate translation.

Joris Ivens (1930)

From the West, where the acted entertainment film thrives, from Holland—a country, which still has no film industry whatsoever—Joris Ivens came to us with a modest quantity of reels of film, in order to show us his work, to learn our attitude towards it, but principally to become closely acquainted, on the spot, with the only revolutionary film industry in the world of the Land of the Soviets.

He declared himself to be a committed advocate of the documentary film and confirmed his position through his work.

Here, the documentary film serves entirely as propaganda and agitation in the struggle for socialism and Socialist Construction. We strive to create objects, socially connected with science, technology, pedagogy, with the essential tasks of the present day. The importance of the non-acted film is accepted by the Agitprop Central Committee, approved by resolution of Sovnarkom. The creation of powerfully functioning factories of the non-acted film, or, as we still call it, the "agitpropfilm" occupies a central place. Here, a whole gamut of workers are working enthusiastically on this front. We would like to review the works presented by our foreign colleague from the point of view of our position on documentary film. He is the camera operator and author of his films. He works with a Kinamo. He showed us films for the most part on themes of construction: *Zuiderzee*, *Pile Diving*, *The Bridge* and the film étude *Rain*. Of these films, only one, *Zuiderzee* had 4 reels, the other short films were around three hundred or four hundred meters long. That would seem to be not very much at all. However, all these works were worthy of serious analysis.

Before anything else, Ivens displayed great cultural knowledge of the work of the camera operator. The Kinamo in his hands shows itself to be the perfect instrument for shooting motion pictures. The particular precision in the handling of the *faktura*[57] of objects shot by him, the camera movement, the ability to function, without deviating from the established goal, to obtain powerfully shot material, proceeding from the targeted objectives of the entire object as a whole, with maximum expressiveness in the construction of a shot: these are the distinguishing characteristics of his work as a camera operator. No sort of trickery. No beauty for the sake of beauty. His camera work recalls the work of our own camera operator Mikhail Kaufman. Though perhaps, Ivens's camera work is distinguished by a greater austerity.

As the author of his films, Ivens is distinguished by the correct choice of objects to film. His perception of men of every disposition, of the technological and natural environment is distinguished by a sharp and nuanced vision. He is strongly grounded,

---

[57] [Trans.]: In the original: фактура, a term promoted by Alexei Gan, Shub's partner during the 1920s, as one of the foundations of Constructivism. It refers to the material aspect of the surface (of an object) though its meaning can be extended to include the inherent qualities of any medium. Here, roughly equivalent to "rendering."

he intelligently understands the processes taking place in front of him, he knows how not only to see, but transfers what is visible onto film, in such a way, that all the events shown on the screen are perceived in the same way they took place in life. In spite of the complex devices for shooting and the, at times, complex montage treatment of the material, he brings to the screen the perception of the richness of authentic, not "cinematified"[58] life. The processes of labor, the behavior of man, the power of industrial facilities, infect us precisely by means of this perception of authenticity, and not through camera or montage tricks, which destroy the reality of the world in which we live and act. This is one of the most precious virtues of Ivens's work. His work is weaker than ours for its lack of social significance, but the film *Zuiderzee* tells us, that Ivens will overcome this and that he knows how to clearly understand material in a social sense, just as clearly as he films it […].

Zuiderzee was carried out as a commission by the trade union of construction workers of Holland and shows the work on the drainage of inland seas. Those commissioning the work laid down this condition: don't shoot everyday subjects. Ivens, before he started shooting, lived with the workers for some time with his camera, he got to know them, he told them about the goals and purposes of his film, he mentioned the processes he wanted to shoot. The workers got used to him and the camera, and only then, did Ivens begin to shoot. (Comrades in non-acted filmmaking! We must struggle for the possibility of working this way ourselves. It will bring precision to our shooting plans,[59] save enormous amounts of film, and raise the quality of our production.)

In *Zuiderzee*, the strongest images show moments of construction work, when the workers, bare-handed, with inhuman tension in their muscles, sweat pouring out because of the weight, knee-deep in the water, struggle with the elements of the sea, conquer the sea, patch after patch, for the earth. With no agitational intertitles, this film raises the question: For what purpose and for whom was this debilitating work done? Who is in charge? And the author manages, alongside the visible processes of labor, to allow this line of thought to be born, he makes this film a remarkable film-document—a Dutch "Dubinushka."[60]

Only inveterate aesthetes are capable of understanding *The Bridge* and *Rain* as objects of a purely formal order. In our cinema, in the definition of formalism, there is an unbelievable confusion, as the criterion for the accusation of formalism sharply transforms how a film is evaluated, depending on whether it is an acted or non-acted

---

[58] [Trans.]: In the original: кинофицированной [kinofitsirovannoi].

[59] [Trans.]: In the original: съемочные планы [s"emochnye plany]. This could also be rendered as "shooting scripts."

[60] [Trans.]: A famous revolutionary song written in the 1860s by Vasily Ivanovich Bogdanov and Aleksandr Aleksandrovich Ol'khin on the basis of a folksong. Chaliapin's performance of it was particularly well known.

film. In my days at the Press Building, I saw a film by the director Okhlopkov, *Way of the Enthusiasts*.[61] In it, living people are transformed into walking symbols. They are not harmed by water, nor fire, nor bullet. They act and speak for the most part against the background of a sky with swiftly moving clouds. Our difficult era, our severe and heroic daily lives, what we are building, the new life, in which people are actually participating, are all recounted to us in symbolic terms. In the end, the film transforms into a not very clever children's play, in which the grownup and, true, the intelligent spectator is made to participate by force. Okhlopov has expended loads of imagination, talent, inventiveness. All of this is submitted as a claim for a new kind of political film and it is valued by the critics voicing their opinion at the screening as a new stage in revolutionary filmmaking. Not a word about formalism. But should the author of a documentary film—where there are still no traditions, where every zone must be conquered over and over again, where, as we work, we are learning and mastering both methods of shooting and methods of organizing material—display the least inventiveness in transmitting nature and human nature, the technological environment, he is immediately denounced as a formalist, or, at best, as an imitator of the acted film. Meanwhile, every worker in the non-acted film strives to learn how to record the world which surrounds us, with maximum expressiveness and precision. We have never abandoned this.

Rain (by Ivens and Franken) shows great mastery in the transmission of real, authentic natural phenomena. Having acquired this mastery, Ivens will undoubtedly make purposeful use of it. The resolution of the civil engineers after a screening of *Zuiderzee*, *Piles*, and *The Bridge* at the Moscow Business Club will serve as proof of the organicity of those films. They expressed the wish that our films, which show individual construction and building processes, should absolutely be made with a similar understanding of the material, as has been achieved in the works of Ivens.

The workers in the non-acted film were happy to learn, that our factory is inviting Ivens to work with us. This is the best guarantee that a great master of the documentary film will also become a master of revolutionary filmmaking.

The facts serve as proof of this. Ivens took away the strongest impression from the Museum and House of the Red Army. He clearly realized, that the Red Army is a class army and the most powerful guardian of the workers' and peasants' state. He considered, that he received the most correct evaluation and critique of his films in the construction workers club.

These facts, more than anything else, attest, that Ivens does indeed want to work among us.

---

[61] [Trans.]: In the original: *Путь энтузиастов* (1930).

[About Creative Method] (1931)

Today, there is a film screening which is somewhat unusual and this unusual character is unique. I quite regularly and quite zealously, as a member of the ARRK,[62] attend all screenings and this year I watched very important pictures—acted, non-acted—which had their merits and their deficiencies. There were pictures by great masters, which, as it were, seemed to respond inadequately to that purpose, or to those concerns which should have been addressed. But the reproaches, which were voiced there concerning non-acted films, were for me completely unexpected. It is utterly inadmissible for a screening to be conducted in this way. I do not know why Comrade Sutyrin decided, that none of us would speak. And no one said anything about it. Why were we obliged to be the first to speak out? Because every worker in acted films represents not a worker, but a direction, each of the workers in acted films have their supporters. And so, here, when there were screenings of acted pictures, there was nothing to be heard: is it obligatory to gang up on Pudovkin and all those who work using the Pudovkin method, and so on. In my opinion it is inadmissible to pose the question in this way.

In essence, there are pictures. About "bankruptcies and dead ends." It seems to me, that "dead ends" and "bankruptcy" were said to appear this year not only among works of the so-called "non-acted filmmakers," but on the entire front of cinematographic art. I think, that at such moments, it is necessary to seriously consider successes as well as failures. Especially now, since it seems that it was agreed at the last conference, that the significance of agitpropfilms is colossal. Besides that, no matter how much they turn a blind eye and say nothing about the depravity or purity of the acted method, 90 percent of agitpropfilms are made according to the non-acted method. For this reason, the agitpropfilm needs to be treated with particular attention. The work of Comrade Kaufman is work of precisely this sort. And it seems to me, that it needs to be treated, not from the point of view of attacks on the non-acted film, but from the point of view of how it achieved established goals. Besides that, now, when the slogan has been put forth by the Party and the RAPP,[63] that we want to see

---

[62] [Trans.]: In the original: Ассоциации работников революционной кинематографии [Assotsiatsii rabotnikov revolyutsionnoi kinematografii] (The Association of Workers in Revolutionary Filmmaking), "organized in Moscow in 1924, it united professionals-workers under the slogan 'Cinema in service to the Land of the Soviets.' The education of the cinema public and assistance to Soviet film production was carried out with the aid of a monthly newsreel *Kino-Zhurnal ARK* beginning in 1925, and from May of 1926 it became *Kino-Front* and through ongoing business relations with kino factories. Work on the improvement of members' skills and the drawing up of current issues of cinema-life was carried out according to sections: production, scenario, musical, peasant, scientific-pedagogical. In 1924, similar associations were established on the model of the Moscow ARK in Leningrad and several other major cities." [Entry from *The Great Soviet Encyclopedia*, 1st Edition, t. iii (1926) Anrio–Atosksil, stolb. 640.]

[63] [Trans.]: In the original: Российская ассоциация пролетарских писателей [Rossiiskaya assotsiat-

on the screen authentic shock workers, authentic life, authentic construction, and the concrete heroes with their full names,[64] the role of non-acted films is rather urgent and significant.

And so, that is why it would be possible genuinely, seriously, quite substantively, and advantageously to analyze what comrade Kaufman did.

What are the merits and the deficiencies of this film? There is one enormous merit: it is beautifully shot. It is beautifully shot precisely using the method of the non-acted film, because comrade Kaufman has mastered the method of shooting real activities, real people, real environments and he does this with enormous virtuosity.

How is this film designed, how is its issue resolved? There, I am not completely satisfied and I think, that this is a misfortune not only for non-acted filmmakers, but this is a misfortune for all Soviet filmmaking for this year.

It is necessary to speak about the deficiencies of all Soviet filmmaking, from which, in equal measure, the films of Vertov, Kaufman, and Pudovkin all suffer.

About the film *Today*[65] (1930)

What happened with the picture *Today* exceeds the framework of a simple critique of this picture. And today's screening at the ARRK was for me personally an extremely important and demanding screening.

What is *Today*? It is a political film, made with the concrete material of our reality. It is appropriate to critique it for a whole series of errors, which I myself sense and know perfectly well. But at the same time, don't attack and denigrate the method that I used. The method is beside the point.

For what and for whom do I make my films? I make my films for the mass spectator and, therefore, all observations in this regard will be seriously studied and incorporated by me.

How was this film made? Why does it have various defects which I too sense?

The film is made with material of authentic facts, authentic events, authentic incidents. Is it possible to believe, that these facts are simply shown, that these are undifferentiated pieces of film, as comrade Sutyrin says? I consider this misguided. The facts are all dated. It is not a simple showing of facts, but a showing of my relation to them.

---

siya proletarskikh pisatelei] (The Russian Association of Proletarian Writers). A writers union which lasted from 1925 to 1932 and was responsible for violent ideological attacks on writers they deemed to have strayed from the path set down by the Party. Among their victims were Mayakovsky, Bulgakov, Zamyatin, and even Maxim Gorky.

[64] [Trans.]: In the original: с именем, отчеством и фамилией (with their first names, patronymics, and family names).

[65] [Trans.]: In the original: *Сегодня*.

Not two years ago, but one, I went to Germany to acquire material. I was shown an enormous quantity and selected only 1,600 meters. From this material, Soyuzkino acquired only 700 meters; the most important and precious shots were not a part of that. Soyuzkino considered, that paying 10 marks per meter of very precious, very relevant negative was expensive, and that buying *A Sailor's Song*[66] was not expensive, it was possible.

The entire picture in its current form cost 39 thousand. During the production of the picture, the budget was considerably reduced. What does it mean, when the budget of a picture is reduced during production? It means, that a whole series of shoots had to be canceled: The Donbass, Sel'mashstroi,[67] night shoots of Moscow. Those are the production conditions, in which I created this film. And only because I did not have enough material, was it impossible for me to make a whole series of moments resound with full force.

Comrade Sutyrin says, that the title of the film *Today* is not right. The film was ready for the Party Congress, but it lay around for five months. A documentary film with the title *Today* lying around for five months! This is obviously an improper, unacceptable state of affairs. This is an enormous amount of time. I would perhaps construct a whole series of shots differently now, I would organize the material differently, its lines of inquiry.

Why do I defend this title? I consider, that the film, which is made of the material of facts, will not lose its relevance with the years. After naming it *Today*, it occurred to me that this is a film report, these are the facts of 1930. And if this film is watched in five, six, ten years, then the value of the documents, which I managed to collect, will undoubtedly increase.

As is possible today, in five months, one could say: that's not right, this is not right, it's not that way, and so on. If there had been the opportunity to give these directives, I would have taken all this into account and implemented them. Then, it would have been possible to sort this out and these directives would not have affected so catastrophically the fate of a film, which is, in essence, useful and politically significant.

---

[66] [Trans.]: In the original: *Песнь моряка*. It is difficult to identify this film. Perhaps she is referring to the 1929 Finnish film, known in English as *A Sailor's Song*. It is clearly not something she thinks to be of great worth.

[67] [Trans.]: A kolkhoz in the Northern Caucasus.

Not only a great master but an innovator as well (1932)

All those who have commented, find, that *Ivan* is a tremendous work of art and at the same time a failure. I do not understand, how an authentic work of art can be a failure of the master. I consider *Ivan* to be an unconditional success, a success not only by a remarkable master, as is Dovzhenko, but a success for our Soviet film industry.

Every creative worker in the film industry is obligated to make their pronouncement about *Ivan* and through this, to help *Ivan* occupy the place on Soviet screens, which is its rightful due.

Ivan is not a discussion film, as many want to portray it, it is an event; I would like to briefly explain, why I, as a principled worker in non-acted film, feel this way about *Ivan*.

For me, the appearance of *Ivan* is an organic continuation of the entire creative path of Dovzhenko. It is a continuation of the line of *Zvenigora* and *Arsenal* (*Earth*, in my view, stands by itself). This is long and difficult to explain. I do not want to spend the time on this now.

What is *Ivan*? and what is the unique destiny of *Ivan*? and what is unique about Dovzhenko? Our Soviet film industry is a great film industry. We have great, authentic, remarkable masters and among these great, authentic masters, a unique path, a unique place in the acted film is occupied by Dovzhenko and yet another master—Eisenstein.

They are not only remarkable masters, they are innovators. And to make an account of Dovzhenko in the film *Ivan* is to make an account of his inventiveness.

What has Dovzhenko invented in this film, and what, from my point of view, makes this film remarkable? After all the work of Dovzhenko, there is no need to say, that Dovzhenko has a wonderful capacity for working with actors, that he has a remarkable capacity for shooting nature. We have long known, that in this regard he is a great master. We know, that he can sharply, very effectively create individual episodes. And for this reason, the storyline of skipping school, which everyone likes so much, is only another demonstration of the usual, acute work with great imagination on this or that episode.

The victory of Dovzhenko in *Ivan* is, that was the first to take the non-hero[68] Ivan and make this non-hero the central character in the film.

The Soviet film industry has given us and continues to give us remarkable pictures about heroes. But to propose and to direct a picture with the theme of a non-hero, one of the 162 million, the utterly unremarkable Ivan—this is new, difficult, and responsible.

---

[68] [Trans.]: In the original: негерой [negeroi], a neologism from ne [not] and geroi [hero or character].

Comrade Shklovsky considers, that to make a film about the utterly unremarkable Ivan, who has no biography, isn't possible.

And I consider, that the most remarkable thing about Ivan is his new biography. It's possible to understand biography in a different way. Dovzhenko was able to show how Ivan loves and many other things of the sort. In *Earth*, in the moonlit Ukrainian night, they kill the hero of the film, some average Ivans, stand by—frozen in place—along with some young girls. It seems to me, this is a new theme, original, very pointed and purposeful.

Someone has said that Dovzhenko loves *Ivan* a great deal. I don't see that. He lovingly shows people constructing socialism, people who lead Ivan, who lead him to the Party, to school. I will repeat it: this is a great, necessary, purposeful, and beautiful theme, an exciting theme, a theme, portrayed expressively, sparingly, starkly. Dovzhenko is not only a great artist, but as well, he is a sincere man. For the present day, he said everything about Ivan, that can be said. And we should rejoice, that a great master has approached a great and difficult theme and through his work proposed a new thematics.

A few words about the critics. Comrade Shklovsky said, that *Ivan* is a failure. One reason he considers it a failure is, that Ivan is not understood by the greater masses. Shklovsky recounted many remarkable things, about how Pushkin was not understood in his era. He could have chosen an example closer at hand. Not very long ago, people spoke about the incomprehensibility of Mayakovsky. For this reason, for the current day, a critic has no right to say, "This is a great work of art, but it is a failure." This is incomprehensible. The task of the critic for the current day is to set the tone. When a remarkable work of art appears, mobilize yourselves and help out using your pen, so that what temporarily is not understood, quickly becomes understood.

What there isn't (1932)

Given the conditions of kinofactories, which have obtained up to now, I have decided *to take no part* in the development of a staff development plan.[69]

Nonetheless, I consider, that a templan[70] can and should be established, but not so mechanistically and from the top down, as has been done up to now.

Creative workers should participate in the establishment of a staff development plan. This is very important, but even more important, is that directors as a group[71] should also participate creatively in the establishment of a staff development plan.

I think, that our lack of preparation for the celebration of the 15th anniversary of the October Revolution was due precisely to the fact that these conditions were not observed.

I am afraid to say, purely and simply, that we are marking these historic days with the release of the usual sort of films, no special films for the October celebrations and in the name of October were created. And it would seem, that this would have been the responsible and essential fundamental arrangement for the formulation of a training plan last year.

Shub during the shooting of *KShE.*

---

[69] [Trans.]: In the original: тематический план.

[70] [Trans]: In the original: темплан, an abbreviation for тематический план.

[71] [Trans.]: In the original: руководство, which can also mean management, but I believe that Shub is referring here to film directors as a group. In *Man With a Movie Camera*, Vertov uses the term руководитель in referring to his role, more precisely автор-руководитель эксперимента.

The theme of my talk (1933)

I would like to tell you how I made my film.

What exactly is *KShE*? For me, it was the theme of the Komsomol for the Komsomol, in order to show how the Komsomol is working in the most urgent of sectors: electrification. So that, the entirety of the multi-million strong Komsomol will understand for themselves the place of electrification in the Construction of Social-ism.[72] That is the fundamental theme of this object [...]

Secondly, for me, this object is organically connected with my preceding objects, as it is a picture about people, who in the complex of materials as a whole, give a distinct representation of the era. This relates it to the pictures *Fall of the Romanov Dynasty*, *The Great Way*, and *Tolstoy*.

The turning point was the picture *Today*. When I arrived at the picture *KShE*, my fundamental task was to show people and Komsomol members in their real activities, working in this sector. This was the theme of my talk, a very difficult and complicated theme as a maker, because up until then, I had worked with material that was already prepared, and for this picture, I tested myself as a person, to whom it was necessary to capture and record real people.

They say, that this is an incorrectly dramatically developed object. I don't know what dramaturgy[73] is being spoken about. I think, that it is not about construction, as in how dramaturgy is constructed in acted filmmaking. I consider, that *Fall of the Romanov Dynasty* and *Tolstoy* of mine are absolutely correctly dramatically resolved. True, then, I had an arsenal of shot material. Here, it was necessary to shoot and I was horribly limited in the amount of film I had, while it is particularly needed, when you are not working with actors, but with people with whom you cannot rehearse.

Why do I consider that this object is properly dramatically constructed? It seems to me, that my picture has a particularly purposeful thematic turn: from the powerplant-supplier to the consumer. I do not know why some have considered, that the DZORAGES[74] sequence was not included organically. I wanted to show, how electrification functions in the most remote locales of construction, and it seems to me, that this is included organically and correctly.

I was surprised by the accusation of Suprematism by comrade Kozintsev in his statement.

I see practically no abstract shots in my picture, except one, when in my film, after the Moscow night scene, electric lamps are flashing. This was on International Youth Day. I meticulously prepared for editing and it was difficult for me to resist having this shot. It seems to me, that this rush of electric lights establishes some kind

---

[72] [Trans.]: In the original, Shub uses the acronym соцстроилтельство [sotsstroitel'stvo].

[73] [Trans.]: In the original: драматургия [dramaturgia].

[74] [Trans.]: An acronym for the Dzoraget River Hydroelectric Station, located in Armenia.

of actual reference points and, as Shklovsky says, it shows Moscow in ten years. All the rest is extremely organic and I allowed myself no purely montage-based combinations.

Comrade Kozintsev spoke about living people. Of course, one must make pictures about living people and it's not particularly necessary to think about a scenario, when speaking about the non-acted film; when you work with actual human material, with the actual facts of life, it's not at all necessary to write a scenario. There is a whole series of things, which are dramaturgically conceived in the process of shooting, that no script writer could write into a scenario. Working with living people brings into question much more deeply how to approach a shoot.

The next thing I want to make is a film about four women. I would like to live alongside each woman with the camera for two to three months. In this way, it would be possible to get a picture about actual people. I want to take on what seems like a narrow theme, but this theme is also organically connected with my previous works.

I have actually made what must be an autobiographical object. Why did it happen this way? While shooting the picture, I was extremely excited by the necessity of shooting sequences of Socialist Construction, that would reflect our remarkable era. This made me feel optimism and even lyricism.

Shooting any sequence, I spent much more time preparing to shoot, than in shooting. A mass meeting in a factory was shot by us in 40 minutes. Katya Paramonova, whom I had to re-shoot, I shot in 25 minutes. This was the typical amount of time I had for shooting the majority of the sequences.

What struck me at the factory? Stressful work was going on for the fulfillment of the Promfinplan,[75] and at all times during the breaks music could be heard, singing, sailors from the Red Navy performed. On the shop floor stood a piano and the Komsomol members played and sang during the breaks. I was struck by the fact, that the whole time, a band was playing. It might seem to you, that I am transmitting this to you subjectively, but in fact, that's the way it was. In the factory, in spite of the stressful work, during the breaks they played and sang the entire time.

At Dneprostroi, initially, our brigade was received quite badly. I had to overcome this, since it was impossible to work with the brigade and the committee from the Komsomol without an organic connection. In the committee, the plan for my work was discussed comprehensively and accepted quite warmly. I had only ten days to shoot the participation of the Komsomol at Dneprostroi.

When the Komsomol not only accepted our plan, but supported it, I was surprised and even proud, especially when the Dneprostroi Committee of the Komsomol entrusted our brigade with advancing the production of turbines, when we were at the factory. We arrived a tiny bit late; the turbine was already ready, but

---

[75] [Trans.]: In the original: промфинплан [promfinplan], an acronym for Промышленно финансовый план [promyshlenno finansovy plan] (Industrial-Financial Plan).

there was a series of deficiencies and I had to do a lot of things in relation to this. For me, a vast labor began with the Komsomol of the factory. I insisted on uncovering everything that had held up the production of the turbine. The Committee of the Komsomol took on this assignment in true Bolshevik spirit. What happened was utterly remarkable, both when shop foreman Savel'ev spoke and in the excitement with which Klimov spoke. I consider this an amazing document of the current day. This is a complete biography of volunteer service to electrification,[76] to which nothing more need be done, neither with intertitles, nor explanation, and I feel it is a victory, which could be set to music.

Perhaps, this is subjective, but this is my autobiography; that's how I view these things.

Our era is so magnificent, so remarkable and so great, that there is nothing to fear in Shub now filming facts and editing them subjectively. Subjectivity, lyricism, this is my exceptional mood, my organic participation in our era through my works; if they are purposeful, then I am learning to speak with the voice of that class, for whom and together with whom, I want to work. And this subjectivity need not be feared.

I want to make a film about Woman[77] (1933)

A number of comrades have been asking me, what I am planning to do.

The majority, for some reason, have formed the belief, that I will make an acted film according to a scenario prepared in advance, with the participation of actors, and

---

[76] [Trans.]: In the original: электрошефство [elektroshefstvo], an acronym, that might be rendered more literally as Electrosponsorship, i.e. Sponsorship of Electrification. The title of the film *Комсомол—шеф электрификатии* [*Komsomol Shef elektrifikatsii*] is probably best translated as *Komsomol: in Volunteer Service to Electrification*, or *Komsomol Sponsor of Electrification*. Шеф [Shef], which literally means "sponsor," or "chief," here refers to volunteer service performed by workers in settings outside their normal one. As explained to a friend by a Russian working in his office in Moscow, office workers, or others not normally engaged in manual tasks, when needed, might go to the fields in order to help with a harvest, or to factories to help meet a production goal. In this case, the members of the Komsomol had volunteered to help in the construction of turbines for the Dneprostroi power plant.

[77] [Trans.]: Shub uses the singular here; and while it could be translated as "a woman," I believe "Woman" is historically and grammatically correct here. This is complicated by the fact that Russian uses neither definite nor indefinite articles. The de-essentializing distinction between Woman and Women does not seem to exist at this point in Russian history, though Shub entitles her plan for the film *Women* [Женщины]. And in the essay, she even gives *Four Women* as the title. However, as Masha Godovannaya points out, this has a feminist component, since in Russian человек means "man" or "person" and is gendered masculine and is used for a person of either gender. To specify it is to be a film about Woman—entitled *Women*—is to step away from a universalizing of personhood or humanity as masculine.

shot in a studio. And remarkably, many, berating me for "documentalism," without waiting for my reply, say something like, "Yes, you know, it's all quite a pity… you had your style, your path…" and so on.

The comrades are right about one thing. I have mapped out work for myself, which, to a great extent, is distinct from my previous work. I am putting aside my historical montage films. There, the construction of an object was appropriate and organically dictated by the specific character of the treatment of previously filmed documentary material. My two latest films *Today* and *KShE* have clearly shown me, that the problem lies not in documentalism, nor in method being the putative hindrance to the creation of a fully-fledged artistic object. The "trouble" with my latest works is common to a whole series of works by acted [i.e. fiction film] directors, but in documentary material of great force, it is perceptible.

It is the lack of a sharp, graphic, dramatically, intensely coherent development of the action. Because of this, the luster of each sequence remains separate and there is a lack of an organic, stirring connection with the whole.

What is new in the plan of the creative proposal I intend to bring to my new work *Four Women*?

1. My deep conviction is, that an individual hero can also be the subject of a non-acted film. Up until now, it was thought, that only the actions of the collective in moments of their organized, or spontaneous presentations, could be the subject of a non-acted film. I have four heroines. Each has her own biography, her own path of struggle and development, and at the same time, they will be representatives of the millions of women of our new life.

2. Up until now, it was considered, that non-acted film was excluded from dramatically developing events, excluded from truthfully developing internally the construction of a story-line of a film. Because of this, it was inaccessible to a general spectator.

In my new work, I am making the attempt to construct a film by cross-cutting the plot. This does not mean, that I need a canonical acted scenario with a construction thought out in advance.

Life in all its complex contradictions, every day and every hour creates endless dramatic situations and resolves them in extremely unexpected and inventive ways.

I will venture in my new work, in this way, to construct and to connect separate sequences, so that, as a whole, this will become a unified, dramatically developed action.

I want to make a film about woman, to allow myself the opportunity to touch upon the theme of love, of birth, of death. These themes, unstaged, can be unusually powerful, emotionally-moving material, and at the same time, a profoundly new device for showing the authentic people of our days, of our new, developing way of life.

I want to make a film about Woman, because this theme is capable of demonstrating with especial credibility, that only the proletarian revolution, new conditions of labor, new social practice are decisively removing "the woman question" from the accounts of history. After the speech of comrade Stalin at the Kolkhoz Congress, after his words about women-kolkhoz workers[78]—the theme of woman, I feel, is an important and necessary theme for the present day and this is the best stimulus for work and I want to work with particular intensity.

It will be recalled (1933)

[...] I want to say a few words about my apprehensions. I fear, that on that basis of previous discussions of questions for the paths of development for the non-acted film, questions about the paths of development for Soviet newsreels—a crucial sector of Soviet filmmaking—they will be either forgotten, or accorded a few vague and uninteresting remarks. All the same, over the newsreel factory hovers a basic unscrupulousness. Management, having taken into account, that work on the newsreel is creative work, that the work of the newsreel journalist in the process of shooting is artistic work, arrived at utterly incorrect conclusions concerning working methods, unscrupulously engaging in the staging and shooting of acted objects, unqualified and unprofessional shoots in the context of the newsreel factory.

We need to get on with shooting our daily living reality, we need to get on with shooting real people: the heroes of historical construction, we need to get on with shooting their harsh, heroic daily struggle for a bright future, for coming days, because there is no force more moving, than the force of fact, presented inventively, with a clear purpose.

The very objective, the treatment of the presentation of the facts of the present day, must be goal-oriented, class-oriented, Party-oriented.

Does the question of cinema dramaturgy enter into the concerns of workers in the non-acted film? Not at any stage.

For non-acted films, a canonical acted scenario with the participation of actors, with events thought-out in advance isn't necessary.

Life in all its multifacetedness, complexity, contradictoriness every day and every hour creates those situations which can be expressive material for the dramaturgical construction of a non-acted object.

It is necessary only to creatively, inventively know how to choose and to shoot the real events of our life, not made-up, but authentic heroes. It is necessary to learn how to show their thoughts and feelings and to connect the selected material, the selected sequences of our reality with each other, so that this will be a unified, dramaturgically developed action.

---

[78] [Trans.]: In the original: женщины-колхозницы [zhenshchiny-kolkhoznitsy] (women-female kolkhoz workers).

The well-known similarity of devices of the acted and non-acted film should not lead to a misconception about the essential differences between them.

While setting for themselves the same tasks and goals, each of them is obliged to work with completely different expressive means.

I want to work (1934)

To the editorial staff of the newspaper *Kino* and at the same time in response to Comrade Katsman:

In the last issue of the newspaper *Kino* an open letter to me was published, signed by Comrade Katsman. I did not find any annotations by the editorial staff to this letter. This gives me the right to think, that the point of view of Comrade Katsman is the point of view of the editors.

First of all, "Concerning the pace of creativity and the pace of our reality," as Comrade Katsman poses the question. It would have been more accurate to say to me directly, "Creative proposals and the schedules for their implementation." A few notes.

It is true, that my desire to work on a film concerning Soviet women had arisen already in 1930. The proposal was accepted by the management of the factory, but subsequently to this, came a further insistence on [my] making an acted film using actors.[79] Such a film about Soviet woman was not necessary. I proposed making *Magnitogorsk*, but this theme was entrusted to a director, who agreed to make a film which was half-documentary and half-acted. As it turns out, an actual film, devoted to this remarkable construction project, never materialized and I am bold enough to think, that I would have succeeded in realizing such a film. It was necessary to expend a great deal of strength, time, and energy, in order to gain the opportunity to shoot by commission of the Central Committee of the VLKSM[80] the sound film *KShE*. The theme of the White Sea Canal passed me by, because at that time I was shooting this large, important film. And so, having finished *KShE*, and rather than sitting idly by, I returned once again in 1932 to the theme of woman.

Comrade Katsman should have known about that, since I have no doubt, that the most sincere wish to put the master "who had strayed" on the correct path, prompted this letter on his part.

---

[79] [Trans.]: In the original: делать игровую актерскую фильму.

[80] [Trans.]: In the original: ВЛКСМ: the abbreviation for the official name of the Komsomol organization: Всесоюзный ленинский коммунистический союз молодежи [Vsesoyuzny leninsky kommunistichesky soyuz molodezhi] (The All Union Leninist Communist Union of Youth).

I have now made three proposals. For one of the proposals, I had already almost prepared a scenario; why "almost" I will explain below.

I maintain, that with correct use being made of me, I could make three films in the course of two years.

By November 1934, I will be able to make a large scale film devoted to the DVK,[81] showing, with what quick strides, the Far Eastern Region is moving forward, how the economic character of the region is being transformed, how the discovery and utilization of all the enormous natural underground wealth of the region is turning the DVK into a wealthy and thriving area, into an outpost of socialism on the shores of the Pacific Ocean. Is such a film necessary right now? I think it is necessary and very much so. In addition, I commit myself along the way to sending back informational material about the region for a newsreel.

Beginning in 1935, I would be fully occupied by work on the pictures *Moscow—Volga* and *Woman and Reporter*[82] (working title of the film). During this time, the newsreel would have accumulated material beforehand and according to my instructions. As everyone knows, I have never rejected the use of newsreel archives. You see, Comrade Katsman, there would be no delay, if correct and timely use were made of me. In actual fact, three of my proposals have not yet been approved. Time passes. Schedules are postponed; the possibility of realizing these proposals becomes more and more problematic with each passing day.

A few words about the scenario for *Woman and Reporter*. Comrade Katsman, you are not only a journalist, but a worker in newsreels, for this reason, I think you know quite well, that this is the first attempt to make a non-acted scenario. This is something new and accomplishing this task is complex and difficult.

So much futile effort and energy has been expended by screenwriters of acted-films and there have been so many failures on this front, though it would seem, that the acted film has a rather well-proven tradition in the matter of the creation of scenarios. The first version of our scenario, which, as is evident, comrade Katsman has read, neither B. Lapin nor I considered completely finished. We intended and still intend to work on it a great deal more, both during the period of preparation and during shooting, which is completely unavoidable, when we are talking about a non-acted film. Precisely our scenario must be examined only as a first compositional draft of a future object.

---

[81] [Trans.] In the original: ДВК: the abbreviation for Дальневосточный край [Dal'nevostochny krai] (The Far Eastern Region), a former administrative entity of the Soviet Union, the capital of which was Kharabovsk and the largest city, Kamchatka.

[82] [Trans.]: In the original: *Москва—Волга* [*Moskva—Volga*] and *Женщина и репортер* [*Zhenshchina i reporter*].

Why is comrade Katsman doubtful, as to whether all the facts, which will enter in to this film, will be "realized with all the force of the graphic means, of which the art of filmmaking is possessed." This is incomprehensible to me.

I think, that to the extent of my powers and my abilities, I have realized this in my previous works. I am utterly convinced, that I can succeed in making a film about Soviet women, by means of a *feature-length non-acted* film,[83] in which the principal figures will be two chairwomen of Village Councils,[84] the Ul'yanov sisters, and one woman worker from the "Ball Bearing" factory—that I have the capacity "to develop deeply and in an interesting way" images of the Ul'yanov sisters—and that I have the capacity "to understand at the level of an artistic synthesis" all the facts, which will enter into this film. Comrade Katsman and many others along with him are frightened of approving in advance the approach of all so-called "documentary films."

He is frightened by the attitude attributed to me, that I see "only facts" and "I do not see their emergence," that my creative motto is "we fight with facts," that "I link facts formally among themselves," and so on.

Comrade Katsman maintains, that there is a perversity of documentalism "in their large canvases," that only the newsreel or short subject films[85] correctly and artistically document and reflect our reality. (There is a lot to be said about the work of the news-reel. I will make a point of doing so in the next issue.) Comrade Katsman thinks, that I should choose precisely this path. I quite think, that before anything else, it is necessary to know and to respect the creative path of a master, whom you really wish to help.

Comrade Katsman maintains, that "inertia, moving me towards… feature-length films,[86] is depriving Soviet filmmaking of a great master," and at the same time, this master grew and developed, working precisely on feature-length films. I will name them (it is appropriate to name them): *Fall of the Romanov Dynasty, Lev Tolstoy and the Russia of Nicholas II, The Great Way, Today, KShE.*

Allow me to grow and to develop further within the framework of my genre, don't impose on me your paths of development.

Some, who sincerely care about me, propose I make films with actors, others—short newsreel films, or short subject films. But not what I know how to and want to, and not what I consider it socially and politically useful to do. I think that I have the right to expect, that I will be given the opportunity to work on precisely that genre, to which I have devoted no small number of years of creative efforts, uninterrupted study, strength, and energy.

---

[83] [Trans.]: In the original: художественная неигровая фильма [khudozhestvennaya neigrovaya fil'ma]. The expanded letter spacing implies emphasis.

[84] [Trans.]: In the original: сельсовет [sel'sovet].

[85] [Trans.]: In the original: киноочерк. This might also be rendered as a film-sketch, or even essay film, but the implication is that it is a shorter film, i.e. "a small canvas."

[86] [Trans.]: In the original: полнометражные фильмы, a term which makes explicit reference to length.

As is well-known, not one of the films named by me set itself the tasks of "fighting with facts," I never linked facts among themselves mechanically and formally. And the Soviet spectator and even the proletarian spectator of the West were never "indifferent" to my pictures, which gives me the right to be proud and I am.

This does not mean, that everything in my films was good. Of course not. I consider, that many of the allegations—notably regarding KShE—were correct, but these errors of mine were also characteristic of the acted films of that period. Much still needs to be creatively overcome, much still needs to be learned and, above all, learned carefully, in a lively fashion, with political purposefulness, we must learn how to transfer our reality onto film visually in its totality. To learn in this way is to make one's pictures, so that the spectator with utterly absorbing interest and with love will follow every frame, in which the new world of socialism is being constructed in the vast spaces of our Union. And for this, there is no need to waste all one's strength and energy on proving one's right to work, there is no need to polemicize, rather, above all, there is a need to work. *I want to work!*

This is the kind of support that I very much expect from the public, from the press, and, in particular, from comrades in the work.

The deeds and the people of our great days (1934)

The entire second half of 1933, I worked with Boris Lapin on a scenario about Soviet woman. The proletarian revolution, the new conditions of labor, the new social practice, the women participating in Socialist Construction have created and continue to create the New Man, the New Woman. This is the New Woman in the process of her emergence and it is the theme of my next film.

The scenario is ready. I will spare no effort to realize and edit this film in 1934. The desire to work on this theme arose in me already several years ago, but only now did the possibility of realizing it seem to present itself. As in all my previous films, in this film there will be no actors. In it, nothing will be preconceived. The protagonists[87] in this film will have a first name, a last name, an address.

I am deeply convinced, that the non-acted film, as a document of our days, has the possibility to speak the truth about the affairs and the people of our great days with great artistic and emotional credibility, with authentic realism.

---

[87] [Trans.]: In the original: действующие лица [deistvuyushchie litsa]. Shub is using a term used in fiction film, but is restricting it to its literal meaning the figures (characters) who perform actions by avoiding references to acting.

This is why after *Woman*, I would like to make the film *Moscow—Volga*.[88] I would like to plan the shooting now, to gather material in an organized fashion, and at the conclusion of this monumental work, to have the completed film: a document about the people and their struggles for the implementation of the Work Plan.

It is indeed upsetting, that none of the stages of the construction of the Belomorstroi[89] were recorded on film. Now, acted scenarios are being created and more will be created, devoted to the remarkable organizers and shock workers[90] of this unprecedented feat. However clever these scenarios may be, however expressive the performances of talented actors may be, such a film is not capable of substituting for the force of impact and comprehension, which authentic film documents about the real struggles of this construction project, would give.

The Metro on the screen (1934)

From the Moscow Kombinat Building, I began filming the Metropolitan. Five short subject films are envisaged. Each short subject film will present an accomplished goal, and at the same time, after the completion of all shooting, it will be a constituent part of a future film on the Metro Construction Authority.[91]

The first sketch *The Metro Construction Authority by Night*, will be made on August 25th. Large scale preparation work has been carried out. The crew has gone over the entire route several times, familiarizing themselves with all aspects of the work on this monumental construction project.

The fundamental theme is the miner-construction worker.[92] The first thing that astonishes one in the pits is the presence of many, many young miners. These are not the usual miners. It's enough to hear their conversations. Day and night under all conditions, in the shafts, on the tunnel faces, on the shield,[93] laying down concrete, in the relentless struggle for quality, for fulfillment of the plan, for the schedule: everywhere you could intensely feel the persistence, the joy of life, the energy, the confidence of youth.

---

[88] [Trans.]: Shub seems to be referring to the Moscow-Volga Canal, connecting the Moscow River with the Volga, which was under construction (1932–1937) at the time of her writing. The labor was furnished by Gulag prisoners. One has to wonder whether Shub knew who was supplying the labor.

[89] [Trans.]: This acronym refers to the construction project of the canal linking the White Sea and the Baltic Sea. It was also constructed by gulag prisoners, referred to euphemistically as "kanaloarmeets" (singular), a word coined on the model of "krasnoarmeets" (Red Army man). The term for the canal workers could be rendered as Canal Army Man.

[90] [Trans.]: In the original: ударник [udarnik].

[91] [Trans.]: In the original: Метрострой [Metrostroi].

[92] [Trans.]: In the original: шахтер-строитель.

[93] [Trans.]: In the original: на щите. In current mining terminology щит [a shield] has various meanings. Here, it may refer to a device used to protect mine workers from rock falls.

These are people who know no barriers to overcoming obstacles, they are victorious people.

Night and pre-dawn shoots of Moscow will be accomplished without lighting equipment. Experience acquired on night shoots while working on the picture *KShE* gives us the right to expect, that new tasks set by us will be successfully accomplished. As with *KShE*, we propose recording sounds, noises, voices, music on location. We will go down into the pit with a microphone. We hope to overcome the fundamental difficulty of shooting separate short films.

We would like to show this remarkable construction project in a detailed plan, but working on short films is also exciting, because it requires, that each shot be constructed utterly economically, thoughtfully, and visually.

Investigating a creative concept (1935)

In light of the enormous importance of the task assigned to workers in the Soviet film industry, the role of film criticism becomes especially significant and crucial.

The purely emotional aspect in the evaluation of a film, the perception of its "tastefulness" by one or another random reviewer is not sufficient for either creative workers in cinema, or the spectator. It is necessary to remark, that if our cinema criticism has shown a notably slow and restricted growth in its creative perception and ability to master the role of associate and mentor to our cinema cadres, then the broad masses of spectators in recent years have experienced colossal growth in numbers and in strength in this regard.

The proof is, at least, that the most accurate, thoughtful, and direct comments concerning that tremendous achievement of ours, *Chapaev*, were given to us, for the most part, not by the professional press, but by spectators. I have in mind the large number of letters from military personnel, from the working men and women of numerous factories, from various representatives of Science and the Arts, and so on.

A critic should be first and foremost a man of great artistic culture. Having seriously set himself the task of providing real help to creative cinema-workers, the critic should not be content with watching already completed films. He should communicate with the director while he is at work, learn the difficulties which are encountered on his path, penetrate to the essence of his creative struggle and achievements in the area of the development and taking control of the scenario and in his artistic design, as well as, in the part of his work with the creative collective.

What goals is the director pursuing in his production, what are his intentions, what is preventing him from realizing these intentions, to what degree and by what means does he take control of the collective, how does the director grow, how does each member of the collective grow—that should be the subject of the observations and study of the cinema critic.

On the other hand, the critic must study the spectator attentively, this new spectator, who has grown so quickly in his demands and evaluations.

Trying to accurately sense the mood of the auditorium, identifying with it, as much as penetrating it, the critic must accurately evaluate the perception of the spectator, be attentive to his emotions, and know how to explain to the director *what* gets through to the spectator, *how* to get through to him, what reaction is provoked and *why* it is provoked.

Being, in this way, the link between the auditorium, which is growing in breadth and depth, and the creative collective, the cinema critic can accurately transmit to the director that persistent "order," which is being sent to him from the auditorium.

At the current time, comments, which through their observations provide real assistance in our work, are extremely useful critical analysis, for those of us, who are participating in the pre-screening of films by cinema directors.

In my work, especially at the beginning, criticism played a great and important role. The reception which the press and spectators accorded my first work in documentary-historical films, *Fall of the Romanov Dynasty*, *The Great Way*, *Lev Tolstoy and the Russia of Nicholas II*, affirmed my conviction of the political and aesthetic validity of this genre, which was new at the time, and was a powerful stimulus to my later work in this field. The creative discussion, which developed around my picture *KShE*, was extremely useful for me as a director, since it helped me to understand the errors I committed and to appreciate my achievements in the sound film, which was new for me.

Unfortunately, I cannot say the same about the critical commentaries on my picture *Today*, which were able, instead, to disorient me and the spectator in the accurate evaluation of this work.

[Our path] (1937)

Cinema is the youngest of the arts and Soviet cinema is even younger. Soviet Literature, Soviet theater, architecture, music, painting inherited the monumental culture of the previous millennia of human genius. For Soviet cinema, it was much more difficult. If you understand this, it will become clear what an extraordinary path Soviet filmmaking has traveled. Within a short time, it achieved brilliant victories. Soviet cinema became an art beloved by the masses of our country.

For me, there are three utterly distinct periods of Soviet cinema. The first stage is the stage of our youth, it is that period, when a group of young artists, born through the revolution, passionately strove to speak out through the screen about the Great October victory of the laboring masses. The films *Strike*, *The Battleship Potemkin*,

The End of St. Petersburg, *A Sixth Part of the World*, *Fall of the Romanov Dynasty*, *Fragment of an Empire* appeared. They used different methods, they took different paths, but these films spoke about one thing.

The second stage is making an advance. The country is taking giant steps forward in constructing socialism. The heroes of labor, under the leadership of the Party, are achieving victories on all fronts of Socialist Construction. A remarkable army of shock workers is growing up. In the countryside, in brutal class struggles, the kulak class[94] is being liquidated. The countryside of the kolkhoz is achieving victory.

We ourselves, the artists of the cinema, did not keep pace with the growth of our country. In our films of that period lies the stamp of naked agitationalism, schematism, formalism, and naturalism. A great wave of feeble imitations flooded the screen. The failure encompassed, in equal measure, acted as well as non-acted films. In spite of a whole series of deficiencies, all the same, in the films of this period, the struggle of artists may be seen to understand cinema art at the level of the tasks, which the Party and the government placed before us.

Precisely what did the errors of principle of the workers in documentary film consist of? Feature[95] documentary film is purely a Soviet phenomenon. It arose from the passionate desire to imprint on film our heroic reality, new social relations, the real activities of the people of our great Motherland, the formidable statements of the masses against our enemies, the celebration of our victory, and to do this all without recourse to staging and by shooting pieces of authentic life.

Can such films have expressiveness in their plot, their own visual emotionally affective structure, their own dramaturgy, their own heroism, and their own spectator? Can such films non-schematically, but with deep faithfulness and in all its many-sidedness, in all its contradictory complexity, reflect our life? I am deeply convinced, that they can. A whole series of documentary films have convincingly proven this.

Can and should newsreels create feature-length film chronicles?[96] At the present time, no. The newsreel has other tasks and a different production infrastructure. In my view, documentary film[97] should be one of the genres of feature-length film.

---

[94] [Trans.]: In the original: кулачество [kulachestvo], a collective noun from кулак [kulak], lumping together and abstracting all kulaks as an implicitly conspiratorial entity. This has the flavor of kulakhood, or kulakry. This word has a distinctively Stalinist ring. The "kulak class" is the standard translation and implies it is an enemy of the peasant class.

[95] [Trans.]: In the original: Художественный [khudozhestvenny], meaning at once artistic, *auteur*, and feature-length.

[96] [Trans.]: In the original: художественно-хроникальные фильмы [khudozhestvenno-khronical'nye filmy]. Here Shub plays on the dual meaning of хроникальные as the adjectival form of хроника: newsreel and chronicle, i.e. an historical record. One could also say: feature-length documentary films, or feature-length chronicle films.

[97] [Trans.]: In the original: документальный фильм.

What does the error of documentarians consist of? The first and principal error consists of the fact, that we have set in opposition documentary film and all acted film-making. We declared: "A Revolutionary Soviet film can only be a documentary film." We suffered all the childhood diseases of LEFism, we pronounced the slogan: "Down with art! Down with the acted film!"

Our second and no less great error was that we fetishized facts. We treated facts as material (it must be clearly said) for montage speculation. Urbanism, formalism, schematicism, plotlessness, subjectlessness found their expression in an entire series of documentary films.

But these diseases also afflicted acted films. Working, making errors, rising above errors, all the same, we grew. For me personally, it has been clear for a long time, that documentary film is not the main path for Soviet film. Personally, I long ago discarded as outdated a fetishism of facts, as I have said repeatedly. Not only the fact, but our relationship to the fact, our class vision of reality, our class understanding of facts—that is the main thing.

I will now turn to the third stage of the cinema: a new stage initiated by *Counterplan*.[98] After that, successively *Chapaev*,[99] *Aerograd*,[100] *Men on Wings*.[101] All these are victories of the acted film.

Documentary film, as a genre of Soviet filmmaking, is considered a perverse genre. They would prefer, that either we become directors of acted films, or newsreel makers, or didn't work at all. Vertov managed to break through and he made a good film: *Three Songs about Lenin*.[102]

I did not receive any commissions to direct during these years, not because I didn't fight for them, but I must have fought badly. I didn't manage to finish my work on the Metro, because I was sent to work in Turkey.

As before, I consider, that feature documentary film is a necessary and a legitimate field of feature filmmaking. Now, in the process of working on Pushkin, I have suddenly clearly understood, that the means of documentary cinema cannot transmit everything. There are themes, which documentarism connects with. There are themes, which I deeply care about as an artist, but it isn't possible to transmit them through the methods of documentarism. I am not a member of a sect. I believe, that as the director of an acted film, I could make some of the artistically valid productions needed by Soviet art.

---

[98] [Trans.]: In the original: *Встречный* [*Vstrechny*] (1932), also known as *Shame* by Fridrikh Ermler.
[99] [Trans.]: (1934), directed by Sergei and Georgy Vasil'ev.
[100] [Trans.]: aka *Frontier* (1935), directed by Alexander Dovzhenko.
[101] [Trans.]: In the original: *Летчики* [*Letchiki*] (1935), aka *Flyers*, directed by Yuli Raizman and Grigory Levkoev.
[102] [Trans.]: *Три песни о Ленине* [*Tri pesni o Lenine*] (1934).

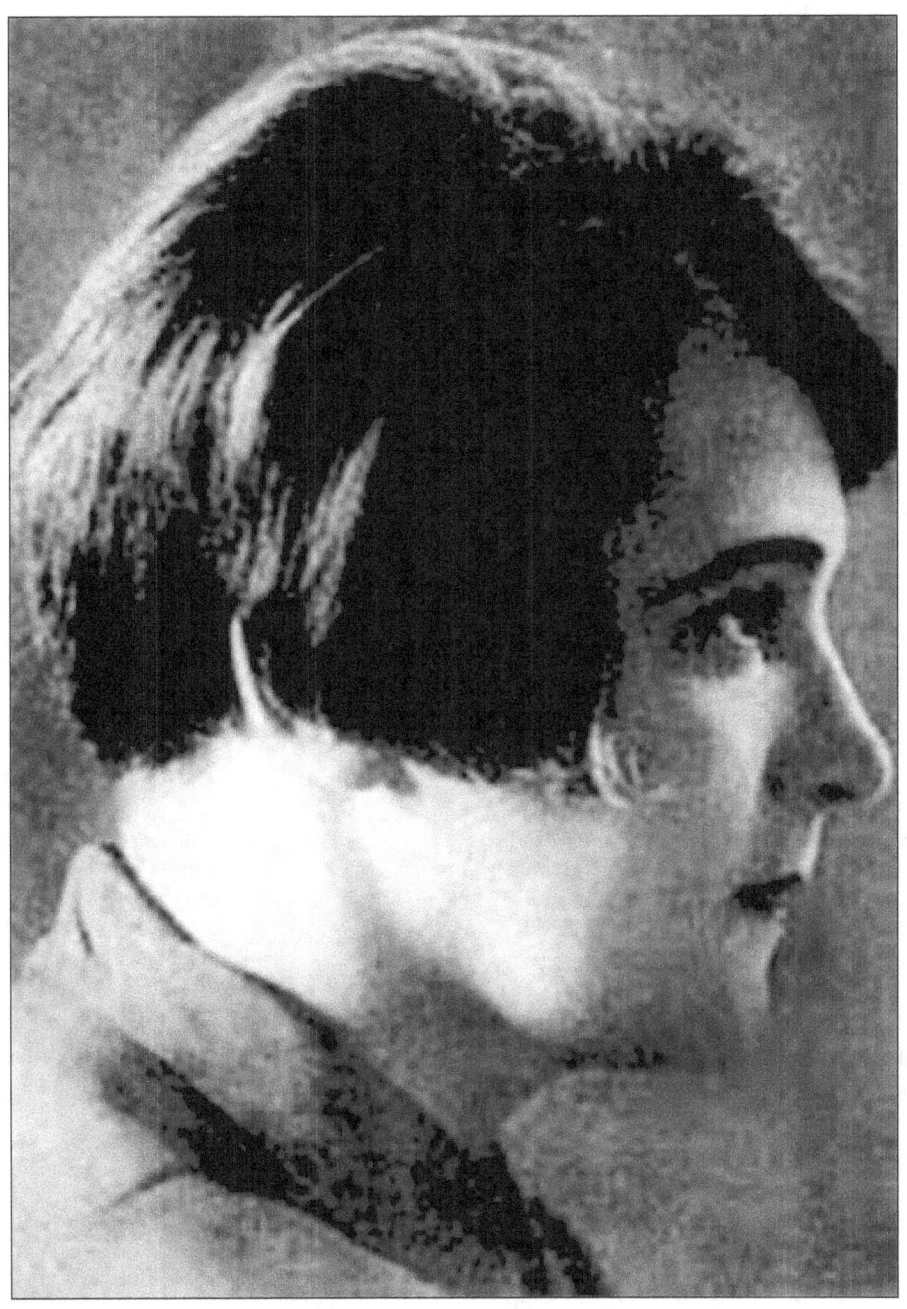

An Important and Urgent Matter (1938)

…More than once, the argument has arisen, whether it is possible for staged material to supplement a newsreel or documentary film. To put it another way: is it possible to place documentary and staged facts side by side, without damaging the veracity and artistic expressiveness of a film. This argument seems trivial to me. It does, however, distract the attention of workers in the newsreel from their principal and pressing task.

The camera operator is, indisputably, the leading worker in the newsreel. On his inventiveness, correct choice of lenses for shooting depends the success of the shoot and the quality of the material shot.

If we had a great deal of well-shot documentary material, the question of staging would fall away. It is necessary to have recourse to staging only in exceptional circumstances. Staging, here, is the result of the lack of factual material and it is produced using the methods of the acted film. Side by side with documentary material, a fact staged using the methods of acted film looks false, unconvincing, damaging artistic authenticity. Shooting a newsreel using "the acted method" renders a shot meaningless.

We need to shoot the many-sidedness of our life in all its complexity and we need to do more of it and do it better. The main thing is: it's necessary to elevate the level of culture of filming. This means, first and foremost, *raising the political level and artistic culture* of the director of the artistic-documentary film and of the newsreel cameraman.

Isn't it hurtful, that we did not accumulate materials for films on comrades Sverdlov,[103] Dzerzhinsky,[104] Frunze.[105] We know what force was achieved by docu-

---

[103] [Trans.]: Yakov Mikhailovich Sverdlov, an early supporter of Lenin in the Bolshevik/Menshevik split in the Social Democratic Labor Party. He took part in the 1905 uprising and was either imprisoned or put in internal exile until the Revolution. Upon return from exile, he was elected to the Central Committee of the Communist Party and eventually became the legal head of state as chairman of the All-Russian Central Executive Committee. He is said to have been instrumental in the execution of the Romanovs.

[104] [Trans.]: Felix Edmundovich Dzerzhinsky. A committed revolutionary since his teens in Poland, his persistent agitational activities took him in and out of many prisons in Poland and Russia, where he suffered great physical and mental abuse. Freed by the Revolution, he quickly rose through the ranks and was eventually entrusted by Lenin with matters of "internal security." He became feared and renowned as the head of various internal security organizations, including the notorious Cheka, where he organized the "red terror" against those perceived to be internal enemies of the revolution. He became, in succession, head of the GPU section of the NKVD and the OGPU and eventually Minister of the Interior and Minister for Communications, all the while maintaining his control over the state security apparatus. Other notable deeds include taking charge of the embalming of Lenin's body and the organization of orphanages for the *besprizornye* (orphans of World War One, the Revolution, and the Civil War), who frequently became incorporated into the ruthless state security apparatus.

[105] [Trans.]: Mikhail Vasil'evich Frunze was another early supporter of Lenin in the Bolshevik/Menshevik split. He took part in the 1905 uprising and was put in a Siberian prison from which

mentary films, which managed to show the great people of our era. The films *Kirov*,[106] *Three Songs about Lenin*,[107] *Land of the Soviets*,[108] show distinctively the rich possibilities given by documentary material accumulated over the years.

Feature documentary films must, in the end, occupy their rightful place in Soviet Filmmaking. Feature documentary films require planning, just as do acted films. They must be shot according to a treatment. They require a period of preparation. The participation of the director in the shooting of a documentary film is mandatory. The ability of the director to see the environment surrounding him in a meaningful way and to select materials, in essence, predetermines the quality of the future film. Those who maintain, that, for the shooting of a documentary film, preliminary organization is not necessary are deeply deluding themselves.

It is clear that the methods of *organization* of shooting, as well as the very *method* of shooting people for documentary films are essentially distinct from the method of shooting and working with actors in acted films. But the process of shooting people in a feature documentary film demands no less complex and careful organization than does shooting in acted films.

The technological facilities for documentary films must be just as well equipped as for acted films. Shooting, in my view, must take place with the technological capacity of a studio for acted films. Only in these circumstances can valid feature documents be created, which will speak in full voice about our great days.

The cinema newsreel in our land must shoot a great deal and shoot well. Newsreel and feature documentary films must be produced significantly more quickly than they are now; this is an important, urgent, Party matter.

A range of themes mentioned in the plan for work in the cinema, in my view, require implementation with documentary methods. These are military-defense and antifascist themes, these are themes about Soviet reality—about kolkhozes, shock workers, Soviet youth, about Soviet woman, about the friendship of the Peoples of the Soviet Union, about the beauty and richness of our nature, about the flowering of the art of our happy Peoples.

---

he later escaped to carry on clandestine Bolshevik agitation. He later became a renowned military commander and was responsible not only for the defeat of the White General Wrangel during the Civil War, but for crushing Makhno's Ukrainian anarchist movement. Widely respected within the Party, he was among the candidates to succeed Lenin and may have been murdered by order of Stalin during a medical procedure.

[106] I have been unable to find a record of any film by that title. A documentary film giving lip service to the importance of Sergei Mironovich Kirov may well have been destroyed later by Stalin, who was behind Kirov's murder. Any documentary might have conflicted with Ermler's more or less official account of Kirov's life story in *A Great Citizen* (1938).

[107] [Trans.]: *Три песни о Ленине* [*Tri pesni o Lenine*] (1934) by Dziga Vertov.

[108] [Trans.]: *Страна Советов* [*Strana Sovetov*] (1937) by Shub.

Notes of a director (1939)

The film *Spain* will soon appear on Soviet Screens. The film is finished, but the particular exhilaration, which took hold of me during work on it, remains. It draws me to the editing table, to the Moviola, to the screening room. It seems, that not everything, is completely done yet, all is not said.

Ten months ago, Roman Karmen turned over to me a list of shots taken by him and Makaseev in Spain. The search for the material began. There was a single goal: to have in my hands as quickly as possible the original negatives of their work. The search was complicated. No small amount of time was required to gather, and with the help of Karmen and Makaseev, to date all of the shots taken by them. Karmen and Makaseev beautifully shot the initial period of the struggle (1937) of the heroic Spanish People with Fascism. Also, in my hands were the work prints[109] of what was shot by Karmen and Makaseev.

With a feeling of legitimate pride in the Soviet Artist, I am happy to say: Karmen and Makaseev are not only wonderful camera operators, they are courageous, brave, and bold comrades and because of this, they succeeded in recording documents of enormous power and truth.

---

[109] [Trans.]: In the original: рабочие кадры. This is not current terminology.

It was immediately clear, that there was little material. Events took their course. Each day brought one new report after another, exciting the entire Soviet People. Camera operators from the Spanish Republic came to our aid. We began to receive beautifully shot material of the events of 1938 and 1939. They sent songs, sound recordings.[110] It also became clear, that it was an enormous theme. The theme of a People struggling for their freedom. A theme such as this required a powerful dramatic resolution, with an expressiveness new for a documentary film.

The help of a writer, of a dramatist was essential. Vsevolod Vishnevsky agreed to provide a scenario. A collaborative labor began. There were daily screenings and study of the material. I was very pleased by Vishnevsky's enormous, professional memory: he immediately memorized every shot, the entire complex semantic and rhythmic particularities of an individual piece of film. He perceived perfectly the kind of composition in which, each separate piece of film would attain the greatest force of expression. This quality of Vsevolod Vishnevsky made it possible to correctly solve a whole series of difficulties, which presented themselves along the way, flexibly, quickly, and on the fly.

Events began to change. The difficult year of 1939 arrived. New material arrived. More and more decisions arose. Individual sequences, entire parts of the scenario changed. New decisions arose during screenings where we were both present, they arose at the editing table, and were immediately and patiently worked out in conversations over the telephone. The entire time, to the very last day, the work was passionate, exciting, collaborative, and enriching to me in many ways. The shots were made by many camera operators. They were not made according to an assigned theme. It was imperative to subordinate the disparate shots to a single design. The material did not subordinate itself. The content within the frame was difficult to shift, it was difficult to compel it to express our theme, our design. We were relentless. We compelled the material to express the content, that we considered solely correct. We compelled it to express the thoughts and feelings of the Soviet People, the thoughts and feelings of Soviet artists. The beautiful music by the composer Gavriil Popov helped a great deal to express these feelings.

In this film, the Soviet spectator sees, how the great Spanish People heroically, over the course of three years, struggled and defended their freedom. In open war against the generals, against the interventionists, the Spanish People always showed themselves to be the victors. Only the blockade and treachery brought temporary defeat. In the film *Spain*, the Soviet spectator will see with their own eyes, what Fascism is, they will see its brutal face.

Death to Fascism! This is our cry, this is what the film documents, recording the bloody deeds of these contemporary Barbarians demand. The group who worked on

---

[110] [Trans.]: In the original: звукошумовые фонограммы. Again, not current terminology.

Spain was overflowing with rapture and love for the Spanish People, who were the first to show heroism and courage in open combat with Fascism.

Vsevolod Vishnevsky and I very much did not want to end the film with the usual title "The End."

We believe, the day will come, and shots showing the triumph and victory of the Spanish people, will come to lie on my editing table. And then, only then, will this film be finished.

The blood of the Spanish People, the blood of the International Brigades was not spilled in vain. The People, who rose up in defense of their rights, in the defense of freedom, cannot be conquered. The defeat is temporary. The End of the film still lies ahead.

About a contemporary theme (1939)

I cannot repeat the entire series of things comrades are saying. I would like to express some reflections about things not expressed by them.

When I think about a contemporary theme and why it has not found full expression in our film industry, sometimes it seems simply obvious, that here a distinct role has been played by the relationship of our organizations towards such a question as the budget of a thing. Among us, such a conception is held by administrators and, unfortunately, even by some directors, that a large budget defines a picture. This is a fact.

A comrade responds:[111] It has turned out this way historically, because these budgets have received more time and more attention.

In what way, how did it happen, that the most responsible leading directors, who, in essence, could and should have presented themes of the contemporary era, were endlessly charged with what are called expensive productions?

What has this led to? It has led to very important themes of the contemporary era, even when they become the order of the day, not being assigned to the most talented screenwriters

Here, it seems to me, that if this question is examined at the root level, then at once the air will be cleared. I know that Dovzhenko and Pavlenko take on themes of the contemporary era; this, of course, singles out this kind of work, this marks some kind of break.

I want to speak about the documentary film, the sort of work that has been considered taboo, flawed.

---

[111] [Trans.]: In the original: Г о л о с. I am informed by Yuri Tsivian and Masha Godovannaya that Г о л о с is used in the minutes of a meeting to preface a statement or objection by someone present at a meeting.

When I made *Land of the Soviets*, I looked at many hundreds of thousands of [meters of][112] negatives and it became clear to me, that the first years of the revolution (when we were very poor, when film stock was scarce) were shot better. Two of our Five-Year Plans were practically not shot at all. This is a fact. Moreover, the first one was shot better than the second one.

Why did this happen, why was the first Five-Year Plan shot and [why does] the material exist? Because not only were short shots taken of the sort associated with a newsreel, but long documentary films were made according to scenarios, as well. And only in this way can material be accumulated.

It is necessary to examine the attitude towards documentary film with the same intensity.

The third Five-Year Plan must be extensively documented on the screen. It seems to me, that no segment [of the film industry] should be as mobilized as the documentary film.

Is it not an outrageous crime, that we did not shoot footage of Hassan?![113]

The proposition that documentary film does not require specific means and possibilities is not correct. The quality and quantity of camera operators, the quality and quantity of cameras, of sound recording equipment, of directors: all this is just as important and should be given equal consideration, as any kind of feature film. It needs to be understood, once and for all, that this is creative work, that this is artistic work, that this kind of work needs to be considered at the level of art, and only then will this be broadly resolved.

Spain was an intriguing case in point. I would like to communicate two facts. One: it was with difficulty, with a great struggle, that they allowed me to have Popov as the composer. They said: this is not important. Why do you need Popov? There are other composers in Moscow. Think about it, it's a newsreel type film.

Now, when we see *Spain* on the screen, we understand, what this composer means for this work by Vishnevsky and me.

There is a second rather intriguing matter concerning the film *Spain*. The text, which accompanies this film, was written by Vishnevsky for himself, with all the particularities of his speech, his sense of expression. And how interesting was such an attempt, such a possibility, that the author of the scenario himself should speak his own text. We know, that in the pacifist film made by Hemingway, the text is spoken by Hemingway himself. He speaks in a husky voice. And this is good. I maintain, that we had very little time and that everything we managed to do when we recorded Vish-

---

[112] [Trans.]: Shub normally specifies the amount of film examined in meters; since this is from a stenogram, I suspect the word for meters was omitted by mistake.
[113] [Trans.]: In the original: Хасан, a locale near the border with North Korea and China, the site of a battle between Japan and the USSR, which deterred the advance of Japanese forces, arguably preventing the opening of a second front against the USSR.

nevsky is good. Much that was intriguing, interesting, and utterly unique was to be found in the way this text sounded.

True, Vishnevsky is not a voice-over artist. There was something which didn't turn out, in the sense of the clarity of pronunciation of certain words. It was simply the matter, that Vishnevsky, if he had heard himself a couple of times on screen, would have understood his deficiencies perfectly. And the film would have profited from this remarkably. However, I was ordered to record a voice-over artist.

Meetings (1940)

I had the pleasure during the last four years of Mayakovsky's life to meet with him rather frequently. In 1927 and in 1928, almost every week, the nearest comrades of the poet from *LEF* and then *Novy LEF* would gather at Mayakovsky's. Aseev, Shklovsky, Kirsanov, Kassil', the artists Rodchenko and Stepanova, and others would come. Film directors would also come: Eisenstein, Kuleshov, Yutkevich, myself. At these comradely meetings, we didn't formally meet. In the modest apartment around the tea table passionate conversations went on about what the new art of the land of socialism should be.

Now, discarding all that was not correct in these arguments, there is only one thing which became deeply imprinted on my memory for the rest of my life: the fiery, committed poet who gave his creative labor to the Party, to the People, to the world-historical cause: the victory of socialism. This was the theme of his entire life, almost the sole theme of his poetry. The evenings will be forever remembered when he read the poems "Vladimir Il'ich Lenin," "Good," "About that." Much needs to be written about this. He was different during these meetings: not the way we knew him, when he was at the podium of the Polytechnical Museum, or the House of the Unions. A muted, strong voice. There was an attentiveness and interest in the work and the words of his comrades. The conversations between him and those around him created a festive atmosphere, something outside the norm, coming from the time spent with him.

He attributed enormous importance to the development of Soviet Cinema as a new means of artistic labor.

He wanted to work closely with us. It seemed, a great deal of time lay ahead. He would live on forever. We would succeed in shooting the poet at the podium, in the Moscow streets, in the factory, at home, we would succeed in recording his voice. But we did not succeed…

We must hurry, while the artists of his generation, his contemporaries, artists who interacted with the poet, are still in possession of their full creative powers, to embody his image on the screen through the most powerful means of the art of the cinema.

About Soviet documentary cinema (1949)

Today, the thoughts of all of us—the workers in documentary cinema—are directed towards a single goal: to do everything within our power, to cause our documentary cinema art to advance, to grow, and to deepen.

What can raise our documentary cinema to the highest heights?

At first glance, it is already understood, that the very nature of our work, the tasks and goals which stand before us, demand from us a Party-oriented attitude towards reality and the ideologically accurate transfer to the screen of the living facts shot by the movie camera.

We all know well, that the power of documentation consists not only in our shooting living facts, but in the choice of events and in our attitude and comprehension of what is shot.

I would like to say a few words about what demands each of us must make of themselves, while critically viewing our given creative path and placing before ourselves the tasks, which are capable of elevating our documentary film art to a higher level.

Documentary, journalistic film is only a Soviet phenomenon; nowhere else, nor as powerfully has it emerged. The bourgeois critics of America and Europe were forced to recognize this. The Soviet Newsreel began its existence with the first few days of the Great October Revolution.

The names of the camera operators Giber, Tissé, Novitsky, Ermolov, the Lembergs (father and son) are inextricably connected with the beginning of the Soviet Cinema Newsreel. They gave it the high level of professional experience gained in the period leading up to the revolution.

Precisely which events of Soviet life were filmed in newsreels and documentary films?

What did our spectator see?

Above all, he saw our leader: Lenin and the inspiring events of the Civil War, the first years of Socialist Construction, the new conditions of labor, the empowerment of women, the solemn days of celebrations, and the formidable statements of the popular masses protesting against international counter-revolution.

Those contemporary with these events appeared on the screen—authentic Soviet People—and this was the most important thing.

In the very first years after the revolution, the camera operators Belyakov, Eshurin, Semenov, Troyanovsky, Glider came to the fore.

In 1925, director Dziga Vertov's *Leninist Kino-Pravda* came out.

Leninist Kino-Pravda opened the road to the journalistic film, which succeeded the so-called *Kulturfilm*, propagandizing for the RAPP. In 1926 and 1927, my films for the tenth anniversary of Soviet Power, *The Great Way* and the biographical film, *Lev Tolstoy and the Russia of Nicholas II*, came out.

In 1928 and 1929, Lidiya Stepanova's[114] film *Gigant*[115] appeared, which was one of the first works to show the arrival of tractors and combines in the Soviet countryside, as did the inspiring film *Shanghai Document* by the director Bliokh.

I am speaking about the older generation of documentary filmmakers and about films, which marked the beginning of this new phenomenon in cinema.

Which tasks stand before us, we directors of documentary cinema?

Above all, to record the new stirrings of socialist daily life, to show authentic Soviet People, to show what has been accomplished in the present day by the builders of the new socialist society. We are striving to make these films finished works, we have set ourselves the task of exposing the interior essence according to the Party of events shown on the screen.

Not only is the innovation of these films now clear to me, but also their errors, which we declared at the time.

The fundamental error was that we spoke out against acted cinema and maintained, that only the newsreel could be revolutionary.

But I myself, up to the time when I began to work as a director of documentary films, edited feature acted motion pictures, such as *Wings of a Serf*,[116] *Abrek Zaur*,[117] *The Skotinins*,[118] *First Fires*,[119] *Trouble*,[120] *Smoke*,[121] and others.

As a director of documentary cinema, I have striven to prove, that montage which avoids over-sophistication[122] can elevate the meaning of a documentary film. I have wanted and have tried to edit my films simply and semantically clearly.

It seems to me, that in my films, the successful ones, as well as the less successful ones, I have succeeded in carrying out this intention.

During the years of the Great Five-Year Plans, during the years of the Great Patriotic War, many talented masters of the documentary film have come of age, both in the field of the camera operator and the in the field of directorial mastery.

---

[114] [Trans.]: Lidiya Il'inichna Stepanova (1899–1962). Soviet film director, notable for *Советская женщина* [*Sovetskaya zhenshchina*] (*Soviet Woman*), *Советская Эстония* [*Sovetskaya Estonia*] (*Soviet Estonia*), for which she received the Stalin Prize of the First Order, and *Москва—столица СССР* [*Moskva—stolitsa SSSR*] (Moscow, the Capital of the USSR), for which she received the Stalin Prize of the Second Order, among others.

[115] [Trans.]: The film is named after the sovkhoz, which it depicts, the name of which means "Giant."

[116] [Trans.]: *Крылья холопа* [*Kryl'ya kholopa*] (1926), directed by Yuri Tarich.

[117] [Trans.]: *Абрек Заур* [*Abrek Zaur*] (1926), directed by Boris Mikhin.

[118] [Trans.]: *Господа Скотинины* [*Gospoda Skotininy*] (1927), directed by Grigory Roshal'.

[119] [Trans.]: *Первые огни* [*Pervye ogni*] (1925), directed by Yuri Tarich.

[120] [Trans.]: *Морока* [*Moroka*] (1925), co-directed Evgeny Alekseevich Ivanov-Barkov and Yuri Tarich.

[121] [Trans.]: *Дым* [*Dym*] (*Smoke*). I could find no film by this title. The closest title of the period is *Два дыма* [*Dva dyma*] (*Two kinds of Smoke*) (1926), directed by Oleg Frelikh, which is believed to be lost. Shub edited Frelikh's 1926 film *Проститутка* [*Prostitutka*] (*Prostitute*), so it is conceivable she could have worked with him on this other film.

[122] [Trans.]: In the original: неизощренный.

Films have appeared, which are varied in form, significant works have appeared, beloved by the Soviet People, and now, no one needs any longer to prove, that documentary film is a kind of new cinematic art.

The works of Vertov, Kopalin, Belyaev, Varlamov, Karmen, Stepanova and others developed and moved forward documentary cinema. During the years following the war, new and talented directors have come to the fore. I am speaking of the work of Kristi, Setkina, Ovanesova, Bubrik, Gurov and Katsman. I would like to believe, that in this lineage, my film *On the Other Side of the Aras*,[123] made in 1947, could occupy a place.

The camera department of the newsreel has an entire constellation[124] of wonderful masters; I will not enumerate them here, but their significance is so great, that today it is precisely the camera operators of the newsreel, who by right, are the leading masters of Soviet documentary cinema.

Many problems have been posed for us by the makers of fiction films in the time following the war; the remarkable film *Vladimir Il'ich Lenin*[125] by Romm and Belyaev occupies a special place among them.

Up to now, documentary film had shown our people in a different way, it has demonstrated considerable success in showing the Republics of the Union. It revealed and brought to the screen extensive pictures of life in full, as we see it in such films as *One Day in Soviet Russia*[126] and *A Day in the Victorious Land*.[127] Documentary films with a broad view have become today an indispensable kind of work of our documentary cinema. But however interesting these films may be, however interesting the material assembled in them, we must seriously consider updating the bent, the point of view, under which this material will be presented.

---

[123] [Trans.]: *По ту сторону Аракса* [*Po tu storonu Araksa*] (1945), a film written and directed by Shub about the short-lived rise and the fall of the National Government of Azerbaijan in Southern Azerbaijan (i.e. Northern Iran), known to me only in a version with Azeri voice-over. It was made a year after the failed 21 Azer Movement (which created the National Government of Azerbaijan) and mixes documentary footage with what is clearly staged footage. One wonders whether it was intended to immortalize that movement for official Soviet History and perhaps provide inspiration for a future uprising to the citizens of the Soviet Republic of Azerbaijan, or to the Azeri-speaking population of northern Iran, where the 21 Azer Movement took place. Stalin had sponsored this uprising via proxies in the Soviet Republic of Azerbaijan in an attempt to gain access to oil in the region.

[124] [Trans.]: In the original: плеяда [pleyad] (Pleiades), alluding to a group of 19th-Century Russian poets.

[125] [Trans.]: *Владимир Ильич Ленин* [*Vladimir Il'ich Lenin*] (1949), a documentary.

[126] [Trans.]: *День нового мира* [*Den' novogo mira*] more literally: *A Day of the New World* (1941) by Roman Karmen and Mikhail Slutsky.

[127] [Trans.]: *День победившей страны* [*Den' pobedivshei strany*] (1949), directed by Il'ya Gutman and Il'ya Kopalin. It was released in German as *Ein Tag in der Sowjetunion*, that is, *A Day in the Soviet Union*.

We still have not learned how to shoot our contemporaries in a new way, though only this can transform the formal monotony of the documentary film.

Only this can help to discover multifaceted genres, only this can help to shoot the broad masses in a new way.

The problem of the biographical film must be solved another way.

These films must be not only about people who have passed away, but about people living now with us, about political figures, workers, kolkhozniks, doctors, teachers, people in the arts and sciences.

These people must be shot lovingly and deeply. I think, that in this, great discoveries lie ahead.

Look at how many significant successes in this direction our Soviet films with actors have achieved and what varied genres and artistic forms have arisen on precisely this basis.

In that, for us, there is no room for complacency.

It is possible to realize a biographical film in a new way, if we set before ourselves the task of showing a person, from among our contemporaries, living with us, having a practical effect among us.

And our archives?[128] I maintain, that it awaits the closest study by directors of documentary cinema, and then, there will be no dogged repetitions of the same clips from film to film, destroying the negatives, on which one event or another appears for the first time.

The point of view that the Soviet archives is our past, is inaccurate.

Yes, it is our past, but not only.

The archives is our present and our future.

What enormous meaning is possessed by films made with documentary material for our younger generation and for the generations of coming days.

Now, when it is no longer necessary to prove, that documentary film is an artistic phenomenon, a phenomenon of art, we must be bold in everything: in shooting, in the semantic construction of a film, and only then, will we succeed in expressing everything that is new, that today's socialist era brings to us.

Soviet daily life, culture, art still await their visual embodiment in documentary cinema.

---

[128] [Trans.]: In the original: А наша летопись? [A nasha letopis'?]. This seems a slightly surprising use of the word летопись, which normally only refers to written records and is more normally translated as "annals," "record," or even "history" or "story," when she is clearly referring to film archives. She uses летопись throughout the rest of the essay, making it clear that she is referring to *film* archives. In a sense, she is admonishing documentary film directors to *pay more careful attention*, to examine the nuances of the films which constitute Soviet History, as they constitute the historical record, the role once played by written records. The etymology of летопись, after all, is a record of the year лето = year and пись = to record, or more deeply: to make colorful, to embellish.

Sources

"About myself"
Printed here according to the text, published in the journal *Rabis* (Moscow, 1929, № 10).

"The Fabrication of Facts"
Printed here according to the text, published in the newspaper *Kino* (Moscow, 1926, № 41).

"To Work!"
Printed here according to the text, published in the newspaper *Kino* (Moscow 1927, № 46).

"Before *February*"
Statement concerning the plan for the future picture *Fall of the Romanov Dynasty* (*February*). Written at the beginning of 1927. Published here for the first time,[129] according to the author's manuscript, preserved in the archive of E. Shub.

["From my experience"]
Material for an article. Published here for the first time, according to the author's manuscript, preserved in the archive of E. Shub. Approximate date of composition the end of 1927.

["We do not reject the element of mastery"]
Statement at the *LEF and the Cinema* conference. Printed according to the text, published in the journal *Novy LEF* (Moscow, 1927. № 12). In the publication in the form of a stenogram, changes were introduced, with which E. Shub did not agree, about which she wrote in a letter to Tret'yakov (see letter № 56).

"The Great Way"
Printed here according to the manuscript (typewritten copy) preserved in the archive of E. Shub. Approximate date, beginning of 1928. The article appeared in the journal *Iskusstvo Kino* (1964, № 11).

"First work"
Printed here according to the text, published in the journal *Sovietsky Ekran* (Moscow, 1928, № 51).

---

[129] [Trans.] The notation "published here for the first time" is that of the Russian editor.

"*Lev Tolstoy and the Russia of Nicholas II*"
Material for an article with the elaboration of a plan for the picture (1928). Printed here according to the manuscript, preserved in the archive of E. Shub.

"This work cries out"
Printed here according to the text, appearing in the newspaper *Kino* (Moscow, 1928, № 11).

"The Newsreel, once again"
Stenogram of a conversation on the motion picture *Lev Tolstoy and the Russia of Nicholas II* (statement and concluding remark), 1929. Preserved at TsGALI (f. № 2494, op. 1, ed. khr 178).[130]

"A film about Tolstoy"
Material for an interview with English Film Critics (1929). Published here according to the manuscript, preserved in the archive of E. Shub.

"Non-acted Film"
Article published as a part of a discussion section in the journal *Kino i kul'tura* (Moscow, 1929, № 5—6). Printed here according to the text published in the journal.

Zrelishcha—a weekly publication on the theater, the music hall, the circus, mass actions, farces, cinema. Editor: L. Kolpakchi (Moscow, 1922, 1923, 1924).

"Towards the arrival of sound in the cinema"
Printed here according to the text published in the newspaper *Kino* (1929).

"First Impressions"
 Article written after arrival in Berlin in the summer of 1929. The original is preserved in the archive of E. Shub.

---

[130] [Trans]: I have transcribed the Russian terms, as they will be necessary to anyone attempting to locate this document or other documents at this archive. It will also require a knowledge of Russian. The terms here might be translated approximately as "collection № 2494, section 1, individual file 178." From here on, archival reference will be transcribed only. TsGALI (Центральный государственный литературный архив) is now RGALI (Российский государственный архив литературы и искусства).

"Joris Ivens"
Published here according to the text appearing in *Kino* (Moscow, 1930, № 11).

["About Creative Method!"]
From a statement in a discussion of M. Kaufman's film *Unprecedented Campaign*[131] at the ARRK[132] in 1931. Stenogram is preserved in TsGALI (f. 2494, op. 1, ed. khr. 388).

"About the film *Today*"[133]
Statement in a discussion of the film at the ARRK on November 12, 1930. The Stenogram of the discussion is preserved at TsGALI (f. 2494, op. 1, ed. khr. 388).

"Not only a great master but an innovator as well"
Printed here according to the text appearing in the newspaper *Kino* (Moscow, 1932, № 55), based on the discussion of the films *Ivan* and *Counterplan.*

"What there isn't"
Printed here according to of the text appearing in the newspaper *Kino* (Moscow, 1932, № 42).

"The theme of my talk"
Statement and concluding words of a discussion of the film *KShE*, in the editorial offices of the newspaper *Kino*. Published here according to the text appearing in the newspaper *Kino* (January 4, 1933).

"I want to make a film about Woman"
Printed here according to the text appearing in the mass-circulation newspaper *For Bolshevik Film* of the Moscow Factory Rosfil'm (April 15, 1933).

---

[131] [Trans.]: *Небывалый поход* [*Nebyvaly pokhod*], a film made during the First Five-Year plan, concerning rapid industrialization and the collectivization of agriculture.

[132] [Trans.]: Ассоциация работников революционной кинематографии [Assotsiatsiya rabotnikov revolyutsionnoi kinematografii] (The Association of Workers in Revolutionary Cinema), a professional association organized in Moscow in the summer of 1924 as ARK (The Association of Revolutionary Cinema), renamed ARRK in 1928.

[133] [Trans.]: The film's title in Russian is *Сегодня* [*Segodnya*].

"It will be recalled"
Published here according to the text appearing in the newspaper *Kino* (Moscow 1933, № 27). Article written in connection with the preparation for the Plenum of the ROS ARRK.[134]

"I want to work"
Addressed to the editors of *Kino* and simultaneously a response to Comrade Katsman. Printed here according to the text appearing in the newspaper *Kino* (Moscow 1934, № 12). An open letter to R. Katsman as a response to his article ("Master and Reality"), which had been published in the previous issue of the newspaper *Kino* (Moscow, 1934, № 11).

"The deeds and the people of our great days"
Printed here according to the text appearing in the newspaper *Kino* (Moscow 1934, № 4)

"The Metro on the screen"
Material for an article for the newspaper *Izvestiya* (July 12, 1934).

"Investigating a creative concept"
Printed here according to the text appearing in the journal *Sovietskoe Kino* (Moscow, 1934, № 3).

"Our path"
A statement in a discussion of the workers of Mosfil'm. Printed here according to the stenogram, preserved in the archive of E. Shub.

"An Important and Urgent Matter"
Printed here according to the text, which appeared in abbreviated form in the newspaper *Kino* (Moscow, 1938, № 26).

"Remarks of a director"
Printed here according to the text, which appeared in *Literaturnaya Gazeta* (Moscow, June 10, 1939).

---

[134] [Trans.]: Российской ассоциации работников революционной кинематографии [Rossiiskoi assotsiatsii rabotnikov revolyutsionnoi kinematografii] (The Russian Association of Workers in Revolutionary Cinema). The name assumed by ARRK as of 1930.

"About a contemporary theme"
Printed here in abbreviated form according to the stenogram, preserved in the
archive of E. Shub. The statement was made at a meeting in the Section of the
Arts,[135] in which a number of questions concerning the cinema were discussed.

"Meetings"
An article written for the ten-year anniversary of the death of V. Mayakovsky.
Printed here according to the text which appeared in the newspaper *Pravda*
(April 14, 1940).

"About Soviet documentary cinema"
Material in the article published in the collection *Twenty Years of Soviet
Cinema*[136] (Moscow, 1940). The last written work of E. Shub. Printed here
according to the manuscript, preserved in her archive.

---

[135] [Trans.]: In the original: отдел искусств. Presumably, this refers to the Section of Visual Arts,
отдел изобразительных искусств, of Narkompros.

[136] [Trans.]: In the original: *Двадцать лет советской кинематографии* [*Dvadtsat' let sovet-
skoi kinematografii*]. This might arguably be translated as *Twenty Years of Soviet Filmmaking*, or
even *Twenty Years of the Soviet Film Industry*, but in practice the meanings of "kino" and "kine-
matografiya" overlap and depend on immediate context, since "kino" can also refer to a movie theater
as well as the institution of "cinema."

Part III
Unrealized Projects

Women (1933–1934)

A film scenario

> *We wanted to create a film document about Soviet women. You will now see the results of our intelligence gathering. Nothing in this film is invented. There are no actors here. Everyone we are showing to you has a first name, a last name, an address. Perhaps these are your acquaintances, your friends, your enemies.*

Reel 1[1]

> *If, in 1914, someone living in the Russian Empire wanted to find out, what woman was, art might give him a precise answer.*

Circus music thunders. The [music for the] grand entrance of the artists into the arena[2] and a flourish.

A woman in light blue and pink appears with a golden hero around her head. In her arms lies a baby.

Here, she is strangely transformed and turned into a completely naked woman with rosy cheeks, on green grass.

She turns into the egotistically smiling beauty of Leonardo da Vinci.

She turns into a Rops[3] woman without any clothes in black gloves and mask, in her hands there is a switch.

She turns into a Beardsley woman. Graphic animation traces out her features.

In this way, in quick succession, pass by before us the colorful Madonnas, Venuses, Gretas, Susannas created by world art.

Once again, from the very beginning, the identical circus music repeats for the grand entrance of the artists into the arena and the flourish.

A film heroine with a child in her arms. An internationally known beauty. The spectator will recognize her. He has seen her in old films. She is shot like a Madonna.

---

[1] [Trans.]: One might arguably translate this as Part 1, but feature filmmakers of the era of photo-chemistry, often thought of their work in terms of reels, which for sound films of that era means units of about 11 minutes, which corresponded both to the maximum available lengths of print stock and to the capacity of older projectors: 1,000 feet, about 11 minutes at sound speed.

[2] [Trans.]: In the original: "парад-алле," possibly from the French, "parade allée," or, "parade, allez." The term is, at best, extremely rare in French and refers to a formal military parade. It may have developed among Russian speakers of French. It is a term used in the circus to describe the grand entrance of the circus artists into the arena. It seems that here, Shub is suggesting the typical music for the grand entrance, rather than an image of the grand entrance of the artists of a circus.

[3] [Trans.]: Félicien Victor Joseph Rops (1833–1898), a Belgian artist associated with Symbolism and Decadence, much admired by Baudelaire. Known for his erotica.

She turns into the worldly beauty from an old French film.

She turns into a painted fairy from an Aumont[4] féerie from 1912.

In her place, a contemporary Gioconda, Francesca Bertini.[5]

In her place, Lisenko[6] or Vera Kholodnaya.[7]

Once again, from the very beginning, the circus music repeats, the [music for the] grand entrance of the artists into the arena and a flourish.

Here the most typical woman with a child in her arms. She is walking down the street. She stops. We see her, just as closely and clearly, as we saw the Madonna.

She turns into a streetwalker.

She turns into an old peasant woman.

The music breaks off and with a bravura cry:

> *Gentlemen, would you like to get to know the ideal woman of the 20th Century? Buy gramophone records! Watch Pathé films!*

Shots from *At the Fireside*,[8] *Forget about Love*,[9] *Malyutka Elli*[10] and others.

—Bravo! Bravo! The spectators began to applaud.

From the screen comes barreling out, the Vyal'tseva[11] song, "Giddy-up troika, the snow is fluffy!"…[12]

---

[4] [Trans.]: Charles Aumont was a French theatrical entrepreneur in pre-revolutionary Moscow. He had a theater, known as the Театр Омона «Олимпия» (Théâtre Aumont "Olympia") along with a restaurant in a pleasure garden, which presented summer spectacles of various sorts. It was known for the severe discipline imposed on its female cabaret stars. Aumont was also the organizer of some of the first film screenings in Russia at the Nizhny Novgorod fair in 1896, reviewed by Maxim Gorky, whose review famously commenced, "Last night I was in the kingdom of the shadows…" Aumont also brought the first sound film to his Théâtre Aumont "Olympia" in 1902, a demonstration of the Joly Biophonographe. Though Aumont left Russia in 1907 to escape his mounting debts, his theater lasted some years more.

[5] [Trans.]: Italian silent movie diva, famous for her starring role in *Assunta Spina*, among many others.

[6] [Trans.]: Natal'ya Andrianovna Lisenko, Russian film star and later spouse of Russian matinee idol, Ivan Mozzhukhin. She left Russia in 1920 with Mozzhukhin and continued to act in films in France until 1939.

[7] [Trans.]: Considered by some Russia's first female film star.

[8] [Trans.]: In the original: У камина [*U kamina*], a 1917 feature melodrama, directed by Petr Ivanovich Chardynin and starring Vera Kholodnaya. It was a massive commercial success, running in cinemas until 1924, when Soviet authorities ordered many of Kholodnaya's films destroyed. Chardynin had directed a number of films between 1909 and 1917 and continued to direct until 1926, though given the success of this film, not in the great numbers one might expect.

[9] [Trans.]: I could find no film by this title. Perhaps Shub is confusing it with the title of another Chardynin film Позабудь про камин, в нем погасли огни [*Pozabud' pro kamin, v nem pogalsli ogni*] (*Forget about the Fireside, the fires have gone out there*) (1917).

[10] [Trans.]: In the original: *Малютка Елли*. A feature of 1918, based on a story by Maupassant, directed by Yakov Protazanov, starring Natal'ya Lisenko and Ivan Mozzhukhin.

[11] [Trans.]: Anastasiya Dmitrievna Vyal'tseva, renowned pre-Revolutionary mezzo-soprano, specializing in Gypsy Art songs. In the Soviet era, the genre was viewed by some as a remnant of decadent bourgeois sensibility.

[12] [Trans.]: In the original: "Гай-да тройка снег пушистый!" Composed by Mikhail Shteinberg,

The tragedy has begun.

A dandy in a tuxedo with a revolver kills a woman, pressed up against the wall in horror.

—Bravo! Bravo!

"A frosty night all around. The silver moon is shining…" continues the Vyal'tseva song. "A couple rushes off, just the two of them…"

In a disordered bed, a prostitute smothers a drunken merchant.

A girl sobs in despair in a back alley.

A wife, with her hands on her hips, screams at her broken, neurotic husband:

—Quiet!

—My God! What can we do? What can we do?

A girl stops at the railing of a bridge. Now she throws herself into the river.

—My God! What can we do?

A lady repeats this, leaning back in a chaise longue. Now, she stands up slowly, goes to the fireplace, she is yearning. There is nothing she can do.

A pre-war orchestra thunders on. Pre-war Negroes dance a cake-walk, the precursor of Negro dances.

—Bravo! Bravo!

> *Cinematographes, Electro-screens,*[13] *and Bioscopes of
> the Russian Empire always showed the Russian woman
> the same way.*

Now she has become frozen in a kiss with some sickly-sweet handsome man. This is the beginning of the film.

Now, at the end of the same film, they are standing facing each other. Now the murder takes place.

—You betrayed me! [he says]

—But I swear to you…

—You betrayed me!

—But I swear to you…

—My God, what can I do… what can I do…

Now shots from an old newsreel. A skating rink, pre-war music. Guardsmen in tall hats, women in tight skirts.

Some full-figured women move around a charity bazaar.

---

recorded by Vyal'tseva in 1903. A recording of this wistful romantic song can be found on her Russian Wikipedia page: https://ru.wikipedia.org/wiki/ Вяльцева,_Анастасия_Дмитриевна.

[13] In the original: электроэкраны [elektroekrany]. I could find no reference to this outside of Shub's writings. Yuri Tsivian suggests, she may have made it up to parody typical cinema hyperbole of the time. Many early British cinemas were called "electric cinemas."

—Each of you, ladies—says the voice of a traveling salesman—can develop your bust, improve it, you can take it from droopy to well-proportioned and sleek, thanks to the new Grenier method.

We see "Gramophone" company brand gramophone records. On the label is written: "The voice of Lev Tolstoy, recorded at Yasnaya Polyana March 3, 1908." The record begins to spin and Lev Tolstoy says,

"The Chinese sage, Confucius, taught, that reason, that is concern for our neighbors, is placed within us. It is the same in men and in women."

A high society lady from the film *Dreams, Dreams*[14] has taken her seat in her Landau. The coachman nods, the horses begin to move.

—To whom do you owe your riches, madame? To your husband, or to your lover…

—To both, answers Sidoniya…

Parisian fashions. A cavalcade of stars from the Pathé-journal.

And so it happened. Who could predict that belts, modest leather belts would again take the stage! It makes you think you have to believe in miracles…

Waistlines once again. Narrow waistlines…Turn your back towards the public!

The bandstand of a café-chantant. One of the variety numbers. A dancer with a vacant face tap dances and sings:

> I frankly admit
> I am a slave to women.
> Before you I am speechless.
> You always make me glad.
> As soon as I see
> One of you
> I tremble and get weak in the knees
> Every single time.

—Bravo! Bravo! cries the public.

> *Give us the answer, what is woman: sphynx, riddle of the ages,*
> *a destroyer passing through our lives, some kind of evil genius!?*

And suddenly Glupyshkin[15] crashes through the ceiling.

—Ha-ha-ha-ha!!

---

[14] [Trans.]: In the original *Мечты, мечты* [*Mechty, mechty*]. I could find no Russian film by this title. Possibly a foreign film such as *Day Dreams* (1919) by Clarence Badger.

[15] [Trans.]: André Deed (1879–1940), the stage name of Henri André Augustin Chapais, a French comic vaudeville star, cabaret star, and film actor and director. He made films in both France and Italy and enjoyed world wide fame during the silent era. In Russia he was known as Glupyshkin, in the English-speaking world as Foolshead, in Italy as Cretinetti. The made-up Russian name takes its root from the word for stupid, or foolish: глупый [glupy].

Glupyshkin strikes his mother-in-law with a rolling pin and freezes. Everything suddenly stops.

— Bravo! Bravo! applause breaks out and dies away.

Silence ensues. Darkness.

Bells can be heard ringing in the distance.

Early morning. In the distance, the headwaters of the Volga.

On the horizon, a village.

Fields.

A man's and woman's voices resound. Once more, silence.

Somewhere a woman's voice is singing a peasant song.

Where are we?

The song grows distant. The fields grow distant. The Volga closer. On the banks of the Volga is a cathedral.

The sound of bells interrupts the song which is growing ever distant. It is clear, musical.

We enter the cathedral. A young priest serves at the altar. The choir is singing. Candles are burning. There are many women here. They cross themselves. They bow. They drop to their knees.

We examine their faces. They are old women. Almost all, old women. Only one young face.

The choir is singing.

We examine the face of the young woman attentively, so unexpected it is among the old women.

And once again the fields, round hills. Again the sound of bells grows distant.

Unexpectedly we hear a voice, as if it is finishing a conversation which had begun: "These are Khlyabinsk lands. Here our MTS[16] operates. Over on the right…," says an unseen voice, "this is the field of the kolkhoz."

We see movement in the surrounding fields. We must be traveling by car: everything suddenly shakes and sinks down. The hum of the motor can be heard.

1934.

A field. A plowed field. A tractor is at work. On each side lamps are lit, in spite of the daylight. The face of the tractor driver is tired. He has been plowing all night. Here the tractor stops. The lamps are extinguished. He plows further. This means morning has begun.

On the edge of the field, the brigade sleeps in tents.

---

[16] [Trans.]: In the original: Машинно-Тракторная Станция [Mashinno-Traktorskaya Stantsiya] (Machine Tractor Station), a rural agency, which supplied collective farms with agricultural machinery.

In the field is a mobile kitchen. Pots are lined up.

We move around the field. An unseen automobile, in which we are apparently located, sounds its horn as it thunders over a bridge above a creek.

A village is revealed in front of us.

It is as if we jump out of the unseen automobile. Everything is swaying. The noise of the car cuts off and we stand firmly on the earth.

We now see, that the automobile is a traveling sound film production facility.

In the automobile, alongside the camera operator, stands a man who says (we have already heard his voice on the screen):

—This is the Khlyabinsk selsoviet.[17] I'm the Head of the Artemovsky Political Department of Klyazin. This is the Headwaters of the Volga, he says. From here, it's 140 kilometers to Moscow.

We look around the village.

We continue our drive through the country morning.

A rooster crows.

—Get up! Get up! someone quickly responds. A little boy is rubbing his eyes.

A man comes out of a peasant hut. Slow morning movements. He pulls off the tarp from the grain separator.

In the back, at the entrance to the garden are young pioneers—girls and boys—on duty. From their appearance, it is evident that they have been standing here since it got dark. They are on the look-out for something, as if they are on watch in the game "Indians,"[18] hiding behind trees. One has even climbed up a birch tree and stares off into the distance.

Here, the cowherd is driving the herd of cows.

Here, the windows of one of the huts is being opened; a young lad crawls out of it. He looks around and runs around back. A woman's hand waves after him.

The patrol of Pioneers stops the lad.

—You can go! says a tiny Pioneer to this tall strapping lad and the tall lad runs on around back.

The country morning continues on its way.

Here, children are going to school.

In a small print shop, the newspaper of the Political Department is being printed.

---

[17] [Trans.]: In the original: сельсовет, the lowest rural administrative unit. The term can also refer to the village council of that administrative unit.

[18] [Trans.]: In the original: в игре «в индейцы». A summer camp game where participants form "tribes" and compete in various ways for the title "Real Indian."

Here is the fenced off courtyard of the MTS, looking like a fortress. Here they left off sleeping a long time ago. Here, a tractor pulses. "Motorized detail to the 3rd section of the Molotovsky Kolkhoz…"

The printshop watchman goes door to door, shoving newspapers in the doors.

In front of one of the houses, the loading of the grain separator begins.

The whole time the distant sound of the bells can be heard.

—This is the house of the Ul'yanov sisters. Have you heard of them? says the voice of the head of the Political Department. In response comes the voice of the camera operator.

—We ask you, comrade Klyazin, to have a conversation with the Ul'yanov sisters for our microphone.

And while we set up the camera and place the microphone, Klyazin knocks on the window and says something.

—Ready! says the camera operator.

Out of the door and onto the threshold of the little house come three young women. The oldest, Varvara, is well known to us. We remember her praying in church. The second oldest is Mariya and the third, the very youngest is Aleksandra.

The head of the Political Department cannot be seen by us. He is standing in the place where we would be located. We can only hear his voice. The Ul'yanov sisters are speaking as if to the viewers. And right here, noting, in an aside,

—Here is the chairwoman of our selsoviet, Mariya Ul'yanova. The comrades are interested, in how you…

The conversation begins, in which it becomes clear that: two Ul'yanov sisters, Mariya and Aleksandra, are Chairwomen of the selsoviet and are Communists. The third sister, Varvara, a member of the kolkhoz, is religious and goes to church. Two sisters will say glibly, that they are used to meetings. The third will be embarrassed. This only helps to make the scene lively. The head of the Political Department will ask them about their way of life, work, about their external world.

—The Fascists say, that women should only learn about cooking pots, church, and children. Do you agree with this?

You can count on a very pointed response here on the part of the women, the chairwomen of the selsoviet.

Skillfully and briefly posed questions will show us at once the life and the psychology of advanced women of the Soviet countryside. This will be the first film interview with the new peasantry of the USSR. It must not be done, so that it comes off as artificial.

The interview will end with the words:

—…now take us to the selsoviet.

A building with the sign "Khlyabinsky selsoviet."

We are in the Office of the selsoviet.

—And so, comrades—declaims one girl—you are starting a mutiny. You cry out, "We don't want a kolkhoz, that's where our kolkhoz stands!"

—This is not correct. "We don't want a kolkhoz. That's where our kolkhoz stands," interrupts another one.

On the lap of the director of the club is a booklet with a play. It is one of the little hack one-act plays, supplied for club theater stages. From it, the text being rehearsed in this episode should be taken.

The club members will make two or three more remarks, during which the discrepancy between the urbanity of the rural Komsolmol members and the stereotyped peasant language the author of the play forces them to use, will jump out at the viewer.

—Comrades, it's nine o'clock, says Mariya Ul'yanova, as she leaves in the company of the secretary.

A day in the Khlyabinsky selsoviet, shot in such and such a month, or such and such a year.

We see the selsoviet at work. Here is Ul'yanova, the chairwoman. Here is the secretary. Here is the clerk.

Everything of interest, which will take place here in a week, we will condense into a day in the picture, which will last five minutes.

The details of this report about the day should be very faithful and based on our observation.

They cannot be provided in advance.

They will come with the advice, with the aid of the chairwomen of the kolkhoz, the brigades, the Komsomol members, the old women, the policemen, the teacher.

Mariya is able, quick, laconic. When necessary, she can get angry, give orders, but she is equally authoritative for everyone.

—I'm not going to talk to you. You don't understand anything. Send your wife, she says to one.

—I'm giving you a fixed assignment. Get it done! she says to each individually.

Reel 2

Four o'clock in the afternoon.

Mariya Ul'yanova leaves the selsoviet building. She locks the door.

Mariya Ul'yanova walks across the fields. She deliberately makes a detour to see how the planting is going.

She walks slowly, pensively. She scrutinizes the fields and the people.

What is Mariya Ul'yanova thinking about now?

Something like this:

A greatly enlarged chamomile flower.

—What is Mariya Ul'yanova thinking about, while she is looking at the chamomile? asks a voice. —Does she like flowers?

Here she walks past a young woman. The woman is breastfeeding a child. Mother and child are blissfully merged.

What is Mariya Ul'yanova thinking about, while looking at the young mother?

Here, she walks past a brigade working in the fields. A brash, funny guy rushes up to meet her. He bows to her.

—What is she thinking about while looking at this guy? asks a voice. —A funny guy? Or something of the sort? A gorgeous guy? Does she like him?

Here is an unplowed piece of land.

Of course. She is thinking about the gaps that have been left.

Here, a young priest comes up to meet her—the very same one who was conducting the service. Wearing street clothes, a tie, a hat, with a cane.

—The father has been visiting someone, comes a comment from the field.

We hear the sound of the bells. Ul'yanova turns around in the direction of the priest, who is moving off into the distance towards the town, and makes a notation in her notebook.

What is Mariya thinking about while looking at the priest out for a stroll in such unusual clothing.

What does this sound bring to mind for her? It's hard to guess… It's hard to guess a person's thoughts. Wait a bit. You'll soon find out!

—Here is my Political Department. That's my assistant.

At this instant, we are already at the door of the building of the Political Department. Once again we see the Head of the Political Department, Comrade Klyazin, whose voice we have been hearing the whole time. He repeats once again:

—Here I am.

In a second, we see him already standing in the courtyard, near a table sunk into the ground. He is presiding over the meeting. The entire staff of the Political Department is here. Including Mariya Ul'yanova.

This brief meeting proceeds even more quickly than the protocol of the day. Hardly has one person begun to speak, when the floor passes to another.

—Does everyone agree?

—Everyone…

Here, finally, Mariya Ul'yanova takes the floor. We now in amazement learn through her words the answer to the questions, which came into our heads, during the time of her walk through the fields.

She says, for example, that the church should be turned into a club.

—Our club is cramped. The number of church-goers in the Sel is small. They are all old women, she says. We see the imploring face of the young Varvara.

—There will be no arguments, says Mariya. Varvara's face once again looks at you.

—There will be no arguments, Maryia firmly repeats. She says, that Perov prevents work getting done with his joking around. We again see the lively guy in the field.

She says, that day nurseries are imperative, absolutely imperative.

—A peasant mother, we see the peasant woman in the field, feeding her child, a peasant mother in the field, doing heavy labor, in a sweat, under the sun, hastily feeding her child is a disgrace.

She says that flowers... We see the enormous field of chamomile.

But here, Ul'yanova grows silent.

Twilight. It is still light, but the shadows are growing dim.

Already another tractor driver is plowing in the fields. He climbs down, turns on the lamps. This means evening has begun.

Here is a village street. People are sitting around the huts in the half-darkness.

It's possible to make out a guy with a guitar. He plucks its strings.

Here, one of those present begins to speak. This must be him.

—In Magnitogorsk we have proved ourselves. We have begun to kinda set the pace, you know, the Khlyabinsk Sel [soviet]. The Head of Construction said to me personally, "Nikolai, I will make something of you. Do you want a thousand arshins of cotton cloth, or to study to become an engineer?" But I turned down these rewards, I worked for the heroism of it...

> Oh these eyes, oh this gaze—
> The whole world will envy you,
> You are a typist in an office,
> And I am on a construction site—
> And I am a foreman on a construction site...

It's getting dark. Here is another corner of the village. On opposite ends of a bench people are sitting, it seems to be an old man with an old woman. We hear their voices, they are arguing.

Young people are going somewhere in a crowd.

We follow them.

The club. Here the play is being performed, the rehearsals for which we heard in the afternoon.

—We don't want a kolkhoz, we're fed up with it, says the prompter loudly.

—We don't want a kolkhoz, repeats the actor after him, this time dressed up as a kulak out of a Lubok print. And the costumes and makeup of the actors are all quite distinct from those which can be seen among the peasants in the auditorium.

—We don't need none of them rattletractors...

A reaction of surprise from the spectators, who haven't seen the kind of village there is on the stage, for a long time...

We watch the performance, we listen to the prompter, we listen to the actors, we observe the auditorium.

As we say goodbye, we glance over at Mariya Ul'yanova.

Mariya is by the window. Her secretary extends to her an enormous bouquet of chamomile through the window.

Now we know: Mariya Ul'yanova likes flowers. She takes the bouquet, she smiles, she takes some kind of booklet from the window, says something to the young guy, but we don't hear the words.

The hut recedes into the distance. The village at night.

> Oh these eyes, oh this gaze—
> The whole world will envy you.
> You are a typist in an office,
> And I am on a construction site,
> And I am a foreman on a construction site...

"And I am a foreman on a construction site..." so the song dies away.

Very close up we see the face of the Head of the Political Department Klyazin. He says:

—We, the Political Department of the Vikhrevskaya MTS, kolkhozniks, and peasants of the Khlyabinsky selsoviet, declare, that here women participate in the construction of a new society. We challenge the world to a competition.

Reel 3

What was it the foreign tourists didn't see?

Music is playing. We are at the Metropole hotel. Here in the club, people are dancing. A group of foreigners is sitting around a large banquet table. We examine them.

An orchestra. The drummer is singing a song. He is dancing.

> Traveling around the Baltic country,
> I got sick and tired of everything.

> I would open up my little suitcase,
> Dance around and sing.

Here, someone, whom we later find out is a guide, approaches one of the foreigners and bends down. He says something.

We examine some of them closely. Here, one bows to us, having noticed that he is being filmed, he smiles and says something.

Depending on the content of his words, the voice of the author translates for us:

—Mr. So-and-so, professor at Columbia University, has told us, that the strongest impression made upon him in the streets of Moscow was the complete absence of the class of wealthy men and their overdressed women, which leaps to the eye when surveying other cities of the world.

> Buy face powder and shoe laces
> And cigarettes and stockings,
> Buy high heels and boots,
> And gramophone records.

A lady sits next to him.

—But I only fear...[19] she starts to speak. Only the movements of her lips are visible from here on, but a voice speaks for her:

—Mrs. Smith, the wife of the American Senator Mr. Smith, fears, that in our country the sense of gentlemanliness will disappear, that respect and reverence for women, which is so characteristic of the citizens of her country.

—Mr. So-and-so, the director of the Allegheny Trust, fears, that the ease of divorce, will lead to mass promiscuity.

Everyone has already gotten up from the table.

—Well,[20] says Mrs. Smith.

—Well,[21] says the director.

—Ladies and gentlemen, tomorrow, you receive exhaustive answers to your questions,[22] says the voice-over.

A Moscow morning.

On the boulevards, the jackdaws have awakened. Sweepers are sweeping the pavement. The sun appears atop the Sukharev Tower.

---

[19] [Trans.]: In transliterated English in the original.
[20] [Trans.]: In transliterated English in the original.
[21] [Trans.]: In transliterated English in the original.
[22] [Trans.]: In transliterated English in the original.

Trucks bring bread out of the gates of the bread factory. Dissolve on a window on the fourth floor of an enormous building where workers live.

A door slams, then another.

The siren of one of the factories sounds.

—Well, says a woman's voice, with imperfect pronunciation.

—Well, Khorosho. Very well. Ochen Khorosho. Bad, Plokho. Very bad. Ochen Plokho.[23]

We see an apartment in a communal residence. Some workers live here. Beds, bedside tables, flowers by the windows, little books, postcards on the walls. Party leaders, girlfriends, buddies, actors.

Morning. Here, they are getting up. We see some women workers, with whom we are going to become acquainted.

They wake up cheerful, joking around, one of them finishes telling a story. Everyone laughs.

Another is getting dressed and washing herself at the washstand, peering into an English language textbook. She is doing gymnastics, tidying up the room, all the while muttering English words.

—Well,[24] says the one we've just gotten to know, pointing at some place in the newspaper.

—Very bad, she says, pointing to different column. She puts on a dress.

—Sof'ya Barsukova, says a voice, is a shock worker at the "Ball Bearing" factory. She is taking English Language courses and courses in Political Literacy at an advanced level.

Through the open window, the sound of the factory siren can be heard.

—Very well,[25] says Barsukova, slamming the door behind her.

Once again we hear English words. But this time the guide is speaking.

A large open car with foreign tourists, with camera operators and camera assistants, is driving around the outskirts of the city. Standing with his back to the driver, the guide gives an explanation in English:

He points to one side, all the tourists look out that side at the same time. He points to the other side and all the tourists look over there.

The faces of the tourists express various things, but most likely, indifference.

The faces of passers-by express interest in the foreigners driving by.

---

[23] [Trans.]: In the original, phrases alternate between transliterated English and their Russian translation.

[24] [Trans.]: In transliterated English in the original.

[25] [Trans.]: In transliterated English in the original.

—Who is that Mrs. Smith? She lives in New York. She has three maids and a Japanese houseboy. She wakes up at 11am. Her toilette is prepared by two chamber maids and a masseuse. She travels at her doctor's insistence, explains the voice.

—Who is this lady? She is an American *artiste*. Her grandfather was a Negro. And she considers herself a Negro.[26] She joined in the excursion to Moscow. Some of the tourists protested against a mulatto traveling with them.

We move around the faces in the car. It would be interesting to know, who precisely among them lodged a protest.

—We bought the tickets… We bought the tickets for the trip, without asking for… without asking for a certificate concerning the color of the skin of the individuals…

With these words we move from face to face; this is a very diverse group of people, from various nations.

This automobile excursion continues, accompanied by music. A building on the outskirts of the city. Workers' housing. Country lanes. Garden plots. Trams.

Sukino Swamp.[27] *A famous Moscow waste land, dumps, overnight homeless shelters.*

To all appearances, the guide says these exact words to the tourists. What we see is something entirely different. We see around us the new buildings of the workers' settlement. The Factory-Kitchen.[28] The vast buildings of the "Ball Bearing" factory. The factory gate with an enormous model of a castor instead of a monument.

And so on, the tourists look indifferently out either side.

It's really a pity, that the tourists drive so quickly around the city…

To the final measures of music, the car drives by the front of a building with the sign "State Factory of Ball Bearings."

The camera operator jumps out of the car. But the car with the tourists does not stop, it continues onward.

—…In our factories, much that is unexpected can be seen. Here, we have happened upon a shop floor. Barsukova, whom we have already met, is working with a complicated Swiss machine tool. We are observing her work. One cannot help but admire the accuracy and precision of the movement of the machine tool.

---

[26] [Trans.]: In the original: негритянка [negrityanka]. This is a noun with a feminine ending, so one might say "Negress," but that would exaggerate the unconscious racism lurking in the term.

[27] [Trans.]: Literally "Bitches' Swamp."

[28] [Trans.]: In the original: Фабрика-кухня. A large facility for preparing food for communal dining rooms, or personal purchase, intended to liberate women from kitchen drudgery and integrate them into the work force.

Barsukova's working day

With the same precision and concentration, with which we observed the day of the selsoviet, we will now scrutinize Barsukova's working day. We will get a clear visual presentation about the process of the work, which Barsukova carries out. She herself, in a few short words: "On the right… I am releasing the handle… Stop… This is the next castor… I am pushing down… (the machine begins to make a sound)… Ready…" gives us a presentation about the work. We compare her quick and accurate movements with the somewhat tentative movements of her neighbor and without a word, we understand, that Barsukova is truly a shock worker.

We see Barsukova on her break on the shop floor next to hers. She is a socially active person. People approach her. She holds half-minute meetings amidst the machine tools, she takes charge of collecting contributions for an airplane, or a loan. She exchanges a few words with a guy unfamiliar to us. In a few days, it would be possible to cover Barsukova's intense working day on film.

Here the foreman approaches her and says,

—Barsukova, free yourself up and go to the cafeteria. A couple of visitors have come to see you.

—What visitors?

The car with the tourists drives by the factory.

There are the visitors, thinks the spectator.

Here, we are already at the entrance to the factory.

The disorganized sounds of the shift change can be heard.

—Pass! Your pass! Pass! Comrade, pass!

—Pass, comrade, they say to us.

—You came with the writers? they ask us.

—What writers?

—Today, there are some writers with us.

—What are the writers doing at the factory?

We are making a short tour around the shop floors. We are looking for the writers. We see the machine tools. Countless rows of people working. Men, women.

The premises of the Factory-Kitchen. Breakfast among comrades. On the tables are jugs of morse. The cafeteria is full.

Here Ermilov gives a speech.

—We have come to the "Ball Bearing" factory, in order to study the intelligentsia… The intelligentsia? The spectator examines a row of workers' faces at the tables in the cafeteria and is surprised.

The writers are looking for the intelligentsia in a factory?!

—…in order to study the new proletarian intelligentsia here, continues Ermilov.

—The editors of the journal *Krasnaya Nov'*[29] often hold such meetings in factories…

We pass over a row of writers who are seated, identifying them in subtitles. We pause on these writers: Shaginyan, Karavaeva, Inber. Then, we see the shock workers, men and women, sitting here, they are identified. Here Barsukova stands up and tells the story of how, in previous meetings with *Krasnaya Nov'*, shock workers told their stories, how she became a literate and conscious woman, how she studies, how she lives.

One of the writers, let's say, Vera Inber, will attentively watch Barsukova. She will note something down in her notebook.

Suddenly, making a vigorous movement, she freezes.

Saying,—I have a very complicated, Swiss machine tool. It's as smart as a person… She repeats this phrase four times in a row.

Again and again, we repeat her characteristic movements, her apt words, the nuances and expressions on her face with more dramatic foreshortening.

Gradually, we notice the connection between these pauses and the attentive gaze of Vera Inber.

(This cinematographic device will help to show us the process of observation.)

—I have already been observing this woman for several days, says Inber to us or to the person sitting next to her.—I will observe her on the shop floor, in meetings, at her home. I want to write about her.

Barsukova stands at the blackboard and responds to an assignment in mathematics. This is some kind of course at the factory.

Here is another lesson: "der Stuhl," "der Tisch," "die Wand," she says, pointing to the chair, the table, the wall.

—At the movies, I like to watch those kinds of things…

And we see the shots, she likes at the movies.

—So tell me, asks Ermilov, which writers do you like? She answers. And the writers note down her answers in their notebooks.

And in just what country will you see such a thing, gentlemen?

The tourists drive on. The streets get busier. They cross the B Ring. In a little while, the tourists' attention is focused on an old church.

The guide continues to recite something to them in English. They once again turn their heads: first to the right, then to the left.

The radio speaker sings an Italian aria, absurd amidst the noise of the street.

---

[29] [Trans.]: *Красная новь* (*Red Virgin Soil*) a substantial literary magazine established in 1921, which featured articles by important Soviet authors as well as essays on politics, economics, and science.

Nel scendo del camin
di nostra acta…[30]

The car approaches a stop. Unexpectedly, the radio speaker begins to recite something in a wooden voice.

—Listen now to a story by the English author Wallace: "Jenny returned upset. Today she was fired from her job. She went out into the street and saw thousands of hostile men's faces."[31]

The ride continued with the story trailing off, interrupted sometimes by a car horn, sometimes by the bell of a tram.

Only at the next intersection, where there is a radio set, we make out the words:

—Will you permit me to escort you, my beauty, a man in a bowler hat said to her…

We are in the center of the city. The sidewalks are full of people, various men and groups of women arrest our attention. Here a policeman turns around and turns out to be a woman. The policeman deftly directs traffic.

The tourists' car continues. Here, on the steps of a tram, a woman with a briefcase energetically struggles with a man for a place, others push her away and she pushes back.

Here, we are inside the tram car. Here is another picture. From the front platform, a pregnant woman has entered. Everyone gets up at once to offer her a place.

The car continues on. Some soldiers in overcoats, with revolvers pass right in front of the car. A sharp blast on the horn. They turn around to look. One of the soldiers is a woman.

But here is the Arbatsky market, we see housewives, exiting the gates of the market with baskets.

The tourists exchange some sort of remarks, not exactly ironic, not exactly impatient.

On the street corner, the radio continues:

—Oh, you vile little hussy! You've had a child on the side, said the old missus and her face was stretched out like the sole of a shoe. Here a young mother pushes a carriage with a child in front of the "Intourist" car.

---

[30] [Trans.]: The original appears to be Italian transcribed phonetically into Cyrillic letters; the passage resembles the beginning of Dante's *Inferno*, but badly transcribed, or perhaps erroneously back-translated into Italian from a Russian translation. If so, it should read: "Nel *mezzo del cammin* di nostra vita." ["In the middle of the road of our life."] Assuming an intentional and somewhat non-sensical variation on the original, it would mean, "In the descent of the road of our beach resort," or "in the descent of the chimney of our beach resort." This assumes a Latin meaning for acta, as it is not current Italian.

[31] [Trans.]: Having been unable to locate the original, which I believe is by Edgar Wallace, I have translated the Russian back into English.

What a pity the tourists saw only the surface of things
Intertitle: "Metro Construction Pit"
Here, we have jumped over to the other side of the fence.
We approach a kind of stairway, for deliveries. And suddenly, we fall rapidly
into the earth.
The tourists did not see what's hidden beneath the surface.
The foreign tourists drive along the surface of the earth.
We are below, in the tunnel where the metro is being built.
Streets, machines, supplies, people passing by. Already the car with the foreign
tourists is turning the corner. It has disappeared.
Below, strenuous labor is going on. Here, pneumatic drills are rattling. Here,
they work, standing under the vaults and crouching in the pit.
Here, we see brigades of young women. One of them gives us an interview. We
find out that five hundred female Komsomol members have been mobilized in the
metro pits. We see some of them at work.
—Sergeeva, says a voice, was a clerk, now she's a miner.
—When we finish the metro, I'm going to study and will be an engineer, says
Sergeeva herself.
These female mine workers are unusual.
Here, they are sitting around during a break and arguing about something.
—Well, I like Mayakovsky, comes in one voice.
—But I don't understand him…
—But why don't you go back to work, my dear… —And in Jenny's hand, the
copper coin began to sparkle—continues the radio at Mosfinotdel.[32]
The foreign tourists have driven through the center of town. They are on Red
Square.
—Here, before us, says the voice of the guide,—is one of the most beautiful
monuments of Russian art, the Cathedral of Vasily the Blessed,[33] constructed by Aris-
totele Fioravanti. His lines are fanciful, the cupolas beautiful. You won't see anything
comparable in Europe…
The car moves into the distance around the square, honking its horn.
You really won't find anything comparable in Europe.
We examine Red Square, the cathedral, the Kremlin wall, the Mausoleum.
But unexpectedly, we start to approach one of the palaces inside the Kremlin. On
the square, in front of the palace, there is an unexpected crowd of men and women.
Women in national dress leap to the eye: Turkmen women, Ukrainian women, women
from the Caucasus, women from the Far North.

---

[32] [Trans.]: In the original: Мосфинотдел, a financial institution, used as a landmark for the location of
the car.
[33] [Trans.]: Also known as Saint Basil's Cathedral.

This is a break from a session of the Central Electoral Commission.
—Salam-Aleikum.
—Va-alekum-assalim.
—Myndy.
—Zhadorov bul'suk.
This is how they greet us, each in her own language.

> *The participants in the session of the CEC of the USSR: Comrade*
> *Semenova traveled for 50 days from Kolyma to Moscow. Comrade*
> *Tadzhikhanova arrived by plane from Pamir in a week.*

Among the delegates we unexpectedly meet some old acquaintances: Maria Ul'yanova and Barsukova.

We pause, we approach each one of them directly. She sees us, she introduces us to the delegates.

—Comrade Astakhova is a former cook, who took part in the Civil War, and graduated from the Promakademia,[34] she says.

As before, the foreign tourists drive indifferently around archaic Zamosk-vorech'e,[35] and as before, turning to the right, then to the left.

—Zamoskvoretsh'e, he says with an English accent, pointing to a street.

Reel 4

The mulatto woman takes a stroll.

> *Miss Mildred asks us to accompany her around the city and to shoot*
> *"life unprettified," as she expressed it. The writer Lev Nikulin (or*
> *another writer) agreed to be her translator.*

A somewhat strange sort of expedition happened in the Park of Culture and Recreation. Ahead of us goes the mulatto woman-tourist, whom we have already met. Behind her, falling behind somewhat, goes a person as yet unknown to us: Lev Nikulin.

Further behind, go two people with a movie camera. They set it on the ground, fiddle around with it, then carry it off. Behind them go two gawkers, laughing and not understanding what is going on.

The mulatto woman gives us the sign as to what to shoot: "This here! This here!"

The line at the lemonade stand and the shooting gallery where they shoot at cardboard Fascists.

---

[34] [Trans.]: In the original: Промакадемия (The Industrial Academy). It educated industrial specialists and economic managers from 1925 to 1941 with branches in Moscow, Leningrad and Sverdlovsk.
[35] [Trans.]: A older part of Moscow on the Right Bank of the Moscow River, colonized in the 14th century.

Boom! An orchestra is playing on a stage.

Now, a kid around twelve years old came up to a park bench and began to sing:

> "Snatch 'n' Skip,"[36] that would be me.
> Listen to me, my friends!
> As my craft, I choose to steal,
> I won't be getting out of prison,
> House of Correction[37] is a bore without me.

The funhouse and other attractions of the park. Here, for the last time, the conductor gives up and the orchestra stops playing.

> *—Look at this park! says Miss Mildred,—and you'll understand that life's the same all over the world.*[38]

But the next instant, she sees something else. She asks us to shoot the mass dances, the carnival procession of the members of the Komsomol, relaxing in a day spa on the banks of the Moscow River. Then, a group of Pioneer-parachutists. A singing delegation of foreign workers.

A couple sits on the bench. They are snuggling close as they sit. She is clearly dressed up in a festive way, in a light-colored dress. He has a flower in his buttonhole, in his hands, a box of candy. Nikulin and the mulatto woman walk along the boulevard, they approach the bench.

—Tell me, please,[39] says the mulatto woman.

—This lady is a mulatto woman from America, says Nikulin.—She wants to know…

At this moment, the orchestra begins to play and not another word can be heard. It's obvious that the mulatto woman and Nikulin are asking about something. The couple on the bench do not answer.

When the orchestra begins to quiet down, the final words of the girl's answer can be heard.

For example:

—When I come here, I study with my father.

---

[36] [Trans.]: In the original: Гоп со смыком [Gop so smykom]. The name of a legendary criminal singing his own familiar ballad, one of the most popular street ballads of the 20th Century in the Soviet Union. Гоп [Gop] can be a thief, house breaker, or pickpocket. There are various glosses for смык [smyk], referencing the m.o. of a quick attack and quick escape as well as смык [smyk] being a tool of the trade such as burglar's tools. Leonid Utesov's version was a favorite of the time.

[37] [Trans.]: In the original: Исправдом [Ispravdom], an acronym for Исправительно-трудовой дом [Ispravitel'no-trudovoi dom], a short term correctional facility intended for non-violent criminals, with mandatory literacy and craft skills training.

[38] [Trans.]: Miss Mildred is speaking Russian.

[39] [Trans.]: In transliterated English in the original.

—Who is your father, a professor?

—No, he's a laborer.

—Oh, very well,[40] we hear the voice of the mulatto woman.

Suddenly, the guy gets up.

—We're going, he says to the girl. And, turning towards Nikulin—We're going to the Registry Office, we're getting married. Nikulin quickly translates.

—Oh, very well, says the mulatto woman.

Here is the small premises of the local Registry Office. It's somewhere off the beaten track. In two or three tiny rooms. There are posters on the wall. The registrars for unmarried women are sitting at a table. There is a line at the table.

—Name? Family name? Age? Which family name do you wish to keep?

—That's all.

Happy newlyweds walk away.

—Oh yes, very strange,[41] says the mulatto woman.

—Very strange, Nikulin translates with the very same intonation as her voice. And he continues like this:—She imagined the Registry Office differently. Of course, without priests and without garlands, but, probably, with more solemnity.

—No, this is all very simple.

—We will celebrate at home, say the newlyweds and invite us and the mulatto woman to come to their place that evening.

Another table. A rather young woman has brought her baby here. She is standing with her back to us.

—Tell me, who his father is?

—Father? It's all the same. The child is mine. The woman registrar registers a new citizen of the country.

—The poor woman,[42] says Miss Mildred.—This is an illegitimate child,—this is how Nikulin translates the words we do not hear.

No, Miss Mildred, the Soviet Land does not recognize a distinction between legitimate and illegitimate children.

We are in a large room. There are a lot of tables. From every corner, children's faint cries can be heard.

Here, women are taken to the operating room. Behind the door, cries of pain can be heard.

Here, a woman who just gave birth is being taken back out. Her face is tired and drawn. Crying babies are taken out into the large room. They are washed and dressed.

In the waiting room the fathers sit silently.

---

[40] [Trans.]: In transliterated English in the original.
[41] [Trans.]: In transliterated English in the original.
[42] [Trans.]: Miss Mildred is speaking Russian.

From time to time, a nurse comes in.

—Everything went well for you... A boy.

The children are already lying in small beds.

There is unremitting whining. There are many children. And all of them appear exactly the same.

> —*See, Miss Mildred, try to distinguish here between the legitimate and illegitimate children.*

Here, we see the table for divorces. Above it, in seemingly mockery, hangs a sign: "The hygiene of marriage."

A gloomy man walks in. His wife has left him for another. He needs a divorce.

—That's it. A notification will be sent to her.

Here, another two walk in. They are young. She is pregnant.

—That's it. Which family name do you wish to keep?

(It goes without saying, that at the time of the shoot, both the people and the words will be different.)

—But, if it's so easy to get divorced, the woman is defenseless! She's abandoned! With a child! She's doomed to poverty![43] says the mulatto woman.

And here, we are at the entrance to a building: "People's Court of such-and-such a District."

We are in the courtroom. The matter of alimony is being addressed.

The room is tightly packed with long benches. On the benches, there is only one group of three. *She* is a domestic worker, quite young, fragile. In her arms is a baby. Next to her is a witness, the woman next door. In the opposite corner of the room *He* is sitting, a policeman (employed).

The Presiding Judge, a secretary, two lay judges are all women. (Later on, present the legal action being decided by means of a court report.)

Judge:—Plaintiff, what are you asking of the court?

She:—That he help, give something for support. I'm by myself. I can't...

Judge:—Is Citizen Falomeev your husband? Is your marriage registered?

She:—No... but I have always considered him my husband... We've known each other for a long time, we grew up together... We're from the same village. I would come to him in his dormitory and later he would come to me in the kitchen.

Judge:—This means, that you are demanding, Citizen, that he pay alimony?

She:—Yes...

Judge:—Citizen Falomeev!

He approaches the judge.

Judge:—Do you recognize your paternity?

---

[43] [Trans.]: Miss Mildred is speaking Russian.

He:—I do not recognize it, because I don't know. I had no relations with her. At the time, it couldn't have happened. I was in the army, in the barracks. I have written proof of it. This little Citizeness, said that somehow I had her come to me in my dormitory and there's no way that could happen. Both rooms are always full of comrades, one unmarried woman. This is nonsense. And to her apartment I never came. I don't even know where it is. The witness Bashmakova said, that Paramonova had her baby with the carpenter.

Judge:—And why did Bashmakova talk to you about Paramonova?

He:—Who knows what one broad can say about another broad. How am I supposed to know someone like Paramonova. I know a lot of people besides her. There was no reason for me to get to know her.

Judge:—Citizen Paramonova, do you know Bashmakova? Is it known to you, how she became acquainted with the defendant, Falomeev?

She:—Marus'ka was my girlfriend. I went with her to see Falomeev in the dormitory. Later, we stopped being friends. I got jealous of her, I told her, "I took you as a friend, and you stole my Sergei from me."

Judge:—Falomeev, do you persist in denying, that you were in the apartment with Paranomova?

Falomeev:—Do you really think, that a person of my rank, would be traipsing around with some kind of cook?

Judge:—Present your witness.

A well-dressed woman walks in. She is very animated and merry. It is evident that she is participating with pleasure.

Witness:—Natasha has lived with me for two years. She is a nice, very modest girl. She always stays at home. It was known to me that Sergei would come to visit her. My bed is situated just at the wall of the kitchen. From time to time I suffer from insomnia and several times it happened that I heard, that on the other side of the wall… Yes, I heard quite perfectly, that their relations were of the most intimate sort.

Judge:—Did you see them yourself?

Witness:—No, I go to the theater early and get up quite late. My husband, son, and daughter saw them many times—they were so much in love. A first love! I warned her, but she laughed: "Sergei will not deceive me. Sergei is mine." But here you see it! I feel horrible for the woman. She was crushed! Sergei, as soon as he realized the thing was serious, disappeared and got married to someone else. What an underhanded thing to do! I am mortified for all of humanity!

The judges retire to chambers. Those involved sit sedately in silence for a few seconds, then, without restraint, quickly sit down across from each other and immediately, unceremoniously begin to have it out with one another.

Falomeev:—What's it to you? Why are you tagging along? Why are you meddling in other people's business?

Witness:—Tagging along, am I? What impudence! What kind of a man are you? You coward! Are you afraid of your own child? A wonderful little boy. Just look: his eyes and his nose are just like yours. Recognize him! What's it going to cost you?

Falomeev:—This isn't going to end here. I'll go to the Supreme Court. I'm not gonna pay.

Witness:—You heard him! What a scoundrel!

The judges return to the courtroom.—In the name of the Soviet Socialist Republic, etc., etc., on the basis of the testimony presented, the court considers as established: the intimacy of the relationship of Falomeev and Paramonova, his cohabitation, and paternity, etc. The court, on the basis of paragraphs 42, 48, 50 has decided to recover from Citizen Falomeev...

(In any alimony case, which happens to be filmed, most often we see the chicanery of the petty bourgeoisie, refusing to be responsible for the life of the child. We will see, how Soviet Law comes to the defense of the interests of the child.)

And here, in front of us once again, the mulatto woman appears. As she approaches us, she speaks a few disconnected words:

—I'm happy I saw this. In your country women love differently, they live differently. The Soviet Union helps them.[44]

Reels 5 and 6

The Good and the Bad
Does this mean, that everything is wonderful? Does this mean, that all working women without exception are happy?

We are seeing the staff of the Emergency Service.[45]

A doctor is on duty. In the garage, a vehicle is at the ready.

A chronograph continuously displays the calls. In them are the life and the anxiety of a big city.

Our sound recording apparatus is connected to the telephone line. The operator has an assistant, who is clearly inexperienced, appears tired.

—Hello! Emergency Service! Send someone to the corner of such-and-such streets! cries a worried voice.

From out of the gate comes the Emergency Service vehicle.

—Hello! Help is needed immediately.

---

[44] [Trans.]: Miss Mildred is speaking Russian.
[45] [Trans.]: In the original: Скорая помощь.

—A premature birth on the street… The baby girl is alive. A tranquil happy voice can be heard.

—A vehicle will be there in four minutes.

—Hello! A drunk has fallen under a tram.

—Hello! A woman has been knocked down.

—Hello! The vehicle has left.

Tearing himself away from the receiver for a second, the doctor on his break between calls gives quick film dispatches:

—Here it is, in order for you to shoot a murder out of jealousy and suicide for love, stay with us for five days, though before the time of the Soviet Union, every day in the papers, there was news about the murders and suicides of women. At that time, there was that notorious Prasolovsky business. A woman was considered the property of a man, jurors considered jealousy as a justification for murder. Now, we don't have those kind of murders…

But precisely then, a policeman is stepping into a phone booth.

—A policeman on duty at such-and-such a post is saying…attempted murder out of jealousy… we hear a worried voice. And the timer shows the calls.

And at that moment, some woman who is out of her mind, screams:

—She's poisoned herself… my daughter has poisoned herself.

For love?

—Vehicle № such and such will be on the scene immediately… the address… The family name… says the doctor on another telephone.

The Emergency Service ambulance is already leaving the gates. A doctor is on the way. In another car is the location film crew. The warning sounds of the siren burst upon the crowd in the city. The Emergency Service ambulance passes cars, trams, runs through red lights.

They arrive. They walk quickly to the entrance of a building.

Outside a crowd is gathering. On the stretcher is a young woman.

Very young and it seems… she is dead. Her face is utterly dead.

And it is nearly Spring.

School children are walking along the sidewalks; they are smiling.

Someone is selling flowers. Radio announcers are giving instructions for gymnastics.

A sports team passes by in a line. They are walking along strong, young, happy. Just ahead is an orchestra.

The sounds of a march fills the street. It appears sunny, festive, happy.

On such a day, there is a dead woman, the young face of a suicide. Utterly senseless!

There is a beer hall in Samoteka. Drunks are crowding around it.

Blind people are singing.

Homeless[46] children are arguing over cards.

All this still exists. Do we know the explanation, as to where at least these homeless[47] children come from?

We examine these homeless and neglected children,[48] we linger on one of them. He is dressed relatively cleanly and not so raggedly.

You can bet this guy is from around the area.

We have another look at the boy.

Afterwards we see a dirty courtyard full of trash.

Back alleys. Cess pits are closing in on the courtyard from all directions.

We see a door, on which a piece of paper is glued: "Fillippov 2, Alekseev 3, Fedul'ev 3 short ones and 2 long ones, Ostapov 2 short ones, Sinyagin 4."

A door opens, along the corridor are bins, a great number of doors, before each one of them is a kerosene stove, a narrow kitchen. In the kitchen, a woman is fussing around, trying to determine whether the food is ready, she gathers up the utensils.

This is his mother…

At the market. There is a crush of people. Stalls of the Cooperatives. Lines for something.

…or here.

And once again we see the homeless and neglected children. They are playing, singing, arguing.

How to approach the boy?

And here, we happen in on the Comones (The Commission for the Protection of Minors MONO).[49] We see in close up a mother, who is communicating with us, as if the camera were set up on the table of the Commission.

—Not sure where you can locate my son, he got beat up, made friends with some hooligans…

The boy.

—I have parents, only I deserted them.

---

[46] [Trans.]: In the original: безнадзорные ребята [beznadzornye rebyata] meaning unsupervised but implying they are out on the street. This is a slight variation on besprizornye, which is etymologically closer to "not looked after," or "neglected" Both terms refer to the same group of children.

[47] [Trans.] In the original: безнадзорные ребята [beznadzornye rebyata].

[48] [Trans.]: In the original: беспризорные [besprizornye]. Shub switches back to the other term here.

[49] [Trans.]: In the original: Комонес (Комиссия охраны несовершеннолетних МОНО) [Kommissiya okhrany nesovershennoletnikh MONO].

In the course of the day, some tens of children pass through the Comones. For the most part, children and parents come in upset, agitated, they say they are worried and nervous.

The women, members of the Commission, speak with the children skillfully, in a lively way, attentively, not raising their voices, without coddling or harshness.

Here's a mother. After the death of her husband, she started to drink. She deserted her two children, for several days she didn't come home, and when she returned, she beat them. The neighbors turned to Comones, they collected material.

The Commission, called the mother in for a meeting, and declared, that because of her drunkenness and violence, her children were being taken away.

Here is a mother, with a thirteen-year-old son, brings home visitors, gets drunk, fornicates with them in the presence of the child. In these circumstances, arguments start between her and her son, then fights, during one of which, the son slashes his mother's face with a knife. The affair is dealt with by the Commission.

Another pair. The tall, skinny mother, a worker at the "Photographic Plates" factory, and her son, to all appearances is a small, clean-cut boy.

Their story is that the mother, who leaves the child alone, has lost any influence over him. The boy has made friends with street thieves, homeless and neglected children, they order him as they wish, force him to steal things and food rations from his mother, involve him in street fights, brawls, and theft. The woman is at the end of her rope because of her child.

—I'm at the point, I'm ready to kill the child, I can't take any more, they will ruin him, they steal, they are teaching him vile things… Help me get out this district. Sometimes you can't hold back—you strike out… And I love him…

They calm her down, they promise to help with an apartment, to straighten out the child.

Tverskaya Street. An empty sidewalk. Some woman passes by.

It is empty. This same woman slowly comes back. We guess, that she is a prostitute. On a side street stands a group of prostitutes.

From the main street, a car with a movie camera operator comes out. The light of floodlights. We begin shooting them. They instantly rush to the side, covering their faces with their hands. They try to escape through the side street.

But at this time, agents from the MUR[50] approach from behind.

—Your documents?

And here the women are detained.

What will happen to these women.

---

[50] [Trans.]: МУР: Московский уголовный розыск (The Moscow Criminal Investigation Department).

Sign on the wall of a building: "Vtoraya Meshchanskaya. Labor Dispensary."[51]
We pass through its workshops. We see machine tools and various rooms for industrial education. It is late. They are already empty.

A bedroom. A woman lies down to sleep.
—Don't be shy, Citizen, I am a woman filmmaker. We don't allow men in here. Just a minute. Tell me about yourself, Citizen Ivanova.
And a woman's voice says:
—What can I do? They sent me to the AMO factory. It's the best factory of them all. I was a prostitute… Khitrov Market,[52] cocaine, wine, prison, the underworld, sent to Siberia. I escaped to Moscow… I happened into the Labor Treatment Center….—A long pause.
—Now I am a shock worker… And in my head, there's still a lot… —she doesn't finish.
Women are lying down. They are shy with the camera. There are practically no conversations.
They turn off the light. The camera wanders between the beds, lit by the light spilling in from the windows.
Very quietly a voice says:
—The woman in charge of the dispensary would talk with me. Often in the evenings here, they talk about what they are going to do when they leave the dispensary. You can study. You can become whoever you want. A worker. A technician. An actress.
—Katya Smirnova….
We see Katya Smirnova, not clearly lit. Up until that time, she didn't know who she would become. She is very young. She wants to be a worker… She wants to be an actress… The clock sounds. It is night…

---

[51] [Trans.]: Vtoraya Meshchanskaya is the name of the street. This would seem to be related to the later Medical Labor Dispensaries for treatment of drug and alcohol addiction, which appeared in the 1960s and provided training in job skills alongside addiction treatment.
[52] [Trans.]: Also known as Khitrov Square, from the 2nd half of the 19th century a notorious locale where criminals and the unemployed would congregate.

Reel 7

It is dark. We hear strange, fantastic music. Incomprehensible flashes of light appear on the screen. Dancing geometrical figures, blurred splotches of light. Monstrously enlarged human faces, a gigantic rotating wheel, a colossal hand are all distorted in convex and concave mirrors.

Gradually, amidst this chaos, we can distinguish a sleeping girl. This is the prostitute Katya Smirnova, with whom the preceding reel ended.

What could come to Katya Smirnova in her dreams, as she dreams about her choice of professions.

The dream continues. We see a geometric chaos in the play of convex and concave mirrors.

In the next instant, we see a starry sky filling the entire screen.

Stars. The Milky Way.

—Do you see Perseus on the right; on the left is the constellation Draco, says a woman's voice. We see a telescope, the open dome of an observatory…

—My profession is the best in the world, if you think about it, we discover, what is happening beyond the solar system.

Clouds. Daytime sky. Now, the sky rushes to one side. The motor gives out a low-pitched drone. The plane heads towards the ground. The stick goes back. The plane heads upwards. Already, the sky is below, above, like a ceiling is the ground. Stick neutral. The plane again flies level. Out of the cabin, a figure of some kind crawls onto the wing. Now, the figure jumps into the air. Now, the parachute opens. Rocking back and forth the woman parachutist descends.

The following instant, we see her land on the ground and unfasten the parachute.

Mikhailova who has finished the Moscow Flight School.

—My profession is the best in the world, because it helps us to defend the USSR, she says.

—We descend from the sky to the ground.

A circus big top. A female acrobat takes off under the big top. She swings on a trapeze. She plunges down.

N. M. Korn is the best shock worker in the Circus School.

—I love my profession, she says, because it provides leisure for workers and teaches us to be strong.

A young female singer sings.

—Being a singer is wonderful, she says and explains why it is wonderful to be a singer.

—Say, comrade, what is attractive about your profession? asks an off-screen voice. This question interrupts a rehearsal of Meyerhold and Raikh's *La Dame aux Camélias.*

Raikh explains, what is attractive about the professions of the director and actress in the Soviet Union.

Alisa Koonen reads a monologue, in the light of a spotlight.

> You accuse Phèdre of lies,
> But the blood of the Kings of Hellas ordered me
> To the strange deed, so that Hellas
> Might pass away in the circle of heroes.

Here she is removing her makeup in the dressing room.

—You want to know why I love the profession of being an actress? she asks and then explains why.

The writer Vera Inber.

—Yesterday I wrote a poem about a woman worker from the "Ball Bearing" factory, Barsukova. Do you want me to read it to you?

She reads the poem about Barsukova, which speaks about the things, that Vera Inber noticed in a scene showing supervision in the factory.

And still more of the various professions accessible to women in the Soviet Union.

A parade of professions.

We are in a metallurgical plant. An enormous rolling mill is controlled by a small woman. Fire. Smoke. From the rolling mill, a red-hot metal bar is drawn out.

—I love my shop floor because… screams the woman. Nothing else is audible to us.

And again fantastic music, fantastic geometry, and flashes of light, and the fire of a red-hot furnace in concave and convex mirrors.

A woman is bent down over the mirrors.

It turns out we are in an optical laboratory.

—I chose my profession… says a woman professor and explains why.

> *This is what Katya Smirnova might dream. However, it's not a dream. It is the authentic reality of our country.*

—Very well,[53] says Barsukova and locks up her machine tool. The shift has ended.—Today, I worked well. And suddenly we hear Chopin's turbulent music.

The door has opened. A festively dressed woman is walking up the stairs of some building or other. She looks at the camera in bewilderment.

—They invited us here, says the voice of the mulatto woman.

And here, we are in a large apartment. Here are the newlyweds, who invited us over and whom we filmed in the Culture and Recreation Park and at the registry office.

In one corner of the room is an amateur factory orchestra.

There are a lot of young people in the apartment.

Among the guests are both adult (male) workers and their wives, smartly dressed. At this evening gathering, there are both old and young.

At first, our appearance causes shyness among those present. It is difficult for us to foresee how the celebration of our two acquaintances among the circle of those near to them will go. Our appearance causes little shyness among the young people. They were waiting for us, in the course of the day they had become accustomed to the insistent observation of our movie camera.

We are good, old acquaintances. They help us overcome the shyness of the guests.

We freely integrate ourselves into the flow of the events of the Party, but we will be on the alert. We will make a record of everything new, that rich Soviet reality has to offer in any one of its manifestations.

We will film the merry din, the witty retorts and the comradely toasts of those present. We will film the games, the dances, the group singing. We will film much more, that it is impossible now to foresee. We promise to catch with camera and microphone those moments of human behavior of young people, which on the screen in the theater should give joy and gladden and instill confidence, that young people are growing, living a new life and loving.

Yes, loving!

If any of the adult guests cry out "Bitter!"[54] and the young people are ready to kiss, we will not be tempted by the opportunity to end the picture with a kiss, but ask someone from among those present to stop the young people and pronounce the following speech:

---

[53] [Trans.]: In transliterated English in the original.

[54] [Trans.]: In the original: Горько! [Gor'rko!]. This is an old Slavic custom, in some circles now avoided, relating to the changes to be expected as the couple leave their old lives, freedoms and families behind as they assume the duties and restrictions of married life. It is a call for the newly wedded couple to kiss. In some circles it is said that the wine served at the wedding feast is bitter until the newlyweds kiss. Their kiss sweetens the wine and the length of the kiss predicts the duration of their happiness. After the kiss, in some circles the cry of Сладко! [Sladko!] (Sweet!) follows the kiss.

—You will have plenty of time to kiss. We wish for you to be good friends and comrades and that your shared life will be full of faith and hope! We will shoot them, comrade camera operator, in such a way that their wedding portrait will hang on the wall their entire lives.

—Oh, these are good words![55] says the mulatto woman.

—Quiet, we are shooting, says the camera operator. There is a pop and a magnesium flash.

The factory orchestra strikes up a fast number. And suddenly we see:

A color portrait of the young people, frozen in a firm handshake.

Then, a color portrait of Barsukova at her machine tool.

A color portrait of Ul'yanova at the window with a bouquet.

The spectator will involuntarily recall the women seen previously by him at the beginning of the picture.

Here, the female pilot frozen in the parachute jump and others.

And once again, the admiring face of the mulatto woman.

—Give us the answer: What is woman? Sphynx? Riddle of the Ages?[56]

—A working woman of our country is a citizen of the Land of the Soviets. All paths lie open before her.

The City Sleeps (1933–1934)

In the night sky, flicker thousands of electric stars: from Poklonnaya Gora, this is nighttime Moscow as it shimmers in distant lights.

The distant sounds of the symphony of the evening rush out from the screen.

In the silent nighttime mirror surface of the Moscow River, the lights of the night are reflected in golden columns.

Loudspeakers transmit the final numbers of the nighttime concert broadcasts.

At the brightly lit Metropole, there is a line of cars.

A car with its lights on starts up now.

The sounds of sirens, nearby and far away.

---

[55] [Trans.]: Here the "mulatto woman" speaks slightly ungrammatical Russian difficult to reproduce in English.

[56] [Trans.]: Since Russian has no articles for nouns, this might also be rendered: "What is a woman? a sphynx, the riddle of the ages?" But the rhetoric here harkens back to the beginning of the film, an essentializing rhetoric Shub seeks to undermine by showing us many different women in many different roles and facing many different life issues. And we are meant to answer with a resounding No!

The final lights of electric advertising signs. And they flicker out.

The rails gleam on the asphalt pavement like black snakes. In the distance, the ringing and the clanging of trams begin to die away as they head off somewhere into the night.

Silence.

In the night sky, the gigantic figure of a mine worker emerges with outstretched hands.

A hand raised high confidently makes a summons and powerfully makes a pledge.

Between the mine worker's helmet and this outstretched hand emerges the distant, bright summit of the Bolshoi Theater with small bronze horses flying and a bronze Apollo.

Close up. Rushing along in a bronze whirlwind, Apollo clearly sees on the gray tower the enormous figure of the mine worker with a pickaxe on his shoulder.

This encounter of the two figures on Sverdlov Square at night speaks meaningfully about time past and time present.

Steps can be heard on the pavement grown quiet and a male voice slowly reads the words, as if for himself, in huge letters inscribed at the mine worker's feet:

All Moscow is building the Metro.

And Moscow sleeps.

Magnificent are the monuments of Red Square in the silvery dawn of a summer night.

The slight contours of the balconies of the House of the Government[57] cut through the evening sky high overhead, and it seems, that alongside, the dark silhouettes of the Kremlin towers are engraved vertically.

The white and empty "Dinamo" stadium sleeps.

Magnificent are the nighttime silhouettes of the poplars at the Palace of Culture of the Leningrad District.

In the silver of dawn sleep the monuments of one street.

The monuments of another street sleep.

Lonely couples, standing at the entrances to buildings, at shop windows, merge with the night.

The emptied square in front of the train station sleeps.

The silence of the night is troubled by the lonely steps of passers-by, the distant sounds of sirens, the fragments of songs, which arrive from somewhere, and the incessant sounds of distant steam engines. In them can be heard the nighttime respiration of an enormous city.

The garage of the Metro Construction Authority knows no sleep.

Trucks leave incessantly in the night.

Watchful and always ready for the call is the Emergency Response Center.

---

[57] [Trans.]: In the original: Дом Правительства [Dom Pravitel'stva].

And once again, the words:

All Moscow is building the Metro.

They are pronounced with a foreign accent by a young man's voice.

—Very well,[58] says a woman's voice. A woman's laughter is heard and the echoing steps moving off into the distance of two unseen passers-by.

On the square, at the Nationale hotel, a wooden tower and fence can be made out where someone has written:

Metro Construction Authority, Pit #10.

We see up close the figure of a young miner. He has a hammer and his arm is extended. This is not a statue. This is a living Komsomol miner. He slowly moves downwards.

And suddenly, we fall rapidly after the miner.

We are flying downwards.

Flashes of light and shadows flicker by, the distinct upper contours of invisible structures rise upwards. And we are flying downwards.

The silence of the night is gone.

The din of human voices grows, pneumatic drills rattle away, growing closer; the clatter, the racket of an as yet unseen mass.

We collide with the concrete.

Concrete, mine cars move away from the camera and revealed before us is Moscow underground in motion. It is filled with labor, motion, sounds, life.

For the Capital of the Soviet Union: the best Metro in the world—

we read, as we move towards a banner which has been stretched out.

The pit passes before us in motion.

Unceasingly, the train of mine cars comes to meet us and moves away from us.

Healthy muscular hands first push, then tip, then grab hold of a mine car.

A Young Male Miner: Take the concrete to the fifth gallery.

A Male Miner: Let's go, let's go.

A Female Miner: You don't need to yell. I'll give you as much concrete as you want. Where am I spose to put it?

Male Miner: Where are you taking it? Stop. Let's go now.

One corridor of the pit after another.

Bright light alternates with dusk. As we go along, we catch various sequences of work.

People are digging.

People are drilling.

People are pushing mine cars away.

Shovels sparkle, as they toss earth.

Here, a mine car goes off the rails.

---

[58] [Trans.]: In transliterated English in the original.

Some young Komsomol members yell, "Little Masha, help!"

Hefty Masha comes up and with a single motion and a smile puts the mine car back on the rails.

—Let's go! she says, loudly issuing a command.

"Not like that, it will go off the rails again."

We go further. Here's the gallery. They are working here, standing under a vault, bent over the pit face.

A miner, leaning into it with all his strength is turning up dirt with a jackhammer.

A well-borer is showing how to use a boring drill.

—Don't yawn. You're dreaming all the time you're working on the caisson.

We move by a finished section. A young miner girl is rolling out concrete.

—Hey, comrade! Watch out for your legs! she yells.

—Take the concrete to the fifth gallery! someone yells to her from someplace.

We go past a guy and a girl.

They are hastily pushing along the delayed concrete.

—Hey, Zinka, don't touch me with those dirty hands, she jokes and the guy keeps teasing her.

We pass by a telephone, there a stern voice, screaming, yells into the receiver:

—Hello, Seregin, two more cartloads of concrete I tell you. You're giving it to me by the teaspoon. Again. Not on schedule again?

We go further. The screen splits in two horizontally.

At the top of the frame: the sleeping masses of the Moscow streets. Below, there is activity, the masses of the underground labor, unaware of the Moscow night.

Din. Racket.

This is the front.

We move towards the English shield.

In its sections, workers and engineers are working. The best Komsolmol brigades are competing. The Kraevsky and Rebrov Brigades. All methods of the latest technology are mobilized here, on the underground front.

(After this, we will track and demonstrate all the work on the shield. We will reveal the winners and the conditions, that led the brigade to their victory.)

We approach an impromptu meeting. Spot lights will pick out the faces of the miners, only snatches of words will be audible:

—You need to write about this in our *Rupor*[59]... comrades, for this reason, I propose to deliver units, so that...

—...this will be a great gain in efficiency... Nothing further will be heard.

We move towards a group of young female miners on their break. Many of them have jackhammers.

---

[59] [Trans.]: In the original: *Pynop*, a Komsomol publication started in the 1920s. The name means, Megaphone, Trumpet, or Voice.

A Male Miner: "Marusya, Marusen'ka," he yells from the distance.

Female Miner: "There's the captain. I'm coming," she answers with a smile and goes towards the calling voice. And once again, shots of the attacks on the stubborn, resistant depths of underground Moscow.

Our final run is to the icy ducts. The miners are covered with frost. Here, it is winter. Here, the machines freeze the loose soil, which is saturated with water.

After these shots, we will show the entire route from an airplane, in the splendor of early morning sunlight.

The entire expanse of space, covered by the socialist labor of the miners will be made visible—labor, knowing neither day, nor night—labor, knowing no barriers in overcoming obstacles—the labor of the victors.

Shots of the route taken from an airplane, will go with a song devoted to the miners, the builders of the Metro of the capital, Moscow.

A New Turkey is on the Move (1934)

A documentary sound film

The majestic music of *Die Götterdämmerung*. A desert mountain range. Ruins of the ancient world. Marble from ruined buildings. A combination of Hellas, Rome, Byzantium. A world gone by.

Pergamon. Marble buildings, paved roads, columns, gymnasiums, temples, a circus. The Temple of Aesclepius with baths, niches, a theater for the entertainment of the sick. A majestic Acropolis, a theater for fifteen thousand spectators with the temple of Dionysos at its base, an aqueduct.

Statues of emperors, of citizens, of noblewomen, of gods. Mosaics. From these ruins and the monuments which have been preserved, you can vividly imagine an entire life, the entire way of life of a city destroyed and buried for centuries. These ruins testify to cyclopean labor, to the genius of humanity of past millennia. Still, uninhabited, dead. High mountain ranges, covered with moss, like a fortress, spiral around this dead city. The burning glitter of the sun. The limitlessness, the boundlessness of the sea in the distance. The crashing of the waves.

A deserted road. The shattered ruins of the Byzantine wall with seven towers. The granite hippodrome, the obelisk, the serpent column, the remains of the tripod from the temple of Apollo at Delphi.

In the distance, the Golden Horn shining silver. The dead city floats slowly by, amidst the Gothic forest of poplars. A world gone by.

Eastern music. A chorale.

The palace of the Ottoman sultan. Topkapı.

The buildings of the palace, the pavilions were spread out amidst tall cypress trees. The splendid interior enclosure of the courtyard.

The fairy-tale view onto the Bosphorus, the Princes' Islands. The Golden Horn. The Throne room.

In the palace treasuries, the dazzling luster of precious stones. A throne, a mass of Persian goldwork, decorated with emeralds and diamonds. A throne of ebony encrusted with pearls, silver, gold. Emeralds the size of a fist—the largest in the world—were hung beneath the baldachin. Persian, Smyrna, Hindu carpets.

In vitrines, mannequins of the sultans have been set up: the Ottoman emperors. On them is lush clothing in brocade, diamond-studded sabers, precious headdresses. And here, as well, are wax figures of mullahs, executioners, and eunuchs.

Topkapı and the entire shore of the Bosphorus with its majestic monuments— its mosques—floats by like a vision. Here is Hagia Sophia, Bayazid, Süleymaniye. Pidyya[60] floats by: a city of palace-mansions.

A monument to the bloody rule of the last tyrant Abdul-Hamid. A world gone forever! And once again, the crashing of the waves, the boundlessness of the sea in the distance. The mountain range in the dawn fog, valleys, the mountain landscapes, a mountain lake and rhythmic, slow Eastern music on instruments recalling sazandars.[61]

On the shores of a mountain lake in a semi-circle sit zeybeks[62] in old-fashioned embroidered clothing and in a line, they dance in time to the music, a rhythmic, warlike dance.

You take in the zeybeks like a picture of the past, somehow filling out the previous theme.

A pan from the zeybeks rises up towards the mountain range. The mountains pile up one range after another.

The face of the country has been transformed. We drive by groves of fig trees, olive trees, vineyards, groves of pomegranates. Railroads cut through the country in the mountain regions. We drive along splendid highways. Steamships travel the sea lanes.

At the foot of two mountains, a new city stretches out with straight roadways. Splendid buildings, banks, schools. Busses, automobiles, monuments, embassies. There

---

[60] [Trans.]: In the original: Пидыя [Pidyya]. I can find no reference to this. I can only imagine it is a mistranscription of Shub's text, or a lapse on her part, or the part of her translator. Istanbul is a city of many palaces and mansions, so it is difficult to know what she might mean. Her next sentence could be taken as referring to the Yıldız Palace, a complex of palace-mansions, from where Abdul-Hamid II ruled for the majority of his reign. Aykan Safoğlu, filmmaker and native Istanbulite, responded to my queries by saying the only Turkish word that might be deciphered from what was is written here, could be Padişah (Ottoman Emperor).

[61] [Trans.]: Sazandars are actually the musicians of a traditional Azeri trio.

[62] [Trans.]: Zeybek is actually the name of the dance, rather than the dancers.

is nothing to remind us, that we are in Asia. This is the new capital of Turkey, a European city, the residence of Kemal Atatürk.

And here, he himself, surrounded by members of the Turkish government, to the sounds of the new Turkish national anthem, walks to the Madjlis.[63] Numerous monuments repeat his outline. Everywhere, he is the commander, leading into battle against the yoke of the sultans and foreign domination. Or, astride a horse, is the *Gazi*,[64] the victor. And everywhere on the monuments in honor of the *Gazi* alongside him is the figure of the Turkish peasant woman. Her face is without a veil. She carries high the banner of freedom, behind her, go soldiers. A woman, having bent down in rapid motion, carries a cannonball to the field of battle. A woman takes the rifle from the hands of her wounded husband to the field of battle.

The face of the country has changed.

Aboard a ship, we pass through the Bosphorus and the Golden Horn. How could these landscapes fail to resemble the engravings and descriptions, which have reached us from Loti[65] and Farrer. The shores are lined with docks, factory buildings extend along the shores. Urban chaos, railroad tracks, factories. The entire shoreline is in smoke, in motion, at work.

Here are the factories for Smyrna figs, raisins, tobacco. Here, for the most part, women work. They sit in long rows, Eastern-style on the floor. Their faces are without veils. Their heads are covered with light white shawls like madonnas. Their fingers sorting raisins, tobacco, figs move with inconceivable speed. The dusky fingers of children can be glimpsed fleetingly as well.

Inside the new mills and factories. Women workers in black dresses and scarves alongside men in the woolen mills. Young women in urban attire and men at the new machines of the textile factories. More women than men at the complicated conveyorized machines of the cigarette factory. In the section for high quality cigarettes, the work is done by hand, at unbelievable speed, exactingly, rhythmically. Mountains of smartly decorated boxes and everywhere the emblem of the crescent moon and the star.

Women and men in the new mechanized liquor factory, that looks like a chemical laboratory.

In the cement factory, in the factories for shoes, clothing, soap, and other things, everywhere there is intense labor. The results of this labor we see in smart kiosks, located in the beautiful sunny halls of a new trade show building in Ankara. Music, crowds of visitors—goods, demonstrating the products of Turkish industry, demonstrating emancipation from foreign markets.

---

[63] [Trans.]: The Turkish Parliament.

[64] [Trans.]: Gazi is a traditional Islamic military honorific; capitalized in Turkey it refers explicitly to Atatürk.

[65] [Trans.] Pierre Loti (1850–1923) A French naval officer and romantic, exoticist writer, known for his exacting descriptions and confessional style.

Everywhere: on walls, on windows, on posters is the figure of Kemal Atatürk and his slogans.

In the cloudy sky, the tops of steamships float by, adorned with the flags of the entire world.

A slow pan revealing the port of Smyrna. American, French, English, German, Greek, Italian, and other steamships. There are a lot of them, quite a lot. Ropes, like strings, stretched out between the shore and the sea. On the embankment, movement. Noise, rumbling, horns: conversations in many languages. From the steamship you see Smyrna: an old Turkish city. Buildings run down from the mountain to the bay. On the summit of the mountain are the ruins of the towers of fortresses.

From here, you see the beautiful Smyrna embankment. On the embankment, the tiny car of a horse-drawn tram rolls along—beautiful busses and automobiles of the latest models pass by the little horse. Everyone is rushing along towards the center of the city: Konak Square.

All the riches of Asia Minor flow together in Smyrna. Trucks constantly arrive at the port, laden with tobacco, figs, raisins, olives. On all these goods is the emblem of the crescent moon and the star.

Under the scorching, sparkling sun work goes on. Stevedores quickly and continuously relieve the arriving trucks of their goods. Cranes are at work, in the holds of ships, the loading goes on.

On the horizon, the smoke of the steamships can be seen as they move into the distance.

The growth in the economy goes hand in hand with the growth in the culture of the country.

On a marble panel engraved in gold letters is this call: "Hey you, Youth of Turkey! Your first obligation is to keep a firm grasp on Turkish freedom. May your freedom and the Turkish Republic live forever! Grow strong and defend yourselves!" Signed, Kemal Gazi.

To the sound of the Turkish national anthem, young men and girls pass by. Their bodies are strong and powerful. Their faces are burnt by the sun. They demonstrate their strength, their youth, their love of country. Turkish youth is strong, beautiful, nimble.

This youth fills the universities. Listens avidly to lectures about new legislation given by the director of the university. Listens with concern to Recep-Bey, as he speaks about the international situation. They experiment with interest and attention in the class of the German professor at the Agro-institute. In the field, they work with tractors. In the Academy of Arts, they study sculpture, painting, architecture. Everywhere young men and girls are together. They study with enthusiasm and they train their bodies with enthusiasm in beautiful gymnasiums. On the snow-white marble square on the rooftops of the new buildings of the institutes.

Little schoolchildren don't lag behind the grownups.

Here, they are lining up in the shape of a star in the schoolyard of a school named for the *Gazi.*

One of the schoolgirls has a flag in her hand. On it, is the crescent moon and star. The courtyard is filled with the voices of the children singing the national anthem.

In a class, very small girls and boys of seven or eight consciously and enthusiastically repeat each word after their female teacher: "I am a Turk... I am true... I must love my country more than myself. I dream of growing up and building a great, new life. My life I give to Turkey."

Here, a charming eleven-year-old girl artfully recites, her class and her teacher listen to her: "I am not a butterfly, I am not a doll of stone. I am not a bee, I am not a flower. I am not a bird. I am a small person. I think, I feel, I live. My blood is pure Turkish blood. You will see, how this little person will grow up."

A new generation is growing, a new youth.

Istanbul stretched out in a vast panorama around the Bosphorus and the Golden Horn. On this sunny day, it seems, the whole city has come out onto the squares and streets. The many shades of green, of fruit, and flowers.

On Karaköy square, an endless stream of automobiles. A line of buggies with well-dressed children, pushed by nannies, rolls along on the sidewalks. Şişli is a wealthy neighborhood in the Pera[66] district. Endless crowds stream along Grande Rue de Péra[67] past beautiful shop windows with beautiful things, past the windows of restaurants. Past shops with lamb carcasses. Past cafes, where Istanbulites sit for hours with a cup of coffee, fingering their prayer beads, drawing smoke from nargiles.

We are quickly swept along the street of stairs, Yüksek Kaldırım,[68] which joins Pera with Galata.

An enormous crowd of students, men and women, walk around the university grounds. A procession of schoolchildren goes by, young boys and girls, in caps, with posters, banners, slogans. Boy Scouts beat drums, athletes march along, troops pass by, their weapons jingling. On the asphalt schoolyard, former homeless and neglected children[69] from the streets of Istanbul fall in line.

Tram bells, car horns, the bells of vendors selling water, little bells in shop windows acting as advertisements, fill the air. The cries of street vendors, the cracking of whips, the thin whistle of polishing, produced in the stores of shoe-shine men.

---

[66] [Trans.]: Now known as Beyoğlu.
[67] [Trans.]: Now known as İstiklal Caddesi.
[68] [Trans.]: In the original, mistranscribed as Юсек-Калорым [Yusek-Kalorym].
[69] [Trans.]: In the original: беспризорные дети [besprizornye deti].

Here tourists and visitors leave their shoes at the entrance to Hagia-Sophia, Beyazıt, Süleymaniye. Remarkable monuments of Byzantine and Ottoman art. Here there is quiet, grandeur, solemnity. Beauty. The marble court of the Beyazıt mosque with a fountain, surrounded by stalls. In them, old men with marvelous faces, as if they had issued from old engravings, sell beads, aromatic oils. Only here, do you still feel in the old, narrow, little streets, with little houses of darkening wood, with Venetian balconies, the exoticism of days gone by. But through the gaps between the columns of the Beyazıt mosque, one can see the square paved in granite, the marble of new buildings, and the noisy, populous crowd, dressed in European clothing, the movement of automobiles, and trams.

Overfilled sherkets[70] head towards Princes' Islands. There, there is tropical vegetation, summer palaces,[71] leisure. Evening shadows descend. A beautiful sunset on the Bosphorus. In the hour before dusk, endless numbers of lights pour out, lighting up the expanse of the city like an amphitheater. In the sky before dusk, the delicate contours of ancient towers, minarets, palaces stand out sharply. Fishing dinghies with white sails ply the smooth waters of the Bosphorus.

The signs of movie theaters light up.

Radio loudspeakers fill the streets with European music.

In a national cultural center,[72] in a beautiful auditorium, a Turkish opera by a young composer is being performed.

On the shores of the Bosphorus, hundreds of couples of women and men move to the sounds of music as they dance.

Fishing dinghies with small lamps throw golden shadows on the still evening waters of the Bosphorus.

At the entrance to a small house, a young woman from the countryside is sitting. She is rocking a child. Her eyes are directed towards the sea. She softly sings an ancient song.

—Is the song an old one? And life? we ask. She becomes silent. She covers her face with her shawl. She opens it slowly and softly says:

—My eyes are unveiled. I have a new life. I am beginning to see my future clearly. And she begins to sing again softly. Her eyes are looking into the distance,

---

[70] [Trans.]: In the original, шеркеты (sherkety). I could find no reference for this in Turkish or English. The closet Turkish word is şirket (meaning firm, company, concern), so this may have been a misunderstanding of some sort. She clearly means some sort of boat.

[71] [Trans.]: In the original, дачи-дворцы [dachi-dvortsy] a coinage combining the plural of dacha, which can be anything from a quite humble summer cottage to something quite luxurious, with the plural of palace.

[72] [Trans.]: In the original: народный дом [narodny dom]. This is necessarily an inexact translation, but the original implies some kind of government sponsored cultural center. Whether it is the only one, or one among many, is ambiguous as Russian has no definite article, but since it is not capitalized we might infer it is one among many.

into the boundlessness of the sea. She is just like the one on the monuments, radiating courage and bravery.

For the film *Native Land* (1942)

Moscow. 1942. I am going to make this film in the empty Mosfil'm studio. I want to finish it by November. My garret has no windows, no doors, just a gaping hole in the ceiling. Through it would come gusts of wind. I am living in the Hotel Moscow. It is the time of the immeasurably heavy fighting for Stalingrad. Moscow, emptied out, is bathing in the sun, it is magnificent. Her silence, peace, and depopulated state pierce my heart and fill it with pride. There are frequent air strikes. They have Mosfil'm in their sights. Twice I go down into a bomb shelter; I want to know how the metro looks under the Hotel Moscow; the second time, was in the Conservatory, during a performance of Shostakovich's symphony.

D. Shostakovich, I. Ehrenburg, V. Vishnevsky, have recently arrived from Leningrad; from the front have come A. Dovzhenko with Solntseva and Dzigan. They are living in the Hotel Moscow.

One memorable evening, after a day of exacting work, Dovzhenko took me with him to Ivan Semenovich Kozlovsky's place. Dovzhenko and Ivan Semenovich were friends.

They sat down at the piano. And the magic began. At the top of their lungs, they sing the songs of their native land, of their childhood and youth. Ivan Semenovich accompanies himself and Dovzhenko puts his poet's heart into every word of the song. They look at each other, smiling slightly. The memories wash over me in waves. I will never forget this song....

I am shooting Shostakovich on the sound stage of the Studio for Documentary Films. He plays two fragments of his Seventh Symphony on the piano. The piano blends in with the orchestra. After the shoot, at night, we walk back through darkened Moscow to the hotel. Neither of us can see very well and we often stumble. On the way, he spoke about the conductors Mravinsky and Ivanov and how he hears the music created by him in concert. He was attentive and kind inside. Quite simply, with no special persuasion, he agreed to the shoot. It seems, we succeeded in filming him well.

I filmed Ehrenburg. In a small room, behind a typewriter, he was typing out his next article for the newspaper *Krasnaya zvezda*.[73] These articles were awaited by

---

[73] [Trans.] *Красная звезда* (*Red Star*). Created by the Politburo in 1923, it was the newspaper of the People's Commissariat of Military and Naval Affairs of the USSR. During WW II, it was a leading source of news across the USSR. It remains the principal newspaper of the Armed Forces of the

hundreds of thousands of Soviet Citizens. During the period of the heaviest fighting for Stalingrad, they helped preserve tranquility, steadfastness, and faith in victory, they showed the face of the enemy relentlessly, its inhumanity, its brutal nature, the horror that Fascism brings to the world. He wrote these relentless articles, but his eyes were blue, peaceful, kind as anything. In them, were tranquility and willpower.

But the most interesting shoots were on a Mosfil'm set and at the airport.

I also shot the old woman, with whom Zoya Kosmodem'yanskaya spent her last night. She was a witness to how a Fascist beast tortured the girl. The camera operator Fel'dman filmed her magnificently. This story rang out with truth—she told everything with an unspeakable inner horror. This story provoked rage.

A Film Chronicle of the Great Patriotic War (1945)

(an excerpt from a working draft)

The task, which stands before the workers who will create the chronicle, is clear.

1. To examine all the material shot during the years of the Patriotic War. I foresee including first and foremost:
   a) Soviet Newsreels
   b) Special news reports
   c) Topical essay films
   d) Films based on real events
   e) Documentary films
Since the best shots in terms of content taken by professional cameramen during the war years were certainly used by the directors of newsreels, they will be found in this material.

I foresee including, as well, film documents not used in the course of newsreel work.

2. The shots must be selected, in terms of their content within the frame, as film documents of recorded facts, events, occurrences, and not as an abstract montage of shots.

These shots must be precisely described in terms of their visual information (shooting location, natural environment and technical means, the people actually participating, etc.) and, if possible, dated.

From material made use of from newsreels, must be taken:

Russian Federation.

a) sequences, which for various reasons, were not included in previous films;

b) individual shots, significant in their content;

c) individual takes used in novel contexts.

3. To examine all new material for the chronicle. In order to do this, attend all general screenings of current material shot by camera operators. Immediately request printing of an inter-positive of all sequences and shots selected.

4. Systematization of the material. 1939. Prologue.

a) Key developments, facts, phenomena, depicting the identity of our Motherland, on the eve of the terrible events. The selected sequences and shots must reflect industrial, kolkhoz, and cultural life, and as well, the way of life of the populations of our Republics.

b) The liberation by the Red Army of Western Ukraine and Belorussia.

c) The war with Finland.

d) The liberation by the Red Army of Bessarabia and Bukovina.

e) The liberation by the Red Army of the Peoples of Latvia, Lithuania, and Estonia.

1941–1945. The Front.

First period. From the beginning of the sneak attack to the battle of Moscow, inclusive. Include here, sequences of heroic battles, the partisan movement.

Second period. The Battle of Stalingrad.

Third Period. The victorious movement of the Red Army towards the West. The Battle of Leningrad, of the Dnepr. People who performed acts of heroism.

Within the periods mentioned above, systematize the selected material into sequences. If possible, do this following government reports. The content of each shot must be described precisely, economically, and visually. Shots must be numbered according to thematic sequence. Within a thematic sequence, a list of shots must be kept.

Such a description should read as written by film historians, that is, as a chronicle of the Patriotic War, and along with that, it must give a complete picture of the work of newsreel workers in the years of the Patriotic War. To the descriptions of the shots, the most vivid descriptions must be attached from *Pravda, Izvestia, Krasnaya zvezda* and *Morskoi flot.*[74]

1941–1945. The Home Front.

The sequences and shots selected must reflect: the life of the Republics, the work of evacuated factories, the creation of new industrial facilities, news about culture, science, art, to show the heroes of the home front—individual incidents, important events, the work of transportation, etc.

---

[74] [Trans.]: *Морской флот* (*Sea Fleet*) was, at the time, a periodical of the Soviet Navy and continues to be a periodical of the Navy of the Russian Federation and includes a website. It first began publication in 1886, some 30 years before the birth of the Soviet Union.

It is difficult now, to give a more detailed account of the system of the thematic categories of shots and their description. The work itself will point to new categories.

To the descriptions of life on the home front, an index must be attached of the most interesting articles in our current press, which coincide with the contents of the shots.

For the descriptions of shots from newsreels, an editorial commission must be created, which should include: representatives of the public (factories, transportation, etc.), a film director, writers, journalists, military consultants, as well as a worker compiling the descriptions of the shots.

A card file for the chronicle must elaborate a system of recording and numbering, which will make possible their speedy location. For this, it will be necessary, first of all, to organize the categories of the card file in numerous and varied ways, taking into consideration, that one and the same shot, may be listed in various categories, in each case, except for the general identification number and the number of the location in this, or that category of the chronicle.

Each shot, named in the card file, must have, if possible, the exact date of the shoot, the place of the shoot, and the name of the camera operator.

5. An outline for shooting and for re-shoots can be worked out only in the process of reviewing and selecting material. The production must be worked out according to the design of the director, in coordination with the newsreel camera operators.

All work on the chronicle must be organized, in such a way, that it will merge organically with current work in the newsreel.

Our principal task is to preserve, in the best possible way, the selected material, which is of enormous historical value. To preserve it, not only for our contemporaries, but for future generations.

It is a matter of preserving the negatives of what has been shot in their original state and completely intact. This is fundamental. Without this, all work on the film chronicle will have only a temporary significance.

What happens to a negative in the system, as it now exists? It is in constant motion, it is subjected to individual tastes in montage cutting, it is worn out in printing and is, thus, destroyed.

The correct thing to do, would be to allow only one positive print for general viewing from a negative and three or four fine grain master positives for selected sequences and shots for current montage work, including the film chronicle. The negative in its original state should be preserved in a special vault, and only, in the case of the wearing out of the fine grain master positives, by special permission of the management or the head [of the facility], should new fine grain master positives be printed. Only this measure can preserve a negative, and thus, preserve historical film documents from rapid destruction.

All of my other concerns, regarding the creation of a film chronicle, as well as the composition of an editorial board, will be elaborated by me, upon approval of the basic work plan.

Victory (1945)

We clearly know: the war is coming to an end. Victory is near. From this unspeakable world-historical battle with Fascism, the Soviet people will emerge victorious. In these days, when the Red Army stands at the border with East Prussia, when the sons of the Soviet Union, together with the Polish Liberation Army, with weapons in their hands, fight for Warsaw, when the Red Army has gone out onto the streets of Bucharest and Sofia, and Czechoslovakia and Yugoslavia know, that our help is near, that it is near the threshold, one can and one must set before oneself the task of making a film, which sums things up, vividly depicting the path our Motherland has traveled, whose glory will not fade with the centuries.

We have made many good films over the years about the struggle on the decisive sectors of the front: the Battles of Moscow, Stalingrad, Ukraine, and others. It is my thought, that the task is to comprehend and to elaborate a newsreel of the Patriotic War through montage, so that the Soviet People will catch sight of the harsh and heavy, sacrificial path traversed by them. This film must show, that the tasks, which the Soviet People set for themselves, they have fulfilled with glory. The world must catch sight of the fact, that the battle with Fascism has been won, because the Soviet People struggled.

It must show our particular strategy and tactics of battle, the unique Soviet heroes, born of the struggle. From soldier to general.

It needs to underscore both the noble goal—the struggle for the liberation not only of our own country, but of brother Peoples from the darkness of the brutal madness of Fascism.

The task is difficult, but there are possibilities for fulfilling it. They have been laid out, both in the material already accumulated, as well as, in the shooting of supplementary material.

It is impossible to bring back events not filmed at the time by shooting now, but the people, who participated in these events, the living traces of the events: the cities, the collective farms, fields, pastures, which have been brought back from devastation and have been brought back to free, working, and creative life, can and must be filmed.

Some directors say, and I myself think, that the first shots of any film determine its figurative and semantic meaning. This is precisely my thought for the beginning of this film.

Moscow, on that joyous day and that evening, when for the first time, the streets, the houses, and windows of the apartments will be flooded with electric light and strangers, grown-ups and children, will greet one another when they meet, as if they were relatives.

Leningrad, Kiev, Minsk, Stalingrad, Sevastopol should then pass before us after Moscow. They will all be listening to Moscow, because:

Moscow is victory.

Moscow is the Red Army.

Moscow is the sword of punishment and of freedom.

And then, Berlin. The lair of the beast, caught in a trap, defeated and awaiting judgment. The victorious Red Army on the streets of Berlin. It is a witness to unspeakable atrocities and a fearsome judge. The events, beginning with June of 1941, will emerge on the screen.

They will pass by with little commentary. Each event must be meaningful and subordinated to the overall theme and to the task set for the film.

They are the following:

The sneak attack.

The face of the enemy.

The strategy and battle tactics of the Soviet Union.

The heroes born on the fields of battle.

The generals: the path from Commander to Marshal.

The Soviet People on the home front during wartime. The supreme sacrifices made by the Soviet People in the name of Victory. The heroes of the home front.

Our tomorrow.

Moscow: 800 years (1947)

800 years have passed since the founding of the city of Moscow.

Throughout the years after the Revolution, Moscow has been the subject of documentary film shoots—in any journal, in any film, one can see shots of the Soviet Capital, but until now, no film has been brought to the screen, which has been entirely devoted to Moscow.

All the same, Moscow—the heart and the brain of the Soviet Union—has become a symbol of the entire Soviet State: the favorite songs of the People have been dedicated to it, plays have been dedicated to it, poets have dedicated their verses to it, millions of people from every corner of the earth have sought to visit it.

Moscow today is a new stage in the history not only of our Motherland, but of all humanity. This is recognized both by those, who sooner or later must exit the stage of history, and by those, who will take the place of those who have exited and will build on our planet a new, a decent life for man.

In this proposal, we would like to outline the individual themes, which should go into the film.

Moscow is one of the most ancient cities, not only of the Slavic world, but in all of Europe. It has played the greatest role in our history.

Film documents about the history of Moscow begin in 1907 and present material of unusual interest. Yet, in contemporary Moscow, as well, at every step we encounter evidence of the history of the Fatherland: in its buildings, in its monuments, in its cultural and scientific institutions. For this reason, documentary cinema possesses a wide range of possibilities for showing how Moscow, over the course of centuries, has governed the civic and cultural life of our country.

It goes without saying, that the film will present to the viewer the most beautiful things to be found in Moscow, in this enormous city, which has been revitalized during the years of the revolution.

But the fundamental task, which we are setting for ourselves, consists of showing Moscow as the center of the Soviet State, a State of a new type, the capital of Socialism.

The fate of the country is being decided here. From here, across the entire expanse from the River Bug to the Pacific Ocean, a guiding will is in motion, moving forward our Fatherland. The best people in the land converge here to participate in governing the State.

Five million people live in Moscow. Who are these people? What are their distinguishing characteristics? How do they spend their hours of labor and hours of leisure? The most varied professions have their best representatives in this city: the world of industry, the world of primary education and higher education, urban planning, in child development, in railroad transport, in the management of urban traffic: in a word, in all fields of human activity. These are the people of Moscow. The same ones who defended their capital during the brutal year of 1941 and are now building life in peacetime, not only in their own city, but in the whole country.

This film will be about Moscow and the people of Moscow.

It will be shot using documentary methods. But its content must exceed the framework of reportage, or pretty pictures. For Moscow is too profound and too precious to the heart of every Soviet individual, to show it superficially, or cursorily. Moscow is the image of our Soviet World and, in this, we see the key to addressing this theme.

B. Agapov
E. Shub

They are 30 years old (1947)

The theme of this film must be to show the powerful, young tribe of people, born during the days of the Great October Revolution. Along with their country, they have traveled a great path of struggle and historical victories. This is a special generation of people. Their willpower, consciousness, purposefulness, their vision of the world around them, their goals were formed by historical events. These events of their childhood determined their consciousness, as they were active participants in these events, beginning in their childhood.

This must be a film about ordinary adults, who are still young, and about their best representatives, who most fully sum up the fundamental qualities of the entire generation. A film about them must instill in the consciousness of the spectator a joyous conviction, that the great work of Lenin has splendid, strong, and dedicated heirs.

The tasks set forth by the Party before our Motherland will be fulfilled by them and our children will live in the bright world of Communism.

Their cradle is October, 1917. Their first word, after mama and papa, is "Lenin." Their fathers are workers or peasants who struggled on the fronts of the Civil War against the intervention, the blockade, against the White Guard; with weapons in their hands, they defended the first State of workers and peasants in the world.

Their fathers are the inspiring glorious red heroes of Voronezh, Tsaritsyn, Perekop, Volochaevsk, who were led by Frunze, Voroshilov, Budenny. In their ranks, the first commanders from the People arose: Chapaev, Parkhomenko, Shchors…

These people conquered the poles, they are the *Serovs* on the battlefields of Spain. This generation showed their best qualities in the battles of Khalkhin Gol and on the battlefields of the Great Patriotic War. These are the finest leaders in the construction sites of the fourth Five-Year Plan, in the cities and in the kolkhozes, in Science and in Art.

It will be the job of the scriptwriter to select from among these people, the heroes of a future film and to address, by means of dramatic construction, the lofty task of the theme proposed.

Oil (1948)

In this proposal, I want to present the author's objective for the film, outline the fundamental themes which it should express, outline the plan for the preparatory work, which is essential for the writing of the scenario.

The theme of oil must be taken broadly, not limiting the film to showing oil as the principal natural resource of Soviet Azerbaijan, and showing the struggles of oil workers for the fulfillment of the commitment taken on themselves to provide the country with 17 million tons of oil. But this, of course, will be reflected in the scenario.

The first theme. To tell why oil is not only a decisive part of the People's Socialist Economy, but one of the fundamental factors in international economics and politics.

In Moscow, there is a collection of captured documentary films and newsreels, from both the pre-war era and from wartime. We will undoubtedly find there recorded facts, clearly depicting the struggle by imperialist forces for oil, the frenzy of capitalist concerns and exchanges for oil. Besides that, in these newsreels, we will find sufficient material clearly depicting the purposes and interests guiding this imperialistic and I would say, "total" offensive on oil.

Second theme. The distant historical past.

In the distant past, the Azerbaijani People, before the Arab invasion, which forcibly imposed Mahommedanism,[75] were fire-worshippers. This is evidenced in ancient monuments and temples preserved on Azerbaijani soil to this day and in a whole series of folk customs.

And how could this People not be fire-worshippers?

The soil of Azerbaijan, the water table, and seabed are impregnated with a mysterious source of fire: oil.

Fire would unexpectedly break out in the soil, in the water, in the air. All this ignited the imagination of man in distant eras and struck a superstitious terror.

Oil is fire.

Oil is black gold.

It is light, it is wealth, it is sometimes a cure for maladies.

A radiant, good, and punishing deity. This is the distant past.

The not so distant past. Attempts by capitalists of all countries to lay their hands on the oil of Baku.

The revolutionary past of the country, of the city, where Kirov, Ordzhonikidze, the twenty-six Commissars, led the fervent struggle for a better future for the Azerbaijani People.

Third theme. Oil production in the post-war years.

This theme must show how successful oil production is contributing to mitigating the aftermath of war, how the timely fulfillment and over-fulfillment of the plan is strengthening the economy and the culture of the country, is contributing to the defensive power of the socialist state. All this must not be resolved in a purely formal manner, but the scenario must find an original and dramatic representation.

It seems interesting to me, to resolve this theme using the following device.

---

[75] [Trans.]: In the original: магометанство.

That the life of the family of a single oil worker be at the center of the film—from the beginning to the end.

In the scenario, it will be necessary to outline the shooting of those events and behaviors of the characters who appear, which will most vividly demonstrate the high cultural level of the concerns of the oil worker, his participation in the governing of the State, his ethical attitude towards the family, his children's future, his fervent love of the Motherland, and the understanding pervading his mind and his heart, that the source of our entire life, the source of our victories is the great teachings of Lenin.

The life of this family must be filmed in such a way, that it becomes a generalized image of the many-thousand-strong army of laboring oil workers, who demonstrate the wonders of industrial perseverance, of innovation in all areas of the struggle for oil.

In the scenario, we will find the means of conclusively proving, that the Soviet Union is a strong oil power and that its oil industry is equipped with the most advanced technology.

We will conclude the film with a rapid montage sequence,[76] economically explaining the peaceful ends served by oil in the Soviet Union. If the Ministry of Cinema finds it possible to sign an agreement with me for the scenario (working title *Oil*), it should entrust me with the viewing of the material of the collection of captured material. For the viewing, I will need a translator. (A translator is on the staff of the Studio of Documentary films in the Ministry of Cinema.)

Lists of the footage selected by me will be described in detail and dated.

As the shots needed accumulate, an interpositive will be struck. In this way, when the scenario is ready, the studio will have the necessary material ready for editing the first two parts.

The artistic director of the studio should allow me to research the heroes appearing[77] in the film.

The fundamental themes of the film will be written (4 or 5 reels), based on the observations and study of the life and surroundings of the family of the oil worker, and a precise editing and shooting plan established.

---

[76] [Trans.] In the original: Стремительной монтажной фразой.

[77] [Trans.]: In the original: действующие герои фильма: approximately: the acting heroes of the film. The normal term for a character is a fiction film is: действующий лицо фильма: literally the acting person of the film, usually translated as "character."

The Motherland in the Art of the People (1949)

The authors of the current proposal have in mind a feature-length film survey of the year 1945. The idea arose of showing our Motherland, this time being guided by a completely new principle. What if we were to take a look at the country in light of the lamp of art, following the sounds of song, admiring the rhythms of dance, looking into how the People see the Motherland, in their inexhaustible and beautiful creative work. We often speak of our native land, as a land of happiness, a land of celebration. This is truly the authentic understanding of the People, this understanding is expressed in the creative arts of the most diverse sorts. There is no field of human activity, which is not, in some way or other, reflected in art. Sometimes, this is a direct representation in word or gesture, sometimes art becomes a part of life, as we observe, for example, in Kazakh or Kirghiz folk poets' competitions,[78] in the folk choirs of the Baltic Republics and so forth. Sometimes, within a song, or verse, or even an instrumental passage, we see a piece of the reality of our creative labor.

The authors are convinced, that with a thoughtful and loving approach, it is possible to show the entire country with exceptional completeness, if we take as a guide, the art of the country, the creative work of the People. After all, it is not born cut off from life; it is not created in ivory towers. It is the flesh of the flesh of the People, it is the radiation of that same spirit of the People as all the rest: buildings, fields, science… And if you discard the traditions of film concerts and revue films and enter deeply into the problem of how its creative work is integrated with the People — through its activities — it would be possible to create a work, which would be a kind of oratorio about the Motherland, the activity of the entire nation, dedicated to our glorious day. In it, will be reflected, the struggle for the Five-Year Plan, as well as the heroic actions in the fields, and the great belief of the People in their bright future, and the pride of the People in what has been truly achieved. The cause of this will not lie in the words of the voice-over text, but in the unmediated expression of art. The compelling shots of documentary cinema, which show our lives, will confirm this.

The authors consider, that this kind of work, which is utterly unusual for our documentary cinema, moving beyond all the usual templates and clichés, could be well received by mass spectators. We, as documentarians, all dream of such a reception as our greatest happiness.

From our point of view, this will become one of the most important conditions for the existence of documentary films. For that, we must search out what is new, we must boldly blaze as yet unknown trails.

---

[78] [Trans.]: In the original: в соревнованиях акынов [v sorevnovaniyakh akynov]. An akyn is a Kazakh or Kirghiz folk poet.

We are convinced, that with a song, our travel along this path will be easier and more joyful.

The film must show the place, the role of art in the country of socialism, that is, not only the folk sources of art, but their use by the entire nation.

Who listens to the best singers of the USSR? Who reads and speaks in person with the best writers and poets? For whom do Uzbek dancers perform, before whom do the Kazakh and Kirghiz folk poets compete, for whom do the many-thousand-strong choirs of Estonians sing?

Art sparkles in the most distant corners of the Soviet Union, it has become the heritage of the broadest popular masses. From the depths of the People arise the new masters of art, its new creators.

We imagine this film as a celebration of music, color, line, as a wondrous spectacle. It must combine documentariness with the most fascinating visual form. This is a difficult, but achievable task. We are convinced, that the efforts will be rewarded a hundredfold: compelling shots of documentary cinema will show around the entire world the joy, the fullness, the spiritual riches of the land of socialism. We will demonstrate the authentic friendship of nations who are equals, united in the Soviet Union, and thus inflict another blow against the slander spread against us by the enemies of democracy and peace.

Sources

Women
Scenario co-authored by E. Shub and the writer B. Lapin in 1932–1933. A typed copy is preserved in the archive of E. Shub.

The City Sleeps
Treatment[79] written in 1933–1934. The film was shot, but not edited, and was never screened. Typewritten original of the scenario is preserved in the archive of E. Shub.

A New Turkey is on the Move[80]
Treatment written in 1934. Printed according to the manuscript, preserved in the archive of E. Shub.

For the film Native Land
Journal entries made at the time of work on the film. The original is preserved in the archive of E. Shub.

A Film Chronicle of the Great Patriotic War
Printed according to the manuscript, preserved in the archive of E. Shub. In the war years, E. Shub worked on the systematization of material shot by camera operators on the front. The published proposal and work plan are the result of her knowledge acquired.

Victory
Proposal, written in 1944. On the basis of episodes[81] proposed by her, selected during the viewing of material for *A Film Chronicle of the Great Patriotic War*. Printed here according to the manuscript preserved in the archive of E. Shub.

Moscow: 800 Years
Proposal for a film scenario, written by B. Agapov and E. Shub in 1947. Published according to the manuscript.

They are 30 years old
Draft proposal for a scenario. Printed here according to the manuscript preserved in the archive of E. Shub.

Oil
Proposal for a scenario. Printed here according to the manuscript preserved in the archive of E. Shub.

The Motherland in the Art of the People
Synopsis of the scenario,[82] written together with B. Agapov (1949). Printed here according to the typewritten text (archive of E. Shub).

---

[79] [Trans.]: In the original: Литературный сценарий.

[80] [Trans.]: A significant amount of the proposed film was shot, but production was interrupted by the Turkish producer and the film was never edited by Shub. The fate of the material shot is unknown. The director's working diary, stills, and other project materials are preserved in the Shub fond at RGALI.

[81] [Trans.]: In the original: сюжеты.

[82] [Trans.]: In the original: Либретто сценария.

Appendices

Appendix I
Correspondence[1]

Letters from S. M. Eisenstein to E. I. Shub

1
S. M. Eisenstein to E. I. Shub

May 15, 1928, Gagra

Dear Esfir' Il'ini... but *no no no* (this vile little machine doesn't have an exclamation point, though, here, a minimum of a hundred to a hundred and fifty of them are required).

no no no

I totally forgot, to whom I am writing. Here, there are *the non-acted* [*film-makers*], here, there are *documentarians*, and there is no place for youthful pathos in letters to them... Not a peep about feelings, O! letter mine, only *documentation*... Not a letter, but an *Abkhaz document*... and in so far as now construction "is no longer in fashion" let this be *work material*[2] as our friend the "Hamburg Scorekeeper"[3] expresses it—*work material*[4] *for the Abkhaz document*, in any case, as he expresses it, "a letter not about love"[5] seems the most lyrical and touching thing of what I have read. [...]

---

[1] [Trans.]: Since I discovered them after having added my own, I have kept the Russian editor's notes for the correspondence as they were for sake of completeness, even where they differ from my own, or where they provide similar information. The format differs as the Russian editor gives all references for a letter in a single note and I have given references at the point in the letter at which they occur. The Russian editor's notes start on page 477.

[2] [Trans.]: In the original: заготовки [zagatovki]. Shushan Avagyan, in her translation of *The Hamburg Score*, uses "provisions." The word has a large range of meanings including industrial blanks, fabricated parts, procurements, work material, and the gathering of firewood. Shklovsky uses it in the context of fixed phrases, clichés, or ready-made components of language and culture.

[3] [Trans.]: Eisenstein is alluding, here, to Viktor Shklovsky's *Гамбургский счет* [*The Hamburg Score*], so I have echoed that language. Eisenstein's remarks are friendly but pointed, as Shlovsky was a friend of his and of Shub's. Shklovsky worked with her as the script writer for several films she edited, notably *Wings of a Serf*. Shlovsky had also pointedly and in print preferred Shub's *Fall of the Romanov Dynasty* to Eisenstein's *October* for the former's documentary qualities. The phrase "Hamburg score," meaning the unvarnished assessment of something, quickly permeated Soviet society at all levels.

[4] [Trans.]: In the original: заготовки [zagatovki].

[5] [Trans.]: In the original: *ZOO, или Письма не о любви* (*Zoo, or Letters not about Love*), another text by Shklovsky.

So… —but erroneous keystrokes prevail over correct ones, temperament holds sway and to hell with the industrialization of the handwritten letter—from here on, we will write by hand, but strictly, strictly, strictly documentarily (as would be said here, if the happy Abkhaz People had any notion of it—here, the frisky Harry Piel[6] holds undivided sway…).

But before anything, I wish to be guaranteed, that you will write me, but not send it and hand it over to me when we meet in person (one still has to save on stamps!), so that it will absolutely and truly reach me. I *cherish* this greatly. For I want to have recorded and documented on paper evidence about your true relationship with me. For, from time to time it all starts to seem to me, that if I die, then you, like the others, will not put on mourning gloves and something in crêpe, but will dress up for the glory of the non-acted—in wedding attire.

And so, the documentation begins.

Year: 1928

Month: May

Place: Gagra

We arrived according to no known pattern, having already had a preliminary taste of displeasure in Tuapse. Think about it: all the mountains covered in clouds, but from every kiosk Lyubimov-Lanskoi[7] postcards are staring at you, smugly blaring out of every crack in the kiosks. Fortunately, they are occasionally interrupted by the wide shots (to the knees) of the Williams Truzzi sort.[8] We are buying a great navigator[9] and will send you this most cherished object of your maidenly dreams. […]

What a painful gravitation towards the accepted pattern of the entire resort: it's painful even to write it. Children, of course, Adochka, Nelli, Galya, Natella, Yurik, and so on. A bit of variation is introduced by the name of a boy called "Givi" (probably not of Christian origin), which is uttered with a piercing cry the whole day long by a series of different Armenian women from the top floor. The boy is very small, but, judging by the piercing quality of the cries, he is not deprived of initiative.

---

[6] [Trans.]: A prolific German film actor, director, and producer (active from 1912 to 1953), known for his action adventure films.

[7] [Trans.]: Evsei Osipovich Lyubimov-Lanskoi. Russian theater actor and director of the 1920s, known for realist productions about the Revolution, combining documentary and emotional qualities.

[8] [Trans.]: Williams Truzzi (1889–1931). Celebrated circus director and circus artist, part of the famous Truzzi circus dynasty, who worked in both the pre-revolutionary and post-revolutionary eras. He was at various times head of the Sevastopol, Moscow, and Leningrad circuses.

[9] [Trans.]: In the original: Покупаем великого навигатора. In the context I believe Eisenstein is referring to a large guidebook, and not without some irony. There would seem to be an additional innuendo, as a navigator can also be a guide to health matters. "The great navigator" is also a phrase referring to Columbus or Prince Henry the Navigator.

Of course, there is a "life of the party." An engineer, of course. […] During the day, he plays tag[10] with the children. In the evening, with the mothers. By night, he concerns himself, with making certain, that the mothers will continue to have children. The chase goes on. There is, of course, a couple, who've come to Gagra solely for this purpose. A belief exists, that the beauty of the place of conception determines the good disposition of the future child. Remember in Gogol, "when momma was expecting, the ram came in and began to bleat," and, the little one—subsequently, it seems, who became the Judge of the District Court,—in the whole lower part of his face, resembled a ram. Because of this, they avoid encountering buffaloes and stare from the dock in a wide shot at Gagra, for that, they even look through the ground glass of a camera. I don't think, they are taking pictures. But that doesn't seem to be helping. She is a bit sarcastic. He is especially anxious. For the same reason, by day, he shoots at the shooting gallery. She watches. According to Freud and this, in my opinion, is clear proof of the painful state… of the hearth. At the same time, the plywood walls of the shooting gallery are penetrated in all directions. Yesterday, they were painted over again in sky blue. But the penetrations aren't improving the color of things. And she remains sarcastic.

There is, of course, here, "an intelligent young man." Alas! You know, that intellectual beauty is always at the expense of the physical… And he is very intelligent. 3rd Floor, Room #42. This is a high class model. He knows, for example, that the worst sort, when speaking of engraving, finds expression in Dürer. In cinema, it is customary to show one's education by inserting into conversation the good name of "Grifschitz"[11]; for that reason, he speaks about Stroheim. At the Hermitage, he neglects Van Dyck but extols Van Eyck. Leonardo's "Dzhiokonda,"[12] of course, is not beautiful, rather the "Madonna Litta," etc. A very educated young man. Today I will have some fun with him on the subject of Japanese prints. I think, he'll "find himself in some trouble." But of course, the most difficult thing is the musicians in the restaurant here! There aren't too many of them. They are traditional to the point of indecency. […] They have one horrible characteristic: when they aren't playing, they wander around everywhere. Moreover, all the others suffer from this [characteristic] as well.

I am not going to run down your enduring ideology of the toiling masses. Otherwise, I would tell you about the class dislike of us, the "raznochintsy,"[13] and the

---

[10] [Trans.]: In the original: горелки [gorelki], which means "burner" but also refers to the game of tag.

[11] [Trans.]: Eisentein deliberately mocks the fashionable, clichéd references to D. W. Griffith by the young man, who mispronounces the name as if it were German. The normal transliteration is Гриффит [Griffit]; instead the intelligent young man says "Грифшитц' [Grifschitts].

[12] [Trans.]: Here, Eisenstein is mocking the young man's mispronunciation of "Gioconda." It is normally transliterated as Джоконда [Dzokonda], a fairly accurate phonetic transcription of the original. Instead, the boy adds an extra и [i] in the pronunciation: Джиоконда [Dziokonda], as if to imply he knows the original Italian Gioconda.

[13] [Trans.]: A 19th-century term for educated people not of the aristocracy.

aristocracy of the "health resort" and "sanatorium" crowd. Here, instead of noble-men's books, you find "health resort booklets." Whoever doesn't have them, walks around as if they were ashamed not to. In addition, he pays more for the same things. I'm not going to talk about the trip to Athos[14] either. I will only say, that "there is something miraculous there." There is much, which is infinitely interesting to be seen there, for 8 rubles, 50 kopeks, there and back; I shall recount upon our meeting in person. I am ending, because at the beginning of your letter you promised to write me just exactly as much in response. And it's necessary to spare your hands and your eyes in the name of victory on the non-acted front!

Farewell, beloved (Thierry Sandre *The Beloved*,[15] a novel, translated from French by M. E. Abkina, "Kniga" editions, Moscow—Leningrad), until our next meeting. In case of my death, do not wear a wedding dress, since I remain faithful to you with my entire soul [...]

S. Eisenstein

During times of "the pervasive sadness of my soul," my signature, which is usually made without a break, is supplied with a cross. As you see, the cross is lopsided, maybe, that's a good sign, I hope it is for you.

S.E.

Grisha,[16] of course, sends his regards.

---

[14] [Trans.] Mount Athos is site of a famed and ancient Orthodox monastery.
[15] [Trans.]: In the original: *Любимая* (*The Beloved*). This does not correspond in an obvious way to any titles by Sandre up to 1928, though his titles are replete with suggestions of romantic intrigue.
[16] [Trans.]: Presumably Grigory Alexandrov, Eisenstein's close friend and collaborator on several of his films.

2
S. M. Eisenstein to E. I. Shub

April 5, 1929, Tselina station

Esfir'!

Ok, here it is:

> I write to you—what would one more?
> What else is there that I could say... [17]

And I can say, that I don't want you to think me worse than ever, because I never managed to run into you [...]

I am writing to you from the most advanced outpost of the Construction of Socialism. From the sovkhoz "Gigant." You will see on the reverse side of this some typical landscapes of this blessed land. It doesn't make it into the frame, because it's keenly efficient.

You now have a complete understanding of our surroundings... (Yes, by the way: Christ is risen! Today is the first day of Easter.)

We live in the above-mentioned mansion. The owner is sharing it with us.

The owner...

She makes ice cream. Sells it at the bazaar. It's nasty.

She makes kvas. Sells it at the bazaar. It's nasty. (I think, that this kvas, by the feeling it produces in the stomach, should be the ideal medium for etching.)

In my opinion, she must have a secret brothel somewhere between the house and the cellar. The daughter, Shurochka. She's nasty.

She is surround by six women, who constantly scratch themselves, splash water around, cook, smoke, and create a hissing sound with the kerosene stove.

She firmly believes in god.

This is extremely useful to us: we comb our hair in the glass on the ikon for lack of mirrors.

Aside from that, the weather is tropical.

---

[17] [Trans.]: In the original: Я Вам пишу, чего же боле,/Что я могу еще сказать. These are the first two lines of Pushkin's "Letter from Tat'yana to Onegin" Book III, of Евгений Онегин (*Evgeny Onegin*). For accuracy, I have used Nabokov's translation, which preserves the rhythms but discards the rhyme scheme. Pushkin ends these lines with a question mark, Eisenstein with an ellipsis. The next two lines, implied by the ellipsis, which rhyme with these, are: Теперь, я знаю, в вашей воле/ Меня презреньем наказать: "'Tis now, I know, within your will/to punish me with scorn." Again, the Nabokov translation.

Animals are to be found here: cows (only a few), horses (many), lizards (very many green and gray ones).

Tractors. For the most part, also green and gray. They make a deafening noise, but they are so far away in the fields, they aren't audible. They plow and sow day and night (though nights are designated for quite different forms of entertainment. By the way, some of them are girls. That is, more precisely, they were that, now they are tractor drivers). It's hard to distinguish between them. They have gotten just as tan. They are just as completely covered in oil, and in just the same way, they cover everyone and everything with curse words. Nice girls.

It's strange to write to you. Like in a well. Or like a dog: I pull its tail from my end. From your end, there will be barking. But, this isn't possible in reverse: in a few days we'll finish shooting and take off out of here.

There's more:

This is how Buddhists pray: they chew paper and spit it at a statue. If it sticks, it's good. If it doesn't stick, it's bad. And Buddha can't answer. In this case, Buddha is sending something. Hopefully, this will stick. But you can't answer: hmmm…

Besides that, there's a driver[18] here: Wheat.[19] That's the last name. Swear to god. And it's quite suitable ethnographically, in terms of flora and fauna. Sometimes gives us lectures on the varieties of religions in the local area.

Imagine what kind of culture this is!

For 25 versts around, not a single church!!! […]

The fact is, that there are no churches, because, here, they are all members of sects. Baptists, New Israelites, Mormons, Pryguny, Molokans, Khlysty.[20]

Because of them, you would have to drag yourself for 30 versts on bad horses in order to receive a blessing in a church !!!! […]

Today we shot echelons of tractors being taken away to other sovkhozes. A great deal of pathos

In a couple of days, we are going to shoot a tractor parade. And on the First of May, we had a parade of troops in Rostov.[21]

---

[18] [Trans.]: In the original: возчик, implying he is driving a horse-driven vehicle.

[19] [Trans.]: In the original: Пшеница.

[20] [Trans.]: These are all rural heterodox sects, who broke away from the Russian Orthodox church.

[21] [Trans.]: In the original: А 1-го мая принимали парад войск в Ростове. As Masha Godovannaya points out, this is oddly ambiguous, or even contradictory. This was written in April, so he seems to be speaking about the future in the past tense. It is also ambiguous whether the subject is we or an impersonal they. So, with the verb used, this could mean: we saw, we shot, we had, we welcomed, or they held. Eisenstein was in Rostov-on-Don in November or December of 1927 during the shooting of *Old and New*. I am unaware of his whereabouts in May of 1928.

Comrade Kovtyukh was in command. He is "Kozhukh" of the *Iron Flood*.[22] The rest of the commanders were all heroes of the Red Cavalry and the *Red Cavalry* of Babel. Babel explained to us about them.

"Wheat" comes up to the window in a gray jacket…

Shurochka brought back from the bazaar the empty ice cream jars…

Our expedition went to shoot at the local shooting gallery.

I'm thinking about you.

…On the other side of the wall, "Wheat" is exchanging the triple kiss (Easter greeting) with Shurochka. They are exchanging "pysanki" (these are painted chicken eggs)…

I am thinking about you…

You must not fail to write me. Put it in an envelope and hand it over to me when I arrive.

S. Eisenstein

PS: In Rostov, I met with Kopalin. Stepanov is here. Almost died of pneumonia. Him, not me. The devil knows why! I can't get away from these neigroviks[23]!

Grisha sends his regards.

---

[22] [Trans]: In the original: *Железный поток*, a short story and then a novel by Alexander S. Serafimovich referring to events in the Russian Civil War, in which Kovtyukh took part. His character in the novel is called "Kozhukh." Eisenstein is said to have made several film proposals based on a stage adaptation of this novel.

[23] [Trans.]: In the original: неигровики [neigroviki], a slightly humorous neologism, to refer to Shub's fellow partisans of the non-acted film. Shub uses it as well elsewhere.

3
S. M. Eisenstein to E. I. Shub

September 19, Frankfurt

Well, how's your *SA*![24]

Yes! architecture! Some very nice people these Frankfurt architects; they took us to have a look at this curiosity and perversion of the principles of architecture! Some quite utilitarian forms and... a church. Will write to you from here to establish some architectural contacts. We spent hours on end here, utterly remarkably.

S. Eisenstein

4
S. M. Eisenstein to E. I. Shub

November 6, 1929, London

Dear Esfir' Il'inishna!

We've already been in London for a week. Of all we have seen so far, this city is the most remarkable. I am writing you now from Parliament: MacDonald has already spoken, as have Henderson and Baldwin. We are drinking tea and going to listen some more.

I've been writing a letter to you.

S. Eisenstein

---

[24] [Trans.]: In the original: *CA*. Contrary to the Russian editor (see their end note for letter #4), rather than Soviet Architecture, I believe it is more likely Современная архитектура [Sovremenaya Arkitektura] (Contemporary Architecture) to which *CA* [*SA*] refers, as it was designed by Shub's husband, Alexei Gan, who was also on the editorial board. Eisenstein says *your SA*; Shub had no connection to the other magazine of which I'm aware.

5
S. M. Eisenstein to E. I. Shub

November, 1929, Paris

Dear Esfir' Il'inishna!
Don't scold me for not writing. With all the complications in my life, things drag on badly. But in the meantime, I am still in Paris. Greetings from lace heaven. Greetings from Richter. We've met five times.
Yours always,

S. Eisenstein

6
S. M. Eisenstein to E. I. Shub

April, 1930, France

Here today, we are making up for the sins of the night before. Don't think, dear Esfir' Il'inishna, that I am forgetting about you, but there is simply no time at all to write— we are racing all around France.
Yours always,

S. Eisenstein

7
S. M. Eisenstein to E. I. Shub

1930, La Sarraz

Dear Esfir' Il'inishna!
We are sending warm greetings from this out of the way place, the palace of MM. Mandrot, where they are playing at having a Congress,[25] and we are resting in the bosom of nature.

S. Eisenstein
Gr. Alexandrov

---

[25] [Trans.]: Here, at the castle of an aristocratic Swiss patron of Modern Art, Hélène de Mondrot, Eisenstein is said to have participated in the making of a short experimental film called *The Storming of La Sarraz*, part of the activities of the 1er Congrès international du cinéma indépendant.

8

S. M. Eisenstein to E. I. Shub

April 7, 1930, England

Dear Esfir' Il'inishna!

Today I stepped onto the deck, to sail along for two weeks to New York, and then, to Hollywood. All the same, it's strange. I waited so long and then everything turned out and it happened in 10 days.

Soon, I will come to my senses and start writing. You absolutely must write me. You are very much in my debt.

Address: Notorious Film Center Paramount—Publix Corporation for me.

Hugs. Yours always,

Eisenstein

9

S. M. Eisenstein to E. I. Shub

May 17, 1930, New York[26]

Warm greetings from Atlantic City, where the Paramount annual meeting is taking place. Greetings to Anechka.[27] Don't forget me.

Yours always,

Eisenstein

10

S. M. Eisenstein to E. I. Shub

May 12, 1930, aboard the "Europe"

In the distance, you can see New York. Well, there you go, dear Esfir' Il'inishna, our journey is nearing its end: we get off in New York. The Atlantic Ocean was affectionate to the point that, "I couldn't take any more": hopefully it won't rock any more, so as not to embarrass the Russian land in the land of the Americas.

S.E.

---

[26] [Trans.]: For reasons unknown to me, the Russian editor has placed this letter of May 17 before the letter of May 12.

[27] [Trans.]: An affectionate diminutive, like "Annie." Presumably Shub's daughter, Anna, from her first marriage.

11
S. M. Eisenstein to E. I. Shub

June, 1930, Hollywood

Dear Esfir' Il'inishna!

It's totally impossible to write – So many things to do and so much to experience. But I don't understand at all, why you don't write anything. I'm current with how your work is going (via Pera), but only in very general terms; and you could, truly, write me about this and about yourself. About me too… You know how I value everything you think about me […]

Write me.

Instead of words, I'm sending you a series of images: pictures are always more expressive than words!

Sending you big hugs and am patiently waiting for letters about you, about cinema, about me!

Yours always,

Eisenstein

12
S. M. Eisenstein to E. I. Shub

May 29, 1930, New York

1. Dear Esfir' Il'inishna!

There's never any time to write! There are too many things to see and these postcards are the living proof of it. The "Institution" which I serve is the "Paramount Board."

2. The tallest building (another building taller than this one has not yet been completed).

3. This very building is drowning in the clouds (not bad!)

Give my regards to Anechka and do not forget the one devoted to you,

Eisenstein

4. The view from the roof of this building in clear weather.

NB: (in the distance, the Statue of Liberty).

13
S. M. Eisenstein to E. I. Shub

1930, New York

Dear Esfir' Il'inishna!

This is a just completed building. It's so tall, that from the seventy-first floor, it seems like I can see you: but that's an optical illusion. It's only the Statute of Liberty.

Four days speeding on an express train between here and the opposite coast, so that in a few days it can finally be decided whether or not *An American Tragedy* will come to be. I think, that this will solve the problem of the duration of our stay in these lands.

I will be sure to write you, whatever is finally decided, and in the meantime, I will get totally drunk on the Negro experience.[28]

Yours always, affectionately,

S. Eisenstein

14
S. M. Eisenstein to E. I. Shub

1930, Hollywood

Dear Esfir' Il'inishna!

I am a pig—but you're already used to that. You wrote me such a good remarkable letter (I heard it directly, like I used to hear your voice regularly on the phone) […] and I still haven't written you: but this is not out of thoughtlessness, on the contrary: I don't want to respond, "just any old way," but to answer really completely, but there's just no time at all. I am working really hard on the scenario for *An American Tragedy*—today we left for New York to consult with Dreiser. Write me what you think about this, but after you have clearly imagined to yourself how I will do it. You know me well enough for that.

Write.

With all my soul, your S. M.[29]

---

[28] [Trans.]: In the original: а пока до отвала напитаюсь негритянских впечатлений.

[29] [Trans.]: S. M.= Sergei Mikhailovich.

15
S. M. Eisenstein to E. I. Shub

July 4, 1931, Mexico

Dear friend Esfir' Il'inishna!

The color of the paper is the degree of the intensity of feelings of friendship towards you raging inside me! I was struck with sorrow by Pera's message that you consider yourself erased from my memory. This is a stupid, utterly dishonest untruth! I would have more grounds to make a similar "unseemly" claim: a lonely stranger in a foreign land, forgotten by you and by your letters.

We have wandered up and down the map of Mexico. Pushkin also wrote about us, "the rains wash them, dust covers them."[30] Work is complicated, difficult, multi-lingual, but fascinating as hell. I don't think about final results: after *General*,[31] I consider myself incompetent to judge the prospective qualities of my own productions. I didn't think I would survive after the fate it suffered, but time heals all wounds and perhaps the only trace that remains of it is, that I am interested in everything except… cinema. Cinema is engaging, as a "small experimental universe" in which it's possible to study the laws of much more interesting and meaningful phenomena than current pictures, which are nowadays accompanied by deafening noise and tiresome chatter. Maybe this is a quite logical period of "purification," because for a cinema, which is advancing, a complete re-configuration is required and not one stone will be left upon another stone of our dearly departed ones, sorry… [our] work. I am surrounded by living ethnography, more fascinating than any fiction film and more than even any documentary. There is a colossally interesting shift taking place in the viewer psychology of the USSR. I am receiving very scanty material, but even by means of it, the most curious changes in the viewer's pulse are making themselves felt… I would even risk writing an article about that, for I think, that it's better to feel that pulse from half-way around the globe. These shifts are not at all taking place where our everyday scribblers perceive them! I am writing all this exclusively for you: on the order of a phone conversation, which, alas, it will soon be two years since one has taken place. What are you doing now? What do you think—Which direction do you think things will go? […]

Sometimes, I feel like I would like to stage things in a theater. In a good one, a genuine one. My reaction to the cinema is just that strong. Although it seems, that I have never worked more earnestly than here and now.

---

[30] [Trans.]: From Pushkin's "Песнь о вещем Олеге" ["The Lay of the Wise Oleg"].
[31] [Trans.]: Eisenstein is here referring to his film *The General Line*.

The problems of montage do not occupy me in any way any longer and I'm afraid to say sound occupies me even less. It's interesting what comes of a picture shot in such circumstances?! Maybe, it will be just what's needed?! What a laugh that'll be!

Mexico is astonishing for me in particular: imagine a country where they crucified... my character. There is a range from one unseemly thing to another and a contrast to all my passions and interests you know! Well, I think, that I have befuddled you enough as punishment for your disbelief in me.

I await your letters: quick and detailed and remain with all my soul, always your

S. Eisenstein

See you soon!

16
S. M. Eisenstein to E. I. Shub

March 23, 1932, Mexico

Dear Esfir' Il'inishna!
Finally, after leaving Mexico, we are rushing home to Moscow.
Want to see you as soon as possible. Yours always,

S. Eisenstein

17
S. M. Eisenstein to E. I. Shub

March 27, 1939, Moscow

It's imperative you read the scenario today. Imperative you read it carefully. And imperative you bring it to me tomorrow at the factory.
I anxiously await your comments.

The old man

18
S. M. Eisenstein to E. I. Shub

December, 1939, Moscow

Dear loving friend Esfir'!

As you have noticed, I haven't written all this time. I didn't want to write, or even to live. I wanted to be like the grasses and grasses don't write letters. Somehow, I started to get better. And again, Mexico with its abominations, sends it all to hell. The people on whom everything depends are such bastards!

I received your kind letter and was deeply touched by it. Essentially, I am afraid to think about the questions raised: perhaps, it's the end after all? The last two days again a monstrous flood of gloom. I'm unlikely to catch a glimpse of the sun sparkling like diamonds...[32]

I want to go to Persia.

Perhaps, it will compensate in some way for the oozing wounds.

[...]

I'm putting the brakes on myself: I'm afraid of letting go—I can't contain myself.

So, don't pay any attention. Maybe it's just a whim... In any case, it's piggish of me to write this to you. You have your own things to worry about.

I'm waiting for letters from you (this time with your own signature and not... Fadeev's signature, like on the first letter. Although I am delighted and touched by it).

Big, strong hugs, dear Esfir'.

Your unhappy brother,

S. Eisenstein

---

[32] [Trans.]: As Masha Godovannaya pointed out to me, Солнце в алмазах echoes the phrase "небо в алмазах," meaning "a happy beautiful life" [heaven glittering like diamonds]. This phrase comes from *Дядя Ваня* [*Uncle Vanya*] by Chekhov from Sonia's monologue: "Мы отдохнем! Мы услышим ангелов, мы увидим все небо в алмазах, мы увидим, как все зло земное, все наши страдания потонут а милосердии...." ("We shall rest! We shall hear the angels, we shall see all heaven sparkling like diamonds, we shall see, how all earthly evil, all our sufferings will be drowned in compassion...") Since Sonya is speaking about what will happen after death, after all life's travails have ended, Eisenstein is adding a note of mocking self-pity.

19
S. M. Eisenstein to E. I. Shub

1946, Moscow

Dear Esfir'!

I was quite delighted by your note. On February 2nd, I made the final "cuts" on the picture, rushed over to the Dom kino and I thought, that starting tomorrow, I would begin to fulfill all my moral obligations: the very first one of which should be to visit you in the hospital, which I could not do earlier. And here it is: almost the "beautiful death" in Circe's embrace… But somehow I managed to get through it and am even getting better. But for the next two weeks, I can't even sit. Just as soon as they let me near a telephone, I will call you.

Get well soon!

An affectionate hug

Greetings

S. Eisenstein

Letters from E. I. Shub to S. M. Eisenstein

20
E. I. Shub to S. M. Eisenstein

November 4, 1929, Alupka (in transit)

Dear Sergei Mikhailovich!

Sending you October greetings! I very much want to know what you've been up to. How are you? What thoughts and plans do you have? Did you receive my letter?

Write me in Tiflis. General delivery. I intend to write you all my thoughts about the victory of unscrupulousness. In *Old and New*[33] no one understood, or caught sight of its deeply-principled nature.

Respectfully,[34] your friend,

E. Shub

21
E. I. Shub to S. M. Eisenstein

August 2, 1930, Moscow

Dear Sergei Mikhailovich!

I visited Pera, in order to write to you […] about myself briefly. I've been working a lot these past few months. The picture *Today* here and in America is, in many ways, typical of my work: curious. I know, that you would approve of it in many ways. If it is sent to Amtorg,[35] I will let you know. Arrange to see it and make sure to show it to some Americans, so that they can see Soviet views of American life.

---

[33] [Trans.]: The title of a revised version of *The General Line* which caused a great deal of criticism for Eisenstein.

[34] [Trans.]: The closing formulas of Russian letters of this period are a minefield for those wishing to bring them into English. One particular example is: жму руку, literally "I shake [your] hand." As Masha Godovannaya informs me, this gesture indicates admiration and respect, so: "Respectfully." Masha insists this should be literally translated, but this just doesn't work for me as a native English speaker. But there are also additional levels of жму руку: крепко жму руку (with great respect, literally: I firmly shake [your] hand), крепко крепко жму руку (with great great respect, literally: I firmly, firmly shake [your] hand) and крепчайше жму руку (and the superlative: with the greatest respect, literally, I most firmly shake [your hand]). And there are, no doubt, others.

[35] [Trans.]: In the original: Амторг [Amtorg], an acronym for Американская Торговля [Americkan-saya Torgovlya], approximately, "American Trade." It was the first trade representative of the Soviet Union in the United States. It acted as a film distributor among other things.

The GRK[36] made the picture Category 1. But the battle continues, and it's not a healthy one: the igroviks[37] vs. the documentalists. I'm very tired. On the 5th (of August) I'm going to take six weeks off to relax. [...] Well now, about you. This is the most complicated thing. You are so far away, you've been living an utterly different kind of life for almost a year. What do I think of you? You are near and dear to me and I have a complex anxiety for you, anxiety with minutes of joy and minutes of complicated and contradictory anxiety.

It's fine to gallop about the world. To see so much, as you have in such a short period, to see with your own eyes, to monitor what you have seen with your own brain. I know, that this year will be recorded as a year in your life of your intellectual growth. I know, that it's not about the pictures, which you made in Paris and will make in New York (although this is, in some way, important for you). It's important, how you will come back, it's important, what and how you want to and will do here.

And it's important, that you didn't live through this year with us.

You haven't lived with what we have. This year is remarkable in many ways: a severe, difficult, but wonderful Bolshevik year. You have been living far away, living differently; and I don't know, what would be more important for you, for your work—what is greater: Hollywood and the opportunities given to you now, or the zone[38] of continuous collectivization, right now, in 1930—even with our handmade, poor technology, a theme taken up and formulated by you in the cinema and not by others, etc. etc.

Do not take everything that I've written to you as the primitive ecstasy of a member of the intelligentsia. I don't know how to write. I love to talk with you and so very, very much has happened this year. Or maybe, we experience time differently here.

But I am your friend. And I want to be proud of you, and so, I do care what you are going to do now, there, with them. I would like for it to be *The Glass House*, but a little different from what we talked about, *The Glass House of 1930*. Without stars and, above all, violating the production traditions of Hollywood in every way. Don't seduce anyone, or be seduced yourself.

Forcefully, in the Eisenstein way, and this time especially, long live Cynicism!— your cynicism! Please, make the Americans a gift: something on the order of *The Glass House*.

---

[36] [Trans.]: In the original: Главрепертком [Glavrepertkom], a division of Narkompros, the People's Commissariat for Enlightenment, controlling the public display of films and stage productions.

[37] [Trans.]: In the original: игровики [igroviki]. This term is a plural and is used by Shub and Eisenstein to refer to those favoring fiction films over documentary films. It means essentially "the partisans of acted films." It is paired with неигровики [neigroviki], that is, those who are against acted films. Here it is the igroviks vs. the dokumentalists.

[38] [Trans.]: In the original: район [rayon].

It was difficult to start. Now, I will write you frequently. And you write me. I want, on arriving in Moscow, to find both a reply and a letter. Don't forget me.
All the best to you,

Yours, Esfir' Il'inishna

22
E. I. Shub to S. M. Eisenstein

October 3, 1930, Moscow

Dear Sergei Mikhailovich!
I rested for two months in the Caucasus. I had hoped to receive an answer to my letter in Moscow. Instead of a letter, I received the photos of you and Chaplin. They made me very happy, but I would have been even happier to receive a letter from you. I'd like to know as much as possible about you, from you directly.

From Pera, I learned, that you selected Dreiser's novel *An American Tragedy* to work on. I know this novel well. You must have been interested in showing the diversity of social and societal layers of America. I think that's right. The truth of life, well, let's say, the fate of the hero of the novel is utterly dependent on all this, in Dreiser's view. There's no way you can escape this, no matter how thoroughly you would like to preserve Dreiser's elevated "spirituality" and "humanity."

From there, comes the fourth to tenth stage of *A Woman of Paris*. Don't get angry, my dear. I love terribly much seeing you and Chaplin looking at each other (Chaplin is remarkable), but this is not a crossroads in your creative path. You are a man of a different kind of fury, different lyricism, different love from Chaplin. And I love your cynicism (there is also something else in you), when, because of some complex inner feelings, with this cynicism, you hide a still utterly youthful romanticism behind the business-minded, tough guy of Soviet days.

It's not entirely clear to me, what you are going to do with sound for this subject. Do you realize, that there is enormous interest in America, growing every day across broad segments of Soviet society. It's revealing, that Ludwell Denny's book,[39] this year had an utterly remarkable success, not only with the reading public, but among political leaders. No point in writing you, I think, about what is dictating this extraordinary interest. Will *An American Tragedy* made by Sergei Eisenstein be capable of satisfying this interest. Think that over. Carefully.

---

[39] [Trans.]: Shub is most likely referring to *We Fight for Oil*, published in 1928.

And one more thing (but this is less important): do you realize the friendly and hostile expectations, which are being assigned to your American work. Forgive me for writing to you about this, without knowing all the circumstances at play. You are to blame. As a friend, I am keenly interested in everything connected with you and your work. It's possible, I am wrong. It will be more evident to you there. Have you been thinking about your adaptation of *An American Tragedy*? There are a lot of interesting possibilities for sound there too. And after that, the citadel of New York, shot by you, would, I think, present enormous interest for Americans as well.

I am waiting for your letter. After I receive it, many things will become clearer and more distinct […].

The "atmosphere" surrounding you has completely cleared up. You have real friends. We are protecting you. We are waiting for you calmly, not impatiently, but we are waiting for you with great anticipation.

Wishing you well in everything,

Esfir' Shub

23
E. I. Shub to S. M. Eisenstein

September 9, 1931, Moscow

Dear Sergei Mikhailovich!

I am finally managing to write to you. The days pass restlessly and in confusion with few hours of quiet. I often think about you, about your work, about your imminent return, about how you will determine your position here, and how your existence here will be determined. I am glad you will soon be in Moscow and more than anything, I fear delays. You need to return to the USSR as soon as possible. This is the first time I've written to you in this way and knowing my love and friendship, you will understand, that I have considered this in many aspects. I know, that you are having a lot of difficulties with your Mexican work, I know, that you are passionate about it, that likely a whole series of your objectives is assuming a particular urgency in the process of realizing them on the basis of material, that is completely new for you. I understand all this quite well and I feel it even more, but I say all the same: you need to return quickly. I know how you put together the material for *The Battleship*, I know about the twists and turns of *October* and *The General Line*, I know the characteristic, which distinguishes you from everyone else: do not remain captive to the initial conception of the scenario, understand and listen to the material in its semantic and filmic quality alone and subordinate it to you, subordinate it to the new concept, which arose in the process of work.

Don't get angry, dear, that I so brazenly, from across the ocean, claim, that the material you have already shot is enough for your new work. I saw all your photos at Pera's. At first, I was waiting for shots connected with my own imagination about Mexico. From everything I know about it, from all I remembered most, what came to mind was *Insurgent Mexico*,[40] by the remarkable John Reed. But after that, I understood and became very interested in what you are doing. I think, that it's all accurate and very interesting.

I believe, that your Mexico will be a discovery and a revolutionary discovery. I would like to explain to you concisely and quite completely, why I am urging you and so insistently asking you to return. It is quite impossible to write about this. It's necessary to speak, in order to understand one another completely, to overcome and to strike out the two immense years, which have separated us, but I somehow think presumptuously, that even at a distance, I know what you are living through, what determines your intellectual daily life, with such an inordinately developed brain. And that is your particular quality.

A small advance party of fellow film directors and allies (I don't know about you but these terms make me cringe), confronted by the great events of recent years, have finally resolved to transform themselves internally, in order to organically connect their creative abilities with the tasks and goals of the country, that is building socialism. […][41]

24
E. I. Shub to S. M. Eisenstein

1934, Moscow

Dear Sergei Mikhailovich!

I have been waiting, waiting for the letter you promised, but you remain silent. Such is women's lot: whomever we love, "we spoil." So, I am writing you. Not so many "events and developments" have taken place during your absence, all the same a few things have taken place. I am going to write to you about them. Perhaps it will entertain you.

First: *Aerograd*.

The press, as you know, praises it. […] Now, my opinion—and this might be of interest to you—*Aerograd* I consider something significant, I consider it an artistic phenomenon, something very Dovzhenko. I am waiting impatiently for a word from you [about it]. I don't want to write in great detail about *Aerograd*. We will talk in person. […] They showed Ehrenburg some excerpts of your work. I don't know

---

[40] [Trans.]: In the original: *Революционная Мексика* (*Revolutionary Mexico*).
[41] [Shub's note]: The letter breaks off here. The final page is not preserved.

which ones. I think, that without you there, it wasn't worth doing. He was in ecstasy about the material of the boy, but he doesn't much like Orlov or Rzheshevsky's lines. Much of what he said to me, it seems, is worthy of attention. But I would like to talk to you about it in person. I so warmly wish you success in your work, that I feel a personal passion for everything, that touches upon it. Hope that's ok. I have been led to a number of conclusions about both *Aerograd* and many other things, which I have been thinking about, the most important of which was the Stakhanovite rally, that I finally managed to attend. All this is directly connected with thoughts about your work. But I want to have a chat with you about this, since in my communications with you in person, you forgive my inarticulateness and always catch onto the main thing that worries me and what I want to get across to you. You see what a lengthy conversation awaits you!

I've tucked away one story for you. I'll give you the pleasure of that later. Writing about myself makes me sad… But I'm completely calm, because more than ever before, *I know*, that I have come to understand many things better, that I've gotten *smarter*, and the most important things are, that my brain and my eyes have not betrayed me, and that I'm always ready to work.

A big kiss,
your *Esfir'*.
When are you arriving?
Send even just a telegram, so that I know you haven't forgotten about me completely.

25
E. I. Shub to S. M. Eisenstein and Pera Atasheva

October 5, 1934, Smyrna

Dear and most warmly beloved friends!
I very much wanted to write to you together. On the 21st, I left for Smyrna. We went through the Bosphorus—through the Sea of Marmara, the Dardanelles, the Aegean Sea. We passed alongside the Isles of Lesbos, alongside Troy. The Governor of Smyrna showed us Smyrna and the surrounding area. Ask Zarkhi to tell you about him and you will understand this trip in all its picturesque aspects.

We shot the ruins of Pergamon for four days and I got completely frantic. In spite of the terrible heat, of working in the mountains, of all of the difficulties of this work, I was happy to see the ruins, which had been preserved for thousands of years, of a city of unfathomable beauty: the temples, the layout of the town, the great halls, the theaters, the Circus, gymnasiums, baths, statues, columns, fortresses, towers—all this, the result of Cycolpean labor and on everything the stamp of genius and beauty—

it is an enormous work of art. A theater for fifteen thousand spectators, an amphitheater running from the base to the summit of a great mountain. Along the mountain range, sitting at the top, a voice coming from the stage is audible. At the foot of the stage is a white marble temple to Dionysos. In the temple to Dionysos, I found a water supply system. I especially thought of you, Sergei Mikhailovich. Among other things, I wanted to hear from you, what sort of spectacles took place in such a theater. A few days ago, we went into the mountains, devil knows where. There, in the mountains, on the banks of a mountain lake, I shot the dances of the zeybeks.[42] As you see, I am traveling a lot, I am seeing much that is interesting, but I am not completely satisfied, as I clearly understand, that a significant work cannot be accomplished—the "boss" is repulsive. He himself doesn't know what he wants. He is a cunning, cruel, tasteless tyrant. He is greedy. He is concerned with arranging his own political and business affairs. I'm afraid I will run out of self-restraint. I will edit Pergamon and Smyrna for him and slip away. I really want to shoot Istanbul. It would be really interesting to do, but I'm convinced, this won't be possible. For personal reasons, the "boss" is less interested in Istanbul. There's a lot I can't write about in a letter.

I've gotten sunburned, bitten by midges, my lips are blistered by the sun and I'm tired.

I want to know about you, dear. What about the theater? Is anything working out yet? What about a book? What's the mood? […] Write to me about yourself and don't forget me.

Pera, I'm not going to tell you what to write about—you yourself know. You know how much I need your letters, you are the closest to me.

Tomorrow, I will begin to shoot Smyrna. I'm leaving here for Istanbul on the 15th or 16th of October. Write me in Istanbul. I am living in our embassy there. You have the address.

A big kiss to you both, individually and together.

yours Esfir'

Greetings to Zarkhi, Ol'ga Viktorovna, and the others.

---

[42] [Trans.]: Zeybek is actually the name of the dance, rather than the dancers.

26
E. I. Shub to S. M. Eisenstein

January 23, 1934, Moscow

Dear friend!

Today is really a festive day for me and, in the midst of my spiritual gloom, it is more than words can say, to tell you how dear you are to me and what a joy it is, that you live in our great world.

May the day not come anytime soon, not even in a fairy tale, when you say, "My plans have strangled me."

You live *three lives*.[43]

Live a long life. Flourish in eternity!

Kisses,

Esfir'

27
E. I. Shub to S. M. Eisenstein

August 25, 1938, Moscow

"Everything, which exceeds the limits of the familiar, receives the harshest interpretation, for your taste runs contrary to what is above it, and what is below it" (de Montaigne).

Dear old man! I wish everything for you, everything that is most remarkable, "which exceeds the limits of the familiar."

E. Shub
The Summer of *Alexander Nevsky*

---

[43] [Trans.]: Shub seems to be alluding to the Russian saying, that you live three lives: the first ends with the loss of naiveté, the second with the loss of innocence, and the third with the loss of oneself.

28
E. I. Shub to S. M. Eisenstein

October 6, 1939, Moscow

Dear old man! Yesterday, I returned from Kislovodsk. I am rested, have gotten healthy, and calm. Pera is still in Kislovodsk. The poor dear is still very ill.

Frequent dizziness and vomiting. The concussion, evidently, was serious.

I have not yet seen anyone in Moscow. At the moment, Moscow is quite strange.

How are you? How is work? When will we see you again? Rumor has it, that the material you sent is very interesting. I'm so glad.

Write me about yourself. I miss you a lot. There's a lot I want to talk to you about.

Warmest greetings to Edouard.

In a few days, I will write you in more detail about Moscow and people here.

With great respect and kisses,

Esfir'

29
E. I. Shub to S. M. Eisenstein

1942, Moscow

Dear Sergei Mikhailovich!

Sending warm greetings. If you only knew, dear, how far behind the front lines you are living!

Here, things are in a state of alarm. Moscow is a wartime city and is at war. I remember the heat in Alma-Ata and the whole measured silence of the life in the countryside, of the residents of the "Laureatnik"[44] as if it were a dream.

I am working hard and a great deal. I go back and forth between Potylikha, the newsreel archive, and the Committee. Potylikha[45] is overgrown with grass and weeds. Utter silence.

---

[44] [Trans.]: Shub is referring to the residence, housing the filmmakers of elite status evacuated to Alma-Ata to work on projects during the war, including Eisenstein and herself, among others. In the Soviet Union, various prizes and decorations were awarded to artists, scientists, and workers who were judged to have made outstanding contributions to the Soviet Union, among them the Lenin Prize, the Stalin Prize, and various ranks, such as Decorated Artist of the Soviet Union. A person who had received such a prize or rank would be referred to as a Лауреат, that is, a Laureate. So, the residence acquired the nickname of Лауреатник "Laureatnik," which might be translated as "Laureate House," but with a touch of irony.

[45] [Trans.]: Shub refers to Mosfil'm using the name of the street on which it is located.

So painful, it makes me sick.

I saw the Ehrenburgs, Fadeev; Solntseva and Agapov were there—there is a lot of news about each of them, but I won't be writing about them. Pera is preparing an American Festival to which she intends to invite you and Kozintsev. Will you come? My view is that it will be worth it. [...]

I see Pera often. Greetings to Magarill and Kozintsev and Marina Ladynina[46] and Raizman.

Kisses,

Esfir'

Are you taking care of my property?

30
E. I. Shub to S. M. Eisenstein

1944, Moscow

Dear Sergei Mikhailovich!

Did you get any nearer Moscow this time? You are greatly missed. And you need to be here. Both to live and to work, in spite of the many difficulties, you will be better off here than in Alma-Ata. Comrade Polonsky already told you all the news about the Cinema Committee. [...] Both Vishnevsky and Dovzhenko were very interested in you and asked about you in detail. [...] Your film is becoming the stuff of legends here. So, continue and appear wielding thunderbolts in a blaze of lightning. Jupiter does, as Jupiter will do.[47] [...]. Pera is quite busy with the Jubilee edition of *25 Years of Soviet Cinema*. I'm sorry, that you are not among the guests at the Narkomindel[48] and VOKS[49] receptions. Don't forget me.

Esfir'. Write.

---

[46] [Trans.] Marina Ladynina was a stage and screen actress, having started with the Moscow Art Theater. In film she worked from the silent period through the sound era, starring in *Tractor Drivers* among many other films. She was a People's Artist of the USSR and received the Stalin Prize five times, among other honors.

[47] [Trans.]: In the original: Юпитер—так Юпитер.

[48] [Trans.]: In the original: Наркоминдел, an acronym for Народный комиссариат по иностранным делам СССР [Narodny komissariat po inostrannym delam SSSR] (The People's Commissariat of Foreign Affairs of the USSR).

[49] [Trans.]: In the original: ВОКС, an acronym for Всесоюзное общество культурной связи с заграницей [Vsesoiuznoe Obshchestvo Kul'turnoi Sviazi s zagranitsei] (The All-Union Society for Cultural Relations with Foreign Countries).

31
E. I. Shub to S. M. Eisenstein

1946, Moscow

Dear Sergei Mikhailovich, my closest and dearest friend!

I returned home and found out what happened to you. I am very upset. I know you are better now and that soon you will be completely fine. You can and must be completely healthy. You must organize your life, so that nothing remotely like what has occurred, can ever occur again.

Everywhere, they are saying, that the color sequence of *Ivan* produces the same stunning impression as *Potemkin* did in its time and they praise all the rest as well. [...].

I have my leg in a cast until the 7th of March, the pain is still intense and I am lying down. My phone number is G 1–14–75.

When you have the opportunity, call me. I think about you a lot. During these two months of illness, I have been doing a lot of thinking. The time and the pain were enough. I have managed to think through some things. Wishing you everything wonderful and the main thing is health, complete health.

Kisses for you,

Esfir'

Letters of A. A. Fadeev to E. I. Shub

32
A. A. Fadeev to E. I. Shub

September 24, 1933

Dear Esfir'!

I write, knowing, that this letter either will not reach you at all, or will reach you in a month and a half. We're sitting here at Nikolaevsk-on-Amur, which we reached by plane—we flew over utterly wild and devilishly beautiful places and tomorrow we leave by sea for Vladivostok. Everything here, in the [Khabarovsky] krai, happens in such an unusual way, it seems so unlike anything Russian, that to write about it in a letter is a sacrilege, it is nearly impossible. It would be possible to write dozens of scripts and novels with this material, but the facts of this reality beat anything you could think up. Our heads are bursting! Dovzhenko and I have already discussed the fact, that it would be possible to properly reflect the Far East, working according to your method, relying only on the facts, and we were sorry, that you were not with us. How are you, my dark-haired one? We think about you quite often and say, "She's going to have a laugh when we tell her about that." Don't fret about life's hardships, my friend! With great respect and hugs.

A.

I will write you from Vladivostok with the details about everything.

33
A. A. Fadeev to E. I. Shub

November 14, 1933, Koshkaroevka

Dear sweet Esfir'!

I have already sent you several letters and telegrams, but whether you have received them, I am unaware, since we are roaming around the kind of forests that no letters reach, nor could reach. Here's a cursory account of our route: Moscow to Khabarovsk, from Khabarovsk by train to Birobidzhan and by car traveling around the Jewish kolkhozes. Next, Khabarovsk to Nikolaevsk-on-Amur by plane (ah! I failed to mention a trip to the Gol'di,[50] on the Tunguzka River by motor boat)—here for a few days we traveled by boat along the Amur Liman (saw fisheries and canning factories) and—from the hills, on horseback we saw our military fortifications. Next,

---

[50] [Trans.]: A previous designation of the Nanai people of the Amur River Basin.

by steamship to Vladivostok by way of Sakhalin (we saw the fisheries). From Vladivostok by boat to a sovkhoz breeding animals for fur (deer, raccoons, arctic foxes) then by handcar to the Kapgauz station (they are building a new branch line of the railroad through the most formidable taiga and hills) and in a coal car (we were coated in dust like devils!) to the mines at Suchan. From Suchan we went over taiga trails (in total 300 kilometers) to the Ulakhin Valley, where I grew up. This trip through the taiga has gone on for more than a month. Winter caught up with us in the taiga, but spirits are high. We are now in Koshkarovka village in fur coats bestowed on us from the manly shoulders of some Old Believers, gray-haired and with intelligent faces, looking like Decembrists in exile. We eat grouse and rabbits, which we kill ourselves, and are planning in the next few days to go for a big game hunt on the taiga for several days with a group of local hunters. In one of the villages, a famous Ussuri hunter, a companion of Arsen'ev and a friend of the Gol'di, Dersu Uzala, became our constant companion: a peasant from Varvarovka village, Vasily Tarasovich Glushak. He is an old tiger and bear hunter (he took as many as 30 tigers alive and, as he himself says, killed "countless numbers" of them). We are quite fond of him. Imagine a fifty-year-old bogatyr with unusually bright, childlike eyes, fists like frying pans, modest and somehow pure both physically and morally. After this hunt, we will travel, most likely, along the border with Korea and China, afterwards, we will return to Khabarovsk by dog sled — we will travel north to the new city of Komsomol'sk, which is under construction, and, only then, on to Moscow. We will be in Moscow around January 1. Everyone sends you their warm greetings. Sending lots of kisses. How is your life there? How is work?

Sasha.

34
A. A. Fadeev to E. I. Shub

January 17, 1935, Vladivostok

Dear sweet Esfir'!

I am writing to you at your Moscow address in the hope that you have already arrived. As soon as I arrived in Khabarovsk from Moscow, I received your note from Odessa with the Istanbul address and sent a letter. A month and a half or more after returning from the trip to the Amur region, I received a postcard. I understood, that my letter hadn't been received by you and that before the postcard, you had written me something, that I also did not receive. It was sad and painful and hopeless, like in a bad dream: they are ascribing awful things to you, you are moving your lips, but you can't be heard, and everyone turns their backs on you. I have to begin again. […]

I traveled around the region a great deal and saw lots of wonderful things and wrote a lot. I think, that at the beginning of March, I will finish the third part. My personal life was destroyed utterly and completely and it looks like I will have to start everything over again from the beginning. It was difficult at first, but now it's easier and I feel, I still have a lot of strength left. And the closer I am to the lives and work of so many, many splendid people, the more I become convinced, that at the end of the day, I am not the worst among them, and that I will still do much that is splendid. [...] I will not leave the [Khabarovsky] krai until I finish *The Udege*.[51] That is my firm decision. Unless the Central Committee calls me. I'm thinking of going to Kamchatka in the spring. How were your travels, dearest Esfir'? And how is work? Starting in my childhood, the word Turkey for me has been connected with something fairytale-like. If I had gone there, I would probably have become disenchanted: the People probably live in poverty, government officials steal, the natural world resembles Crimea, there are no more clever people than there are in other countries. Don't you think? Write me in great detail about everything. I think of you often, dearest Esfir', and I think that with your mastery, what is most important and interesting remains for you to create. With great respect and kisses.

A.

Don't be discouraged, don't be discouraged about life.

A.

35
A. A. Fadeev to E. I. Shub

1935, Vladivostok

Dear sweet Esfir'!

I received your telegram long ago and I answered, but came down with the flu (for the second time this month) and only now have had the opportunity to write. I am very grateful to you for the books, especially for Belinsky. I have been studying the questions of theater and dramaturgy rather seriously (in the secret hope of writing some sort of play) and in these questions Belinsky has been particularly indispensable and useful to me. The fact is, I have no opportunity to write you which books would be desirable for me to have. Firstly, I have no idea where, when, and what is getting published and secondly, the scope of my reading is currently rather strictly limited to questions of political economics and philosophy (I deliberately set this up for myself with the most honest, "local"[52] and "self-educational" goals) and I read little for my

---

[51] [Trans.]: An indigenous people living in Primorsky Region and Khabarovsk Region. Here Fadeev refers to his uncompleted novel, *The Last Udege*.

[52] [Trans.]: In the original земский [zemsky] which Fadeev places in quotation marks. It is an adjective referring to a zemstvo, an elected local district assembly. This post-Emancipation reform allowed a zemstvo to function semi-autonomously to deal with local issues. During the Soviet era, this system

own pleasure. The nicest thing which has happened in my life recently, is that I have finished the third part of *Udege*. I sent more than half of it to *Krasnaya Nov'*,[53] the remainder I will clean up a bit and send along in the next few days. It's possible, I will start on part 4 right away, if not, then I'll write a story for *Pravda*. No later than the 20th of June, I am leaving for Kamchatka, and, as a result, our correspondence will be interrupted until the middle of August. By the way, you are mistaken when you write, that I somehow didn't answer your letter. […] I sent you a telegram immediately. […] However, until this letter of yours from Sochi, I had no answer. That you are alive, I can only guess by the absence of obituaries in the newspapers; I had been thinking, that you […] had gone off somewhere and I was very happy to receive your letter. I recently saw *The Peasants* by Ermler and I got upset, that I had a different assessment of the picture than Eisen[stein]: with the exception of two, or three good moments, all the rest is intolerably false, a lie, and boring. And the animation insert is just a cheap trick. For all its shortcomings, there is, in *Maxim's Youth*, great realism and an inner generosity. For the most part, I actively dislike all Ermler's pictures, though he seems very nice to me; so this dislike, clearly, is not accidental. Dear sweet Esfir', send me a telegram, when you receive this letter; I think that a telegram will still get to me here. When I return from Kamchatka, I will write you. With great respect and hugs. I wish you good cheer, success in life.

Greetings to Eisen[stein] and Pera.

A.

36
A. A. Fadeev to E. I. Shub

March 1, 1935, Vladivostok

Dear sweet Esfir'! I received your letter about the characteristics of the Turks: a lot of fun was had (at least they weren't groping each other, were they, the devils?) And above all, I was glad, that your travels went well, that you are working, that the tone of your letter is cheerful, and even in your handwriting a firmness can be felt. If this is (more or less) the defining tone in all aspects of your life now, then I'm very happy for you. A couple of days before I wrote you a letter at the address of the GUKF,[54] I wrote to Eisen[stein] (I forgot the exact apartment number), did he receive it? It's marvelous, that he took on the picture. I believe in the talent of this man, like a cliff of granite, because his talent inheres in the quality of his great mind, besides all the

---

was replaced with local soviets, i.e. councils.
[53] [Trans.]: In the original: *Красная Новь* (*Red Virgin Soil*), a thick, monthly Soviet literary magazine.
[54] [Trans.]: In the original: ГУКФ, an abbreviation for Главное управление кинофотопромышленности [Glavnoe upravlenie kinofotopromyshlennosti] (Chief Directorate of the Film and Photo Industry).

other qualities. And talents of this kind are as hardy and indestructible as life itself—they come to an end only with the death of the vehicles, which carry them. Talents of this kind are able to pass through—or more truthfully, cannot fail to pass through—periods of doubting their strengths, of suffering, of mistakes (of seeking in the wrong directions), of "crises" and silence, but inevitably declare themselves again and again, at times when no one is waiting for anything anymore from them, it is often difficult to determine, which hole they will spring out of again: alive, enriched, rejuvenated, and pugnacious as the devil himself. Eisen[stein] is one of those. I sometimes feel, that he doubts himself and confers power on others and makes them superior: "How is it," he says, "that they live peacefully and confidently, when I suffer so much!" But the still courageous old man Goethe (whose verses I cannot abide) said: "Our [artists'—A. F.] imagination, by its very nature, is inclined to carry around elevated [one should say, great—A. F.] thoughts, nourished by the fantastical images of poetry, and fabricates for itself an entire series of sublime beings, below which we stand, and everything except us, is magnificent, and every other individual, besides us, is perfect. And this is completely natural. So often we must convince ourselves, that we lack much; and it is precisely what we lack, that we attribute to others, whom we endow in this case, not only with everything we ourselves possess, but as well, with some ideal satisfaction and tranquility. And there you have the lucky individual, the product of our own fantasy. On the contrary, if we, in our weakness and sluggishness, start calmly to work, it often turns out, that we, with our maneuvering and swaying from side to side, achieve more than others, with their sails and oars, and then we come to the authentic consciousness of our own strengths, being convinced, that not only are we not lagging behind the others, but from time to time we even overtake them…" Frankly, the old man, though verbose, was honest and hardly stupid. Eisen[stein] is now going through all this in order "to calmly set to work" and not only to arrive "at an authentic consciousness of his own strengths," but as well, to once again *show his strength to others* […]. Do I need to say, Esfir', how much I wish you success and how happy I am, that you are living and working, you are so smart and such a beauty! My life is monotonous: I write, I stroll around in the woods, I read Shakespeare, whom it's possible to properly understand [only] after the age of 30, when in human experience, in aggregate form, one's own thoughts, passions, and nastiness emerge. Here, it's spring: pussy willows are scattering into the air, the daffodils are coming out from under the leaves, sometimes loose warm snow falls and melts right then; Red commanders (I live not far from the Red Army sanatorium) press their girlfriends against the trees, embracing them with their huge hands—the girlfriends emit dove-like cooing and I envy the commanders. Sometimes I travel to Vladivostok and stroll around the places of my childhood. […] I'm even-tempered, hardworking, but I'm getting too old for my mood to be "serene" and expressing myself Byronically:

...Everywhere, the year sounds out a mournful groan
And demon thought disturbs me...[55]
Write, dear sweet Esfir'. Kisses. You will make me happy with just the books.
Send them. Stay healthy, go to the baths, don't drink wine, and don't put money in a
savings bank.[56]

A.

37
A. A. Fadeev to E. I. Shub

January 16, 1935, Sukhumi

Dear sweet Esfir'!
I only received one letter from you. I didn't answer at once because I was
lying in bed: I was knocked down by a truck, but for the most part, everything has
turned out fine and now I'm quite healthy again. Due to this forced break, my work
has also stalled somewhat. Currently, it's difficult to "get back into form." At least I
have been reading Hamsun to my heart's content (I had already read all of Hamsun's
early work) and have been under his influence for a long time. And this, in spite of
his extraordinarily wretched attempts to philosophize on the manifestly reactionary
quality of "ideals." I have even become convinced, that he is a bit dull-witted, in the
larger human sense (not pretending to be in Pushkin's sense, but just a bit dull-witted).
But he is possessed of good common sense and an enormous, natural, animal talent.
This, combined with neurasthenia (and the cunning of a Norwegian muzhik[57]) is
what constitutes his individual peculiarity. The old man read a whole lot of Nietzsche
(whence *Pan*,[58] whence all the philosophy of *Mysteries*). But all these considerations

---

[55] [Trans.]: This is a prose translation of Fadeev's slightly altered version of the sixth stanza of a poem
called TO INEZ inserted between stanzas LXXXIV and LXXXV of Canto the First of *Childe
Harold's Pilgrimage* by Lord Byron. Byron's original lines are these: "Still, still pursues, where'er I
be,/The blight of life—the demon Thought." One Russian version is as follows: "Везде звучит мой
скорбный стон.../И демон дум меня тревожит." The Russian verse maintains the meter and rhyme
scheme of the original. A prose translation of this version would be: "Everywhere, sounds out my
mournful groan.../And demon thought disturbs me." Fadeev has altered this slightly, inserting лет
[let] (the year).

[56] [Trans.]: I am informed by Masha Godovannaya and Yuri Tsivian that this bit of advice about wine
and money seems to be an echo of Il'f and Petrov.

[57] [Trans.]: In the Soviet Era and especially in the era of Agricultural Collectivization, a muzhik is a
grasping, selfish devious kind of peasant, holding on to the old ways, as distinguished from the heroic
крестянин [krestyanin].

[58] [Trans.]: The original has Глан [Glan], which seems to be a mistake by the compositor for Пан
[Pan], the title of one of Hamsun's novels, since Глан [Glan] has no meaning in Russian and there is
no work by that title by Hamsun.

come afterwards and when you read him, you'll be blinded by tears. I read *Fiesta* and *Death of a Hero* again. The former is really great! The latter I didn't finish; because the "hero" is of very little interest, and the author takes him too seriously; mainly, it gets boring. But certain parts are good, especially what relates to the hero's parents and his wife. I got together with the Dovzhenkos here. They aren't staying at the Sinop,[59] but nearby, at the resort: Ordzhonikidze. [...] Tomorrow I'm leaving for Sochi to meet Valya. [...] Valya's arrival is a great joy for me.

I'm glad, dear sweet Esfir', that you are working. It's foolish, that you didn't put your name on that work,[60] which is insignificant (*from your* point of view). It would be useful for you in a *social* sense. Convey my warmest greetings to Eisen[stein] and write to me in detail about how his efforts are going.

With great respect and hugs, dear Esfir'

A.

38
A. A. Fadeev to E. I. Shub

April 7, 1936, Sukhumi

Dear sweet Esfir'!

I haven't written you for a long time; this is explained by the fact that I have been pushing and pushing forward on the fourth part and am completely crazy with work. I can no longer stand it here (unlike in the Far East, my life here, if I weren't writing, would be meaningless), and I can't yet see the end of this part, though almost. My nerves are so worn out, that I, literally, cannot engage in anything else and I don't even read anything. The only relief was at the end of March, when Kolya Shengelaya, who was suffering from pneumonia, came here for a few days. [...]

With enormous labor and boredom, I got through Tynyanov's *Pushkin*. Not because it's badly written — it's well written — but because in the novel, there is no motivating conflict, everything is descriptive, static, there is a monotonously ironic tone, and even in the language, there is some sort of monotonous, tiresome sense of rhythm (although the language, as it were, isn't bad: quite balanced in its archaic quality and in its simplicity). But the main thing, when I finished reading it, I understood, that all this was well known for a long time. But there is much which is good

---

[59] [Trans.]: Judging by Fadeev's reference in a later reference (letter #40) to the Hotel Sinop, it would seem he is referring to the hotel here.

[60] [Trans.]: It would be interesting to know which work this refers to, or how often she resorted to this practice. She also neglected to put her name on her 1949 hymn of praise to Comrade Stalin, *От чистого сердца* [*Ot chistogo serdtsa*] (*With Heartfelt Sincerity*).

and even beautiful: Vasily L'vovich and Sergei L'vovich: this is quite nuanced work, it is amazing how one feels, that they are different and they are brothers; the old man Gannibal.[61] There is much which is particularly tangible, everyday, that in application to the historical novel constitutes an indisputable advantage. Speransky wasn't bad while I was reading, but now, when I put the novel aside, Tolstoy's Speransky blots things out and I no longer see Tynyanov's. With regard to Pushkin himself: only in the "Lycée" chapter does one begin to get a feeling for character, but in "Childhood"— no. This isn't good. This is the principal shortcoming. Children, for the most part, have their own individual identity and children of genius especially. But, all in all, this work is, undoubtedly, of great significance and clearly has an entire future ahead of it. Concerning boredom, I, myself, have committed this sin.

Here spring is in full swing. Lots of trees have become white in color. And besides that, there's the sea. Dolphins. Little dolphins. But none of this is for me. I am vividly imagining sitting in your attic and tormenting you for three or so hours with a reading of *Udege*. […]

The debates of the cinema, the theater, literature, I have followed as best I could, laughed a lot, got a little angry. Later, I understood, that all this would be of benefit to those who have a love of art, which is inseparable from a love of country and the People, and who have a head on their shoulders and a spine in the bodies. And whoever does not have all this, let them go their own way.

With great respect and kisses, Esfir'!

A.

39
A. A. Fadeev to E. I. Shub

December 20, 1936, Sukhumi

Dear sweet Esfir'!
In effect, this letter could have begun this way:
…The First iron night.
At nine o'clock the sun sets. A whitish mist descends upon the earth. A few stars flicker. In two hours, the crescent moon appears. I light a fire and the light from my fire glints off the trunks of the pine trees.
"The first iron night," I say. And a mad, passionate joy cuts through me with a strange trembling at thoughts of the place and the time.

---

[61] [Trans.]: As Masha Godovannaya informs me, this is Pushkin's grandfather, Abram Petrovich Gannibal, a Chief Military Engineer, General-in-Chief, and nobleman of African origin.

You: people, beasts, and birds! I raise a glass to a lonely night in the woods! To darkness and the whispering of God among the trees, to the simple, delicate consonance of silence, ringing in my ears! To the green foliage and to the yellow foliage! I drink to the sound of life, which I hear, to the muzzle snorting in the grass, to the dog, to the ordinary soil! A stormy toast: to the feral cat, who has pressed her chest to the earth and is ready to leap onto a sparrow in the darkness! To the brief silence in the earthly kingdom, to the stars, and to the crescent moon. Yes, to them and to it!...

Gratitude for a lonely night, for the mountains, the darkness and the murmur of the sea, it resounds in my heart! Gratitude for my life, for my breath, for the happiness, that I am experiencing through this night, I give thanks for this with all my heart! Listen to the East and listen to the West—no, listen! This is the eternal God. This silence, dear Esfir'! Are you healthy? Are you working? What are you drinking? "A Napareuli?[62] A Tsinandali?[63]" or, as they say, "the bitter cup of life"? Has Eisen[stein] returned? and how is his work going? I'm staying here because I don't want to leave the work half-finished. [...]. But all the same, I miss the Far East. The maximum, I can remain in Sukhumi is until January. After that, of course, I will be in Moscow for at least all of February. People from the Far East probably say bad things about me.

Write me anything at all, Esfir', my friend. ("My friend is a woman," Jack London used to say.) Did you like the views of Prague? Bratislava? Slovakian tapestries? (Unfortunately, they are poorly reproduced.) What are you reading now? I have with me all your Balzac with your citations from Pushkin. With great respect. I wish you all the best,

A.

Sukhumi, Hotel Sinop

---

[62] [Trans.]: A Georgian wine from Kakheti.
[63] [Trans.]: Another Georgian wine from Kakheti.

40
A. A. Fadeev to E. I. Shub

1937, France

Dear Esfir'!

Greetings to you from Saint-Malo. I am vacationing here with the Tolstoys[64] for a few days. On the postcard are our marvelous surroundings. On this trip, I went swimming in the Mediterranean Sea and now I am swimming in the Atlantic Ocean. I will leave for Moscow near the beginning of August. Many impressions. A whole series of stories are ready for you. I am eagerly awaiting the arrival of the Moscow Art Theater in Paris, to have a stroll with them. Lots of kisses. Greetings to Eisen[stein].

A.

41
A. A. Fadeev to E. I. Shub

April 2, 1938

Dear Esfir'!

I am sending you a ticket to the Assembly of the Moscow Society of Writers[65] at the Polytechnical Museum. It is beginning today at five o'clock in the evening. Drag Eisen[stein] along with you. He can enter on a member's ticket. Greetings.

A. Fadeev

42
A. A. Fadeev to E. I. Shub

February 25, 1941

Dear Esfir'!

I didn't send the books, I wanted to find a free day and give them to you personally. But business and domestic woes do not allow for the possibility of coming to you happy, but, at least, not depressed. Of course, once again, I haven't written to you for a long time and I am quite sad. It's a pleasure to be sending you my book. Get better. Lots of kisses.

Sasha

---

[64] [Trans.]: Possibly Alexei Tolstoy, the science fiction writer, and his then current partner.
[65] [Trans.]: In the original: Общемосковское собрание писателей.

43
A. A. Fadeev to E. I. Shub

February 7, 1954, Pakhra

Dear sweet Esfir'!

And so, I am living on the estate of one of the Sheremet'evs, Count Sergei
Dmitrievich. I am living in an ancient, immense palace with high windows and ceil-
ings, with large and small rooms, halls, storerooms, stairways, entresols, corridors,
and passageways: all with 120 furnaces, of course, with tiles. It was all badly damaged
during the war, and afterwards converted to central heating. There was remarkable
antique furniture, an art gallery, museum quality mirrors, a library of ancient books
and manuscripts. Gradually, all of this was removed to museums and galleries and
during the days of the war, a large part of what remained was burned, destroyed by
our soldiers in anticipation of the Germans—the front was 12 kilometers away. The
Germans, however, did not reach it.

One of the ancestors of the above-mentioned count, concerned himself with
planting dense forests all around, on the banks of the Pakhra: the rows of pines and
spruce trees show, that the pine forest was planted, although quite old and, therefore,
densely overtaken by undergrowth, which gives the impression of something wild.
The park on the estate is a special story: large with allées of lime trees, lime trees with
intentionally twisted trunks and normal lime trees, a poplar, quite old, something
like a hundred and fifty years old, which grew freely, mighty, spreading out, a spruce
just as old with a bench around it, a larch, mighty beneath the sky—in a word, a park
worth seeing. One of his ancestors buried his favorite trotter in a field, nearby, and,
as a monument, planted spruce trees around the grave in the form of a horseshoe. The
spruce trees are now a hundred years old and this gigantic, green horseshoe covered in
snow, unknown to anyone (except me!), grows in a field.

The manor house, situated on high ground, overlooks a wonderful view of a
rolling Russian plain. Below, the small River Vyaznikovka, no, Vyazovka, flows into
the Pakhra. It is dammed up, and on the ice, some lively young people are skating
now. The estate, in a word, as an estate of its kind, shows that the landowners lived
better under feudalism than under socialism and the descendants of their former serfs,
who now enjoy recreation on this estate, without a doubt, live better under socialism
than under feudalism.

Sergei Dmitrievich, the last count, was caught off guard by the revolution,
being already quite an old man, and he was given the right to continue to live on his
estate—no longer with the rights of a landowner, but simply with the rights of an old
man. He passed his days in the company of former political prisoners, resettled exiles,
and old Bolsheviks, who were given this estate after the war. He was buried right here,

but among those living there, there is no longer anyone who could point out where his grave is. He was a devout man; on the grounds of the estate, two stone chapels were preserved (in one of them, there is now an x-ray facility) and he always gave food to around a hundred "wanderers" and monks. Besides that, he was a great patron of the arts and there were always several Russian artists of the second-rank living with him. And something of them remains. I really love precisely these artists of the second-rank, since their paintings are less obscured by mass reproductions and postcards and suddenly remind me how original and beautiful old Russian painting is, in fact. Here, in those long sorts of galleries, hang paintings by Sokolov, Maksimov, Orlovsky, Kryzhitsky, and from among the top-shelf items, are preserved one Aivazovsky, one Vereshchagin ("Mtskhet") and one Klodt. One of the daughters of Sheremet'ev was also a painter; not too important to judge by surviving examples of her work. She was rather more engaged in copying. She worked under the direction of the famous Bogdanov-Bel'sky, who lived on the estate for quite a while. And, as a trace of his stay here, a remarkable portrait remains of that same daughter, almost life-size. She is still young, delicate, shapely, she is looking towards us, with bright, light-gray eyes, she has a pretty little Russian nose, she is wearing a light blue blouse with puff shoulders and long sleeves tightly fitting her arms below the elbow and with a standing collar trimmed in white lace, surrounding her long neck. In one hand is a brush, in the other, a palette. And she will remain standing until the end of the world, never aging. Bogdanov-Bel'sky, you must know well by his pictures dedicated to a village school—I have forgotten their names, especially one of them, where in the background there are kids from the village in various poses in the classroom grouped next to the teacher and there is a blackboard with numbers on it and in the foreground stands a little boy in bask slippers, in a coarse white cotton shirt and pants, and holding the back of his head with his hand, with great concentration, tries to solve the problem. When they showed me the former school building here in the village of Mikhailovskoe, which was more than a hundred years old, I thought to myself, that maybe, Bogdanov-Bel'sky actually made these famous idyllic and enlightening little pictures right in this school, living quite well off the landowner's bread and tending to this beauty with the little Russian nose, wearing this sort of blouse and dress, which were characteristic of your mother and mine and so adorned their era.

Now here, in this house, for the most part, live miners (men and women) from the Moscow region coal basin, some from the Donbass and even the Kuzbass, a lot of engineers from the same places, a lot of young people from the Mining Institute, a few professors. These people are very happy, lively, uncorrupted. The young students celebrate the holidays, there's lots of singing and dancing. It's very pleasant to live among these people. I walk a lot and write a lot.

How do you feel in your garret, which was so dear to me, my dear Esfir'? Are you writing? What are you reading? Have you learned how to manage your heart condition? Who comes to visit you? Has Anya gotten better? You don't have to answer any of these questions since writing anything is a labor for you; these questions characterize, as it were, the range of my primary interests concerning you. To go beyond this primary range, then my interests concerning you (you know that yourself) are so immeasurably broad and varied, that letters cannot satisfy them, neither mine, nor yours.

We will surely see each other soon! Now, as always, above all, I wish you health, at the very least. You must and you will regain it. Affectionate hugs and kisses,

Yours, Sasha

44
A. A. Fadeev to E. I. Shub

May 10, 1954, River Shosha

Dear and sweet Esfir'!

Do not be surprised, or offended, that I have not phoned you for such a long time.

I left the hospital on April 30th, spent the May holidays with my family, and left to live on the River Shosha, in Zavidovsky region, next to the Moscow Sea,[66] from where I am writing to you.

I stayed in the hospital so long because of illness. Sometime in the first half of April, I underestimated my age and the cold spring, I sat out late in the hospital court-yard and caught "lumbago," not single but double: one in the place put there by the good lord and the other in the shoulder. I lay there for nearly two weeks without even the strength to turn my head, or even move. Lying there, moaning in pain, I wrote my novel, something, with which, you, unfortunately, are familiar; the time, however, was not without its uses. With the double lumbago somewhat diminished, I was able to move, but I understood, that lying with it in the hospital was a hopeless affair. After my dire requests, they let me go home on the 30th. But, by this time, clouds were gathering over me, capable of laying me low for a long time. Already during the second half of April, various literary figures and personalities, suffering because of their activities, began to make their way to me for an appointment. Organs of the press were swamping me with requests to publish articles in anticipation of the congress. And at that time, I started calling up my good comrade, the director of a factory, with whom I studied at the Academy and to whose place I go every year to go hunting, to see whether or not he might put me up at his dacha next to the factory (his factory is in the Kalininskaya oblast'). We are living there with him now.

---

[66] [Trans.]: The informal name of the Ivankovskoe Reservoir, located some 130 km north of Moscow.

During this time, I have been to Moscow twice by unavoidable necessity: I went to pay my Party membership fees and to receive a new Party card, but I didn't spend more than an hour and a half there. I might have run by, but I was afraid of agitating you by the lack of warning and the situation prevented my calling. But I think of you all the time and the main thing is, I'm eager to read what you have written (I crossed out the words "for me"—the presumption of a literary figure, imagining, that everything is written for him, and ultimately—being accustomed to intimate letters: neither one is good). Firstly, as a man over fifty, this is simply very, very interesting to me and important somehow for myself alone to read about the times, which were for me, times of development. Secondly, I actually dream, that I have forgotten something in Moscow, that I forgot to do something, after which, it's uncomfortable to go on with my life. In a word, listen to me and do the following:

Either you yourself, or have Anya for you, call my secretary, Angelina Osipovna's sister: Valeria Osipovna Zarakhani, at this number: G 6–43–37, best between 9 and 10 in the morning and say, "When can you send a package for A. A.—Shub is calling" (or someone is calling on behalf of Shub). Valeria Osipovna, who is a careful and tactful person, will not read anything, but will send it to me by car. It's necessary to say, that besides her and the driver, no one knows my address.

I will read it immediately. Either I will reply with an extremely detailed letter, or, when the occasion presents itself, I myself will go, and it will be at a time when I can remain in Moscow for a while, so that I can call you beforehand and then drop by your place. And we will talk to our heart's content.

Are you in good health, my dear precious friend?

I would so like to see you active, happy! But you must reach the point, that for those suffering from your disease, there is a peculiar compensation: they achieve a kind of equilibrium, already at the level of the capabilities of their heart, when they are able to get up and go out. Write to tell me when you are able to send the manuscript; living outside the city, I wouldn't be able to help you during the summer. In this sense, I have a light touch, and perhaps I could come up with something suitable for you. Write me.

Heartfelt greetings to Anya and to all the friends you can consider as ours in common.

An affectionate hug,

your Sasha

45
A. A. Fadeev to E. I. Shub

November 8, 1954, Moscow

Dear Esfir'!

I'm sending you *Ogonek*.[67]

Among these chapters—gathered together by me under the heading "The Street during the morning hour," one is being published. It will be printed soon in *Litgazeta*.[68] In my novel, this chapter from *Litgazeta* will be chapter VIII, and the one that appears in *Ogonek* as Chapter VIII will be number IX. But in order for this chapter VIII to appear more or less self-sufficient, I had to add to it a small piece of chapter VI, when it was printed in *Ogonek*.

I am writing you about this, so the chapter in *Litgazeta* doesn't cause you any confusion. Happy holidays, once again!

An affectionate hug,

Sasha

46
A. A. Fadeev to E. I. Shub

March 28, 1955, Moscow

Dear Esfir'!

And so, we are living in different hospitals and, unfortunately, for rather a long time. Frankly, I didn't imagine, that they would keep you there so long (not to mention myself: I've lived too long in this golden cage).

You, of course, know, that I regularly speak with Anya about you and I am very concerned about your ills. But you must fight and don't give up; in summer, in a sanatorium, it'll be better for you: you'll be able to write again, you'll see good people, who love you, you'll see the grass and the sky and the leaves on the trees and much else that is different, pure, and good. Among the good people, who love you, of course, I include myself. I miss you very much.

I fell ill on the 3rd of February and by the 9th I was in the hospital. I began to have a cardiac arrhythmia, a bravura cardiac discoordination, resembling contemporary music. Now, this is all long in the past and I am once again living in the world of melodies. They would have already discharged me a long time ago, if there were room

---

[67] [Trans.]: In the original: *Огонек*, a Soviet literary magazine. The name means spark, or little flame.

[68] [Trans.]: Short for *Литературная газета* [*Literaturnaya Gazeta*] (*Literary Gazette*).

in the sanatorium. But they don't want me to go home immediately. It seems, that in a few days a place will open up and I will be in "Barvikha."

Of course, during this wondrous, boring isolation, I have been writing quite a bit and, it seems, with some success. And I read. And I often think about whether they are allowing you to read? If yes, then really, it is a great outlet. Ask them to get you *Independent People* by Halldór Laxness. This is a great and authentic writer. The Icelandic countryside, the people, nature are filled with poetry, all the more astonishing for the grim hopelessness of life. Among western contemporaries, it is difficult to find his equal in literature. And he is very Scandinavian. During the day I write, at night I read. I am reading Stendahl, London, Fast, the pre-revolutionary Sergeev-Tsensky, Ibsen (*Peer Gynt*). I could not finish André Stil: good, but boring and I couldn't manage *The Seventh Cross* by Seghers: it's quite heavy going. Of course, I have read a good half of the Belorussian prose of the decade and have reviewed it from the hospital. Generally here, I'm swamped with manuscripts and business mail; I have to live according to a schedule, in order to have time for everything. But, sometimes, I get lazy and that's when I start thinking about people, about life, and I often get sad. It isn't possible not to agree with the marvelous remark of Stendahl: "People who possess a physician, in the person of their own imagination, who have challenging affairs lying before them, should work a lot, and not think too much." In the end, what is most necessary for others and the happiest for you and I to do, is to write. And you must summon all of your spiritual strength, in order to finish the book.

I am now reading *The Art of the Actress* by Pashennaya: it is her life in art. How interesting this is and how much it is needed! And I often think about how the world of your life is immeasurably more vast—how much more people are in need of what you have the possibility of telling them and how you underestimate yourself! Get well, dear good Esfir', tender kisses.

Your A.

I will continue to write to you, until we have the possibility of seeing one another.

47
A. A. Fadeev to E. I. Shub

April 7, 1955, Moscow

My dearest Esfir'!
Here I am in "Barvikha" already. Here, is it still winter, really winter. In the afternoon, the sun is dazzling, the air is both frosty and spring-like, and here, I immediately got better. The truth is, I spent two days at home—I had to do this, for family

and, in particular, for institutional reasons—and I started to feel so physically weak, that I even got a bit "frightened." My plans included talking with Anya on the phone, then, with the hospital, in order to try to visit you. I had hoped to visit Marshak as well, who has fallen ill with pneumonia for the fifth time in the past year (he's staying at home). But all this turned out to be impossible. In the hospital I was already walking around every day, so, when I got home I tried… to walk to the savings bank. But I didn't feel like I was walking, but swimming, and I had to go back. This did not prevent me from meeting with three unwanted acquaintances and adding three more matters to my affairs; and the horrible conveyor belt of these small and large matters, of which I've lost the habit, was really doing me in—I had to lie and do everything by lying, using my wife, my secretary, and my son. I suddenly felt, that I was not a man, but an institution and not a contemporary institution—I wasn't too happy about this.

Right now, on my table, is my manuscript, which seems so appealing to me, a little volume of *Tales of the North* by Jack London and *The Soul of Freedom* by Howard Fast,[69] and my soul is at peace and I want it to live like that the entire remainder of my life.

If they allow you to and if you would be able to write even the shortest, most "pro forma" little notes, just about the state of your health, I would be unspeakably happy. It's difficult for me to consult with Anya about your health from here: it is even more difficult to reach you by phone (because of the number waiting in line), the audio quality is bad, and they don't allow one to use the phone until 10am. Of course, over time I will get around all these difficulties, but it would be good to catch a glimpse of your handwriting. My address is the following: c/o Barvikha, Moscow region, poste restante. If this is at all difficult for you, don't force yourself, I will completely understand.

I forgot to write you in my last letter, that after the award to Dovzhenko of the order,[70] I phoned him to say, "God sees the truth, but doesn't speak it quickly," and congratulated him. And he said, that he loved me.

---

[69] [Trans.]: The Russian title *Душа свободы* [*Dusha svobody*] is not a literal translation of the title of any of Fast's works. The most likely candidate would seem to be *Freedom Road* (1951), translated into Russian as *Дорога свободы* [*Doroga svobody*], assuming Fadeev, or the Russian editor slightly misquotes the title. Fast, a member of the Communist Party USA since 1943, had been imprisoned for Contempt of Congress in 1950 for refusing to divulge the names of contributors to a fund for an orphanage for children of those killed in the Spanish Civil War. He was blacklisted for several years, publishing successfully under his own imprint. He received the International Stalin Prize in 1953 for "Strengthening peace among Peoples."

[70] [Trans.]: In 1955, Dovzhenko received the Order of the Red Banner of Labor. At the time the letter was written, Dovzhenko had already made all of his remarkable features, including *Zvenigora, Arsenal, Earth, Ivan,* and *Aerograd*. Fadeev would seem to be referring to the gap between Dovzhenko's last finished film, *Мичурин* [*Michurin*] (*Life in Bloom*) (1949) and the awarding of the Order of the Red Banner of Labor, six years later.

God, how I long to communicate only with good people who are dear to me, to write books and read books. But the world, with its imperfect organization, it seems, does not afford this possibility to even a single person. One must fight. You, for example, must fight for your health and do everything, in order to emerge victorious. And I, it seems, will get out of here, but the price of my getting out of here will be to stop writing books, because I will be starting to fight for peaceful coexistence.

Writers are so overloaded with things, that they can only write well, when they fall ill, or when they make mistakes. Pavlenko[71] became a real writer when he fell ill with tuberculosis and settled in Crimea. Vishnevsky wrote his best play after they filmed him and he fell ill.

I write now, only when I am ill. If you could achieve such a state of health, that you could write your book, breathe fresh air, and communicate with good people, your situation could be considered ideal.

Forgive me, my good and dear one, this soldier's joke ("If a soldier can't make a joke, then what does he have left?").

An affectionate hug and a kiss, dear Esfir'. Get better, don't lose your spirits, fight for your health and the sooner it strengthens, the more confident and calm you will grow about your work in the past, the present, and the future and about your entire life, which you so generously devote to people, who are near to you. This confidence and calm should make you conscious, that you are a hardworking person, a person with a bright, clear mind and such deep feelings, which pour out towards everything in your life, even though, not everyone sees this. For deep feelings, in the words of Flaubert, are like respectable women: they fear, they might be found out and go through life with eyes lowered. The main thing is, you are a great and extraordinary person and must see and understand yourself as such.

Another kiss, dear Esfir',

Sasha

48
A. A. Fadeev to E. I. Shub

April 14, 1955, Moscow

How glad I was to receive your little letter, dearest Esfir'! It was as if I were seeing you and I was glad, that you are feeling better and doing well. With some well-placed professional jealousy, as I read through your letter several times, I thought again and again about your ability to say a great deal in a few words. And the truth is:

---

[71] [Trans.]: Petr Andreevich Pavlenko. Soviet writer, screenwriter, and war correspondent. Shub addresses letter #84 to him.

both in your book and in your letters, you possess the almost magical ability to say everything that you need to, both outwardly and in its very essence, avoiding unnecessary "justifications" and "transitions" (quite according to B. Tomashevsky, whose textbook is no longer being reissued, as it is considered formalistic, which is why everyone is writing worse and worse).

I will venture to send this little note to you at the hospital, although you know how happy I would be to finally hear your voice. Recently, I've been talking with Dovzhenko on the phone occasionally. He's threatening to come in the next few days and I'm quite happy about that.

Tender kisses, hoping to see you soon,

Sasha

49
A. A. Fadeev to E. I. Shub

April 21, 1955, Barvikha

How upsetting to me was your second letter; it was upsetting, not of course, because you shared your condition with me—no, you always write me the truth about your health and the main thing is: don't hold back about your desires, when you feel the need to share with me even the most burdensome ones—it was upsetting in its very essence. I'm sad I can't be with you and I can't help you, or at least somehow raise your spirits. I can only tell you, that all during this time, the heart patients (both here, in the sanatorium and in the city—I'm judging by Dovzhenko, who in the last few weeks is spending more time in bed) are suffering from unusual blood pressure due to the especially late, wet, dank spring. At the beginning, until I got stronger, it had an impact even on me. I am surrounded by more seriously ill patients of precisely this type. The doctors, along with them, are hoping for more tolerable weather and are promising improvements when sunny days arrive. I want to believe, that you will get better as well. Then, you will move back home and later to a sanatorium. Right now, however unpleasant it may be, in my opinion, you need to be in the hospital a bit longer, where you can receive doctor's care and specialized medical treatment. You must hang on for just a bit longer. There will be sunlight for you and we will see each other soon. I will be leaving the sanatorium no later than the 10th of May. If fate holds, that we will see each other while you are still in the hospital, then to hell with fate, it doesn't really matter—of course I will come by, once having agreed to this with you in advance through Anya. And we might even see each other again in your garret, which will probably seem wonderful to you too, after such a long absence. And it is, in fact, wonderful.

I write less now than I did earlier (but no worse)—less, because the spring mood for roaming is really bubbling up in me—it draws me to the forest, to the river (here the Moscow River is starting to stir a bit), you want to go somewhere to swim, to sing, to shoot. I'd like to see you very soon and have some fun. (It would be wonderful to have a drink or two in good male company.) But, by and large, all this isn't possible for me, I simply walk a bit more. I've even begun to read less and sleep more. I have no regrets about this, of course. Somewhere around the 20th of May, I have to go to Helsinki…

My friend, do not write me when it's physically difficult for you, but write me always and about everything, when you want to and when you have the strength. Don't give in to bleak moods and the main thing is: don't give up. You are not the Faustian type of person, but simply a very good and dear person to me—so please "give it a try."

Affectionate hugs and kisses on your hands.

Sasha

50
A. A. Fadeev to E. I. Shub

April 29, 1955, Barvikha

My dearest Esfir',

I wish you a happy holiday. I haven't spoken on the phone with Anya since last week, so I don't know how things are with you?

I have the following news: the attending and the chief physicians have filed a request for the extension of my stay in the sanatorium for all of May. If they don't extend it for a month, then for half a month, in any case. And while I'm bored out of my mind here, objectively speaking, all the same, it's better than anywhere else. What's more, the weather has improved.

If you happen to end up at home during this time, I will visit you and, perhaps, more than once.

I am working a little bit more now—all the same, it's boring to take walks alone. I read *Blackout in Gretley* by Priestley with a great deal of pleasure (I love adventure novels, and this also has a social aspect). While not particularly deep, it is interesting, all the same. I am now reading the utterly stunning stories of Maupassant; even at my age, these are dangerous to read, the more so in spring. The main thing is, I have understood, that one must never lose heart. Dearest Esfir', Until we see each other again. An affectionate hug for you.

A.

51
A. A. Fadeev to E. I. Shub

November 24, 1955, Moscow

Dear Esfir', God knows how long it's been since we've seen each other and spoken. I know nothing about your health, your work, about your state of mind—I often think, that, perhaps, in your soul there is a feeling of bitterness or resentment towards me. But, of course, I think about you not only in connection with this, but I often just think about you.

The last time we saw each other was when I was preparing for the report in the Assembly Hall of Moscow State University for the heads of Departments of Social Sciences in higher education. It was difficult for me to give it, since too much needed to be read. And I did not succeed in finishing the whole thing, but only half, although, by my request the report was rescheduled from the 24th to the 27th of August. All the same, I managed a successful presentation. But I was dissatisfied with my own report—precisely in the part, where it was necessary for me to speak [rather than read]. The report could not be printed in this form, and that, for me, in fact, was the main point of the report. And somehow, it became clear, that for writers little was said in it and what was said was inarticulate about the books of recent years, and about many of them nothing was said at all. *Litgazeta*,[72] which helped me with material and with books for the report, was hanging over me, demanding it for publication. My enthusiasm had already dampened. I had to sit down to write my novel; many urgent institutional and personal matters were being neglected. Nonetheless, the work of anathematizing had to be carried out: first, the report itself had to be corrected for the transcript and for the Central Committee; second, what, in essence, was a new article had to be written, on the basis of the report, including everything new: both new materials and books. As always, when you are forced to do something, the thing did not go well, took a great deal of time, I was dissatisfied with myself and with life, I slept badly, I was irritable, and the main thing is, that I felt very alone at the dacha: towards the first of September, the whole family left for the city. And, as always, when I force myself and am forced to do something where my heart is not in it, I immediately became ill [...] right after the final parts of the article got turned in to *Litgazeta*. This happened at the end of September, [...] the matter dragged on and on the 15th of October, I ended up in the hospital in precarious physical condition and with extremely low morale. Against the background of my years and everything which had been lying around in my system—especially for the last ten years—it is more difficult, of course, for me to stand up to all these diseases. I almost didn't sleep, not to mention

---

[72] [Trans.]: A familiar abbreviation of *Literaturnaya Gazeta* (*Literary Gazette*).

the wretched state of my heart and my liver. As concerns these organs, I'm still like that doll you knock down and it pops right back up,[73] they recovered pretty quickly, but as for the nerves, both on the physical level (polyneuritis) and on the psychological level, the matter dragged on. They put me in maximum isolation from the outside world, which was fine with me, for I was simultaneously experiencing extreme psychological agitation and unbelievable mental fatigue.

This, in fact, is what tore us apart—there was no possibility of visiting you in the sanatorium and none of getting in touch with you in the hospital (and not only with you). Of course, I sometimes managed to break through with the odd letter and more rarely with telephone calls, but I myself chose, what not to allow to agitate me and simply what was utterly unavoidable for business reasons. So, this is how I have been living through this time, since the last time we saw each other, chained to the wheel—at first, with painstaking, unloved labor, and later—cut off by illness from friends and even simply from interesting people. The only good thing—this was in the final days of September, when I had already fallen ill, but was still strong enough on my feet and in my head, I went by Fedin's,[74] and he read me a marvelous excerpt— around two pages—of a new novel.

I have now returned to my normal state, I sleep, though not quite enough (this has been my normal state for the past ten years), but my spirits are up and I am simply calmer.

I am writing you and taking up your time with my personal matters and perhaps you're just not up for that. I don't even know whether you're at home? Many times I have returned to your work in my mind, thinking how much it is needed, needed for a new generation in art, who knows nothing of all this, nourished on dogmatism, ignorance and bureaucratic distortions, and all the same, they have kind hearts, they also seek and they need to be told about people for whom art is both love and devotion. Here, I read Ermilov's manuscript about Dostoyevsky (a great, remarkable work) and there, he perfectly evokes the memories of Dostoyevsky in *Diary of a Writer* of how Nekrasov and Grigorovich came to see him at 5am after reading *Poor Folk*, when he was young, alone, unknown, and how afterwards he was at Belinsky's[75] place. God, how beautiful this is.

Since October 15th, I haven't met with anyone from the literary milieu or the milieu of art, I have not read either *Litgazeta* or *Soviet Culture*, in order not to become irritated. But I overheard some patients say, that Meyerhold might be rehabil-

---

[73] [Trans.]: In the original: "ванька-встанька" [van'ka-vstan'ka], which might be rendered as "Johnny Standup."

[74] [Trans.]: Konstantin Aleksandrovich Fedin, novelist and literary official, recipient of various Soviet honors, including a Stalin Prize, First Class in 1946. From 1959 until his death in 1977 he served as chair of the Union of Soviet Writers (Союз писателей СССР).

[75] [Trans.]: He is referring, here, to Dmitri Grigorovich, a writer and friend of Dostoyevsky, the poet Nikolai Nekrasov, and the influential literary critic Vissarion Belinsky.

itated? Probably, if this is true, you won't be able to avoid him in your book. Given the complexity of his path in art and tragic fate, it is very difficult to write about him — even difficult in a psychological sense. But "as a minimum," one must not — it would simply not be good to avoid mentioning his name. I hope to speak about all this with you in person. These are my last few days here in the hospital. It's not worth writing to me here, because it isn't possible for a letter to reach me. It's possible, I will leave on the 28th, Monday. I will phone you at once.

Affectionate hugs and kisses.

Sasha

I'm in a ward where the reception desk phone is used [to call out], there's always lots of people, phoning from here is difficult and I don't want to.

52
A. A. Fadeev to E. I. Shub

March 14, 1956, Moscow

Dear Esfir'!

Again and again, as I return in my mind to the plan for your book, I find it ever more harmonious. Precisely this word comes to mind. In the book, everything is imbued with the authentic, the great individuality of the author. In the views and the tastes of the author are reflected, therefore, both what of her and what already of history, of the entire great generation, born of the revolution, has now, in part, passed away, or is passing away. And the trace, left by her, is suddenly so meaningful, so great! The book says precisely: I lived not in the midst of what sparkled for a moment on the surface, but in the midst of what had the recognition of the world and at the same time, came about through suffering and frequently — through a disavowal and a rejection on the part of what is temporary. But it is precisely that, which has entered into the future and is the source of the significance acquired by these several blocks of individual portraits, arising, as if out of the flow of life of the author's generation (of the life in art of that *great* time!), which then returns (the flow, that is) to its course and so, once again, the character profiles, the encounters bear the natural character of fleeting, precise, expressive sketches. And then — there is the result of thoughts, arising from *personal* labor in art. It is, therefore, not a result in the sense of a rational explanation of the content of the book, but the concentrate in art of the book *itself*, formed according to natural laws over the course of the book. This is your trace amidst the small and the great and is the utterly natural "ending" for such a book from the point of view of form.

I have already told you, that everything you do is done with unusual economy. Now I can say, that this is well structured. And, therefore, harmonious as a whole.

With great pleasure, would I take on the role of the kind of editor and friend, who understands everything well in its essence, but is able to see it all from the outside—(since he is not the author)—the small things in their relation to the whole, infelicitous expressions and so on. And afterwards—when the book is passed on to the publishing house, where I could give it my final review—I will be able to prevent the "corrections," which might arise, from stupid editors.

I am sending you an excerpt from my report to the 2nd Congress of Proletarian Writers from 1928, which, as far as I remember, took place in the hall at Narkompros. And my report was called "The Mainstream of Proletarian Literature," under which title it was printed in some journal or other, and afterwards came out as a separate brochure, then two years later, in a small booklet containing three other rather imperfect opuses: "Down with Schilller," "Against Superficiality," and "In favor of the artist of the materialist dialectic" (sic—as they used to write in the old days). As you can see, this is also a part of history.

The extract I am giving you is the version as it was—I apologize for the sharpness of the characterization of Vertov, but at that time, there was not yet any abhorrent institutional consequences,[76] and besides, I did recognize his talent.

I had to go under quarantine for the flu, but, evidently, tomorrow, or the day after tomorrow, they will release me and I will phone you, my good and sweet little friend.

I wish you everything good. Affectionate hugs.

Sasha

---

[76] [Trans.]: The word Fadeev uses here is оргвыводы (orgvyvody), a Soviet-era compound (still currently in use) of org- (short for организационный [organizatsionny] (organizational or institutional) and выводы [vyvody] (consequences). The term currently refers to institutional decision-making. Given Vertov's public humiliation by Zhdanovists and Fadeev's personal role in the persecution and death of various writers, one wonders at the disingenuousness of this euphemism. He is clearly playing to Shub's sympathy for Vertov as a comrade, which, in spite of Vertov's poor treatment of her, extended to her repeatedly expressions of support, admiration, and gratitude for Vertov's contribution to non-acted filmmaking in this volume. She even, at some risk, slipped images from *Man With A Movie Camera* into a transitional sequence of the compilation documentary she made with Pudovkin in 1940 called Кино за 20 Лет [*Kino za 20 let*] (*Cinema 20 Years On*), an official history of Soviet Cinema, which makes no overt mention of Vertov, who, by that time, had been utterly anathematized.

Letters from various years

53
A. S. Khokhlova to E. I. Shub

August 23, 1927, Tiflis

Dearest Esfir'! First of all, the burning question for me is: what's the current title for *Zhurnalistka*?[77]

How many and what were the titles? Who made suggestions? Are there any concerns, or is everything finished?

I'm asking you to really answer me as soon as possible, i.e. immediately. If only the words strictly necessary to answer my questions.

Also, tell me what stage of printing is it in? [...]

Now, about traveling. Theoretically, I hate traveling. But I am looking out the window with curiosity at the Donbass I used to know and at what's new: Baku, oil wells, the sea. [...]

How is your "October"? How is the work coming along? Tell me about everything. If it's difficult for you to write about everything at once, then write to me about *Zhurnalistka* and, after you've had some rest, about everything else...

I completed your assignment concerning the newsreel on the very first day and Arustangov said, that he will send it in a couple of days. When I see him, I'll remind him again.

I'll finish for now. That'll do for a start. [...] Kisses,

yours, Khokhlova.

---

[77] [Trans.]: This seems to refer to the film directed by Khokhlova's husband, Lev Kuleshov, in 1927 called *Ваша знакомая* [*Vasha Znakomaya*] (*Your Acquaintance*) *also known as* Журналистка [*Zhurnalistka*] (*Newspaperwoman, i.e. Female Journalist*). Khokhlova plays the title role of the journalist.

54
A. S. Khokhlova to E. I. Shub

November 30, 1927

Dearest Esfir'!

If I were capable of it, I would make a jealous scene. You write to Fefer,[78] and I get nothing!...

How was your trip? How are you feeling? How are you feeling about the trip in general? How's the weather and the climate?

Yesterday, I spent 14 hours on the shoot on the street[79] (not literally on the street, but in an open field). The whole day, I managed to get inside just once for an hour to have lunch. I was really tired. For the most part, it was due to the weight of the fur coat, and today my neck, back, and shoulders hurt—it's the kind of muscle pain you get in your legs, when you go out skiing for the first time. When we are leaving—I can't say more precisely, but tomorrow, or the day after tomorrow, things should finally be cleared up [...]

Sending you kisses, and waiting for your letter.

yours, Khokhlova

55
G. M Kozintsev to E. I. Shub

1927

I saw *The Great Way*. Totally great. Transmit to Shub my sincere congratulations.

Kozintsev

---

[78] [Trans.]: Most likely, Itzik Fefer, a prominent Soviet Yiddish poet and Party apparatchik, executed on the Night of the Murdered Poets, one of Stalin's late purges.

[79] [Trans.]: What Khokhlova says is "на улице," which literally means "in the street" but idiomatically means "outside"; she plays on the literal and figurative meaning of the phrase here.

56
E. I. Shub to O. V. and S. M. Tret'yakov

1927

Dear Ol'ga Viktorovna and Sergei Mikhailovich,

Today is the first day, I've been able to move around my room. Thanks for sending us *LEF* № 11–12. I read it attentively. I want you to know, that I value your relationship to me as friends a great deal. I would never want to do anything to destroy it. You, better than anyone, know how directly I strive to defend my point of view about the cinema. And for this reason, I was quite surprised, and even more, hurt by the inaccurately transcribed stenogram, which appeared as a report of the *LEF* meeting. I anticipated and almost knew in advance, that you would discard what I said about *LEF* and the Party meeting, about *LEF*, Vertov, and Eisenstein, and other things, but it was difficult for me to imagine, that you, Sergei Mikhailovich, having under-taken to edit my stenogram (although I never refused to edit it), would put it in the form in which it was printed.

Is it really possible to rely on the record of a stenographer, in which basic "conversational" logic is often disregarded?

I consider it absolutely indispensable to put the text of my presentation in the next issue of *LEF*. The text must be revised by me and have an explanatory note from the editors, if the latter find it necessary.

Greetings.

I will phone.

E. Shub

57
G. M Kozintsev to E. I. Shub

November 2, 1931, Leningrad

My dear, dear Esfir' Il'inishna!

I understand quite well, that you have a premiere and that you don't have time for me, but the first snow has fallen in Leningrad, I am finally feeling pretty good and can't think quite logically. I really want to write you, that I really admire you and that you are one of the few, whom I trust, and with whom I can be open and forget, that irony is quite a useful thing in life. […] I really want to and really need to have a chat with you. I want and hope, that you will come here with the picture. Are you satisfied with it? My wish for you is, that this will be the most remarkable picture of the season.

We are on stand-by here. We start shooting on the 10th. And I'm not looking forward to it. […] It is possible, that everything will work out and I will see the sky sparkling like diamonds,[80] or with something else just as remarkable.

In the meantime, with great respect and eagerly awaiting your letter.

Kozintsev

Greetings to Natasha.

58
V. Gusev, A. Piotrovsky, M. Romm to E. Shub

1932, Leningrad

We, in long and cruel disputes
Have learned to give you our respect.
We have taken all your classes,
Brilliant master of montage.
Success for you will surely follow,
We, with each film more clearly see:
Fact with rehearsal is much better,
than it is, when there is none.

Congratulations without falsehood,
The three of us ask but one thing:
That you rehearse and even more
that you transform into a "wizard."

Your flag in film they'll raise on high.
But there is one more thing we ask:
The document
that's called *Today*
Tomorrow
will become
a fiction![81]

V. Gusev, A. Piotrovsky, Mikh. Romm

---

[80] [Trans.]: Another mildly ironic allusion to Sonya's monologue in *Uncle Vanya*. Not quite as pointed as Eisenstein's in letter #18, but more direct.

[81] [Trans.]: For this occasional verse, I have tried to keep the original meter, but have discarded the possibility of imitating the rhymes which occur every other line, in the interest of preserving meaning. The style of the original echoes Pushkin, for example, parts of Клеветникам россии (Klevetnikam rosii) ["To the Slanders of Russia"]. The final word in the film in the original is игровым [igronvym] (acted). The three who composed this poem of congratulations are all associated with acted, i.e. fiction

59
N. M. Shengelaya[82] to E. I. Shub

1932, Leningrad

CONGRATULATIONS ON TEN YEARS OF GREAT PRINCIPLED
CREATIVE WORK I SINCERELY REGRET I CANNOT KISS MY DEAREST
COMRADE STOP[83] I DELEGATE THAT EXCLUSIVELY TO NATASHA
SHENGELAYA

60
G. M Kozintsev to E. I. Shub

1932, Khot'kovo

Dear Esfir' Il'inishna!
I really want to see you. Or, worst case, to write you a letter. I'm afraid to do
that, since I'm not certain you're in Moscow. If you've already arrived, please do write.
Where is Natasha and how are things with her?
Greetings,

Kozintsev

Write as soon as possible!

---

films: Viktor Gusev was a poet, translator, playwright and screenwriter, Adrian Piotrovsky,
a dramaturg and artistic director of the Leningrad Film Studio, and Romm, a director of fiction films.
The polemical terms of the era oppose the "acted" or "played" film to the documentary ("non-acted"
or "non-played") film. They are playfully suggesting Shub bring the talents as a director she has
shown in her film *Сегодня* (*Today*) into the world of fiction film, which is where Shub started, as a
re-editor of foreign films for the Soviet market and editor of Soviet fiction films.
[82] [Trans.]: Nikoloz Mikhailovich Shengelaya was a Soviet Georgian filmmaker. His wife, Nataliya,
better known as Nata Vachnadze, referred to in the last line of the telegram, was a celebrated film star
of the early Soviet cinema, renowned as much for her acting as for her beauty. When beautiful leading
ladies fell out of favor in Soviet cinema in the late 20s and early 30s, she acted as Shub's assistant,
notably on Shub's film *KShE* (1932). In 1934, she resumed her acting career, making her last film in
1952.
[83] [Trans.]: The word translated as STOP is тчк (tchk) which is short for точка (tochka) meaning stop
in a telegram.

61
S. I. Yutkevich to E. I. Shub and P. M. Atasheva

November 29, 1933, Istanbul

My dear and beloved Pera and Eddi!

Don't be surprised, that I am sending you a "coupled"[84] letter and don't be angry, that I haven't written anything for so long.

I never expected, that it would be so difficult to write from abroad. There are so many impressions every day, that they can't be contained in a single letter and they are so numerous and interesting, that they could only be transmitted in person, comfortably seated in the "luxurious sitting room" at Pera's or in Eddi's white cell with a nice bottle of old wine, but simply to write them, just isn't necessary or interesting.

Besides that, both fatigue and anxiety take their toll—every day I fall into bed like the dead, because, all the same, I'm working and not loafing around.

But, in spite of all this (besides, there's a fast approaching in-person meeting, because I'm counting on leaving Istanbul on the 14th by steamship), all the same, I'm writing, unconcerned with stylistic beauty, for the sole and honest purpose of this letter is to admit (without fear of reproach for excessive sentimentality), that I really, really love you both very much, in different ways, but in the same way, you are near and dear to my heart and that I care about your friendship and am grateful for it.

I am not afraid of these words, for everything I am saying is quite serious and thought-through—because, only here, when cut off from the [Soviet] Union (which, by the way, is experienced, without exaggeration, as painful, I never thought, that nostalgia was such a serious illness, that I would be pining away—all this would seem unusual, given my dry, Leningrad nature, made even harder by squabbles in the film world!). So only here, when you can look at everything and everyone from a distance, from a different angle, can you begin to understand, what a magnificent thing our socialist Motherland is and that it's starting to become something specific even in the people (you do know my deep attraction to the criminal theory about "the living man"![85]) many of whom you start to love less and less and some of whom (sadly, they are fewer and fewer) you begin to value and to love all the more strongly, all the more truly.

And so it is with you, my dear, beloved friends!

I have thought about you quite a lot (and often in the least appropriate places and times!).

---

[84] [Trans.]: The word Yutkevich uses спаренное (sparennoe) can be taken in a mechanical sense of linked, coupled, dual, paired, or mated, but in giving it emphasis, he is also playing on the less innocent "coupling."

[85] [Trans.]: He seems to be alluding to Lombroso's theory of criminal physical "anthropology."

That's all I wanted to say.

It isn't much, is it?

But for me it is a colossal amount, for, evidently, within my deeply rotten nature there arose an even bigger idealist, which smells of utter catastrophe, taking into consideration the purge lying ahead for me…

In general, as for my travels, the infamous Ostap Bender[86] said it best: "It's not exactly Rio de Janeiro for you."

Brilliantly stated! I will elaborate on the details upon arrival.

Meanwhile… here, we still didn't agree with your evaluation, Eddi, of our pet project of a scenario by Natan and me, in vain am I trying to follow in your footsteps, o wise Esfir', and I'm obsessing on a film about Ankara, a most interesting city.[87]

But Yutkevich the documentarian is quite a spectacle, and besides that, just 5 days ago I won the ambassador's tennis championship and now rain and wind have begun.

Besides that, I think if one were to take all of your documentary difficulties, Eddi, and the agonies associated with shooting one and multiply that, at a minimum, by 1,000, even then, you wouldn't get a clear picture of the demands of working here. An old actor (the only one in the whole city!) who, in the course of his small role as a partisan, was to give a tiny comic (synch sound) monologue, addressed to the donkey (on which he had arrived) flatly refused to do it, arguing that, this demeaned his dignity, to have such a "partner."

This, of course, is a small thing, but when millions of such small things come pouring out, you immediately remember your knowledge of the Turkish language, in which an innocent glass is referred to using the word "bardak"![88]

"Bir bardak su" my guys are yelling ecstatically (which means, "one glass of water!"), when they crawl into a local restaurant, which has the sonorous name of "Lohanto" and which was immediately christened "lokhanka."[89]

Well, I will have to tell you in person about how I was in a tuxedo and once danced the rumba with some ladies from the embassy, because you'll die of ecstasy and envy! And there is so much else, both painful and hilarious, that I can regale you with in vast quantities, once I break off the excessive embrace, in which I will hold you, when we meet quite soon.

---

[86] [Trans.]: Ostap Bender is the anti-hero of a series of novels by Il'ya Il'f and Evgeny Petrov, including *The Twelve Chairs* and *The Golden Calf*. These novels have been turned into films in several countries.

[87] [Trans.]: Yutkevich is referring to his film *Анкара — сердце Турции* [*Ankara — serdtse Turtsii*] (*Ankara is the Heart of Turkey*), released the following year, and to Shub's unfinished project *Идет новая Турция* [*Idet novaya Turtsiya*] (*A New Turkey is on the Move*).

[88] [Trans.]: In the original: бардак, meaning "a hell of a mess."

[89] [Trans.]: In the original: лоханка, meaning wash-tub, renal pelvis, dumbass, among other things.

And while the gentleman carrying this letter is rushing me, this page is coming to an end. Huge kisses. Don't forget your loving friend Sergei.

Greetings to all our friends (if any remain)—little Macheret[90] especially—tell him not to get angry, that I didn't write him: all will be explained upon my arrival!

62
G. N. Popov to E. I. Shub

November 30, 1933, Leningrad

Dear Esfir' Il'inishna!

I very much regret, that we didn't manage to meet in Moscow in August. [...]

I would very much like to have a conversation with you, to become acquainted with your creative plans, your endeavors, and your current work. What is the fate of *4 Women*? Will Vachnadze be appearing in this project? Are you going to Turkestan? I remember your proposal for me to go there with you. I suppose now all of this has been disrupted. But going to the South would be great!...

I heard that Eisenstein left the Film Factory? Or is this gossip? Give him my warm greetings. I'm planning to be in Moscow in the middle of December [...]

The Leningrad Radio Center is extremely eager to perform our music for *KShE*. They keep asking me to give my assistance in getting sheet music material for all the music from the factory.[91] That is: 1) a score and 2) the orchestral parts for the music for *KShE*.

I'm writing to ask you to arrange the transfer of this material to the Len. Radio Center for a concert, which is supposed to take place on the 16th of December. If the official request from the Len. Radio Center is delayed, I would really like you to direct all the sheet music material to me at Detskoe.[92] I think, it would be enough for you to call the right person and the factory would send out the material to me. I want to express my gratitude to you in advance for the attention you will give to this matter. After all, the two of us have long dreamed of a public concert of our music. Its performance is also planned for the Len. Philharmonic this season.

Esfir' Il'inishna, be a dear and write me as soon as possible about this matter, and about your creative work, and about Eisen[stein].

I very much want to see you and him.

I send my warm greetings and kisses on both cheeks.

Yours, Gavriil Popov

---

[90] [Trans.]: Likely Aleksandr Veniaminovich Macheret, a contemporary film director, actor, and screenwriter.

[91] [Trans.]: That is, the film studio.

[92] [Trans.]: Detskoe Selo, now Pushkin. Masha Godovannaya points out to me, that from 1918 to 1937 it was known as Detskoe Selo. Previously to 1918, it was Tsarskoe Selo.

63
G. N. Popov to E. I. Shub

July 15, 1934, Leningrad

Dear Esfir' Il'inishna!

On my return to L[eningra]d, I fell ill with an inflammation of the periosteum and remained in bed for an entire week. Yesterday, for the first time, I made it into the city for urgent business. I read your article in *Izvestia* about *Metrofilm*.[93] From it, I learned of there being "5 essays." I knew about there being 2 parts.[94] The overall plan seems to have changed these last few days, or has it? Or have you simply expanded your two-reel project into a feature-length film. The scenario, of course, I have not yet received. And have you given a commission for the poetry to a good poet? Kirsanov[95] would have a good approach to this theme. [...]

How's Dovzhenko? I read his article in *Liter. Gazeta*. I completely agree with him, that "writing a good scenario is no less difficult, than a good play." And I'm very glad that he raises the question of "the serious work of the writer in the cinema." And what's the news about his shoot in Sevastopol?

And "Metrostroi"[96] could be brought to the screen brilliantly if the theme is approached not naturalistically, but if a way can be found for it, through a whole series of events, showing the development of the great and profound culture of our Union. For this, it seems to me, one would need to take the related branches of industry serving "Metrostroi," to take the people, who are managing this idea, and show the participation and energy of the masses in this construction project. But perhaps, it would be better to speak about this idea, since, in a letter, you always feel the inadequacy of words for the full development of a thought.

Read Pushkin attentively. I really love his verses. I will definitely write the music for voice and orchestra for them.

Kisses.

PS: Write.

Greetings to you from Irina.

From me to Dovzhenko and Eisen[stein].

---

[93] [Trans.]: This would seem to be either a working title, an abbreviation in Soviet style, or a mistake for *Москва строит метро* [*Moskva stroit metro*] (*Moscow Builds a Metro*), now considered lost.

[94] [Trans.]: The word часть [chast'] can mean either a part or a reel; in practice, films tended to be composed by the reel, so the two were in practice synonymous. Each reel for a sound film was about 11 minutes long.

[95] [Trans.]: Possibly Semyon Isaakovich Kirsanov, a highly decorated Soviet poet, a disciple of Mayakovsky, by some considered his literary heir. Stalin Prize, Order of Lenin, Order of the Red Banner of Labor, Medal "For the Victory over Germany in the Great Patriotic War 1941–1945."

[96] [Trans.]: In the original: "Метрострой." Metrostroi was the name of the organization responsible for building the Moscow Metro. It is now known as Мосметрострой (Mosmetrostroi), an acronym for Moscow Metro Construction Authority.

64
P. M. Atasheva to E. I. Shub

September 29, 1934, Moscow

Dear Esfir'!

Write me about where you are living, how the sun is in Smyrna, what people are around you. Think about Moscow less and concentrate fully on yourself. Once the trip has started, it means breaking with the old way of life, and this is already wonderful for you.

I saw the film by Legoshin and Donskoi *The Waters Flow;*[97] in my opinion it's a very cultured and gentle film. Not a bad response to *Jolly Fellows.*[98] Mar'yamov is happy; this is their film. Next, Legoshin is going to do *The Way of the Samurai*[99] with Yutkevich as director.

In Moscow, there's rain. Another summer has passed by. And another winter is upon us. That's how it goes.

I would like to stick my finger on some point or other on the map of the Union and go there. And disappear for no less than a year… and return with a book…

Well, Esfir', my dear, hope your work goes well.

Send us a photo of some working moments.

Big kisses,

Yours, Pera

65
P. M. Atasheva to E. I. Shub

November 5, 1934, Moscow

Dear Esfir'!

My precious friend,

I write you very little, but from your letter, it's clear, that you have not received even half of my gloomy letters with little substance. How familiar to me are the feelings you are experiencing in Smyrna. Mine in Moscow are not worth writing about. You know yourself, it's not a matter of geography.

---

[97] [Trans.]: In the original: *Воды текут* [*Vody tekut*]. It would seem that Atasheva is referring to *Песня о счастье* [*Pesnya o schast'e*] (*Song about Happiness*), which saw its public release two days later.

[98] [Trans.]: In the original: *Веселые ребята* [*Veselye rebyata*] by Grigori Alexandrov, 1934. A popular musical comedy.

[99] [Trans.]: In the original: *Тропа самураев*. No information available about this title.

[…] I am working at a journal. Zarkhi has almost finished his play; work proceeds on the finishing touches. Gavrik[100] is writing the music. S. M.[101] and he have become friends. The best evening of my life for some time was an evening at Gavrik's, when he played quite a lot. What a delight to hear music that way, when they break it down into parts and a fragment of a world, which is completely unknown to you and its particular laws, opens up, and you suddenly experience the same patterns in them, the same laws of birth of timeless values, as in the art which is dear to us.

And speaking of cinema—the Dovzhenkos arrived yesterday; it seems, everyone is satisfied with everything. I didn't see them. Tomorrow, I will go to the Dom Kino for a screening of *Chapaev*[102] (they say, that the Vasil'evs' film has been a success) and I will probably see everyone there.

Gavrik praises *Metro*, and, judging from the pieces he played, he wrote good music. He loves you very much. I hope you received our collective telegram.

The old man[103] has decided to put *Москва Вторая* (*Moscow II*) in the cinema immediately after the play and, in this way, the theater will appear to be our pre-production period. It's already practically completely settled and Shumyatsky is pleased.

They postponed his book until May, but I'm still not convinced, he will finish it by that date. You yourself know: the theater, the GIK, the Kino Academy from December on, then the film plus everything else, and the qualification courses of theatrical directors for the cinema, where such geniuses as Tairov[104] and Zavadsky[105] will be studying. This is an initiative of Kul'tprop,[106] and Dinamov[107] will also be studying there. S. M. is, of course, terribly proud, that precisely he will be teaching them [film] direction. On the 8th, he leaves for Leningrad, where Ermler is summoning him for help. The old man got a spring in his step and it's a pleasure for him to go.

Good night, dear Esfir'. […] There's a lot of work tomorrow and I will be seeing a lot of people. Take care of yourself.

Yours, *Pera*

---

[100] [Trans.]: She is referring to Gavriil Popov; Gavrik is a nickname for Gavriil.

[101] [Trans.]: That is, Sergei Mikhailovich Eisenstein.

[102] [Trans.]: In the original: Чапая from Чапай; a familiar way of referring to Chapaev.

[103] [Trans.]: Pera seems to be referring here to Eisenstein and his proposed project for a film on Moscow. A proposal for a film called *Москва во времени* (*Moscow Over Time*) was published on July 11, 1935 in *Literaturnaya Gazeta*.

[104] [Trans.]: Possibly Aleksandr Yakovlevich Tairov. People's Artist of the RSFSR, Order of Lenin.

[105] [Trans.]: Possibly Yuri Aleksandrovich Zavadsky. People's Artist of the USSR, State Prize of the USSR, Hero of Socialist Labor.

[106] [Trans.]: In the original: Культпроп, the Department of Culture and Propaganda of Leninism under the Central Committee of the All-Union Communist Party.

[107] [Trans.]: Possibly Sergei Sergeevich Dinamov, a literary scholar specializing in Shakespeare.

66
G. N. Popov to Esfir' Shub

December 9, 1934, Leningrad

Dear Esfir' Il'inishna!

I received your 2nd postcard on the 23rd of November. I wrote you a letter immediately and with great enthusiasm. But a number of circumstances prevented me from sending it and I am writing to you once more, as I hope to reach you in Istanbul. I hope to see you in Moscow soon and to hear the many details of what you saw, that is new, colorful, and unexpected in your exotic journey around sunny Turkey.

While I was generally extremely pleased and touched by the warmth, friendliness, and the "pulse" of your postcards, I would, all the same, very much like to receive a detailed, descriptive letter. But I am fully aware of how difficult it is to set aside a couple of solid hours for letter writing, in the midst of a constant stream of business matters, work, creative efforts. It is very difficult for me to make time for a letter, when a thought feverishly, in a state of excitement is occupied by an entire formation of not yet completely clear artistic images insistently demanding the most rapid materialization in clear-cut musical forms, in thoroughly logically sound and emotionally conscious and justifiable faktura.[108]

From the first of May to the first of December, owing to a series of serious creative obligations on films (*Chapaev*, *Metro*, *A Severe Young Man*[109]), I had no opportunity to continue work on a violin concerto begun on April 17 of this year. In recent days, owing to a delay in the completion of the play by N. Zarkhi, *Moscow II*, for which, at the request of S. M. Eisenstein, I will be writing the music, once again, I took up my concerto. [...] A little bit about the past. In the summer, I was concerned about *Metro*, since I was sitting in Sevastopol for a month and a half, not knowing a thing about this film. Now, the first part is already ready and I have been left with the best impression about collaborative work with Filonov[110] and Solodovnikov.[111] I think, that if you had participated in this work to the end,[112] a number of the struc-

---

[108] [Trans.]: In the original: фактура, a highly charged term, sometimes translated as "texture" in the context of painting and cognate with "facture." It refers to giving attention to the inherent qualities of an artistic material, something like "realization" or "form."

[109] [Trans.]: *Chapaev* is by the Vasil'ev brothers, *Metro* could refer to Shub's *Moscow Builds a Metro* (now believed lost), and *A Severe Young Man* is Строгий юноша [*Strogy yunosha*] by Abram Room.

[110] [Trans.]: Possibly Pavel Nikolaevich Filonov. Soviet painter, art theorist, and poet. Founder of the Analytical Realism movement.

[111] [Trans.]: Possibly Aleksandr Vasil'evich Solodovnikov, a figure in the Soviet theater world, director of the Moscow Art Theater and the Maly Theater.

[112] This implies that Shub was no longer fully participating in the film and that responsibility for completing it may have been turned over to Filonov and Solodovikov.

tural montage plans would have been significantly more pointed and clearer. I wrote the music according to two plans: 2 numbers in a jazz style and 2 in the classical manner of "Concerti grossi" for strings and brass. The jazz is for the shots of the predawn awakening of Moscow and for the evenings. The "concerti grossi" are for the shots of brutal, intense work underground. I am thinking of making these pieces of brutal music the basis of a 2nd piece for a large symphony orchestra, again, in the same manner for strings and brass (without woodwinds or percussion).

The music was recorded perfectly. This is the best recording of my film practice. The jazz numbers sounded on the screen like the best records from abroad. I parted ways with the management of the factory on the best possible terms and I should especially emphasize the attentive and solicitous attitude shown towards me while we were at work, both on the part of the collective and on the part of management. […].
I bring the pleasant news, that work has begun with Eisenstein on the staging of a play by Zarkhi in the Theater of the Revolution. The play is quite incisive and promises to bring a good jolt on the theater front. […]

At the beginning of November, during the time *Metro* was being delivered, I had a wonderful meeting with Eisen[stein] and Pera (or is it Piera?). There was food, chocolate, fun, a lively time, marvelous books (at Eisen[stein]'s place), then a taxi, rain, fruit and music, music and dancing (the music for *Metro*, a suite for phonograph by Gershwin: jazz songs). This was on Khlebny Lane, in my brother's apartment. I liked Pera quite a bit. A marvelous girl. She mentioned you and spoke about you extremely warmly, and with "great feeling" (and without a drop to drink). It was clear that all of those present—Eisen[stein], Pera, and I—respect you, and highly value your purity[113] and your principles (what strengths!) in art, not to mention, loving you and wanting to see you as soon as possible. Meanwhile, wishing for you to fully and in the best way possible accomplish your creative plans and bring us more impressions of things unfamiliar.

There are a number of things I would like to speak with you about. Namely, *Chapaev* and the method of working on music for film, and so on. But that's for when we meet. It is amazingly good to speak with you about art. You are intelligent and profound.

Write me as soon as possible. If there's no time to write, just send a few interesting postcards about Turkey.

Don't forget my request: bring me something spicy, if, you are not, however, overburdened with such requests. And bring me a couple of cigars, if good ones are to be had in Turkey. But the main thing is: come back as soon as possible.

With the greatest respect, my courageous friend.[114]

Greetings to you from Irina Vladimirovna.

---

[113] [Trans.]: In the original: чистота [chistota]. Literally, purity. Something like a combination of sincerity and integrity.
[114] [Trans.]: In the original: Крепчайше жму Вашу мужественную руку.

67
G. N. Popov to Esfir' Shub

September 12, 1936, the Caucasus

Exactly 32 years ago, that is, 9/12/1904, your friend and humble servant was born.
A year ago on this day, we met in the evening at Shebalin's and I clearly remember that
evening. Remember: Eisen[stein], you, Fadeev, Oborin, Polovinkin, Shebalin, and my
two brothers were there [...] Afterwards, Tchaikovsky's 6th Symphony for four hands.

Not like today. Silence. The courtyard is heavy with garlands of grape vines,
with nearly ripe, ripening clusters of grapes. In front of the window are oleanders
(flowering), a banana tree, fig trees, peaches, mandarin oranges, a lemon tree, plum
trees, right next to the garden, and two steps away is the sea. Today, it is harsh, noisy.
The wind is not too strong, but the waves are big. The surf is forbidding. Today I
didn't even swim. No one did. I went down, treading water in the surf. [...]

I really, really want to capture in a symphonic image a trip to Ritsa. I spent the
night deep in the forest, where the Yupshara[115] River comes out of the ground. A warm
night. The moon. A campfire. Suddenly, clouds. Lightning. Thunder. Darkness.
A downpour. I moved my campsite to under a huge rock. I moved the campfire. Felt
the cold. In the morning, a difficult ascent along a wooded, mountain trail. Then,
a marvelous lake. Eagles, high above the lake, over the summits of the surrounding
mountains, rugged mountains, going up to the clouds, situated above the zone of the
alpine meadows. Small craft, skating over the lake in the rain. The gloomiest weather,
clouds. Cold. Then the moon—dazzling through the clouds. Night. The long road
back. [...] But I found neither any real rest, nor any peace. [...]

To learn to work, "for the future, firmly relying on the present," this is what I
am drawn to. I want my music, the further it goes, to resonate more clearly and more
comprehensibly. I don't want to create perishable things. Art must be judged *by society
over time,* within the movement of life, within history. The more decades and centuries
an aria endures, the better.

Esfir', dear, there are authors who are forerunners, they give answers to questions not yet posed. Today, they are overlooked, tomorrow is for them. Among the
generation alive today and those who will come to replace them, these writers are a
bridge, they sustain a hidden continuity—they are essential, although at times also
misunderstood, they are the destination of literature. Esfir', write me. I value you and
love you so very much.

Greetings to you from Irina. With great respect and kisses.

---

[115] [Trans.] In the original: Юншара [Yunshara]. This is clearly an error.

The most heartfelt greetings to Fadeev. If the cigars are still intact, please put them aside for me.

What do you hear about Eisen[stein]'s work?

Gabriel'[116]

68
G. N. Popov to E. I. Shub

February 28, 1938, Leningrad

Dear Esfir'!

For a long long time, I've been intending to write you about everything, but, apparently, letters are so difficult for me—it's hard to find the momentum. […] This whole period (starting from 12/21) has proceeded under the sign of intensified, creative efforts to engage with work systematically. But only at the end of January, did I start to manage this. […] Now I am proceeding to expand and alter the score for *A Severe Youth* into a suite for orchestra, opus 19: "10 miniatures for orchestra." It's turning out to be rather large and varied. […]

I very much want to write an opera based on the scenario for *Rus'*. Find out from Eisen[stein], Esfir', whether he has spoken with Pavlenko about my desire to obtain from them a libretto for an opera on this subject. If he hasn't, then hurry Eisen[stein] up, as it's important for me to have an agreement in principle, or a refusal. I am seeking out specific material for a Soviet opera, and I don't want to waste time. Of course, I would be ecstatic to write the music for the film *Rus'*, but as Mosfil'm has not invited me to do so, I don't want to impose myself. In general, it's nice to work with directors in the cinema, whose creative idiom you know well and love. Isn't it?

I am also interested in the creative plans of the director E. Shub. What is she thinking up? Does she intend to invite a composer to participate in the composition of the scenario, in order for the scenario to turn out organically musical? I heard, that you intend to make an acted film? So, I am waiting for a letter from you, both about your projects and with a response to my request about an opera version of *Rus'*. Get Eisen[stein] and Pavlenko to hurry up with an answer.

I love you lots and lots. I want to see you. If I get some cash, I'll quickly arrive in Moscow for a couple of days. But don't wait for my arrival and answer me as quickly as possible. You yourself said, that you also love and think about me!

Kisses to you. Esfir', big ones.

---

[116] [Trans.]: In this single instance, the Russian editor has transcribed Popov's signature as Габриэль.

Here's wishing you creative success.
Yours,

Gavriil

Heartfelt greetings to Eisen[stein]. Let him know, that I love him very much and send him hugs.
Heartfelt greetings to you from Irina.

69
B. N. Agapov to E. Shub

1938, Crimea

Here, it's almost dark. Storm: magnitude 8, wind: magnitude 10, snow: magnitude exceeding scale, joyful sense of freedom 20.

83 years ago, 129 thousand people were killed here. It is difficult to walk around the city, in which 129 thousand dead soldiers live. They were killed with cast-iron balls, the program was carried out, over the course of 10 months. What pitiful technology! Contemptible. Now this can be done in 2–3 days.

Boulevards here pass through the places of these senseless deaths. Sailors stroll around them and there stands a monument to some German, Totleben, who built the fortifications, next to which these 129 thousand Russian guys were slaughtered.

Near the monument, I saw a dog in a gas mask and rubber clothing. It's interesting, that it had a tail piece out of rubberized fabric. It had a Paleozoic look.

Maybe, someone should make a movie about it.

And the most beautiful thing in the world is what was untouched by Man. For example, a storm or a rock. I'm just thinking about them… Here, trees will blossom, the smells of the earth will arise… No, Esfir', I'm already old and I am beginning to understand things like tenderness towards children and a love of nature. In ten years, if I survive, I am going to write poetry. Old age! Why is it that no one has sung its praises, as they have sung a million times the praises of filthy youth with its sweaty hands and wandering eyes?

Free from lust and teeth! Then will I write you a script!
Kisses
Yours,

B. Agapov

70
E. I. Shub to V. V. Vishnevsky

March 3, 1939, Moscow

Dear Vsevolod! Salud!

I finished reading your scenario. It's all good. It could work, but I want to share with you a series of my comments.

The overall composition of the scenario on the whole is correct. My reservations, for the most part, concern specific devices for fragmenting the material, working on a single theme (for example, Galicia and the University campus, etc.), by means of different material, at times the semantic content and the construction of the shot don't match. A number of times, this device weakens the impact of the theme as a whole and does not afford the possibility of revealing it fully.

This especially pertains to the introduction. Eliminating the voice-over text, the theme of the introduction appears as follows:

1. Landscapes (various views) Galicia once
2. Barcelona (various views)
   Valencia (various views) a plant
3. Madrid (various views) Galicia twice
4. Landscapes (various views)
   For the first time people appear and the theme of labor.
5. The countryside in Valencia, some vegetables characteristic of the North and popular musical instruments typical of Galicia.
6. Once again, shots of Galicia (3 times)

And the children swimming can't be put there as they are Spanish Pioneers shot in the Crimea, which is clearly obvious. I imagine it would be very interesting to use the device you yourself found for the introduction.

A rough outline for the introduction, I envision in the following way:

An introductory title about the Spanish People, their life, labor (the theme of your first voice-over texts).

Then come images. On screen immediately: people in nature, at work, laboring.

The North. Galicia. The whole theme is accompanied by Galician folk songs about labor.

The South. Sun. Palm trees. Orange trees. Labor. Folk songs and motifs distinct from those of the North (only this arrangement of pieces [of film] will give a sense of space and expanse).

Lots of sun. A radio announcement: "All over Spain, not a cloud in the sky" (voice-over text and messages from radio broadcasts).

This message is spoken over:

Sunny Valencia.

Over Madrid.

In Madrid, a demonstration by the Popular Front.

A workers' meeting.

A bazaar (Galicia).

And immediately afterwards, this decryption of the radio messages.

The voice-over says, "This message meant the beginning of the mutiny and was a signal." The theme of the Fascist advance begins. P.8[117]: "About various forms of beauty." Lions, chariots, goddesses, which, in the opinion (of the translator) comrade Albert, are very characteristic of Madrid: they are found the first time we see Madrid before the mutiny. P.11: Develop the entire theme of the defense of the University campus without fragmentation. After the University campus, present Casa del Campo (P.15). That way, we will be able to simultaneously show the International Brigades together with the Republican units in the defense of Madrid. Follow up the actions on the Madrid Front with the actions in Guadalajara, where the enemy was stopped in its movement towards Madrid.

After this, present the prisoners (P.13).

P.14. The field hospital: not necessary (bad material, staged).

P.15. According to the translator, comrade Albert, Líster, during this episode, encourages the peasants to continue at their work. The Army is on their side. The Army is defending their interests.

P.16. The oath needs to be moved to the final sequence, so that the enormous regular army of recent times is visible in motion following the banner.

There are a lot of dead people already.

There are too many of the dead in any case.

P. 17. Show the theme of aerial combat (Caballero and ours are everywhere).

The end of the 6th reel needs a different resolution. (Beginning with the words, "once again the Fascist barrage.")

The departure of the International Brigades from Barcelona should be concluded with their arrival in Paris.

The whole theme of Spring has been omitted: the material is exciting and inspiring. These shots must be shown before the departure of the International Brigades. Spring on the front consists of the trenches and the International Brigades. In my view, this theme must find its place before the blockade. The 7th reel needs a different resolution. This is especially noteworthy after the speech by Dolores, which appeared in *Pravda* today.

The frequent repetition of the same material (Fascists, battles, etc.) makes me uneasy. There is very little material. And there are no alternate takes. It would be

---

[117] [Trans.]: The references to pages are unexplained; it would seem they refer to pages of the current version of the Vishnevsky's scenario, on which she is proposing revisions.

better to make two or three good, strong episodes of combat, than to endlessly repeat the same material.

So far, the voice-over text is in large part informational-illustrative in character and is frequently placed over shots, which are expressive even without any text, because of their meaning and because of their content within the frame. These shots would be more correctly accompanied by music, songs, sounds.

The length of some texts exceeds that of the images.

The voice-over text fundamentally should ring out independently of the shot, as a force functioning organically alongside the shot and with the shot giving form to the entire composition of the object as a whole. The blockade is very good.

Respectfully,

Esfir' Shub

71
B. N. Agapov to Esfir' Shub

1939, KISLOVODSK

GOING TO UZBEKISTAN TO MAKE AN EPIC FICTION FILM DIRECTORS WET-BEHIND-THE-EARS THIS THREATENS TO DISRUPT THE MAGNIFICENT PROJECT TELEGRAPH YOUR WORK PLANS I KISS YOUR GOLDEN HANDS[118]

AGAPOV

72
B. N. Agapov to Esfir' Shub

October 14, 1939, Tashkent

Dearest Esfir',

Just a few words—I'm diabolically busy. I saw Eisen[stein]—he is courageous as always. […] He won't release the picture earlier than the autumn: location shoots begin here only in April. He was touched by the letter, as always, hiding his feelings under a joke. But it seems, this has become second nature to him.

---

[118] [Trans.]: It isn't clear to me whether this was an actual telegram or a letter written in the style of a telegram, that is, without punctuation marks. I have taken the liberty of emphasizing the telegram trope.

At the moment, I have my hands in everything. Or better said, my hands do everything for the group.[119] There's a scuffle for every reflector, I have to fight for every truck and for gasoline for a month-long expedition to Fergana. I've managed to get 40 full days of shooting without a scenario approved—we will shoot whatever we see.

Take me on as production manager for your next picture.

What are your plans?

Is it true about Mayakovsky?[120] No, don't say a word!

Write me, for God's sake, and right now, before I leave and disappear. If only you were here. What an epic we would cook up!

I'm waiting for your letter—Yours, Boris

73
B. N. Agapov to Esfir' Shub

October 23, 1939

Dear Esfir',

I don't know how things are for you, although I am constantly thinking about you and having a mental conversation with you, both about the picture and about life. Tomorrow, I will go on an expedition to Fergana, which I organized literally with my own hands—from the gasoline to the people. I think, that something will come of it. The construction of the Fergana Canal is now particularly harsh and difficult for me. It was not being filmed here. All the materials (nearly 12 thousand meters) were shot by Soyuzkinokhronika[121] and are located in Moscow. Khronika[122] will release a film about this, and as always happens, the material will go missing. [...]

This recorded material should be preserved, regardless of whether it goes into the film produced by Khronika, or not, and transferred to the Tashkent studio. [...]

I know, that this material is extraordinary, unlike anything you or I have ever seen in the cinema. Here, I am begging you to do this for me. Look at the material and make selections, make a record of the shots. My dear little Esfir', the success of the

---

[119] [Trans.]: In the original: Я сейчас—на все руки. Лучше сказать—все руки группы это—я. Agapov is playing on the sense of being on the one hand, a jack-of-all-trades, and on the other, of having to do everything for the group.

[120] [Trans.]: In the original: Ах, не надо! Agapov may be referring to Mayakovsky's rehabilitation and canonization after his death, or simply expressing incredulity and distress at some information which has recently come out concerning his death, which took place nine years earlier. He is also alluding to the fact that whatever she might say will be read and could be compromising.

[121] [Trans.]: Literally Union Newsreel, a Soviet organization charged with documenting important news events throughout the Soviet Union. It had four regional centers (Moscow, Leningrad, Rostov, Kharkiv) and one mobile center.

[122] [Trans.]: In the original: Хроника, meaning Newsreel.

picture and my pathetic life at this stage depends on this. A representative of Uzbek-film, Boris Aleksandrovich Chechikov, will set up everything, and you need only sit, watch and dictate the sequences [of interest].[123] If you are free and love me even a little bit, do this.

Write me whether you agree, at this address: Agapov c/o Tashkent Shaikhantaur Shteinberg. I eagerly await your letter. If I don't answer you at once, it means that I am on the road, but I will immediately be contacted and I will receive your letter, wherever I might be.

Kisses, sunshine, I will send you a little warmth from Tashkent in a letter, of which there is here no small amount.

Yours,

Bor. Agapov

74
B. N. Agapov to Esfir' Shub

February 9, 1941, Leningrad

Esfir',

The film was already finished, when I arrived. My God, how bad it is! Such things make obvious the level of your culture and mastery. I am remembering our work together and I see, that we had only one shortcoming: we acted slowly. And generally speaking, no one, except you and I, understands, what a documentary film is.

I did the text in three days. Everything that was good in it was thrown out.

"There is too much of a feeling of your individual character in it," they told me

[...]

What are your plans?

Write me at the Astoria,[124] room 108.

Yours,

Bor. Agapov

---

[123] [Trans.]: In the original: диктовать эпизоды.

[124] [Trans.]: A landmark hotel in Leningrad run by Intourist, hosting mostly foreign visitors and Russian dignitaries. During the Great Patriotic War it served as a field hospital.

75

B. N. Agapov to Esfir' Shub

March 16, 1941, Moscow

Happy Birthday!

My dear,

Your letter made me happy, since I had had no greetings for a long time.

It would be good to preserve our friendship for many long years! It is a rare thing and, so often, we are thoughtless about those things which are precious, which seem too natural for us to cherish. Only in losing them, do you understand this.

There will be many quarrels between us. We are both intolerant, egotistical, greedy, and envious. We are very passionate guys. But let's make an agreement and sign it in blood, that quarrels are quarrels and friendship is friendship.

I will fight, lose hope, walk away. […] You will take offense, become contemptuous, shrug your shoulders. Over a single phrase, we will smash dishes against one another. But let's agree to gather up the pieces and sweep the floor.

Because everything passes, and only What one does, Creative Work remains. We must not sacrifice it to the wild beasts, who lie within us.

And, in the same way, we must not kill these wild beasts—they give us blood, rage, ecstasy—like lightning, they clear the air and force the rain to pour down and fertilize the soil.

I live in my labors.

When you left, I wrote the first page of a scenario about agriculture.

Tomorrow, I will write the last.

Each morning, I get up at 8 o'clock, pour ice water over myself, and sit down to write until 5. […]

And you? They are pawing you, soaking you, drying you, shining lights on you, warming you, cooling you, feeding you, spraying you down, moving you around, and generally torturing you!

Go for a walk! That's the main thing. Walk, walk, use your imagination, and watch the clouds. Observe the birds. Study water. Imitate the cries of the roosters. Read Krylov's fables aloud… Above all, breathe deeply: first imagine, you are breathing in roses. Then, the whole sky, then the mountains. They will find a place within you, if you raise your arms to your sides at shoulder height and stand up on your tiptoes. Blow your nose harder: squeeze one nostril, then blow out air from the other one forcefully. God preserve you from handkerchiefs—a nasty invention of decaying Europe. This very night, forgive everyone all their offenses: this kind of streptococcus is especially harmful. Do all this and you will achieve health, strength, and beauty.

Yours,

Bor. Agapov

76
E. I. Shub to S. K. and V. V. Vishnevsky

April 27, 1942, Alma-Ata

My dear friends Sonya and Vsevolod!

First of all, I want to explain my silence. I was ill all winter. Twice, I suffered pneumonia and pleuritis. Only at the end of March, did I begin to get out and work. During my illness, I wrote the scenario for a jubilee film. It's been approved here. All April I waited to be called to Moscow. It's possible I'll leave for Moscow any day now. I wanted to write you from there. My existence here is difficult. Everything is strange and incomprehensible. There is a pronounced feeling of isolation. I feel myself pushed up against the white mountains with no way out. My homesickness for Moscow is deadly. I don't want the war to pass me by. The whole time I was writing the scenario, you were with me in my thoughts—I wanted to feel with particular clarity, how Vsevolod would write it, to catch sight of Leningrad through your eyes—I was writing with the dream, that Vsevolod would help me make the film and how his voice would sound coming from the screen. The film must be about our Great People, liberating humanity from Black Fascism, through incredible efforts and difficulties.
I am filled with the profound conviction, that on the great anniversary of the October Revolution, we will meet in Moscow, and the Requiem in memory of those who have perished for our Motherland, with which the film will begin, will sound in solemn celebration and in victory.

My precious, beloved friends, if you only knew, how my thoughts about you comforted me in moments of spiritual and physical suffering. I do not know, dearest Sonya, whether you received my letter. I wrote to you in Kuibyshev and in Moscow—I know, that it is difficult for you, but I am happy, that you are now with Vsevolod and I am proud of you.

In Alma-Ata, the spring days are hot. The studio has taken on a life of its own—work goes on. Eisen[stein] will soon begin *Ivan*. Pudovkin is finishing a film based on Brecht's novella.[125] Gerasimov[126] is shooting a film about the defense of Leningrad,

---

[125] [Trans.]: *Убийцы выходят на дорогу* [*The Muderers are Coming*] released 1942. Alternate title *Школа подлости* [*School of Infamy*]. Yuri Tarich is credited as co-director.
[126] [Trans.]: Sergei Apollinarievich Gerasimov. The film would seem to be *Непобедимые* [*Neobed-imye*] (*The Invincibles*), released 1942.

Kozintsev, *A City Surrounded*,[127] Ermler,[128] a film about partisans. Alexandrov and Orlova left for Baku. Alexandrov is quite ill. Dzigan had a great deal of difficulty surviving. People are very lonely here. And you don't feel the shoulder of a comrade is nearby. I think that cinema people generally suffer from this. I live in the same apartment with Eisen[stein]. He, too, lives a lonely life. I live for a single desire: to leave for Moscow and to work there. Pera left for Moscow a few days ago. She was also quite ill here. Zoshchenko[129] is here, Mikhalkov[130] is coming back again. They are all for me like "slanting rain."[131]

Don't forget me. I am always with you. I love you, I am thinking about you. Yours,

Esfir

77

S. K. Vishnevetskaya to E. Shub

1942, Leningrad

Dear Esfir' and Pera!

That's how things go. From Alma-Ata far away, you think of friends—and from near Moscow (though in my mind quite far away) you no longer ever write. From Bol'shakov's telegram and from Edouard's letter, I found out, that Esfir' is in Moscow, too. I'm happy for her. What shall I write about myself to you? I recently finished 5 pictures about Fort N.[132] This was my first large scale work in painting here. In *Pravda* you saw a photo of it. It was mistakenly labeled as a drawing. Without color and at such a small scale, it is almost unrecognizable. All five pictures were approved by my

---

[127] [Trans.]: *Город в кольце* [*Gorod v kol'tse*] (*A City Surrounded*). I could find no information about this film. The two films listed in Kozintsev's filmographies for 1942 were never released and neither would seem to have any relation to this title, as one is a comic lecture about Nazi anthropology and the other is set on a collective farm.

[128] [Trans.]: *Она защищает Родину* [*Ona zashchishchaem Rodinu*] (*She Defends the Motherland*). English release title: *No Greater Love*. Released 1943.

[129] [Trans.]: Possibly Mikhail Mikhailovich Zoshchenko, a writer and satirist, denounced in the Zhdanov decree of 1946.

[130] [Trans.]: Possibly Sergei Vladimirovich Mikhalkov, writer and lyricist. He wrote the words for the Soviet National Anthem. Hero of Socialist Labor. Order of St. Andrew.

[131] [Trans.]: Here Shub alludes to a poem by Mayakovsky of 1925: Я хочу быть понят родной страной, а не буду понят—что ж?! По родной стране пройду стороной, как проходит косой дождь. (I want to be understood by my native land, and I will not be understood: What of it?! I will pass through my native land obliquely, the way slanting rain passes through.)

[132] [Trans.]: This may be the series known as "Балтика в дни Отечественной войны" ("The Baltic in the days of the Great Patriotic War"), which refers to the Baltic Fleet. Форт [fort] is used in Russian not only to refer to a fortress but to a naval base.

superiors. They thanked me, they shook my hands. I'm happy because this gives me the right to do more of what I need to continue to do: to live in the conditions of the front and to draw. Now, the things are in an exhibition. The Deviz. comis.[133] wanted to take them away to Moscow, but I pleaded against this: I painted them with my heart, under very difficult conditions, I painted what I saw and what I lived through, right there for the Baltic and for Leningrad. I will send things to Moscow, if I will be alive, for the October Jubilee Exhibition. After completing this work, I helped organize an exhibition of all the artists, commanders, and Red Fleet sailors of the Baltic: on the Sunday of the commemorations, there will be openings and on Monday, I will leave again. This time, I will leave again for the sea, I will work with the submarine chasers, go with them on patrol and make paintings about them. I have learned how to paint the sky, with the sea it's been amazingly difficult—but somehow it works out. Of course, I'm sorry about one thing: I would now like to paint everything that has happened at the fort all over again—this is my material. I really liked everything there, but since I am nearly the only artist who can go to the front and draw (others are designated for ships, for newspapers), it demands working in a very short amount of time and with great efficiency. For that reason, it requires making what are effectively sketches and not authentic things. And all the same, I'm convinced it's the best thing I have done. A crazy lust for life, work, love, victory! It's all so pointed: since everything I want to do, all dreams and plans begin for us with the words: if I will be alive. For this reason, you hurry as much as possible to succeed at sketching, capturing, doing. Perhaps you saw my winter cycle about Leningrad. I gave a photo to Vera Inber; these things I consider weak, as they were not done from nature, but under the very difficult conditions of cold and hunger. But these are documents. Even now, my hands are still swollen. My sweet girls, I am very happy. I love Muffin,[134] but unfortunately, I rarely see him, since everyone is either on the road, or I have been painting locked up in Inber's husband's apartment; but we have a wonderful friendship and he is proud of me and calls me a little "worker-fighter." He also works like an ox. […] We have been mourning the loss of E. Petrov.[135] Here, the fleet and the Leningrad front and every citizen of Leningrad loves Vsevolod. You can be proud of him, your friend, and he will write a great work of art, if he will be alive, how else would he write! But now, both physically and because of the conditions of the constant need for operational work, this is impossible. Unfortunately, not all of this will be understood where you are […].

---

[133] [Trans.]: In the original: Девиз. комис. [Deviz. komis.] This is an abbreviation for Дивиз[ионный] комис[сар], that is, Divisional Commissar. In the armed forces of the USSR, this was a special rank for senior military-political officers of the Red Army and Navy from 1935–1942. Vishnevsky is mentioned as a Brigade Commissar in the next to the last paragraph of letter #79.

[134] [Trans.]: In the original: Мася [Masya], a term of endearment. Vishnevsky uses the same term for her.

[135] Possibly Evgeny Petrovich Kataev, know as Evgeny Petrov. One half of the team of satirical writers known as Il'f and Petrov. Their main character was the previously mentioned Ostap Bender. Petrov died in July 2, 1942, the same year this letter was written.

There are some quite bitter moments, it is painful, pitiful for our country, our people, but I myself have learned of and seen here such beautiful examples of courage, such amazing fighters and commissars, such endurance and steadfastness in our People, that I know, I believe, that whatever the cost, we will smash the damn bastards. Oh, how I hate them, for every round they fire into the city, and this is still going on. For every horrible thing, that we have lived through here, that has been lived through by everyone, who has felt the breath close by of this utterly heinous enemy. I learned how to shoot a revolver and a TT,[136] and it is my fever dream to make at least one authentic picture about the Baltic and to kill at least three Germans. I don't want to leave here for anywhere else. I feel I belong here. Although I had to work hard to earn that. In the beginning, I was Vishnevsky's wife — now I am someone new and in the Baltic, I'm Vishnevetskaya. I'm glad about that. I feel really good here — I knew, what I was saying, when I argued with you, Esfir', that I needed to go to the front, to war. Maybe we will see each other again — it will be a wonderful — and if not, well, what can you do? But in my soul, I am at peace and along with the heavy hardships of Leningrad I lived through, perhaps, the most colorful, brilliant moments as a person and as a woman, as an artist. Until we see each other again. Answer as soon as possible.

When I returned from the front, there were letters waiting for me from you, from Eisen[stein], from Tairov. It was a delight. In 2 weeks I hope once again to return and find nice letters from both of you. Lots of kisses to you and Lyuba too.

Sonya

PS: I'm glad, that Vsevolod and Fadeev became friends here. If you see Sasha, give him my warm greetings.

My crazy man just rushed over, having decided, that now was not the time to relax. Through an insane effort, by order of Director L. U., we managed to get him admitted to hospital, but it was too much for him and today with all his belongings he came down on my head like snow. […]

---

[136] [Trans.]: TT also known as a Tokarev (after its designer Fedor Tokarev) was a series of semi-automatic pistols developed in the late 1920s as a service weapon for the Soviet Armed Forces. There are a number of models designated by a number: TT–30, TT33, etc.

78
N. G. Vachnadze to E. I. Shub

January 27, 1942, Tbilisi

Dear Esfir' Il'inishna!

I am so very glad to receive a letter from you. We are living here quite settled into our situation. The [film] factory is catastrophically idle. In the course of six months, nothing has been shot except 3 very average shorts. We now have 5 feature-length scenarios actually ready, but, alas, their approval will probably require as much time as their writing, considering that Bol'shakov is in Moscow, and Room is in Tash-kent, and still someone else is in Novosibirsk. This is all so stupid, but in light of the current day, perhaps, it's not so important, the question of motion pictures is hardly compelling. Much more importantly, we have been healthy lately.

Kolya is planning to do a scenario on the theme of the home front and the battle front. The scenario is ready. I will probably act in it. Meanwhile, I am working in the cinema school as an assistant.

My children are all growing and healthy. Kira is working among the actresses at the [film] factory. Chiaureli[137] is shooting *Saakadze*.[138] Well, that's everything. Life is going forward in gigantic steps and nothing makes any sense. I will be very happy, my dear, if you should happen to wind up here in Tbilisi. Lots of kisses. Kolya sends greetings and kisses. Where is Anya?

Yours,

Natasha

79
S. K. Vishnevetskaya to E. I. Shub

January 27, 1942, Leningrad

My dear friends (Esfir', Pera, Verochka, Edya, Grisha, Sergei Mikhailovich),

I have written all of you a single letter, just to reiterate. Finally, I am in Lenin-grad. You yourselves understand, that clawing my way from Kazan to Moscow was rather difficult and flying over here was even more difficult. Of course, none of the "friends" helped… I managed it all myself. Vsevolod was very sick. Now he's in pretty

---

[137] [Trans.]: Mikhail Edisherovich Chiaureli, Soviet Georgian actor, film director and screenwriter. Stalin Prize 1941, 1943, 1946, 1947, 1950.

[138] [Trans.]: *Георгий Саакадзе* [*Georgy Saakadze*] 1942 an historical drama based on Anna Anton-ovskaya's Stalin Prize-winning novel *Великий Моурави* [*Veliky Mouravi*] (*The Great Mouravi*), based on the life of the 17th-century Georgian political and military leader.

good shape. He won't hear about resting. Having lived through two weeks here, I understood him profoundly. A day is a month; a month is a year. Frozen over, under siege, the city has suffered through the sixth month of a blockade. The courage of the people is beyond measure. There is one person in cinema art, who would be able to immortalize, to catch sight of, to read through these pages of life in Leningrad; that is Eisenstein, but, alas, he is far away from us. It is sad—to the point of tears—that nothing is being set in the record with a movie camera. It is gone forever. Unfilmed by anyone. [...] It is impossible to describe the daily feats of hundreds of thousands of people in a letter. The city is astonishing and terrifying with a particular, terrible beauty. Everything is under snow, tangled wires in huge knots have been hanging over the streets, houses ripped apart gape open, trolleybuses and trams, which have been shelled, lie frozen in the snow. The shimmering of the moon, silhouettes of ships; hoar frost; corpses in the streets; gunfire; the music of Tchaikovsky; perseverance!... The monument of Peter the Great by Falconet and the other monuments stand like pyramids of snow, in their impenetrable casings; it sometimes seems, that you are seeing the hand of Peter [the Great] beneath the sand, beneath the snow. Fortunately, all the best buildings in Leningrad are intact. And everywhere people go on foot with sleds, on which they are transporting wood, water, etc., and these people have infinitely great strength, patience, and faith.

I am proud and happy, that I am here, that I did not attempt to take Vsevolod away after his illness, but instead came here myself. My place is here; my fate is here. I believe we will get through it. I am hoping, that the wait for a break in the Leningrad blockade will not be too long. Write us at Krasnoznamen Baltic Fleet, Naval Post Office № 1101, Box 176. To Brigade Commissar Vs. Vishnevsky, or to my name. I love you, I'm thinking about you, S. K.

It turned out: all the things, which happened before the siege of Leningrad, were "test runs"; this is the epic of total war here!... Long live great Leningrad, which taught the country and the world how to stop Hitler. We will fulfill our duty and go West...

Greetings—Vs. Vishnevsky

Sonya

80
M. I. Aliger[139] to E. I. Shub

November–December 1942

My dear Esfir' Il'inishna,

I don't know when my letter will reach you; I am writing it, not from Moscow, but from the front, where I am now working for the army gazette. I left Moscow quite soon after your departure and all this happened quite quickly and unexpectedly. I think, that this is better for me, if it's at all possible now for anything to be better for me. [...][140]

If you knew how I missed you, if you only knew! Sometime when we meet again like we used to, I will spend a few hours telling you everything. You will understand this. [...]

But the most important thing for me is, that, in spite of everything, I am at peace in my heart, there are no anxieties, no doubts... Your absence is so difficult for me and it is so difficult for me to write you. This amounts to so little, compared to all I want to say to you. It will be a long time before I find out what you think, before I hear your harsh and direct words, that are so necessary for me now.

The New Year is slowly approaching and I wish you happiness, my dear, and I miss you so much, lots of kisses,

Margarita

Using the date of this letter, decide where it is best to write me, here, or in Moscow, where I will be around the middle of February, if nothing happens to me.

Be my true friend always and never betray me... This is infinitely important and precious to me. I love you a lot and I trust you deeply,

Margarita

---

[139] [Trans.]: Margarita Iosifovna Aliger, distinguished Soviet and Russian poet, translator, and journalist.
[140] [Trans.]: She may be referring to the fact, that the year before, her husband, Konstantin Makarov-Rakitin, had been killed at the front and her infant son had died.

81
M. I. Aliger to E. I. Shub

February 11, 1943, Moscow

My dear Esfir' Il'inishna!

Once again—as I have so many times already—I read through your letter that I received only today. What a person of integrity you are, so true to yourself. I am not reading your letter, I am listening it. Everything in it is yours, your voice, your intonations. As if I were sitting in a hotel room on a still warm September evening and listening to you. And once again, you are saying things, that are harsh and direct and again I am listening to them intently and warily and again, in the end, they are helping. My dear friend, my lovely soul, thank you for your ruthlessness, your truth, your loyalty. […].

The other day, I sent you a letter, I wrote to you there about my wish to come to you. I very much want that, but now I am already doubting the desirability of this. I don't know. What do you think?

What new work are you thinking about? May god grant you success this time. I was so full of my own woe and misery in the fall, that I could spend very little time with you on your grief over the picture and this still weighs on me.

I live a thoroughly solitary life, keeping to myself. […]

I saw Tvardovsky[141] in passing. He also called me to come visit, but now this is somehow pointless. All the same, as I was writing this phrase, I understood, that I did want to see him and in a few days, I will do so. I will write then.

I met with Marshak.[142] It's so interesting to speak with him about poetry and about a lot of other things.

Good old Pavlik Antokol'sky[143] remains faithful to me. He wrote a remarkable poem, "Son."

I won't be receiving any more prizes. Some authority or other rejected "Zoya" for one, but this didn't upset me much. "Zoya" came out as a little book. I'll send one at the first opportunity.

---

[141] [Trans.]: Possibly Aleksandr Trifonovich Tvardovsky, Soviet poet and writer, chief literary editor of *Novy Mir* (*New World*) literary magazine. Stalin Prize 1941, 1946, 1947. USSR State Prize 1971. Lenin Prize 1961.

[142] [Trans.]: Possibly Samuil Yakovlevich Marshak, writer of children's literature. Translator of foreign literature, including Shakespeare, Eliot and Heine.

[143] [Trans.]: Possibly Pavel Grigor'evich Antokol'sky, Soviet and Russian poet, translator and theater director. The nickname Pavlik implies friendly familiarity.

What shall I do with this letter? Obviously, I can't mail it, it's too bulky. It will be necessary to actively search for the occasion—all the same, that's faster... Write as soon as possible, my dear.

Margarita

82

M. I. Aliger to E. I. Shub

March 1943, Moscow

Dear Esfir'!

On the 15th of February, I sent an enormous letter to you and the actress Tat'yana Kondrakova.[144] And my little book. Did you receive all that? I'm sending you "Zoya" and some of my new verses, which I don't even know whether I will publish. How do you like them and do you consider they are worth publishing?

Nothing has changed with me. In Moscow, it is deserted and lonely and I, perhaps, without any options, yearn for my favorite people. But this manifests itself violently, very rarely, since I leave practically no time for my own feelings. I live keeping to myself and occupied. I work a lot, I write (I almost have a new book of verse ready), I am reading, and I am studying the English language.

> And my courage remained as well
> as the voices of those not returning,
> and also the sinless paper,
> the sails of fleeting song.[145]

Besides that, two months from now, I'll be anticipating the arrival, finally, of my little daughter, who is already quite big and smart and who also misses me.

Lots of kisses, my dear. Write me as soon as possible.

Margarita

Your Anechka[146] called me and we agreed to keep in touch.

---

[144] [Trans.]: Tat'yana Nikolaevna Kondrakova. Soviet theater and film actress.
[145] [Trans.]: A small excerpt of her long poem "Zoya," about the courage of the teenage partisan, Zoya Kosmodem'yanskaya, tortured to death by Germans during the Great Patriotic War.
[146] [Trans.]: Another diminutive from Anna, Shub's daughter.

83
N. G. Vachnadze to E. I. Shub

January 25, 1949, Tbilisi

Dear Esfir' Il'inishna!

You are probably quite surprised, that I have erupted with a letter. And, the truth is, now life is so dreary and everyone in the circle of our art is so sad, that there is hardly time enough or nerves, to maintain connections and friendships with such close friends, as you are to me.

We are in utter gloom at the film studio. Complete strangers are in charge. For them, there is nothing precious in what Soviet art has carried forward all this time. They value neither the people and what they have previously accomplished, nor anything at all, which touches the heart and the life of the people, who have devoted themselves—their whole lives—to our work. And in this environment, they are celebrating my 25 years of work in the cinema.

At the beginning of March, there is to be an evening at our Grand Opera Theater celebrating my creative work. They are shooting a sketch about me, then they are doing a montage of the 22 pictures in which I acted. I would very much like to get one episode from *The Living Corpse*, so that this piece of film could also go into the montage. It would be ideal for me to have one piece of film with the Uhlan lancers and one with Pudovkin and me. You could probably advise me, as to whom our studio should address itself, to request that one of my pieces [of film] be found and printed and the prints sent to me. The negatives are probably stored somewhere. It's from 1929, release date 1930, at Mezhrabpom-Rus'.

I would really appreciate it, dear Esfir', if you could look into this for me and, perhaps, arrange for someone to find this for me, or determine who should be contacted directly.

My life is very hard.

You know that my mother died. Now, I am alone with the children. My youngest son has heart problems. It's very scary. My oldest is finishing university. I am just sitting this out. You yourself understand what this means and there is no light at the end of the tunnel. Dear Esfir' Il'inishna, I would really appreciate it if you could help me, answer me at this address: Tbilisi, Tskhakaya ul. 13, apt 4, N. G. Vachnadze.

Lots of kisses.

Perhaps, in this way, I will learn the details of your life.

Yours,

Natasha Vachnadze

84
E. I. Shub to P. A. Pavlenko

1949, Moscow

Dear Petr Andreevich,
I learned, that today you are returning to Moscow. I would like to meet with you to express my gratitude for your wonderful story "The sun of the steppes."[147]
I read the story and my heart was overflowing with joy and a particular gentle sadness from being close to something beautiful. You read and live in a world of great love for our fellow man.

I won't congratulate you on your fiftieth birthday. Why? I know how little joy there is in this.
Wishing you everything remarkable!
Kisses to you and Natasha.

Esfir' Shub

85
M. I. Aliger to E. I. Shub

January 13, 1952, Yalta

Dear Esfir',
They phoned me today from Moscow, the weather there is nasty. How are you feeling? [...]
I have been living here for two weeks already in such an extreme state of tension, which, in my opinion, the human heart cannot withstand. Nonetheless, it does withstand it. I am working quite a lot—this is the only physical regimen of existence, in which my heart lets go a little and I stare in great surprise at what is obtained as a result of this work: is it possible I can still write verses? And at the same time, I, as a poet, now feel wonderfully strong and confident. I feel, that I can do it all, that everything will turn out substantial and serious. If I now again had the freedom of spirit, which I have not had for a long time, not a constrained, but a free heart, I would probably work ten times better. And then, who knows?! From the time of my arrival from Moscow, I have written a lot, even I didn't imagine, that I would manage so much, perhaps, precisely because only at work do I still feel human. [...] I miscalculated my strengths, I overestimated them, and they are coming to an end. Well, one

---

[147] [Trans.]: In the original: «Степное солнце» ["Stepnoe solntse"].

should never write about that, never, probably, nor talk about it and precisely because I work so much, that only in work using my head, at least, not my heart, of course, do I get distracted. [...]

We are all very upset, that it's so difficult to get to us, because if we were to bring you here, you would immediately feel better. Really, ask the doctors, whether perhaps, it's still worth doing? Finally, it's only 26 hours to Simferopol' in a comfortable train car, and from there to Yalta 3 hours by car with an experienced driver, perhaps, this is not too difficult [...]

Lots of kisses. I wish you health, strength, and courage.

I will be glad to hear from you.

January 12, 1952. Crimea. Yalta.

Yesterday, at our place it poured down torrential rain and today is a bright, sunny day, 23 degrees, in the sun. I re-read the letter and today I will send it.

M.

86
V. I. Mukhina[148] to E. I. Shub

January-February 1953, Moscow

Esfir' Il'inishna, dear, I felt so good yesterday and the day before. I slept well. Today, I feel very bad, I didn't sleep the whole night [...]

Yesterday, I vividly imagined a bluebird in the corner and today it flew far away. I am so sad. How are you? Write, I want desperately for you to be well.

V. M.

---

[148] [Trans.]: Vera Ignat'evna Mukhina. Distinguished Soviet sculptor, a member of the Four Arts association. She is famous for, among others, the iconic "Рабочий и колхозница" ("Worker and Kolkhoz Woman"), adorning the entrance to the Russian Exhibition Center in Moscow, which became the logo for Mosfil'm Studio. Order of the Red Banner of Labor, The Badge of Honor, Medal For Valiant Service during the Great Patriotic War of 1941–1945, Medal in Memory of 800 Years of Moscow, Order of Civic Merit, Honored Artist of the RSFSR, People's Artist of the USSR, Stalin Prize (5 times).

87
V. I. Mukhina to E. I. Shub

April 2, 1953, Moscow

Dear little one,[149] they are saying that you are already on your feet. How happy I am, in spite of the fact, that you have bested me in Socialist Competition.[150] Dear, lovely one, claw your way out as quickly as possible. I so want to know, that Esfir' Shub has already left and, in spite of everything, is already working. Quickly, quickly. Kisses.
Yours,

M.

88
E. I. Shub to V. I. Mukhina

April, 1953, Moscow

Dear Vera Ignat'evna!
How have you been spending your nights and days?
And I am particularly anxious today. […]
I keep thinking, that I haven't succeeded in doing in art for my Motherland even a tenth of my share of what I wanted, since my life is the cinema.
I wasn't lucky enough and now it's too late.
I wish you many more years to work and to make more beautiful works again.
It will be so. You are my favorite and a wonderful artist.

E. I.

---

[149] [Trans.]: In the original: Милуша [Milusha], an affectionate diminutive from милий [mily] (dear).
[150] [Trans.]: In the original Mukhina uses the official acronym: соцсоренование [sotssorevnovanie], short for социалистическое соревнование [sotsialisticheskoe sorevnovanie]. This was a official policy instituted originally by Lenin. The term is used here in a darkly jocular way. The official translation into English, socialist emulation, is, somewhat misleadingly, meant to distinguish the competition to excel to the benefit of all in socialist countries from exploitative capitalist competition, in Russian: капиталистическая конкуренция [kapitalisticheskaya koncurentsiya]. In practice, according to Kravchenko and Heller, the competition in the East Bloc on an individual and enterprise level was quite brutal. Winning the competitions for over-completing Five-Year Plans eventually led to cheating, to waste, and double accounting, since the stakes were high. Winners could receive trips to resorts, permission to travel abroad, housing, vehicles as well as various public honors and medals.

89

I. V. Meyerhold[151] to E. I Shub

July 21, 1958, Moscow

Dear Eddi!

On July 13, on the eve of my flight to Dnepropetrovsk, Anyuta[152] called and, very upset, half-choking, told me, that you shouted at her for my passivity in relation to Meyerhold's affairs.

At first, I too got upset, but later, being in possession of great optimism, which helps me to live, I quickly calmed down. [...]

I know, that my conscience is clear in connection with father, my passport has never known a surname other than his.

My children know, that the memory of their grandfather is sacred to them.

I write a great deal about father, when my health does not prevent me from doing so.

But I do not intend to make an outcry about this, and in my own time, when it is ready, I will transmit it, where it is appropriate.

I have turned 53. My head still works well enough.

My heart has been destroyed by all the terrible experiences connected with father. I cannot hold onto the "legacy" with the same indifference, that many of his "friends" and "relatives"[153] do. If you don't understand this, it means, that you have forgotten me, which makes me very upset.

Kisses, be well,

Yours,

Irina

---

[151] [Trans.]: Presumably Irina Vsevolodovna Meyerhold. Daughter and student of Vsevolod Meyerhold. Soviet actress, director, teacher. Honored Artist of the Chechen-Ingushetia ASSR 1978.

[152] [Trans.]: Irina's daughter Anna.

[153] [Trans.]: In the original, Irina Meyerhold uses the word родственники [rodstvenniki], which she puts in quotation marks along with the word "friends." It is difficult to say whether she is referring to members of her own family, who may have actually changed their surnames to avoid sanctions associated with Vsevolod Meyerhold, or to persons who had previously considered themselves part of his extended artistic "family." On June 20, 1939, Vsevolod Meyerhold had been arrested in his flat in Leningrad, then repeatedly tortured. To end his suffering under torture, he made a false confession to being a British and Japanese spy. In 1940, he was executed by firing squad along with a group of 345 others, by an order of the Politburo, signed by Stalin himself. In the 1980s, documents revealed that their bodies were cremated and thrown into a mass grave. Shortly after Meyerhold's arrest, his wife, actress Zinaida Raikh, was stabbed repeatedly in their flat by KGB agents, and died of her injuries soon after. During the first wave of de-Stalinization in 1955, The Soviet Supreme Court cleared Meyerhold of all charges. So, there had previously been incentives, if not moral courage, in dissociating oneself from the gifted and influential theater director. This letter was written three years after his "rehabilitation," so there was more than adequate cause for Irina Meyerhold's scorn and anger.

90
A. I. Medvedkin[154] to E. I. Shub

1959

Dear Esfir' Il'inishna!

I think about you always as someone who wishes me well and as my friend.

I sincerely wish you the most speedy recovery!

I am now living a full life. I worked in Alma-Ata for around four years.

Now I am returning to Moscow. I am doing a scenario for a film comedy for Mosfil'm, and when it is written, I will give it to you for critique with pleasure.

Once again, With great respect.

Get well as soon as possible!

Yours,

Medvedkin

91
Letters from A. M. Gan to E. I. Shub[155]

End of July 1927

Edi!

I've been thinking a lot these past few days. I've been thinking about myself and about you. I've been thinking about our relationship. I've come to a conclusion: our—that's you and I—, who love one another, man and woman and... two workers, working in the same school, working for the social order.

---

154 [Trans.]: Aleksandr Ivanovich Medvedkin. Soviet Russian film director, best known for his feature *Happiness* (1935) and his stewardship of the Agitprop Кинопоезд [Kinopoezd] the Cinema Train of the 1930s. It was a mobile film studio on a train complete with cameras, a film laboratory, editing facilities, and projection equipment. It traveled across the USSR, showing rural communities their own images on the screen. They would shoot one day, process and edit, and project the next day. USSR State Prize (1974).

155 [Trans.]: These two letters from Gan to Shub and one from Shub to Gan were not published in *My Life is the Cinema*. They were published online by *Киноведческие записки* under the heading Письма Алексея Гана Эсфири Шуб in *Киноведческие записки*. № 49. 2000. The link at the *Киноведческие записки* website is now broken. They are available as of November 2025 at https://chapaev.media/articles/7385 and should be part of the Shub fond 3035 at RGALI. Most likely, as part of the collection of letters of Gan contained at ф.3035 оп.1 ед. хр.105 or, ф.3035 оп.1 ед. хр.106. Shub's letter to Gan would have come from ф.3035 оп.1 ед. хр.79. These three letters seem to represent only a small fraction of their correspondence.

I have thought it through and come to the conclusion: it can't be this way. This isn't right.

Without factionalism, art is an inkblot, without factionalism, without partisanship, the struggle for new forms of artistic labor is social eclecticism. With that and with its assistance, the social order is not realized. For the second week now, I have been alone. I read and I think. I remember and go through things. I draw conclusions.

No, no, and no! I don't agree, I disagree.

From the time that you, "objectively," began to work independently, you decided, as did many of my former comrades and collaborators, that you were free to act separately, as you found… the necessary and appropriate way to go towards your goal.

This must never be forsaken, for it prevents us from doing. Go.

But I must be honest and in this case, that is, ours: loving and working must be put in their proper places. I love you, but I can't do things with you, I won't, for betrayal does not make friends, but creates feuds; those who love, answer betrayal with hatred. I hate your work, as much as I hate the work of the creators of *Potemkins*, of *Sixth Parts of the World* and other speculators of our time. I love and I approve the work of great culture, even if it is not within my camp. Chaplin and Kuleshov will always remain friends for me, for this work that they do and because they aid me, in what I call production ingenuity and production culture. Khokhlova and Harry Carter[156] will always remain for me great friends, for they point the ways for me on which it is simpler to seek a method, with the help of which, I can genuinely approach each living person, in order for him to become a better demonstrator[157] of everyday life and of life itself.

Your versatility—that you can speak with me today (and agree), the very same day speak with Eisenstein (and be fascinated) and the very same day speak with Kuleshov (and understand) and the very same day with Vertov (and become interested) and the very same day with Rodchenko (and be thrilled in boundless friendship) and, finally, accommodate English language transcribers, reporters from the fucking film press [word missing] in lively fashion, lackeys à la Trainin[158] and much more—all this has cut you off from me, all this prevents me from speaking with you about the school and social work.

---

[156] A prolific American film actor, appearing in 84 films between 1914 and 1934.

[157] [Trans.]: In the original: демонстрант [demonstrant], a Constructivist term, implying an example.

[158] [Trans.]: Il'ya Pavlovich Trainin, director of Sovkino (1926–30). In the early 1930s, he left the film world to become a legal scholar, earning several Orders of the Red Banner of Labor in the 1940s.

But I love you. You have given me too much and have already borne way too much from me, for me to simply be able to walk away from you, like I have from so many.

We will probably meet in Leningrad. I am traveling to Leningrad on the night of the 31st of July. And I don't want for us to return to these questions. They will be resolved over time, by facts and by our behavior.

All this needed to be written, and not spoken about, for the conversations of lovers, who have betrayed one another, lead to nothing. Each is convinced they are right… and then, they kiss one another.

Your first and second letters don't sit right with me. The worst thing is when words do not match deeds.

Til soon,

Gan

I'm not sending you Anichka's letter. It's really too good! I read it every day. What an intelligent and good little girl. Loving her is fantastic.

Shub and Gan in happier times.

92
Letters from A. M. Gan to E. I. Shub

Undated

Edi!
You will read this, on the condition, that you accept my request, that from this day forward, we will not speak about this subject again, to clarify things again and again, to somehow forget, so that... to once again bring our failures out into the open.

As bitter as it may be, I must leave home. I am leaving. On Wednesday, I am going away for the summer and during this time I will move out altogether. Tomorrow, I am going to the housing authority and I will ask that they give me and my father accommodations in the front annex. I don't want to interfere with your work, to unsettle and make your life difficult. It's difficult for you to be with me—I know this. It's hard to be with someone who is ill. I didn't find you healthy either. But I helped you, not only to heal but to work. I helped you heal, because I knew what made you ill. I made of you a productivist, for I had the culture to do so. Not only you and not only Vesnin[159] began to do things that way, and not some other way. I have many more such comrades. But of all of them, only Vesnin widely and honestly, here and everywhere, will say, "I began to do things in a new way, only because Gan showed me the way."

It is hard to live with people who are ill in general. But even more difficult, when you don't know why they are ill. And you do not know why I am ill. You think, that I am an alcoholic. It seems to you, that I need to go to a sanatorium. Kanabikh[160] told you all about it. You've come to a conclusion: I'm breaking with everything and hurting even myself. No, it's not like that.

I really am ill, but my illness is of a different order. Again and again, I will say: I can't give birth to anything. I can't take up any work until I decide on the main thing: what I need to do. You have decided everything about how you need to act, but I can't decide what to do. Our era is devilishly complicated. We have lived through a revolution in the social order. It is essential to understand this in actively participating in construction. I understand this and I am resolving it. But that is precisely my illness. But besides all this, the fury, the coarseness, and the unshakable desire to bring all my

---

[159] [Trans.]: Most likely, Viktor Aleksandrovich Vesnin. Neo-classical architect who, under Gan's influence, became a Constructivist architect along with his brothers Leonid and Alexander. After the suppression of Constructivism in the early 1930s, Viktor remained the highest-ranking architect in the Soviet system.

[160] [Trans.]: Possibly, Yuri Vladimirovich Kannabikh. Prominent Russian and Soviet psychiatrist and psychotherapist. It appears Gan has misspelled the surname.

failures into the open has led me to want to leave. This is not words. This is already action.

Forgive me all this grief. I love you and I am leaving in love with you, though I am carrying away a lot of bitterness after the end of our relationship.

I'm asking you one more time, don't insist, don't speak to me about this subject.

Farewell
your Gan,
who will never again have a wife.

93
Letter from E. I. Shub to A. M. Gan

Undated

1
Gan! If this is your final letter, that's really bad.

2
It sounds like a threat and an accusation.

3
The word "ravings" is not a petty jab.
You understand things badly.

4
I believed it for two months
and don't believe it any more.
To me this is sick and scary,
And you write "jab."

5
You are leaving too hastily.
People don't leave like that.

6
I'm sick, I haven't seen you for 8 days—
You got completely drunk a second time during those 8 days
your way of checking out—

7
I want to be truthful to you to the end:
If I had any money now,
I wouldn't give you a single ruble.

8
So, if you want my help—
Wait a day or two—
I will do all I can for you.
I will go get the ticket myself
And I will give you as much money as I can when the train leaves.
As painful as it is, that's the way it is—
I don't believe you—
I don't believe your note at all either.
I feel really bad.

9
I don't have either money or rations,
Which means, all I can do,
I definitely want to do. That's it.

10
And another thing:
I now know for a fact,
That you don't care for me a bit as a human being.
E.

Sources and notes by the Russian editor

1. This letter, like all the additional published letters between S. M. Eisenstein and E. Shub, is published according to the original manuscript, preserved in the archive of E. Shub. Printed with omissions noted with square brackets and ellipses. This letter was sent from Gagra [in Abkhazia] where in May of 1928 S. Eisenstein and G. Alexander were on vacation.

"our friend the 'Hamburg Scorekeeper'" has in mind V. B. Shklovsky author of the book *Hamburg Score.* (L[eningrad]. Izdatel'stvo pisatelei, 1928).

"a letter not about love" again refers to V. B. Shklovsky and his book *ZOO, or Letters not about Love* (L[eningrad]. *Atenei, Sovetsky pisatel'*, 1924).

Grisha is the film director Grigory Vasil'evich Alexandrov.

2. From the Tselina Station of the Severo-Kavkazskaya Railroad at the Gigant sovkhoz near Rostov. S. Eisenstein was shooting additional material for his film *Old and New.*

3. The first postcard sent from Europe, where S. Eisenstein, G. Alexandrov, and E. Tissé were on an official trip to learn about contemporary film technology.

4. *SA* is the journal *Sovetskaya Arkitektura.*[161]

5. *Richter, Hans.* German film director, who created a series of experimental films in the 1920s, constructed according to a rhythmic montage of documentary material.

7. In La Sarraz, S. Eisenstein gave a presentation to the Congress of Independent Filmmakers.

16. The last letter of Eisenstein from Mexico; on May 9, 1932, Eisenstein returned to the USSR.

17. *"It's imperative you read the scenario today."* S. Eisenstein is asking E. Shub to read the scenario of *Ivan the Terrible.*

18. *"And again, Mexico with its abominations…"* refers to the film *¡Que viva Mexico!* (December 1931). Having shot 60,000 meters [of film], S. Eisenstein was obliged to break off shooting and return to the Motherland. There were conversations about the material which had been shot being sent [to him], but they were not successful.

19. *"I made the final 'cuts' on the picture…"* refers to part one of S. Eisenstein's film *Ivan the Terrible.*

20. This letter, as well as all further published letters of E. I. Shub and S. M. Eisenstein, are published according to the original manuscripts preserved in the TsGALI[162] (f. 1923).

---

[161] [Trans.]: I believe the Russian editor is mistaken. It is more likely *Современная архитектура* (*Sovremenaya Arkitektura*) [*Contemporary Architecture*] to which *SA* refers.

[162] [Trans.]: TsGALI refers to the Центральный государственный архив литературы и исскуства (The Central State Archive of Literature and Art), now РГАЛИ [RGALI] Российский государственный архив литературы и искусства (The Russian State Archive of Literature and Art) in Moscow. f. refers to the fond фонд, or collection.

21. This letter from the USA is preserved in the TsGALI (f. 1923) *GRK* Gosudarstvennaya repertuarnaya komissiya [The State Repertoire Commission]. *The Glass House* refers to a project by S. Eisenstein which he was describing to E. Shub. Eisenstein was proposing to make a satirical comedy about bourgeois society, the action of which, would take place in a huge, completely transparent house.

22. *Ludwell Denny* is an American writer.

23. Letter to Mexico, published without the following pages, which apparently are missing.

24. Letter, apparently sent to Yalta, where S. Eisenstein became acquainted with the work of the Film Factory.

25. Letter from Smyrna.
    Ol'ga Viktorevna is the wife of the poet Sergei Tret'yakov.

26. Note sent to S. M. Eisenstein on his birthday, January 23, 1934.

27. Note sent August 25, 1938, when S. Eisenstein was shooting the film *Alexander Nevsky*.

28. Letter sent to Fergana, where S. Eisenstein was working on the film *Большой Ферганский канал* (*The Great Fergana Canal*).

29. Letter sent to Alma-Ata.

30. Letter sent to Alma-Ata.
    Polonsky, Konstantin Andreevich, at that time the head of the Chief Directorate for Feature Film Production.

32. Letters between A. A. Fadeev and E. I. Shub are printed here according to the originals, preserved in her archive. As with all the letters, omissions are noted with square brackets and ellipses. All letters are dated.

33. In September and November of 1933, while in the Far East, A. Fadeev was working with A. Dovzhenko on the scenario of the film *Aerograd*.

34. This letter was written, as were the two following ones, during the time of work on *Последний из Удэге* (*The Last of the Udege*).

37. Letter from Sukhumi, where A. Fadeev often went for work and leisure.

42. "*I didn't send the books…*" A. Fadeev was starting the publication of a chapter from his novel *Черная металлургия* (*Ferrous Metallurgy*).

49. Letter sent from the Barvikha sanatorium near Moscow.

53. *Zhurnalistka* (*Newspaperwoman*) working title of the film *Your Acquaintance*.
    L. Kuleshov and A. Khokhlova were working together in Georgia on the film *Паровоз № 1001* (*Steam Locomotive № 1001*). The work was not completed.

57. "*come here with the picture…*" refers to E. Shub's picture *KShE*.

58. A humorous poem in celebration of ten years of creative work by E. Shub, sent by M. Romm, V. Gusev and A. Piotrovsky. The original is preserved in the archive of E. Shub.

61. *"I'm obsessing on a film about Ankara"* refers to the documentary film *Анкара—сердце Турции* (*Ankara is the Heart of Turkey*), which S. Yutkevich shot in Turkey (scenario by S. Yutkevich and N. Zarkhi, camera operator Zh. Martov).[163]

86. In January and February of 1953 the famous Soviet sculptor Vera Ignat'eva Mukhina and E. I. Shub were both in Botkinskaya Hospital; confined to their beds, they were forced to communicate by letter.

90. Letter from the film director Alexander Ivanovich Medvedkin was sent to E. I. Shub in the hospital.

---

[163] [Trans.]: Zarkhi is nowhere credited for this film directed by Leo Oskarovich Arnshtam.

Filmography

Паление династии Романовых [*Padenie dinastii Romanovykh*], *Fall of the Romanov Dynasty*. A chronicle of the years 1917–1927. 7 reels, 2,080 meters. Sovkino and the Museum of the Revolution, 1927. A work by Esfir' Shub, consultant M. Tseitlin. Silent.

Великий путь [*Veliky Put'*], *The Great Way*. A ten-year chronicle 1917–1927. 9 reels, 2,350 meters. Sovkino and the Museum of the Revolution. 1927. Author-Director Esfir' Shub, camera operator N. Sokolov, consultant M. Tseitlin, assistants to the director L. Felonov, T. Kuvshinchikova. Silent.

Россия Николая II и Лев Толстой [*Rossiya Nikolaya II i Lev Tolstoy*], *Lev Tolstoy and the Russia of Nicholas II*. 5 reels, 1,700 meters, Sovkino, 1928. A work by Esfir' Shub, intertitles by M. Tseitlin, assistant director L. Felonov, camera operators for supplementary material E. Shneider, D. Fel'dman, G. Blyum. Silent.[164]

Сегодня [*Segodnya*], *Today*. 6 reels, 2,090 meters. Soyuzkino, 1930. Scenario Esfir' Shub and M. Tseitlin, director E. Shub, camera operators Stepanov and Stilianudis. Silent.

КШЭ (Комсомол—шеф электрификации) [*KShE (Komsomol—shef elektrifikatsii)*], *KShE (Komsomol in service to Electrification)*.[165] 6 reels, 2,750 meters. Soyuzkino, 1932. Scenarist and director E. Shub, assistant directors L. Felonov, N. Vachnadze, camera operators V. Solodovnikov, A. Barkovsky, music composer G. Popov. Sound.

---

[164] [Trans.]: In her essay, "The Newsreel, again," Shub explicitly says, that the film was not preserved. She juxtaposes that with expression by Repertkom of the concern that the film might help to canonize Tolstoy and because of his late antinomian views, might become a rallying point against authority because of his great popularity and the respect accorded him. I take these two adjacent mentions as a kind of montage, meaning that the film was deliberately destroyed, in spite of the fact that Shub, by her account, includes an explicit narrative of Tolstoy as the product of his aristocratic class background and thus fatally flawed in his social critique. Since the film was seen abroad, it is remotely possible that a print not returned, or purchased abroad may still exist. Efforts up to now to locate a print have been unsuccessful, as far as I am aware. The only existing material with which I am familiar is an extremely fragmentary trailer for the film at Krasnogorsk.

[165] [Trans.]: A more literal rendering of the title might be *Komsomol, Patron of Electrification*, but that obscures the meaning in its context. According to a co-worker of a friend and longtime Moscow resident, Rick Witt, her father and other citizens of the Soviet Union were regularly called upon to render service outside their normal positions. Office workers or engineers might find themselves pitching in with the harvest. In English, the word Komsomol has wrongly taken on the meaning of a member of the Komsomol. "Komsomol" refers to the organization, the members were referred to as a "Komsomolets" (male), or a "Komsolmolka" (female).

Москва строит метро (Метро ночью) [*Moskva stroit metro (Metro noch'yu)*],
Moscow Builds a Metro (The Metro by night). 1 reel, 400 meters. Moskovsky kino-
kombinat, 1934. Director Esfir' Shub, composer G. Popov, camera operator
V. Solodovnikov. Sound.

Страна Советов [*Strana Sovetov*], *Land of the Soviets*. 8 reels, 1,945 meters.
Mosfil'm, 1937. Treatment Boris Agapov and Esfir' Shub, director Esfir' Shub, back-
ground music L. Shteinberg and N. Kryukov, editor L. Felonov, song and lyrics by
Mikhail Svetlov, music of a song N. Kryukov, camera operators E. Tissé (Ukraine and
Georgia), B. Krylov (Crimea), D. Fel'dman (Moscow). Sound.

Испания [*Ispaniya*], *Spain*. 10 reels, 2,090 meters. Mosfil'm, 1939. Scenarist, author
of voice-over text Vs. Vishnevsky, director Esfir' Shub, co-director A. Frolov, camera
operators R. Karmen, B. Makaseev, composer G. Popov, text read by Yu. Levitan.
Sound.

20 лет советского кино (Наше кино) [*20 let sovetskogo kino (Nashe kino)*], *20 years
of Soviet Cinema (Our cinema)*.[166] Tsentral'naya studiya dokumental'nykh fil'mov,
1940. Authors of the scenario and directors V. Pudovkin and Esfir' Shub. Sound.

Фашизм будет разбит (Лицо врага) [*Fashizm budet razbit (Litso vraga)*], *Fascism
will be crushed (The Face of the Enemy)*. 6 reels. Mosfil'm, 1941. Scenario B. Agapov
and Esfir' Shub, voice-over text B. Agapov, director Esfir' Shub. Sound.

Страна родная [*Strana rodnaya*], *Native Land*. Tsentral'naya studiya dokumental'nykh fil'mov, 1942. Author of the treatment, director and mise-en-scène Esfir'
Shub. Sound.

---

[166] [Trans.] Gosfilmofond holds a film with the title *Кино за 20 Лет* [*Kino za 20 let*] (*Cinema 20
Years On*). It would seem to be the same film under a different release title as it is credited to both
Pudovkin and Shub. The Production Company is listed as follows: произббодвсво МОСКОВСКОЙ
ОРДЕНА ЛЕНИНА киноьстудии Мосфильм (A Production of the Moscow Order of Lenin Cine-
ma-Studio Mosfil'm). The release date is also 1940. The credit for Pudovkin and Shub differs slightly.
In the Filmography for *My Life is the Cinema*, it runs: Авторы сценария и режиссеры В. Пудовкин
и Эсфирь Шуб (Authors of the scenario and directors V. Pudovkin and Esfir' Shub). In the titles to
Kino za 20 let, it runs: работали: над планом и монтажом — режиссеры: орденосец В. ПУДОВКИН
и заслуж. арт. республики ЭСФИРЬ ШУБ (The directors V. PUDOVKIN, holder of an Order and
Decorated Artist of the Republic ESFIR' SHUB worked on the scenario and editing). The following
credit carrying over from the one just mentioned is as follows: над планом и текстом Ю. ОЛЕША
и А. МАЧЕРЕТ (Yu. OLESHA and A. MACHERET [worked] on the scenario and text). This film
represents a canonization of the approved classics of Soviet Cinema up until 1940. Its primary
interest is as a representative Stalinist canon of Soviet film. In this context, it is notable that Shub and
Pudovkin slip in, without identifying them, a shot or two from Vertov's *Man With a Movie Camera*.
Vertov's place in official histories was then at a low point and this subtly subversive gesture did not go
without some risk.

Суд в Смоленске (спецвыпуск) [*Sud v Smolenske (spetsvypusk)*], *Judgment at Smolensk (Special bulletin)*. Tsentral'naya studiya dokumental'nykh fil'mov, 1946. Author of the treatment, director and mise-en-scène Esfir' Shub. Sound.

По ту сторону Аракса [*Po tu storonu Araksa*], *On the Other Side of the Aras*. 6 reels, 1,496 meters. Bakinskaya kinostudiya, 1947.
Author of the treatment and director of mise-en-scène Esfir' Shub, director I. Efen-diev, camera operators M. Dalyshev and O. Badalov, author of the text N. Shpikovsky, text read by L. Khmara, composer Niyazi. Sound.

От чистого сердца [*Ot chistogo serdtsa*], *With Heartfelt Sincerity*. 2 reels. (16 min 53 sec. at 24fps. = approx. 463 meters). Tsentralnaya ordena Krasnogo Znameni studiya dokumental'nykh fil'mov, 1949. Deputy Director of the Studio B. Shumov, director E. Shub, assistant director P. Plotnikova, treatment S. A. Garin, voice-over text by E. A. Dolmatovsky.[167] Sound.

---

[167] [Trans.] Although no credits appear on the film, the *montazhny list* at RGALI (ф 3035, оп.1, ед. хр. 40) gives the credits for Shumov, Shub, and Plotnikova listed above. The credits for S. A. Garin and E. A. Dolmatovsky made be found in RGALI document (ф. 2487 оп. 1 ед. хр. 513).

The gifts to Comrade Stalin in the Hall of Gifts to Comrade Stalin in the Museum of the Revolution in Moscow and some of their many admirers. From Shub's film *От чистого сердца* (*With Heartfelt Sincerity*) (1949).

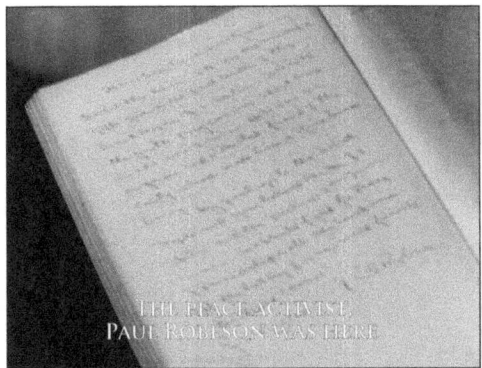

THE PEACE ACTIVIST,
PAUL ROBESON WAS HERE

A SKILLFUL MOSAIC OF VARIOUS KINDS
OF WOOD IS A GIFT FROM SAILORS

THERE ARE SO MANY TALENTS WITHIN
THE SOVIET PEOPLE

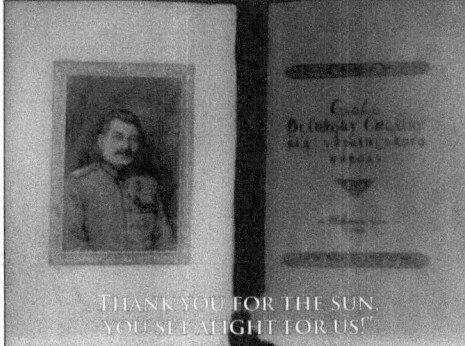

THANK YOU FOR THE SUN,
YOU SET ALIGHT FOR US!"

TURN TOWARDS THEIR GREAT
LEADER AND TEACHER.

"She's No Dziga Vertov"
An Afterword by Keith Sanborn

Esfir' Shub's difficult path to recognition, her formal style, and her ability to survive, if not to thrive, under Stalin have painted one picture of her in official histories—mostly one of neglect. Dziga Vertov, her chief rival and comrade-in-arms in the "non-acted film," after his self-propelled rise to fame as a formal and political innovator under Lenin—which brought him as much blame as praise—was utterly anathematized under Stalin. This has painted a film-historical picture of martyrdom. These contrasting narratives have led many to the conclusion, that Shub "is no Dziga Vertov." Just what that might mean, however, is the subject of this essay.

Besides this brief introduction, this text has two main parts: first "The Quality of what we perceive" and second, "The Quantity of what we see."

By way of review, since you will have come to this essay at the end of the translation of her writings, Esfir' Ilyinichna Shub lived from 1894 to 1959. She was active in film from the 1920s until she fell ill at the end of her life. She was a Soviet documentary filmmaker and was recognized officially with the title "заслуженный артист РСФСР," "Decorated Artist of the RSFSR." She came from the provincial bourgeoisie, and unusually for a woman of her generation, she attended an institute of advanced studies for women in Moscow, where she studied literature. During her student years at the Moscow Women's Advanced Studies, through her classmates, she made the acquaintance of some of the literary elite of the old regime and visiting foreign luminaries, including Edward Gordon Craig, the visionary English theater director.

After her coursework, through her employment at the Theater section of Narkompros, she became acquainted with the Moscow intelligentsia of her era. She grew to be on friendly terms with Mayakovsky, Eisenstein, Vertov, Kuleshov, Shklovsky, Khokhlova, Brik, Gan, Meyerhold, Lunacharsky and later, Vishnevsky and Fadeev. Though she sometimes disagreed with them quite vocally and publicly, she almost always spoke of her comrades in terms of the highest respect.

I. The Quality of what we perceive

Esfir' Shub and her most widely-known work, *Паление династии Романовых* (*Fall of the Romanov Dynasty*), in the past century since its appearance, have mostly been defined either indirectly or negatively. When introducing her achievements, she is identified as "the person who taught Eisenstein how to edit," or as Eisenstein's "collaborator" on a re-edit (*peremontazh*) of Lang's *Mabuse, the Gambler*, which for Soviet distribution was retitled *Позолоченная гниль* (*Gilded Decay*). It is less well known, that she was his (uncredited) collaborator on the scenario for *Strike* and it was, in fact, Eisenstein who was the understudy in the re-edit of *Mabuse*. Though it has not gone unnoticed, it is less frequently remarked, that Eisenstein's *October* was unfavorably compared to her *Fall of the Romanov Dynasty*: she showed Lenin in actual newsreel footage, whereas Eisenstein used an actor to *play* Lenin. This was seen as a clear victory for the non-acted film неигровая фильма [neigrovaya fil'ma] over the "acted" film игровая фильма [igrovaya fil'ma].[1] Within the realm of the non-acted film, Vertov's *A Sixth Part of the World*, which appeared around the same time, was also publicly and unfavorably compared to Shub's film, much to Vertov's chagrin.

A. A. Fadeev, the novelist and Stalinist arbiter of writers' literary and personal fates, expressed this opinion about Vertov's film, in his report to the Congress of Proletarian Writers in 1928:

> How are we to apply the theory of "the precise fixation of facts" in practice? There is a director, Dziga Vertov. In all probability, he is a talented person, but, in creating his picture *A Sixth Part of the World*, he, as an orthodox follower of LEF, avoids all philosophy and instead of *A Sixth Part of the World*, he presents an eccentric mishmash, such a superficial mixing together of facts, the result is simply a boring picture… The LEF group loves to refer to the beautiful film work of Esfir' Shub, which presents a montage of old, pre-revolutionary films. But the LEF group sees, that Shub has taken the line of art and not the simple fixation of facts, because she has brought facts into a well-defined system, she has taken the most typical one and transformed those very ones into artistic symbols…

Fadeev later, in a letter to Shub, claimed to have modified this damaging and polemical view and to have had different thoughts about Vertov in private. In any case,

---

[1] [Trans.]: It should be noted, that although it was later to be reassigned as masculine in gender, in Russian during Shub's initial years, "film" was at least *grammatically* gendered feminine, even if women, in their overwhelming majority were relegated to secondary roles, seldom achieving recognition as authors. Shub was a rare example of a woman who achieved that status.

this public statement contributed to Vertov's difficulties, some of which were of Vertov's own intransigent making. It is significant to me, that Fadeev was a confidante of Shub as she wrote her memoir, *My Life is the Cinema*, translated in this volume, though in what precise way remains to be unraveled. Since Fadeev was extremely powerful as the head of the writers' union, their friendship would certainly have been helpful to Shub in navigating the treacherous waters of the Stalin era, at their high point.

Fadeev was not the only one, on the occasion of the release of Shub's *Fall of the Romanov Dynasty* on March 11 of 1927, to take the opportunity to make both veiled and explicit criticism of Dziga Vertov and his methods. Vertov had been dismissed from Sovkino in January of 1927, allegedly, for going over budget on *A Sixth Part of the World* and for refusing to conform to the requirements of submitting scenarios in advance of production. Shub, as she became involved in shooting her films—rather than creating her films out of preexisting material—and became more aware of the unpredictability of documentary production, expressed some cautious sympathy with Vertov's view, though never wholly subscribed to it and later strategically repudiated it.

Osip Brik, in an article in *Novy LEF* entitled "Against Genre films," also compared Vertov's work unfavorably to Shub's, saying that by abstracting shots into generalities, Vertov, in *A Sixth Part of the World*, had completely failed the cause of the хроника [khronika] (the chronicle or newsreel) and the non-acted film: "In point of fact, we didn't get a finished film at all; what we got was some individual pieces of footage forcibly glued together." Vertov had participated in LEF earlier and published articles in the journal, but past or present association with the LEF group did not exempt anyone from the strictest criticism. In his response to Brik, "Against Levist Phrases," which doesn't seem to have been published by Vertov during his lifetime, he refers to "*Dynasty*," as he calls it, as "illiterate" (or "ungrammatical") [неграмотная] and "completely unedited" [никак не смонтированная.]

While Vertov spends more time in "Against Levist Phrases" attacking Brik than Shub, his feelings ran considerably deeper.

On March 7, 1927, four days before her film's public release, Vertov sent the following typed note to Shub:

> It is, unfortunately, not appropriate for me to praise this film, insofar as its cinematic construction is at a so extraordinarily low, pre-revolutionary, even pre-war level.

> To berate it for illiteracy [lack of grammaticality] is not in the interest of the thing we are fighting for at the current moment: the matter of non-acted filmmaking, which has not yet gained strength.

In order not to damage (even indirectly) the whole of our growing movement for the non-acted film, I will refrain from a public appraisal of this film work and for this reason I limit myself to a greeting <u>as a matter of principle</u>.[2]

March 7 (1927)
Kinok Dziga Vertov

Хвалить эту фильму я, к сожалению, не вправе, так как ее кинематографическое построение на чрезвычайно низком, дореволюционном и даже довоенном уровне.

Разнести ее за безграмотность–это в <u>настоящую минуту</u> не в интересах дела, за которое мы боремся: дела еще неокрепшей неигровой кинематографии.

Чтоб как-нибудь (даже косвенно) не повредить все растущему движению за неигровую фильму, я воздерживаюсь от публичной оценки этой киноработы и поэтому органичиваюсь лишь <u>принципиальным</u> приветствием.

7/III
Кинок Дзига Вертов

Shub's response is handwritten on Vertov's typed note:

What a small person you are; how pathetic! Esfir'

Маленький ты человек—жалко! Эсфирь

While it's unclear whether Shub ever sent a response, her feelings are clearly expressed. She was disappointed in his pettiness as she looked to him as a pioneer of

---

[2] [Trans.]: My translation. The original text follows from *Дзига ВЕРТОВ ИЗ НАСЛЕДИЯ Том второй СТАТЬИ И ВЫСТУПЛЕНИЯ*, Редактор С.М.Ишевская. Российский Государственный архив литературы и искусства Эйзенштейновский центр исследований кинокультуры, москва, 2008. Фонд 3035 (Э. И. Шуб), оп. 1, ед. хр. 198, л 1, машинопись, датирована 7 марта 1927 г., на листе приписка–Шуб : «Маленький ты человек—жалко! Эсфирь ». Фильм вышел на экраны 11 марта 1927 г. [Fond 3035 (E. I. Shub), op. 1, ed. khr. 198, l. 1, typewritten note, dated March 7, 1927, note added to the page by Shub: "What a small person you are, how pathetic! Esfir'." The film was released on March 11, 1927.] Apparently Vertov had been invited to a preview screening.

the non-acted film. Vertov had been published in the Constructivist journal *Кино-фот* [*Kino-fot*] in which she had actively participated and which was edited by her husband, Alexei Gan. Vertov had been a part of the LEF group with her. Shub even employed some distinctive common terminology in her writings, such as кино-вещь [kino-veshch'] (cinema-object), both before and after this incident.

In fact, Vertov's private judgment of Shub's film ran even deeper. In an extensive note unpublished during his lifetime, he summed up his feelings this way:

Conclusion[3]

Fall of the Romanov Dynasty is a third-rate student picture, pulled out of the ranks of similar things and inflated into the appearance of a substantial film out of commercial and special considerations of the management of Sovkino.

The film is [simply] not edited; it requires a fundamental reworking, and first and foremost, a literate cinematic construction.

The female editor Shub, having come to the newsreel from feature filmmaking, before <u>completely changing direction</u>, ought to have registered the difference between the construction of acted and non-acted film.

It's not too late to do this and right now, so as not to remain in the position of blind apprenticeship, in the position of dull, albeit self-satisfied, imitation.

Вывод

«Падение династии Романовых»—третьеразрядная ученическая картина, выдернутая из ряда подобных ей и раздутая, по коммерческим и особым соображениям администрации Совкино, до видимости значительной фильмы.

Фильма не смонтирована, требует коренной переработки и, в первую голову, грамотного кинематографического построения.

Монтажерше Шуб, пришедшей в хронику из художественной кинематографии, раньше, чем <u>сменить вехи</u>, следовало учесть разницу между построением игровой и неигровой фильмы.

---

[3] [Trans.]: This is reproduced from *Дзига ВЕРТОВ ИЗ НАСЛЕДИЯ Том второй СТАТЬИ И ВЫСТУПЛЕНИЯ*, Редактор С.М.Ишевская. Российский Государственный архив литературы и искусства Эйзенштейнавекий центр исследований кинокультуры, москва, 2008. Фонд 2986 (М.А.Кауфман), оп. 1, ед. хр. 145, лл. 1–4, рукопись, печатается с указанием разночтений с рукописным наброском из архива Вертова, ед. хр. 167, лл. 1–2 об. [Fond 2986 (M. A. Kaufman), op. 1, ed. khr 145, ll. 1–4, handwritten manuscript, printed with indications of discrepancies from the handwritten draft in the Vertov archive, ed. khr. 167, ll. 1–2 ob.]

Это не поздно сделать и сейчас, чтоб не оставаться в положении слепого ученичества, в положении тупого, хотя бы и самодовольного, подражания.

In his note, Vertov uses the word Монтажерша [montazhersha], which I have translated as "female editor." With this word, I went down the translator's rabbit hole. Монтажер [montazher] is the usual word for an editor then and now. It is used indifferently to refer to men or women, though it is of the masculine grammatical gender. Editing credits for women were never done using монтажерша then or now in the Russian film industry. In Shub's era, if any credit was given at all, the usual credit is simply монтаж, that is: editing [by], or sometimes монтажер [editor]. That said, Yutkevich, who was a member of the same generation as Shub and Vertov, also uses the word монтажерша in his introduction to this volume praising Shub's work on *The Wings of a Serf*, though in terms that could be considered condescending: догадливая и неугомонная [cunning and restless]. However, these words entail a range of meaning from cunning to perceptive and restless to indefatigable. Perhaps, some unconscious gender bias echoes here. In an earlier paragraph praising her innovations, Yutkevich notes that the term режиссер-монтажер [director-editor], notably masculine in gender in both components, is the term now recognizing the kind of work repurposing previously existing material Shub invented.

As Yuri Tsivian and Daria Khitrova have informed me, understanding the import of the word монтажерша in this context is somewhat complicated, since the primary meaning of adding -ша [-sha] to a word denoting a profession gives it the meaning: the wife of, as in генеральша [general'sha]: the wife of a general. This usage, in Russian Literature, as Masha Godovannaya points out, can be disrespectful. Respectfully one would say, жена генерала [zhena generala]. Though Pushkin makes it endearing, notably in *Капитанская дочка* (*The Captain's Daughter*), where one of the most sympathetic characters is referred to as капитанша [kapitansha]. But things get messier since, as Daria Khitrova points out, this ending could mean either the wife of a man pursuing a profession, *or* a woman pursuing that profession and in some cases has come exclusively to mean a woman pursuing that profession, for example бухгалтерша [bukhgaltersha] (female bookkeeper). Other women, to avoid the possible lack of seriousness implied, prefer to simply use the grammatically masculine form of the word denoting their profession. So, Vertov's use of the word, while somewhat unusual, is not in itself pejorative, though in the context of his excoriation of Shub's film, it is suggestive of something less than objectivity in noting her profession in the fiction film world.

It could also be argued, that using the feminine form of the word was actually grammatically necessary in order to avoid an infelicitous grammatical confusion as to her gender in the subordinate clause. And Vertov is not utterly unique in the use of the word. Professor Khitrova kindly provided me with a few uses of the word by other Soviet era industry insiders.

Tellingly for me, Vertov's credit for Svilova in *Man With a Movie Camera* is Ассистент по монтажу [Assistent po montazhu], that is, Assistant in editing. Not only does he avoid the terms монтаж [montazh], монтажер [montazher], or монтажерша [montazhersha], but he can't quite give Svilova full credit; it has to be as the *assistant* to the Автор-руководитель эксперимента Дзига Вертов, that is: assistant to the Author-manager of the experiment Dziga Vertov. Although it could be understood in the opposite way: that by making her the assistant to the Author-manager of the experiment, he has elevated her position to part of the creative team from the often-denigrated position of editor. She was, after all, part of the Council of 3. And, in the copies I have seen, her position and name appear in the same point size as Vertov's. For himself, Vertov, here, pointedly avoids the term режиссер [rezhisser], a transliteration of the French régisseur, a term used for the director of a fiction film at the time in the Soviet Union. For *The Eleventh Year*, Svilova's credit is simply ассистент [assistent] (assistant) in a smaller typeface than the Автор-руковадетель in period copies. For *A Sixth Part of the World*, she is "promoted" to асситент режиссера [assistent rezhissera] (assistant director), though again in a smaller typeface than the Автор-руковадетель in period copies. This is a curious choice for Svilova's title, as it echoes the language of mise-en-scène, rather than montage and would make Vertov, by implication, a режиссер. Режиссер is the term Yutkevich, a fiction filmmaker, uses as part of the hybrid term referenced above for Shub's work, режиссер-монтажер (director-editor).

During the 1920s, Shub was well-known in the Russian film world and was much sought-after as an editor of feature-length fiction films. For *Fall of the Romanov Dynasty* she refuses any title for her role in creating this unique film, but claims authorship of the labor involved by simply saying Работа Э. Шуб: [A] Work [by] E. Shub.

Alla Gadassik has pointed out, that for International Women's day of 1927, Shub wrote on the role of the монтажница [montazhnitsa] referring to her assistants in her own work in *peremontazh* (the re-editing of over 200 foreign films for Soviet distribution), her editing of numerous feature fiction films, and her recent work on *Fall of the Romanov Dynasty* and *The Great Way*. Монтажница, in Gadassik's words, refers to the "ubiquitous gender-specific job title of a person supporting the film editing process," entailing a range of jobs from inspecting and repairing rental prints, sorting and organizing footage according to a director's instructions, and matching workprints to negatives and cutting the negatives—all jobs requiring rigorous organizational skills and dexterity in the handling of materials. This would not, however, be used for a screen credit in a film for the principal editor of a film, though it was sometimes used within the industry to refer to an editor, according to Khitrova. In this text of 1927, Shub distinguishes between the supervisory role of the directing editor (her) and the монтажница, and, in her film *Today*, gives the screen credit of монтажница to Tat'yana Kuvshinchikova. In exemplary fashion, Gadassik contextualizes and translates Shub's essay on the монтажница here: https://www.apparatusjournal.net/index.php/apparatus/article/view/125/304. This article appears in the informative issue of *Apparatus* on recognizing women's work in film edited by Adelheid Heftberger and Karen Pearlman, who have both worked extensively on these issues.

Masha Godovannaya informs me that, although it is not accepted industry terminology and ridiculed by some, a number of feminist filmmakers use the term монтажерка [montazherka] for a woman who edits. This denotes a feminine agent, but does not in itself imply a diminutive.

In sum, the term used by Vertov for Shub, монтажерша, lies somewhere between an industry term of art and industry slang for the Soviet era. The context in which he uses it, however, is important. So many rabbit holes, and the rabbit nearly always seems to slip away.

The release of Shub's first work of her own was not the first time Shub and Vertov had come into conflict. The year before, when Vertov in *Pravda* famously called for the total centralization of non-acted film production under the Kinoks in his manifesto "The Factory of Facts," [Фабрика Фактов], Shub had responded in *Kino* with, "The Fabrication of Facts." [Фабрикация фактов]. She took issue with Vertov's declaration, that there was only one way to move the non-acted film forward and that the Kinoks were the only ones to do it and control it.

In part 6 of his private notes on *Fall of the Romanov Dynasty*, Vertov gives a clue to an additional source of his excess of scruples regarding Shub's film:

6.

The struggle for the non-acted film obliges those who struggle for it to be of the highest standards in appraising this or that non-acted film, it requires not allowing slipshod organization of valuable historical film material, it requires a struggle for quality in the production of non-acted films. In this honorable struggle, all personal sympathies or secondary considerations must be discarded. It's appropriate to recall this in connection with the circumstances, that *Dynasty* received the benediction of Sovkino management, that it was highly and lavishly promoted in major theaters (unlike the dozens of earlier and better-made non-acted films, hidden away and allowed to decay in institutional vaults, or, by whims of distribution, thrown into the most godforsaken parts of the country).

6.

Борьба за неигровую фильму обязывает ее борцов быть на высоте при оценке той или другой неигровой работы, обязывает не допускать халтурной организации ценнейшего исторического киноматериала, обязывает бороться за качество продукции неигровой фильмы.

В этой честной борьбе должны быть отброшены всякие личные симпатии или же служебные перспективы.

Об этом приходится вспомнить в связи с тем обстоятельством, что «Династия» получила благословение от администрации Совкино, благосклонно и щедро продвинута на большие экраны (не в пример десяткам прежде и лучше сделанных неигровых фильм, спрятанных и сгноенных в ведомственных подвалах или заброшенных, по прихоти проката, в самые глухие углы страны).

In short, Vertov was jealous. *Fall of the Romanov Dynasty* was heavily promoted and was screened in first tier theaters; *A Sixth Part of the World* had received second tier distribution and promotion and he was jealous. In these same notes, he refers to *Fall of the Romanov Dynasty* this way: "It is impossible not to agree with the opinion of those comrades who describe *Fall of the Romanov Dynasty* as a crappy little commercial film, building its supposed success on exhibiting the tsar and the empress." [Нельзя не согласится с мнением тех товарищей, которые отзываются о «Падении династии Романовых» как о кассовой фильмочке, строящей свой мнимый успех на показе царя и императрицы.]

Vertov says of her editing: "The very construction of the film is on such an extremely low, pre-war level. It only shows the raw material, *mechanically glued together in chronological order. What we have in front of us is the work of a warehouse manager, more than the work of an editor*" [my emphasis]. [Самое построение фильмы на чрезвычайно низком довоенном уровне. Налицо лишь сырой материал, механически склеенный в хронологическом порядке. Перед нами скорей работа кладовщика, чем работа монтажера.]

Though this note is undated, it clearly echoes the accusations leveled against him by Brik. Ironically, these same charges might be leveled against his own recently resurrected two-hour-long *Годовщина революции* [*Anniversary of the Revolution*] (1918), about the first year of the revolution. It would be informative to consider the public reception greeting that film.

If I have allowed so much space to Vertov's negativity, it is as a preamble to the observation that many people, in the past 50 years, have privileged a similar judgment of *Fall of the Romanov Dynasty*, perhaps without even knowing of Vertov's private spleen: *She's no Dziga Vertov.* If more recent critical reception of the film has not been blinded by Vertov's monomaniac jealously, it has been blinded by Vertovolatry and an attempt to settle scores against the Soviet authorities with whom Vertov seemingly inevitably came into conflict in the internal strife over игровая vs. неигровая фильма *even before* the promulgation of Socialist Realism as the official Party aesthetic. More narrowly, at this point (1927) it is a matter of the фабрика фактов (the factory of facts) (Vertov) vs. the фабрикация фактов [the fabrication of facts] (Shub's critique of Vertov). Brik had also chimed in near the end of 1926 with "Фиксация Фактов" ("The Fixation of Facts").

I want to point out, that I use the word "inevitably" with caution since successions of events always appear inevitable in the rear-view mirror of history; this point has been made repeatedly in the attempt to establish the historical uniqueness of the so-called "Primitive Mode" and the so-called "Institutional" mode of filmmaking in protecting the former against the teleological and totalizing narratives of the latter, which would subordinate the "Primitive" to the "Institutional," rather than recognizing their differences. I realize that many scholars consider this distinction outmoded; in any case, this basic understanding of the course of film history remains tied to a basic distinction of a similar order, whatever it might be called.

The fact is, that there is much to be regained in examining the particulars of the initial reception of *Fall of Romanov Dynasty.* Kuleshov's praise for it was unstinting, as was Brik's and Shklovsky's. And it was not only by way of attacking Vertov. Though their loyalty to a fellow member of the LEF group should not be ignored—Shub was a member of that group—but they also critiqued Eisenstein—one of their own—comparing *October* unfavorably to *Fall.*

If we are to compare Vertov and Shub as practitioners of the non-acted film, perhaps the best place to start is Shklovsky's suggestion, in "On the fact that Plot is a Constructive Principle and not One from Daily Life," in his text *Their Present Time [Их Настояшее]* (1927), that Vertov has a predilection towards parallelism, towards equivalences, towards copulas, as Devon Fore has more recently phrased it, in short, towards the rhetorical figure of metaphor and equivalence. Shub, by contrast, in most of her work and most of all in *Fall of the Romanov Dynasty*, privileges metonymy and a logic of association. The intertitles of Shub's film narrate the progress of the images, but seldom entirely duplicate them as Shklovsky criticizes Vertov for doing. Not that Shub is incapable of creating meaning via metaphor; rather, she uses a slow burn, which ignites only after a long period of kindling, not an immediate conflagration, born of quick sparks as we might characterize Vertov's method.

The celebrated sequence of *Fall*, which begins with royals and nobles dancing on shipboard and one elegant lady finally cooling herself with a lace handkerchief, another delicately wiping her brow and a third fixing a few strands of hair poking out from under her tremendous hat after the exertion of the dance—with the space just after the

... до поту.

Complex montage in *Fall of the Romanov Dynasty*.

end of the dance and before the waving handkerchief and fixed hair punctuated by an intertitle, "Until they sweat" [...до поту]—and cuts to a peasant digging a ditch, taking a moment to wipe the sweat from his brow with his hand and spitting on his hands before he grasps the handle of his shovel again—actually begins well before we board the ship where the dancing takes place and carries on well after. As the preposterous length and complexity of the preceding sentence will imply, Shub gives extraordinary attention to detail, something her detractors have missed, or at least undervalued. Shub's sense of montage is subversive in its indirect quality. Even when inserting that intertitle at the critical moment, it appears as a physical observation, not an abstract conclusion. It's implication only becomes clear afterwards, when we see a different quality of exertion and a different quality of sweat. If for Eisenstein—who has more in common with Shub than one might initially suspect—every cut must be seen and felt as a collision, for Shub the best cuts remain invisible. As she describes it in the chapter of her memoir called "My film school":

Gradually, at the editing table and in the viewing room, I acquired the knowledge essential for every director. I learned how to properly assess the construction and composition of a shot. I cultivated a memory for shots, for the content and motion within the frame, for the rhythm and pacing of things as a whole. I interiorized when it was necessary and appropriate to change from a wide shot to a medium shot, from a medium shot to a close up and back again. I realized the magical power of the scissors in the hands of a person possessing mastery of the grammar of montage. I began to try to make the changes imperceptible, so that one shot would replace another in a continuous motion. All this was basic, but I realized it and conceptualized it myself.

What I would like to point out is, that in comparing Shub and Vertov, we have a classic example of Roman Jakobson's well-known opposition between metonymy and metaphor, that is, relations of contiguity and relations of similarity. This insight, by which he links the structure of language disorders in aphasia with literary theory, he would later extend to mapping brain functions, on the one hand, and into film theory, on the other.

In a sense, Shub's work—at least in 1927—was invisible to Vertov or perhaps unpleasantly redolent of his earlier work. Shub's work has remained invisible to many, not only for polemical reasons, but also because criticism, as Jakobson further points out, privileges the pole of metaphor, since it offers a mirror image of itself: criticism, as metalanguage, is overwhelmingly metaphoric in nature. As a result, Jakobson notes, the critical literature on lyric poetry (the pole of metaphor) vastly outweighs in sheer bulk the literature on literary realism (the pole of metonymy). As the twentieth century moved forward, claims to "realism," as a correspondence between literature, or film and reality, became more and more problematic, but not before the demand for so-called "Socialist Realism" became deadly.

Shub's mission is deceptively modest; she is a kino-chronicler. Хроника means "chronicle" as much as it means "newsreel." Her кино-хроника, *Fall of the Romanov Dynasty*, is as much a cinema-chronicle as a newsreel, though it certainly consists of many newsreels brought strategically together. To reiterate her words, it is a "montage of historical filmdocuments" [монтаж исторических кинодокументов].[4] And yet, much is to be read between the lines. In place of parallelism, she emphasizes complex disjunction, a kind of negated logic of parallel trains of associations. The famous sea

---

[4] [Trans.]: She titles *The Great Way* "an historical chronicle. A Montage of authentic film-documents" [историческая хроника. Монтаж подлинных кино-документов] and titles her Tolstoy film "a montage of authentic film-documents" [Монтаж подлинных кино-документов]. The titles for the Tolstoy film are preserved in her fond РГАЛИ, ф. 2965, оп. 1, ед. хр. 2 and may be accessed at: https://www.kinozapiski.ru/ru/print/sendva.

The tsar and his son review sailors, whose heads turn in military precision as they pass.

cruise sequence—mentioned as early as Kuleshov and mentioned above—which ends in the disjunctive juxtaposition of members of the gentry dancing on the deck of a ship "until they sweat," [до поту] with men digging ditches, is carried on after the ditch diggers in an extended logic of association into other workers and peasants laboring in subjection and was preceded by an elaborate exposition including the tsar reviewing sailors aboard ship, their heads turning in military precision as he passes. There is a kind of dissonant visual rhyme between the elegant ladies fanning themselves with their handkerchiefs (Kuleshov identifies them as the tsar's daughters) and the ditch-digger wiping the sweat from his brow. This too is montage: a collision of sorts, as Eisenstein formulates it, though the friction creating the sparks builds gradually in the details observed within a medium wide frame, the frame characteristic of the newsreel footage and the "Primitive Mode." The result is not so much a visual shock as a social insight, an Ah-ha moment. This understanding of montage places Shub in Eisenstein's camp in their shared predilection towards metonymy, yet a negated parallelism of associations is still a form of parallelism: one of these things is NOT like the other and yet they inhabit parallel worlds. As Mayakovsky recognized, as Shub recalled his words, "You interpreted all the material well; it was especially good, that you turned material that was counter-revolutionary in its essence (he had in mind the tsarist news-reels), so that it resounded with a revolutionary denunciation."

One could argue that this is, in embryonic form, what the situationists would later call *détournement*—though the analogy would be inexact: Shub's purpose is explicitly an ideological critique, while the situationist project is a critique of ideology. Several historical reversals would have to be taken into account in order to trace such a lineage, not the least of which would be the process of de-Stalinization, which would leave Shub on a different side of history, in spite of the parallels of method.

If we scan it frame by frame, in *Man With a Movie Camera*, we will find cuts of a single frame; Shub never approaches that even remotely in this film and Eisenstein only goes to a minimum of two frames in the famous machine gun sequence of *October*.

Esfir' Shub (right) in the editing room with a montazhnitsa.

Vertov's cuts—or should we say Svilova's[5]—of a single frame allow the images to merge in consciousness; Eisenstein's two-frame cuts remain disjunctive and percussive. They retain their successiveness. Shub approaches those limits only once I know of, in *Сегодня* (*Today*). In one sequence, accelerating to 2-frame cuts of a capitalist in formal attire, alternating with 2-frame cuts of falling bank notes, she creates an aggressive visual association, re-thinking Vertov's and Eisenstein's methods of synthesis and collision, while remaining explicitly ideological. Her sensibility is that of *перемонтаж* (re-editing), rather than simple *монтаж* (editing). She travels through materials and methods to create new forms of meaning, but meaning grounded in historical actualities.

Shub's repeated insistence on a first name, a last name, and the date of a shot, her catalogic impulses are indexical of a worldview driven by the pole of metonymy, of linearity, of historicity. In comparison, Vertov's consistent refusal to submit scenarios, or shooting plans as unnecessary or even counterproductive is part of his utopian drive towards the simultaneity, the eternal present of metaphor, the instantaneity of the single frame. This drive Shub critiques, saying "this kind of montage helps the conception of the scene very little and leads the spectator to fall in love with the device itself." It leads, she says, "to the annihilation of documentation," placing the shot "outside of time." Shub must constantly direct the spectator beyond the events on the screen and into the world, into history, "according to the Party."

To sum up, Shub is no Dziga Vertov, nor is she Sergei Mikhailovich Eisenstein and yet the historical conflict of Vertov vs. Eisenstein has largely overshadowed Shub's important role, which at the very least, suggests greater complexity than the usual dichotomies: acted or non-acted, the factory of facts vs. the fabrication of facts, or for that matter, metaphor vs. metonymy. There is a kind of parallel here to the way in which Alice Guy forces a triangulation of the film historical dualism of Lumière vs. Méliès.

---

[5] [Trans.]: It might be interesting to explore the exact nature of the relationship between Svilova and Vertov. What is clear, is that Vertov *did not* edit his major works—Svilova did, though under his immediate supervision. Shub and Eisenstein, whatever assistants they might have had, *did* edit their own films. Whether posed or not, when Shub and Eisenstein are pictured at the editing bench, it is with film in their hands and both often refer to handling film. And that tactile relationship to the film strip is the stuff of metonymy. I have encountered such an image of Vertov only once and it is posed in a slightly different way than that of Eisenstein seen in the chapter of Shub's memoir devoted to Eisenstein. Vertov gazes intently into the visionary distance while looking *through* the film strip; Eisenstein, at least to me, whatever the comic exaggeration of the image, appears to be looking quizzically *at* the film strip. Though this comparison pushes the limits, it's safe to say, that when Vertov is pictured at the editing bench, it is Svilova who almost always handles the film. Svilova appears as editor in *Man With a Movie Camera*; Vertov plays the role of demiurge. Perhaps, Vertov did edit *Anniversary of the Revolution* himself; this would account for its plodding pace of assemblage; he simply has no *feel* for the physicalities of editing. Though that pacing may be due to the condition in which we find the reconstructed film. Whatever the case, Vertov is a visionary in the narrow and the wider sense and that is his most important quality.

Elizaveta Svilova in *Man With a Movie Camera*,
Svilova and Vertov editing a sound film, Vertov gazes through the film strip.

And while we are discarding these familiar dualisms, it might be of interest to observe that Shub is accomplishing something—in fact several things—in *Fall of the Romanov Dynasty*, which are extraordinary, novel, and largely invisible, or at least difficult to articulate without an understanding of the historical context. She is creating an historical narrative out of fragments, which are highly resistant to re-contextualization. She is, in a sense, creating a work in a Mode, which already stands as a critique of the Institutional Mode and its economic and social structures, out of fragments from the Primitive Mode. The autarky and unicity of the frame, to use the descriptive terminology of Noël Burch, which keeps the newsreel footage she uses closer to the Lumières than to D. W. Griffith, or to Eisenstein—for that matter—is distilled and subtly juxtaposed in such a way as to yield a global overview; insights arise from the particular, but are clearly within the domain of the intellectual and the emotional. She allows the shots to play out at length, so the details within the nearly unvarying wide frame of the medium wide shot can rise to the surface to keep a social perspective always in view.

As she says in "Первая работа" ("A First Work"), she allows the meaning to emerge from the material. Nor is she afraid to deemphasize cuts, to use the scalpel instead of the cleaver, to make them less obvious, less visible, rather than more. In fact she sees making the cut invisible as a virtue. This is ironically a logic we associate with the Hollywood dictum: the best cut is the one you don't see and it is certainly at variance with the work of Eisenstein, Vertov and even Kuleshov of the 1920s, who were influenced by the energetic visual experiments of the Hollywood of the teens.

Shub's shaping of the arc of the film—the slow pace and gradual build-up of pressure, which lead to a series of eruptions, ending in the appearance of Lenin—comes to be seen as the result of the inevitable weight of history. One could say, that Lenin replaces the tsar, but this would be misleading: things have changed utterly. Within the visual and intellectual logic of the film, it is rather, that the context in which the tsar could rule over a hierarchical empire of fragmented, oppressed subjects, gives way, under the weight of history—exploitation, starvation, war, death,—to a new world of vastly greater equality. Vladimir Il'ich emerges with the proletariat as first among equals, as Orwellian as that may rightly sound. Lenin is seen amongst the People, engaging with them passionately and familiarly; the tsar creates ritual pageantry, mostly for his own amusement, a spectacle the masses may only watch from behind police lines.

Paradoxically, to many, this may appear as an obvious party-line truism, but we should recall that under the rule of the tsar, as Yuri Tsivian points out, the public film projection of images of the imperial family was initially forbidden, but when finally allowed, that projection had to be strictly segregated from images of any other sort, in order to avoid untoward juxtapositions—those accidents, which might associate the tsar with anything vulgar, comic, or critical: what I call "Brechtian hiccoughs," or unintentionally meaningful glitches created by juxtapositions, by untoward associations. Shub, then, in *Fall of the Romanov Dynasty* is specifically violating an enforced taboo of autocratic autarky, which lasted in Russia until the actual fall of the Romanov Dynasty and coexisted with films solidly in the Institutional Mode, both domestic and foreign. It is a taboo of which few except specialists are aware. And context is everything to a logic of metonymy.

Shub transforms newsreel "views" into elements, which can participate in the larger narrative project of making meaning of the whole, but without precisely functioning as what we might understand as a "shot." In a sense, in *Fall of the Romanov Dynasty* we are witnessing a film historical transformation at the same time as a world historical transformation. Put another way, there are almost no close-ups and few medium close-ups in this film; the vast majority of the visual elements of the film are "medium wide shots,"—that paradoxical nomination which Burch uses to characterize the most common element of the "Primitive Mode." Vertov, for all his fierce intelligence, is blind to this subtlety, or irritated by it; he sees only, "the work of a warehouse manager, more than the work of an editor." And, in fact, goes further to claim, in his summary:

The film is not edited; it requires a fundamental reworking, and first and foremost, a literate [grammatical] cinematic construction.

Фильма не смонтирована, требует коренной переработки и, в первую голову, грамотного кинематографического построения.

Vertov's word is грамотный [gramotny], which means both literate and grammatical. Since Vertov lives in the world of metaphor, metonymy does not even count as a form of language, cinematic or otherwise. His is a world, unruled by the metonymic domain of syntax—which for him equates negatively with hierarchy—but rather by grammar and metaphor. Shub remains outside his horizons and, unfortunately, outside the horizons of the majority of film historians.

We might also add, that the criticisms leveled at Vertov display a parallel incomprehension: the pole of realism, of documentariness or fictional narrative demands syntax, that is, a subordination to linear narrative, narrowly understood. We have only to remember Eisenstein's famous characterization of *Man With a Movie Camera* as "formalist jackstraws and unmotivated camera mischief." This echoes the mutual incomprehension around narrative Hollis Frampton frames for the avant-garde of the 1970s in "A Pentagram for Conjuring the Narrative." He finds his way out of the impasse of the valorizing or devalorizing of narrative through mathematical abstraction, positing narrative as equivalent to succession in time. In the Soviet Union of the early 20th century, we find no such exit.

One final note on Shub's relationship with Vertov: I find it appropriate to record, that Shub retained a considerably wider and more generous view of things than Vertov. In 1940, in collaboration with Pudovkin, Shub made a compilation film entitled *20 лет советского кино* (*20 years of Soviet Cinema*), released by Mosfil'm as *Кино за 20 лет* [*Cinema 20 Years On*]. In spite of his numerous attempts to demean her work and in spite of the fact that Vertov was considered—and for good reason—utterly beyond the pale of the reigning aesthetic of Socialist Realism, she and Pudovkin managed to sneak a shot or two—without identifying them—from *Man With a Movie Camera* into an early transitional sequence in this official film history.

In her memoir, Shub also expresses her dismay at the humiliation suffered by Vertov in his groveling retractions of his earlier "errors." From the perspective of current academic Vertovolatry, where Shub is remembered in Russia by film historians of considerable standing only as one of Eisenstein's lovers, or someone who used too much text, these might seem like small, or even grudging acknowledgments, but in the Soviet Union ruled by our helmsman, leader, and teacher, Joseph Vissarionovich Stalin, these were gestures of considerable risk. Examples of perceived artistic trespass and their fatal consequences were not lacking among her friends Meyerhold and Zinaida Raikh. This was something Shub would experience even closer to home in the disappearance and execution of her former husband, Alexei Gan. His death sentence for "counter-revolutionary activities" was supposedly the result of a remark uttered in an angry moment in a far eastern part of the Soviet Union, referring to comrade Stalin as a "pockmarked bastard" [рябая сволочь].[6]

Though marginalized and frustrated in her ambitions, Shub survived Vertov's fate by what we might, not without irony, call "strategic cooperation." In 1949, Shub seems to have received an offer she couldn't refuse: to document the Halls of Gifts to Comrade Stalin in the Museum of the Revolution. This took the form of a short

---

[6] This information is reported by Shub's granddaughter, A. B. Konoplev, in her "Короткое вступление к воспоминаниям моей мамы, А.И.Коноплевой, об Алексее Гане." "A short introduction to the memories of my mother, A. I. Konoplevaya about Aleksei Gan." This note was written at the request of RGALI and may be found in the Shub fond.

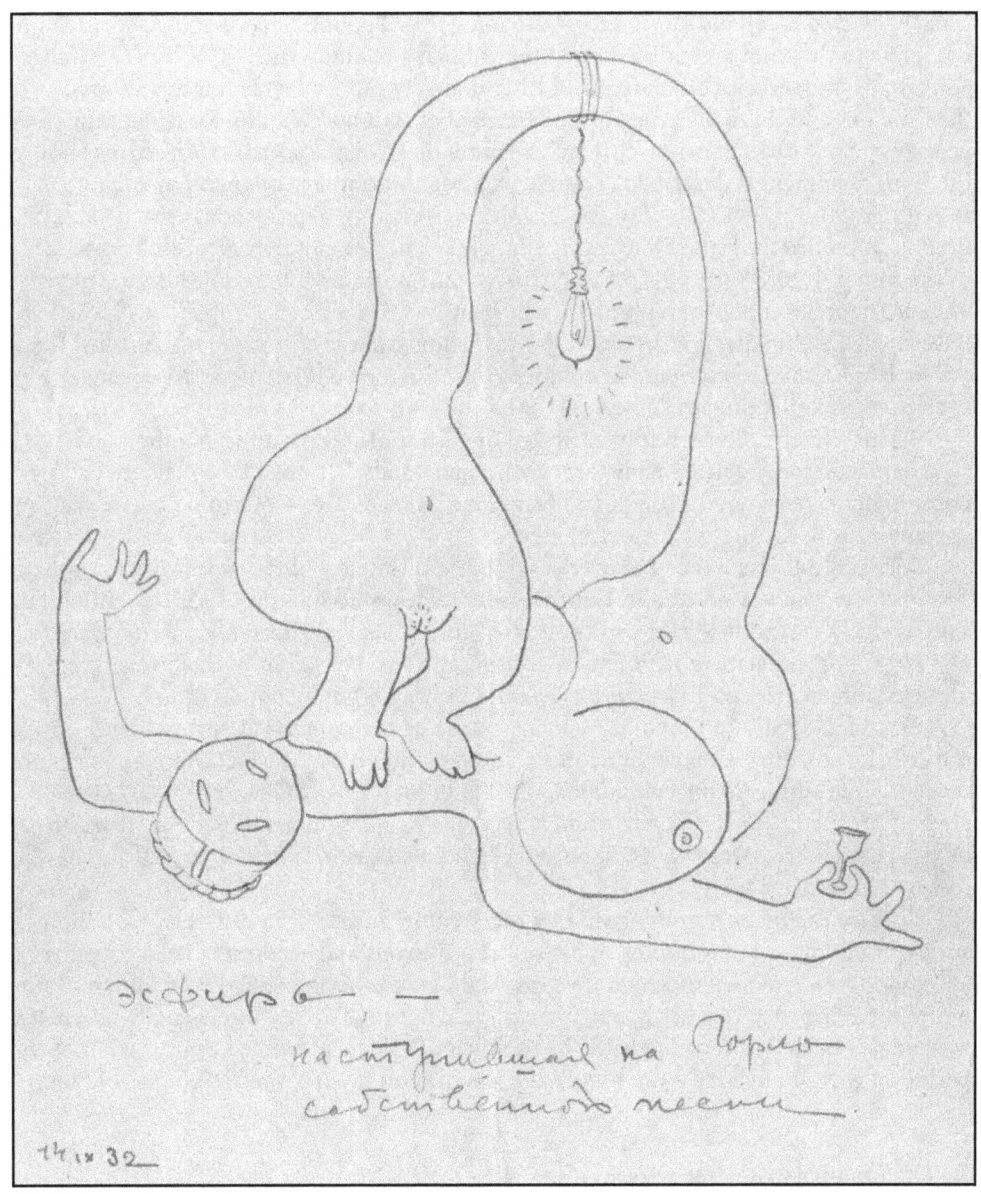

эфиръ —

наступившая на горло
собственной песни.

14 ıx 32

Eisenstein's drawing of "Esfir' Shub having stepped on the throat of her own song."
Dated April 14, 1932

film *От чистого сердца* (*With Heartfelt Sincerity*). Though Shub declined to attach her name to that film and at least one other film as yet undiscovered, *With Heartfelt Sincerity* is unquestionably hers. RGALI contains two documents linking Shub to the film: one is ф.3035 оп.1 ед. хр.40, described as Вариант концовки сценария, режиссерский план съемки, that is: Variant ending for the scenario, director's shot list. This document is described as Автограф, Машинопись с правкой автора, that is: Autograph, Typewritten with the author's corrections. The author is listed as Шуб Эсфирь Ильинична: Shub Esfir' Il'inichna The second document linking Shub to the film is ф.3035 оп.1 ед. хр.41. Фотография кадра из фильма Э.И.Шуб "От чистого сердца" a photograph of a frame from the film of E. I. Shub "With Heartfelt Sincerity." The film itself is archived at Krasnogorsk in the collection of her films there at The Russian State Documentary Film & Photo Archive [Российский государственный архив кинофотодокументов].

This nearly unknown film, stripped of authorial credits, appears miraculously, an acheiropoieton: an ikon made "not by human hands." It must be considered a low point in her career—she chose not to recognize its maternity—but to deny it a place in her output is to distort the historical record.

That Shub was a true believer singing the ultimate righteousness of triumphant communism, there is no doubt, but then, the same could be said of Vertov, though in a different key. And his later works show a similar decline. *With Heartfelt Sincerity* of 1949 is not a deviation from, but a continuation of her belief in the Soviet system under Stalin, evidenced in *Испания* (*Spain*) (1939), *Страна родная* (*Native Land*) (1942), and allegedly in *Страна советов* (*Land of the Soviets*) (1945), which I have not seen. According to her grandson, in conversation with Masha Godovannaya and myself, Shub's film *По ту сторону Аракса* (*On the Other Side of the Aras*) (1947), created problems for her due to some misplaced or mistimed sympathies. It was to be her last feature. Afterwards, she was relegated almost exclusively to editing newsreels.

There can be no summing up of a life, or a life in art; I can only say, that Shub survived a number of monumental historical upheavals and accomplished a considerable amount in circumstances where slips could mean social or physical death, but not without paying the price for it. She is a complex figure in Soviet intellectual and artistic life and a consideration of the path she took should open a nuanced examination of the period of Russian history from before the Revolution to after the "triumph" of Stalin.

II. The Quantity of what we see

Given the current state of film preservation and the recurrent myth of film's capturing the world for all eternity, it is important to note just what we actually see, on the rare occasions, when we "see" one of Shub's films. I will use as my example, the only film by her known to any considerable extent in the West: *Падение Династии Романовых* (*Fall of the Romanov Dynasty*).

So, what is it exactly that we "see" when watching *Fall of the Romanov Dynasty*. It will be something resembling *Падение Династии Романовых* as Shub made it, but not precisely identical with it, either in time or in space.

A. Time

As recorded in the 1972 edition of *Жизнь моя—Киноматограф* (*My Life is the Cinema*) and as recorded by Gosfilmofond, the original length of the film was 2,080m. No print known to me of this length currently exists. Even if the original negative, were to be found, it would not be of this length, since as her friend Jay Leyda records in *Films Beget Films*, and as Vaisfel'd affirms in his introduction to the 1959 edition of *My Life is the Cinema*, Shub's negatives were constantly pillaged by other filmmakers. They would plead emergencies and promise to restore the footage taken, but never did. Gosfilmofond does not list the length of its silent copy, but Krasnogorsk has a silent copy, which undoubtedly comes from Gosfilmofond (though it is printed on a sound aperture), which is 1,823m. Eye Film Museum in Amsterdam, who has the only known full silent aperture print of *Man With A Movie Camera*, has a copy listed as 1,840m. The distressing Gosfilmofond sound version, prepared by Yutkevich, runs to replace with 1,803m. without intertitles. The Pacific Film Archive holds a silent print from Gosfilmofond of around 1,767m. The Austrian Film Museum has a print of only 1,533m (79 min at 16fps), but of exquisite quality. The print typically seen in the United States is the MoMA 16mm rental reduction print, with English intertitles. This seems to be the source of the many digital copies currently in circulation. But even greater unhappiness lies in the considerations of space: All copies I have seen (which does not include the EYE Museum copy) are printed on sound aperture, with the possible exception of the print of the Austrian Film Museum.

The longest available copy is 240m short of the 2,080 original, which is approximately

≈ 13 mins short @ 16fps
≈ 11.54% missing in footage
≈ 88.46% complete.

Comparing a DVD from the MoMA print and a DVD from the AFM print with the cleanest most complete copy of the subtitle list, the montazhny list in the Shub fond at RGALI, it seems likely that the vast majority of the missing footage is in the last reel, reel 7. In fact, almost the whole last reel is missing from the AFM print and 2 or 3 titles at the end of reel 6. In reel 7, 24 subtitles are missing, several are changed and

4 are added. But given the various discrepancies, there is no guarantee that the uncorrected montazhny list was the final one: the final edit of a film could be less than, but not more than, the montazhny list.

It also seems likely, that the final reel would have been the most controversial one and most subject to pillage since it portrays the foundational role of the Bolsheviks, making it the reel containing the historical footage of greatest interest to later chroniclers of the October Revolution. It should also be noted, that the subtitles of the montazhny list spend quite a bit of time identifying members of the provisional government, whose very existence later Soviet historians might have been keen to deny. And Trotsky, among other revolutionaries, would have later been seen as more than disposable; many disappeared and not only from official "historical" photographs.

This table summarizes the known prints of the film I have been able to identify. All prints are 35mm except the MoMA print.

Archive Projection length/speed	metrage
Original Length (*My Life is the Cinema*)	2,080m
Gosfilmofond listing	2,080m
Gosfilmofond Sound Print (Yutkevich redaction)	1,803m
Krasnogorsk Silent Print (from Gosfilmofond)	1,823m
Pacific Film Archive 78 min @20fps	≈1783m
MoMA 16mm	725m
EYE Film Institute Amsterdam	1,840m
Austrian Film Museum (78–79 min) 16fps	1,533m
Swedish Film Institute	not public
Cinémathèque Française (90 minutes)	not public
Cinémathèque de Toulouse	1,794m
Cinémathèque Québecoise	1,793m
Cinémathèque Royale de Belgique	1,534m
Cineteca di Bologna	1,841m
Kino by Jay Leyda	1,700m

Longest print 240m short of Original ≈ 13 mins short @ 16fps

≈ 11.54% missing in length
≈ 88.46% complete

B. Space

If we compare a frame from a DVD of the AFM print, the best quality print—at least that I have seen—with the same frame from the DVD based on the MoMA print, we will find that on the DVD from the MoMA print a great deal is missing: nearly 23.1% of the frame. While Shub does use awkward gestures and framings of her subjects as a comic device and an index to authenticity, it is not nearly so prevalent, or extreme as this print would seem to show.

One instructive example comes from an early section of the film showing two members of the State Duma, Shulgin and Krupensky.

Aspect ratios do not correspond precisely, as the DVD has taken the approach of stretching the already cropped sound aspect ratio to fill the screen and the AFM print shows doubling artifacts caused by the rotating prism of the Steenbeck, on the digital copy I have seen. I have attempted to match the two as closely as possible by reformatting the image from the DVD of the MoMA print.

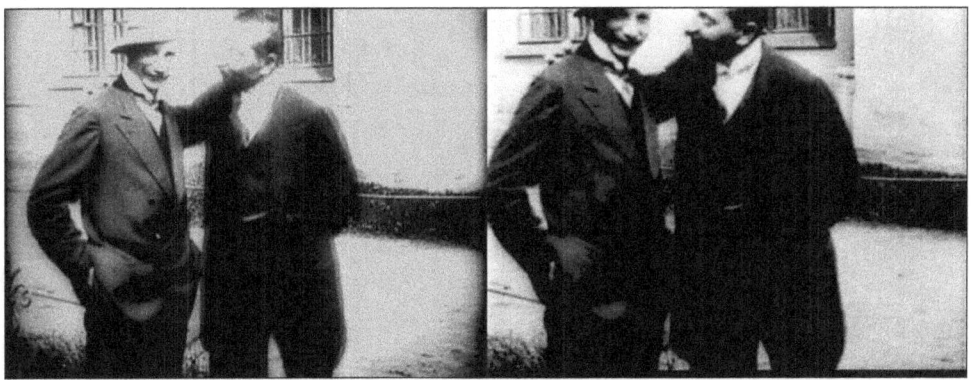

Left: DVD of AFM print rephotographed from Steenbeck.
Right: DVD likely from MoMA 16mm reduction print, 76.9% of AFM frame.

By keeping the normal tonality of the DVD of the AFM print and by inverting the tonality of the MoMA DVD image, we arrive at a more graphic visual comparison: We can now overlay the DVD on top of the AFM print to see the extent of the loss.

Left: AFM print. Right: DVD of MoMA print inverted.

Reducing the overlay to the appropriate scale we see:

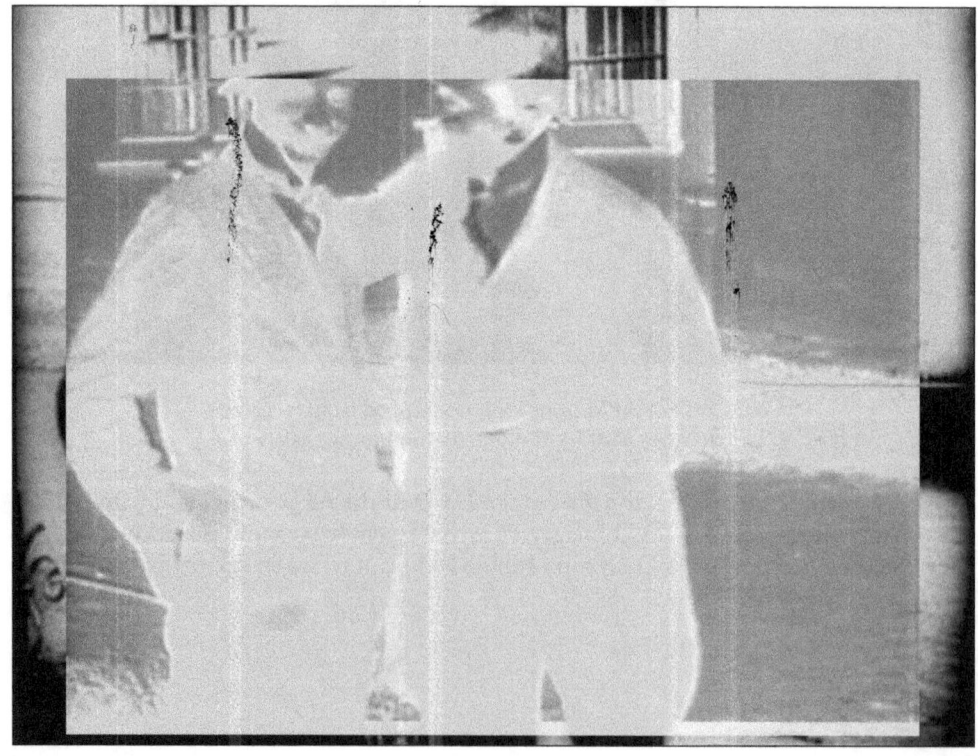

MoMA print inverted superimposed on AFM print.

Using some slightly preposterous math, we might conclude, that when we "see" *Fall of the Romanov Dynasty*, we are typically seeing something like 88.4% of the duration x 76.9% Space = 68% of the total Space/Time of the film. This should at least give us pause when making inferences on the basis of what we "see" in this film. After all, only recently were we able to see a more or less complete, full frame version of Vertov's *Man With a Movie Camera* presented on the original silent aperture, a film which has received considerably more attention since the 1970s than *Fall of the Romanov Dynasty*. Saint Augustine cautions us that the literal level of a text must be true, before we can move on to allegorical, moral, and anagogical interpretations.

No stranger to strange math, Hollis Frampton once summed up for me the material mortality of film in two words: "*Triste cinéaste*." But as he also used to remark, with considerably greater frequency: "Better than a poke in the eye with a sharp stick."

Both the cautions of St. Augustine and Frampton's perspectives on the mortality of film have guided the efforts of the extended archaeology of this translation by my friends, my colleagues, and myself.

Now, on to the work on what remains of the films themselves.

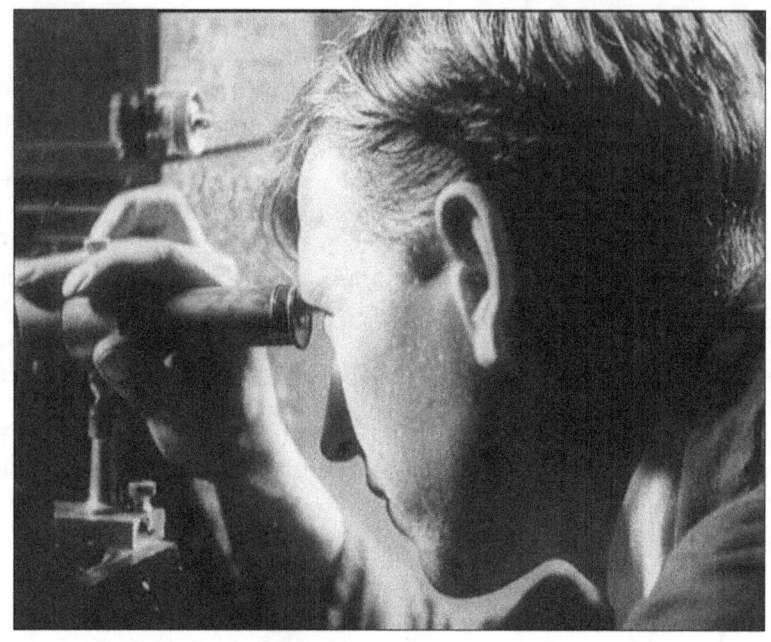

A sound operator views the image of sound as it is recorded on the Shorin system.
From *KShE* [*КШЭ*] (1932).

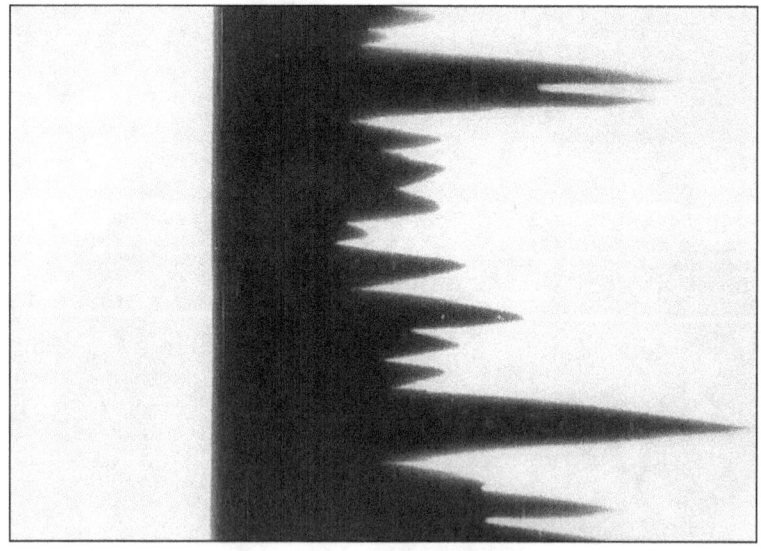

On *Esfir Shub: Pioneer of Documentary Filmmaking* by Ilana Shub Sharp (Bloomsbury, 2022) by Keith Sanborn

That Esfir' Shub is deserving of greater recognition in the annals of documentary filmmaking, there is no doubt, but this exaggerated and falsified hagiography by Ilana Shub Sharp is not the way to get there. Having spent decades researching Shub and having carefully engaged with translating her writings, I was appalled at many of the claims of Shub Sharp's book. Here, I will limit myself to discussing just one, which is sadly symptomatic of the entire book.

This most egregious and falsified claim by Shub Sharp is that Esfir' Shub edited Eisenstein's *Strike*. This claim is not only speculative at best, but is directly contradicted by Shub herself. That Shub's explicit statement to the contrary is omitted from this discussion, is a deliberate deception. Shub wrote:

> This year [1924] came to an end with what was for me a noteworthy event. S. M. Eisenstein proposed that I work with him on the shooting script for *Strike*. It was proposed that after this I would become part of the production team.[1] This determined my subsequent career in filmmaking. We were by that time the greatest of friends. We were brought together by the common views on filmmaking we held. We worked for at least two months at my home on *Strike*. The shooting script was approved and accepted for production. But I did not become part of the production team.[2]

And later:

---

[1] [Trans.]: In the original: С. М. Эйзенштейн предложил мне работать с ним вместе над режиссерским вариантом сценария «Стачка». Предполагалось, что после этого я войду и в съемочную группу.

[2] [Trans.]: In the original: Но в съемочную группу я не вошла.

I was distressed, that I was not part of the production collective of *Strike*. Now I think, that perhaps, this was helpful.[3] What interested me most of all in art, was its connection with our reality, everything that reflected and strengthened it. I was finding my own way. At that time, I became acquainted with Dziga Vertov; I became interested in his activity.

To eliminate any ambiguity about the phrases "production team" or "production collective," Shub, as a renowned editor, would have been included in any group described as such. As Shub describes, in her account of editing of *Wings of a Serf*, she assembled dailies into a rough cut during production. This remains common practice for any feature-length film. Shub Sharp, who repeatedly refers to *In Close Up*, deliberately omits Shub's explicit statement that she was *not* part of the production team, instead relying on three questionable pieces of circumstantial evidence.

First, on an undocumented assertion by R. C. Williams (who could not have been present, since he was born in 1938) on page 179 of his *Artists in Revolution: Portraits of the Russian Avant-Garde* (Indiana University Press, 1977). This is possibly an inference based on a misreading of Shub's text, as he uses the phrase "Shub did most of the editing at her home in the autumn of 1924." In the chapter of *In Close-Up* called "First Years in the cinema (1922–1930) My film school," Shub does mention a small editing set up and projector at her apartment at one point, during the period of 1922–1925, which she used for experiments with trims from her *peremontazh* work. At her editing studio and screening room at Goskino, she and Eisenstein did screen newsreel footage, some of which later ended up in *Fall of the Romanov Dynasty* and which she insists influenced Eisenstein in making *October*. *At no time, however, does she say, or infer, she edited* Strike *either at her home or anywhere else.*

Esfir' Shub describes her Kuleshov-inspired experiments, with Eisenstein in attendance, this way:

S. M. Eisenstein—already at that time a theater director at Proletkult— was very interested in my work in re-editing.[4] More than once he came

---

[3] [Trans.]: In the original: Я огорчилась, что не попала в съемочный коллектив «Стачки». Сейчас, я думаю, это было, может быть, и полезно.
[4] [Trans.]: In the original: перемонтаж [peremontazh]. The Russian word does not emphasize repetition, but rather the sense of through or across. The Russian word for translator переводчик [perevodchik] uses this same prefix. A translator is someone who leads across. Though the idiomatic translation of *peremontazh* is re-editing, the sense of *peremontazh* is more *transformative* editing or *transformative* montage, giving the sense that a work undergoing *peremontazh* is being thoroughly transformed. And indeed, this applies to Shub's own work with preexisting material, such as *Fall of the Romanov Dynasty*. She transforms it. This is quite distinct, for example, from Eisenstein's sense of montage as "the collision of the shots." Shub strives for a subtle sense of inevitability where her strategies are *not* immediately visible. As she says later in that same chapter, "I began to try to make

to my editing studio and viewing room. There, for the first time, we would screen huge reels of mixed pieces of film, which would turn out to be newsreels of the events of February [1917] in Leningrad and Moscow.

This material made a huge impression on us. I returned to it when I became a director of documentary films, and in Eisenstein's case, in his film *October*, the scene of the events of July in Leningrad was unquestionably worked out under the influence of this viewing.

Serial films had one particularity: each successive serial began with a quick summary of the previous one. The summaries were edited together out of very small bits of film and each one contained shots of various episodes. I would cut out the introduction, so that in the process of re-editing, many shots would drop out. When rather a large number of these short reels from various films would accumulate, Sergei Mikhailovich and I would engage ourselves over at my place (in my apartment at that time there was an editing table and a small projector) in thinking up new studies, elaborately splicing together the shots once again. This was a useful and lively activity, borrowed by us from L. V. Kuleshov.

Second, Shub Sharp bases her assertion on a questionable listing allegedly in the database of the British Film Institute. Buried in footnote 89 to Chapter 1, Shub Sharp writes: "Yet in the archives of the British Film Institute, Shub is in fact listed as *Strike's* co-editor with Eisenstein." Shub Sharp presents no reference for this listing and no justification for it from the BFI.

And third, Shub Sharp bases her assertion on the claim, that Valerian Pletnev is credited as co-editor of the film and that he had no editing experience. That he had no film editing experience may be true, however, Pletnev is, in fact, *not* credited as the co-editor of the film at least on the copies I have seen, including the authoritative Kino Academia HyperKino DVD, which seems to use an archival source. The credit with Pletnev's name reads: Сценарий ПРОЛЕТКУЛЬТА под общей редакцией В. ПЛЕТНЕВА (Scenario by PROLETKULT under the general management of V. Pletnev).[5] It is a kind of general managerial credit, not a credit for a technical role, though Pletnev, a playwright, was part of the collective responsible for the scenario, the other members of which, were Eisenstein, Alexandrov, and Il'ya Kravchunovsky.

---

the changes imperceptible, so that one shot would replace another in a continuous motion." This is *not* the "eccentric" style of editing in *Strike*. Eisenstein strives for in-your-face shock value, so that every shot and every cut stands out, at least in his work of the silent era.

[5] Perhaps the origin of this misinterpretation is the sequence of two English subtitles in the Hyper-Kino disk, which are: "Screenplay by PROLETKULT," then "Edited by V. PLETNYOV." The second subtitle is clearly meant to refer to the editing of the scenario, which, in any case, Eisenstein, who had come into conflict with Pletnev during the creation of the scenario, discarded during shooting, according to Shub.

Pletnev's credit does not come *over* Eisenstein's credit as director [режиссер] but does precede it. Also preceding Eisenstein's credit, is the credit for the players: Исполнение коллектива 1-го рабочего театра (Performance by the Collective of the 1st Worker's Theater). These are credits which focus on the collective nature of the project, something Eisenstein was at pains to emphasize. Other credits emphasize the intellectual project of the film. I can only conclude, that either Shub Sharp has access to information I do not, she does not read Russian, or that she has made yet another fabrication of facts in the service of the unnecessary burnishing of a halo for Esfir' Shub. *No one* is, in fact, listed as the editor of the film, but as Esfir' Shub points out, Eisenstein strongly believed that only a director *who edited his own films* fulfilled his role as a director and Sergei Mikhailovich can hardly be accused of slacking.

Having also worked with Shub to re-edit Lang's *Mabuse* into a version more ideologically suited for Soviet release called *Позолоченная гниль* (*Gilded Decay*), Eisenstein had served a rigorous apprenticeship as an editor and was likely by then quite capable of cutting *Strike* by himself. He had also already directed *Glumov's Diary* for his theater production of *Enough Stupidity in Every Wise Man*, though it is unclear what other technical role he might have assumed. In any case, Eisenstein learned rapidly and thoroughly; he was a student who "surpassed his master." This phrase came to him in a note from Zinaida Raikh, a Meyerhold theater actress and Meyerhold's wife, who described Eisenstein's relationship with Meyerhold in this way. Shub uses the phrase about Eisenstein and herself and Eisenstein about Sergei Vasil'ev (one of the co-directors of *Chapaev*) and himself.

A more distressing example of deception on the part of Shub Sharp is the fact that on page 32, she quotes the passage where Shub expresses her distress at not being included in the production collective and suppresses Shub's reason for being distressed, i.e. that she was not included in the production collective. Shub Sharp writes:

> In retrospect, pondering on her non-inclusion on the final film credits of *Strike*, Shub was to conclude: "I was saddened... Now I think that this might have been a good thing. What interested me most of all in art was everything connected with our reality, everything that reflected and supported it. I was seeking my own way."

Shub Sharp translates as "saddened" what I prefer to translate as "distressed." Both are reasonable translations of Esfir' Shub's words, but for Shub Sharp to pretend that Shub's feelings were being caused by her not being credited as the editor of *Strike* when Shub says no such thing, and for her to suppress Esfir' Shub's own words— "I was distressed, that I was not part of the production collective of *Strike*"—goes beyond even what Esfir' Shub would call "the fabrication of facts."

Eisenstein editing *Strike* (1924). Courtesy of the Eisenstein Center (Moscow).

To make things worse, Shub Sharp strategically selects Esfir' Shub's words here: "We worked on *Strike* in my house for at least two uninterrupted months." This remark is deliberately taken out of context in the middle of the paragraph to support the theory that Shub edited *Strike*. In the first sentence of the same paragraph, which I have quoted above, Shub explicitly says, "S. M. Eisenstein proposed that I work with him on the shooting script for *Strike*." Shub Sharp's citation comes from later in the same paragraph. And the sentences following the one quoted by Shub Sharp leaves no doubt as to the nature of their work together on *Strike*: "The shooting script was approved and accepted for production. But I did not become part of the production team." I have quoted the entire paragraph above.

For context, we should consider the chapter of *In Close-Up* devoted to Eisenstein, where Esfir' Shub recounts the following event, which she calls an "attraction":

The second "attraction" was staged for me. Sergei Mikhailovich called me to hear one of his lectures and precisely indicating the time, when I should arrive, said sternly: "Don't be late."

Having arrived at the appointed time, I was embarrassed, to find that the lesson had already been going on for around ten minutes. I knew, that Eisenstein did not like to be interrupted. All the same, I took the risk of opening the door, going into the auditorium and under the stern gaze of Sergei Mikhailovich, of taking a place by the door.

And suddenly, with a kindly smile, he turned towards his students: "This is the director Esfir' Shub; stand up and raise a cheer for her. From her hand, I took my first strip of film and she gave me my first lessons in montage."

The students stood up and cheered me. The lessons continued. Brilliant sketches in chalk completed in an instant on the blackboard accompanied the lecture.

I was embarrassed and happy. This was also a case, when the "student" had greatly outstripped the "teacher." Sergei Mikhailovich taught me so much, and communicating with him greatly enriched me.

The first "attraction," which Shub describes, is a ceremony conducted by Eisenstein to honor Sergei Vasil'ev, another student who had surpassed the master. In this case Eisenstein casts himself, rather modestly, as the master who had been surpassed. This ceremony is depicted on page 177 of the present volume.

Finally, let me reiterate, that, in describing Eisenstein's pedagogy, Shub notes, that Eisenstein "considered that a director, who did not edit his own film, had not fully realized his work as a director."

For Ilana Shub Sharp to make the claim, that Shub, rather than Eisenstein edited *Strike*, is not only implausible, it is a contradiction of the facts as Esfir' Shub herself recounts them. This claim is sadly typical of Shub Sharp's entire project. Esfir' Shub, known for her sometimes abrasive integrity, as well as for her generosity, deserves better.

Keith Sanborn is a media artist, theorist, curator and translator. His work has been seen in numerous one-person shows and been included in major surveys: The American Century, the Whitney Biennial, Monter/Sampler, and festivals: OVNI, Video Vortex, Rotterdam, EMAF, Oberhausen, and Hong Kong Videotage. His theoretical work has appeared in *Artforum*, *Kunst nach Ground Zero* and catalogues of MoMA, Exit Art, and the San Francisco Cinematheque. He has translated into English the work of Debord, Viénet, Wolman, Bataille, Napoleon, Bouhours, Shub, and Gioli, among others. He has curated for Oberhausen, Exit Art, Artists Space, the Pacific Film Archive, and CinemaTexas. He has taught at various colleges and universities, including Princeton University, Columbia University, Bard College, SUNY/Buffalo, the San Francisco Art Institute, the University of Wisconsin, Milwaukee, UC, San Diego, the Smolny Institute of Liberal Arts and Sciences, The New School, New York and elsewhere. He earned his undergraduate degree in English Literature at Rice University, an MA in English and Comparative Literature at Columbia University, and an MAH at SUNY/Buffalo in film, photography, and digital arts.